D1585317

THE
GUITAR
HANDBOOK

THE GUITAR HANDBOOK

Ralph Denyer

with
Isaac Guillory and Alastair M. Crawford

Dorling Kindersley London

The Guitar Handbook was conceived, edited and designed by Dorling Kindersley Limited, 9 Henrietta Street, London WC2

Special contributors
Isaac Guillory, Alastair M. Crawford

Editor **Alan Buckingham**
Assistant editor **Tim Shackleton**
Designer **Ron Pickless**
Assistant designer **Nick Harris**
Art director **Stuart Jackman**

First published in Great Britain in 1982 by Dorling Kindersley Limited, 9 Henrietta Street, London WC2

Second impression 1983
Third impression 1985

Copyright © 1982 by Dorling Kindersley Limited, London
Text copyright © 1982 by Ralph Denyer

All rights reserved. No part of this publication may be reproduced, stored in a retrieval system, or transmitted in any form or by any means, electronic, mechanical, photocopying, recording or otherwise, without the prior written permission of the copyright owner.

Denyer, Ralph
   The guitar handbook.
   1. Guitar—Methods—Self-instruction
   I. Title
   787.6'1'0712   MT588

ISBN 0 86318 004 3

Typeset by Rowland Phototypesetting (London) Limited
Reproduction by F.E. Burman Limited and Dot Gradations Limited
Printed in Italy by A. Mondadori, Verona

CONTENTS

The Guitar Innovators 7

Acoustic Guitars 33

Electric guitars 49

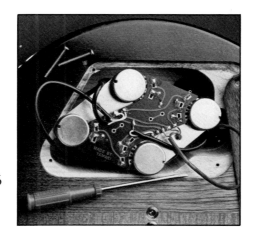

FOREWORD

When I was given my first guitar – a battered old Spanish thing – it had only five strings. The much-needed sixth string did not arrive until half a year later, at which time the possibilities of actually tuning the thing were slowly dawning on me. My first E, B and A seventh chords were learned by desperately trying to memorize the funny shapes I had seen older, more sophisticated youths playing in the yard at school – to which accompaniment they lustily sang a song called "Worried Man".

Despite the anxiety and desperation which dogged my first untutored steps on the guitar, I was nevertheless utterly seduced, and my mother's pleas to "stop banging that bloody thing and get on with your homework" fell upon deaf ears. Slowly, in the confines of the small bedroom I shared with my younger brother, I made progress. Within eighteen months or so I was, maybe naively, attempting to copy Django Reinhardt's solo on "Nuages" – the record of which I had stolen from my older brother.

As time passed, I met more and more guitar-mad kids with whom I was able to trade tricky chord shapes and the inevitable Hank Marvin lick. Naturally, I used these to my advantage with the girls and also as a means of one-upmanship with rival guitar players.

The point I am trying to make is that, had a book like this existed then, I would have saved myself a great deal of time and trouble. Now it is here. This book will provide you with a solid foundation for the basics of playing and the workings of the guitar. It took me many years to acquire the information presented here, and I envy those of you who can start with this wonderful advantage. I suggest that you take it step by step and have fun on the way: what we are climbing here is a mountain – and it never ends!

It is important to realize that the goal we are seeking is one which eventually transcends all considerations of plectrums and strings, etc. It is the realm of pure music. It is my belief that this book will provide you with the foundation and doorway into a world where wonders never cease.

Bon voyage!

Andy Summers

THE GUITAR INNOVATORS

A whole book could have been written on guitar innovators. Selecting which players to include and which would have to be omitted has been a difficult task. The final list should not be considered in any way complete – more as a personal choice. The guitarists who do appear here have all, in some way, made an original contribution to guitar playing. The range of their personalities, attitudes and backgrounds just goes to show that there is no single "ideal" way to play the guitar. The important thing to realize is that, glorious though the guitar's past may be, all the major innovators have simply used the guitar as a vehicle for their own individual musical self-expression. This is the common factor that links Frank Zappa with Django Reinhardt and Robert Fripp with Charlie Christian. The fifteen profiles contained in this chapter act as an introduction to the art of guitar playing. Listening to the recordings made by these players will give you a taste of what is possible on the acoustic or electric guitar, and will perhaps inspire you to make new advances in your own playing.

Django Reinhardt

Since he first came to prominence in the 1930s, the Belgian acoustic jazz guitarist Django Reinhardt has provided inspiration for generations of guitarists, as well as exhausting many a writer's stock of superlatives.

Jean Baptiste "Django" Reinhardt was born into a nomadic, caravan-dwelling gypsy family on 23rd January 1919. They travelled through Belgium and France during Django's early life, though Paris later became the centre of most of his musical activities. Django displayed an early interest in music and, by the age of thirteen, he was playing banjo or banjo guitar at the Bal-Musette, a notorious hangout of Parisian low-life during the 1920s. Django played distinctly European music, with a strong Spanish flavour, until he was about fifteen. It was then that he heard American jazz for the first time. He was converted instantly.

The now legendary tragedy struck when Django was just eighteen: he was severely burned when he accidentally started a fire in his caravan. After months of treatment, the 3rd and 4th fingers of his left hand were left permanently deformed and paralyzed. However, he not only fought and overcame the disability but also developed a unique range of techniques and a new style of playing.

In 1933, when Django and the violinist Stephane Grappelli were playing together in the same band at the Hotel Claridge in Paris, they decided to form their own group. In 1934,

it consisted of Django on guitar, Grappelli on violin, Django's brother Joseph and Roger Chaput on rhythm guitars, and Louis Vola on double bass. They were to become internationally famous as the Quintet du Hot Club de France. At their first concert, they created such a strong impression that the newly formed Ultraphone recording company offered to record them on a trial basis. This was before tape recording, so the session was cut direct-to-disc. The first title they recorded was "I Saw Stars" followed by "Lady Be Good", "Tiger Rag" and "Dinah". The company was impressed and gave them a firm contract. The quintet continued to work together until the outbreak of the Second World War.

In 1946, Django made his debut in America, touring the country with Duke Ellington. His records and his reputation had preceded him and he was received enthusiastically.

To this day there is a strong interest in Django's guitar playing, and records on which he is featured have sold steadily for the past fifty-five years. He has had thousands of imitators, but none have ever equalled his combined virtuosity, projection, expression and inventiveness on the acoustic guitar. Both his rhythm and single-note playing were devastating. Guitar strings are literally meant to "drive" the soundbox, and Django – probably using fairly heavy-gauge strings – had the power to make them do just that. He played

with such force that he wore out a guitar about every six months.

Django's name is synonymous with that of engineer and guitar designer, Mario Maccaferri. The distinctive acoustic guitars which Django was frequently seen playing (along with other guitarists in the quintet) were made by the Henry Selmer company of France to Maccaferri's individual designs (see p. 47). They were designed to give the maximum power, and were therefore ideally suited to Django's requirements – playing as he did in noisy clubs without the aid of amplification.

It is hard to list the qualities that went to make up Django's ability. The emotional content of his music was just as impressive as the technical skills he had at his disposal. His strong vibrato, individual octave playing (see p. 149) and exciting rhythm work have inspired generations of guitarists. His compositions rank among the best ever written for acoustic guitar. He didn't read music, and it is thought that he couldn't even read or write. Yet, at a private party, he astounded Segovia with his playing. When the father of the modern classical guitar asked him where he could buy the music for the piece, Django laughed and explained that he had just been improvising.

Django died at the age of 43 – in May 1953. He left a rich heritage of guitar music on record that continues to delight, confuse, confound and stimulate guitarists the world over.

Django Reinhardt with a Gibson electric (*above*)
Later in his career, Django experimented with electric guitars as well as his Maccaferri acoustics.

The Quintet du Hot Club de France (*right*)
The unique jazz "string quintet" formed by Django and Stephane Grappelli in 1934.

Charlie Christian

Although there were guitarists who had played amplified guitars before him, it was jazz musician Charlie Christian who established the electric guitar as a serious proposition. He developed the style of single-note, melodic electric guitar playing that placed the instrument on a par with the saxophone, trumpet, clarinet and other solo voices in jazz. He also combined a rhythmic percussive style with diminished and augmented chord structures in an original way that gave birth to what he and his co-innovators called "modern" jazz – though the form has since become widely known as "bop" or "bebop".

Charles Christian was born in Dallas, Texas, in 1919, though some jazz historians place his year of birth earlier, in 1916. His father was a singer-guitarist and his four brothers are all thought to have played musical instruments. The Christian family moved to Oklahoma when Charlie was just two years old.

He started off his interest in music by playing the trumpet at the age of twelve, but he also learned to play acoustic guitar, double bass and piano, thought not necessarily in that order. It was as a double-bass player that Christian got his first professional gig with Alphonso Trent's band in 1934. He played in several other bands before coming into contact with Eddie Durham sometime around 1937. Durham was an arranger, trombonist and pioneering electric guitarist with Count Basie.

Christian had been impressed with Durham's electric guitar work, and also by that of Floyd Smith who had been playing an amplified Hawaiian. When he met Durham, he quizzed him on his playing technique. At the time, Christian did not own a guitar, and, when Durham told him to get one of his own, he turned up with a five-dollar instrument that was just about as rough as they come. Durham was amused by the instrument but impressed with Christian's insatiable desire for information and his instant ability to assimilate all he was shown.

By 1938, Christian had acquired an "Electric Spanish" Gibson ES-150 guitar (see p. 54) and, in all probability, a Gibson amplifier. The guitar was the first model sold complete with a fitted magnetic pick-up. Suitably equipped, he rejoined Al Trent's band, but this time as a guitar player. The response to his playing, from both audiences and other musicians, combined astonishment with admiration. Though other guitarists – not least Django Reinhardt – had mastered the *acoustic* guitar as a solo voice, this was the first time an *electric* guitar had taken on such a role.

The pioneer of the electric guitar solo
A rare photograph of Charlie Christian – seen here playing a Gibson ES-150 fitted with the pick-up that was named after him. Almost single-handedly, Christian revolutionized the role of the guitar, and influenced the generation of guitarists that followed.

Christian was something of a local hero in Oklahoma by the time he was discovered by influential jazz entrepreneur John Hammond. He first met him on his way out to the West Coast to record jazz clarinettist and bandleader, Benny Goodman. He wired ahead to let Christian know he was coming and was met off the plane by the entire band, apart from Charlie, in an ageing Buick. At the Ritz, he met Christian, dressed in a ten-gallon hat, bright green suit, purple shirt, string bow-tie and pointed shoes that apparently hurt his feet. However, as soon as the band started to play, Hammond realized he was hearing something special. Christian was producing a seemingly endless flow of inventive musical ideas, playing a style unheard on electric guitar.

Hammond thought that Christian would be perfect for Benny Goodman's small jazz group, and he was flown to California for an audition. However, Goodman, displaying a "good musicians are a dime a dozen" attitude, showed no interest in Christian, claiming to be pre-occupied with more important things. That evening, Hammond sneaked Christian's guitar amplifier on stage while Goodman was having dinner prior to playing. When the band was ready, the kitchen door opened and the band-leader saw Christian heading for the band-stand. Enraged but forced to let the guitarist play for at least one number, Goodman counted the band into "Rose Room", a tune

that a black guitar picker from Oklahoma was unlikely to know. Of course, he was unaware that Christian needed to hear a chord sequence just once in order to improvise with total ease. Instead of being caught out, Christian played superb solos on chorus after chorus. Forty-five minutes later, the band finished the number to be greeted by the greatest ovation that Hammond had ever seen a Goodman group receive. That night the Benny Goodman quintet became a sextet.

Christian stayed with Goodman until his death less than two years later. But, after playing with Goodman in the evening, he would frequently head for Minton's Playhouse, a jazz club in Harlem. There he would play for hours with such formative jazz musicians as Dizzy Gillespie, Thelonius Monk and Charlie "The Bird" Parker. In fact, these four are considered to be the founders of bebop jazz, and Christian has been described as its "spiritual father".

Between 1940 and 1941, Christian was very busy. It is surprising that he packed so much activity into a period of less than two years, and fortunate that he was recorded so often.

In July of 1941, he collapsed and was admitted to Bellevue Hospital, New York, with tuberculosis. By the early part of 1942 while at Seaview Hospital, Staten Island, he was reported to be making progress towards some kind of recovery, but on 2nd March 1942, after contracting pneumonia, he died.

Chuck Berry

Charles Edward Berry was born in St Louis, Missouri, on 18th October 1931, or in San José, California, on 15th January 1926. Interviewers who have tried to ascertain which date is correct have been told by Berry, "that's personal and nobody's business".

He is a witty, sharp and suspicious man who makes a policy of avoiding interviews. He appears to loathe the media and love his audiences. No doubt his various clashes with the law – commencing with two years at reform school as a teenager for armed robbery – have a great deal to do with this attitude.

He is the most important founder-figure in the story of rock'n'roll guitar playing. His instantly recognizable guitar riffs, solos and rhythm playing complement perfectly the witty scenarios of teenage life in America during the fifties and sixties contained in his lyrics.

It would appear that Berry grew up in Elleardsville, St Louis, one of six children in a family, and that he sang at the Antioch Baptist Church Sunday School at the age of six. On the subject of his earliest influences, and what actually turned him on to music, he says:

"I suppose I could say music itself, because I was singing at the age of six – in church it began. Then the feeling to harmonize began to be a desire of mine. To get away from the normal melody and add my own melody and harmony was imperial, and I guess that grew into the appreciation for music. Rock'n'roll. Actually I don't think it was . . . matter of fact I know it wasn't called that then."

His most important early guitar influences were T-Bone Walker, Carl Hogan and B. B. King. He also listened to jazz and mentions a liking for Charlie Christian's work with the Benny Goodman band.

"Ah yes, jazz musicians. Well you could call Les Paul . . . I suppose he's a jazz musician. His "How High The Moon" is just beautiful. I wish I could run upon some musicians who knew it; we'd surely do it in one set."

His early vocal influences included Frank Sinatra, Little Richard and Nat King Cole. The latter's influence can be heard quite clearly on some of Berry's slow blues, in particular "The Wee Wee Hours".

Berry had "played around" on guitar while at High School but had not taken the instrument seriously until a local R&B performer by the name of Joe Sherman made him a present of a Kay electric. In the early fifties, Berry had a trio which played at small local functions. He had studied and at that time worked as a hairdresser in case his guitar playing could not always pay the rent. In fact, he hung on to his hairdressing booth right up until the time he was paid an advance on his first recording contract. He used to do a wide range of material in his efforts to get work, playing ballads and country music alongside his first love, the blues. His repertoire included both Nat King Cole and Hank Williams material.

During 1955, Berry admits to being thrilled when Muddy Waters let him sit in with his band one night to play a song. Waters was impressed by Berry's guitar playing and told him that he should go to see Leonard Chess at Chess Records in Chicago and "get him to record you". Berry went to Chess courtesy of the Waters introduction and took with him a demo tape of six songs that he had written and recorded on a cheap mono tape recorder. Chess was impressed and immediately offered Berry his first recording contract.

Though Berry was apparently keen to promote himself as a blues singer and guitarist (through a slow blues on the tape – "The Wee Wee Hours"), Leonard Chess saw greater sales potential in the up-tempo song "Maybellene" which brought elements of country music and the blues together in a new and accessible way.

Chess put out "Maybellene" as an A-side, and it became a top-ten hit almost immediately.

The importance of "Maybellene" cannot be over-estimated. Its success was obviously good for Berry, but it was also good for Chess Records. The sales of their previous records – those by Muddy Waters, for example – had been limited to a dominantly black audience. "Maybellene" was certainly one of the very first rock'n'roll songs to break through to white audiences on a large scale. It was not until January of 1956, the following year, that Elvis Presley had his first major national hit with "Heartbreak Hotel".

Berry followed his success by going on to write, perform and record a series of songs which collectively made up the greatest contribution any individual has made to rock'n'roll. The succession of gems include "Roll Over Beethoven", "Johnny B. Goode", "Sweet Little Sixteen" and "Brown Eyed Handsome Man".

At the height of his powers, at the end of the fifties, Berry had another run in with the law.

The original rock'n'roller (*left*) Although it is impossible to point to one single record as representing the birth of rock'n'roll, Chuck Berry's song "Maybellene" – released in 1955 – must certainly be one of the contenders. It combined elements from both country music and blues in a completely new way, and its success opened up a huge market for the new music. As Leonard Chess (the owner of Chess Records) is credited as having said – "the big beat, the cars, and young love: it was a trend and we jumped on it".

The showman (*right*) Chuck Berry in performance – combining theatrics, stage presence, distinctive lyrics set to simple blues-based chord structures, and what, at the time, was a brand new guitar style.

He was charged with violation of the Mann Act which prohibits the transportation of a minor across a state line for immoral purposes. The racialist attitudes displayed at his first trial were so flagrant that a re-trial was granted. But two years later the verdict finally went against him, and he found himself unable to get out of serving a two-year prison sentence.

However, he had not been idle during the time he had been waiting for the re-trial. He had added to a stockpile of recorded masters that Chess were to continue to release during his incarceration. The titles included "Bye, Bye Johnny", "Our Little Rendezvous", "Worried Life Blues", "Route 66", "Talkin' 'Bout You", "Go, Go, Go", "Come On", "Down The Road Apiece", "Too Much Monkey Business", "Memphis, Tennessee" and "Reelin' and Rockin'".

Throughout most of his playing career, Berry has chosen to work with resident bands, travelling alone with his guitar and making the promoter responsible for arranging for an amplifier and backing band. This produced some interesting performances, such as the time he turned up to discover The Steve Miller Band were to provide the backing for a gig that was to be recorded. On other occasions, devoted followers have been sadly disappointed by a poor performance, due mainly to the standard of the musicians with which promoters frequently fobbed him off. Berry rarely rehearses with a band. If he does, it is likely to be for a maximum of thirty minutes. He'll tell musicians that if they're playing when he brings his foot down, they stop, and if they're not playing when he brings his foot down, they start.

Berry's principal aim is and always has been to "entertain", whether in front of 200 or 200,000 people. He shows little preference as far as amplification is concerned: if it works, that seems to be OK. He has nearly always played Gibson semi-acoustic guitars, frequently an ES-335 stereo model.

While it is true to say he has always been an entertainer, it is also true to say he is one of the most important rock musicians of all time. The surprising point is that he seems aware of his value as the former but not the latter.

The "duck walk" (right)
This is how Chuck Berry describes the first time he did the "duck walk" at the Paramount Theater in 1956:

"I had to outfit my trio, the three of us, and I always remember that the suits cost me 66 dollars – 22 dollars apiece. We had to buy shoes and everything. So, anyway, when we got to New York, the suits – they were rayon – but looked like seersucker by the time we got there . . . so we had one suit, we didn't know we were supposed to change. I actually did that duck walk to hide the wrinkles in the suit. I got an ovation, so I figured I pleased the audience. So I did it again, and again, and I'll probably do it again tonight."

Bo Diddley

Bo Diddley, an ex-boxer, was a contemporary and stablemate of Chuck Berry, also recording on the Chicago-based Chess label. His music was heavily influenced by post-war Chicago blues, but what separated him from all other performers in the idiom was his totally unique "jungle rhythms", as he called them. He rarely played twelve-bar blues, choosing instead to make the verses of his songs long and remaining for some time on one chord, changing only for the chorus or hook lines. His distinctive rhythmic style tended to rely on the line-up of his band. It featured Diddley on guitar and vocals, Jerome Arnold on maracas, Otis Span on piano, Billy Boy Arnold on harmonica, and Diddley's half-sister, the "Duchess". Diddley's rhythm guitar, along with Jerome's maracas, the bass drums and piano, fused together to create the rhythms.

Diddley heavily influenced some of his contemporaries and his first record release, "Bo Diddley", has been recorded and performed on stage by a wide spectrum of artists, most noticeably by Buddy Holly. The Rolling Stones and many others featured note-for-note arrangements of many of his songs on stage and on record. Diddley's influence is further underlined by the fact that David Bowie used the basic structure of Diddley's "Cops and Robbers" when he put together "Jean Genie" years later.

Bo Diddley was born Elias McDaniel in McComb, Mississippi, on 29th December 1928 but grew up in Chicago where he was exposed to post-war blues. As a boy he played violin before switching to guitar. In the best tradition of the early rock'n'roll performers, Diddley had a visual gimmick. He had his guitars made for him by Gretsch in an amazing assortment of sizes, shapes and finishes. These included oblong guitars and some that were even covered with fur.

Vintage Bo Diddley (*above*)
One of the "gutsiest" of the early rock'n'roll guitarists, Diddley's classic records were heavily blues-based and featured his distinctive, syncopated "jungle rhythms". His style found its way into the sound of many of the most successful sixties rock bands in America and in Britain.

A connoisseur of guitar design (*right*)
Having made up his mind that he "always wanted a guitar that was different", Diddley got Gretsch to build him a series of custom-made instruments. Of the various different models – each with its own level of eccentricity – the oblong-shape was the most enduring. There are only four in existence, and he owns them all.

B. B. King

B. B. King was born Riley King on 16th September 1925 in Itta Bena, Mississippi. From the age of eight, he worked full time on a plantation, walking miles to a schoolhouse on the days when it rained. He was paid 35 cents for every hundred pounds of cotton he picked. King first got hooked on the blues through hearing records by Blind Lemon Jefferson, T-Bone Walker and Lonnie Johnson which a teenage aunt would bring home. He was also strongly influenced by Gospel music.

By the time he was fourteen he got his first guitar – a three-quarter sized Stella costing fifteen dollars. Since that was his monthly salary at the time, he paid seven dollars and fifty cents down and the balance the following month. His next guitar was a Gibson acoustic which he bought with some help from a country cousin – the legendary blues bottleneck player, Bukka White – and on which he put a DeArmond pick-up. He also had an early Fender Telecaster but has been using Gibson ES-335 guitars since around 1958. The instrument he is currently playing is a custom-built guitar made by Gibson. It is based on a 335 but has a closed body with no f-holes to reduce the amount of uncontrolled feedback. Previously, King had stuffed the insides of his 335s with towels in order to overcome the problem. The

tailpiece is a Gibson TP-6 which is tuned at the back of the instrument. He claims this new style doesn't snag his cuffs and hands the way the old ones used to. His first choice for amps is Gibson. He now uses Gibson 740XL strings.

B. B. King developed the ability to play several instruments with varying proficiency, and reads music though he is not a fast sight-reader. He is also a "musicologist" and now owns a collection of 30,000 records, the beginnings of which date back to his days as a DJ.

He acquired the initials "B. B." early in his career when Sonny Boy Williamson II (Rice Boy), hosting the American King Biscuit, gave him a ten-minute, unpaid DJ spot on the show. They nicknamed him "The Blues Boy from Beale Street" which was eventually abbreviated to the initials B. B. Between shows, B. B. would play guitar with visiting jazz and blues musicians.

B. B. King was a great fan of Charlie Christian and Django Reinhardt, and their influence can be heard in his playing. He combined some of the raw elements of the blues with the cleaner, more concise, melodic approach of the jazz players. King still claims that he can only play single-note leads, though he knows a few chords. He says he has never played rhythm and isn't very good at it. He also

finds it impossible to play guitar and sing at the same time.

B. B. King is thought to be the originator of the vibrato technique of moving the finger in small movements across the string rather than along its length. Asked about this, he said ". . . I won't say I invented it, but they weren't doing it before I started". He was also one of the pioneers of note-bending techniques, first developed to simulate the bottleneck style of players such as Elmore James, and now regarded as an integral part of blues and rock guitar playing.

B. B. King's first record release was "Miss Martha King" on the Bullet label in 1949. Then, after recording for a number of small labels, he had his first national hit on the R&B charts in 1950 with a song called "Three O'Clock Blues". Successes that followed included "Woke Up This Morning", "Sweet Little Angel", and "Eyesight To The Blind". In the early sixties, he recorded the "Live At The Regal" album which is generally regarded as his finest. Two highly-rated albums followed. They were "Alive And Well" and "Completely Well". King's own personal favourite is the next album he recorded, "Indianola Mississippi Seeds", with Leon Russell, Joe Walsh and Carole King in support.

Making the guitar "sing" (*right*) When a critic once said in a review of one of his performances that B. B. would sing and then he would make Lucille sing, King regarded it as the greatest of compliments. His whole approach revolves around making his playing as expressive as possible. And he achieves it, not by playing as many notes as quickly as he can, but by injecting a maximum of feeling into his music – sometimes with just one note, bent, twisted and shaped with faultless control.

"Lucille" (*left*) During 1949, King played some weekend dates at a place named Twist in Arkansas. One night a fight broke out and there was a fire. Everybody rushed to get out of the building, including King, but once safe he realized he had left his guitar behind. He rushed back inside and managed to get out with it just before the building collapsed. The next day he learned that the fight had been over a girl named Lucille. Ever since he has called his current guitar "Lucille" – to remind himself that there are plenty of guitars around but only one B. B. King.

The inveterate tourer (*far left*) This shot shows B. B. King on stage in 1981. Like many of the great blues players, he thrives on live appearances, and still does around three hundred every year. During his career, he has recorded over three hundred titles and fifty albums.

Freddie King

Freddie King was born in Gilmer, Texas, in 1934. His mother and his uncles played guitar, exposing Freddie to blues and gospel music when he was just a small child. He started to play guitar at the age of six, and his first instrument was a Silvertone acoustic. His influences included many of the major blues players. He mentions Lightnin' Hopkins, Robert Johnson, T-Bone Walker, Muddy Waters, Jimmy Rogers (who played in Waters' band), B. B. King and many others as being players he listened to at one time or another. He moved on to electric guitar during his early teens. Before long, he was making trips to Chicago to seek out the guitar players he had heard on record. In 1975, he told me:

"Well, that was a Blues Town. It was the bluesiest town I ever knew! Every youngster you'd see there was playing the blues. There were a lot of players but they were from all over the country. From Mississippi, Louisiana, yeah . . . Alabama, Arkansas. All those guys livin' and playin' there but they were from the South."

King says that he played on a number of sessions with some of the major players before recording under his own name. He mentions Howlin' Wolf, Muddy Waters, and harmonica player Little Walter in this context. He had a great deal of respect for Howlin' Wolf:

"Well, Wolf, he played some rockin' stuff, man. He's just not a laid-back cat all the time. He'd get up and move, you know? . . . So I put my style right between T-Bone, Muddy Waters, Lightnin' Hopkins and B. B. King. Now T-Bone, he's the first cat that started this style on electric, and he was followed by B. B. King."

Though he recorded under his own name as early as 1956 (on the El-Bee label), it was not until 1961 that he had his first major success on record. At the time, he had been making a living by driving a bulldozer during the day and playing the blues at night.

"Yeah, that was "Hideaway". Well, the first release was "Have You Ever Loved A Woman" and "You've Got To Have Love With A Feelin' ". Then came "Hideaway". Then just some pickin' on things like "San José". At that time I made a whole album of instrumentals. People think it was my first album, but it wasn't. My first album was "Freddie King Sings" and it was all vocals. Then the all-instrumental one was second."

The inventor of many classic "blues licks"
Freddie King, seen here shortly before his death, was one of the most imaginative and consistent of the great blues players. One way or another, his blues licks have found their way into almost every rock guitarist's style.

As he points out, his first album release was "Freddie King Sings" and was all vocal. The instrumental "Let's Hide Away And Dance Away With Freddie King" followed. Incredibly, it was also subsequently re-packaged and marketed as "Freddie King Goes Surfin' ".

After some recordings for Leon Russell's Shelter label he finally signed with RSO Records. His last two albums were recorded for that label with production by Mike Vernon. The titles were "Burglar" (with a guest appearance by Eric Clapton) and "Larger Than Life".

While playing a gig in Dallas on Christmas Day 1976, Freddie King suffered a fatal heart attack. He played a number of Gibson guitars throughout his professional life. For "Hideaway" and most of his influential instrumental recordings, he used a vintage Gibson Les Paul. On stage he also used a Gibson ES-335, ES-345 and an ES-355. His top three strings were light gauge and unwound, and he used Gibson medium gauge for the three bass strings. Since his early days in Chicago, he wore a plastic thumbpick and a steel fingerpick on his 1st finger, using the thumb to pick out bass lines and the fingerpick for treble lead lines. At one time, people thought mistakenly that Freddie and B.B. King were brothers.

Duane Eddy

The fact that dazzling technique is not necessarily an integral feature of good rock'n'roll guitar playing is exemplified by the remarkably successful career of Duane Eddy during the late fifties and early sixties. In England during 1960, *New Musical Express* readers voted him "The World's Top Musical Personality" ahead of Elvis Presley and Frank Sinatra. At the time, wherever rock'n'roll was popular, village halls, ballrooms and clubs reverberated with the sound of thousands of guitarists imitating Duane Eddy's sound.

Duane Eddy was born in Corning, New York, on 26th April 1938 but did most of his growing up in Arizona. He took up guitar at the age of five, learning first on an old Martin acoustic. For his thirteenth birthday, he was given a Gibson Les Paul which he had traded in for a Gretsch Chet Atkins by the time he was fifteen, when he was sitting in at local road-houses with Al Casey's band. He was influenced by jazz, country and blues guitarists including Chet Atkins, Les Paul, Howard Roberts, Charlie Christian, B. B. King, and also Barney Kessel whom he particularly admired.

Much of the music he was to record was a true development of what many of these guitarists had been playing, but it appeared only on later albums and B-sides of singles. His "Three-Thirty Blues", for example, was a test piece for aspiring guitarists that was also a unique example of blues guitar playing in a rock setting. In Britain, his influence on young guitar players was enormous.

However, for his initial success, he had to severely limit his playing ability to record-producer Lee Hazlewood's concept of a simple, saleable format. Duane Eddy's commercial success was all about sound, feel and basic melody. He reaped considerable benefit from the enforced discipline, becoming the biggest-selling instrumentalist of his day.

At the time, many people thought that he tuned his guitar right down. In fact, Eddy would write and play most of the tunes in A and E, allowing open-string root notes to ring on. The problem was that these were not necessarily good keys for Plas Johnson who played the fiery sax solos which were an important part of the records. Therefore, Eddy would tune his guitar down a semi-tone so that his fingerings would be the same but he could play in A flat and E flat, or he would tune *up* a semi-tone to play in F and B flat. Tuning variations also avoided the monotonous effect of successive songs in the same one or two keys. Later, he experimented further.

"On the "Twangs The Thang" album I used the Danelectro which was an octave lower than a regular guitar, all bass strings. They were the first to come out with all six strings an octave lower than a regular guitar. It was a six-string bass guitar."

Duane Eddy was nineteen years old when, in 1957, he cut his first hit with Hazlewood at Audio Recorders Studio, Arizona. According to the guitarist, the sound and concept should be jointly accredited to Hazlewood, Casey and himself. The simple melody lines played on the bass strings were greatly enhanced by Hazlewood's pioneering recording techniques. A grain silo (an airproof chamber used for storing grain) was used to create the reverberating "big sound". Eddy's use of the tremelo arm to create vibrato and sliding notes was integral to the sound, as was the use of a fairly slow electronic vibrato, probably built into the amp.

Eddy stuck to playing his original Gretsch Chet Atkins most of the time, in spite of the fact that he worked with Guild on the development of a "Duane Eddy" model that sold quite well. He, himself, only used the guitar on stage for a while. He was unhappy with the pick-ups that Guild used on the early models and appears to have lost interest in the endorsement deal.

In the early days, he used a souped-up Magnaton amplifier. Later, Tom Macormack of Phoenix built him a custom-made 100-watt model which he used virtually throughout the influential period of his recording career. By 1975, he was using solid-state amps on the road for convenience.

The instrumental era (*below*) Duane Eddy's "twangy" bass-string style influenced a tide of instrumental bands.

The "Guitar Man" (*above*) Best known for his Gretsch Chet Atkins, Eddy also used a classical guitar.

Eric Clapton

Eric Clapton was born in Ripley, Surrey, on 30th March 1945 and was raised by his grandparents. In his early teens he was given a guitar but was unenthusiastic about playing it at the time. After a fairly uneventful early education, he went on to attend Kingston College of Art but was eventually asked to leave – due to his total lack of interest and because he was considered a subversive influence on other students.

After hearing blues tunes on the radio, he developed an interest in the music. He sought out records by American musicians including Muddy Waters and Big Bill Broonzy, and was soon playing along with the records on his previously discarded guitar. Like others of his day, he also cites Chuck Berry and Buddy Holly as major influences along with the ethnic blues players.

When asked if B. B. King was a strong influence when he began playing, Clapton replied:

"Always was in those days, yeh. Not as much as Freddie King, I don't think, because Freddie always had a funkier style of playing. B. B. was always clean – Freddie always had that distorted style even right at the beginning."

1963 was to be a hectic year for the British R&B scene. Alexis Korner was the father figure of the movement, but the Stones had taken over as the focus of attention, particularly when their single of Chuck Berry's "Come On" made the national charts. Halfway through the year, the Yardbirds emerged, and, although Clapton had joined a band called the Roosters, he accepted an offer to join them. The Stones had just moved on from the small club circuit, and, at the Crawdaddy Club in Richmond, the Yardbirds took over the Stones' previous Sunday-night residency. Eric recalled:

"I used to live there, it was incredible. It was better when they (the Stones) were playing there because they took half the crowd with them when they left, and it took us quite a while to build up our own sort of following. It was never really the same though. Obviously it wasn't the same for us anyway to be on stage after having been part of the audience."

At the time, Eric was a self-confessed blues purist – quietly serious about his music and unwilling to compromise. Although rock historians paint a picture of the Stones as having been the commercially-inclined band while the Yardbirds were the purists, this just was not so. As far as records were concerned, the Stones' first single was laden with slide guitar, harmonica and Chuck Berry guitar riffs, whereas the Yardbirds' first single (released in 1965) was the pop-mainstream "For Your Love". Clapton described the circumstances:

"It stemmed from the fact that Georgio (the Yardbirds' manager) or maybe even us, decided that we were going to have a hit single. And everyone started to contribute ideas of what they thought was going to be a good hit single. It finally came down to a split choice as to whether we did this Graham Gouldman song "For Your Love", which was Paul Samwell-Smith's idea, or this Otis Redding song which was my idea. I'd never heard of Otis before and I'd just got this one single which Georgio had given me and I just wanted to do that."

"For Your Love" was chosen, recorded and considered by all but Clapton to be the perfect single. The result was that Clapton left. A teen magazine called *Rave* quoted him as saying at the time, "For me to face myself, I have to play what I believe is pure and sincere and uncorrupted music. That is why I had to leave."

In later years he found the remarks amusing and reflected that he had probably been childish over the affair. None-the-less, the magazine interview caught the eye of blues crusader, John Mayall, who led his own band, the Bluesbreakers. He contacted Clapton, and soon after (in 1965) the guitarist joined his group.

By this time, Clapton had already built up a considerable personal following. Though one or two guitarists were already playing good blues guitar, Clapton was outstanding. He had perfected the feedback-assisted sustain and the overdriven valve-amp sound with Marshall amplifiers. At the time, there was no such thing as a set of light-gauge strings with an unwound 3rd. Clapton improvised his own, using a banjo string to replace the traditional wound 3rd string. This extended his treble soloing range and assisted note-bending. With the American blues players as his inspiration, he developed a superior blend of technique and control, producing guitar solos which had an unequalled power and emotion.

Sound systems then consisted of 100 watt amplifiers used with a pair of column speakers. Instrument amplification was also generally limited by today's standards, yet Clapton's guitar always seemed to cut through. If the Bluesbreakers played for more than twenty minutes or so without featuring Clapton, the audience would begin to call to Mayall, "Give

Cream's final performance (*left*) Jack Bruce, Ginger Baker and Eric Clapton on stage at the Royal Albert Hall in London in 1968 for their last live performance as Cream.

Beyond the myth of the guitar hero (*right*) No other guitarist has ever been saddled with super-star status to quite the same extent as Clapton. Since the early seventies, his career has been marked by a concerted – and partially successful – attempt to break out of the restrictions that the adulation imposed and to change the direction of his music.

God a solo", and he would give the OK for Clapton to launch into a blistering version of Freddie King's "Hideaway" or something similar. Graffiti started to appear on the walls of clubs up and down the country – "Clapton is God". For better or worse, the age of the guitar hero had begun.

Examples of Clapton's superb playing at this time can be heard on the album "Bluesbreakers: John Mayall With Eric Clapton" which was recorded live at Klooks Kleek Club in West Hampstead, London. By the time Clapton left the Bluesbreakers in 1966, his following was such that Mayall had a severe problem trying to find a replacement. Although hundreds of up-and-coming guitarists were already emulating Clapton's playing, none had quite the same impact. Eventually some fine players did emerge as Bluesbreakers. They included Peter Green (who later formed Fleetwood Mac) and Mick Taylor (who went on to join the Stones).

By 1966, certain musicians had acquired the sort of individual reputation previously associated more with jazz. Two who had become very highly rated indeed were bass guitarist Jack Bruce and drummer Ginger Baker. Baker suggested to Clapton that they should get a bass player and form a trio to play blues. Jack Bruce was the obvious choice, and together the three formed Cream.

The group were to do far more than play straight blues. Jack Bruce had a classical music background and had played in various blues, R&B and jazz groups. His songs, with lyrics supplied by the poet Pete Brown, were impossible to fit into any category. And Baker, though he played in the heavily R&B influenced Graham Bond Organisation with Bruce was essentially a jazz drummer. Clapton, of course, had his roots firmly planted in the blues. Each of the three took it in turns to display their individual virtuosity on different numbers. On other occasions, they would fuse together brilliantly, frequently finding their strongest common ground on the blues-based numbers featuring Clapton's guitar playing. Heavy guitar riffs, sometimes played in unison with the bass guitar, became one of Cream's most recognizable and most often-copied trademarks. "Sunshine Of Your Love", for example, featured the famous combined guitar-and-bass riff that launched a thousand bands. Other classic tracks include "Politician", "I Feel Free", "Crossroads", "Strange Brew", "I'm So Glad" and the later "Badge".

Cream's initial success was in America, where they took rock music to the huge venues. Jack Bruce once told me:

"We were the first to do Madison Square Gardens, for instance. Hendrix did it next. We made so much money out of it: it was great because they didn't realize how big our audience was so they didn't charge us much to hire it. They thought maybe three hundred people would turn up, and it was jampacked full. It was fabulous."

On stage in Philadelphia in 1975
Clapton was back touring again. This was the year of the album that was originally to be titled "The Best Guitarist In The World – There's One In Every Crowd". The first phrase was dropped when Clapton was persuaded that too many people would miss the joke he intended.

The three members of the group have given different reasons for the disbanding of Cream. Clapton claimed that, among other things, he had grown tired of mediating between the feuding Baker and Bruce. He was also bored by the whole "God" thing. He complained that it made no difference how well or badly the band played; the audience adulation continued unabated. When *Rolling Stone* magazine reviewed a Cream concert and described Clapton as the ". . . master of the cliche", that was the last straw. Moreover, he was beginning to feel the need of a change in direction.

"Another interesting factor was that I got the tapes of "Music From The Big Pink" (the first album by The Band) and I thought, well, this is what I want to play, not extended solos and maestro bullshit, but just good funky songs. The combination of the "Rolling Stone" thing and hearing "Big Pink" decided for me that I was going to split Cream."

Early in 1969, Eric Clapton and Ginger Baker joined forces with bass guitarist Rick Grech and Clapton's close friend Steve Winwood to form Blind Faith. It was a case of the total not being

equal to the sum of the parts. After the band split up, there followed a short spell during which Clapton, in a reaction against the superstar tag, played as a backing guitarist with Delaney & bonnie and Friends. Later he was to describe his decision to do so as a "mistake".

In 1970, Clapton formed his own band for the first time. It included top American musicians Carl Radle (bass guitar), George Terry (guitar) and singer Yvonne Elliman. Clapton insisted that his name was not to be featured, and the band was called Derek and the Dominoes.

Clapton took his band to Criteria Studios, Miami, to record an album. After three days, they decided to take an evening off to go to a nearby open-air concert being given by the Allman Brothers. Eric had heard Duane Allman's impressive guitar work on record and wanted to see him live. Afterwards, Clapton invited the Allmans back to the studio for a jam session. Duane Allman stayed, and at the end of ten days they had completed enough material for the double album "Layla and Other Assorted Love Songs". Clapton later described Duane Allman as "the catalyst for the whole thing".

The recording of the album was punctuated by regular and open drug-taking. But Clapton paid little heed to warnings, and, back in England soon afterwards, he was living the life of a reclusive addict in his home in Surrey, supporting a £1,000-per-week heroin habit. During his addiction – which he later called "a waste of three years" – he turned in a well-below-par performance at George Harrison's Madison Square Gardens concert for Bangladesh. Caught out in New York, unable to obtain heroin of sufficient purity to be taken orally, he spent most of the week that had been set aside for rehearsals in his hotel fighting withdrawal symptoms. Pete Townshend, concerned about Clapton, later stepped in and was the driving force behind the so-called "Come Back" concert at London's Rainbow Theatre on 13th January 1973.

It was not until the early part of 1974 that Clapton finally beat his addiction by taking an electro-acupuncture cure. He went back to work, recording his highly rated "461 Boulevard" album and returning to live work. The live album "E. C. Was Here" recorded during 1975 had Eric demonstrating that his guitar playing was in fine shape.

Clapton's guitars and amps

While playing with the Yardbirds, Bluesbreakers and Cream, Clapton developed the style of American electric blues guitar which used valve amps virtually as an extension of the instrument. As well as being used purely for amplification, it contributed to the actual sound. Up until he left the Bluesbreakers, he used a combo amp. With Cream, he moved on to stacks consisting of separate 4 x 12 speaker cabinets in conjunction with individual amps.

Initially, he used a variety of electric guitars – in particular, Gibsons which, with their distinctive humbucking sound, were ideally suited to blues-based guitar playing. In fact, he was one of the first British guitarists to discover how perfect the vintage Les Paul guitars were for this style of playing.

When, in 1968, he heard the Band's "Music From The Big Pink" album, he was influenced both by the way they worked as a tight, co-operative unit and by the guitar playing of Robbie Robertson. Robertson used Fender Stratocaster and Telecaster guitars, with their characteristic cleaner sound. Soon after, Clapton was seen playing Strats more than any other models. By the 1980s, Clapton was using three Stratocasters for stage work. His favourite he dubbed "Blackie", a black 1956 instrument. The other two are 1954 and 1965 models.

Clapton has a collection of acoustics including a wood-body Dobro, a huge custom-built Tony Zemaitis twelve-string, and a Martin D–28 fitted with a Barcus Berry Hot Dot.

He uses a Music Man HD–130 Reverb amplifier with special open-back cabinets. He also has a Leslie speaker cabinet fitted with JBL speakers. The only effects he uses are a faithful old Cry Baby wah-wah, and an MXR analog delay unit.

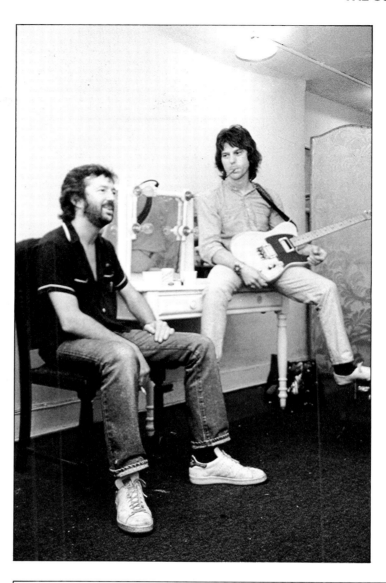

Clapton with Jeff Beck Shot backstage in London in 1981, Clapton and Beck appeared together as part of The Secret Policeman's Other Ball – a concert in aid of Amnesty International.

The background to the British blues boom

During the 1950s, the club scene in Britain was dominated by musicians emulating New Orleans and Dixieland traditional jazz bands, with forays into American blues. Chris Barber's jazz band, for example, had a banjo, guitar and an occasional vocalist named Lonnie Donegan. On a live album of the band, Donegan performed a couple of blues songs as a "novelty feature". One of them was the traditional song associated with Leadbelly, "Rock Island Line". When it was released as the A-side of a single, it was a huge hit, making Donegan a star in his own right. He went on to become the figurehead for a brand-new musical craze called "skiffle".

Concurrently – but attracting far less attention – singer, guitarist and "bluesologist" Alexis Korner was performing his versions of the ethnic blues originated by Muddy Waters, Big Bill Broonzy and others. He started the London Blues and Barrelhouse Club at the Roundhouse pub in central London in the late 1950s. At the time, the music did not attract an audience big enough to sustain the venture. In March 1962, he tried again and started the Ealing Club in London. On this occasion, he got the timing just right. The main attraction at the club was the band he formed called Blues Incorporated. Initial line-ups included pioneer electric blues guitarist Jeff Bradford, and drummer Charlie Watts, soon to be a founder member of the Stones.

Not only was there a new audience developing for the music, but Korner was inundated with musicians who wanted to join his band or just sit in for a couple of numbers at the club. They included Mick Jagger, Paul Jones, Long John Baldry, Eric Burdon, Dick Heckstall-Smith, Graham Bond, Jack Bruce, Ginger Baker, Brian Jones, Keith Richards, John McLaughlin, John Surman, Davey Graham, and many others. The movement mushroomed, dominating the club scene and taking over from revivalist, traditional jazz. A guitarist who sang in local pubs for pints of beer and who would occasionally cover at the Ealing Club for Mick Jagger "when he had a sore throat" was Eric Clapton.

Jeff Beck

Jeff Beck, born in Surrey, England, in June 1944, first gained attention as an important guitarist when he joined the Yardbirds in 1965 as Eric Clapton's replacement. At the time, the Yardbirds were going through a transitional phase, relying less on the inspirational thrust of American blues music and moving on to develop their own ideas. Beck was later to describe them as "the first psychedelic band" Though Beck and Clapton had similar blues roots, Beck was far more suited to the Yardbirds' increasingly experimental approach. As time passed, he proved to be a musician constantly on the lookout for new sounds, textures and means of expression through his guitar playing. Clapton remains, to this day, essentially a blues guitarist.

During 1966, the Yardbirds managed to lure Jimmy Page away from the lucrative session work he had been doing as a guitarist and persuaded him to take up bass with the group. When Beck became ill at one point, Page did a quick switch to lead so that the group could continue. When Beck recovered and rejoined the band, there was a short spell during which the Yardbirds featured both Page *and* Beck playing lead guitar. However, on a particularly gruelling tour of America in the same year, Beck again claimed to be ill. The band didn't buy it, and he was sacked. There is a certain amount of confusion over whether he jumped or was pushed. The Yardbirds continued with Keith Relf (vocals/harmonica), Jimmy Page (lead guitar), Chris Dreja (bass guitar) and Jim McCarty (drums) until 1968. Page was then left as the only original member in the group he put together to fulfil outstanding tour dates as "The New Yardbirds". Almost immediately, they changed the name to Led Zeppelin.

In the meantime, Beck had embarked on a solo career, and had some initial success in the singles charts with the aid of producer Micky Most. The vocal "Hi Ho Silver Lining" was the most successful, though its B-side, "Beck's Bolero", was far more interesting – featuring as it did Keith Moon, Jimmy Page, John Paul Jones and Nicky Hopkins.

As a result of his earlier work with the Yardbirds, Beck became established as a highly rated guitarist – as well as something of a mixture of pop star and cult-figure. From that position, he was able to form what was to be the first of a long line of Jeff Beck Groups. However, whether it was due to their diverse personalities or their different musical backgrounds, the first line-up never even got past the rehearsal stage. Beck, who by this time had a reputation for being abrasive and difficult, at least deserves an award for the optimism of his attempt to put himself, Rod Stewart, Jet Harris, Viv Prince and Ron Wood together in one band. Be that as it may, when drummer Aynsley Dunbar joined Stewart, Wood and Beck, cohesion was achieved, and Beck was on

The Yardbirds
Seen here performing live in front of the cameras for the British television series "Ready Steady Go", the Yardbirds were one of the most interesting of the mid-sixties groups. Beck is on the right playing the sunburst Gibson Les Paul. In his early days in the band, the Yardbirds made a cameo appearance in Antonioni's movie *Blow Up*. Beck can be seen rather unconvincingly smashing a guitar in the manner of Pete Townshend.

his way. The albums "Truth" and "Beckola", along with the band's live appearances, enhanced Beck's reputation as an outstanding guitarist and established him as a major performer. Stewart and Wood remained with Beck until 1969. Stewart has admitted to the trouble he had pandering to Beck's somewhat overbearing attitude, but suppression of his own egotistic tendencies paid off: it was the recognition he gained while singing with Beck that provided him with the launch pad for the Faces and then his own mega-star success.

By the end of the sixties, the parallel development of Clapton, Townshend, Beck, Page and the mighty Hendrix had established the broad base of British rock guitar playing. But, in terms of commercial success, Beck was at least partially eclipsed by the others. There was no doubt that the powerhouse guitar, bass and drums trios were more popular. This disparity looked as though it might be overcome with plans for the formation of the cooperative trio Beck, Bogert and Appice.

Beck had been quite close to Tim Bogert (bass) and Carmine Appice (drums) ever since their early days as half of the American band Vanilla Fudge. The association dated back to Beck's days as a Yardbird. While in New York to record a jingle for Great Shakes, he went to a club to hear Vanilla Fudge, and, when their lead guitarist failed to show up, Beck accepted an invitation to cover for him. Beck, Bogert and Appice enjoyed working together enough to want to do it again, but the idea was shelved until the end of the sixties when they were all free at last. However, in 1969 Beck was in a serious car crash and sustained injuries bad enough to keep him out of action for over a

year. Bogert and Appice joined Cactus and, when Beck recovered, he formed another band of his own. Two albums – "Rough And Ready" and "Jeff Beck Group" – followed. It wasn't until 1972 that Beck, Bogert and Appice finally formed their trio.

Unfortunately, Beck's obsession with the idea of the band seems to have blinded him to the fact that time had marched on and that the concept of the powerhouse trio was outdated. Almost as soon as the group was formed, Beck appeared to realize this. They recorded two albums, but only one was released. The experience brought a few truths home to Beck. His style of playing had been adopted by countless imitators. The whole "guitar hero" thing had been played to death. Although Beck had always been an experimenter and an innovator, a master of texture, sound and control, he now needed a new inspiration. He withdrew from the rock scene altogether and began a period of self-examination and experimentation. By this time, he was well aware of the handful of musicians – in particular, Stevie Wonder – who were able to combine a high level of musicianship with popular appeal. And when John McLaughlin's Mahavishnu Orchestra emerged, Beck was taken aback by the keyboard and synthesizer playing of Jan Hammer. He came under the influence of Hammer, just as he had with the early blues players some ten years earlier. For a time, he even considered changing to keyboard synthesizers. He also tried a guitar synth – but without success.

In 1975, with the release of his "Blow By Blow" album, produced by George Martin, Beck appeared as a very different guitarist, combining elements of the newly emergent jazz-rock with a dash of funk and a pinch of soul. Max Middleton, the keyboard player who had been hired to work with Beck, Bogert and Appice, joined Beck on "Blow By Blow" rehearsing with him and stimulating fresh ideas.

Although many of Beck's followers were disappointed with his new style of music, others were not. "Blow By Blow" was a big seller. As far as Beck was concerned, it marked the end of a period of frustration and the beginning of a period in which he could play music he believed in.

More of the same followed with another album produced by George Martin. "Wired" featured both Max Middleton and Jan Hammer. On this recording Beck moved further into jazz-rock. The music was less accessible than on "Blow By Blow". It was, however, also less individual and original.

Beck consolidated his association with Hammer by touring with his group. This produced the "Jeff Beck With The Jan Hammer Group – Live" album. Beck's guest appearances on other people's records bear out the fact that he had become a highly respected musician. Two outstanding examples are "Lookin' For Another Pure Love" on Stevie Wonder's "Talking Book" and "Hello Jeff" on Stanley Clarke's "Journey To Love".

In 1978, Beck formed another group with Simon Phillips (drums), Tony Hymas (keyboards) and Stanley Clarke (bass). They toured Japan, but no recordings with Clarke were released. Just why is not clear. Indications are that, although Beck regarded Clarke as an inspirational musician, things didn't work out when it came to their playing together on a regular basis. Effectively, it was a band with two lead guitarists and no bass player. Exactly how they parted company is, again, not clear.

Beck retained the services of Hymas and Phillips and, on the recommendation of the latter, gave top session bassist Mo Foster an audition in the studio. This was after other big-name bass players had been tried and rejected. Hymas and Phillips relieved the tension of the audition by holding up score cards, which Foster could see through the control room window, after each take. With some bass lines recorded by Jan Hammer (guesting on mini-moog) and the remainder played by Foster, the "There And Back" album was released in 1981. Subsequently, the band toured extensively with the same line-up.

Over the years, Beck has used a variety of guitars and amplifiers. In 1975, at the time of "Blow by Blow", he played a vintage 1954 Les Paul Standard fitted with two humbuckers and, on occasions, a Fender Stratocaster. The guitars went through the 100 watt Marshall amplifiers with Fender speaker cabinets. He used a pre-amp to get an overdriven valve sound and a wah-wah pedal. He also used a "voice box" on "She's A Woman". By 1980, he was favouring a standard Stratocaster and a Telecaster fitted with Gibson humbuckers.

The jazz-rock changeover (*above*) The album "Blow By Blow", released in 1975 and produced by George Martin, famous for his work with the Beatles, marked a transitional point in Beck's career. It was his first, highly successful excursion into jazz-rock and contrasted strongly with the former style of the powerhouse trio Beck, Bogert and Appice.

A constant experimenter (*left*) Jeff Beck must be acknowledged as one of the greatest rock guitar players. His stormy career serves to prove that he can never be accused of resting on past glories or of allowing himself simply to play it safe.

Pete Townshend

Pete Townshend was born in Chiswick, London, on 19th May 1945. His grandmother gave him an acoustic guitar when he was twelve years old. Gradually he broke the strings until he was left with only three – the D, G and B. At that point he found he began to see how chords are constructed and, in the following months, learned quite a number. Armed with this basic understanding, he replaced the missing strings and was on his way.

Though Townshend's father is an accomplished saxophone and clarinet player and has worked as a band leader and session musician, Townshend reacted in the traditional way – with teenage rebellion. Right from the start, he was more interested in sound, in songwriting and in self-expression than in music theory.

He did, however, learn the banjo and joined a traditional jazz band playing revivalist New Orleans jazz. The trumpet player in the band was John Entwistle, who later formed groups with Townshend before becoming the Who's bass guitarist.

Townshend's first electric guitar was a single pick-up Harmony Stratocruiser. But when he became a member of a group called the Detours, the lead guitarist – Roger Daltrey – sold him an Epiphone solid on "easy payments". By the time the group were calling themselves the High Numbers they were, in all but name, the Who. Their one and only single as the High Numbers was "Zoot Suit/I'm A Face" – the latter written around the basic format of Slim Harpo's "Got Live If You Want It". The single was not a sales success and is now a rare collector's item, but it established the group as a "mod" band. They accepted the mod image to a degree – combining it with flamboyant "op-art" fashion. The result was a flashy image with which young mod audiences could identify. Their raw, high-energy music, strongly influenced by American R&B, reflected and also expressed their generation's youthful frustration. By the time they changed their name from the High Numbers to the Who, the band had become synonymous with the mod movement.

Townshend was to channel his self-expression through the group's overall sound, the songs he wrote for them, his rhythm guitar work, and his visual approach on stage. This separated him from his contemporaries: Jeff Beck and Eric Clapton, for example, were very much *lead* guitarists. Townshend wasn't. Frustrated because he simply could not get the kind of sounds out of a guitar that Clapton and Beck could, he discovered his own solution.

One night when strutting about on stage at the Ealing Club in West London, he accidentally put the head of his Rickenbacker through the false ceiling above him and snapped off the neck. When the audience started to laugh, Townshend smashed the rest of the guitar to pieces, picked up a twelve-string for the rest of the show, and continued as if nothing had happened. The next night, the club was packed. Subsequently, ritualistic equipment-smashing became the climax of all the Who's stage and television appearances.

By this time, Townshend, the inventor of the "power chord" and a pioneer in the use of controlled feedback, had developed his own unique playing style. Laced with on-stage acrobatics and windmilling arm motions, it nevertheless provided a solid, powerful foundation for the rest of the band. The basic format of guitar, bass and drums, uncluttered by excessive soloing, allowed John Entwistle and Keith Moon much more freedom than they would have had within the tight constraints of a conventional rhythm section. From a mêlée of semi-contrived image, staged violence and personal expression came the Who's early hit singles – "Anyway, Anyhow, Anytime", "I Can't Explain", "My Generation" and "Substitute" – raw, uncompromising music that contrasted sharply with other bands of the day and that spanned the divide between pop and rock. The Who became one of the most emulated of the sixties rock bands.

Managers Chris Stamp and Kit Lambert played an important role in the initial development of the Who. It was Lambert who suggested to Townshend that he try writing an

The art of rhythm guitar Townshend's guitar playing always differed from that of his contemporaries. Instead of adopting the conventional role of the lead guitarist, he concentrated on developing a unique, powerful rhythm style that was an essential part of the Who's sound. He himself claims that he is happier when driving the rest of the band (see p.88).

The Who
From left to right, John Entwistle, Keith Moon, Roger Daltrey, and Pete Townshend, shot in an American TV studio in the late sixties. As normal on such recordings it was a mimed session: Townshend's guitar is not plugged in.

extended piece to "pad out the playing time" when they ended up about ten minutes short of material for their second album. Still convinced that the three-minute format was the standard framework for pop records, Townshend at first said that he couldn't see it. Lambert suggested that he link together several short songs with an overall concept. The result was "A Quick One" which appeared on "The Who Sell Out" album. When, in 1968, the Pretty Things extended the idea to a whole album with "S. F. Sorrow", Townshend was impressed, and started work on "Tommy".

The framework provided him with a stimulus for new ideas. He had developed considerably as a guitarist, and was by this time playing keyboards and writing his songs at the piano. The music on "Tommy" is ambitious and is acknowledged as one of the major achieve-

ments in rock music. It featured some of Townshend's strongest material – including the classic "Pinball Wizard".

During the early days of the band, John Entwistle obtained one of the first 4 x 12 speaker cabinets made by Marshall for bass guitar. Townshend noticed that he was getting twice as much volume and projection as before, and promptly got hold of one for himself. He followed it with a second cabinet, stuck one on top of the other, and thus probably created the first "stack". Because the top cabinet was at ear level, he could hear himself more clearly, and because the speakers were in line with his guitar pick-ups, it was easier to employ controlled feedback. He initially used the Marshall cabinets in conjunction with Fender amplifiers, and he claims that he never really liked Marshall amps. Subsequently, he

settled down with the same set-up but using Hi-watt amps and cabinets. Sometimes he uses dummy cabinets with no speakers at the bottom. He tends to have the amps turned up loud and adjusts the volume level on the guitar. He also uses combo amplifiers, such as the Boogie, for recording.

The strong individual personalities of the Who members has meant that the band's history is punctuated with argument. At one time, bitter recriminations were regular and public events. Yet the Who stayed together. They survived the death of Keith Moon in 1978 and continued with drummer Kenny Jones (from the Faces) and "Rabbit" Bundrick on keyboards. Though they now tour less often, and have all pursued individual interests, the Who still play. And Pete Townshend is still regarded as one of the key rock guitarists.

The Townshend power chord The windmill arm motion became Townshend's trademark. An impressive stage gimmick, it underlined the energy of his playing, and led the way for the heavy-metal "power chord". With both guitar and amp flat out, often on the verge of feedback, Townshend's guitar playing was the driving force behind the Who's music. He has played (and smashed up) many different makes and models of guitar in his time. They have included Rickenbackers, Gibson SGs, Gibson Les Paul Customs, and, more recently, Telecaster lookalikes made to order from Schecter parts (see p.179). He has said that he chooses his guitars to suit his amplifiers and not the other way around. His power-chord style means that he has to use heavy-gauge strings and change them frequently: "If I'm lazy and decide to keep strings on, then always in the first or second number they break. I've actually had strings break on the first chord."

Jimi Hendrix

James Marshall Hendricks was born on 27th November 1942. He inherited Indian blood from his mother, his grandmother being a full Cherokee, and negro blood from his father's side. From the word go, Hendrix was exposed to blues and R&B music through his father's record collection. He was given a harmonica at the age of four, an acoustic guitar at ten, and went "electric" a year later when his father bought him his second guitar. Initially, major blues guitarists Elmore James, B.B. King and Muddy Waters were among his influences.

While still in his teens, Hendrix was already gaining a considerable word-of-mouth reputation as an outstanding guitarist playing back-up for touring acts which included Ike and Tina Turner, The Isley Brothers, Little Richard, and one of his idols, B.B. King.

After his medical discharge from the US Army, Hendrix adopted a stage name and formed his own band, Jimmy James and the Blue Flames. This was in 1965, when the British music invasion of the States was well under way. Hendrix was already barnstorming wherever he played his guitar. Bob Dylan, who saw him play in Greenwich Village, had taken over as his main inspiration but, at the same time, the guitar playing of Pete Townshend and Eric Clapton was also making a considerable impression. Even at this early stage, Hendrix could walk into a club, sit in with a pick-up band, and deliver an awe-inspiring performance. When the Animals' bass guitarist, Chas Chandler, heard him play in a New York club he offered to bring Hendrix to London.

With the release of his first single on Polydor, Hendrix reverted from Jimmy James to his own name, although with the modified spelling. Chas Chandler had hastily put Hendrix together with a guitarist called Noel Redding – who played bass just to get the gig – and a drummer called Mitch Mitchell. They formed the Jimi Hendrix Experience. The single "Hey Joe" (written by Tim Rose) was released in December 1966, and by the early new year it was a number 4 hit. In the space of nine months during 1967, he followed the record with three more hit singles that stand out as all-time classics. They were "Purple Haze", "And The Wind Cries Mary", and "The Burning Of The Midnight Lamp".

Hendrix returned to play in America with the Experience in 1967 at the Monterey Pop Festival. The festival featured big names of the day, including Janis Joplin, Otis Redding, and the Mamas and Papas. Hendrix was there on the recommendation of Paul McCartney, and Brian Jones of the Stones flew to the States just to introduce him. Hendrix did his show, to unanimous acclaim, and culminated his spot by setting fire to and smashing his guitar. While English co-manager Mike Jeffreys is reported to have complained bitterly about damage to equipment, top promoter Bill Graham eagerly

booked the band to play at his prestigious Fillmore West venue. They were booked for several nights with Jefferson Airplane. On the first night Hendrix was unstoppable. The Airplane dropped out of the following shows.

The first Hendrix album was "Are You Experienced". It was a showcase for his multitude of talents, and is now regarded as one of the all-time classic rock albums. In 1968, it was followed by "Axis: Bold as Love" and then the double "Electric Ladyland" set.

By 1969, Hendrix was dissatisfied with his music. Eventually, in order to do more justice to himself, he disbanded the Experience, and recorded a live album called "Band of Gypsies" with Billy Cox on bass and Buddy Miles on drums. It was not very successful. He then falteringly reformed the Experience, and also worked with Mitchell and Redding on separate occasions. He seemed to dither between doing what he should in order for his music to progress, and maintaining personal loyalties to Redding and Mitchell as well as the many people who wanted him to keep the Experience together. He began to shy away from live performances because it was on stage that his dilemma would come to a head. He had his own "Electric Ladyland" studios constructed in New York and was thinking far more in terms of recording than live gigs. The month before he died, he said:

"I've turned full circle. I'm right back where I started. I've given this era of music everything, but I still sound the same. My music's the same and I can't think of anything new to add to it in its present state.

When the last American tour finished I just wanted to go away and forget everything. I just wanted to record and see if I could write something. Then I started thinking. Thinking about the future. Thinking that this era of music, sparked off by the Beatles, had come to an end. Something new has to come and Jimi Hendrix will be there.

The main thing that used to bug me was that people wanted too many visual things from me. When I didn't do it, people thought I was being moody, but I can only freak when I really feel like doing so. I wanted the music to get across, so that people could just sit back and close their eyes, and know exactly what was going on, without caring a damn what we were doing while we were on stage.

I think I'm a better guitarist than I was. I've learned a lot."

Hendrix died on 18th September 1970. Within days, he was to have started work with orchestrator and arranger Gil Evans, who had collaborated with Miles Davis on "Sketches of Spain" and other albums.

Most of the time, Hendrix played right-handed Fender Stratocasters turned upside-down and with the strings reversed. He also used a Gibson Les Paul for blues and, later on, a left-handed Gibson Flying V which he called his "Flying Angel".

His amplification usually consisted of six Marshall 4×12 cabinets, one 4×12 monitor, and four souped-up 100-watt Marshall amp heads. Road crews were at times hard-pressed to keep his equipment going during a performance as he simply had everything turned up full, driving it well past the limit, as well as frequently attacking it.

Hendrix's guitars (*left*) Despite being left-handed, Hendrix preferred right-handed guitars. This meant that he was able to use the controls and tremelo arm – then at the top – in his own unique way. Here, he is playing a Fender Jaguar turned upside-down.

Live on stage (*right*) In terms of showmanship, Hendrix could "out-Townshend" Townshend – playing his guitar with his teeth, setting fire to it, and smashing it to pieces while still extracting sound from it. At the same time, he completely re-defined the musical possibilities of the electric guitar. There was no precedent; his style and the effects he created were totally new.

Frank Zappa

Frank Zappa is a person who makes you wonder, is he out of step with the rest of the human race or is everyone else out of step with him? Whichever it is, he's unique. He's survived rock music's most turbulent years, remaining at almost total odds with the conventional music-business image. Paradoxically he is one of rock music's most prolific writers and performers, with over thirty albums to his credit to date.

Next to talent, paradox is in fact the key word when it comes to talking about Zappa. His music brings together a kaleidoscope of influences from American black music to European classical composers such as Edgar Varèse. His musical parodies of life in America – particularly during the sixties – are bitingly satirical and yet poignant at the same time.

Born Francis Vincent Zappa Junior on 21st December 1940 in Baltimore, Maryland, his family moved around until settling in Lancaster, California, in 1956. Zappa started making music playing drums at the age of twelve. In an interview in 1979, I asked him what music had inspired him to play.

"When I was twelve? I didn't listen to any music, I just wanted to play drums. My parents couldn't afford a record player. There was nothing good on the radio, I just wanted to play the drums, I liked the way they sounded."

The progression from playing drums to playing guitar didn't take long.

"I changed to guitar when I was in Senior High School. My brother had bought this guitar for a dollar-fifty at an auction. He wasn't using it much so I started messing around on it. By that time I had gathered a bunch of records. You know, on most records in those days the instrumental or solos were always played by saxophone. It was very rarely that you would hear a good guitar solo but I searched around and found some. I thought: I really want to do that, make those sort of noises. The guitar I had to begin with wasn't electric, just one of those arched-top f-hole models. I didn't know any chords, I just started playing blues straight away."

When I asked if he listened to players like Scotty Moore or James Burton on the early Elvis records, Zappa immediately put me straight on his feelings about the popular white music of the period.

"You mean session guitarists? That's not what I would call a guitar solo. A guitar solo is like "Three Hours Past Midnight" by Johnny Guitar Watson or "The Story Of My Life" by Guitar Slim. That's a guitar solo, nothing freeze-dried. Something really stinkin', that's what I was looking for."

Zappa also mentions Clarence "Gatemouth" Brown and Matt Murphy as guitarists he listened to in the early days. Later, he rated quite highly the playing of Jeff Beck, John McLaughlin, and Brian May of Queen.

While still at school, Zappa had a band called the Blackouts. From there, he went on to do various jobs to support himself and his interests in music. He worked in advertising on and off for about a year and a half, he had a spell of ten months playing cocktail-lounge music, and he also wrote the music for a couple of less-than-celebrated movies. The second, *Run Home Slow*, gave him the money to buy a small recording studio where he recorded a band called the Omens – whose members went on to form both the Mothers of Invention and Captain Beefheart's band.

Zappa has, to say the least, positive ideas about the way an electric guitar should sound.

"From the very beginning when I used to hear those solos on those old records I used to say: now here is an instrument that is capable of spewing forth true obscenity, you know? If ever there's an obscene noise to be made on an instrument, it's going to come out of a guitar. On a saxophone you can play sleaze. On a bass you can play balls. But on a guitar you can be truly obscene . . . Let's be realistic about this, the guitar can be the single most blasphemous device on the face of the earth. That's why I like it . . . The disgusting stink of a too-loud electric guitar: now that's my idea of a good time."

It was in 1966 that Zappa's breakthrough came. Tom Wilson, record producer for Bob Dylan and many others at the time, heard Zappa's band playing at the Whiskey A Go-Go club in Los Angeles and wanted to record them. The result was the first Mothers of Invention album, "Freakout". The line-up was Zappa and Elliott Ingber on guitars with Ray Collins, Roy Estrada and Jimmy Carl Black. Ingber left soon after the album was completed, and Zappa subsequently brought in Don Preston, Bunk Gardner, Billy Mundi and Jim "Motorhead' Sherwood. This was the line-up for the second album, "Absolutely Free", released in 1967.

The Mothers had moved to New York in 1966 and, during November of that year, they started a six-month season of fourteen shows a week at the Garrick Theatre. The overt theatricality and outrageous nature of their shows has become a part of rock legend.

The guitarist as composer/performer/producer Zappa himself has said that what differentiates him from the conventionally acclaimed guitar hero is that he is primarily a composer "who happens to be able to operate an instrument called a guitar". In the studio, where he assumes the additional role of being his own producer, his multitalents are even more evident.

After the first two Mothers albums, Zappa released his first solo record – "Lumpy Gravy". Looking back, he now considers it his favourite. But the one that followed, "Hot Rats", with the extended guitar soloing that was to be a feature of much of his subsequent work, is perhaps the most highly rated in terms of guitar playing.

Through the seventies, Zappa's live concerts gradually began to feature more music and fewer theatrics. As ever, he continued to drill his bands to perfection, and by the end of the seventies, Zappa concerts consisted of two hours of tightly arranged music with one song segued into the next. He insists on the very highest standards, and, as a result, the tag "ex-Frank Zappa band" is one of the most sought-after credentials for a rock musician.

Zappa has a heavy right-hand technique and uses heavy Fender plectrums. He employs a wah-wah pedal like a tone or distortion control, leaving it set in one position, not rocking it back and forth. On stage he generally plays clean extended lead lines, using valve amps and the wah-wah pedal to give a regular, slightly distorted rock sound. In the recording studio on the other hand, he is always experimenting with different sounds and musical ideas.

"I think any device that's been manufactured for usage is worth messing around with, but I try to find applications for them that are unusual. The biggest challenge in making a record, though, is just trying to get the best possible sound from the instrument, to make the instruments sound as good as possible without flanging the piss out of them."

Over the years, Zappa has used a variety of amplifiers. When the Mothers first started, he was using a Fender Deluxe, but he has often recorded with a Pignose. Recently he has expressed a liking for Boogie amps. He has also used an Acoustic 270 amp on stage but generally seems to prefer Marshall 100-watt tops used in conjunction with 4×12 cabinets containing JBL speakers.

As far as guitars are concerned, he used a Gibson ES–5 Switchmaster for the first three albums. After a spell with a Gibson Les Paul, he was seen playing Gibson SGs on stage more often than any other instruments. He also has two Stratocasters – both with additional built-in pre-amps. One has out-of-phase switching, and the other (which once belonged to Jimi Hendrix) has a Barcus-Berry contact transducer embedded in the neck. This allows finger and plectrum noises to be mixed in with the signal from the pick-ups when recording – in spite of the fact that most other people try and minimize such sounds. For similar reasons, and to get different effects when recording, he frequently fits contact transducers to various other parts of semi-acoustic and solid body guitars. Zappa also has a one-off prototype fretless guitar made by Acoustic. Stylistically, he has always been equally at home mimicking a third-rate blues guitarist or playing a complicated, extended rock solo.

On stage in the late seventies (*left*) Nowadays, Zappa's live concerts are music, not theatre. The image that surrounded the Mothers (and which he more than anyone else created) no longer obscures the fact that for years he has been one of rock's most interesting and innovative guitarists.

Zappa speaks (*below*) Deliberately outspoken, Zappa maintains a consistent reputation for controversy and outrage that goes right back to the days when the Mothers played the Garrick Theater in New York. On one occasion, Zappa persuaded a number of US marines to get up on stage and mutilate toy dolls. Another night, Jimi Hendrix sat in with the band.

Stanley Clarke

Stanley Clarke was born in Philadelphia in 1951. He regards his mother as his first artistic influence. She was a professional operatic singer, so, as a child, he often heard her singing around the house. He started violin lessons at around the age of twelve, but being very tall and having long fingers caused problems. When he tried cello, he had the same difficulties, but a double bass one day convinced him that it was the right-sized instrument for him. He wasn't too keen on the "rough sound" but decided he could work round that.

By the time Clarke was sixteen, he had started playing bass guitar. His interests in music encompassed Wagner, Bach, James Brown, Sly, Jimi Hendrix and the Beatles, as well as jazz greats like Miles Davis. While continuing his classical music studies, he was also playing all kinds of popular music with local groups at various clubs and functions. From High School he went to Philadelphia Musical Academy, taking a course covering symphonic double bass playing. Just over two years later he left the Academy and moved to New York. He successfully auditioned for jazz pianist Horace Silver's group and stayed for a year. He worked with several jazz/improvisational groups before meeting Chick Corea at the beginning of the seventies. In 1971 they led the first line-up of Return To Forever and recorded the album of the same name.

One night while playing at the Boarding House in Los Angeles with Chick Corea, Clarke felt a tap on the shoulder and turned to find a little man telling him that his playing was great but his sound was lousy. The next night, the same man – Rick Turner – turned up at the club with one of his early two-octave Alembic bass guitars. The instrument, with its long scale, active electronics, long sustain and rich sound, convinced Clarke, and Turner made him a custom instrument, thus initiating the combination that resulted in his distinctive sound.

Return To Forever enjoyed considerable success, particularly with the Stanley Clarke, Chick Corea, Al Di Meola and Lenny White line-up. By 1976, Clarke – now a multiple poll-winner – had become something of a legend. His "Stanley Clarke" solo album is accepted as an all-time masterpiece. He went on to form his own group, as well as work with Jeff Beck, George Duke, and The Barbarians with Keith Richards.

Stanley Clarke's playing is a synthesis of classical, jazz, soul and rock music. He believes that the bass guitar can be played as both a rhythm and solo instrument at the same time. He never uses a plectrum, since he prefers using two or three fingers.

By the early 1980s, almost every bass player seemed to be influenced by Clarke's melodic, rhythmic and percussive playing style, as well as his active-circuitry bass and his solid-state amplification (see p. 200).

The Stanley Clarke finger technique (*above*) Clarke utilizes aspects of double-bass technique on bass guitar – for example, resting the thumb of his right hand on the *edge* of the fingerboard to give an anchor point and to enable him to play *pizzicato* (Italian for "pinched"). This means that he is pulling and then releasing – as opposed to striking or plucking – the strings. The effect of their slapping back against the frets and fingerboard creates a unique percussive sound that has been widely copied.

The Stanley Clarke "sound" (*left*) The combination of Alembic bass (with its built-in active electronics) and solid-state amplifciation has helped to create Clarke's distinctive and immediately recognizable sound. (For more details, see p. 63 and p. 200.)

Andy Summers

"A guitarist for all seasons" would be rather an apt title for Andy Summers. Over a period of two decades he has worked in numerous bands and in many different styles. He first came to notice playing slick, soulful licks in Zoot Money's Big Roll Band in the sixties and stayed with them during their subsequent foray into psychedelia as Dantalion's Chariot. Later, he moved on to the more aggressive Animals Mk II, to the free-improvisational Soft Machine, to the Kevin Ayres band and to the Kevin Coyne band. He's been involved in countless recording sessions, and is currently working with Robert Fripp.

During 1977, Summers met drummer Stuart Copeland and singer/bassist Gordon Matthew "Sting" Sumner when all three were booked for the same recording session. Impressed by what they told him about their group, the Police, Summers sat in with them at the Marquee Club in London. As Sting tells it, "he demanded to be in the group, so he was in".

Summers describes the Police as "a challenge to try and do something new with a three-piece band". Instead of turning the amps on full, thrashing the hell out of the drums and squeezing as many notes per second out of the lead guitar as possible, he told me in 1980 that "we approached it the other way, much more of a minimal thing, trying to use a lot more space — and that's where reggae really helped us a lot . . . we fused reggae with rock".

His playing has helped to re-define the role of the guitarist in a rock band. Consciously drawing on as many different musical styles and influences as possible, and aiming to do away with the conventional concept of a rhythm section simply providing a backing for a soloist, he explained to me:

"It's a linear rather than a horizontal thing. I think we would regard it — in broad terms — as three soloists going along three parallel lines, creating a fabric rather than a straight line upwards . . . I can change the way I play the guitar all along that line, in terms of playing fragmented chords, whole chords, changing the progression, and playing solos, depending on what is happening with the bass and drums in the space that's available. I can also colour all my sounds with contemporary modifying devices".

Anyone who has listened to his playing will be familiar with the formidable range of sounds and textures that Andy Summers creates from a skilful blend of technique and sophisticated electronic effects.

A lesson in the use of new sound technology
Seen here with his main stage guitar, a 1961 Telecaster fitted with a Gibson humbucker, on-board pre-amp and phase switching, Summers also uses many other instruments — including Roland guitar synths. He has a custom-built pedalboard.

Robert Fripp

The sixties saw the emergence of many great rock guitarists. Most followed a more-or-less parallel development, based heavily on the music of American blues guitarists. However, Robert Fripp – born in Wimborne, Dorset, in 1946 – took rock guitar playing in a totally different direction from that of the mainstream. Though he uses both acoustic and electric guitars to produce a wide variety of musical textures, it is through his forceful solo electric playing that he has had the greatest impact as a guitarist. His frequently distorted, overdriven guitar sound is combined with a flowing, unrestricted playing style gained from years of study into the scales, chordal structures and harmony of musical cultures from all over the world. His chosen and well-thought-out path has enabled him to break new ground through the seventies and into the eighties.

It was as a founder member of King Crimson that Fripp first gained attention, though he had previously recorded with the group Giles, Giles and Fripp. The impact of King Crimson was immediate and substantial. In the vanguard of "progressive rock" bands, they combined classical and symphonic concepts with elements of rock. Fripp's experimental playing, accentuated by the insistency of his raw, distorted, lead sound, was one of the highlights.

Fripp was the one constant member of King Crimson from its origin in 1969 to its demise in 1974. Plagued by frequent personnel changes and by problems associated with Fripp's uncompromising, somewhat dictatorial stance, King Crimson nevertheless made some excellent recordings – "Larks' Tongues In Aspic", "Red" and "Starless and Bible Black". After the band broke up in 1974, Fripp also put together the double compilation album "The Young Person's Guide to King Crimson".

At the beginning of the eighties, a Fripp band was briefly reincarnated: originally called Discipline, they suddenly changed their name to King Crimson, recorded a superb album entitled "Discipline", and promptly disappeared again. Between 1974 and 1978, Fripp withdrew from the music scene "to pursue alternative education". When he returned, he began the execution of a carefully planned strategy. In a series of articles written for *Musician, Player and Listener* in America and *Sound International* in Britain, he expressed his highly individual views on music and the music industry. He also announced that in the future he intended to operate as a "small mobile intelligence unit". As such, he has acted as record producer, "guest" guitarist, solo performer and occasional bandleader. His well-placed guitar work has provided inspiration for a whole new generation of guitarists and other musicians. His self-labelled "Frippertronics" and his solo album, "Exposure" are particularly interesting and influential.

The "guest" guitarist (*left*) In recent years Fripp has made numerous guest appearances on other people's albums. Outstanding examples of his guitar playing can be heard on David Bowie's "Heroes" and "Scary Monsters", Peter Gabriel "II" and "III", several of Brian Eno's albums, Talking Heads, and the track "Fade Away And Radiate" on Blondie's "Parallel Lines". When Fripp wrote in a magazine article that he had been "spraying burning guitar over David Bowie's new album" ("Scary Monsters"), his choice of words was quite apt.

Frippertronics (*below*) Using two Revox tape machines, Fripp records layer after layer of repeated guitar to use as a backdrop for improvised soloing. He adopted the basic recording technique during his association with Eno and labelled it "Frippertronics". There is a whole album of Frippertronics entitled "Let The Power Fall".

ACOUSTIC GUITARS

Modern acoustic guitars come in two forms – those with steel strings and those with nylon strings. Although nylon-string guitars are always used for classical and flamenco music, and steel-string guitars are more common in folk, blues and even jazz and rock, there are no real rules. It is impossible to say that one kind of guitar must be used only for a certain type of music. From model to model there are, of course, countless variations in design, shape, construction, sound characteristics and usage. Yet the basic idea of the acoustic guitar has remained more-or-less the same for over a century. The steel-string guitar is the direct descendant of the "Spanish" or "classical" guitar – a masterpiece of design in terms of both physics and craftsmanship. All modern guitar-makers owe an incalculable debt to Antonio de Torres Jurado, the man whose nineteenth-century guitar designs are still closely followed for classical instruments. The major part of the development of the steel-string acoustic as we know it today was carried out by American guitar-makers – most notably by the Gibson and Martin companies. In recent years, the Japanese have applied their manufacturing skills to the acoustic guitar, with the result that excellent instruments are now well within reach of most people. This chapter deals with all the different types of acoustic guitar available, detailing the important stages in their development and describing how they are designed and constructed.

The anatomy of the acoustic guitar

The principle by which all acoustic guitars produce musical sounds is generally agreed to be the same. When you strike a guitar string, you apply energy to it and make it vibrate. However, this string vibration alone is not sufficient to create sound waves in the surrounding air that can be clearly heard.

In this respect, a guitar string can be thought of as being similar to a tuning fork. A tuning fork also vibrates when struck, but it is virtually inaudible until you bring it into contact with a mass of lower density which can transmit the vibrations to the air more efficiently.

It is for this reason that acoustic guitars have a hollow body. The body is a carefully designed "soundbox". The energy of the vibrating strings is transferred to the soundbox via the saddle and the bridge over which the strings pass. The soundbox then vibrates in sympathy with the guitar strings to create "amplified" – and therefore audible – airborne sound waves that can be heard up to a reasonable distance from the guitar. In other words, it is the soundbox that is responsible for the guitar's projection and volume.

A simple way of illustrating this point is to play an acoustic guitar alongside a solid-body electric guitar which you have not plugged into an amplifier. The un-amplified electric guitar is much quieter. Its solid body is mainly just a mounting block for the bridge, pick-ups and controls. Because it has no soundbox, the sound waves it generates are much weaker.

To sum up then, an acoustic guitar amplifies the sound of the vibrating strings *acoustically* – through the design of the body or the soundbox. But the sound of a solid-body electric guitar must be amplified *electronically* – through an amplifier and loudspeaker.

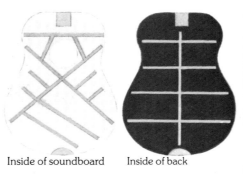

Inside of soundboard   Inside of back

The soundboard and back
Shown above are typical patterns of "strutting" or "bracing" for the soundboard and back of a flat-top acoustic guitar. The design of the struts must strike a compromise between strengthening the wood to prevent it from distorting and allowing it to vibrate in such a way as to give the best tone.

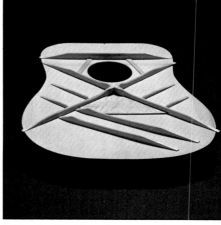

"X-bracing" inside an Ibanez soundboard.

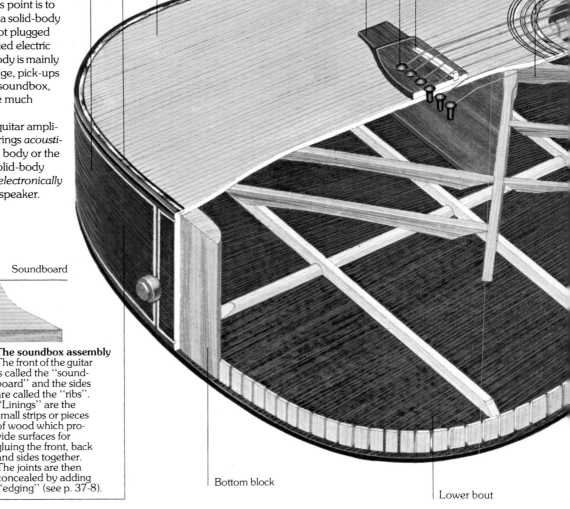

Rib

Edging

Soundboard

Saddle

Bridge pins

Bridge

Bottom block

Lower bout

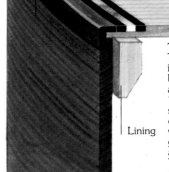

Rib   Edging

Soundboard

The soundbox assembly
The front of the guitar is called the "soundboard" and the sides are called the "ribs". "Linings" are the small strips or pieces of wood which provide surfaces for gluing the front, back and sides together. The joints are then concealed by adding "edging" (see p. 37-8).

Lining

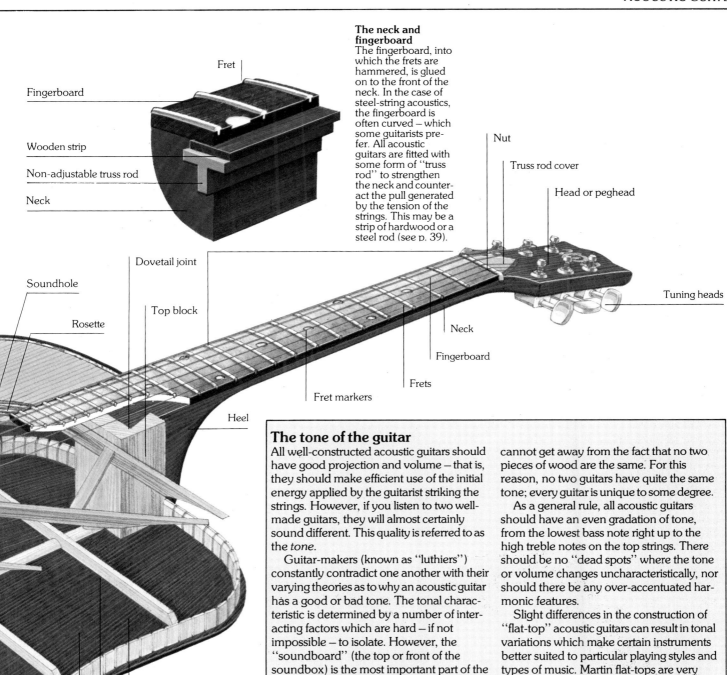

Fret

Fingerboard

Wooden strip

Non-adjustable truss rod

Neck

The neck and fingerboard
The fingerboard, into which the frets are hammered, is glued on to the front of the neck. In the case of steel-string acoustics, the fingerboard is often curved – which some guitarists prefer. All acoustic guitars are fitted with some form of "truss rod" to strengthen the neck and counteract the pull generated by the tension of the strings. This may be a strip of hardwood or a steel rod (see p. 39).

Nut

Truss rod cover

Head or peghead

Tuning heads

Dovetail joint

Soundhole

Top block

Rosette

Neck

Fingerboard

Frets

Fret markers

Heel

Upper bout

Struts or braces

Back

Waist

Lining

The tone of the guitar

All well-constructed acoustic guitars should have good projection and volume – that is, they should make efficient use of the initial energy applied by the guitarist striking the strings. However, if you listen to two well-made guitars, they will almost certainly sound different. This quality is referred to as the *tone*.

Guitar-makers (known as "luthiers") constantly contradict one another with their varying theories as to why an acoustic guitar has a good or bad tone. The tonal characteristic is determined by a number of interacting factors which are hard – if not impossible – to isolate. However, the "soundboard" (the top or front of the soundbox) is the most important part of the guitar with regard to tone. In fact, legend has it that, to prove this, the nineteenth-century Spanish luthier, Torres (see *Classical and flamenco guitars*, p. 42), once made a guitar with a body that consisted entirely of papier-mâché except for the wooden soundboard. Guitarists who played his experimental instrument were apparently amazed by its fine tone.

Theoretically, you might think it would be possible to build a series of different guitars with slightly varying construction details in order to establish one way or another what determines the tone quality. In practice, many top guitar-makers do exactly this – by changing their design slightly to produce an instrument with the sound characteristics requested by a particular customer. But you cannot get away from the fact that no two pieces of wood are the same. For this reason, no two guitars have quite the same tone; every guitar is unique to some degree.

As a general rule, all acoustic guitars should have an even gradation of tone, from the lowest bass note right up to the high treble notes on the top strings. There should be no "dead spots" where the tone or volume changes uncharacteristically, nor should there be any over-accentuated harmonic features.

Slight differences in the construction of "flat-top" acoustic guitars can result in tonal variations which make certain instruments better suited to particular playing styles and types of music. Martin flat-tops are very popular with fingerstyle guitarists because they suit that style of playing especially well. They have a clarity which gives a clearly defined bass pattern when a melody is played simultaneously on the top strings. Gibson flat-tops, on the other hand, are frequently used by country-music guitarists since they give a chunky, rhythmic sound when chords are strummed on them. Gibsons are also highly suited to flatpicking guitar styles.

Both Gibson and Martin are makers of high quality guitars and, although both makes of instrument have their own tonal characteristics which give them an edge when played in particular ways, both will also sound excellent when played in any number of styles.

How acoustic guitars are constructed

As soon as you start to look at the enormous variety of acoustic guitars which are available you will see that different types are constructed in different ways. As far as "flat-top" acoustic guitars are concerned, the differences – which are quite often subtle – are beyond quantification. There are, however, basic limits of practical design which make certain features common to them all.

We will begin by examining the choice of materials used in the construction of guitars and then move on to look in detail at the individual parts of the instrument.

The choice of wood

A guitar made from properly "seasoned" or "kiln-dried" wood will stand up to remarkable changes in temperature as well as humidity and – with just a reasonable amount of care and attention – will have a quite surprising life-span. The use of poor materials in guitar construction usually results in a poor sounding instrument and one that may soon become distorted from its original shape.

A guitar made of "green" timber straight from the tree and not seasoned or kiln-dried at all would be a complete disaster. In fact, the timber would probably shrink and distort so much while still in the hands of the guitar-maker that even the most modest standards would be impossible to attain.

So why use wood at all if it tends to be so problematic? The fact is that wood really has quite a lot going for it. For a start, no other material has been found to give anywhere

near as good a tone. But wood also has a warm feel, and when well finished is very attractive.

What are the criteria for choosing woods best suited to guitar-making? First, the wood – in particular that used for the soundboard – must have the required tonal quality. Second, it must have the required strength and stability. Third, the wood must lend itself to being finished or varnished for protective and decorative purposes.

Why does wood have to be seasoned or kiln-dried? The answer is simple. A tree and a guitar make totally different demands on their basic material. A tree is a complex living entity which must remain subtle enough to stand up to over two hundred years of changing seasons. The tree has a complex hydraulic system which pumps water around to where it is needed to cope with dramatic changes in weather conditions.

As soon as a tree is felled it starts to dry out. The way in which a tree is sawn and shaped into planks and pieces of timber, as well as the way in which it is stored, will affect the qualities of the wood finally used in the making of a guitar.

Seasoned wood is timber that has been carefully stored in controlled conditions with good ventilation for the period during which it gradually loses most – but not all – of the moisture it contains. After being exposed to the varying temperature and humidity changes of several seasons of spring, summer, autumn and winter, the wood becomes

relatively stable. Thus the term, "seasoned". However, the process is long and expensive, and traditional seasoning of timber has become increasingly rare.

It is *kiln-dried* wood that meets most of the demands for timber in the twentieth century. Kiln-drying is a process by which the moisture is removed from new timber far more quickly than by seasoning. The wood is placed in a kiln which acts virtually like a slow oven. The time involved is therefore closer to weeks than to the months or years required for traditional seasoning.

Most guitars are now manufactured from kiln-dried wood. Nevertheless, individual guitar-makers may allow the wood to season for a further period – depending on their standards – and it is not at all rare to hear of a maker keeping kiln-dried wood for several years before using it for a guitar.

Some of the very best guitar-builders flatly refuse to accept kiln-dried timber for their instruments – in particular for the soundboards. Yet good timber is in very short supply generally – regardless of whether it is kiln-dried or seasoned. As a result, the last ten years or so have seen some of the best European makers travelling to Switzerland and Germany to seek out what they consider to be the ideal spruce or pine tree. The Spanish-born master guitar-maker, Romanillos, has been known to have a Swiss pine felled and sawn to his own requirements before seasoning the wood for a further five or more years.

The shape and size of the guitar

The majority of acoustic guitars all have the same basic shape: the characteristic figure-of-eight comprising the *upper bout*, the *waist* and the *lower bout*. However, the relative dimensions of the upper bout, waist and lower bout often vary. The smaller upper bout enhances the treble frequencies while the larger lower bout enhances the bass frequencies. Dropping a plectrum

through the soundhole into the soundbox of the guitar and shaking the instrument so that the plectrum rattles as it moves around from bout to bout demonstrates this quite clearly. The overall size of acoustic guitars also varies from one type of instrument to another. Flat-top steel-string acoustic guitars range from a "standard" size up to the larger "jumbo" and "Dreadnought"

sizes. The standard instrument is very similar to a classical guitar in both shape and size. It is a common practice with major guitar manufacturers to use a standard "scale length" (see p. 40) for a complete range of different-sized instruments.

"Three-quarter-sized" guitars are intended for children or adults with small hands and are not considered here.

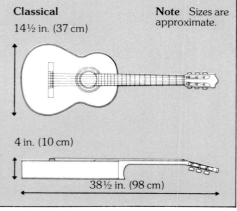

Standard flat-top
14½ in. (37 cm)
4½ in. (12 cm)
40¼ in. (102 cm)

Dreadnought/jumbo flat-top
16 in. (41 cm)
4⅞ in. (12.5 cm)
40¾ in. (103.5 cm)

Classical
14½ in. (37 cm)
4 in. (10 cm)
38½ in. (98 cm)

Note Sizes are approximate.

The soundbox

The body of an acoustic guitar is called the *soundbox*. It is made up of the *soundboard* at the front, the *ribs* (its sides) and the *back*. These pieces of wood are joined together with *linings* and the joints are then finished with decorative *edging*.

The soundboard

The most important part of the soundbox as regards the tone of the guitar is the *soundboard* – also known as the "table".

The very best soundboard would theoretically be made from best-quality, unblemished, "quarter-sawn", "book-matched", well-seasoned, straight-grained pine or spruce.

The term *quarter-sawn* refers to the way in which the timber is cut when the tree is initially sawn into planks.

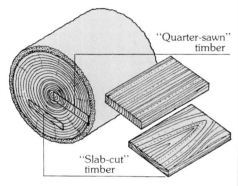

"Quarter-sawn" timber

"Slab-cut" timber

As far as soundboards and backs are concerned, the term *book-matched* describes two pieces of wood which have been sawn from one piece so that the grain of the two pieces matches.

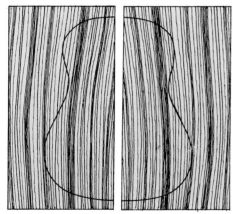

Two pieces of "book-matched" timber.

In practice, you will rarely see a soundboard of this quality. In fact, any pine or spruce which is unblemished and fairly straight-grained will make a fine soundboard for a flat-top steel-string guitar. Other woods also used include cedar and redwood. Redwood is popular with American guitar-makers as it is easily available in the United States.

In some cases, guitar soundboards are made from "plywood" or "laminated" tim-

bers. *Plywood* consists of thin layers of wood which are glued together so that the grain of each alternate layer runs at right angles. Such a piece of wood is likely to be extremely strong – much stronger than a solid piece of pine or spruce – but it will be much more rigid, will not vibrate in the same way and will therefore not produce as good a tone.

The term *laminated* is used for a type of plywood sheeting made with better quality veneers. It also differs in that the grain of each layer sometimes runs in the same direction. Parallel-grained laminated soundboards are used mainly by manufacturers of lower-priced instruments.

Contrary to expectation, not all "flat-top" steel-string acoustic guitars actually have flat tops. The soundboard is in fact often given a slight curve or "arch". The reasons for this are as follows. From a structural point of view, giving the soundboard and the back of the guitar body a slight curve will make it stronger and help prevent cracking and distortion of shape. Such soundboards are also less likely to be affected by extreme changes of humidity and temperature. Some guitar-makers also claim that a curved soundboard gives the instrument a better tone; this is, of course, a subjective judgement.

All guitar soundboards are strengthened by a pattern of struts and braces on the inside of the soundbox (see p. 34). However, the designs for internal strutting and bracing vary considerably. Ideally, a soundboard should vibrate in a uniform way, with the strutting giving only structural support and strength. The strutting pattern can radically affect the sound of a guitar.

To give extra strength to the bridge area of the soundboard, a piece of wood is usually fitted to the underside directly beneath the bridge. Some makers also glue a thin veneer of timber to the underside of the soundboard around the soundhole/rosette area to add some extra strength.

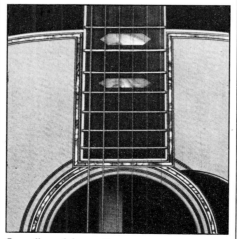

Soundboard decoration
The soundboards of Martin's top guitars are made from best-quality, solid spruce. The D-45 shown here has abalone inlaid by hand around the soundhole, fingerboard and linings.

The *rosette* is the decorative inlay around the soundhole. Traditionally, it is made in a similar way to the edgings, with a series of wood veneers which may be in natural colours or dyed to provide contrasting colours. However, synthetic materials are being used more and more frequently. The rosette is generally regarded as purely decorative, but it in fact strengthens the area of the soundboard weakened by the soundhole. Design themes featured in the edgings and other parts of the instrument are frequently continued with the rosette.

The ribs, back and body construction

The *ribs* of an acoustic guitar are the shaped sides which follow the curved outline of the soundbox. Whereas the soundboards of quality instruments tend to be made only from spruce, the less crucial ribs and back can be made in various timbers with good results. The ribs and back are usually made in a matching hardwood. At the top end of the market, Brazilian rosewood remains the first choice – in both classical and steel-string guitar construction. However, many makers settle for Indian rosewood as a close second since the Brazilian variety is in increasingly short supply. Other hardwoods frequently and successfully used include African walnut, mahogany, maple and sycamore.

In ideal terms, the guitar back should be made using two pieces of book-matched timber. However, designs do vary – even to the extent of making the back from three pieces of wood.

The standard two-piece back is made by butting the two pieces of timber together with a glued joint. This joint is usually strengthened on the inside surface with a fairly flat-section strip of hardwood which should have its grain set at right angles to that of the back. The back is then strutted or braced in a similar way to the soundboard, and it is quite often curved in the same way by making the struts to a slightly convex shape. Sometimes a decorative inlay is set along the joint in the centre of the back.

The ribs are made up of two pieces of hardwood which meet at the point where the neck will be fitted onto the soundbox (the *top block*) and again at the opposite point at the tail end of the soundbox (the *bottom block*). The join at the top block will eventually be covered by the neck and its heel. The join at the bottom block is dealt with in a variety of ways. Some makers set a wedge-shaped piece of wood at this point. Others decorate or disguise the join using inlays. Some lower-priced instruments simply have a butt joint.

The top block is usually far more substantial than the bottom block as it has to accommodate the female slot of the dovetail joint by which the neck is attached to the body. Honduras mahogany is a popular choice for both blocks but the choice of wood varies. The top block is traditionally made from one solid piece of timber, but many makers prefer to use a laminated block which will give far more strength.

The most common method of forming and assembling the body of an acoustic guitar involves the use of a *mould* or *former*.

When the ribs have been cut to shape and prepared, they have to be formed or shaped into the curves that follow the shape of the body. To achieve this, the wood is first soaked in water until it becomes pliable. The ribs are then bent into shape around a metal *bending pipe* which is heated so that, as the ribs are placed against it, the water turns to steam and the dried-out wood retains the shape it is given. After shaping, it is common practice to clamp the ribs in the mould overnight or at least for a few hours to prevent them from losing the shape they have been given.

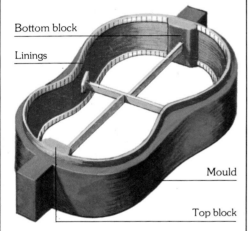

Bottom block

Linings

Mould

Top block

Construction moulds
Guitar-makers usually have a number of different moulds which will give them a variety of body shapes and dimensions. Moulds are traditionally made in one piece, using hardwood for maximum stability, but in recent years metal moulds (as here) and two-piece moulds have become more common.

This is the point at which the guitar soundbox really starts to take shape. With the ribs in position in the mould, the top and bottom blocks are glued and clamped into place – thus joining the two ribs and forming the outline shape of the guitar soundbox. The "linings" are then glued and clamped to the ribs so that finally the soundboard and back can also be glued and clamped in place.

The linings
Linings are continuous strips of wood employed solely for the purpose of making good joints inside the soundbox – between the soundboard, ribs and back. Without them, the thickness of the soundboard, ribs and back is not sufficient to allow reasonable joints to be made. To aid the bending of the linings and so that they match the shape formed by the ribs, they are "kerfed". This means that a saw cut is made through the bulk of the lining every ¼ in. (6 mm) or ½ in. (12.5 mm) along its length.

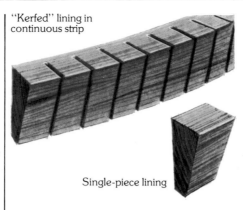

"Kerfed" lining in continuous strip

Single-piece lining

Small wedge-shaped pieces of wood are an alternative to continuous linings. They are fixed in exactly the same way – by gluing and then clamping. Whichever method is used, the wood is tapered or rounded to do away with superfluous timber. By doing this the maker can keep the weight of the linings down and also ensure that their shape will have a minimal effect on the internal dimensions of the soundbox.

Top-class hand-made instruments might be made with pine linings joining the soundboard and the ribs and hardwood linings joining the ribs and back. Some American makers prefer to use basswood for linings. Mass-produced guitars are sometimes made with linings which are in fact laminations of two or three strips of wood.

The edging
Edging, *edge binding* and *purfling* are names given to the protective strip fitted along the outside edges of the soundbox of the guitar, where the soundboard and back join the ribs. It should be made of a durable material so that it can withstand the bangs and knocks that any guitar is bound to receive. Edging also acts as an *effective moisture seal* for the vulnerable end grain and forms an attractive finish to conceal the joints that would otherwise be visible.

Edging is traditionally made from thin veneers or strips of hardwood laminated together. First-class instrument-makers still employ rosewood, maple and other hardwoods for the edging on the guitars they

A selection of decorative edgings.

make, but plastic edging is by far the most widely used material on the majority of guitars being made today.

The edging pattern is sometimes repeated at the bottom of the instrument to camouflage the joint there between the ribs. The same pattern used in the edging – or a variation of it – is sometimes repeated along the edges of the neck and on the head of the instrument.

Some makers choose to elaborate on edgings by using such materials as mother-of-pearl; they may actually put more effort into edging and decoration than others put into making an entire instrument. This is, of course, all a matter of personal taste. Other makers feel that decoration should be kept to a minimum for aesthetic and tonal reasons.

Fingerplates
Also known as "scratch plates" or "pickguards", *fingerplates* have no function other than to protect the soundboard from the scratching and wear caused by the guitarist's plectrums and fingerpicks. Classical guitars do not have fingerplates, but they are almost always added to steel-string guitars.

The traditional material used for fingerplates has always been tortoise-shell but more than adequate man-made imitations are readily available nowadays. Fingerplates are sometimes decorated with engraving and inlays.

The fingerplate is really a compromise. Ideally the soundboard should be as flexible as possible and should be allowed to vibrate freely. This is why fingerplates should be moderately thin and made from a material that will not inhibit the sound of the instrument. Of course, some famous guitars have very large, very thick fingerplates (Gibson "Everly Brothers", for example); the amount by which this affects the tone is open to debate.

Decorative fingerplates
This large, elaborately embellished tortoise-shell fingerplate is one of the most distinctive features of the Gibson J-200 Artist.

The neck and truss rod

The construction of necks for acoustic guitars varies considerably. The simplest type is shaped from a single piece of wood – usually a hardwood such as mahogany, maple, rosewood or African walnut. But this method is expensive, and a far more popular alternative is to make the neck up in its rough, unshaped form by using three pieces of wood. A further variation involves building up the section from which the *heel* will be formed by means of laminated layers of wood.

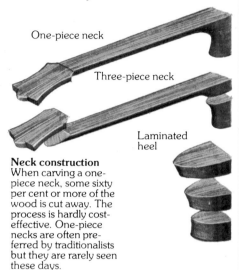

One-piece neck

Three-piece neck

Laminated heel

Neck construction
When carving a one-piece neck, some sixty per cent or more of the wood is cut away. The process is hardly cost-effective. One-piece necks are often preferred by traditionalists but they are rarely seen these days.

Laminated necks are highly regarded because of their strength and stability.

A dovetail joint is the most common method used for fitting the neck of a flat-top steel-string guitar to the body of the instrument. The end of the neck and heel are shaped into the male part of the dovetail joint. The recess or female slot is cut out of the top block. The neck is then inserted and the joint is glued.

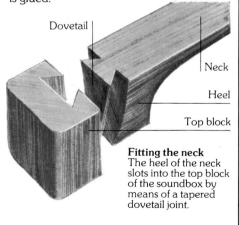

Dovetail

Neck

Heel

Top block

Fitting the neck
The heel of the neck slots into the top block of the soundbox by means of a tapered dovetail joint.

Some classical guitar-makers choose to fit an additional hardwood strip set into a groove in the neck underneath the fingerboard. This is to provide more strength against the pull of the strings. Steel-string guitars, however, have a far greater string tension so something stronger is needed. In the early days of flat-top guitar construction it became common

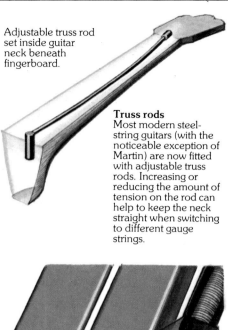

Adjustable truss rod set inside guitar neck beneath fingerboard.

Truss rods
Most modern steel-string guitars (with the noticeable exception of Martin) are now fitted with adjustable truss rods. Increasing or reducing the amount of tension on the rod can help to keep the neck straight when switching to different gauge strings.

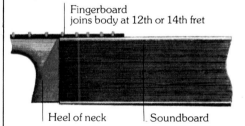

Martin T-bar

Martin hollow bar

Gibson adjustable truss rod

practice to fit a metal strip, tube or "T" section into a similar groove running along the length of the neck just below the fingerboard. This metal strengthening piece is called the *truss rod* or *neck rod*.

During the 1920s the Gibson company came up with an *adjustable* truss rod which they fitted to their arch-top f-hole guitars with great success. Gibson-type adjustable truss rods – and subsequent developments of them – are fitted to the vast majority of steel-string guitars being made today.

The rod is situated in a central groove or channel running along the length of the neck in more-or-less the same position as the hardwood strip or steel section fitted in non-adjustable guitar necks. A further strip of wood is often fitted to close the top of the channel before the fingerboard is added (see p. 35). The truss rod is usually fixed securely in the heel. Because the head of the guitar is tilted back at an angle to the neck, the truss rod can be made to finish below the surface of the head and yet still be accessible for adjustment. With most guitars, a small cover-plate which butts up to the nut is all that has to be removed to reveal the adjusting nut of the truss rod. The end of the truss rod is threaded to accept the adjusting nut and washer. (Some guitars have a slightly different arrangement which may mean they are adjusted with a screwdriver, Allen key or a special tool provided by the guitar-maker.) See p. 168 for how the adjustment is made.

The fingerboard

The *fingerboard* or *fretboard* is the piece of wood fitted to the front of the neck. The frets are set into it. Traditionally, ebony is the first choice of material, but rosewood and other dark hardwoods are more common today.

When the neck is jointed onto the guitar soundbox, its front surface is finished flush with the soundboard. The fingerboard is then glued on so that it runs along the front of the neck and the front of the soundboard. On steel-string guitars, the 12th or 14th fret is usually in line with the join between the neck and body, and there are usually a further six frets on the part of the fingerboard that fits onto the soundboard. On classical guitars, the neck is shorter and joins the body at the 12th fret. This fret is called the *body fret*.

A series of saw cuts are made in the fingerboard to accept the frets. The frets are "T" shaped in section. The top of the fret is rounded so there are no sharp edges to damage the fingers or strings. The upright stem of the "T" is serrated which means it has a roughened edge that grips the sides of the slot in the fingerboard when it has been gently hammered into place. Most steel-string guitars also have *fret markers* inlaid into the fingerboard. They are simply a visual aid to help the guitarist identify fingering positions.

Classical and flamenco guitars usually have flat fingerboards, but many steel-string guitars

Fingerboard joins body at 12th or 14th fret

Heel of neck

Soundboard

have fingerboards with a slightly convex curve to the fretted playing surface.

All fingerboards are narrower at the nut (where the strings are closer together) than they are at the other end. But the actual width varies quite a bit from guitar to guitar.

In my experience, I have found that a preference for different widths and shapes is very much a matter of personal choice. Some guitarists are very adaptable and feel totally at home playing different instruments with varying widths of fingerboard. Others go into a state of depression if they lose their number-one guitar and claim that they feel uncomfortable even with an exact replacement model. Beginners tend to become used to the instrument on which they learn to play and usually feel awkward when forced to change to a different guitar. The only advice I can give is to learn on different types – for instance, an electric guitar with a relatively narrow neck and a classical guitar with a fairly wide neck. You should then find it easy to pick up virtually any guitar and play without difficulty.

The bridge

The vibrations or energy from the guitar strings are transmitted to the soundboard through the saddle and bridge. The bridge must be efficient in the transmission of this energy and strong in both its construction and the way it is attached to the soundboard. There are two basic types of bridge. One is the *floating bridge* (usually used on f-hole guitars) and the other is the *fixed bridge* (generally the type fitted to flat-tops).

A floating bridge is so-called because it is not actually fixed to the soundboard but is held in place simply by the tension of the strings which pass over it. The strings are secured to a fixed *tailpiece*. Floating bridges can therefore be moved backwards and forwards to correct the intonation if necessary.

Fixed bridges are glued to the top of the soundboard and cannot be moved. There is usually no separate tailpiece; instead, the strings are anchored directly to the bridge. The joint between the bridge and the soundboard must be first class. Both surfaces are usually "toothed" or "keyed", meaning that the surfaces of the wood are roughened in order to make the joint stronger.

The traditional and by far the best material for fixed bridges is ebony. It has a high density which aids sustain and the transference of vibration. Substitute woods used to good effect include rosewood, masonia, mahogany and walnut.

On flat-top guitars, the strings are usually secured to a fixed bridge by *bridge pins*.

These hold the ends of the strings in place in the *bridge pin holes*. They are tapered so that when they are inserted in the holes in the bridge a snug fit is achieved without the pins becoming too tight. There should be a small groove in the bridge at the point where each string comes out of the bridge pin hole and turns at a sharp angle towards the saddle.

The *slotted bridge* is a fairly recent innovation and differs from a standard fixed bridge only in the way the strings are attached. The bridge pins and holes are replaced by slots through which the strings are passed. The slots are large enough to allow the strings to pass through them but small enough to catch the metal "barrels" or "end-pieces" attached to the ends of the strings.

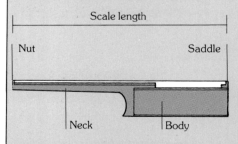

Floating bridges
Bridges of this kind are usually found on arch-top f-hole guitars.

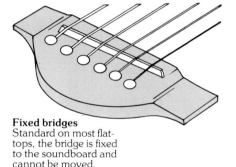

Fixed bridges
Standard on most flat-tops, the bridge is fixed to the soundboard and cannot be moved.

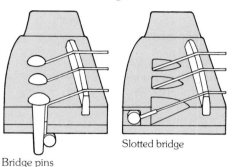

Bridge pins

Slotted bridge

The scale length and string-tension allowances

Scale length is the term used for the total length of the vibrating open string and it is measured from the inside edge of the nut to the point at which the top E string comes into contact with the saddle.

Scale length

Nut   Saddle

Neck   Body

Scale lengths of most flat-top steel-string acoustic guitars range between 24 in. (61 cm) and 26 in. (66 cm). String tension increases with scale length. This is not very noticeable on six-string guitars but it is on twelve-string and bass guitars. It is generally considerably easier to fret notes on a short-scale bass than on one with a standard scale length.

Fret positions can be arrived at by a mathematical formula called the "rule of eighteen" – though it should really be known as the "rule of 17.835". The application of the formula is as follows. First, decide on the overall scale length. To find the distance between the nut and the first

fret, divide the scale length by 17.835. To find the distance between the first fret and the second fret, divide the remaining distance by 17.835. This procedure is followed until the position of the final top fret is determined. Problems sometimes arise because the calculations have to be rounded to the nearest measurable fraction. With a figure like 17.835 some compromise must be reached. But there are checks which can prevent accumulative errors: the twelfth fret should be precisely in the centre of the scale length; the seventh fret should be precisely two-thirds of the way between the nut and the twelfth fret.

When a fretted note is played – as opposed to a note played on an open string – the action of pushing the string down onto the fret increases the string tension. This is because the string is being stretched slightly. If no correction is made, the increase in tension will make each note played on a higher fret progressively sharper. The "intonation" of the guitar, as it is called, will then be inaccurate. Makers generally overcome this problem by moving the bridge/saddle slightly further away from the soundhole – thus increasing the length of vibrating string. The actual distance varies between makers and will vary with different scale lengths and with the height of the guitar's "action". The lighter the action, the more

the string is stretched when fretted (see *Setting the intonation*, p. 171).

On most flat-top steel-string guitars, the saddle is set at an angle so that the bottom E string is between $3/_{16}$ in. (4.8 mm) and $\frac{1}{4}$ in. (6.4 mm) longer than the top E string. This also relates to string tension and intonation. With any given set of six guitar strings, the top E string increases in tension the least when fretted. The B string increases slightly more because it is a slightly heavier gauge. In other words, the heavier the gauge of the string the longer it must be to avoid its pitch going up higher than the required interval when it is pushed down onto the frets. The saddle is therefore sloped as a standard procedure with flat-tops to compensate for this increase in string tension towards the heavier and thicker bass strings.

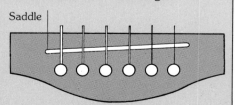

Saddle

The slanted saddle
The "sloping" saddle is designed to make the thicker bass strings slightly longer than the treble strings and therefore to maintain correct intonation when their pitch rises as they are pushed down onto the frets.

The saddle

The *saddle* slots into a groove in the bridge. The strings pass over it and it provides the point at which the vibrating section of each string begins. The saddle also transmits the vibrations from the strings through the bridge to the soundboard. Though it may look rather insignificant, the saddle can have a definite effect on the tone, volume and tuning of the guitar. In the past, the best and traditionally used material has been ivory. Bone is also regarded as a good material, though it does have a tendency to yellow with age. Plastic and synthetic materials are being used more and more by the bulk of manufacturers – although they are still avoided by the makers of top-quality hand-built instruments. This is because plastics do not transfer the energy or vibration as efficiently and because a bridge made of bone or ivory will give more volume than one made from most alternative materials.

Saddles usually have a set of six (or twelve) small notches or semi-circular grooves along their top edge. The strings sit in these so that they do not slide about over the saddle when played fairly hard.

Guitars with flat fingerboards must have flat saddles; guitars with curved fingerboards should have saddles with a matching convex shape. The saddles on better-made guitars

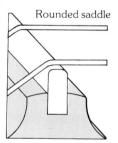

Rounded saddle

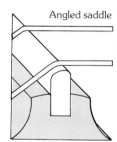

Angled saddle

also tend to be shaped or "angled" at the top (instead of rounded) so that the highest point – where the saddle comes into contact with the strings – is toward the fingerboard.

Some steel-string guitars have adjustable saddles which can be raised or lowered to alter the "action" (see *Setting the action*, p. 166). Others are supplied with a number of small spacing pieces. One or any number of these can be inserted in the slot in the bridge underneath the saddle to increase the height of the strings in relation to the fingerboard.

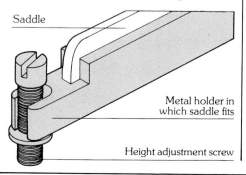

Saddle

Metal holder in which saddle fits

Height adjustment screw

The nut

The *nut* is situated on the head of the guitar at the end of the fingerboard. With the majority of flat-top steel-string acoustic guitars the nut is the point at which the scale length and the vibrating part of the string ends. As with the saddle, the traditional materials used for the nut are bone and ivory, but, as a result of cost and lack of availability, plastic and other synthetic materials are more commonplace now.

Usually, the nut is simply a piece of material with slots or grooves in which the guitar strings sit. As with the saddle, the grooves may have to be set on a curve to match that of the fingerboard. The depth of the grooves is crucial. Ideally, they should be such that fretting notes on the first fret is no harder than fretting notes on the second fret if a capo is placed on the first fret. However, if the grooves are too shallow, the strings may rattle and cause "fret buzz" and the open strings may not even sound at all. Needless to say, altering the height of the nut or the depth of the grooves will affect the "action".

On some other guitars, an extra "zero fret" is employed in conjunction with the nut. In this case, it is the extra fret – not the nut – that sets the string height and scale length. The grooves in the nut are deeper so that a downward pull is created which makes the strings sit firmly on the extra fret.

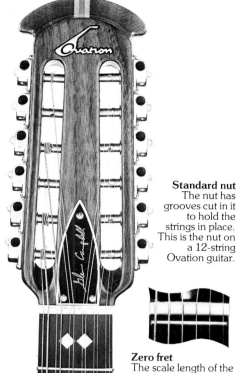

Standard nut
The nut has grooves cut in it to hold the strings in place. This is the nut on a 12-string Ovation guitar.

Zero fret
The scale length of the strings begins at the fret instead of at the nut.

The tuning heads

The *tuning heads* or *machine heads* increase or reduce the tension exerted on each string, thus raising or lowering its pitch and allowing the guitar to be correctly tuned. The tuning heads generally fitted to flat-top steel-string acoustic guitars consist of a capstan, a worm gear and a tuning button on a metal shaft, all mounted on a metal fixing plate. Some tuning heads have individual fixing plates – which means that you can replace a single tuning head should one develop a fault. Others consist of two pairs of three tuning heads which are mounted on a pair of fixing plates so that each group of three tuning heads are at set distances apart.

Any quality tuning head should have a metal bush inserted into the hole in the headstock through which the capstan passes. This prevents undue wear and stops the capstan from binding against the wood of the head. Some kind of gearing is necessary to facilitate fine tuning, to allow the tuning button to be turned with relative ease and to prevent the string tension from turning the capstan. Gear-ratios can differ considerably, but anything in the region of 10:1 will make re-stringing and tuning relatively easy. Top-line manufacturers of tuning heads (such as Grover, for instance) have the gearing section totally enclosed to allow permanent lubrication.

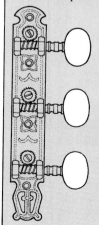

Tuning head design
On the left are three tuning heads set on a single fixing plate. This plate is attached to the side of the headstock. Most often used on classical guitars, they are of the "open" type, which means that the cogs are exposed. On the right is an exploded view of a single Ibanez tuning head. It is enclosed in a sealed housing.

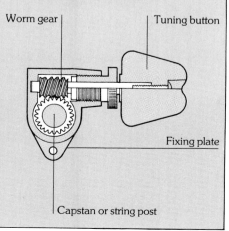

Worm gear

Tuning button

Fixing plate

Capstan or string post

Classical and flamenco guitars

Although volumes have been written on the history and origins of the "classical" or "Spanish" guitar, no precise documentation of the instrument's early development exists. Fragmented information from ancient times clearly indicates the existence of plucked and bowed stringed instruments, but the point at which the guitar as we know it first appeared is not recorded. The indications are that a form of guitar has been made and played since at least the twelfth century. Whether or not the *rebec*, lute, Moorish guitar, North African *aud* (or *al'ud*) or any of the many other stringed instruments to be found in medieval Europe were the direct antecedents of the modern classical guitar remains unproven.

What is certain is the fact that Spain was at the centre of its development. Of the handful of great men who truly shaped the history of the classical guitar, most were from Spain. The influence of one of the greatest – guitarist, composer and teacher José Ferdinand Sor (1778-1839), better known as Fernando Sor – is still felt to this day. Born in Barcelona, he took up the guitar after studying violin, cello, harmony and composition. By the age of sixteen he was able to play his own compositions on the guitar with a virtuosity that set new standards. He went on to compose over 400 pieces, many of which are considered essential to the contemporary classical guitarist's repertoire. Sor was also known as a teacher and as the author of his famous "Method", an extensive work which documented his style and technique in great detail.

Sor travelled extensively in Europe. In Paris he met the French guitar-maker, René-François Lacôte, and in London he met another well-known luthier, Louis Panormo. Both were impressed by the superior tone and quality of the Spanish-made guitars that he played, and both began to employ Spanish methods of construction and design in their own workshops. In fact, Panormo's instruments were subsequently given labels stating "The only maker of guitars in the Spanish style – Louis Panormo".

Nevertheless, Panormo and Lacôte were exceptional in their adoption of Spanish methods. In general, guitars made in other European countries had their own regional characteristics. The English, French, Italians and others were making finely crafted and beautifully decorated instruments, but when it came to tone, projection and sustain Spanish guitars were far superior.

The instruments played by Sor and his most famous contemporaries – Dionisio Aguado (1784-1849) and Matteo Carcassi (1792-1853), for instance – were, however, far inferior to the guitars at the disposal of today's players. All that changed – with a quantum jump in the development of classi-cal guitar construction – at the hands of a carpenter from San Sebastian de Almería, Antonio de Torres Jurado (1817-1892). Better known simply as Torres, he was without a doubt the most important figure in the history of guitar design and construction. Musicians who played his guitars immediately discarded those of other makers. Throughout Spain luthiers adopted Torres' designs. In fact, to this day, classical guitar-makers still construct their instruments almost exactly in the manner of Torres.

Torres first learned the principles of guitar-making in the Grenada workshops of José Pernas. His friend and guitarist, Julian Arcas, suggested that he work on ways of improving the tone of the guitar. This he did. By the middle of the nineteenth century he was making guitars bearing his own name, and over a period of years he gradually refined his ideas, building experimental instruments of varying

The classical guitar
Classical guitars now have nylon strings (though they were originally gut) as these give a more appropriate tone. The system of internal bracing still owes a great deal to Torres. In spite of slight variations and modifications (for example, the famous classical guitar made in 1956 by the Frenchman Robert Bouchet), his basic fan-shaped pattern is still widely used.

Tuning heads   Worm-gear tuning heads with ivory, bone or plastic capstans on which strings are wound.

Fingerboard   African ebony or dark rosewood.

Neck   Usually mahogany or cedar. Classical necks are shorter and wider than those on steel-string guitars; they have only 19 frets and join the body at the 12th fret.

Soundboard   European spruce or pine.

Ribs and back   Rosewood – although maple, walnut, birch and other hardwoods are often used successfully.

Bridge   Nylon strings threaded through holes and then knotted.

Guitar made in 1854

Guitar made in 1888

The development of Torres' guitar designs
Two of Torres' guitars illustrate how he evolved the basic design of the modern classical guitar.

sizes and shapes and trying constructional methods which were quite revolutionary.

He increased the area of the soundboard and the size of the soundbox, making his guitars "deeper" (the soundboard-to-back measurement of the guitar had previously been 2 in. (5 cm) or less). He rounded the bouts and changed their relative proportions. He reduced the thickness of the timbers used for the soundboard, ribs and back, and used lighter and more flexible woods. He evolved a system of "fan" strutting that allowed the soundboard to vibrate far more efficiently, he arrived at the 65 cm (approx. 25½ in.) scale length, and he improved guitar varnishes.

By completely re-defining the science of guitar construction, Torres improved the instrument to such a degree that major musical advances were almost inevitable. It was another Spaniard who was to utilize these advantages. His name was Francisco Eixea Tárrega (1852-1909). Tárrega is universally considered to be the father of all modern classical guitar technique.

He evolved the posture, hand positions and use of the foot-stool to raise the left foot that are taught to every student of the classical guitar today. He also transcribed the works of such great composers as Bach, Beethoven and Mozart for the guitar, and, although he was not the first to adapt music written for other instruments, he was the first to challenge the long-held opinion that the guitar was an inferior instrument incapable of doing justice to such music.

It is of course impossible to talk about the development of the classical guitar without acknowledging Andrés Torres Segovia (b. 1893). Having made his concert debut in Paris in 1924, by the 1930s Segovia's name was known around the world. Perhaps more than any other single player, he has been responsible for the acceptance of the guitar as a valid concert instrument for the performance of classical music.

Andrés Segovia
Segovia is an avid student of every aspect of the guitar and its most knowledgeable historian.

Flamenco guitars

Flamenco is the music of the gypsy people of Andalucia, the region of Spain bounded by Cordoba in the north, Cadiz in the south, Almeria in the east and Huelva in the west. The origins of flamenco are obscure, although it is generally accepted to have North African (Moorish) influences. It emerged towards the end of the eighteenth century when it was always played as a combination of dance, song and guitar accompaniment. Later, the original form gave rise to two subsequent developments: *cante flamenco* (based on different song forms) and solo flamenco guitar. The man credited for the birth of the solo guitar form is Ramón Montoya (1880-1949).

The flamenco guitar
Flamenco guitar construction is based on the design of the Spanish classical guitar, with modifications to suit the requirements of flamenco. Once again, Torres is the key figure: he evolved the basic design to which today's makers still adhere. The flamenco guitar is usually slightly smaller than the classical guitar. Its back and ribs are made from Spanish cyprus tooled very thinly to produce a more brilliant, more penetrating sound and to give the instrument greater volume. This does, however, result in a loss of mellowness and tone which explains why some solo flamenco guitarists play classical guitars.

Flamenco has traditionally been passed from generation to generation without the aid of musical notation. The music is frequently regarded as a loose, undisciplined form. In fact, this is not so. It is a combination of improvisation and strict rhythmic structures, of which there are many. Flamenco is no simple man's music. The *soleares*, for example, one of the four most important structures, has a rhythm based on a twelve-beat form, with accents on the third, sixth, eighth and tenth beats, and is played in ¾ time. Several of the other song forms have rhythmic patterns that are considerably more complex, and a guitarist often specializes in only one of them.

Tuning heads Traditionally, wooden pegs are considered to give a better tone than geared.

Fingerboard Usually African ebony.

Neck Various hardwoods – often mahogany.

Strings Set closer to the body to give a faster "action". Flamenco guitars are often strung with higher tension strings.

Soundboard European spruce or pine.

Ribs and back Spanish cyprus.

Golpe Special "tap" plates to protect the face of the guitar – since "golpe strokes" (striking and tapping with the fingers) are an integral part of the rhythm and sound of flamenco music.

Bridge Most flamenco guitars have the same style of bridge as those fitted to classical guitars. For details on how to fit and tie the knots on the strings, see p. 165.

Steel-string acoustic guitars

The steel-string guitar as we know it today evolved in America, though the majority of the instrument makers who contributed to its development were European or of European descent. During the latter half of the nineteenth and the early part of the twentieth century, America had become a huge cultural melting pot. For a number of reasons – including racial, religious and political persecution – thousands of European, Russian and other emigrants were crossing the Atlantic and seeking a new life in America. Among them were highly skilled musical instrument makers who were to dominate the construction and production of the steel-string acoustic guitar.

Two distinctly different methods of con-struction evolved. The first led to what is known as the *flat-top* guitar and, basically, adapted European classical guitar-making techniques. The second method produced the *arch-top* (or *f-hole*) guitar, with a con-toured or arched soundboard and back carved from a solid piece of wood. Its design and construction were derived from Euro-pean violin-making techniques.

Any history of steel-string acoustic guitars must begin with the names Martin and Gibson, the most influential of all the manu-facturers. Over the next few pages we will take a look at the Martin Organization and its guitars, at the Gibson company, and at a few of the other manufacturers who have made, and still make, excellent and lasting guitars.

Martin guitars

In 1833, Christian Frederick Martin (1796-1873) emigrated from his native Germany to America and opened a combined workshop and music store in New York. He was already an accomplished instrument maker, having worked as foreman for the highly regarded luthier, Johann Stauffer, in Vienna. The first guitars Christian Frederick made in New York were heavily influenced by Stauffer's gut-string classical instruments. They featured a floating fingerboard, an adjustable neck and all six machine heads on one side of the head-stock. They were also quite narrow, as was typical before the influence of Torres (see p. 42). Before long, however, Martin evolved more personal and more original designs and

How to identify Martin guitars

The system Martin uses for cataloguing its guitars is quite complex and has been fur-ther complicated by a long history during which models have been refined, altered, discontinued and re-introduced. However, in simple terms, this is how it works.

Each guitar has a two-part "code". The first part (either a letter or a number) indi-cates the *size* of the guitar, and the second part (a number) indicates the *style*. A Martin OO-18, for example, is therefore a "OO" size guitar made and decorated in the "18" style. A D-28 is a "Dreadnought" size, "28" style guitar. It follows that "45" style guitars

– those with spruce tops, rosewood backs and sides, ebony fingerboards and the famous abalone pearl inlays – can be found in various different sizes. They can – the OO-45, OOO-45, OM-45 and D-45.

There are, of course, exceptions to the rule. There are also further complications such as the addition of a "12" to indicate a 12-string guitar, a "K" to distinguish one with a koa wood body, or a "C" which can mean either "classical", "carved-top" or "cutaway". Many early Martins had a number as the first half of their code, and some still do (e.g., the 7-28 or the 5-18).

What the letters mean	
O	Concert size
OO	Grand concert size
OOO	Auditorium size
D	Dreadnought size
DS	Dreadnought with a slotted headstock and 12 frets to the body not 14
M	Grand auditorium size
MC	Grand auditorium with cutaway
OM	Orchestra model
C	Classical or carved-top model
N	"European-style" classical model
F	F-hole model
T	Tenor or "Terz" 4-string banjo guitar
K	Koa wood soundbox instead of the customary spruce plus rosewood or mahogany

O-16NY
First introduced 1971 as new, authentic version of original pre-1929 "New York Martin". Small "O" size and "16" style. Spruce top, quarter-sawn mahogany back and sides, slotted head-stock, wide rosewood fingerboard, no fret markers or fingerplate.

OO-18
"OO" size guitars date back to mid-1800s and "18" style first appeared 1857. Current "18" style features 14-fret neck, solid headstock, white dot fret markers, "belly" bridge, dark edgings and fingerplate.

OOO-28
"OOO" size guitars also go back to mid-19th century. The famous "28" style emerged some-time before 1874 and remains almost un-changed. Rosewood back and sides, spruce top, white edging.

OM-45
When first introduced between 1929 and 1933, "OM" series were first Martin guitars to have 14-fret necks. Size is same as current "OOO" 14-fret guitars. "45" styling dates from 1904 and includes inlays of pearl abalone all around soundbox, rosette, fingerboard and headstock.

M-38
First appeared in 1977 as updated version of vintage 1930s Martin f-hole guitars (the F-7 and F-9) – but with flat top and round soundhole instead of original carved top.

MC-28
Same size as "Grand Auditorium" M-38 and M-28, but with a body cutaway allowing easier access to the high frets. Also features an oval soundhole. This is Martin's newest guitar.

One of Martin's earliest guitars
This gut-string instrument was built by C.F. Martin in about 1834 and its distinctive shape owes a lot to his former boss, Johann Stauffer. The angle of the neck can be adjusted by means of a clock key inserted in the back of the heel.

gained himself a reputation as a fine maker of classical guitars in his own right.

Christian Frederick did not enjoy New York city life and so, in 1839, he moved to Nazareth, Pennsylvania, which has remained the home of the Martin factory to this day. Initially, an agency called C.A. Zoebisch & Sons acted as sole New York distributor for Martin after the move. Christian Frederick, his son Christian Frederick II and a nephew, Christian Frederick Hartman, all worked together in the company until Christian Frederick Senior died in 1873. When, in 1888, Christian Frederick II also died, his son Frank Henry Martin took over the company. He terminated the unsatisfactory distribution agreement with C.A. Zoebisch and from that time sold instruments directly from Nazareth.

Under Frank Henry Martin, the company continued to grow – modifying and improving designs and introducing new models and new instruments (mandolins, ukuleles, mando-cellos and "tenor" guitars). In fact, the 1920s and 1930s were a time of considerable innovation.

It was at the beginning of the 1920s that the company started making steel-string guitars in earnest. To some extent, this was in response to the increasing demand for steel-string guitars fuelled by the popularity of folk and country and western music. At first, Martin simply strengthened their highly regarded classical guitars in order to make the switch from gut strings to steel strings. Later, other changes were made – the "belly" bridge and truss rod were introduced to give additional support against the increased string tension, the saddle was slanted, and the dimensions of the bracing were re-designed.

Like Gibson, Martin made a variety of stringed instruments at different times to meet changing popular demands. But it was their flat-top steel string acoustics which set the standards of excellence and which became probably the most copied guitars of their type.

Martin "Dreadnoughts"

These are perhaps the most legendary of all Martin guitars. Named after the British battleship, *Dreadnaught*, they were first introduced by Martin in 1931. In fact, however, they date back to 1916 when the company made a range of guitars for the Ditson company of Boston. The design of these "Ditson Spanish Models" was agreed between Harry Hunt of Ditson's New York showroom and Frank Henry Martin. They all had the now-famous wide waists and narrow, sloping shoulders. When the Ditson company folded in the late 1920s, Martin realized that there was nevertheless a considerable demand for the largest of the Ditson guitars. They therefore began making prototype instruments using designs closer to their own guitars. They changed the "fan bracing" – which was a feature of the Ditsons – to the "X-bracing" used on most Martin soundboards.

The first true Martin Dreadnoughts were the D-18 and D-28. They were based on the existing "18" and "28" styles but were built to the enlarged "D" (for Dreadnought) size. The original models had necks which joined the body at the 12th fret, but by about 1934 customer demand had made 14-fret necks the standard feature (partly because a lot of banjo players, changing over to the guitar at the time, were used to slightly longer-necked instruments).

Dreadnoughts have had an enormous influence on acoustic guitar design. Their somewhat "bassier" tone has made them popular in folk, country and bluegrass music, as well as rock. They have been copied in some form or another by just about every other guitar manufacturer. Vintage D-45s (with their beautiful abalone inlay) and HD-28s are highly coveted, very rare and very expensive.

Close-up of herringbone inlay

Martin HD-28
The first prototype for the HD-28 was made in 1931 for a country singer called "Arkie". It was a 12-fret model and was called the D-2. Over the next few years, the guitar went into production as the HD-28 – the "H" standing for the famous herringbone pattern edging – and it became one of Martin's most highly regarded instruments.

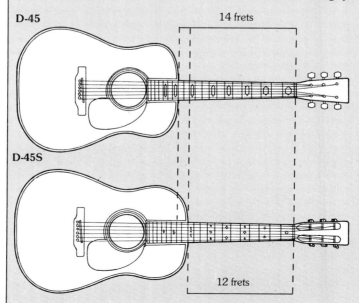

D-45

D-45S

14 frets

12 frets

Neck lengths
When, in 1934, Martin introduced their new 14-fret Dreadnoughts, the term "DS" was used to designate the superseded, original 12-fret models. These drawings illustrate the difference.

However, Martin themselves – as well as most discerning guitar players – were in fact aware that the 12-fret guitars, with their longer sound-boxes, actually had a superior tone.

Finally, in 1967, the original style was re-introduced as an alternative in the form of the D-18S, D-28S, D-35S and, later, the legendary D-45S.

Arch-top guitars

These instruments (also known as "cello", "plectrum", "orchestra" or "f-hole" guitars) came into their own during the 1920s when jazz was a vibrant, evolving musical force and the "Big Band Era" was in full swing. As the guitar began to overtake the banjo in popularity, guitarists were looking for an instrument that produced enough volume to be heard clearly – not only as part of a relatively small group playing "loud syncopated jazz music" but also in big bands such as the Duke Ellington Orchestra. Since regular flat-top or gut-string classical guitars did not project sufficiently, they turned to the new arch-top steel-strings like Gibson's Master Tone L-5.

The fundamental difference between an arch-top and a flat-top acoustic guitar lies in the construction of the soundbox or body. Traditionally, the soundboard and back of an arch-top are carved from fairly thick, solid pieces of wood – a technique which allows for much greater "arching" or "contouring" than on flat-top guitars.

In fact, as arch-top guitars gained in popularity, the Gretsch company started using a different process. Instead of carving the soundboard and back, they laminated them. The soundboard and back each consisted of several thin layers of flat wood which were held in a former or mould while being glued together. When the glue had set and the wood was removed from the mould, it retained its required arched shape.

Gibson's arch-top guitars also saw the introduction of the "adjustable two-footed floating bridge" – a design adapted from the violin family. The strings are fixed to a "tailpiece" and merely pass over the bridge instead of being anchored to it. Moreover, the floating bridge itself is not glued to the face of the soundboard but is held in place simply by the tension of the strings.

In the very early days, some arch-top guitars were made with round or oval soundholes. But, following the example of Gibson's L-5, most makers switched to the now-standard "f-hole" design – another feature borrowed from the violin.

All arch-tops have a much simpler system of internal bracing than flat-top guitars. Essentially, this is because they require fewer struts. Firstly, the arched shape of the soundboard makes it intrinsically stronger. Secondly, the strings are anchored via the tailpiece to the bottom block, not via the bridge to the soundboard.

Arch-top acoustic guitars are no longer as dominant as they were in the twenties and thirties – partly due to a decline of interest in the music for which they were made, but mostly due to the subsequent emergence of the electric guitar. However, some of the most famous models (including early instruments produced by Gibson, Martin, Epiphone, D'Angelico and Vega) are highly regarded and keenly sought by collectors.

Gibson guitars

If Martin is the first name in the history of flat-top acoustics, then Gibson is the most important when it comes to arch-tops.

Orville Gibson was born in Chataugay, New York, in 1856. Keen on wood-carving as well as being an accomplished mandolin and guitar player, he made experimental mandolins that utilized violin construction methods. In the 1890s, he applied the same principles to guitars – producing some fine arch-top, oval-soundhole instruments and pioneering the use of steel instead of gut strings. He carved their arched soundboards and backs from relatively thick pieces of wood, matching the tone of front and back by tapping them and carving the wood until he felt they were compatible.

In 1902, a group of businessmen from the township of Kalamazoo entered into an agreement with Orville Gibson, and the "Gibson Mandolin-Guitar Manufacturing Co. Ltd" was formed. In 1903, the first catalogue appeared and by the time Gibson died in 1918 his company had a solid and formidable reputation.

The death of the founder did not put a stop to the company. In 1920, Lloyd Loar joined Gibson. During the four years he worked there – and before he left to form the unsuccessful Vivi-Tone company – he was responsible for the invention of the famous Gibson L-5, introduced in 1924.

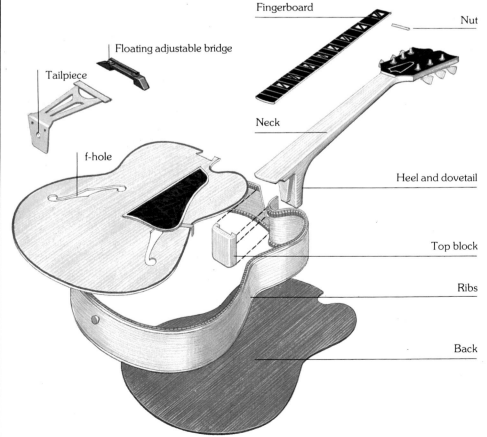

Fingerboard

Nut

Floating adjustable bridge

Tailpiece

Neck

f-hole

Heel and dovetail

Top block

Ribs

Back

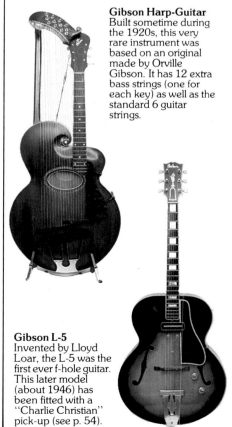

Gibson Harp-Guitar
Built sometime during the 1920s, this very rare instrument was based on an original made by Orville Gibson. It has 12 extra bass strings (one for each key) as well as the standard 6 guitar strings.

Gibson L-5
Invented by Lloyd Loar, the L-5 was the first ever f-hole guitar. This later model (about 1946) has been fitted with a "Charlie Christian" pick-up (see p. 54).

The L-5 replaced the single oval soundhole with two "f-holes". It had an adjustable floating bridge which could be raised or lowered, an improved neck design which made it easier to play, and a raised fingerplate. It was also one of the first guitars to be fitted with Ted McHugh's adjustable truss rod. The L-5 was a huge success. It virtually replaced the banjo as a rhythm instrument, but it also had sufficient volume to trigger a new musical era in which the guitar was used for playing single-note solos.

Further innovations were to follow. In 1934, Gibson introduced their Super 400 – so-called because at that time 400 dollars was what it cost. In 1939, in reponse to the growing use of the guitar for lead playing, both the L-5 and Super 400 were brought out with a single "Venetian" cutaway.

Gibson entered the flat-top acoustic guitar market during the mid-1930s with their "jumbo" size guitars, designed to compete with Martin's Dreadnoughts. The successful SJ-200 went into production in 1936-7. In following years it was joined by the J-45 and J-50, and later (in 1962) by the Dove, Hummingbird and Everly Brothers guitars.

Spurred on by strong competition from Guild, Ovation and many smaller companies, Gibson produced a new series of "Mark" flat-tops in 1977. Unfortunately, the guitars have not been a success.

Gibson Super 400
This guitar was introduced in 1934 as Gibson's top-of-the-line f-hole acoustic. It was larger than the L-5, more elaborately decorated and more expensive. This is one of the post-1939 guitars with the cutaway body.

Gibson SJ-200
One of the largest flat-tops ever made, this guitar was once owned by John Lennon. It has the current-style fingerplate and fingerboard inlays but an original bridge in the shape of buffalo horns.

Other American guitar-makers

Martin and Gibson have not been allowed to dominate completely the manufacture of acoustic guitars. Back in the 1890s, the Washburn company was a strong competitor to Martin, and Washburn guitars are still made today. At around the same time, the Vega and Harmony companies were also started. Vega made small numbers of excellent arch-tops; Harmony, in contrast, concentrated on mass production. They claimed to have built 10 million guitars since 1945.

Following the success of Gibson's L-5, Epiphone built a reputation as makers of fine arch-top guitars – with the mid-1930s

D'Angelico New Yorker (left)
Hand-built by John D'Angelico in the 1930s, only about 300 of these superb guitars were ever made.

Guild F-512 (right)
Guild's 12-strings are among their best-known flat-top acoustics. This is their top model.

Japanese guitar-makers

During the 1960s, an influx of well-made, considerably cheaper guitars from Japan posed a grave threat to American manufacturers. Although Martin, Gibson and Guild have all survived the competition – either by

Emperor and Triumph, in particular. On a smaller scale, the now-legendary guitars made by John D'Angelico also appeared.

As the flat-top guitar gained in popularity – reaching a peak in the 1960s – Epiphone and Guild (a company formed in 1952) began producing in very large numbers.

Maccaferri guitars

Mario Maccaferri deserves a special mention. His most famous guitars – those which he designed for the French Selmer company between 1932 and 1933 – are identified in most people's minds with Django Reinhardt. The early models had the distinctive body cutaway, a D-shaped soundhole, and an extra sound chamber *inside* the soundbox.

A very rare 1932 Maccaferri/Selmer guitar.

---

concentrating on the higher price range or by getting their cheaper models manufactured under licence in Japan – Japanese guitars now make up a large percentage of the market in both Europe and the United States.

Yamaha FG-375
One of the first Japanese manufacturers, Yamaha make a wide selection of flat-top acoustics. More expensive now than they once were, they are nevertheless all excellent guitars.

Ovation guitars

In recent years, Ovation have been responsible for by far the most significant new development in the design and construction of acoustic guitars. The Ovation company, a division of the Kaman aerospace organization, was founded by Charles Kaman in the 1960s. Kaman believed that guitar design could be radically improved if he and his engineers could apply to it some of the principles of vibration and acoustics that they had learned from their work with helicopters and other aircraft. Aware of the fact that in a conventional guitar much of the sound is either "trapped" in the corners of the soundbox or absorbed by the wood, he began building instruments whose back and sides were replaced by a one-piece, rounded bowl made of a fibreglass material called "Lyrachord". This shell-like, moulded back has no corners, requires no struts and reflects more of the natural sound. Ovation guitars have wooden soundboards made of sitka spruce tapered from the neck to the bridge. The bracing pattern varies from one model to another and is specially designed to give the sound best

suited to the style of music for which the guitar is intended. The neck is built up from separate pieces of mahogany and maple integrated with a steel tension rod set inside an aluminium channel.

Since their first model, the Balladeer, was introduced in 1966, Ovation have produced various nylon-string and 12-string guitars as well as a complete range of different 6-string instruments. All of these are also available in "acoustic-electric" versions with Ovation's own built-in piezo-electric pickups and battery-operated pre-amp.

The company's newest models are the highly expensive "Adamas" (with a special soundboad made from a laminate of birch veneer and carbon fibre) and a cheaper line of "Matrix" guitars (which have necks made from polyurethane and aluminium).

Ovation guitars have been very successful. Their distinctive tone – together with their strength and the versatility of the acoustic-electric models – appeals to many guitar players and more and more performers are using them both on-stage and in the studio.

Ovation Custom Legend 12-string
The photograph below shows clearly the round-back shape of the fibreglass bowl which has become Ovation's trademark. Because of the strong, five-piece neck construction Ovation employ, the necks on their 12-string guitars are built to the same, easy-to-play dimensions as those on their 6-strings.

Lyrachord bowl

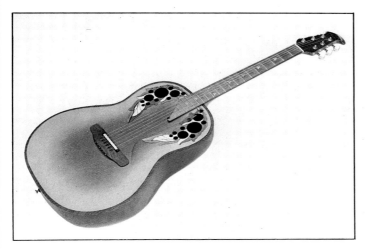

The Adamas
This guitar is Ovation's most expensive model. The soundboard is made from a sheet of birch veneer sandwiched between two layers of "carbon prepreg" (carbon fibres embedded in epoxy resin). The conventional soundhole is replaced by 22 smaller holes set on either side of the upper bout. This design is intended to minimize feedback when the guitar is amplified. There is also an acoustic-electric version of the Adamas.

Resonator guitars

Metal resonator or resophonic guitars are a variation on the theme of the acoustic guitar. Also known as "National" or "Dobro" guitars, they were first developed in the 1920s when the Dopera brothers founded their "National Guitar Company" and, later, their "Dobro Company". Resonator guitars have a distinctive, metallic, "jangly" sound and effectively project a lot more volume than conventional acoustic instruments. This is because the vibrations of the strings are transferred through the bridge to a round metal dish or cone which acts as a resonator within the guitar and which "amplifies" the sound. Early National guitars had all-metal bodies and a single resonator that was cone-shaped. Early Dobro guitars were wooden-bodied and had a bowl-shaped resonator. Eventually, in 1934, the two companies merged.

Resonator guitars have always been considered ideal for bottleneck slide playing styles. In fact, they were built with both square-section necks as well as conventional round-section necks. They were at their most popular in the 1920s and 1930s during the boom in Hawaiian and country music, but they were also used by many famous old blues players.

National "Duolian"
Made in the early 1930s, this well-used, metal bodied National now belongs to Rory Gallagher. It is an original 12-fret model.

ELECTRIC GUITARS

The history and development of the electric guitar, like that of the steel-string acoustic, began in America. The feature that unifies all electric guitars is the *pick-up*. It is the pick-up that converts the sound of the instrument or the vibration of the strings into an electrical signal. This signal is then fed to an amplifier and converted back into sound by a loud-speaker. Key names in the evolution of the modern solid-body electric guitar are Lloyd Loar, Adolph Rickenbacker, Leo Fender and Les Paul. Much of the experimental work was centred around the Fender and Gibson companies — still among the market leaders today. In recent years, Japanese and Far-Eastern manufacturers have established reputations for inexpensive guitars that represent excellent value for money. Their top-line electrics offer a combination of quality and low cost that keeps the whole industry on its toes. The huge variety of instruments, ranging from vintage American models to the most up-to-date Roland guitar synthesizers, can make choosing an electric guitar something of a nightmare to the uninitiated. For this reason, this chapter sets out the history of the instrument, and describes in detail the most important of the many different types and models — explaining how they work, how they are built, and how they differ.

The anatomy of the electric guitar

The solid-body electric guitar developed from early, amplified acoustic guitars. These were simply acoustic instruments with pick-ups attached to them. Like so many innovations in the history of the guitar, it came about as a result of the quest for greater volume.

The heart of the solid-body electric guitar is the magnetic pick-up. It responds directly to the vibration of the strings and transforms this energy into electrical impulses which are then amplified and fed to a loudspeaker (see p. 52). To do this efficiently, the pick-up should be as stable as possible and should not be disturbed by vibrations from the body.

When a pick-up is fitted to the soundboard of an acoustic guitar, two problems can arise. First, the pick-up may move as the soundboard vibrates. Second, speaker "feedback" may be generated. With electric guitars, the solution is to increase the *mass* of the guitar body so that its ability to receive and transmit vibrations is reduced. If this idea were taken to its logical conclusion, the body might be made from concrete or perhaps even lead. In practice, a compromise is reached. Through experiments with various prototype instruments, pioneer makers of electric guitars found that a solid body made of high-density hardwood reduced the problems to a manageable level.

The solid body

There is far more scope for solid-body guitar design than there is for acoustic guitar design. This is because an acoustic guitar has to be constructed within certain design parameters if it is to produce sufficient volume and an acceptable tone. As long as the solid body of an electric guitar keeps the pick-ups fairly stable and provides a mounting for the necessary components, its shape is limited only by practicability and the designer's imagination. Gibson's Flying V and Explorer (see p. 59), the Vox Phantom and the Ovation Breadwinner illustrate some of the endless possibilities that are available.

Well-seasoned or kiln-dried hardwoods such as mahogany, walnut, ash, alder and maple are frequently used in solid-body construction. However, laminated timbers are also common. The original Les Paul guitars actually had a mahogany body with a maple "cap" or front (see p. 58). Several other materials have also been successfully employed – Dan Armstrong's plexiglass guitars, for example.

The material used in the construction of a solid body can in fact affect the sound of the guitar. The denser the material, the longer the natural (not feedback-assisted) sustain the instrument will have. The tone can be altered by changing the wood used for both the body and the neck.

The bridge/saddle
Many different types of bridge are fitted to electric guitars. This one is based on the Gibson "Tune-O-Matic". The height of the whole bridge can be raised or lowered, but each string also sits on its own individually adjustable saddle.

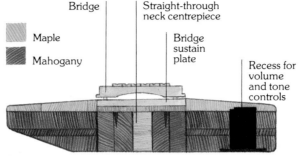

Bridge

Straight-through neck centrepiece

Maple

Mahogany

Bridge sustain plate

Recess for volume and tone controls

The body
This guitar, the Yamaha SG 2000, features a sandwich construction body and a laminated, straight-through neck. The backbone of the guitar is a laminated block made from a strip of maple in between two pieces of mahogany. This runs from the end of the headstock to the bottom of the body so that there is no join between body and neck. The bulk of the body is then made up of mahogany with a carved maple top on the face of the guitar. A solid piece of brass is set directly beneath the bridge to increase sustain.

Pick-up selector or "toggle" switch

The nut
The nut on an electric guitar is much the same as that on an acoustic – although sometimes it is made from metal (such as brass) in order to aid sustain.

Tuning heads

The fingerboard
On most guitars, the fingerboard is a separate strip of wood – often rosewood or ebony – fixed to the front of the neck. On other guitars, the frets may be set directly into the neck. Some guitarists (e.g., Ritchie Blackmore) use "scalloped" fingerboards. The wood between the frets is carved to form concave dips. This makes note bending easier.

Fret marker

The strings
Electric guitars usually have lighter gauge strings than acoustic guitars. This makes solo lead playing easier.

Fret

The neck
Electric guitars tend to have narrow necks. In recent years, considerable thought has been put into neck design. Kramer and Travis Bean, for example, have introduced aluminium necks for greater stability.

Truss rod cover

The head
Most heads (or head-stocks) follow the traditional style of three tuning heads on each side (as here). Fender's distinctive head, however, has all six machine heads on one side.

Front pick-up

Back pick-up

Fingerplate

Tailpiece

Volume control for back pick-up

Volume control for front pick-up

Tone control for back pick-up

Tone control for front pick-up

Output socket
Usually a standard jack plug socket.

The construction of the neck

In themselves, solid-body guitar necks are very similar to those of acoustic guitars. However, there is far more latitude as to where the neck joins the body. The solid-body electric guitar has evolved as a solo lead instrument, frequently played above the 12th fret. Consequently, to allow the guitarist easier access to the upper part of the fingerboard, a single or double cutaway is usually incorporated into the body design and the neck joins the body at a much higher fret. The point at which the joint occurs is sometimes called the "body fret". The neck on the Gibson SG Deluxe, for example, effectively joins the body at the 20th fret.

There is a great deal of controversy concerning the best method of attaching the neck to the body. Most of the arguments revolve around *sustain* – the length of time that a note continues to sound after the string has been struck. Of the three different construction methods, a glued-in neck (similar to the traditional dovetail of acoustic guitars) is felt to give a better joint and therefore more sustain than a bolt-on neck. And a neck constructed from a single piece (or laminated sections) of wood which goes straight through the body is, in turn, considered to give more sustain than a bolt-on neck. The arguments are not conclusive. Sustain also depends on the mass or density of the wood, the material used for the nut and saddle, and the output of the pick-ups.

With fewer design constraints than acoustic guitars, a number of different adjustable truss rods have evolved. Fender guitars have the adjustment screw at the body end of the neck instead of at the headstock end. Rickenbacker developed a double adjustment truss rod to allow the correction of a twisted neck.

Glued-in neck
Les Pauls are constructed in this way. The end of the neck is shaped to fit into a slot in the guitar body, and the joint is then glued permanently.

Bolt-on neck
Fender were responsible for introducing the detachable neck, bolted or screwed to the body. On the Stratocaster, a "neck-tilt" system allows changes to be made to the neck angle.

Straight-through neck
The point of this design (used by Yamaha, Aria and Alembic, among others) is that both ends of the strings are attached to one piece of wood.

Pick-ups and controls

"Transducer" is the name given to any electronic or electro-magnetic device used to convert forms of physical energy into electrical energy. *All* guitar pick-ups are transducers of one kind or another. They convert the energy produced by the vibrating guitar strings into AC (alternating current) electrical pulses which are fed to an amplifier. The amp magnifies these pulses many times before the loudspeaker transforms them back into sound waves.

Electric guitars are generally fitted with *magnetic* pick-ups, although acoustic guitars are often amplified by means of a so-called *contact transducer*. Since magnetic pick-ups only function if they are close to the guitar strings, they are mounted on the body directly beneath the strings. Electric guitars may have one, two or three pick-ups. This means that, by means of the selector switch or volume controls, an individual pick-up or a combination of pick-ups can be used to get different sounds. The rhythm pick-up (which is nearer the centre of the strings) has a more mellow sound than the cutting treble of the lead pick-up (which is close to the bridge).

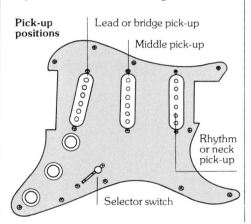

Pick-up positions
Lead or bridge pick-up
Middle pick-up
Rhythm or neck pick-up
Selector switch

The Fender Stratocaster pick-up
Fender Telecasters and Stratocasters are the guitars most often identified with the single-coil pick-up "sound" – clear and punchy but with a penetrating treble. Instead of using a single bar magnet, Leo Fender employed six individual, magnetic pole-pieces, each slightly staggered in height to help equalize the amplified volume of the six strings. The coil is actually wrapped around the pole-pieces. Originally, it was made with 8,350 turns of copper wire, although modern Strat pick-ups now use only 7,600 turns.

How the single-coil pick-up works

The simplest form of magnetic pick-up consists of a permanent bar magnet with a continuous length of insulated copper wire wrapped around it several thousand times. This winding is an electrical *coil*. The wire is extremely fine – about the same thickness as

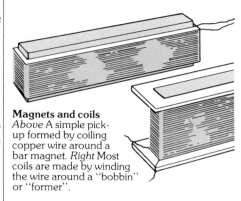

Magnets and coils
Above A simple pick-up formed by coiling copper wire around a bar magnet. *Right* Most coils are made by winding the wire around a "bobbin" or "former".

one single strand of human hair.

The magnet generates a magnetic field around itself, and the pick-up is mounted on the guitar body so that the guitar strings actually pass through the magnetic field – and, because the strings are made of steel, they interact with the magnetic field. While the strings are at rest, the field maintains a regular shape and nothing happens in the coil. But, as soon as a string is struck, its movement alters the shape of the field.

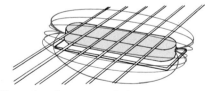

The pick-up's magnetic field
The sole purpose of the magnet is to provide a magnetic field through which the strings pass.

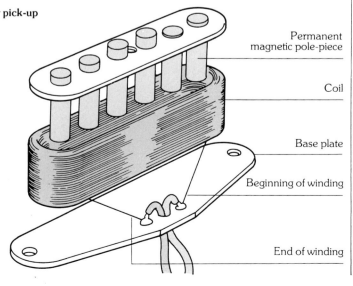

Permanent magnetic pole-piece
Coil
Base plate
Beginning of winding
End of winding

Some of the "lines of force" which make up the magnetic field intersect the coil and, when the vibrating string causes the lines of force to move, small pulses of electrical energy are generated in the coil itself. If the coil is connected to an amplifier, these pulses will travel to the amp in the form of AC.

The precise pattern in which the string vibrates depends on the construction of the guitar and the way the note is sounded. Let's say the pattern is a figure-of-eight as shown below. If the string is an open A tuned to concert pitch, it will vibrate at 440 cycles per second. In other words, it will complete the figure-of-eight 440 times every second. This means that the magnetic field surrounding the pick-up will also be "altered" 440 times.

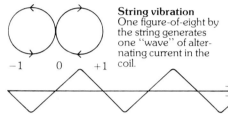

String vibration
One figure-of-eight by the string generates one "wave" of alternating current in the coil.

As the volume of the note dies away, the distance between the points +1, −1 and 0 becomes shorter until the string is at rest again. Nevertheless, throughout the duration of the note, the actual number of cycles per second remains the same. This tells the amplifier the *pitch* of the note – whether it is an A or a B, for example. The size of the vibrating figure-of-eight pattern tells the amplifier the *volume* (or "amplitude") of the note. The detailed shape of the figure-of-eight tells the amplifier the *tone* of the note.

Magnets in pick-ups

Most pick-up magnets are made of Alnico, an alloy of aluminium, nickel and cobalt. However, some manufacturers – such as Alembic – employ alternative "ceramic" or "piezo" magnets. The shape of the magnet varies according to the design of the pick-up. The basic bar magnet may have a "fin" which extends one pole of the magnetic field, taking it closer to the strings; it may have six individual pole-piece extensions – one for each string – and it may be possible to alter the height of each one separately; or it may contain six individual magnets.

In simple terms, the stronger the magnet (and the more windings there are in the coil) the louder the amplified sound will be. However, past a certain point, a strong magnet will "choke" the strings – that is, it will actually restrict the vibratory patterns and create a loss of sustain or a tonal distortion.

For more information on magnets and coils – and on how they can affect the tone and output of the guitar – see p. 186-96.

How the twin-coil pick-up works

All pick-up coils are vulnerable to interference from "electro-magnetic radiation". This means they tend to pick up a noise or "hum" when amplifiers or other electrical appliances are nearby. The hum-neutralizing or *humbucking* pick-up first invented by a Gibson engineer called Seth Lover in 1955 was designed to eliminate this problem.

Humbucking pick-ups have two coils instead of one. They are wired in series (so that the current flows first through one, then the next) but out of phase with each other. This means that any rogue interference is sent by one coil as a positive signal and by the other as a negative signal. The two opposite currents, flowing in different directions, therefore cancel each other out, and the "hum" is not passed on to the amplifier.

To guarantee that the two coils do not cancel out the currents generated by the vibrating strings as well, the sets of pole-pieces within each coil have opposite magnetic polarities. The result is that when the secondary coil inverts the signal from the disturbed magnetic field it *duplicates* – instead of cancelling – the electrical pulse. When the two signals are the same, they are said to be "in phase". When the two signals are opposing each other, they are said to be "out of phase" (*see* p. 192).

Since the mid-1950s, Gibson have been fitting twin-coil humbucking pick-ups to most of their electric guitars. As well as reducing rogue, unwanted interference, the "humbucker" has a sound which is distinctly different to that of the single-coil pick-up. The humbucker's twin-coil design results in less overall sound definition and a decreased response to high frequencies. The fact that Gibson use humbucking pick-ups on their guitars whereas Fender use single-coil pick-ups is one of the major reasons why the clear sound and biting top-end of a standard single-coil Fender is quite different from the "fatter" sound of a standard Gibson fitted with twin-coil humbuckers.

The Gibson pick-up
The "humbucker's" main coil has adjustable pole-pieces which can be screwed up or down. Those in the secondary coil are fixed. Both sets of pole-pieces come into contact with the same magnet, situated below and between them on the base plate. The polarity of the secondary coil is opposite to that of the main coil because the two sets of pole-pieces are in contact with the opposite poles of the bar magnet.

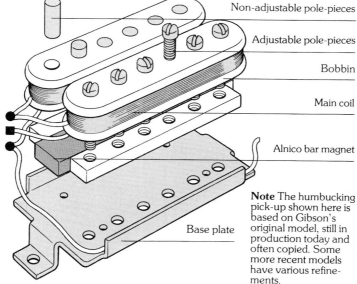

Non-adjustable pole-pieces

Adjustable pole-pieces

Bobbin

Main coil

Alnico bar magnet

Base plate

Note The humbucking pick-up shown here is based on Gibson's original model, still in production today and often copied. Some more recent models have various refinements.

The volume and tone controls

The signal generated in the pick-up coil can be controlled before it reaches the amplifier in two ways: by the volume control and by the tone control. Both are wired in between the pick-up and the guitar's output socket.

The volume control can modify the output by means of a *variable resistor*, commonly known as a *potentiometer* (or "pot"). The volume knob on the face of the guitar is attached to the spindle of the pot. The pot contains a resistive track, usually in the shape of a horseshoe, and a wiper contact is connected to the end of the spindle so that as the control knob is turned the wiper contact moves around the resistive track.

The two wires from the pick-up are connected to each end of the resistive track. At the earthed end of the track the voltage is zero; at the other end it is at maximum. Mov-

ing the sliding wiper contact along the track therefore increases or reduces the voltage fed to the amplifier.

Most guitar tone controls are a combination of a potentiometer and a *capacitor*. They operate by effectively tapping off the high, treble frequencies and sending them to earth. The capacitor acts as a kind of "filter". High frequencies (treble) pass through it, while low frequencies (bass) do not.

The pot (with its sliding wiper contact connected to the tone control knob) determines the amount of high frequencies earthed.

When the tone control is turned full on for maximum treble, the complete signal generated by the pick-up is sent to the amplifier. As the tone control is turned down, an increasing number of the treble frequencies filtered off by the capacitor are earthed by the pot.

Tremelo arms

The *tremelo arm* is, in fact, an incorrect name for a device which is actually a "vibrato unit". *Tremelo* in a note is achieved by rapidly and regularly changing its volume. *Vibrato* is a rapid and regular variation in the pitch of a note.

The device works in the following way. At the bridge or tailpiece, the guitar strings are anchored to a spindle or block which is able to move. When playing normally, this is held in position by springs so that a regular string tension is maintained. But, as the tremelo arm is depressed by the right hand, the string tension is slackened and the pitch of the note drops. As soon as the tremelo arm is released, the springs return the spindle or block to its original position and the note goes back up to its original pitch.

This, at least, is the theory. In practice, tuning problems can arise if the unit is not balanced exactly and if the strings drag on the bridge. Special bridges with rocker or roller arrangements are available to reduce these problems.

The two best-known and most widely used tremelo arms are made by Fender and Bigsby. Fender units are fitted to various guitars in their range. Bigsby units can be bought separately and mounted on almost any guitar, including some acoustic models.

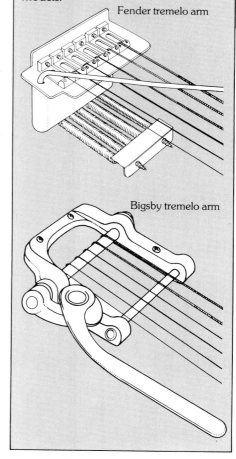

Fender tremelo arm

Bigsby tremelo arm

Hollow-body electric guitars

The story of "electric-acoustic" guitars is thought to have begun with a man called Lloyd Loar. Between 1920 and 1924, when he worked for Gibson, Loar experimented with various prototype pick-ups designed to amplify the sound of an acoustic guitar. Unfortunately, he left Gibson to form his own Vivi-Tone company and his idea disappeared until the 1930s.

It was then that the Rowe-DeArmond company began manufacturing the first commercially available magnetic pick-up simply designed to clip onto the soundhole of a flat-top acoustic guitar and therefore to amplify its natural sound.

It was the Gibson company who, in 1935, took things a stage further by introducing their ES-150 "Electric Spanish" model. This was essentially an f-hole, arch-top guitar fitted with a massive pick-up. Two strong magnets housed inside the guitar body were in contact with a single-fin pole-piece which was set beneath the strings. The fin, not the magnets, passed through the coil.

Gibson ES-150
Jazz guitarist, Charlie Christian, used this guitar to such effect that the pick-up became named after him.

"Charlie Christian pick-up"

Other Gibson ES models followed during the 1940s – the single pick-up ES-125 and the twin pick-up ES-300 and ES-350. In 1949, they introduced their three pick-up ES-5, hailed as the "supreme electronic

Gibson "Johnny Smith" (1961)

Gibson "Howard Roberts" (1974)

version" of the original L-5 (see p. 46), and in 1952 it was joined by the Super 400-CES, an electric version of the Super 400 acoustic guitar. During the 1950s and 1960s, many famous guitarists endorsed Gibson electric-acoustics, and the company produced several "named" guitars – the "Johnny Smith" and "Howard Roberts", for example.

From the end of the Second World War onwards, other companies competed with Gibson for the hollow-body electric guitar market. The most successful were Epiphone (until they were bought by Gibson in 1957), Gretsch and Guild.

Gretsch "Country Gentleman"
Designed with the help of Chet Atkins, this 1960 Gretsch has fake f-holes painted on the body.

Gibson Byrdland
This guitar was first developed in 1955 and gets its name from the two guitarists who designed it – Billy Byrd and Hank Garland. Shown above is a 1968 model; the original instrument had "bar magnet" pick-ups instead of modern humbuckers.

"Semi-solid" electric guitars

Feedback has always been a problem with hollow-body electrics. In the late 1950s, Gibson brought out a range of guitars which were designed to minimize this. They were called thin-bodied or "semi-solid" guitars to distinguish them from the ordinary deep-bodied "electric-acoustic" guitars. The first to appear (in August 1958) was the ES-335T, although others in what became known as the "300" series – the ES-355, 345 and 325 – soon followed. They all had double cutaways and thin bodies with arched soundboards and backs made from laminated maple. They were true "acoustic" guitars in that they were hollow and had f-shaped soundholes, but they each had a

solid block of wood set down the centre of the body. This was intended to increase sustain and prevent unwanted soundboard vibration from causing feedback. The aim of the guitars was to blend the sustain qualities of a solid-body electric with the warmer, more mellow sound produced by an acoustic instrument.

Semi-solid guitars were very successful. The modified ES-355 TD SV, first introduced in about 1959, had stereo wiring (which meant that the rhythm and lead pick-ups could be played through different amplifiers) and "varitone" circuitry (which allowed the treble cut-off on the tone control to be varied).

Gibson ES-335 TD
The 335 was the first of the Gibson semi-solids. The earliest models had "dot" fret markers on the fingerboard; in mid-1959, the dots were replaced by block inlays like those shown here.

The first solid-body electric guitars

The development of the truly "electric" guitar – one with a solid body and no soundbox – owes a great deal to the popularity of Hawaiian music in America during the 1920s and 1930s. Hawaiian guitars are solo instruments, played with a metal slide used in the same way as a "bottleneck". Electric Hawaiian guitars were the first commercially available instruments that depended almost entirely on their sound being amplified electrically, not just acoustically.

One of the key figures in their design was Adolph Rickenbacker. He was originally approached to make metal components for the Dopera Brothers' National resonator guitars (see p. 48). At National, he met George Beauchamp and Paul Barth who had been working on the principle of the magnetic pick-up. Together, they formed the Electro String Company and, in 1931, they went into production of their first electric Hawaiian guitars – the A-22 and A-25. The figures 22 and 25 referred to the scale length in inches. The pick-up, with its strong magnets and six individual iron pole-pieces, was rudimentary but effective, and the guitars' success prompted other makers – such as Gibson and National/Dobro – to start producing equivalent instruments.

The Rickenbacker "Frying Pan" The A-22 electric Hawaiian guitar, which became popularly known as the "frying pan" or "pancake", was cast in a single piece of solid aluminium. The pick-up was a high-impedance device with two tungsten-steel chrome-plated horseshoe magnets of considerable power.

By about the 1940s, Gibson's new electric-acoustic models were firmly established, and it is hardly surprising that a number of people were working on ways of applying the solid body of Hawaiian and steel guitars to regular instruments.

In 1944, Leo Fender – who ran a radio repair shop – teamed up with "Doc" Kauffman, an ex-employee of Rickenbacker, and formed the K & F Company. They produced a series of steel guitars and amplifiers. Leo Fender felt – quite rightly – that the massive pick-up magnets in use at the time need not be so large. He had a new pick-up which he wanted to try out and so he built it into a solid-body guitar which was based on the shape of a Hawaiian but which had a regular, properly fretted guitar fingerboard. Though only intended to demonstrate the pick-up, the guitar was soon in demand with local country musicians. In fact, it became so popular that there was a waiting list of people wanting to hire it. When Leo and "Doc" Kauffman parted in 1946, he went on to form his own Fender Electric Instrument Company, and within two years he introduced the now-legendary Broadcaster (see p. 56).

In the meantime, Les Paul was working in the same direction. Although he had experimented with his own pick-ups throughout the 1930s, he was still experiencing the same feedback and resonance problems with amplified f-hole guitars as everyone else. But hearing about a solid-body violin made by the American inventor, Thomas Edison, set him thinking about making a solid-body guitar. He was convinced that the only way to avoid body feedback was to reduce pick-up movement – and the only way to do that was to mount it on a solid piece of wood.

In 1941, he persuaded Epiphone to let him use their workshop on Sundays. There, he built his historic "log" guitar, about which he later said: "You could go out and eat and come back and the note would still be sounding. It didn't sound like a banjo or a mandolin, but like a guitar, an electric guitar. That was the sound I was after." The story of his later role with Gibson is taken up on p. 58.

In 1947, Paul Bigsby (inventor of the Bigsby tremelo arm, p. 53) built a solid-body electric guitar designed in consultation with the renowned guitarist, Merle Travis. It shares certain design features with the Broadcaster that Leo Fender introduced in 1948 – for example, the way the strings pass through the body, and the design of the headstock, with all six tuning heads on one side. In fact, Bigsby and Travis worked on their guitar in

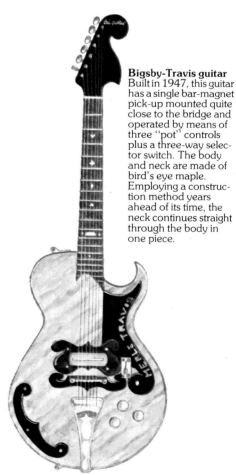
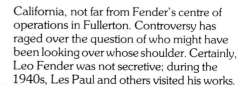

Bigsby-Travis guitar Built in 1947, this guitar has a single bar-magnet pick-up mounted quite close to the bridge and operated by means of three "pot" controls plus a three-way selector switch. The body and neck are made of bird's eye maple. Employing a construction method years ahead of its time, the neck continues straight through the body in one piece.

The Les Paul "log" Despite its looks, this guitar was the first real solid-body electric guitar. Les Paul simply cut an Epiphone f-hole acoustic guitar down the middle and inserted a 4 in. by 4 in. (10 cm by 10 cm) block of solid maple on which he mounted two single-coil pick-ups and a Gibson neck.

California, not far from Fender's centre of operations in Fullerton. Controversy has raged over the question of who might have been looking over whose shoulder. Certainly, Leo Fender was not secretive; during the 1940s, Les Paul and others visited his works.

Fender guitars

Following the success of his experimental solid-body steel guitar in the mid-1940s (*see* p. 55), Leo Fender split with his partner "Doc" Kauffman, set up on his own, and got to work immediately on the design of a new instrument. Fender was concerned with utility and practicality, not aesthetics. He wanted to make a regular guitar with a clear sound similar to that of the electric Hawaiian but without the feedback problems associated with a vibrating soundboard. The result of his labours was the "Broadcaster", which he started manufacturing in 1948.

The Broadcaster had a detachable neck – similar to the banjos of the time. This was simply a question of convenience; Fender felt that the neck was the part of the guitar most likely to cause problems, and his "modular" design meant that it could be replaced in the space of just a few minutes. The choice of maple as the wood from which it was built was apparently due to the popularity of blonde-finish instruments at the time. Natural-wood bodies were made from ash, painted ones from alder. The headstock was designed with all six tuning heads on one side. This made tuning easier and avoided having to fan out the strings.

Fender Broadcaster (1948)
This guitar, one of the first solid-body electrics, belongs to Dave Gilmour of Pink Floyd.

The Broadcaster was fitted with two single-coil pick-ups. These were wired through a three-position selector switch which could be set to either the bridge pick-up, the neck pick-up, or the neck pick-up plus a special capacitor that gave a very bassy sound.

The original guitar featured the same adjustable bridge design still fitted to Telecasters today: three bolts adjust the height and the scale length of the strings in pairs. The Broadcaster also had a clip-on cover-plate

that snapped into place over the bridge and bridge pick-up. This, too, is still fitted to Telecasters, but it is rarely seen on working guitars since most players find that it hinders their technique.

In 1954, Fender went into production with the "Stratocaster". Together with the Telecaster – and with the instruments Les Paul was then making for Gibson – these two guitars must be regarded as having set the standards for solid-body guitar design.

During 1955, Leo Fender contracted a strep infection that was to trouble him for ten years. By the mid-1960s, he was convinced that he had only a short time to live and so he decided to wind up his business affairs. In 1965, he sold the entire Fender company to CBS for thirteen million dollars. Shortly afterwards, he changed doctors and was cured. Within a couple of months, he was working again – this time as a design consultant for CBS Fender, operating from his own research laboratory. This arrangement continued for five years. Since then, through his own CLF Research Company, Leo Fender has worked on Music Man guitars (although not the amplifiers) and, more recently, on G & L guitars.

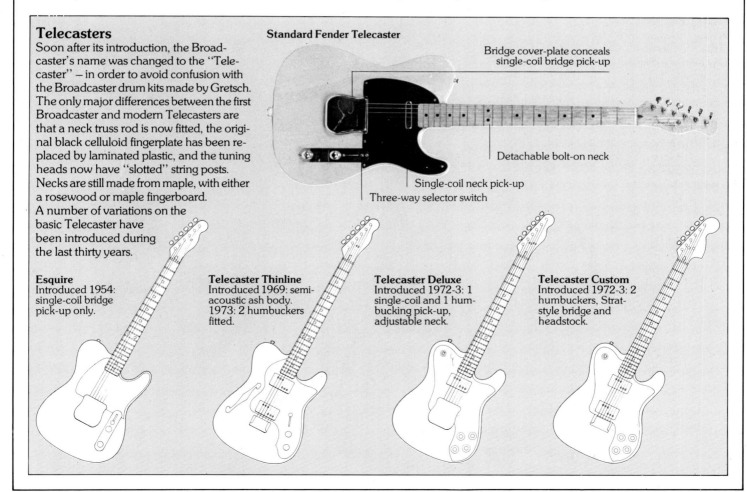

Telecasters

Soon after its introduction, the Broadcaster's name was changed to the "Telecaster" – in order to avoid confusion with the Broadcaster drum kits made by Gretsch. The only major differences between the first Broadcaster and modern Telecasters are that a neck truss rod is now fitted, the original black celluloid fingerplate has been replaced by laminated plastic, and the tuning heads now have "slotted" string posts. Necks are still made from maple, with either a rosewood or maple fingerboard. A number of variations on the basic Telecaster have been introduced during the last thirty years.

Standard Fender Telecaster

Bridge cover-plate conceals single-coil bridge pick-up

Detachable bolt-on neck

Single-coil neck pick-up

Three-way selector switch

Esquire
Introduced 1954: single-coil bridge pick-up only.

Telecaster Thinline
Introduced 1969: semi-acoustic ash body. 1973: 2 humbuckers fitted.

Telecaster Deluxe
Introduced 1972-3: 1 single-coil and 1 humbucking pick-up, adjustable neck.

Telecaster Custom
Introduced 1972-3: 2 humbuckers, Strat-style bridge and headstock.

The Stratocaster

Three features immediately distinguished the Fender Stratocaster as being a revolutionary new guitar when it was introduced in 1954. First, it had a contoured, double-cutaway body designed to make it more comfortable to play. The corners were bevelled and the back had a dished recess. Second, it featured the brilliantly engineered Fender vibrato or "tremelo" unit built into the special "floating" bridge design (see p. 53). Third, it was the first solid-body electric to be fitted with three pick-ups. These were all single-coils and they were wired to a three-way switch which selected one at a time. However, as guitarists soon discovered, the switch could be balanced between two positions to give a unique "out-of-phase" sound. Realizing the attraction of this, Fender changed the three-way switch to a five-way switch.

Like the Telecaster, the "Strat" has remained virtually unchanged – although in 1972 the Fender "micro-tilt" neck and "bullet" truss-rod adjustments were added. Stratocasters are available in various different finishes and colours, and with or without a rosewood fingerboard. In 1981, "the Strat" appeared in Lake Placid Blue and Candy-Apple Red.

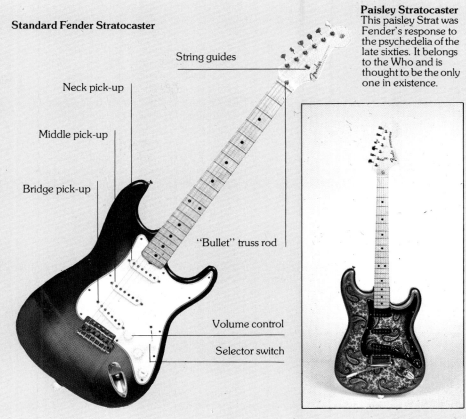

Standard Fender Stratocaster

String guides

Neck pick-up

Middle pick-up

Bridge pick-up

"Bullet" truss rod

Volume control

Selector switch

Paisley Stratocaster
This paisley Strat was Fender's response to the psychedelia of the late sixties. It belongs to the Who and is thought to be the only one in existence.

Other Fender guitars

With the success of the Telecaster and Stratocaster, Fender continued to experiment with new models – the Musicmaster, Jazzmaster, Jaguar and Mustang, for example. These have fluctuated in popularity, as did their less successful excursions into the field of semi-acoustics (the Coronado, Antigua, Montego and, more recently, the Starcaster). When CBS initially bought out Fender in 1965, many guitarists felt that quality standards were allowed to slip, and what became known as "pre-CBS" guitars were more and more prized. Early problems were soon overcome, however, and standards were regained.

Musicmaster
Introduced 1956: 1 single-coil pick-up only.

Jazzmaster
Introduced 1957: 2 single-coil pick-ups with separate tone and volume controls, "floating tremelo".

Jaguar
Introduced 1961: shorter scale length than Jazzmaster, toggle selector replaced by slide switches.

Electric 12-string
Introduced 1965 until 1969: based on Jazzmaster/Jaguar, 2 split pick-ups, "hockey-stick" head.

Mustang
Introduced 1966 to replace "Duo-Sonic": 2 single-coil pick-ups, 2 three-position pick-up and tone slide switches, tremelo arm.

Starcaster
Introduced 1975: semi-solid body with centre block, bolt-on neck, 2 humbucking pick-ups.

Lead I
Introduced 1979: 1 humbucking pick-up, coil-tap and series/parallel switches.

Gibson guitars

The story of Gibson guitars stretches right back into the nineteenth century. Gibson pioneered the arch-top acoustic guitar (the L-5 in 1924, see p. 46) and also the hollow-body electric guitar (the ES-150 in 1935, see p. 54). However, their involvement with solid-body electrics came slightly later – *after* Fender's introduction of the Broadcaster – and owes a lot to the renowned Les Paul.

Following his successful weekend experiments with the "log" at the Epiphone factory (see p. 55), Les Paul took his ideas to Gibson. Unfortunately, they were not interested; they called his prototype "the broomstick with a pick-up on it" and turned him down. But, in 1950, they sought him out again and signed him up, agreeing that he would be paid a royalty on every electric guitar with his name on it that the company made.

At Gibson, Les Paul went on to develop his ideas, eventually working through fifty to sixty prototype guitars before he felt happy with his final design. In 1952, the "Gibson Les Paul" guitar went into production. At first, Maurice Berlin, the company president, thought that they should be called simply "Les Paul" guitars and that they should not bear the "Gibson" name in case the company's reputation suffered. Before long, he changed his mind, saying "maybe we should put the Gibson name on it, just in case it goes anywhere". Time proved him right.

Les Paul wanted the guitars to have a natural twenty-second sustain – which is why they are relatively heavy. The body was made from solid mahogany with a ½ in. (12 mm) maple "cap" or facing on top. The profile of the carved top was, in fact, a Gibson suggestion intended to make it hard to copy.

In 1962, Les Paul's contract with Gibson ended. Occupied by his divorce from Mary Ford at the time, he decided he did not want to be involved with guitars for a while, and the association ended. Les Paul talks with some bitterness about the "Les Paul" guitars Gibson went on to make without his name on them. Nevertheless, in 1967, when rock musicians were paying thousands of dollars for vintage 1957-60 Les Pauls, he contacted Maurice Berlin again and once more became actively involved in Gibson guitars.

In recent years, Gibson have introduced several new guitar lines – the RD series and the man-made "Resonwood" Sonex series, for example – as well as reissuing old favourites, both in their original and in new forms. One of their most recent new guitars is called the 335-S. Somewhat confusingly, it is a solid-body electric guitar loosely based on the shape of the ES-335 semi-solid (see p. 54).

Gibson Les Pauls

The original 1952 Gibson Les Paul had two high-impedance single-coil pick-ups with cream cover-plates (see below). It was fitted with a three-way pick-up selector switch and separate volume and tone controls. At first, Les Paul used his own distinctive "trapeze" tailpiece and bridge. But this caused problems, and in 1955 it was replaced by the new, adjustable "Tune-O-Matic" bridge and tailpiece.

In 1957, the single-coil pick-ups were replaced by the new humbuckers developed by Gibson's Seth Lover and Ted McCarty (see p. 53). Until 1960, the humbucking pick-ups were referred to by the initials "PAF" (Patent Applied For). These 1957-60 Les Pauls are now among the most highly regarded electric guitars ever made.

Les Paul Standard
In 1960, when this guitar was made, Gibson introduced the term "Standard" to distinguish ordinary Les Pauls from Customs, Juniors and Specials. This Standard has a "tigerstripe" sunburst finish.

"Gold-top" Les Paul
The first Les Pauls had a gold-lustre finish with ivory edging. This is a 1954 model with a "stop" tailpiece.

A short guide to the Les Paul range

Over the thirty years since 1952, the basic Les Paul guitar had been modified, added-to, re-modelled, re-named, withdrawn and reissued countless times. This information is a simplified breakdown of the differences.

Les Paul Standard   Introduced 1952; 1954 stop tailpiece instead of trapeze; 1955 Tune-O-Matic bridge; 1957 two humbuckers replace single-coils; 1958 "sunburst" finish; 1960 discontinued; 1974 reissued.

Les Paul Custom   Introduced 1954, nick-named "Fretless Wonder"/"Black Beauty", flat body, two single-coil pick-ups, Tune-O-Matic bridge; 1957 three humbuckers; 1960 discontinued; 1966 reissued with two humbuckers; 1977 three humbuckers optional.

An unusual "silverburst" Les Paul Custom

Les Paul Junior   Introduced 1954, flat body, one single-coil pick-up; 1959 double cutaway; 1960 discontinued.

Les Paul Special   Introduced 1955, same as Junior but two single-coil pick-ups; 1959 double cutaway; 1960 discontinued; 1966 reissued with carved top.

Les Paul TV   Introduced 1957, same as Junior but slightly different finish; 1960 discontinued.

Les Paul Deluxe   Introduced 1969, two-humbucker version of 1966 Special, carved top.

Les Paul Personal   Introduced 1969, low-impedance pick-ups, gold-plated.

Les Paul Professional   Introduced 1969, low-impedance pick-ups, nickel-plated.

Les Paul Recording   Introduced 1971, replaced Personal and Professional.

The Les Paul   Introduced 1976, solid maple reissue of Les Paul Custom.

Les Paul Pro Deluxe   Introduced 1977, reissue of early Standard, two 1952-style single-coil pick-ups.

The development of the Gibson SG

Incredible as it may seem now, Gibson found that their Les Paul guitars were not selling well during the late 1950s. They decided that a completely new design was needed. Their first move was to re-model the Les Paul Specials and Juniors, giving them rounded, double-cutaway bodies that many people associate now with the Melody Maker shape. A limited number of these "prototype SG" guitars were made during 1959. Then, in late 1960, they went further. They discontinued the old Les Paul range altogether, and introduced completely new Standards, Customs, Specials and Juniors with the sharp, horn-like double cutaways of the true SG style.

Much of the confusion that arises over these guitars stems from the terminology. Though Les Paul worked on the early design of the double-cutaway models, he never liked them as much as the original Les Paul shape, but it was not until 1961 that Gibson finally removed his name and officially designated them the "SG" (solid guitar) series.

Les Paul shape
The original Les Pauls were all built to this single-cutaway shape.

Les Paul SG shape
The rounded double-cutaway shape of 1959 which marked the transition. Les Paul's name still appeared on these guitars.

Gibson SG
In 1960, the Standard, Custom, Junior and Special were all issued with two re-designed, sharp body cutaways. This shape has been used for all Gibson SGs ever since then.

The Gibson "exotics"

The SG was not Gibson's only response to the problem of flagging sales in the 1950s. Ted McCarty, then company president, and his designers sat down with the following objective: "we wanted to do something really different, something radical to knock everyone out and show them that Gibson was more modern than all the rest". The results of their work appeared in 1958 – the Flying V, the Explorer and the Moderne. Of these three guitars, the Flying V was the most successful; it is still made today. The

Moderne disappeared almost immediately. At the time, the Explorer fared almost as badly; it is estimated that only about 100 were ever made and these are now extremely rare (although Gibson reissued them as a limited edition in 1976).

In 1963, Gibson came out with the Firebird, a "toned-down" version of the unsuccessful Explorer. Unfortunately, there was a legal problem with Fender over the design of the offset body, and in 1965 Gibson changed the shape of their guitars.

This has led to the 1963-65 guitars being known as "reverse-body" Firebirds to distinguish them from the 1965-67 "non-reverse-body" Firebirds. Original reverse-body guitars are highly sought after.

A series of new guitars, first introduced in 1977, harks back to the Explorer and non-reverse Firebirds. Gibson call them the "RD" series. The RD Artist is the top-of-the-line model, and it features two humbucking pick-ups, "active" electronics (see p. 194-6) and a fine-tuning tailpiece.

The Gibson Flying V
This is one of the earliest Flying Vs and was made in 1958. It can be distinguished from later models by the shape of the fingerplate and by the way the strings pass right through to the back of the body.

The Gibson Explorer
Production of the Explorer stopped sometime in 1959. It was considered too "futuristic" by most guitarists of the time. However, this guitar is one of the reissue models that Gibson made available during the 1970s.

The Gibson Firebird
This is a 1972 Gibson reissue of the original "reverse-body" Firebird with a Maestro vibrola unit. It has the original "backward-facing" headstock fitted with six banjo-style tuning pegs.

Nonreverse-body Firebird

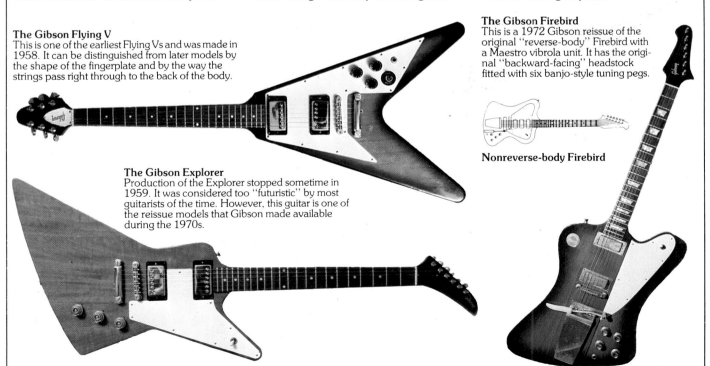

Other American and European guitars

For almost all the established guitar manufacturers, the 1950s were a time of change and experiment – as they worked on their new semi-acoustic and solid-body designs, trying to keep pace with the popularity of jazz and the emergence of rock 'n' roll.

The Gretsch, Guild and Harmony companies were all making hollow-body electric guitars during the fifties. In 1955, Gretsch introduced their first solids (the single-cutaway Jet guitars), but their reputation was strongest among country players who were great fans of their semi-acoustics – in particular, the Chet Atkins and the White Falcon.

When Epiphone was bought by Gibson in 1957, much of their machinery was sold to Guild – and a lot of their staff went with it. But, from 1959, Gibson began manufacturing Epiphone guitars from their Kalamazoo factory. They produced electric versions of their well-established acoustic guitars and, in the early 1960s, a series of solid electrics.

Two other American companies – Rickenbacker and Danelectro – were both working on new designs during the fifties. Their most popular guitars, however, were sold during the sixties. Danelectro went out of business in the early seventies.

In Europe, during this period, the guitar market was still dominated by the Americans. Almost the only companies of note were Burns, Watkins and Vox (British), Hofner (German) and Hagstrom (Swedish).

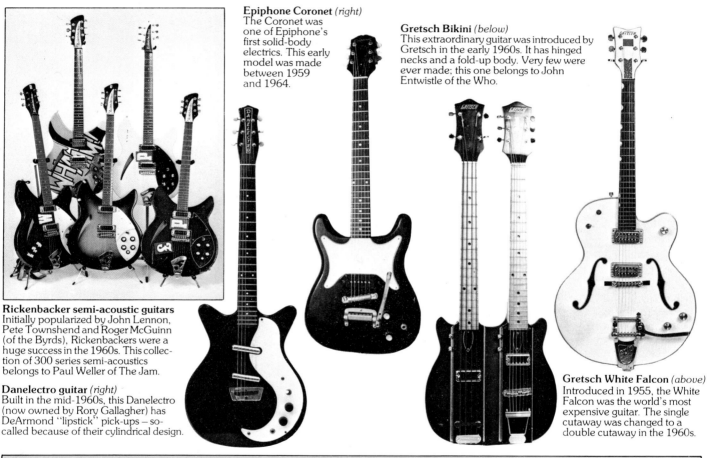

Epiphone Coronet (right)
The Coronet was one of Epiphone's first solid-body electrics. This early model was made between 1959 and 1964.

Gretsch Bikini (below)
This extraordinary guitar was introduced by Gretsch in the early 1960s. It has hinged necks and a fold-up body. Very few were ever made; this one belongs to John Entwistle of the Who.

Rickenbacker semi-acoustic guitars
Initially popularized by John Lennon, Pete Townshend and Roger McGuinn (of the Byrds), Rickenbackers were a huge success in the 1960s. This collection of 300 series semi-acoustics belongs to Paul Weller of The Jam.

Danelectro guitar (right)
Built in the mid-1960s, this Danelectro (now owned by Rory Gallagher) has DeArmond "lipstick" pick-ups – so-called because of their cylindrical design.

Gretsch White Falcon (above)
Introduced in 1955, the White Falcon was the world's most expensive guitar. The single cutaway was changed to a double cutaway in the 1960s.

Contemporary guitar design

Several guitars appeared during the fifties and sixties which demonstrated the design freedom that the solid body allowed – Gibson's Explorer and Flying V, Danelectro's Longhorns, Guild's Polara and Thunderbird, etc. But, in the late 1960s, Dan Armstrong went one step further with the transparent plexiglass guitar he designed for Ampeg. The seventies saw even further experimentation: companies such as Travis Bean, Kramer and Veleno introduced the use of aluminium in their guitars; Alembic, Peavey and Ovation (among others) began using different woods and built-in "active" electronics.

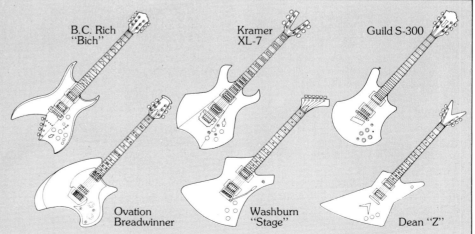

B.C. Rich "Bich"

Kramer XL-7

Guild S-300

Ovation Breadwinner

Washburn "Stage"

Dean "Z"

Japanese guitars

Yamaha was one of the first Japanese companies to make an impact on the guitar market-place. In the 1960s, they produced a range of flat-top acoustics based on Martin designs. To begin with, their range consisted mostly of inexpensive guitars that cost only a fraction of the price of the American originals. The sound was surprisingly good, especially considering that most of the guitars had laminated soundboards. Their value for money was exceptional and Yamaha acoustics served thousands of singer-songwriters perfectly well. Before long, Yamaha were also making some top-line, hand-built instruments which measured up favourably alongside American Martin, Gibson and Guild guitars but which were much cheaper.

As the demand for acoustic guitars decreased towards the end of the 1960s, the Japanese were quick to turn their attention to electric instruments. Again, they began with replicas of the successful American makes. The Gibson Les Paul now has the reputation of being the most copied guitar of all time. Since the late 1970s, it has been possible to find almost thirty different copies of the Les Paul. And the Fender Stratocaster and Precision bass are not far behind.

Often these copies cost as little as a sixth of the price of the genuine article. This has brought them into the reach of thousands of players – both amateurs and semi-professionals. Of course, standards vary. It has to be said that some copies are dreadful. Others, while not matching the originals, are much better instruments. The Columbus, Aria, Antoria and Shaftesbury models are all good value, as are the new Tokai range of Fender and Gibson copies.

In recent years, customizing and upgrading good Japanese copies has become quite popular (see p. 178). Many musicians have found that fitting American-made pick-ups and quality machine heads can turn a good copy into a guitar of a professional standard.

During the 1970s, a few Japanese manufacturers moved on from mere replicas and began to gain a high reputation for making more original guitars. Generally, these are still less expensive than top American instruments, but they stand up very well in comparison. Ibanez and Aria, for example, both make fine guitars that are *not* simply copies, and the Yamaha SG-2000 is probably the most highly rated solid-body guitar made outside the United States.

Several American manufacturers – such as Washburn and the Gibson-owned Epiphone company – now cater to the lower end of the market by getting Japanese companies to build their guitars in Japan and then marketing them throughout the world. The same is now true of the British Vox company.

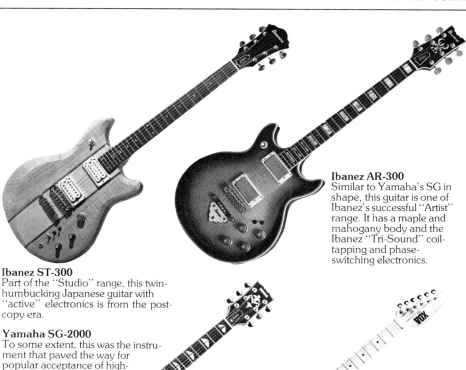

Ibanez ST-300
Part of the "Studio" range, this twin-humbucking Japanese guitar with "active" electronics is from the post-copy era.

Ibanez AR-300
Similar to Yamaha's SG in shape, this guitar is one of Ibanez's successful "Artist" range. It has a maple and mahogany body and the Ibanez "Tri-Sound" coil-tapping and phase-switching electronics.

Yamaha SG-2000
To some extent, this was the instrument that paved the way for popular acceptance of high-quality Japanese guitars (see p. 50).

Vox Custom 25
The British Vox company now makes its guitars in Japan. Since the recent spate of guitars with "active" electronics has not proved as popular as expected, this model has advanced "passive" circuitry, offering a wide tonal range.

Tokai guitars
Tokai, one of the newest companies, have taken the Japanese art of guitar copying into a new league. Their copies of Fender and Gibson guitars are made with painstaking attention to detail. In defiance of the fact that the Japanese have in the past run into legal problems over patents, the headstock of their "ST" series originally claimed that "this is the exact replica of the good old Strat".

Tokai TE-70
Replica of original Fender Custom Telecaster.

Tokai ST-50
Replica of 1964 Fender Stratocaster.

Tokai LS-220VF
Replica of 1958-60 Gibson Les Paul.

Bass guitars

By the end of the 1940s, amplification was playing a dominant role in popular music. Amplifiers, PAs, pick-ups and the Fender Telecaster guitar were the main elements of a trend towards louder music.

Some bass players – limited to their huge acoustic double basses – fitted pick-ups to their instruments and put them through adapted amplifiers. Others followed Les

Paul's example and played bass runs on the bottom strings of electric guitars.

It was Leo Fender who first came up with the idea of a solid-body bass guitar. Realizing the problems that bass players were facing, and feeling certain that they would prefer a less cumbersome, more manageable instrument, he went to work on a prototype bass guitar in 1950. By changing from the "stand-

up" design of the double bass to the idea of a bass guitar supported by a shoulder strap, he thought that guitarists would be better able to "double" on bass when necessary.

The bass is tuned to E, A, D and G – like the bottom four strings of a guitar, but one octave lower. This means that all basses need a longer "scale length" (see p. 40) and consequently extra strengthening.

Fender basses

Leo Fender's first solid-body electric bass guitar – the Fender Precision – went into production in 1951, and within a couple of years he had a runaway success on his hands. The name was chosen because his bass had frets on the fingerboard – unlike the fretless double bass – and therefore

allowed guitarists to play notes with "precision". The first Precisions had a single-coil pick-up and were fitted with single volume and tone controls. In 1957, the pick-up was split into two halves, each with four pole-pieces, and staggered slightly. This was designed to prevent the signal of the vibrat-

ing string from fading and to reduce its "attack" – thus cutting down on loud-speaker casualties.

Although other bass guitars have been produced by Fender and other manufacturers, the Precision still continues to provide the pulse of most rock music.

Precision basses
During the first years of production, the Precision was very similar to the Telecaster in design – as the 1953 model on the left illustrates. In 1954 the body was re-styled to look more like the Stratocaster, and the shape has not changed since then. However, in 1968, Fender brought out their Telecaster bass, almost an exact replica of the pre-1954 Precision. The bass on the right is a Precision from the early 1960s with a rosewood neck. Fender's latest model, the Precision Special, has "active" tone circuitry.

Jazz bass
Introduced in 1960 as a 2 pick-up alternative to the Precision, this Jazz is one of the early models: it has dot fret markers instead of the later slab inlays. The Jazz bass has the same scale length as the Precision, but the neck is narrower at the nut. Many bassists find that this makes it slightly easier to play.

Bass VI
A 6-string bass, tuned an octave lower than the guitar, produced in 1962 with 3 single-coil pick-ups and a tremelo arm. The body shape was similar to that of the Jaguar, as was the layout of the controls. However, the Bass VI was never very popular and Fender discontinued it early in the 1970s.

Gibson basses

Gibson's answer to the Fender Precision appeared in 1953. It was designated the EB-1, but Hofner's copy of it – the model used by Paul McCartney in the early days of the Beatles – made it more popularly known as the "violin bass". Gibson followed it in 1958 with the EB-2, a bass version of their successful ES-335 (see p. 54).

In 1960, the EB-0 and EB-3 basses appeared with the new Gibson "SG" body – the sharp, horn-like double cutaway. The EB-0 had one humbucking pick-up and the EB-3 had two. When Gibson introduced their Firebird guitars in 1963, they had a bass equivalent – the Thunderbird.

Other Gibson basses have included the Melody Maker bass (1968), the Grabber (1974) with its single sliding pick-up, the Ripper (1974) and the RD series (1977).

EB-1
The famous violin-shaped body was built from solid mahogany; the body is not, in fact, hollow. The f-holes are fake, and are simply painted on.

Thunderbird
This original 1963 model, owned by John Entwistle of the Who, is a twin-humbucker Thunderbird 4. The Thunderbird 2 had only one pick-up.

Other important basses

Among the other manufacturers that pioneered the development of the electric bass guitar, Rickenbacker stand out as being almost as important as Fender. Their first bass guitar, the 4000, was introduced in the late 1950s. Several years later, it was joined by the twin pick-up 4001, which has become one of the most popular (and most recognizable) of all basses. Listen to any early recording by Yes to hear the distinctive Rickenbacker sound.

During the 1970s, the American Alembic company established itself as one of the leading makers of bass guitars. Alembic were among the first manufacturers to build pre-amps and "active" electronics (see p. 186-92) into commercially available instruments. Their guitars are very expensive – due to the fact that they are hand-crafted to the highest

specifications, using the best possible materials and components. Some Alembics might be accused of "gimmicky" features – for example, the "dummy" middle pick-up or the LED (light-emitting diode) fret markers inset into the side of the fingerboard. However, this does not detract from their undoubted quality. Stanley Clarke is the most prominent user of Alembics.

The story of Japanese manufacturers holds as true for bass guitars as it does for standard electrics. No longer written off simply as producers of cheap copies based on Fender and Gibson designs, Aria, Ibanez and Yamaha have all moved on to make bass guitars that are excellent in their own right. The American companies, Guild, Kramer and B. C. Rich, and the British companies, Shergold and Vox, all produce good, popular basses.

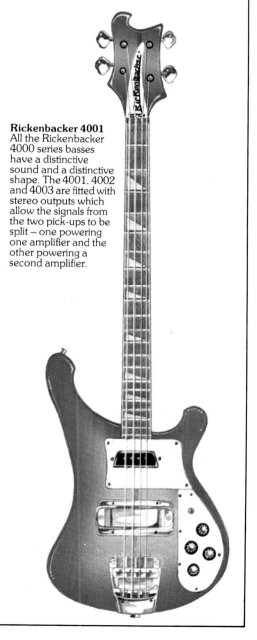

Rickenbacker 4001
All the Rickenbacker 4000 series basses have a distinctive sound and a distinctive shape. The 4001, 4002 and 4003 are fitted with stereo outputs which allow the signals from the two pick-ups to be split – one powering one amplifier and the other powering a second amplifier.

Standard Alembic
Hand-made and therefore expensive, Alembic basses are made from unusual woods and feature "active" electronics. This model is the one which Stanley Clarke has made familiar.

Alembic "Explorer"
This Alembic, based on Gibson's Explorer body shape (see p. 59), was built for John Entwistle of the Who. Alembic have also made a bass for him in the shape of a Flying V.

Guitar synthesizers

A *synthesizer* is an electronic instrument that creates a basic tone and forms it in a variety of ways to produce a wide range of different sounds. Once they have been set to give a particular sound, synthesizers are played by means of a "controller". The early synthesizers were all operated by a keyboard controller. The first production "synth", designed by Dr Robert A. Moog and introduced in 1964, was connected to a keyboard. Guitar synthesizers differ in that they use a guitar as the controller instead of a keyboard. The best-known are the Roland, ARP, Korg and 360 Systems.

There are three basic approaches to music synthesis. The synthesizer can be used to simulate the sound of any instrument, to produce a sound which can only be created on a synthesizer, or to create sounds which incorporate elements of both.

There are many different types of synthesizer – with components and circuits of varying complexity.

How the guitar synthesizer works

All true synthesizers are controlled by varying levels of voltage. Therefore, if a synth is to be operated by a guitar controller, the first thing that is required is a *pitch-to-voltage converter*. This simply tells the synth – in terms of voltage – what note you are playing on the guitar. The synth then uses this voltage to control the basic tone by means of a device called a *voltage-controlled oscillator* (VCO).

VCOs are complicated components which work in a number of ways: they produce "sawtooth", "square", "sine" and "triangular" waveforms which are then shaped further to produce the required musical (or non-musical) sound. This is one of the reasons why a synth can produce such a wide variety of sounds. It follows that the more oscillators a synth has, the more versatile it is.

Synthesizers also incorporate a further means of producing sound. This is the so-called *noise generator*. It generates what is known as either "white" or "pink" noise. White noise is a mixture of sound waves taken at random from across the frequency spectrum. Pink noise is the same thing but with more bass. Both white and pink noise can be added to the basic synthesizer sounds.

Once the VCO has generated the basic tone, a *voltage-controlled filter* (VCF) "tailors" the sound. The VCF can be thought of as working in a similar way to a tone control or a graphic equalizer; it cuts down some of the frequencies so that others are accentuated (this is the process actually defined as *subtractive synthesis*). In a similar way, the strength or loudness of the sound is shaped by a *voltage-controlled amplifier* (VCA).

Synthesizers also have controls which operate the *envelope shaper* or *envelope generator*. These, in conjunction with the VCA, can be used to pre-set the "envelope" of the sound. In other words, they control the note's attack, decay and sustain (ADS) or its attack, decay, sustain and release (ADSR).

When the guitar synthesizer is set to synthesizer only, the sound you hear is not a processed version of the sound from the guitar strings. The synth generates its own sound; the guitar merely triggers it off.

Monophonic, multi-voiced and polyphonic synthesizers

Some synths – including all early models – are *monophonic* which means that only one note can be played at a time. Systems vary, but one of the most common works on the basis that, if the first note is still sounding when the second note is played, the second note takes over and the first note is silenced. Multi-voiced synths allow a certain number of notes to be played at the same time. They can be two-voice, four-voice, six-voice or more. True *polyphonic* synths have a tone-generating circuit for each note.

Using a guitar synthesizer

Even the most basic synth is a relatively complicated piece of equipment compared with most other things guitarists are likely to encounter. There is a complex interplay between the various components – some of which perform more than just the functions described above. If you want to get involved with synthesizers, you will certainly benefit from a careful analysis of the *structure* of notes produced by different instruments.

However, the only way to build up a good understanding of the guitar synth is to work with one for a few months, gradually developing the techniques and background knowledge. No doubt most guitarists could get a few sounds out of the device fairly quickly, but worthwhile results take time to achieve.

Roland synthesizers

By the beginning of the 1980s, Roland had virtually taken the lead in the manufacture of guitar synths. Several noteworthy musicians (Andy Summers and Jimmy Page, for example) use Roland guitar synths both on stage and for recording.

The Roland GR-300 – like its predecessor, the GR-500 – is specifically designed to work with a guitar as its "controller". In fact, Roland synths will only work with Roland guitars. At present, Roland produce four different guitars – the G-202, G-303, G-505 and G-808. They are all standard guitars fitted with standard pickups that can be played through a normal amplifier, but they also have special "hex" pick-ups for use with the synth. The natural sound of the guitar can therefore be blended or mixed with the sound of the synth. Because the "hex" pick-up has a separate channel for each string, and because the synth has six string-selector switches, only the strings that are switched will have a synth sound. This means that it is possible to have, for instance, a bass synth sound on the 5th and 6th strings with a standard guitar sound on the other four.

Roland also produce a simpler synth, the GR-100 for use with its 6-string guitars, and a bass guitar synth, the GR-33B.

"Hex" synthesizer pick-up

Roland G-303 guitar

Roland GR-300
The latest Roland guitar synth is polyphonic and has six individual string-selector switches. It will respond to finger vibrato on the guitar but will also produce an electronic vibrato by means of low-frequency oscillators.

PLAYING THE GUITAR

The guitar is one of the easiest instruments for the beginner to learn but one of the most difficult to master. For millions of people, a handful of simple chords is all that is needed to work out how to play many of the popular songs we hear every day. But, at the same time, the guitar also offers limitless scope for musical expression to those willing to devote the time and practice to it. The great guitarists will all tell you that the guitar constantly presents you with new challenges and rewards as long as you are willing to seek them out. Learning to play the guitar cannot be done overnight. Our aim in this book has been to set out as clearly as possible – often in easily accessible chart form – a structured system of reference information ranging from the basic to the advanced. This chapter can therefore be used either as an introductory guide to the first steps of learning to play the guitar or as the basis for a more serious study of music theory, music notation and more advanced techniques. Either way, it contains a wealth of information which can be referred to time and time again. No matter at what level you play, use this book for reference and as a source for new ideas. Pick up your guitar and let your hands and ears lead the way.

THE BEGINNER

One of the things that makes the guitar unusual as an instrument is that most people who play it are self-taught. Classical guitarists are an exception, since they usually work with a teacher and follow a set course of training and development. But most rock and folk guitar players simply pick up things as they go along – copying songs from records and trading chords and licks with friends. In fact, some of the world's most influential and innovative guitarists were self-taught. Many of them therefore employ unconventional – but nonetheless effective – techniques.

A complete beginner can pick up a guitar and, within a very short while, produce something that sounds musical. This, together with the guitar's adaptability to so many different styles, is what makes it such a remarkably popular instrument.

All that's needed to get started is enthusiasm. What you play, and where you learn it from, is entirely up to you. The important thing is simply to begin playing.

"I'd play whenever I could get my hands on an electric guitar; I was trying to pick up rock'n'roll riffs and electric blues – the latest Muddy Waters. I'd spend hours and hours on the same track, back again, and back again."

Keith Richards

Where to start

The first thing to do is to get yourself a decent guitar. Initially, it doesn't matter whether it has steel strings or nylon strings, or whether it is electric or acoustic. What does matter is that it is playable. Cheap guitars are often a false economy. If they are badly set up – if the action is too high or too hard (see p. 166), if the neck is out of alignment (see p. 168), if the frets are uneven or poorly finished (see p. 170) and if the intonation is inaccurate (see p. 171) – then even an experienced guitarist will have trouble. Probably more beginners are discouraged by trying to learn on a bad guitar than by any other single factor. So, buy the best guitar you can afford, and check that it has been properly set up.

The next most important thing is *tuning*. Guitars go out of tune all the time – especially if the strings are new, if the temperature changes suddenly, if they get knocked or dropped, and if you play them hard. You must learn to tune the guitar yourself. It is not as difficult as it first appears (see p. 70).

Begin with simple open chords. On p. 74, you will find a *Beginner's chord vocabulary* containing fifteen basic chords. Concentrate on learning these shapes until you can get to them without having to think about it. Make sure that you finger them correctly – so that each separate note sounds clearly – and then go on to develop speed and accuracy.

By this time you should already be starting to explore what happens when you put these chords together in different orders. On p. 76, we explain how *chord sequences* work and show how certain progressions form the basis of hundreds of popular songs. At the heart of this lies the "Roman numeral system". It provides you with a way of analyzing chord progressions and also allows you to "code" them so that they are easier to understand, memorize and transpose to another key. It will help enormously if you learn from the outset to think about what key you are in and what the role is of each chord you play.

Experiment with different right-hand techniques. Try playing with and without a plectrum. Let the strings ring when you play chords, then see what happens when you deaden them – either with your left hand or your right. When you strum, notice the different effects produced by upstrokes and downstrokes. Finally, try *flatpicking* (see p. 79) and *fingerpicking* (see p. 80).

Barre chords are the next step on from simple open chords (see p. 82). Their importance cannot be over-stated. Mastering barre techniques is a major breakthrough point, instantly placing many more chords at your disposal. And, once you understand how they work, they will open up the whole fingerboard to you.

The importance of practising

Learning to play the guitar is largely a process of committing skills to instinct, of developing the necessary motor skills or what is sometimes known as "finger memory". And the only way to achieve this is by practising – repeating the same thing over and over until it becomes automatic. As Howard Roberts, one of the great jazz guitarists and a respected teacher, has said:

"Learning to play the guitar is a combination of mental and motor skill acquisition. And to develop motor skills, repetition is essential . . . Whenever musicians have trouble executing a passage, they generally tend to blame themselves for not having enough talent. Actually, all that's wrong is they don't know where their fingers are supposed to go . . . You should learn the piece in your head before you play it. And when you do play it, play it so slow that there's no possibility of making a mistake."

Howard Roberts

However, this tends to make practice sound like unrelenting hard work. It needn't be. There are as many different approaches to practising as there are guitarists. Some practise regularly, at certain times of the day; others pick up the guitar only when they feel like it. The only real advice is to play as often as you can, either on your own or with other musicians. Think about what you're doing while you are playing, and listen to what it sounds like. Stop and take a break when you become bored or when playing turns into too much of a chore. Any extra work you want to put in on studying scales, chords and harmony will always pay off; it can only help you to improve as a guitarist.

"Practise, practise, practise. Practise until you get a guitar welt on your chest . . . if it makes you feel good, don't stop until you see the blood from your fingers. Then you'll know you're on to something!"

Ted Nugent

Ted Nugent

The basics of music notation

Conventional music notation is a complete, self-contained language. It allows music to be written down on the page and thereby recorded or communicated without its having to be heard. Many rock and folk guitarists never learn to read music. Indeed, many of the best-known and most respected players have got by without it. This is unfortunate not because their music would have been any better if they had learned to read, but because it tends to make beginners think it is not worth the effort. In fact, there are four major reasons why being able to use music notation is a good idea: first, it means you can go into any music shop, take any piece of sheet music, and work out how to play it without ever having heard it before; second, it means you can keep an accurate and permanent record of any of your compositions; third, it means you can convey musical ideas to other musicians without having to play them; and, lastly, the very way in which music is written often helps to explain the theory and principles of how scales, chords, melody, harmony and rhythm are constructed.

In this book, we have not made the ability to read music a prerequisite. We do, however, encourage you to learn. Where possible, we have used music notation alongside other methods of conveying the same information – chord diagrams, fingering patterns, photographs, charts, etc. This leaves the choice up to you.

Basic music notation is not difficult to understand. But, like any language, it takes time and practice to become fluent. Sight-reading is not something you can pick up overnight. However, simply learning what the symbols mean is relatively easy.

The system is essentially very simple. Music notation is plotted on a five-line grid called the *staff* or *stave*. Extra lines (called *leger lines*) can be added as the range of the piece of music dictates. The vertical placement of a note tells you its pitch: the higher the note, the higher its symbol will be placed on the staff. The horizontal placement of the symbol tells you when the note is to be played, simply by reading the notes across the page from left to right.

A *clef* at the start of each line of music indicates the pitch of each line in the staff. A *key signature* tells you what key you are playing in. And a *time signature*, together with the *bar lines* that divide up the staff into smaller units of time, tells you what you need to know about the rhythm.

All these elements, plus those that have not been mentioned, are explained in detail later in this chapter, under the relevant topic. The illustration below, which identifies the most important symbols, can be used as a visual key or summary.

How music notation works The diagram here shows the basic "grid" on which all music notation is written – the five-line staff, divided into bars, and "labelled" with a clef, a key signature and a time signature.

Example This shows the scale of G major written out in standard music notation. The key signature indicates that an F♯ is to be played.

Key signature See p. 108. This is the key of A major or F♯ minor.

Time signature See p. 90. This means that each bar contains 4 beats and each beat is equal to one quarter-note.

Staff See p. 103.

Bar line See p. 90.

Repeat sign See p. 91.

Treble clef See p. 103.

One bar

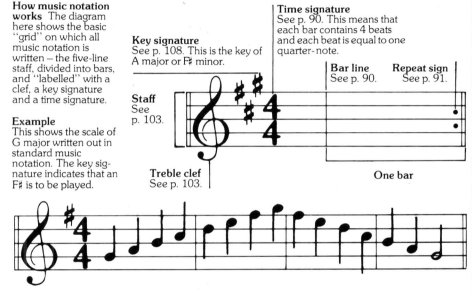

Guitar tablature

Tablature is a system of writing down music for the guitar as well as for other fretted instruments. It has existed in various forms through the centuries and has been used for flamenco, folk and lute music. It simply sets out the fingerings for a piece of music in a sort of shorthand. The system relies on you being able to hear the piece of music so that you are familiar with the rhythmic structure of the piece and the timing of the individual notes. In other words, it is used in conjunction with memory. Compared with music notation, it is easy to understand.

However, tablature cannot convey precise information about timing and the duration of notes. Nor does it help you to understand the harmonic structure of a piece in the way that notation can. Don't fall into the trap of thinking you can do everything with tablature that you can do with notation. Treat it for what it is – a form of shorthand.

Tablature is based on a six-line grid (as opposed to the five-line grid of music notation), but the major difference is that each line represents one of the guitar strings. The top line is the 1st (top E) string, and the bottom line is the 6th (bottom E) string. The numbers that appear on the lines are fret numbers. So, a number 3 on the 2nd line from the top, for example, tells you to play D on the 3rd fret of the 2nd string. An O on the same line indicates that you play the open 2nd string.

How tablature works This diagram shows the basic tablature "grid" – six lines, each representing one of the guitar strings. The numbers indicate at which fret the note is to be played.

Example As above, this shows the scale of G major. It starts on the G at the 5th fret on the 4th string.

Play 2nd string open (unfretted).

Play 3rd fret of 2nd string (the note D).

Hammer on from open string to 3rd fret (see p. 141).

Play two notes together. The melody note is B on the open 2nd string; bass note is G at 3rd fret of 6th string.

Pull off from 3rd fret to open string (see p. 141).

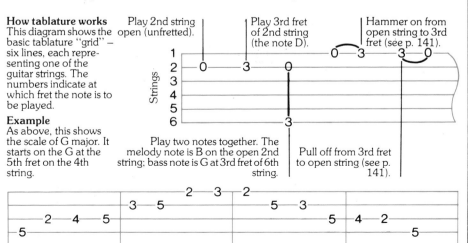

How the guitar is tuned

If you strike a guitar string, the "pitch" of the note it produces depends on three things – its length, its thickness and the tension it is under. Since all the open strings on a guitar are the same length (although see *Setting the intonation*, p. 171), one variable is removed and only two are left – thickness and tension.

On a six-string guitar, each string is of a different thickness or "gauge" (see p. 162). The thickest, heaviest string gives the lowest note of the six, and the thinnest, lightest string gives the highest.

It is by adjusting the tension of each of these six strings that you can control exactly what the pitch of the notes will be. The tuning heads increase or reduce the tension on the strings. Tightening a string will raise the pitch of the note, and loosening it will lower the pitch.

What we now call "tempered tuning" was established around the time that Bach wrote his *Well-Tempered Clavier* (1722-44). Before then, music was approached differently: each key was considered in terms of its own tonality and for its own distinctive atmosphere. In tempered tuning, all semi-tones are at equal intervals; in the pre-Bach "mean tone temperament", they were not. Since the design of the Spanish guitar pre-dates *The Well-Tempered Clavier*, the instrument has inherited the legacy of being difficult to play in tune. In contrast with the piano, the guitar does have a different atmosphere in each key. This occurs most notably when the guitar is tuned in only one key, and is largely due to the different basic constructions of popular chord shapes and to the response of the strings at different parts of the fingerboard. However, a modern guitar, of good quality and in good condition, can play in tune with any other instrument tuned or calibrated to standard or "concert" pitch.

There is a reference standard for concert pitch, used by most orchestras and recording studios (see opposite). It is also used as a standard by guitar and string manufacturers to judge the intonation and accuracy of their products. It is therefore essential, if your guitar is to play in tune in any key and in any position on the fingerboard, that you begin by tuning to concert pitch.

Standard open-string tunings

Over the years, a standard has evolved for how the six open strings of the guitar are tuned in relation to one another. The thickest or 6th string is tuned to E, the 5th to A, the 4th to D, the 3rd to G, the 2nd to B, and the thinnest or 1st to E. The two Es are the same note but they have a different pitch: the top E is two octaves higher than the bottom E. In other words, this convention establishes the difference or "interval" that there is between each string – E to A to D to G to B to E.

Twelve-string guitars are tuned to the same standard pattern. However, they are sometimes set a tone lower, and the tuning of each pair of strings varies. The 1st and 2nd strings are tuned in "unison", giving identical notes of the same pitch; the other four pairs are each tuned to give the same notes but an octave apart.

Of course, this standard tuning is not the only way a guitar can be tuned. There are many variations and alternatives which might be better suited to a particular tune or style, or which might be used to create a specific sort of "sound". Some of these are covered on p. 158.

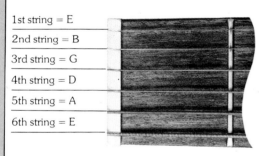

1st string = E	
2nd string = B	
3rd string = G	
4th string = D	
5th string = A	
6th string = E	

Six-string tuning
(left) With top and bottom strings both tuned to E, there are 2 octaves between high and low open strings.

Twelve-string tuning
(right) Although the tuning is the same, a twelve-string guitar produces a much fuller, richer sound.

1st strings = E+E (unison)
2nd strings = B+B (unison)
3rd strings = G+G (octaves)
4th strings = D+D (octaves)
5th strings = A+A (octaves)
6th strings = E+E (octaves)

Fretted notes

Horizontal *frets* are set into the fingerboard throughout its length and at right angles to the strings. When you press a string down on to a fret you are effectively shortening it. As we have seen above, the length of the string is one of the variables which determines the pitch of the note it produces. The shorter it is the higher the note, and the longer it is the lower the note. So, "fretting" a string will give a note with a pitch higher than that of the open string.

Frets are spaced out according to a particular mathematical series (see p. 40) which means that each fret produces a note a "semi-tone" (or "half-step") higher than

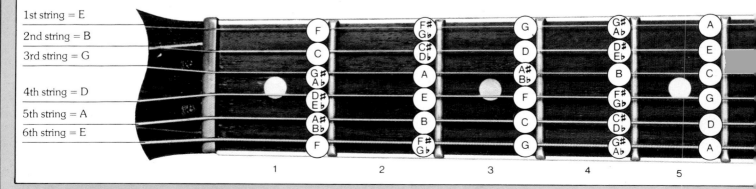

1st string = E	
2nd string = B	
3rd string = G	
4th string = D	
5th string = A	
6th string = E	

Tuning a guitar to concert pitch

The pitch of a note is determined by the *frequency* of the sound waves generated in the air. Frequency is measured in cycles per second or "Hertz" (Hz). A vibrating string producing a note with a frequency of 220 Hz, for example, will be completing 220 cycles of its particular vibration pattern every second.

Concert pitch has been standardized by establishing that the note of A (above middle C on the piano, and on the 5th fret of the 1st string on the guitar) should have a frequency of 440 Hz. The frequency is doubled for a note one octave higher, and halved for a note an octave lower. So, A on the 17th fret of the 1st string vibrates at 880 Hz, A on the 2nd fret of the 3rd string vibrates at 220 Hz, and A on the open 5th string vibrates at 110 Hz.

It is possible for a guitar to be in tune with itself and yet still be above or below concert pitch. But it is a good idea to get into the habit of keeping your guitar at concert pitch; it is better for the accuracy of the instrument and vital when you play in a band with other instruments.

Tuning a guitar to concert pitch can be done by taking reference notes from a well-tuned piano and tuning up or down to them. The open E (1st) string should sound the same as the E that can be found two notes above middle C on the keyboard.

Bear in mind, however, that guitar music is written an octave higher than written keyboard music. Therefore, a middle C played on the guitar (3rd fret of the 5th string) is actually an octave lower in sound than middle C on the piano.

Concert pitch can also be taken from a set of "pitch pipes" (probably easier for beginners, since they produce all six different notes) or a "tuning fork". Most tuning forks give an A of 440 Hz. Tune the 1st string (5th fret), 2nd string (10th fret) and 3rd string (14th fret) to this note, and then tune the other strings in relation to these. The A from the tuning fork also corresponds to the 5th fret harmonic on the open 5th string – that is, the harmonic A two octaves above the open A (see p. 71).

The recent introduction of electronic guitar tuners is a godsend not only to guitarists who wish to play in tune but to any musician who realizes that tuning is an art in itself and to any player who wishes to bring out the best sounds that the guitar can possibly produce.

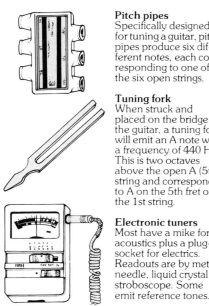

Pitch pipes
Specifically designed for tuning a guitar, pitch pipes produce six different notes, each corresponding to one of the six open strings.

Tuning fork
When struck and placed on the bridge of the guitar, a tuning fork will emit an A note with a frequency of 440 Hz. This is two octaves above the open A (5th) string and corresponds to A on the 5th fret of the 1st string.

Electronic tuners
Most have a mike for acoustics plus a plug-in socket for electrics. Readouts are by meter needle, liquid crystal or stroboscope. Some emit reference tones.

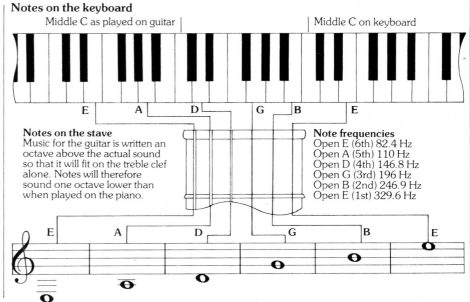

Notes on the keyboard
Middle C as played on guitar | Middle C on keyboard

Notes on the stave
Music for the guitar is written an octave above the actual sound so that it will fit on the treble clef alone. Notes will therefore sound one octave lower than when played on the piano.

Note frequencies
Open E (6th) 82.4 Hz
Open A (5th) 110 Hz
Open D (4th) 146.8 Hz
Open G (3rd) 196 Hz
Open B (2nd) 246.9 Hz
Open E (1st) 329.6 Hz

---

the fret below it. If you hold down the open E (1st) string on the 1st fret you get an F, if you hold it down on the 2nd fret you get an F♯, and so on. Similarly, the first fret on the open G (3rd) string gives you a G♯, the 2nd

fret an A, and so on.

The 12th fret is situated about midway between the nut and the saddle of the guitar – that is, it divides the length of the vibrating string in half. This means that the note on

the 12th fret has the same pitch as that of the open string but is an octave higher. The fact that there are twelve frets representing twelve notes in an octave is fundamental to the formation of scales and chords.

Enharmonic notes
Certain notes (the black keys on a piano) are known by more than one name and are therefore called "enharmonic". The note between F and G, for example, may be referred to as either F♯ or G♭ (see p. 103).

The 12th fret and beyond
Notes on the 12th fret have the same names as notes on the open strings, but they are exactly one octave higher in pitch. Fretted notes above the 12th fret simply repeat the pattern shown here. On the open E (1st) string, the 13th fret gives an F, the 14th fret an F♯, etc.

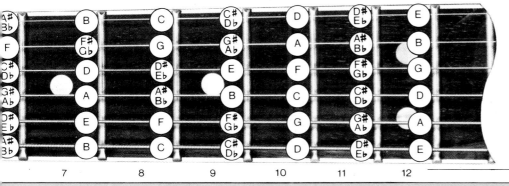

Tuning methods

Many beginners find tuning difficult. The technique depends on the ability of your ears to perceive slight differences in pitch between two separate notes, and also to recognize good intonation when you hear it and the difference when you do not. Although the immediate visual reference provided by electronic tuners is a great help, there is no substitute for the traditional skill of tuning a guitar using just a single reference tone and your ears. Some people find the ability to judge pitch easier than others. If you are one of those who find it difficult, take consolation in the fact that your sense of pitch will develop and improve, along with your technique, the more you play. A good musical "ear" can be learned and is a skill which develops with experience.

One of the secrets of good tuning is to take it slowly and calmly. If you are tense or in a hurry, you will not be able to relax, concentrate and listen objectively, and you will find it hard to recognize whether a particular string is sharp or flat.

You should always use the tuning heads to bring the string you are tuning *up* to pitch. Never try to tune *down* to pitch. Instead, slacken the string so that it goes slightly flat and then tighten it to bring it up into tune. This will help to keep it stable at the right pitch. String slippage is a major problem for all guitarists. It can be more-or-less prevented, however, by fitting the strings properly in the first place (see p. 164) and by "stretching" them – hitting them fairly hard, bending them or pulling them away from the guitar so that you give them a chance to settle down – before you begin playing.

The problem of strings going out of tune is often worse for a lead guitarist who uses light-gauge strings and plays a lot of solos with bent notes than it is for an acoustic guitarist with heavier strings and a lighter fingerstyle technique. Strings also tend to go out of tune if the guitar is suddenly taken from a cold room to a warm room, or vice-versa.

The tuning methods described here will all allow you to tune the guitar to itself. This is called "relative tuning". However, if you want the guitar to be tuned to standard concert pitch – and it ought to be – then you must start by tuning at least one string to an accurate reference note.

Most guitarists use a combination of some or all of these methods. Generally, it is a good idea to start by going through all six strings and getting them approximately to the correct pitch. You can then go back and make slight adjustments where necessary to ensure that each string plays in tune with the others. One should consider tuning in two stages: first, a rough, "general tuning" and then a much more precise "fine tuning".

Method 1

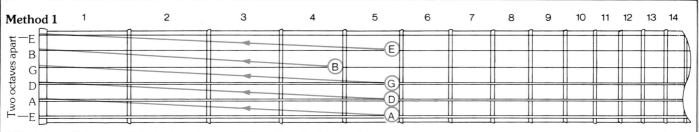

1 Beginning with the open E (1st) string at the right pitch, tune the open E (6th) string to the same note but two octaves lower.
2 Play an A on the 5th fret of the 6th string and tune the open A (5th) string to it.

3 Play a D on the 5th fret of the 5th string and tune the open D (4th) string to it.
4 Play a G on the 5th fret of the 4th string and tune the open G (3rd) string to it.
5 Play a B on the 4th fret of the 3rd string and

tune the open B (2nd) string to it.
6 Finally, play an E on the 5th fret of the 2nd string and check the open E (1st) string against it. Do not move on to the next string until you are certain that the one you are tuning is correct.

Method 2

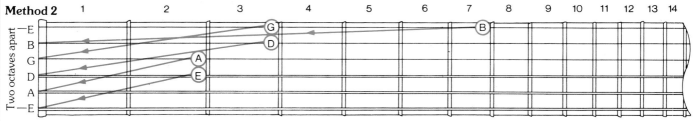

1 Beginning with the open E (1st) string at the right pitch, play a B on the 7th fret and tune the open B (2nd) string to it.
2 Play a G on the 3rd fret of the 1st string and

tune the open G (3rd) string to it.
3 Play a D on the 3rd fret of the 2nd string and tune the open D (4th) string to it.
4 Play an A on the 2nd fret of the 3rd string and

tune the open A (5th) string to it.
5 Play an E on the 2nd fret of the 4th string and tune the open E (6th) string to it.
6 Finally, check the open 1st and 6th strings.

Method 3

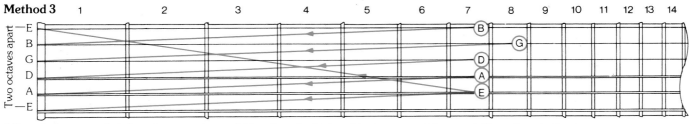

1 If you have a tuning fork, begin by tuning the open A (5th) string to it.
2 Play an E on the 7th fret of the 5th string and tune both open E (1st and 6th) strings to it.

3 Play a B on the 7th fret of the 1st string and tune the open B (2nd) string to it.
4 Play a G on the 8th fret of the 2nd string and tune the open G (3rd) string to it.

5 Play a D on the 7th fret of the 3rd string and tune the open D (4th) string to it.
6 Finally, play an A on the 7th fret of the 4th string and check the original open A (5th) string.

Tuning to chords

All guitars tend to sound perfectly in tune in one chord and to be slightly out of tune in all the others. It is in the nature of their construction. Unlike the violin or double bass (which are fretless), the intervals between the notes are fixed by the frets.

In an attempt to minimize the effect of this, the precise positioning of the frets is designed to spread out across the fingerboard any inaccuracies in the intervals between one note and the next, whatever key you are playing in. This means that, to all intents and purposes, the guitar will sound correctly in tune in every key. It is called "tempered tuning".

Tuning to chords is a good way of checking and, if necessary, adjusting this compromise in the tuning. Once the open strings are in tune with one another, play a chord—sounding each individual note and listening carefully to the intervals between them. If you are going to play in the key of C, for

example, begin by playing an open C chord and check that it sounds right. Then play some of the other chords in the same key—F and G, for instance—to see whether they are also in tune. It is also a good idea to play each chord in different shapes up and down the fingerboard to check the tuning in different positions. (Details of how to play these chords, and how they are related to one another, appear on p. 74-7 and 82-3.)

Fine tuning chords as they are being sounded is a useful technique for checking your tuning while actually performing—although it calls for good judgement in recognizing which string is the offender and the ability to tell how far out it is. With your left hand in position holding down the chord, and while the strings are still ringing, reach across with your right hand and adjust the tuning head. This is a little easier on guitars with all six tuning heads on the top of the headstock.

Tuning to a chord while playing

Tuning with harmonics

"Harmonic" notes are described on p. 116, together with instructions on how to play them. They are often used to check tuning and intonation due to the fact that they have a purer sound than open strings or fretted notes and because of the phenomenon of *beat tones*. Beat tones are generated when two pitches are close but not quite the same. If one note is an A vibrating at 440 Hz and the other is just a little flat, vibrating at, say, 436 Hz, you will be able to hear 4 beat tones or pulses per second when you play the two notes together. As you bring the second note up to the pitch of the first, the beats will slow down – and will eventually disappear when the two notes are in tune with one another. Recognizing the beat tones may be slightly difficult at first, but, with practice, you will quickly develop an "ear" for them. The method is as follows.

Checking 5th and 7th fret harmonics

● Play a 5th fret harmonic E on the 6th string quickly followed by a 7th fret harmonic E on the 5th string so that both notes are ringing together. Tune the strings by bringing the beats together.

● Play a 5th fret harmonic A on the 5th string and a 7th fret harmonic A on the 4th string. Tune these two together.

● Play a 5th fret harmonic D on the 4th string and a 7th fret harmonic D on the 3rd string. Tune these two together.

● Finally, play a 5th fret harmonic B on the 2nd string and 7th fret harmonic B on the 1st string. Tune these two together.

Checking 7th and 12th fret harmonics

● Play a 12th fret harmonic E on the 6th string and a 7th fret harmonic E on the 5th string. Tune these two together.

● Play a 12th fret harmonic A on the 5th string and a 7th fret harmonic A on the 4th string. Tune these two together.

● Play a 12th fret harmonic D on the 4th string and a 7th fret harmonic D on the 3rd string. Tune these two together.

● Finally, play a 12th fret harmonic B on the 2nd string and a 7th fret harmonic B on the 1st string. Tune these two together.

Double checking

To prevent a gradual accumulation of error when tuning, here is an excellent check for ensuring that the two top strings (1st and 2nd) are in tune with the bass string (6th). First, play the 5th fret harmonic E on the 6th string against the 12th fret harmonic E on the 1st string. Next, play the 7th fret harmonic B on the 6th string against the 12th fret harmonic B on the 2nd string.

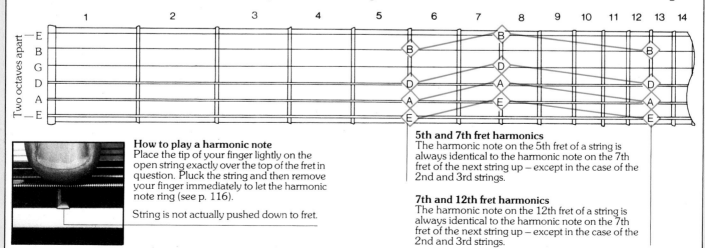

How to play a harmonic note
Place the tip of your finger lightly on the open string exactly over the top of the fret in question. Pluck the string and then remove your finger immediately to let the harmonic note ring (see p. 116).

String is not actually pushed down to fret.

5th and 7th fret harmonics
The harmonic note on the 5th fret of a string is always identical to the harmonic note on the 7th fret of the next string up – except in the case of the 2nd and 3rd strings.

7th and 12th fret harmonics
The harmonic note on the 12th fret of a string is always identical to the harmonic note on the 7th fret of the next string up – except in the case of the 2nd and 3rd strings.

Left-hand technique

The function of your left hand is to press the strings down on to the frets in order to sound the required notes. Before your right hand strikes the strings, your left hand must be in position, creating a specific selection of fretted notes for your right hand to play.

Many of the lead guitarist's left-hand techniques – for example, hammering-on, string-bending, slides and vibratos – are part of the arsenal of tricks associated primarily with the sound of the modern guitar. In contrast, the rhythm guitarist's left hand tends to be more concerned with fingering chord shapes. However, modern rhythm guitarists also use many syncopation and "chop" techniques that rely on the left hand for damping effects. It is, after all, left-hand damping that creates specific time values by releasing the string when it has sounded for the required duration, and that cancels unwanted notes when several strings are played at once.

There are various rules and conventions about how the left hand should be positioned and how the fingers should fret the strings. Classical guitarists are taught to use a specific left-hand technique which allows them to play without altering their basic hand position or posture. Some rock guitarists, however, will use any trick in the book.

Thumb position

The classical approach is that your thumb should always be in the middle of the back of the neck. This means that there should be a clear space between the neck and the palm of your hand, and that your wrist will be slightly bent so that your fingers will rest comfortably on the strings. Your thumb then acts as a fulcrum, allowing you to deliver just the right amount of pressure to your fingertips in order to fret the notes clearly. Many chord positions

are difficult unless your thumb is providing pressure from the back of the neck. This position will give you maximum precision, flexibility and speed.

Many guitarists place their thumb too high on the back of the neck, and end up cradling the neck in their palm. It is an easy habit to slip

Thumb centred on the back of the guitar neck.

into, since it provides extra support for rock and country techniques. However, regardless of technique, if you sit your guitar on your lap or wear it from a strap, the neck should always be balanced so that it stays in the same position when you take your left hand away.

In some modern styles, the thumb is hooked over the top of the neck to fret notes on the bottom E (6th) string. This may be done either when extending a "barre chord" (see p. 82) or when playing separate melody and bass lines. Although condemned by classical guitarists, the technique does open up other fingering possibilities. It is also useful for getting extra "leverage" when bending strings (see p. 142).

Finger positions

To play a single clear note without touching any other strings, your fingers should be arched so that the tips come down on to the fretboard more-or-less at right angles to it. This obviously means that your fingernails should not protrude beyond the ends of your fingertips. If they are too long, you will probably find that you cannot fret the strings firmly or that, when you do, you accidentally deaden other strings.

When you fret a string, you should hold it down between two frets, but just *behind* the one you want. The vibrating length of the string will then be the distance from the higher of the frets to the saddle.

Use only as much finger pressure as is necessary to make the note sound clearly. Pressing too hard will tire your fingers and may well hurt. Beginners often experience this immediately – especially with steel strings – since it takes a little while to toughen the fingertips and learn how to apply just the right amount of pressure to the strings.

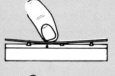

Correct
Fingering the string just behind the fret will produce a clean, ringing note.

Incorrect
Placing your finger too far back may allow the string to rattle or buzz against the fret.

Incorrect
Putting your finger actually on top of the fret will almost certainly muffle the string and dampen the sound.

The "one-fret-per-finger" rule

Classical guitarists approach the fingerboard with the concept that each finger on the left hand should have a fret space to itself and that it should be responsible for all six strings (and therefore all six notes) on that fret. In this way, one hand position will cover four frets; and, theoretically, three hand positions could cover all twelve frets up to the octave.

As a beginner you will find it difficult to use your 4th finger. Nevertheless, it is important to persevere. It will become easier with practice, and strength and independence in your 4th finger is invaluable for advanced chords and fast lead patterns.

Because the guitar is one of the few instruments on which it is possible to play many notes in more than one place, deter-

mining the best position to use is the first consideration of most guitarists learning a new piece of music (see p. 102). However, whatever the position on the fingerboard, playing a melody line is usually easier if you follow the one-fret-per-finger rule. When

you have to change your hand position, each finger moves to cover a new fret.

Sometimes, classical guitarists keep each finger down on the last note it played until it is needed to play a new note. This can produce a "ringing-on" harmonic effect.

Covering twelve frets in three fingering positions

1st fret position
The four fingers cover the four frets from 1st to 4th.

5th fret position
The four fingers cover the four frets from 5th to 8th.

9th fret position
The four fingers cover the four frets from 9th to 12th.

Right-hand technique

Right-hand control is a combination of timing and accuracy. The more you practise, the sooner your right hand will become an extension of your sense of rhythm, and the easier it will be to concentrate on accuracy.

At first you may find it helpful to provide support for your right hand. Your forearm should rest lightly across the upper face of the guitar, leaving your hand free to move and in the right position to play. For even more stability, you can rest your palm on the bridge behind the strings.

The golden rule for all right-hand technique is "minimum movement for maximum effect". Speed, versatility and the energy required for striking the string come from rotating the forearm and wrist. The hand should move only to select the strings and to control the plectrum or fingers.

Generally, the playing area is considered to be the space between the bridge and the body end of the fingerboard. The sound varies according to the exact point of contact: it is sharp and trebly close to the bridge, and becomes progressively more mellow as you move towards the middle of the string.

Whether you choose to play with your fingers or with a plectrum is a personal decision based on the style of the music and the sound you want to produce. With notable exceptions, most blues, rock and jazz guitarists use plectrums. On steel-string guitars, plectrums produce more volume and a clearer tone (due to their sharper attack). In contrast, classical, flamenco, Latin-American and many folk guitarists generally play only with their fingers. It requires considerable fingerstyle technique to match the speed of a plectrum when playing melody lines, but considerable plectrum technique to match the rhythmic versatility of the fingers.

Plectrums

The choice of plectrum is a matter of personal "feel". Thin plectrums, which offer less resistance to the strings, produce a small "click" that emphasizes the treble content of the attack, and they make fast strumming or "mandolin" picking easier. Hard picks produce more volume and a firmer tone. They also offer better control at high speed because they make a more definite contact with the strings.

The plectrum is held between the tip of the thumb and the side of the 1st finger – with the thumb and finger at right angles to one another. There are three ways in which the plectrum can be used to strike the string: as a *downstroke*, as an *upstroke*, or in the form of *alternate strokes*. Each produces its own sound. The basic goal of all plectrum technique should be the ability to use each with equal ease and control.

Plectrum exercises

These exercises are all designed to develop fast and accurate alternate plectrum strokes. Begin by establishing a steady count of 1–2–3–4. On the count, play each open string four times – first with downstrokes, then with upstrokes.

Now, at the same tempo, say the word "and" between each count. Play a downstroke on the count and an upstroke on the "and" – hitting each string eight times over each count of four.

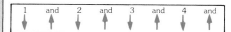

Slow down the tempo and, this time, play a downstroke and an upstroke on each count as well as on each "and". You should now be play-

ing sixteen alternate strokes over each count of four. Try changing chord after each sixteen.

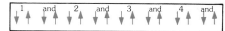

In addition to simple time divisions of four, you should also learn to play alternate strokes in threes. These are called "triplets" (see p. 94). Establish a count of four, as above, but say 2–3 between each count and play the string once for each number spoken.

Maintain a strict down-up movement so that the plectrum never plays two downstrokes or two upstrokes in succession. Finally, try playing different strings for each count or "beat".

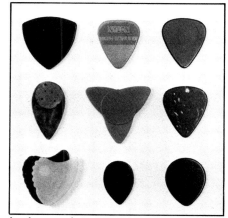

A selection of plectrums
Also called "picks" or "flatpicks", plectrums are made in a variety of materials – plastic, nylon, tortoiseshell, rubber, felt, and even stone. They come in various shapes, sizes and thicknesses.

Fingerstyles

Most popular fingerstyles are a product of traditional folk styles, and they employ every conceivable application of the four fingers and the thumb. There are few rules and only some similarities between styles since most techniques have developed through tradition, imitation and instinct.

All fingerstyles rely on the thumb to play the bass strings and the fingers to play the top strings. With the thumb playing the downstrokes and the fingers playing the upstrokes, four or five notes can be sounded simultaneously or one after another, as an "arpeggio".

As regards the position of the right hand in relation to the strings, the "classical" technique gives the most freedom and the best response from the guitar.

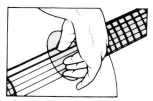

"Classical" hand position

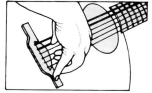

"Anchor" hand position

"Muting" hand position

Thumbpicks and fingerpicks
Many fingerstyle guitarists keep the nails on their right hand fairly long and use them to strike the strings. Others use metal or plastic fingerpicks which fit over the ends of the fingers and thumb.

Open chords

The first goal of any guitarist wanting to play popular music is to build up a chord vocabulary. This is largely a question of teaching the left hand to remember the various shapes. It does take time, but the more often you use a particular chord, the quicker you will be able to find it and the smoother your playing will sound.

The fifteen simple chords shown here comprise the beginner's chord vocabulary. Using these fifteen, in various combinations, it is possible to play a simplified arrangement of many popular songs.

Begin by looking carefully at each chord and try to memorize its shape or pattern. Get your fingers into position one at a time. then play each string separately to check that all the notes are sounding. If a fretted note does not ring properly, it will be due to imprecise fingering or insufficient pressure. If an open string does not sound, one of your fingers will be getting in the way and damping it.

Simple chord construction
It takes a minimum of three notes to make a chord, and *any* combination of three or more notes – however "discordant" they may sound together – can be considered as a chord of some sort. On the guitar, it is possible to play chords with as many as six different notes in them (one for each string), but all the chords shown here are made up of just three

or four notes – some of which are repeated or "doubled" (see p. 123).

Simple three-note chords are called *triads*; two notes are known as an *interval*. All chords convey to the ear two important musical statements. The first is the "key" or "tone centre"; this is the principal note of the chord and it is the one on which it is built. For this reason, it is called the *root* note. The second is the "harmony"; this is the effect produced by sounding the other notes in the chord *in relation to* the root note. It is the particular sound of the chord, and it is determined by the intervals between the root note and the other notes.

Take the three E chords – E major, E seventh and E minor – as an example. All three have E as their root note, but each has a different sound and therefore a different use. E major is a simple three-note triad comprising E, G and B. But, when you play E seventh, you are introducing another note into the chord, a D. This is what makes it sound different to E major. Now play E minor and consider how this differs from E major. Both are three-note triads, but the major chord has a strong, stable sound, whereas the minor chord is slightly sadder, more melancholy. In each case, it is the interval between the root note and the third note in the scale of the chord that determines whether it is a major or a minor (see p. 104-7).

The beginner's chord vocabulary
Learning these fifteen chords should be your first job. The three E chords are probably the easiest with which to start: first, all six strings are played; second, once you can play E major, you need to remove only one finger to play E seventh or E minor. The C chords and the B seventh call for slightly more precise fingering if all the notes are to sound clearly. And to play the F chord, you must use your 1st finger to hold down two strings at once. This is a simple "barre" (see p. 82). Your thumb should be behind your 1st finger, providing pressure directly opposite the barre.

E major
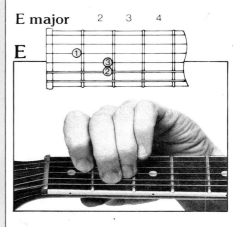

E seventh
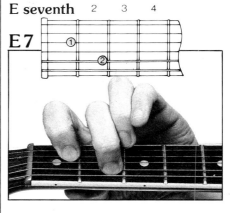

E minor
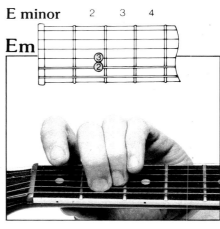

How to read chord diagrams
To learn these fifteen basic chords, you must understand how to read chord diagrams. These are simply box grids representing the strings and the frets on the fingerboard. The six horizontal lines are the strings, with the top E (1st) at the top and the bottom E (6th) at the bottom. The vertical lines are the fret wires, and the spaces in between are numbered to indicate which

part of the fingerboard is being shown. Finger positions are indicated by circles on the strings. The numbers in the circles tell you which finger to use. A circle without a number in it indicates an optional note. If there is no circle on the string, it should be played open (unfretted). If there is an "X" on the string, it forms no part of the chord and should not be sounded at all.

Example: C major

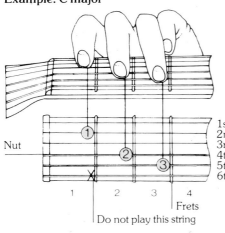

Nut

1st string
2nd string
3rd string
4th string
5th string
6th string

1   2   3   4 | Frets
| Do not play this string

Chord diagram
The circles indicate that the 1st finger plays the 1st fret on the 2nd string, the 2nd finger the 2nd fret on the 4th string, and the 3rd finger the 3rd fret on the 5th string. The 1st and 3rd strings are played open, and the 6th string is not played at all. The thumb should be in the middle of the back of the neck, somewhere level with the 1st fret, so that there is a clear space between the palm and the guitar neck.

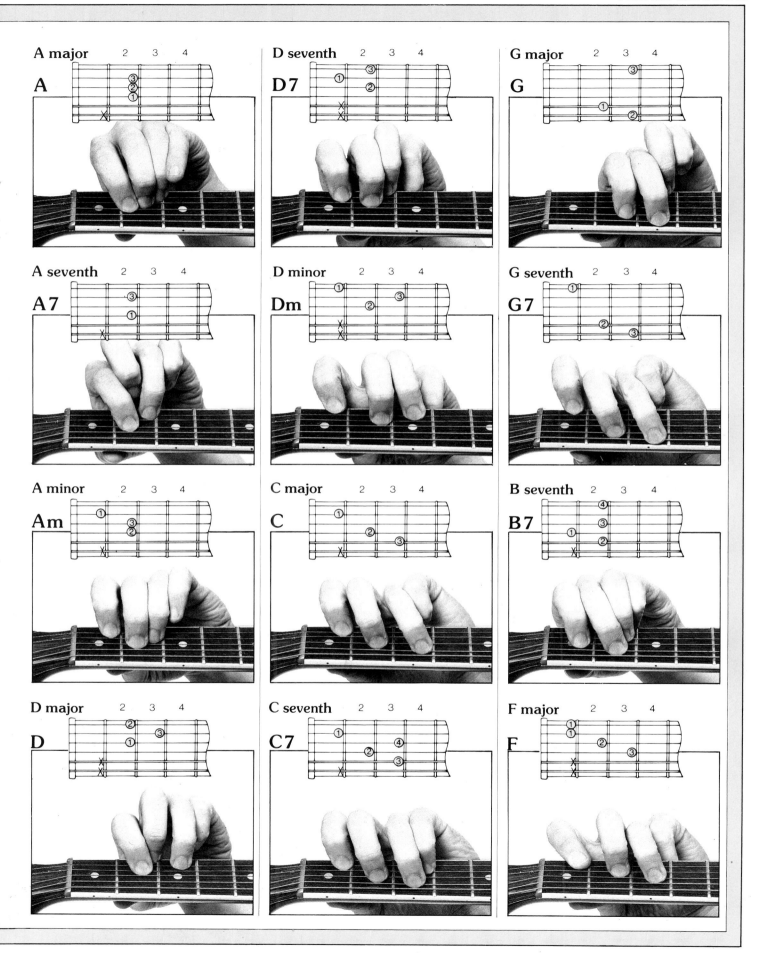

The three-chord theory

As soon as you are able to play the fifteen beginner's chords, it will become obvious that some sound better together than others. In any key, there are three chords which appear in virtually every basic progression. They will always sound good together, whatever order you put them in and whatever key you play them in. They are called the *primary chords*, and they represent the building blocks of all composition.

You can find these three chords in any key by looking at the major scale. Take C as an example. The key of C major has no sharps or flats in it. So, in one octave, the notes are:

C D E F G A B C.

The note of C itself is the root note, and the chord built on this note is C major, called the *tonic* chord. The other two primary chords are the 4th and the 5th in the scale. Counting up four notes, including C itself as the first, brings you to F, and counting up five notes brings you to G. The 4th chord (built on the note of F) is called the *sub-dominant*, and the 5th chord (built on the note of G) is called the *dominant*. F is therefore the sub-dominant chord and G is the dominant chord in the key of C. (For more details on scales, see p. 104, and on chord construction, see p. 121.)

In any key, these three chords have the same relationship to one another. Together, they comprise the "three-chord theory".

Finding the I, IV and V chords

Example: key of C major

I	II	III	IV	V	VI	VII	I
C	D	E	F	G	A	B	C

I chord (C major)
Built on 1st note of major scale.

V chord (G seventh)
Built on 5th note of major scale.

IV chord (F major) Built on 4th note of major scale.

The Roman numeral system

There is a system in music theory which can identify each chord in a key by a Roman numeral. The 1st chord, the one built on the root note, is I, the 2nd chord is II, the 3rd is III, and so on up to VII. Chord number VIII is the same as chord number I but an octave higher.

Each chord also has a name according to its position in the scale and its Roman numeral – whatever key you are in. We have already seen that the I chord is the *tonic*, the IV chord is the *sub-dominant*, and the V chord is the *dominant*. The other names are given below, and their function in chord progressions is explained in the following pages.

I	Tonic (root)
II	Supertonic
III	Mediant
IV	Sub-dominant
V	Dominant
VI	Sub-mediant or relative minor
VII	Seventh or leading note
I	Tonic (octave)

Chords built on the major scale in five common keys

Key of C major		Key of D major		Key of E major		Key of G major		Key of A major	
No sharps		2 sharps		4 sharps		1 sharp		3 sharps	
I	C	I	D	I	E	I	G	I	A
II	D	II	E	II	F♯	II	A	II	B
III	E	III	F♯	III	G♯	III	B	III	C♯
IV	F	IV	G	IV	A	IV	C	IV	D
V	G	V	A	V	B	V	D	V	E
VI	A	VI	B	VI	C♯	VI	E	VI	F♯
VII	B	VII	C♯	VII	D♯	VII	F♯	VII	G♯
I	C	I	D	I	E	I	G	I	A

Chord progressions based on the three-chord theory

The best way of taking in this information and of understanding how the three-chord theory works is to familiarize yourself with the *sounds* behind the rules. And the only way to do this is to play the chords one after another, in various combinations, while listening to the effects they create.

On the right is a chart which sets out many of the most common I–IV–V chord progressions using the fifteen beginner's chords from p. 75. The tonic (I) and sub-dominant (IV) chords may be major, minor or seventh forms, but the dominant (V) chord in these examples is always major and is usually played as a seventh.

You will soon discover that many of these chord combinations are familiar and that most of them form the basis of popular songs. What makes one different from another – apart from the order in which the chords are arranged – is the length of time you stay on each chord and the rhythm you give to the sequence.

Try playing them. Give each chord an equal count of anything from one to four, and try all the permutations shown within one key so that you can hear how major, minor and seventh chords will sound in combination.

	I	IV	V	I
Key of **E**	E	A	B7	E
	Em	A7	B7	Em
	Em	Am	B7	Em
Key of **A**	A	D	E7	A
	Am	D7	E7	Am
	Am	Dm	E7	Am
Key of **D**	D	G	A7	D
	Dm	G	A	Dm
	Dm	G7	A7	Dm
Key of **G**	G	C	D7	G
	G7	C	D7	G
Key of **C**	C	F	G7	C
	C7	F	G7	C

Blues chord progressions

The blues is a musical form based almost entirely on the three-chord theory. Although the blues was certainly not analyzed by its creators, its formula has survived to become the structure of popular music, the accepted roots of jazz, and the heart of rock.

The most common blues pattern is probably the one known as the *twelve-bar blues*. It gets its name from the fact that it takes twelve "bars" to complete each cycle of the chord progression. "Bars" are explained fully on p. 89-90, but for now we can say that one bar equals a count of 1-2-3-4.

The blues is difficult to categorize, however. There are many variations on the theme and many different ways of arranging the three chords. Sometimes the chords are majors and sometimes they are sevenths; sometimes the progression is not even twelve bars long, but may be just eight. The blues is characterized just as much by its rhythms (see p. 97) and its vocal and lead solo styles (see p. 144) as by the construction of its chord progressions.

Below are four typical blues chord sequences in the key of E. The first represents what is usually considered to be the basic twelve-bar pattern. The second shows the same progression but with sevenths introduced. The third is a common variation. And the fourth is an eight-bar rather than a twelve-bar sequence.

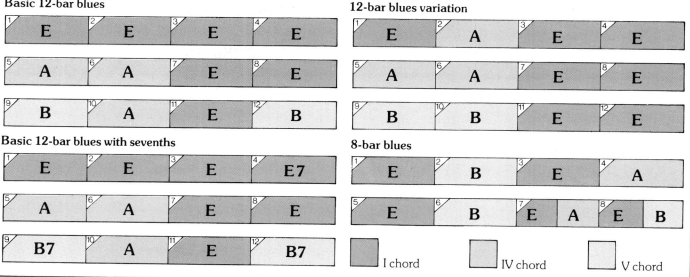

Basic 12-bar blues

1 E	2 E	3 E	4 E
5 A	6 A	7 E	8 E
9 B	10 A	11 E	12 B

12-bar blues variation

1 E	2 A	3 E	4 E
5 A	6 A	7 E	8 E
9 B	10 B	11 E	12 E

Basic 12-bar blues with sevenths

1 E	2 E	3 E	4 E7
5 A	6 A	7 E	8 E
9 B7	10 A	11 E	12 B7

8-bar blues

| 1 E | 2 B | 3 E | 4 A |
| 5 E | 6 B | 7 E A | 8 E B |

I chord   IV chord   V chord

Further chord progressions

On p. 76, we showed how to find the I, IV and V chords built on the 1st, 4th and 5th notes of a "harmonized" major scale. We now move on to introduce the chords built on the 2nd, 3rd and 6th notes. These are called the *secondary chords*. Roman numerals are used to indicate on which note of the scale each chord is based.

The VI chord is built on the 6th note of the major scale in any key, and is called the *relative minor*. Its natural form is as a minor chord, but it can also be played as a major or a seventh. (For more details on its special relation to the tonic or I chord, see p. 106.)

The II chord is built on the 2nd note of the major scale, and is called the *supertonic*. It, too, is usually minor but can be played as a major or a seventh.

The III chord is built on the 3rd note of the major scale, and is called the *mediant* – so-called because it lies midway between the tonic (I) and the dominant (V) chords. It is generally played as a minor but can be a major chord as well.

Because it has no sharps or flats, take the key of C major as an example again. As you can see from the chart on the right, the II chord is a D, the III chord an E, and the VI chord an A. These chords can be worked out in other keys using the same method of counting up the notes in the appropriate major scale. The chart on p. 76 shows them in the five most common keys.

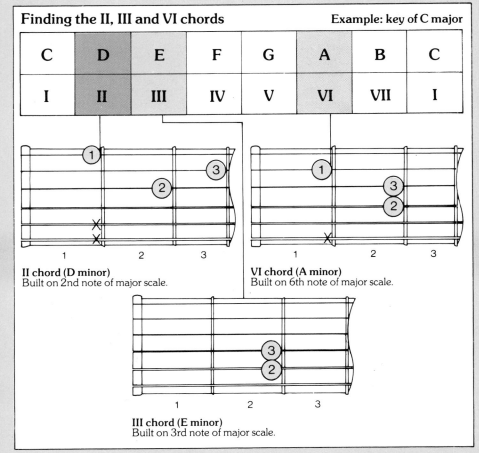

Finding the II, III and VI chords
Example: key of C major

C	D	E	F	G	A	B	C
I	II	III	IV	V	VI	VII	I

II chord (D minor)
Built on 2nd note of major scale.

VI chord (A minor)
Built on 6th note of major scale.

III chord (E minor)
Built on 3rd note of major scale.

Common progressions using the six scale chords

You now have six "scale" chords from which to create chord sequences. The progressions shown here represent most of the variations used in simple popular songs.

Note The last two progressions in the key of G contain a B minor chord. This is usually played as a "barre" (see p. 83 and the *Chord Dictionary*, p. 230).

	I	II	VI	V	I
Key of C	C	Dm	Am	G	C
Key of G	G	Am	Em	D	G

	I	VI	IV	V	I
Key of C	C	Am	F	G	C
Key of G	G	Em	C	D	G

	I	III	II	V	I
Key of C	C	E7	Dm	G	C
Key of G	G	B7	Em	D	G

	I	VI	II	V	I
Key of C	C	Am	Dm	G	C
Key of G	G	E7	A7	D	G

	I	III	VI	V	I
Key of C	C	Em	Am	G	C
Key of G	G	Bm	Em	D	G

	I	II	IV	V	I
Key of C	C	Dm	F	G	C
Key of G	G	A7	C	D	G

	I	III	IV	V	I
Key of C	C	E7	F	G	C
Key of G	G	Bm	C	D	G

Strumming and flatpicking

Basically, strumming is an instinctive action which either comes easily or it doesn't. Most guitarists strum with plectrums, since these give a crisper sound with a clearer "attack", but it is not unknown for players to strum with their fingers, with their thumb or with a thumbpick. As with all right-hand technique, it is important for the overall feel of your playing that you are able to maintain a steady, fluid strum, alternating between downstrokes and upstrokes. Upstrokes produce a sharper sound because they emphasize the top strings; downstrokes produce a fuller sound because the bass strings receive most of the impact of the stroke.

At the same time, you should be aiming to emphasize accents on various beats. Until you can do this, it will be impossible to establish either downbeats or backbeats. As we explained on p. 73, you can use your right-hand palm to mute or deaden the strings by resting it on top of the saddle. You can also use your left hand to dampen strings. This not only provides "space" where required but is also useful for establishing accented beats.

At this point, it should come as no surprise that only practice makes perfect. And the best way to practice smooth strumming is to play with other musicians, with recordings, and with metronomes or rhythm machines.

Flatpicking

A style used chiefly in acoustic folk and country styles, *flatpicking* is a plectrum technique in which you combine open-chord strums and single-string bass notes.

In its simplest form, this consists of alternating the bass notes of any open chord. These are almost always the root note and the "5th" (see p. 121), and the chord diagrams below show you which they are in six of the most commonly used open chords. First play the bass note of the chord, then the chord itself, then the alternate bass note (the 5th), then the chord again. Over the count of four, this produces a bass note on one and three, and a chord on two and four. The technique evolved partially because it gives the left-hand fingers time to form the rest of the chord when you are playing at fast tempos and making quick chord changes.

When you have mastered these alternate bass notes, the next step is to introduce simple bass lines and fills to connect open chords in a progression. A selection of different connecting patterns is given below. They are written out in tablature, instructions for reading which appear on p. 67.

Alternate bass notes for open chords

C major
Bass notes: C and G.

G major
Bass notes: G and D.

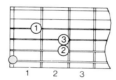

E major
Bass notes: E and B.

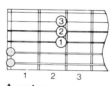

A major
Bass notes: A and E.

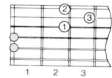

D major
Bass notes: D and A.

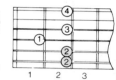

B seventh
Bass notes: B and F♯.

Single-note bass runs and fills

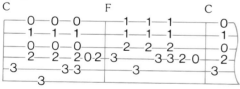

Connecting bass line for chords C to F to C
Count "1-and-2-and-3-and-4-and". Play linking bass notes on "and-4-and" of each bar.

Bass fills for open D major chord
This simple bass line includes either the B or the C on the 5th string. These notes are "hammered on" from the A on the open 5th string (see p. 141).

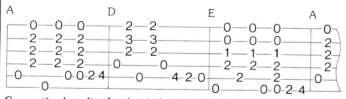

Connecting bass line for chords A to D to E to A
Same principle as above except that the last four counts of the second bar are used to descend from D to E.

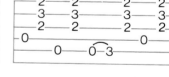

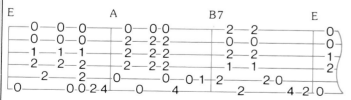

Connecting bass line for chords E to A to B7 to E
At the end of the second bar a B♭ is used in the ascending run that links A and B seventh.

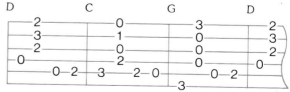

Ascending and descending bass runs
The first example connects the chords D, A and E; the second connects D, C and G. Both have four counts to the bar: the bass notes are on 1, 3 and 4.

Fingerpicking and fingerstyles

The basis of most fingerpicking or fingerstyle guitar playing is the development of independent movement in your right-hand thumb and fingers, so that you can play a rhythmic bass line on the bottom strings at the same time as a melody line on the top strings.

There are countless subtleties and variations in more complicated fingerstyle playing, but, initially, it is better to stick to basic pieces in which your thumb plays the bass line and your fingers play the melody.

Much of the music that features American fingerstyles is written with four beats to the bar. These beats are often played as alternating bass notes — so that there are two groups of two in each bar (see *Folk and country rhythms*, p. 96). Though something of a trademark in American folk, country and ragtime music, such alternating bass lines are never a feature of classical music nor, necessarily, of advanced fingerstyles.

For fingerpicking, you can use the basic classical right-hand position or adopt any of the others developed through American folk, blues, country, ragtime and rock styles (see p. 73). It is generally accepted that the correct right-hand position is essential to achieve a good tone and technique for classical playing. But the steel-string guitar will produce an acceptable tone with the right hand in various positions. The most common is to rest the edge of the palm on top of the bridge. The palm then acts as a steady anchor point, and it can be used to dampen the bass strings in order to create more of a contrast between the rhythmic bass line and the melody. This works chiefly because muting the bass strings prevents them from ringing on as long as the melody notes.

American fingerpicking styles

The *clawhammer* is just one of many American fingerstyles, but it forms the foundation of much of the technique. It gets its name from the fact that the right-hand position looks something like a curved claw hammer used for pulling nails out of wood. The thumb plays the rhythmic bass notes with downstrokes, while the 1st and 2nd fingers play the melody with upstrokes. The clawhammer was a characteristic of Rever-end Gary Davis's style — as it was of many other early blues players. Some guitarists use a three-finger, rather than a two-finger, style. In this case, one finger plays each of the top three strings.

Infinite variations are possible, including playing several strings at once instead of separately (in order to sound chords), and using the thumb to play upstrokes and the fingers to play downstrokes.

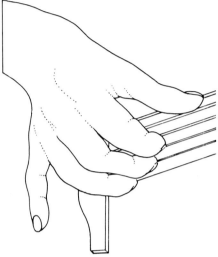

The two-finger clawhammer
The thumb plays the bass line, usually with downstrokes on the bottom three strings (the 6th, 5th and 4th). The 1st and 2nd fingers play melody notes, usually with upstrokes, on the top three strings (the 3rd, 2nd and 1st).

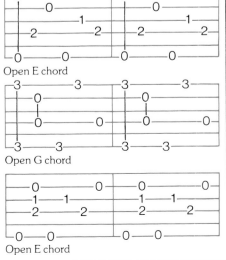

The three-finger technique
Again, the thumb picks the three bass strings, but the 3rd finger is also used so that the 1st finger picks the 3rd string, the 2nd finger picks the 2nd string, and the 3rd finger picks the 1st string — that is, one finger for each of the top strings.

Fingerpicking patterns

The examples shown on the right will give you an idea of how fingerpicking works, will help you to develop independent finger control, and will provide you with a starting point for discovering your own patterns. They are all written in "tablature" form (instructions on how to read this appear on p. 67) and use simple open chords. Although the bass string may vary, the patterns remain basically the same whichever chord you choose.

The first three examples have a very simple bass line, against which the notes on the top strings tend to give a sort of "ripple" or "arpeggio" effect. In the other three examples, the thumb plays an alternating bass, rocking from the 6th string to the 4th string. Begin by playing the exercises slowly, and gradually increase the tempo when your right hand has learned the pattern.

Arpeggio-like patterns

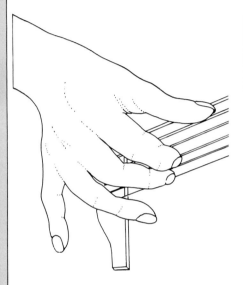

Open E chord

Open G chord   Open C chord

Open A chord   Open E chord

Alternating bass patterns

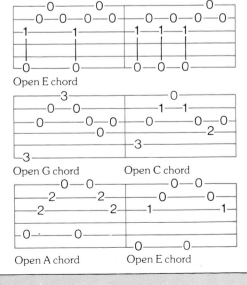

Open E chord

Open G chord

Open E chord

Changing chords while fingerpicking

Once you have mastered a few of the basic fingerpicking patterns, the next step is to combine them with some of the basic chord progressions you have worked out from p. 76-8. As with strumming, the most important thing is to keep the rhythm steady while you make each chord change. Playing along with a metronome or a rhythm machine may help you with your timing.

The example below is one of the most common of all chord progressions, a descending sequence of Am, G, F and E. The fingerpicking pattern has a solid alternating bass and is played to a rhythm of 1-and-2-and-3-and-4-and. You stay on each chord for two bars and play the pattern once for each bar. When you change chord, your thumb should change to a new bass string, so that it plays the root note of each chord – the 5th string for A minor, the 6th string for G, the 4th string for F and the 6th string again for E. When you get to the end of the sequence, you can change from E to A minor and start again.

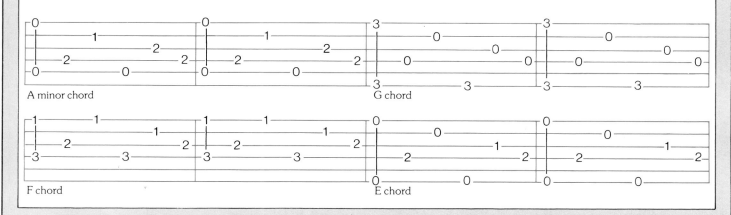

A minor chord   G chord

F chord   E chord

Combining melody and bass line

As well as providing a style for simple chord accompaniments, fingerpicking also gives you the possibility of combining complete bass and melody lines at the same time, so that you can play a two-part arrangement on your own. This sort of style – of which ragtime tunes are a good example – represents steel-string fingerpicking at its most sophisticated. The example given here – a simple arrangement of "When the Saints Go Marching In" – has a regular, unfaltering alternating bass of four beats to the bar. The melody is played on the 1st, 2nd and 3rd strings, and the bass on the bottom three.

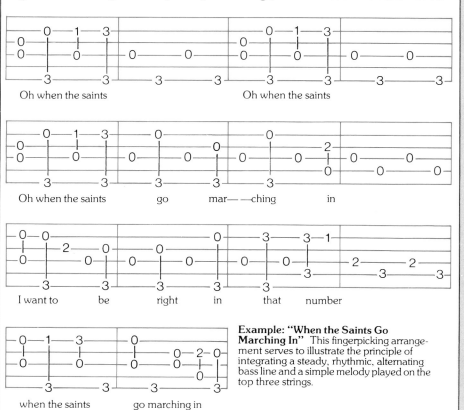

Oh when the saints   Oh when the saints

Oh when the saints   go   mar——ching   in

I want to   be   right   in   that   number

when the saints   go marching in

Example: "When the Saints Go Marching In" This fingerpicking arrangement serves to illustrate the principle of integrating a steady, rhythmic, alternating bass line and a simple melody played on the top three strings.

Plectrum-style fingerpicking

This slightly more tricky but versatile style evolved amongst country and rock guitarists. It is used by countless top players and means flatpicking and fingerpicking can be combined. You hold your plectrum between your thumb and 1st finger (as for normal plectrum styles), but at the same time use your other fingers to play notes on the higher strings.

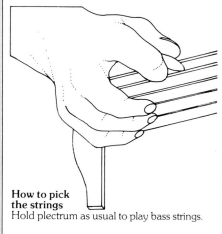

How to pick the strings
Hold plectrum as usual to play bass strings.

Example: two-string run
Playing one string with a plectrum and one with the 2nd finger is ideal for this two-string run, one of the best known country rock licks. The first two notes in each group of three are played as a "slide" (see p. 142).

Barre chords

On p. 75, we showed you how to play fifteen basic beginner's chords. Over the next four pages, we introduce what are called *barre* chord shapes. Learning the simplest of these will increase your chord vocabulary from fifteen to over 150 chord fingerings.

Barre chords take their name from the role of the 1st finger. It acts as a "bar" across all six strings, replacing the nut, and thereby enabling you to adapt open-string chord shapes to any position on the fingerboard.

The key to understanding barre chords is to realize that they are *movable* forms. The same shape can be moved up and down the fingerboard, from one fret position to another, without altering the fingering at all, to give you any one of twelve different chords. The note at the fret on which the shape is built

determines the name of the chord.

As soon as you start to work through the examples that follow, you will also see that, by using the various barre shapes, you can play one chord in several different places on the fingerboard. This demonstrates an important characteristic of the guitar. Being able to choose where you place a chord means that you can play any progression in a variety of ways, each producing a different sound.

There are four basic barre shapes, each derived from an open chord. The "E shape" is based on an open E major, the "A shape" on A major, the "C shape" on C major and the "G shape" on G major. The E shape and A shape can easily be adapted to give minor, seventh, minor seventh and major seventh barre forms.

The 1st finger "barre"
The essence of E and A shape barre chords is that the 1st finger replaces the nut of the guitar – thus creating chord shapes which can be played anywhere on the fingerboard.

E shape barre chords

The principle of all barre chords is to take an open-chord fingering and transform it into a shape that can be moved up the fingerboard. Begin by playing a simple E major chord, the way you were shown on p. 75. Now, in order to release your 1st finger so that it can play the barre, you must change the fingering of the open chord. The second step is therefore to hold down the notes of the chord with your 2nd, 3rd and 4th fingers. The third step is to move this whole shape up one fret, bringing your 1st finger down behind the others and laying it right across the 1st fret so that it covers all six strings. This is the barre. The shape you are now holding is a chord of F major, the chord one fret up from an open E major. The F on the 6th string tells you its name.

Re-fingered open E major
In order to play a barre, the 1st finger must be free, so the chord is re-fingered: 2nd finger on the 1st fret of 3rd string; 4th finger on 2nd fret of 4th string; 3rd finger on 2nd fret of 5th string.

Barre F major
The basic E shape is moved up one fret and the 1st finger holds down a barre behind the other fingers: 1st finger plays barre on 1st fret of 1st, 2nd and 6th strings; 2nd finger on 2nd fret of 3rd string; 4th finger on 3rd fret of 4th string; 3rd finger on 3rd fret of 5th string.

How the E shape moves up the fingerboard

The root note of all E shape barre chords is on the 6th (E) string. When you play a simple open E major, the 6th string is played open – and the bottom E is the root note of the chord. When you play a barre F major, the 6th string is held down on the 1st fret. This gives the note F – and F is the root note of the F major chord.

On the guitar fingerboard, *every* fret represents a "semi-tone" (see p. 68). This means that, *every* time you move a barre shape up one fret, the name of the chord rises by a semi-tone. Moving the F barre shape up one fret gives you F♯ major; moving it up two frets gives you G major, and so on. At the 12th fret, you are playing E again.

Alternative fingering

Many modern guitarists choose to use their thumb to fret the 6th string and play just a two-string barre on the top strings with their 1st finger. The thumb moves from its standard position in the middle of the back of the neck and is hooked over the top of the fingerboard as shown below. This allows the bass note to be damped or altered as well.

The position of root notes for E shape barre chords

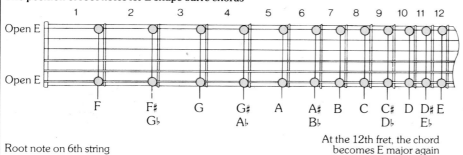

	1	2	3	4	5	6	7	8	9	10	11	12
Open E												
Open E	F	F♯ G♭	G	G♯ A♭	A	A♯ B♭	B	C	C♯ D♭	D	D♯ E♭	E

Root note on 6th string

At the 12th fret, the chord becomes E major again

A shape barre chords

The simple open-string form of the A major chord is also a movable form which, when played with a barre, can be positioned anywhere on the fingerboard to produce any one of twelve different chords.

As with the E shape, the A also has to be re-fingered slightly in order to free the 1st finger so that it can play the barre (see right). Start with the re-fingered form, and then slide the whole shape up one fret so that your 1st finger plays a barre across the 1st fret. This will now have transformed the chord from an A major to a Bb major.

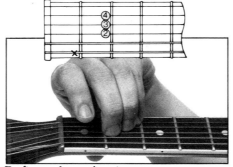
Re-fingered open A major

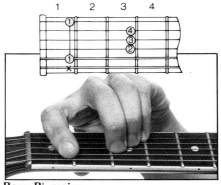
Barre Bb major

How the A shape moves up the fingerboard

The root note of all A shape barre chords is on the 5th string. When you move up from an open A major to a barre Bb major, the 5th string is held down by your 1st finger on the 1st fret. This gives the note Bb — and Bb is the root note of the Bb major chord. Moving the

Bb chord up one more fret will give you a chord of B major, and so on up the fingerboard. In short, the note you are holding down on the 5th string will always tell you the name of the chord. At the 12th fret, you will be playing A again.

Alternative fingering

The A shape barre chord is often played with a 3rd finger barre. The three notes on the 4th, 3rd and 2nd strings are held down by flattening the 3rd finger into a smaller "half" barre as shown below.

The position of root notes for A shape barre chords

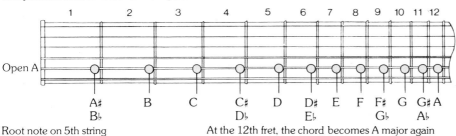

	1	2	3	4	5	6	7	8	9	10	11	12

Open A

| A# | B | C | C# | D | D# | E | F | F# | G | G# | A |
| Bb | | | Db | | Eb | | | Gb | | Ab | |

Root note on 5th string   At the 12th fret, the chord becomes A major again

Barre minors and sevenths

Movable barre shapes of minor and seventh chords are possible in exactly the same way as they are for the major chords. In some cases, they are even easier to play.

The simple E minor and E seventh chords shown in the beginner's chord dictionary on p. 75 are, in essence, slightly altered forms of the open-string E major chord. By re-fingering them slightly and using a 1st finger barre to take the place of the nut, they can be played anywhere on the fingerboard. The same holds for the A minor and A seventh chords; they, too, can be played as adapted forms of the A shape barre chord.

If you learn to play each bar chord variation in each position — and also memorize the notes on the 5th and 6th strings — you will find your chord vocabulary easily expanded to include twelve major chords, twelve minors and twelve sevenths based on the barre E shape, and twelve majors, twelve minors and twelve sevenths based on the barre A shape. Together, this gives you a total of 72 chord shapes — for 36 different chords. The *Chord Dictionary* (p. 225-49) shows these chords in their correct positions, using all the barre shapes.

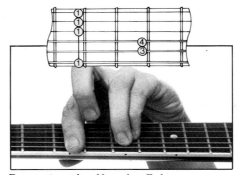
Barre minor chord based on E shape

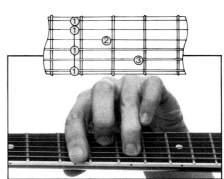
Barre seventh chord based on E shape

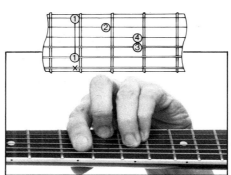
Barre minor chord based on A shape

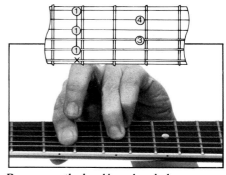
Barre seventh chord based on A shape

C shape barre chords

The third movable barre form is derived from the simple open C chord (see p. 75). The technique is the same as when building other barre chords. You simply re-finger the basic shape so that your 1st finger can play the barre behind your other fingers. The root note of all barre chords based on this shape is on the 5th string and it is played by the 4th finger, not the 1st finger. C shape barre chords are more difficult to play than those derived from the E shape or A shape. The relatively weak 4th finger has to hold down the bass string – involving a considerable stretch, especially at the lower end of the fingerboard where the frets are noticeably further apart.

Re-fingered C major
This form frees 1st finger so that it can play barre. As with standard form of open C major, 6th string is not included in chord.

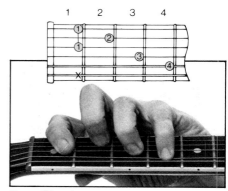

Barre C♯ major
Moved one fret up, with two-finger barre on 1st and 3rd strings. Root note on 5th string is played by 4th finger.

G shape barre chords

The fourth, and last, of the different movable barre forms comes from the simple open G chord (see p. 75). However, the 1st string is not used. All G shape barre chords have their root note on the 6th string – played by the 4th finger, not the 1st finger. Instead, the 1st finger holds down a barre only on the 2nd, 3rd and 4th strings.

Of the four movable barre chords, the G shape is probably the least used, but it is worth learning, if only to understand how it works. It can be handy when used with the C shape, it is a useful shape from which to move to other chords nearby, and it is a good basic position on which to build various "extended" chords.

Re-fingered G major
1st finger is freed to play barre, but 1st string is deadened.

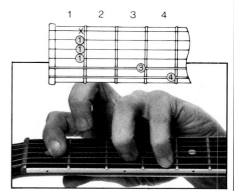

Barre G♯ major
Moved one fret up, with three-finger barre on 2nd, 3rd and 4th strings. Root note on 6th string is played by 4th finger.

The four barre chord shapes summarized

By now, it should be apparent that, by using the four barre chord shapes, any major chord can be played in four different places on the fingerboard – more if you go beyond the 12th fret and repeat the fingerings an octave higher. All you have to do is locate the root note and build the right barre chord shape around it.

By way of an example, the illustration below plots out on the fingerboard the positions in which you can play the chord of D major. Its simplest open form is shown at the bottom of the fingerboard. At the 5th fret on the 5th string, the D note can be used as the root note for an A shape barre, and, at the 10th fret on the 6th string, another D forms the

root note for a G shape barre and an E shape barre. The C shape barre is rooted on the D at the 17th fret of the 5th string. This gives a chord one octave above the simple open form. Compare these two shapes and you will see how the open D chord fingering is, in fact, a part of the fingering based on the C shape barre form.

Example: five ways to play D major

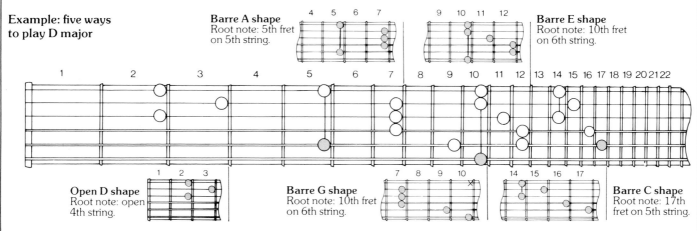

Barre A shape
Root note: 5th fret on 5th string.

Barre E shape
Root note: 10th fret on 6th string.

Open D shape
Root note: open 4th string.

Barre G shape
Root note: 10th fret on 6th string.

Barre C shape
Root note: 17th fret on 5th string.

Barre chord relationships

The best way to incorporate barre chords into your playing is to start using them immediately in chord progressions. And the best way to do this is to go back to the "three-chord theory" (see p. 76). As soon as you apply the I-IV-V rule to barre chords, you will come up against a surprising – and useful – fact: the root notes are always within three frets of each other, whatever key you are in and whether you build the I chord on the 5th string or the 6th string. The diagram below illustrates this principle with the I-IV-V chords in the key of C major.

The second diagram shows where all the other chords built on a major scale can be found in relation to the tonic (I) chord – again in C major, since it has no sharps or flats. It is worth remembering that the VI chord, the "relative minor" can always be found three frets below the I chord on the same string. So, as an example, A minor is played with its root note on the 5th fret of the 6th string – three frets below its tonic (I) chord, C major, played on the 8th fret.

It should now be obvious that you *must* learn the names of the notes on each fret of the 5th and 6th strings. Once you have memorized these, you should have no problem putting together sequences of barre chords in any key.

The position of root notes for I-IV-V barre chords
Using C major as an example, this diagram illustrates how the three most important chords in any key – the I, IV and V – can all be found within the space of three frets. This applies whether the I chord has its root note on the 5th or on the 6th string.

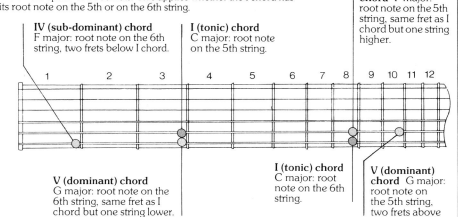

IV (sub-dominant) chord F major: root note on the 6th string, two frets below I chord.

I (tonic) chord C major: root note on the 5th string.

IV (sub-dominant) chord F major: root note on the 5th string, same fret as I chord but one string higher.

V (dominant) chord G major: root note on the 6th string, same fret as I chord but one string lower.

I (tonic) chord C major: root note on the 6th string.

V (dominant) chord G major: root note on the 5th string, two frets above the I chord.

The names and positions of all root notes in the C major scale

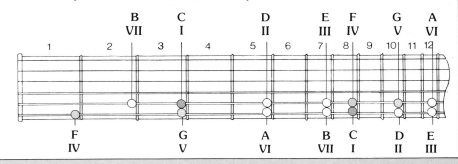

B	C		D		E	F		G		A
VII	I		II		III	IV		V		VI

F		G		A		B	C		D	E
IV		V		VI		VII	I		II	III

Barre minor sevenths and major sevenths

So far we have only dealt with three types of chords – the major, the minor and the seventh. But, if you look at any page in the *Chord Dictionary* (see p. 225-49), you will see that there are five different chords in the first column of each key. Generally, these are the five most commonly used chords.

The two we have not yet covered are the *minor seventh* and the *major seventh*. They can both be played as movable barre forms, with their root note on either the 5th string or the 6th string.

The minor seventh chord is derived from the minor chord by introducing an extra note. It therefore becomes a four-note chord instead of a three-note "triad". You can see from the illustrations here that this can be done simply by making a slight alteration to the fingering of the standard barre minor shapes.

The major seventh chord is also a four-note chord. It is derived from the major triad, but differs from the ordinary seventh chord in that the "interval" between the root note and the extra fourth note is not quite the same. It, too, can be played by slightly altering the barre major shapes.

More details of the construction of these and other new chords appear later on p. 126-9.

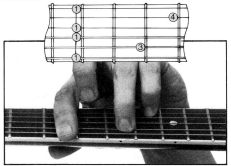

Barre minor seventh chord based on E shape
Movable form with root note on 6th string.

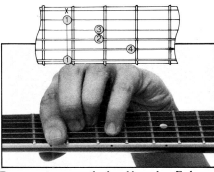

Barre major seventh chord based on E shape
Movable form with root note on 6th string.

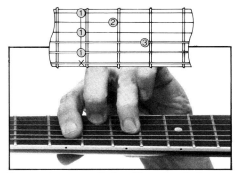

Barre minor seventh chord based on A shape
Movable form with root note on 5th string.

Barre major seventh chord based on A shape
Movable form with root note on 5th string.

Analyzing and transposing songs

Once you master barre positions, you will be able to play major, minor, seventh, minor seventh and major seventh chords. From here it is a simple matter to analyze and "transpose" any simple song. *Transposing* a piece of music (a chord progression, say, or a melody) means playing it in any key that is different to the one in which it is written or the one in which you originally learned it.

There are two reasons why you might want to transpose a chord sequence. First, you may want to sing along with it but find that it is too low or too high for your voice. Second, you may want to use chord shapes or add melody notes which are difficult to play if the music remains in its original key. Transposing the chord progression to an appropriate new key can help to solve both these problems.

Assuming you can play the chord progression you want to transpose, and that you have written down the chord names in

sequence, the first step is to convert – or "code" – it into Roman numerals (*see* p. 76). Music theory and analysis uses these numbers to describe the position of a chord (or note) in the context of its particular key. The numbers are free of any specific note or "pitch" value; they simply convey in theoretical terms a sequence of sounds. The secret to understanding the Roman numeral system is realizing that the sequence of sounds is the same, whatever key it is played in. The relationships between the individual chords described by the sequence of numbers remain intact and will sound the same in all twelve keys – only the actual pitches change.

As we have seen, the Roman numerals are derived from counting the number of steps up the major scale – from the tonic or root note of the key (which is always I) to the root note of the chord in question. The Roman numerals then identify the same "distance"

or number of steps from the tonic or root note in any key. Transposing requires you to find the specific notes or chords in the key to which you are moving. This is done by "decoding" the Roman numerals – translating them back into real notes or chords – using the same kind of scale in the new key. When the new tones or chords are played in the same rhythm and with the same "feel" as the original, the music will have been transposed, with its characteristics completely unchanged, to another key.

Two examples are given below to illustrate exactly how this works. More details of keys – how they are constructed and how "key signatures" are used to label them – are given on p. 108-9. Transposition should never be confused with "modulation". Modulation involves deliberately moving into a new key in the course of a single chord progression or melody, and it is explained on p. 138.

How to transpose chord progressions

Transposing from, say, C to D is easy – you simply raise the pitch of each chord by one whole-tone. But larger "steps" are more complex. The first thing to do is therefore to "code" the chords by changing them to a series of Roman numerals. This can be done using the chart at the top of the opposite page. You simply look along the top row until you find the key in which the original

chord progression is written. The column beneath it will give you the notes in the major scale and their Roman numerals. Now write out the chord progression using numbers instead of chord names.

To find the names of the chords in the new key, the procedure is simply reversed. You find the vertical column which represents the new key and "de-code" the

Roman numerals by reading off against them the names of the notes in the new major scale.

If you use a major scale to make the original conversion to Roman numerals, you must use the major scale of the new key to de-code them in order to arrive at the correct equivalent notes. Similarly, you must work from minor scale to minor scale.

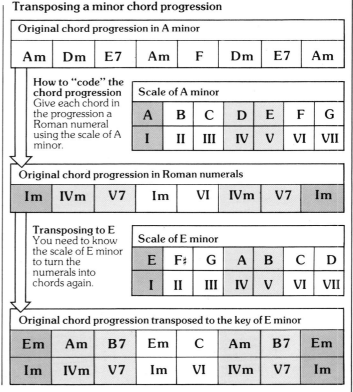

Transposing a major chord progression

Original chord progression in C major							
C	Am	Dm	G	F	Dm	G7	C

How to "code" the chord progression Give each chord in the progression a Roman numeral using the scale of C major.

Scale of C major

C	D	E	F	G	A	B
I	II	III	IV	V	VI	VII

Original chord progression in Roman numerals							
I	VIm	IIm	V	IV	IIm	V7	I

Transposing to G You now need to know the scale of G major to turn the numerals into chords again.

Scale of G major

G	A	B	C	D	E	F♯
I	II	III	IV	V	VI	VII

Original chord progression transposed to the key of G major							
G	Em	Am	D	C	Am	D7	G
I	VIm	IIm	V	IV	IIm	V7	I

Transposing a minor chord progression

Original chord progression in A minor							
Am	Dm	E7	Am	F	Dm	E7	Am

How to "code" the chord progression Give each chord in the progression a Roman numeral using the scale of A minor.

Scale of A minor

A	B	C	D	E	F	G
I	II	III	IV	V	VI	VII

Original chord progression in Roman numerals							
Im	IVm	V7	Im	VI	IVm	V7	Im

Transposing to E You need to know the scale of E minor to turn the numerals into chords again.

Scale of E minor

E	F♯	G	A	B	C	D
I	II	III	IV	V	VI	VII

Original chord progression transposed to the key of E minor							
Em	Am	B7	Em	C	Am	B7	Em
Im	IVm	V7	Im	VI	IVm	V7	Im

Major scale transposition chart

Note For details of how to use this chart, see opposite.

Twelve keys

I	A	A# / B♭	B	C	C# / D♭	D	D# / E♭	E	F	F# / G♭	G	G# / A♭	**I**
II	B	C	C#	D	D# / E♭	E	F	F#	G	G# / A♭	A	A# / B♭	**II**
III	C#	D	D#	E	F	F#	G	G#	A	A# / B♭	B	C	**III**
IV	D	D# / E♭	E	F	F# / G♭	G	G# / A♭	A	B♭	B	C	C# / D♭	**IV**
V	E	F	F#	G	G# / A♭	A	A# / B♭	B	C	C# / D♭	D	D# / E♭	**V**
VI	F#	G	G#	A	A# / B♭	B	C	C#	D	D# / E♭	E	F	**VI**
VII	G#	A	A#	B	C	C#	D	D#	E	F	F#	G	**VII**
I	A	A# / B♭	B	C	C# / D♭	D	D# / E♭	E	F	F# / G♭	G	G# / A♭	**I**

Roman numerals for each note of major scale

Using a capo

The capo is a clever little device which allows you to play a chord progression in different keys while still retaining the same chord shapes. It works because it acts like a sort of artificial "barre" (see p. 82-5). The capo fits around the neck of the guitar and raises the pitch of all six strings. The amount by which it raises them is determined by the fret on which it is placed. Putting a capo on the 1st fret will raise the open strings by one semi-tone; putting it on the 2nd fret will raise them by two semi-tones; and so on. This means that an open chord of C major played with a capo on the 1st fret becomes C# major, and the same shape played with a capo on the 2nd fret becomes D major. In other words, the fingering remains the same, but the notes are different.

Let's take an example to show how the capo works. Suppose you want to sing a melody to go with the fingerpicking accompaniment shown at the top of p. 81 – the chord progression of Am – G – F – E – but you find that the key in which it is written is too low for your voice. You would feel more comfortable if it were raised a semi-tone to the key of B♭ minor. If you transpose the chord progression using the chart above the sequence becomes B♭m – A♭ – G♭ – F. Now, these four chords can *only* be played as barre forms, which makes an easy chord progression suddenly more difficult – especially if you are fingerpicking. The capo provides the solution. By fitting it to the 1st fret, you can raise the pitch of the whole sequence to the key of B♭ but still use exactly the same chord shapes as in the original key of A minor. This will make the fingering much easier.

Capo with spring attachment

Capo designs
Some capos are clamped into position over the strings by a spring arrangement; others rely on elastic or an adjustable strap. Guitars with curved fingerboards need a capo with a curved bar; guitars with flat fingerboards, on the other hand, need a capo with a flat bar.

Capo with screw fastening

Capo with nylon strap

How to fit capos
The capo is clamped over the fingerboard of the guitar just behind the chosen fret so that it raises the pitch of any chord you play.

THE RHYTHM GUITARIST

In the context of most modern music, the drummer and the bassist are considered to be the rhythm section. Both the guitarist and the keyboard players are therefore free to choose between playing *with* the rhythm section or playing *on top of* it.

"What interested me about Chuck Berry was the way he could step out of the rhythm part with such ease, throwing in a nice, simple riff, and then drop straight into the feel of it again. We used to play a lot more rhythm stuff. We'd do away with the differences between lead and rhythm guitar. You can't go into a shop and ask for a "lead guitar". You're a guitar player, and you play a guitar."

Keith Richards

This attitude has its roots in the days of the big bands, when the guitarist and pianist were always thought of as part of the rhythm section. It was the brass and woodwinds that played the melodies and harmonies, while the rhythm section concentrated on providing the pulse and timing for the rest of the band. Playing this kind of rhythm guitar was best summed up by Freddie Green, Count Basie's guitarist for nearly forty years.

"You shouldn't hear the guitar by itself. It should be part of the drums so it sounds like the drummer is playing chords – like the snare is in A or the hi-hat in D minor. You only notice the guitar when it's not there."

Freddie Green

Most modern music still depends heavily on a rhythm guitarist who understands the traditional responsibility of the instrument.

Keith Richards on the Rolling Stones 1973 European tour.

"I don't think I even approach being a lead player; I think I'm very much part of a band and a riff-maker. I enjoy backing people up and letting people ride on top… I'm musically happiest when I feel I'm driving everyone else to do good things, when I'm not being the pin man."

Pete Townshend

Most guitarists play by ear, relying more on their sense of rhythm than their knowledge of scale and chord theory. This means that when they play they concentrate primarily on their left hand – switching their right hand on to "auto-pilot" and strumming instinctively.

It is the left hand that chooses the notes and chords, and therefore dictates the general direction of the right hand. When playing rhythm, another important contribution of the left hand is *damping*. By holding down or releasing fretted notes, the left hand acts as the sustain control, and may also allow certain notes to ring while damping others.

Its two functions of selecting the notes and controlling their sustain make the left hand comparable to a piano. If this is the case, then the right hand is like the drummer. Playing fingerstyle or with a plectrum, the four right-hand techniques – downstrokes, upstrokes, alternate strokes, and right-hand damping – give the guitarist control over timing, volume

and dynamics. Combining the effects possible with both hands produces the wide variety of rhythm styles for which the guitar is so well known.

The musical identity of each rhythm style results from a combination of six basic factors: the choice of plectrum or fingerstyle; the choice of chords – their complexity and application; the degree of sustain or damping; the sub-division of the bar into a rhythmic pattern; the beats that are accented or emphasized; and the tone of the guitar.

In this section of the book, we begin with an analysis of what rhythm is and explain how it is made up of four components – the tempo, the time signature, the note or rest values, and the accented beats. This will give you a solid understanding of how rhythm works, and will allow you to both write and play from written chord charts or rhythm charts.

The section ends with an examination of various rhythm styles – divided into five general sources or categories: folk and country; blues and rock; Spanish and Latin; soul, funk and reggae; and jazz. Listen to as many of these styles as you can, and try to isolate how the rhythm is constructed and what the role of each musician is. You will find that, in rhythm guitar playing, the spaces between chords are as important as the chords themselves.

Pete Townshend on stage with The Who.

Tempo, rhythm and timing

Timing is the ability to play a piece right through without speeding it up or slowing it down. It also involves the ability to keep up a rhythm and to emphasize certain notes (or rests) at precisely the same moment as other musicians in the band.

Timing can be difficult, especially in the early stages of learning to play the guitar, when you are concerned primarily with getting your fingers into the right positions and with sounding the notes or chords that you want. But timing is a skill that grows the more you play; it is directly related to confidence and experience. And, like tuning (see p. 68-71), it is a basic discipline which will spoil the effect of your music if it is not up to standard. If your timing is out and your playing speeds up and slows down, your audience will certainly notice it, even if you do not. In fact, it will probably be more obvious than the odd "bum" note.

Although timing is an "instinctive" thing, it can be analyzed and communicated in terms of written musical notation. Over the next few pages, we devote quite a lot of space to the ways in which timing can be written down. Since most guitarists learn to play by ear, this may seem unnecessary, but there is no doubt

that understanding the components of rhythm will help you learn more quickly, be more aware of what you are doing, and play better. Moreover, a knowledge of rhythmic notation is vital if you want to work out how to play a piece from sheet music or lyric sheets, or if you want to write down songs, chord progressions or arrangements that you have made up yourself.

Timing breaks down into two components – tempo and rhythm. *Tempo* is the speed (or rate) of a piece of music. Any specific tempo is measured as a number of beats per minute – and, generally, one beat is represented by one "quarter-note" (see *Time values*, p. 92). This means that music can be speeded up or slowed down by changing the tempo – that is, by playing more or less beats to the minute. Musical instructions that tell you what tempo to establish are explained on the right. For machines that measure tempo, see below.

Rhythm is the way in which a tempo is played. Whereas the tempo states how long it will take to play a set group of notes, the rhythm dictates which of the notes are emphasized (or "accented") and which are not. The rhythm is, therefore, what produces the "feel" of the music.

Tempo instructions
If the tempo has not been specified as a number of beats per minute – such that it can be set on a metronome – it is the responsibility of the conductor or the drummer to establish the correct tempo. In classical music, Italian phrases are used to describe various tempos.

Italian	English	Beats per minute
Presto	Very fast	168-208
Allegro	Fast	120-168
Moderato	Moderate speed	108-120
Andante	Moderate walking speed	76-108
Adagio	Slow (literally "at ease")	66-76
Largo	Slow and solemn	40-66

$\downarrow = 90$

Tempo instruction
This sign means that the music has a tempo of 90 beats per minute.

Developing a sense of timing
There is no question that by far the best way to improve your timing is to play with good musicians. It is the most effective way of learning to keep up the same tempo right through a song – but it also teaches you about rhythm and how it is established. In any good band, the drummer, bass player and rhythm guitarist create rhythms by playing *different* parts, not by playing on the same beat. This creates a much more complex and more interesting "composite" rhythm, and it is only possible if each player has a good sense of timing and a good feeling for what the other members of the band are playing. A band who have put in a lot of practice and have got their timing right will sound "tight" and effective.

However, not all guitarists either choose or are able to practise with other players. It is when playing on your own that timing is most difficult. Although varying the tempo is sometimes done deliberately – to create a special effect – as a beginner, you should concentrate on aiming for regular, steady tempos. There is a very real danger of losing your timing when you come to a difficult chord change or a tricky run. This is where metronomes and drum machines come in. They make invaluable practice aids – bringing it to your notice when your timing goes wrong and giving you a steady beat to help you keep your timing accurate.

These days, most guitarists are more likely to use a "drum machine". Originally

simple electronic metronomes, drum machines have developed rapidly in the last few years. The cheapest models are battery operated and plug into an amplifier to produce so-called "standard" rock rhythms. They are not very versatile, nor in any way realistic. They can best be used simply as the source of a steady beat. In contrast, the more expensive drum machines are highly versatile and can produce an almost infinite variety of complex rhythms. Many have built-in micro-electronic circuitry which allows them to be programmed, and they can create surprisingly realistic sounds.

Playing along to records or tapes is also an excellent way of developing accurate timing and understanding rhythm.

Roland CR-78 *(left)*
Sophisticated programmable "compurhythm" unit with built-in microcomputer.

Boss Dr Rhythm DR-55 *(below)*
A medium-priced drum rhythm unit.

Metronome
This simple clock-work device emits a sharp click on every beat. Its tempo can be adjusted by moving a small counter-balancing weight up or down the arm that swings from side to side. Sometimes metronomes also include a bell that will ring on the off beat.

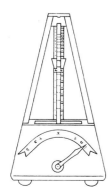

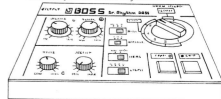

Time signatures

In written music, any tempo (a succession of regular beats played at a fixed speed) can be divided into small, manageable "chunks". Each chunk contains a certain number of beats or pulses and is called a *bar* (see p. 67). Grouping beats into bars in this way allows you to measure and count a tempo much more easily than if your only information was how many beats there were to every minute.

A *time signature* or *metre* is used to tell you how the bars are organized – that is, how many beats are grouped into each bar, and how long each beat lasts. Each piece of music begins with a time signature. It is always written as two numbers, one on top of the other, in the form of a fraction. The top number determines how many beats there are in one bar, and the bottom number determines the time value of each beat.

In the following explanation of different sorts of time signatures, it is important to remember that the numbers refer to *beats* not to note or time values. Any combination of notes or rests can be played in a bar as long as their total time value adds up to the total time value of the number of beats in the bar. This is explained in detail on p. 92.

Simple time signatures

Take the simplest time signature as an example – 4/4. This is called "four-four time", and is often abbreviated to "C", meaning "common time". In this time signature, there are four beats to the bar, and each beat has the time value of a quarter-note – since it lasts for one quarter of a bar. Music in 2/4 time has beats of the same time value (quarter-notes) but has only two of them in each bar. It is therefore essentially the same as 4/4 but with twice as many bars. The only difference is in the "feel" produced by the way the music is counted and played.

Besides 4/4 time, the most common time signature is 3/4. In 3/4 time (also called "triple time" or "waltz time"), there are three beats to the bar, and each beat has the time value of a quarter-note.

All time signatures based on "duple", "triple" or "quadruple" time are called *simple time signatures*. Compound time signatures are multiples of these.

○ = **Accented or emphasized beat**

2/4 Two beats per bar. Each beat is one quarter-note.
2/4 has same tempo and rhythm as 4/4 but twice as many bars.

3/4 Three beats per bar. Each beat is one quarter-note.
Two bars of 3/4 can be counted and heard as one bar of 6/8.

4/4 Four beats per bar. Each beat is one quarter-note.
Often written as "C" – as a symbol of a half circle – and meaning "common time".

Compound time signatures

If the pulse of a piece of music is not felt as single beats but as groups of three beats, it is said to be in *compound time*. Take, as an example, 2/4 time played in groups of threes: each of the two beats in a bar of 2/4 is divided into three beats. This now produces six beats to a bar, and the time signatures that describe this are 6/4 and 6/8. In the same way, 3/4 time played in three groups of threes becomes 9/4 or 9/8, and 4/4 time played in four groups of threes becomes 12/4 or 12/8. These groups of three beats are called "triplets" (see p. 94).

When music has five, seven or eleven beats in each bar, it is said to be in *asymmetric time* – since these numbers are not divisible by two or by three. However, "accents" still tend to be placed on the beats to form them into groups of two, three or four which then add up to the required five, seven or eleven. This means that 7/4 time, for example, can be played as a group of three plus a group of four, as a group of four plus a group of three, or as a group of two plus a group of three plus another group of two. The way the beats are subdivided should follow the musical phrase and the "accents" on individual notes (see p. 94). An 11/8 bar can be counted as three groups of three beats followed by a group of two, with a pulse or emphasized beat felt at the start of each group.

6/4 Six beats per bar. Each beat is one quarter-note.
Duple time played as 2 groups of 3 beats each, with accents on 1st and 4th beats.

6/8 Six beats per bar. Each beat is one eighth-note.

9/8 Nine beats per bar. Each beat is one eighth-note.
Triple time played as 3 groups of 3 beats each.

12/8 Twelve beats per bar. Each beat is one eighth-note.
Quadruple time played as 4 groups of 3 beats each.

5/4 Five beats per bar. Each beat is one quarter-note.
Can either be played as 3+2=5 or as 2+3=5 beats.

7/8 Seven beats per bar. Each beat is one eighth-note.
Can be played as 4+3=7 or as 3+4=7 or as 2+3+2=7 beats.

11/8 Eleven beats per bar. Each beat is one eighth-note.
Can be played in several ways – for example, as 3+3+3+2=11 or as 6+5=11 beats.

Using chord charts

Now that you know what a "bar" is and how to count it, you are ready to read charts that plot out the complete chord progression for any song. A *chord chart* is a sequence of chord symbols written to indicate their relative time values. A lyric sheet with the chord symbols written above the appropriate word or syllable can convey this information – if you know the melody and rhythm – but a chord chart will give it to you, usually in much less space, using bars instead of lyrics to indicate time.

The first thing to do if you want to write a chord chart is to decide on the tempo and the time signature. This establishes the speed at which each bar is to be read. All chord charts should be written with a time signature.

The next thing is simply to decide how long each chord lasts and on which beat of which bar there is a change to a new chord. Vertical strokes indicate beats instead of notes.

Chord charts in this form represent the standard means of communicating information to a guitarist. They leave it up to each player to select an appropriate chord inversion and to choose a rhythmic pattern that gives the right sort of "feel".

How to read chord charts

Chord charts always begin with a time signature to establish how many beats there are in each bar. Chord symbols are then used in the bars, along with other standard forms of musical notation such as rests (see p. 92) and repeat signs (see below).

One chord per bar

If there is just one chord written in each bar, the chord is played for the duration of the bar. As an initial aid, the "count" for the beats is shown in circles above the bars.

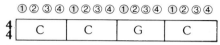

Each chord played for 4 beats

More than one chord per bar

Two, three or four chords in the same bar may be given an equal number of beats – unless vertical strokes indicate otherwise. Each stroke represents one beat of the chord that it follows.

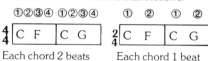

Each chord 2 beats   Each chord 1 beat

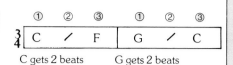

C gets 2 beats   G gets 2 beats

Rests

Conventional rest symbols indicate silence – no chord is played (see p. 92).

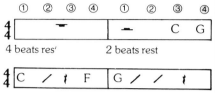

4 beats rest   2 beats rest

1 beat rest in each bar

Repeats

Chord chart repeat symbols tell you to play the previous bar again. A figure 2 or 4 above the symbol indicates that the previous 2 or 4 bars are to be repeated.

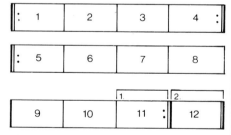

Repeat 1 bar   Repeat 2 bars

Playing directions

We have seen that the time signature is used to define the bar, and that the bar is the basic counting unit of music. However, if you wanted to write down a four-minute song, played at a tempo of 120 beats per minute, you would have to write out 120 bars of music. In fact, most music involves a fair amount of repetition, and conventional notation has a number of symbols that will tell you which parts of the basic theme are to be repeated and in what order. These symbols are the *repeat signs, first and second endings, capos* and *codas*. They act as the "signposts" or "traffic signals" of all written music.

What the symbols mean

Repeat signs When you come to the second sign, you go back to the first and repeat the section in between the two double bar signs.

First and second endings The first time through, you play the section marked 1. Then go back to the beginning and, on the second time through, play the section marked 2 (omitting section 1).

Da capo Often abbreviated to D.C., *da capo* means "from the head". When you see this sign, you must go back to the beginning of the piece of music.

Dal segno Instead of going right back to the beginning, go back only as far as the sign. *Dal segno* means "from the sign" and is abbreviated to D.S.

Al coda Meaning "to the tail", this tells you that you must go the the end section, which starts with a coda sign.

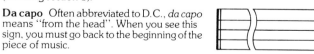

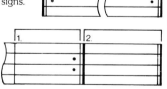

Example: repeat signs and endings

How to play
Play bars 1 to 4. Go back to the beginning and play bars 1 to 11. Go back to the start of bar 5 and play bars 5 to 10, omit bar 11, and finish with bar 12.

: 1	2	3	4 :
: 5	6	7	8
9	10	11 :	12

Example: segnos and codas

How to play
Begin by playing bars 1 to 12. When you reach the *dal segno al coda*, go back to the sign at the beginning and play bars 1 to 8. When you reach the *al coda*, go to the start of bar 13 and play bars 13 to 16, repeating them but gradually fading them out (R + F).

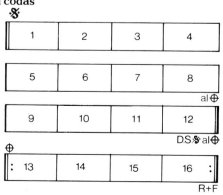

Time values

To play any note, you have to know three things about it – what pitch it has, when you should start playing it, and how long it should last. The question of its pitch is considered on p. 103. The question of its duration is determined by its *time value*.

Basically, there are seven different time values in musical notation – from the "whole-note" (which lasts the longest) to the "sixty-fourth-note" (which is the shortest). However, like the bar, time values are strictly related to the tempo and time signature of a particular piece of music. We have already seen that the bar is the basic unit of time in all music. And we know that the time signature divides it into a certain number of beats, and the tempo determines the speed of these beats. You can therefore give a time value or duration to a note only when you know the tempo and the time signature of the music in which it is to be featured.

Rests

A rest is a direction *not* to play. It is designed to create silence in between separate chords or notes. In all rhythm playing, where what you do not play is always as important as what you do, rests are crucial.

For *every* note symbol, there is a rest symbol with an equal time value. So, like a note, a rest will tell you when to stop playing and for how long. In a bar of 4/4 time, a whole-note rest will mean that you stop playing for four beats, and a sixty-fourth-note rest will mean that you stop playing for just a sixteenth of a beat. Clearly, the value of a rest symbol depends entirely on the time signature.

The rest symbols are shown below. Note that the last four have the same number of "flags" on their stems as their equivalent note symbols.

Rest symbols		
Rest	Time value	Note
▬	Whole-note rest	𝅝
▬	Half-note rest	𝅗𝅥
𝄽	Quarter-note rest	𝅘𝅥
𝄾	Eighth-note rest	𝅘𝅥𝅮
𝄿	Sixteenth-note rest	𝅘𝅥𝅯
𝅀	Thirty-second-note rest	𝅘𝅥𝅰
𝅁	Sixty-fourth-note rest	𝅘𝅥𝅱

Notes

Of the seven different notes in conventional music notation, each has its own relative time value and its own name. However, the terminology differs. The English system calls the longest note a "semi-breve" and the shortest note a "hemi-demi-semi-quaver", whereas the American system has a "whole-note" and a "sixty-fourth-note" as the two extremes. Since the American terminology is becoming increasingly common in Europe, it is the one used here.

The only note not included here is the "breve". It lasts for twice as long as the semi-breve (that is, for the length of two whole-notes) but it is now used only rarely.

Note symbols, shown in the chart below, are based on an open circle for a whole-note. As the time value decreases, the circle acquires a "stem", then becomes solid, and then has one, two, three or four "flags" attached to its stem. In most time signatures, either a "quarter-note" or an "eighth-note" represents one beat. It is probably easier to understand time values if you consider one beat as equalling one quarter-note. Notes that last for longer than one beat are then *multiples* of a quarter-note (for example, half-notes and whole-notes), and notes that

do not last as long as one beat are then *sub-divisions* of a quarter-note (for example, eighth-notes, sixteenth-notes, and so on). This means that in one bar of 4/4 time (where there are four beats to every bar) a whole-note will last for the whole bar, and a sixty-fourth-note will last for a mere sixteenth of the bar.

Equivalent values

All notes are simple multiples of one another. Two half-notes last as long as a whole-note, two quarter-notes add up to a half-note, two eighth-notes are the same as a quarter-note, and so on. It is vital that you understand how these values work if you are to learn how they are counted.

Take one bar of 4/4 time as an example. It can comprise one whole-note, or two half-notes, or four quarter-notes, or any combination of notes and rests that adds up to exactly four beats. In one bar of 3/4 time, the same would apply as long as the total number of notes and rests added up to exactly three beats. In one bar of 5/8 time, the notes and rests should add up to exactly five beats – but each eighth-note (not each quarter-note) would represent one beat.

Note symbols							
Note	𝅝	𝅗𝅥	𝅘𝅥	𝅘𝅥𝅮	𝅘𝅥𝅯	𝅘𝅥𝅰	𝅘𝅥𝅱
American name	Whole-note	Half-note	Quarter-note	Eighth-note	Sixteenth-note	Thirty-second-note	Sixty-fourth-note
English name	Semi-breve	Minim	Crotchet	Quaver	Semi-quaver	Demi-semi-quaver	Hemi-demi-semi-quaver

How notes are related
This "family tree" of note values shows clearly that one sixty-fourth-note lasts only for a sixty-fourth of the time that a whole-note lasts. However, notes have no actual time value in themselves; their duration must be taken from the tempo and time signature.

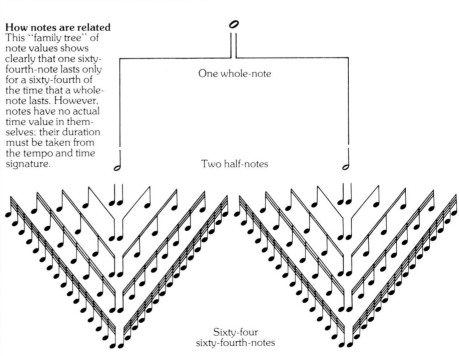

One whole-note

Two half-notes

Sixty-four sixty-fourth-notes

Note divisions

If we take one quarter-note as being equivalent to one beat, then the chart below shows that a whole-note lasts for four beats, an eighth-note for half a beat, and a sixty-fourth-note for a sixteenth of a beat.

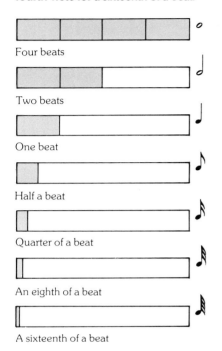

Four beats

Two beats

One beat

Half a beat

Quarter of a beat

An eighth of a beat

A sixteenth of a beat

Note One quarter-note is equivalent to one beat. Each line represents one bar in 4/4 time.

Bars in 4/4 time

All the notes in each bar, whatever their individual time values, must add up to a total of four beats of one quarter-note each.

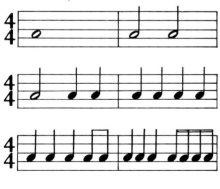

Bars in 3/4 time

All the notes in each bar, whatever their individual time values, must add up to a total of three beats of one quarter note each.

Dots

If a note is followed by a *dot*, its time value is increased by half again. A half-note normally worth two beats (in 4/4 time), when written with a dot, becomes worth three beats. A whole-note written with a dot would be worth six beats and could therefore only be used in a bar of 6/4 time. In the same way, a "dotted" quarter-note would have the combined value of a quarter-note plus an eighth-note, and a dotted eighth-note would have the value of an eighth-note plus a sixteenth-note.

Dots can also be added to rests. The principle is exactly the same: the dot increases the time value of the rest by half. Examples are given below.

Examples of dotted note and rest values

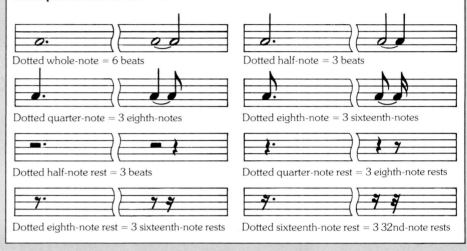

Dotted whole-note = 6 beats

Dotted half-note = 3 beats

Dotted quarter-note = 3 eighth-notes

Dotted eighth-note = 3 sixteenth-notes

Dotted half-note rest = 3 beats

Dotted quarter-note rest = 3 eighth-note rests

Dotted eighth-note rest = 3 sixteenth-note rests

Dotted sixteenth-note rest = 3 32nd-note rests

Ties

So far, all the timing directions have worked within the confines of a bar. To extend an uninterrupted note across a bar line – that is, to play a note which lasts for longer than the time represented by one bar – requires the use of a *tie*. A tie is indicated by a small curved line connecting two notes of the same pitch. It means that the note should be held for the duration of *both* note values. A tie can be used with any pair of notes, either across a bar line or within a bar, but ties are not used with rests. Besides combining two note values into a longer one, ties are used to clarify a complicated phrase so that you can see how it is constructed and where the main beats fall.

Examples of ties

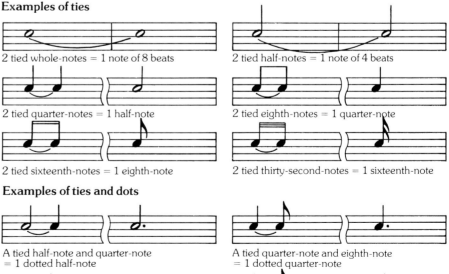

2 tied whole-notes = 1 note of 8 beats

2 tied half-notes = 1 note of 4 beats

2 tied quarter-notes = 1 half-note

2 tied eighth-notes = 1 quarter-note

2 tied sixteenth-notes = 1 eighth-note

2 tied thirty-second-notes = 1 sixteenth-note

Examples of ties and dots

A tied half-note and quarter-note = 1 dotted half-note

A tied quarter-note and eighth-note = 1 dotted quarter-note

A tied eighth-note and sixteenth-note = 1 dotted eighth-note

A tied sixteenth-note and thirty-second-note = 1 dotted sixteenth-note

Triplets

Any group of three notes, in which each note is played with the same time value and the same "stress" or "accent", is called a *triplet*. The three notes are linked with a curved line called a "slur" (similar to a tie) and the number 3 is written over the top or at the bottom.

Triplets are usually used to describe the effect of three notes being played in the space of two. They are a necessary device because there is no other way to indicate dividing a time value into thirds. There are no such note values as a third-note, a sixth-note, a ninth-note, and so on — yet these time values do obviously exist.

In 4/4 time, where one beat equals one quarter-note, a triplet of quarter-notes represents three notes played in the space of two beats, and a triplet of eighth-notes represents three notes played in the space of one beat. The best way to play four triplets of eighth-notes (which make up four beats) is to count *one*-two-three, *two*-two-three, *three*-two-three, *four*-two-three.

In 6/8 or 9/8 time, triplets of eighth-notes can be written without having to add the slur and the number 3. This will produce the same musical effect and "feel".

Examples of triplets

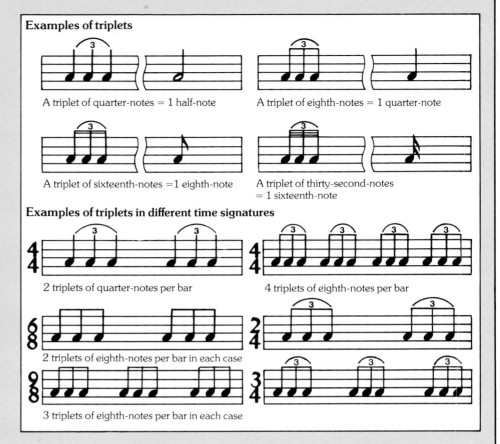

A triplet of quarter-notes = 1 half-note

A triplet of eighth-notes = 1 quarter-note

A triplet of sixteenth-notes = 1 eighth-note

A triplet of thirty-second-notes = 1 sixteenth-note

Examples of triplets in different time signatures

2 triplets of quarter-notes per bar

4 triplets of eighth-notes per bar

2 triplets of eighth-notes per bar in each case

3 triplets of eighth-notes per bar in each case

Additional symbols

There are three further symbols used to give precise instructions on the execution of specific notes or phrases – the *staccato*, the *portato* and the *accent*.

The *staccato* is a dot either above or below a note. It should not be confused with the dot which increases a note's time value (see p. 93). *Staccato* means "short and sharp", and it tells you to play the note for only half as long as it is written — while still keeping to the rhythm specified. A series of *staccato* notes should be clearly separated from one another. In other words, the symbols create an effect which, otherwise, could be achieved only by inserting short rests in between each of the notes.

Portato symbols have exactly the opposite effect. They comprise short horizontal dashes written above the note, and they tell you to stress its full value — leaving only as short a gap as possible between it and the note that follows.

Accents mark out notes that are to be emphasized more strongly than they would otherwise be. You should therefore hit the string or strings harder so that the accented note or chord stands out from surrounding un-accented ones.

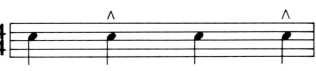

Staccato
A dot below or above a note shortens its time value by a half.

Portato
A horizontal dash above or below a note means that it must be held for its full time value.

Accent
An arrow-head above a note indicates that it must be emphasized or "accented".

Dynamic directions

Although not strictly a part of rhythm playing, musical notation includes a system of "dynamic" instructions. These concern the volume at which you are to play a sequence of chords or a phrase of notes, and they affect the overall "sound".

Most of the directions are in the form of abbreviations of Italian words — as shown below — but there are also symbols to indicate a *crescendo* (meaning that the music should get gradually louder) and a *diminuendo* or *decrescendo* (meaning that it gets gradually softer).

Symbol	Italian word	Direction
ff	*Fortissimo*	Very loud
f	*Forte*	Loud
mf	*Mezzo forte*	Moderately loud
mp	*Mezzo piano*	Moderately soft
p	*Piano*	Soft, quiet
pp	*Pianissimo*	Very soft

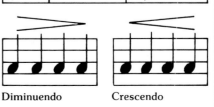

Diminuendo

Crescendo

Rhythm charts

There is a standard "shorthand" method for writing down the *rhythm* of a series of chords or notes without referring to their pitch. It is most often used with chord progressions and forms a compromise between a simple "chord chart" (see p. 91), which conveys only limited information about rhythm, and full musical notation, which conveys all the information you need but which takes much longer to write out.

Rhythm charts do vary somewhat – as do all shorthand styles – and you may come across slightly different symbols, but the basic principle remains the same. All rhythm charts use bars and time signatures in the standard way. Chord names are written either in, above or below the staff. The precise rhythm in which they are played is indicated by just the "stems" and "flags" of the ordinary note symbols.

The only two notes that cannot be represented by rhythmic shorthand are the whole-note and half-note – since the note symbol itself is needed to indicate the time value. The way around this is to use the vertical strokes representing quarter-notes and "tie" together as many of them as necessary.

Counting out rhythms

Complex rhythm patterns can be very difficult to count – especially if they contain short notes and rests. To help you analyze them and so that you can clearly see and understand what is going on, it is a good idea if you slow down the tempo and divide the number of beats in the bar so that the shortest note has a value of one count. A bar of 4/4 time is shown below written out so that there are eight counts – one for each of the eighth-notes. If the bar had contained sixteenth-notes, it could have been counted out in sixteen separate counts to the bar.

Original notation
This bar is in 4/4, which means that it contains four beats. But, because the eighth-notes and rests have only half a beat each, it is easier to count if written out in eights.

Re-written rhythm chart
The structure of the rhythm becomes more obvious when seen in terms of eight counts to the bar. The green circles indicate the beats to play, and the white circles are rests.

How to read rhythm charts

Rhythm charts observe the basic rule of all music notation: each bar should total the correct number of beats specified by the time signature. These beats can be made up from any combination of notes and rests.

The examples below show various rhythms in different time signatures. On the top line is the conventional notation, and on the bottom line is the equivalent rhythm chart. Play them through using any chords.

Folk and country rhythms

The acoustic guitar dominates folk and country music – largely as a result of its musical versatility and its portability. In the absence of a bass player or drummer, the guitarist frequently assumes the role of the rhythm section. The guitar then becomes a primary source of time and harmony.

The "ballad" is the most common form of this music. By definition, it is played at a slow-to-moderate tempo – with any combination of plectrum, thumbpicks, fingerpicks and fingerstyle (see p. 73). Time signatures are usually 3/4 or 4/4, and the songs use simple chords and basic progressions such as those shown on p. 76-8. The chords are almost always played with full left-hand sustain – which means that they are allowed to ring without being damped. The most common right-hand styles are either full, open strumming, alternate bass notes with strumming, or alternate bass notes with arpeggios. The strums may be either upstrokes or downstrokes, but, since an uninterrupted flow of the hand is the most important element in playing a smooth, steady rhythm, the most common pattern is a downstroke on the 1st beat, an upstroke on the 2nd, down on the 3rd, and up on the 4th.

Folk and country styles played at faster tempos are often related to some kind of dance. American bluegrass and mountain music, country and western, western swing, and Irish jigs and reels all share common elements, so the rhythm guitar roles have many similarities. They are based on simple chords and progressions played with full sustain. One of the most important differences lies in which beats are accented – the "downbeat" or the "backbeat". For example, in a bar of 4/4, the 1st and 3rd beats are the downbeats, and the 2nd and 4th beats are the backbeats. The Americanization of Irish music can be heard as a process of evolution in which different beats are emphasized. So, in 4/4 time, with two bass notes per bar, one pattern might be: 1 bass, 2 chord, 3 bass, 4 chord. Each beat is played with a downstroke, and, because the chords sound louder than the bass notes, the effect is of a natural backbeat.

In fact, Irish and American bluegrass tunes are usually played at a fast tempo, and the rhythm is in either eighths or sixteenths. As the examples show, the principle of the accented beats remains the same. Bars in eighths are best counted as 1–and–2–and–3–and–4–and; bars in sixteenths become easier to follow if you count four groups of four – 1–2–3–4, 2–2–3–4, etc.

Patterns like this are almost always played with an alternating bass. For a C major chord, for example, the 3rd finger would move from the note C (3rd fret, 5th string) to the note G

(3rd fret, 6th string). This technique is explained under *Flatpicking* (see p. 79).

Traditional ballads and Irish jigs and reels arranged for solo guitar represent a highly sophisticated folk guitar style. The bass lines, chords and melodies are interwoven in the same way as they are in much of classical guitar music, and the tunes are always played fingerstyle (see p. 80-81). Based on modal harmony, alternative tunings (see p. 158), or using as few as two chords, the bass is often sounded to resemble the pipes from which the music originated. The left-hand techniques of hammering-on and pulling-off (see p. 141) are a strong rhythmic feature.

How to read the rhythms

All the rhythm styles set out in the following pages are written in the form of standard rhythm charts (see p. 95). Circled numbers appear above each bar and indicate how the bar should be counted.

② Standard count

⊕ Plus sign indicates a count of "and" (as in 1–*and*–2–*and*)

③ Green circles indicate the beats that should be accented or emphasized.

Examples of folk and country rhythms

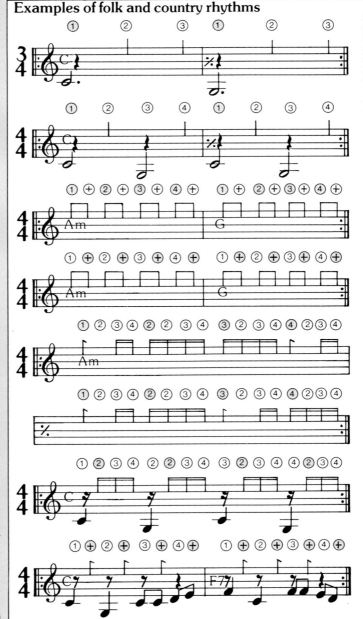

3/4 ballad rhythm with alternating bass Bass note is played on 1st beat, chord on 2nd and 3rd. Bass note changes from C to G.

4/4 ballad rhythm with alternating bass Bass is played either on 1st beat or on the 1st and 3rd, as here.

Downbeat An emphasis on 1st and 3rd beats is characteristic of Irish rhythm guitar styles.

Backbeat An emphasis on 2nd and 4th beats tends to identify American country styles.

Fast Irish fiddle tune rhythm In this example, each bar is divided into sixteenths – best counted as 1–2–3–4, 2–2–3–4–, etc. The accent is played on the downbeat – that is, the 1st of each 4 sixteenths.

Fast American country rhythm The bar is divided into sixteenths. The chords emphasize the backbeat.

Country rhythm with moving bass This style often includes a simple bass line as a lead-up to each change of chord (see p. 79).

Blues and rock rhythms

Most forms of modern music have their roots in the blues. In fact, the evolution from blues to rock is the story of the modern guitar. Broadly speaking, any music in 4/4 time based around simple I–IV–V chord progressions (see p. 77) can be considered to have evolved from the blues. Any discussion of where blues stops and country, folk, rock or jazz begin must acknowledge the fact that the styles overlap and divisions have long been blurred.

In its simplest form, a slow blues is played by sounding the chord on the first beat of the bar, leaving it to ring, then playing it again on the second beat and either damping it or cutting it off so that an accent is created. The third and fourth beats repeat the first and second so that a backbeat results. The pattern can also be reversed to produce a sustained chord on the backbeat.

One of the most common of blues rhythms is based on a simple alternating "riff" played on the damped bass strings (see below right). Whatever the tempo, this pattern forms the basis of the "shuffle" feel. It produces the pick-up effect of the bass line striking just before and on each beat, with a slight hesitation (the rest) immediately after each beat.

The basic pattern or riff can be varied in countless ways, and it often is – for example, by varying the number of beats on each pair of notes, by playing the strings individually, by including the note on the 5th fret of the higher string, and so on.

In a small blues band containing a drummer and a bass player, the simplest rhythm guitar patterns are based on one or two chords per bar, or on a steady repetition of a bass-string riff. The riff is usually played with downstrokes, heavily damped, in time with the bass and the bass drum. Chord patterns are usually played as upstrokes, cut off by left-hand damping, in time with the snare.

Rock and roll emerged when musicians increased the tempo of blues patterns, incorporated elements of country and popular music, and changed the lyric content of the songs. Musically, there is not much difference between fast blues and early rock and roll or rhythm and blues. A Chuck Berry guitar solo is a classic example of blues triplets, and the accentuated backbeat is a fixture of all rock and roll. However, what differences there are, though subtle, are important to the guitarist. Many changes of style occurred in the transition from blues to rock. Of these, the most noticeable were perhaps the replacement of the triplet feel by even eighths or sixteenths when playing at a fast tempo, and the use of more sustained chords, often accented on beats other than the downbeat or backbeat.

Examples of blues and rock rhythms

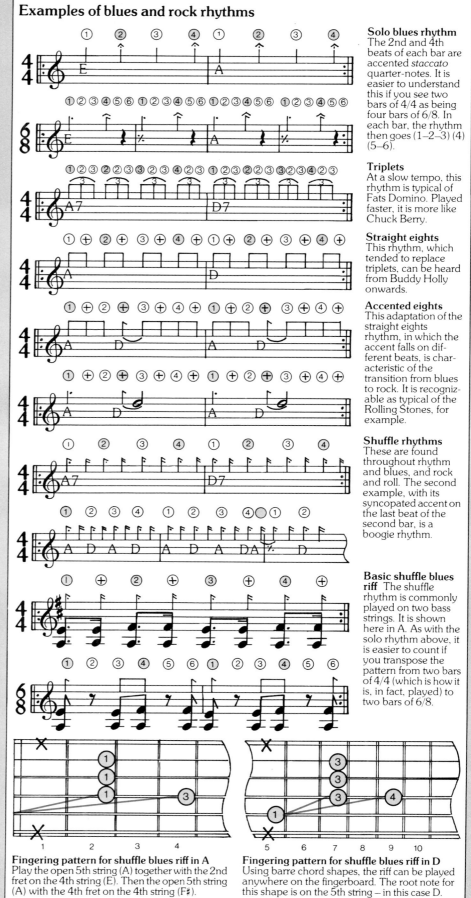

Solo blues rhythm
The 2nd and 4th beats of each bar are accented *staccato* quarter-notes. It is easier to understand this if you see two bars of 4/4 as being four bars of 6/8. In each bar, the rhythm then goes (1–2–3) (4) (5–6).

Triplets
At a slow tempo, this rhythm is typical of Fats Domino. Played faster, it is more like Chuck Berry.

Straight eights
This rhythm, which tended to replace triplets, can be heard from Buddy Holly onwards.

Accented eights
This adaptation of the straight eights rhythm, in which the accent falls on different beats, is characteristic of the transition from blues to rock. It is recognizable as typical of the Rolling Stones, for example.

Shuffle rhythms
These are found throughout rhythm and blues, and rock and roll. The second example, with its syncopated accent on the last beat of the second bar, is a boogie rhythm.

Basic shuffle blues riff The shuffle rhythm is commonly played on two bass strings. It is shown here in A. As with the solo rhythm above, it is easier to count if you transpose the pattern from two bars of 4/4 (which is how it is, in fact, played) to two bars of 6/8.

Fingering pattern for shuffle blues riff in A
Play the open 5th string (A) together with the 2nd fret on the 4th string (E). Then the open 5th string (A) with the 4th fret on the 4th string (F♯).

Fingering pattern for shuffle blues riff in D
Using barre chord shapes, the riff can be played anywhere on the fingerboard. The root note for this shape is on the 5th string – in this case D.

Soul, funk and reggae rhythms

Soul and funk are fusions of various roots, and are both recent styles by comparison. Soul gained popularity in the sixties, and funk in the seventies, both as dance music.

The term "rhythm and blues" accurately describes the two key ingredients in early rock and early soul music. Like rock, soul music was born with a rhythm section. Following the tradition of big-band guitarists, the role of the guitarist playing soul music is predetermined by what the rhythm section play. The two strongest characteristics of the style are the "chop" and the "stab".

The *chord chop* is played on the backbeat in time with the snare drum. It is usually an upstroke (played with a plectrum) and requires quick left-hand damping if the sound is to have the same "attack" as the snare.

Accented *chord stabs* can be used to imitate a horn section. They are short, sharp patterns, often played while sliding the whole chord up and down over one fret. Try them with any ninth chord (see p. 142).

The crossover from soul to funk has a lot to do with the rhythm section – in particular the bass player – creating a different kind of "space" for faster tempos. There are no traditions in funk other than welding all the instruments into a precise rhythm that is as steady as a rock.

The rhythm guitar part usually involves playing a repetitive pattern in a mid-to-high chord inversion. There is a classic pattern that can be considered a crossover "lick" common to soul, rock and funk styles. A bar of 4/4 is divided into sixteenths – so that there are four groups of four, each group lasting for one beat. In its simplest form, the chord is played only four times in the bar, but on different sixteenths of each beat (see right). This rhythm can be played either as individual upstroke chops punctuated by rests or as fast, continuous alternate strokes, all deadened except for the accented sixteenths. The latter is particularly characteristic of funk. It demands skilful left-hand damping and a steady right-hand motion. But once you get the hang of "squeezing" the chord with your left hand so that it sounds on just the right accent, you will produce a "busy", highly syncopated rhythm.

The chords used in funk represent an evolution of the harmony found in soul music. Ninths and elevenths (see p. 132-5) are commonly used where the chord remains basically the same for many bars. And, when the chords do change more often, they are often structured around the I-IV-V formula.

The key to funk is that the rhythm guitar style should be *sparse*. At its simplest, this may mean no more than quick backbeat chord stabs, but it can also involve single-string patterns damped with the right hand.

Reggae, which began as a combination of early American rhythm and blues, calypsos, and a Jamaican rhythm called "blue beat", is also a style that depends heavily on the bass line. As far as the rhythm guitarist is concerned, the backbeat is even more important. The difference is that the drummer need not play the backbeat at all; often, the job falls solely on the rhythm guitarist, who may end up not playing a single downbeat.

The technique is a "chop" again – usually played as a hard downstroke on the second and fourth beats of every bar. The aim is always to create a steady, hypnotic pattern that changes as little as possible. However, damped single-string patterns may also be included, usually in the form of short bursts of triplets to compliment the bass pattern.

Examples of soul, funk and reggae rhythms

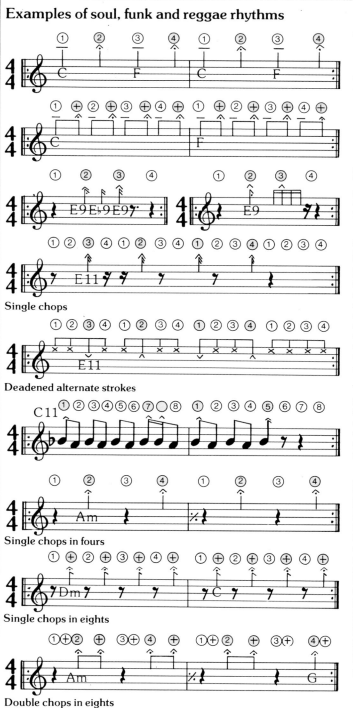

Single chops

Deadened alternate strokes

Single chops in fours

Single chops in eights

Double chops in eights

Chord chops
Emphasizing the backbeat with a sharp upstroke or "chop" is characteristic of all soul music. The first rhythm is in fours and is similar to a blues feel; the second is in eights, at a faster tempo.

Chord stabs
These horn-section riffs for rhythm guitar are ideal for sliding ninth chords.

Soul/funk crossover riffs The pattern is based on dividing a bar of 4/4 into sixteenths and accenting only the 3rd, 6th, 9th and 12th of these. It can either be played as single chops or as continuous, alternate strokes deadened except for the accented beats.

Single-string funk riff Over a C eleventh chord, play a heavily damped single-string riff, alternating from B♭ to A.

Reggae chops
Regular chops on the backbeat are the foundation of all reggae and ska rhythms. These examples, all in 4/4, show the variations produced by counting in fours and eights and by playing single or double chops. Harmonically, reggae is one of the simpler forms of music – primarily based on the familiar I–IV–V–VIm chord progressions (see p. 78).

Spanish and Latin rhythms

Until fifty years ago, the Spanish guitar (see p. 42) was still the instrument played by the vast majority of guitarists around the world. It is rarely played with a plectrum, since it is generally accepted that the fingers produce a better sound in the styles of music for which the guitar is used. The stylistic range of the Spanish guitar is still wider than that of steel-string guitars, and it is still the only type accepted as a legitimate classical instrument.

The original Spanish flamenco, as well as the songs and ballads related to it, uses mostly simple open chords and is based on a I–V–I structure. An important feature of flamenco is the right-hand technique called *rascuedo*. Starting with the hand clenched, the fingers are "thrown out" so that the fingernails play three or four downstrokes across the strings in quick succession. The palm comes down to provide an immediate damping effect. The thumb alternates with the fingers and plays bass notes independently.

Many former Spanish colonies in Central and South America feature ethnic styles strongly based on the techniques of Spanish music. Simple open chords and open-hand strumming and damping, for example, are the primary techniques of Spanish Portuguese and Latin American guitar styles.

African and Caribbean musicians playing essentially Spanish-influenced music transferred the accent of the rhythm from the downbeat to the backbeat. The backbeat is an established structure in ethnic African rhythms, and in the earliest examples of American blues and Caribbean music you can hear it clearly.

"Syncopation" is used to describe accents that do not fall on the beat, and it is the chief characteristic of various Caribbean and Latin American rhythms. The patterns are played with a backbeat, which is created by damping the chord with the palm on the third and seventh beats (if you count each bar in eighths). This damped backbeat provides a contrast to the syncopated accents so that they have a stronger effect.

Bossa nova (meaning "new style"), the term used for Brazilian jazz, is the most sophisticated of the Latin styles. The thumb almost always plays syncopated bass notes, and the fingers play chords. The chords either fill the spaces between the bass notes with a pattern of their own or play *with* the bass notes, creating a rich harmonic and rhythmic texture equalled by few other styles.

Latin American rhythms such as the *bossa nova*, *samba* and *montuno*, and Caribbean rhythms such as the *rumba*, *mambo* and *cha-cha*, are all part of the repertoire of modern music. To help you learn to identify and use these rhythms, some of the better-known patterns are written out here.

Examples of Spanish and Latin rhythms

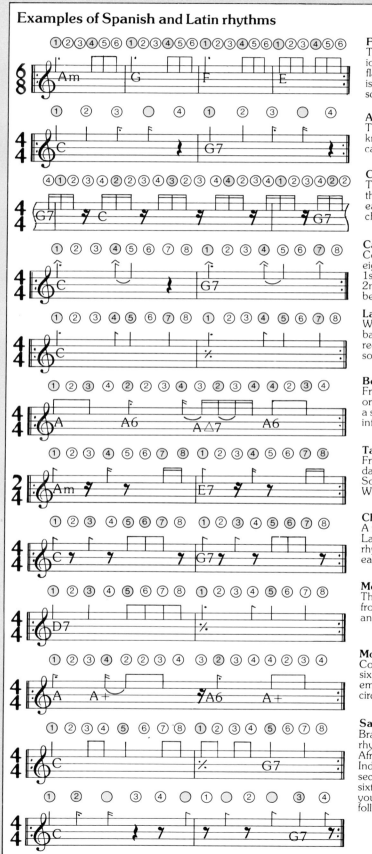

Flamenco
This chord progression is standard in flamenco music, and is used with minor scales (see p. 106).

Afro-Cuban
This rhythm is best known as the dance called the "conga".

Caribbean
The accents fall on the middle beat of each group of three chord strokes.

Caribbean/Latin
Count each bar in eights and stress the 1st, 4th and (in the 2nd bar) the 7th beats.

Latin/soul crossover
When played with a backbeat, you should recognize this as a soul rhythm.

Beguine
French West Indian in origin, this dance has a strongly Spanish-influenced rhythm.

Tango
From Argentina, this dance combines South American and West Indian rhythms.

Cha-cha
A fast West Indian/Latin American rhythm derived from earlier "mambos".

Merengue
This rhythm comes from a Dominican and Haitian dance.

Montuno
Count the bar in sixteens and emphasize the green circled beats only.

Sambas
Brazilian dance rhythms with a strong African and West Indian feel. Count the second example in sixteens to each bar if you find it difficult to follow.

99

Jazz guitar styles

Of the many descendants of the blues, jazz is the form that represents the state of the art in terms of the evolution of popular music. Musically, it is the most sophisticated, the most demanding and, some would say, the most rewarding of popular styles. During the last fifteen years or so, the increasing amount of crossover between mainstream jazz and electric rock has produced the variety of fusion forms that include jazz-rock and jazz-funk. As a result, the distinction – if there ever really was one – between a rock guitarist and

a jazz guitarist has become more and more blurred and increasingly meaningless.

In the history of jazz, the guitar has come from nowhere to being accepted as one of the front-line instruments. Its career can be seen in terms of two phases: first, its gradual replacement of the banjo in the rhythm section, and, second, its emergence as a solo instrument. The key factors in this development – chiefly the introduction of amplification and the playing of guitarists like Django Reinhardt and Charlie Christian – are plotted

below. The guitar is now established as a major rhythm and solo instrument.

At the heart of jazz lies the concept of *improvisation*. And countless influential guitarists have proved that the guitar is an instrument that allows improvisation rhythmically, melodically and harmonically: *rhythmically* in the choice of accents, emphases and syncopations; *melodically* in the choice of notes for a solo; and *harmonically* in the choice of chords, chord voicings and substitutions.

The role of the guitar in jazz

In the earliest forms of jazz, the guitar played virtually no part at all. The music coming out of New Orleans around the turn of the century featured collective improvisation based on the interplay of three instruments – the trumpet (or cornet), the clarinet and the trombone. These "melodic" instruments were supported by a rhythm section consisting of banjo, drums and bass or tuba. Although the steel-string guitar was around by this time, the banjo tended to be used instead because it had a sufficiently loud "attack" to cut through the volume of the rest of the band.

This, essentially, was the line-up of the Original Dixieland Jazz Band, who in 1917 became the first group in history to make a commercial jazz recording. Their "Dixieland" style, with its roots in Gospel, ragtime and the New Orleans sound, featured a strong, alternating bass line on the downbeat (the 1st and 3rd beats of each bar) and accentuated, damped chords on the backbeat (the 2nd and 4th beats of each bar).

The first evidence of a change came in the mid-twenties in Chicago. The King Oliver Band, which included Louis Armstrong, made a series of recordings containing the earliest examples of written jazz. The King Oliver line-up had grown to three reed instruments (clarinets and saxophone), four brass instruments (two trumpets or cornets, trombone and tuba), banjo, drums and piano. There was still no place for the guitar.

It was the introduction of the arch-top acoustic guitar (see p. 46) that gave guitarists their first opportunity to challenge the role of the banjo in the rhythm section. Though still not quite as loud, it had a smoother tone and greater harmonic potential. Slowly the guitar started to replace the banjo. By the early 1930s, Duke Ellington, Count Basie and Benny Goodman had established a big band line-up with three trumpets, three trombones, four reeds, and a rhythm section of piano, bass, guitar and drums.

Eddie Lang is often credited as being the

first jazz guitarist. Playing with Benny Goodman, Lang inspired musicians everywhere to regard the guitar as a serious jazz instrument rather than one associated mainly with blues, folk and country music. His duet work with another key guitarist, Lonnie Johnson, also demonstrated the potential of the guitar in a small setting.

By this time, the acoustic rhythm guitarist needed a high-quality guitar and considerable technique and musicianship. The chord vocabulary was further expanded, and the guitarist played a continually moving melodic chord pattern, observing the effect of the harmonic progression and often changing the voicing of the chord on every beat.

In smaller groups, where the acoustic guitar could be heard more clearly, several prominent guitarists were beginning to establish their reputations as soloists. This was a major advance for the guitar. But it was the introduction of pick-ups and amplifiers that really gave the guitarist a new status. With the new sound, a new role emerged. The guitarist was confined less to time-keeping and began to move out of the rhythm section into the front line, playing improvised solos or sustained melodic and harmonic phrases.

Nowhere was this more apparent than in the playing of Charlie Christian (see p. 9). In 1939, John Hammond brought the young guitarist to the attention of Benny Goodman and, during the three years until his death, Christian eclipsed every other guitarist and opened the door for a new musical era. Considered the first jazz soloist on electric guitar, his melodic ability and his new sound proved that the guitar was the equal of any sax or trumpet in the art of the improvised jazz solo. What he played is widely regarded as the first sign of the new direction in jazz – "bebop" – and as the beginning of the end for the "swing" era.

Something of an anachronism at around this time was Django Reinhardt (see p.8). A

Django Reinhardt with Maccaferri acoustic

self-taught gypsy guitarist, he was more-or-less the only influential guitar player to come out of Europe until years later. Playing his distinctive Maccaferri/Selmer guitars (see p.47), he demonstrated a complete mastery of melody and the new sophisticated harmony. In the mid-1930s his music established milestones that endure to this day.

By 1940, it was clear that the guitar was equally adept at providing a rhythmic chord backing and at soloing. Playing guitar in the Count Basie Band, Freddie Green epitomized the guitar's harmonic development through the swing era. His superb timing and the flowing sense of harmony he created, helped to establish the role of the rhythm guitar as an important part of every rhythm section.

Just before the war, Charlie Christian's solos served as an inspiration to musicians who were growing frustrated at having exploited the diatonic system to its fullest. The music of Duke Ellington was conclusive proof that the essential spirit of improvisation could be orchestrated and directed to new heights. Soloists from Louis Armstrong and Coleman Hawkins to Lester Young and Johnny Hodges, and composers from

Developing an approach to jazz guitar playing

It's difficult to give advice on playing jazz guitar – as it is on any form of improvisation. One thing that *can* be said, however, is that, of all the forms of modern music, jazz is the one that demands the highest level of musicianship – in terms of both theory and technique. By the end of the bop era and the beginning of "modern jazz", the role of the guitarist required the following skills.

● A quick "ear", trained to monitor what each member of the band is playing.
● A solid understanding of scales, chords, harmony and fingerboard theory.

● An ability to play any combination of rhythmic accents or syncopations.
● A single-string picking technique capable of handling sixteenth-notes and triplets.
● A good instinct and an imaginative feel for improvisation.

Any guitarist wanting to follow in the jazz tradition should certainly start with the music itself. Get hold of the recordings and, if possible, the sheet music to as many classics as possible. In a small jazz band consisting of, say, sax, keyboards, guitar, bass and drums, the guitarist must be con-

stantly aware of the other musicians. The interplay between the bass and the drummer will suggest certain rhythmic accents, the bass and the keyboards will suggest different approaches to the harmony, the sax and the keyboards will suggest voicings of the harmony, and the combined rhythmic patterns of the other four players will establish the general "feel". Just how the guitar fits in is virtually limitless. The only real way of deciding what to play and when to play it is to use your ears. There are no rules: just listen, then play.

Fletcher Henderson and Jelly Roll Morton to Count Basie and Duke Ellington, had thoroughly explored the possibilities of the eighteenth-century system. Pianists like Earl Hines, Teddy Wilson and Art Tatum had led the way for further variation – largely within the system – and big bands were on the road playing dance music to a new generation of jazz audiences. But the beginning of the war saw the demise of the big-band era, and the end of the war heralded the true arrival of bebop. The diatonic system exploded into a new concept of chromatic harmony, and melodic and rhythmic theory were completely re-evaluated. Small groups appeared everywhere with a new look and a new sound.

The new generation, now able to work from the complete tonal palette, and represented by Charlie Parker, Dizzy Gillespie and Thelonius Monk, arrived at a form which served as a vehicle for exploration. A recognized chord sequence – usually from a pre-war standard – could be given a new melody or top line, and could be played as fast as possible, with liberal extension and alteration of the original chords. The first chorus was played in unison, a chorus was then reserved for each soloist, and the final chorus was the theme in unison again.

Although the guitar did not have a regular role in a bop line-up, developments in theory and technique over the next few years established a new standard for the instrument. Players such as Johnny Smith, Jimmy Raney, Barney Kessel, Tal Farlow, Jim Hall, Herb Ellis, Kenny Burrell, Wes Montgomery, Joe Pass and Howard Roberts have all contributed to the evolution of modern jazz guitar playing.

The "cool jazz", which followed on the heels of bop, demonstrated the speed with which the new chromatic concepts were accepted by musicians. Miles Davis gave jazz a new mood by improvising over a modal instead of a harmonic system. However, the absence of identifiable diatonic

key-centres meant that audiences found it difficult to follow the harmony. The new style became largely musician's music. Ornette Coleman made the break into "modern jazz". In his search for soloist's freedom, he said that musicians must be free to produce any given sound at any given time.

The jazz world was now split into three different "schools": first, the traditionalists who preferred the pre-war diatonic music; second, the "hard bop" era of Parker, Monk and Mingus; and, third, the many variations producing new forms of modern jazz. John Lewis, founder of the Modern Jazz Quartet, combined elements of classical music and jazz, Dizzy Gillespie introduced Afro-Cuban rhythms, and Dave

Brubeck popularized a more commercial stream with the hit "Take Five".

The next major influence on the course of jazz came with Miles Davis's album "Bitches Brew", released in 1970. It introduced jazz to the power of the modern electric rhythm section, and it introduced audiences to the guitar playing of John McLaughlin. Like many great soloists before him, he came blazing in with a new sound and a new style that showed a mastery of past concepts and a vision of a new one. When, in 1971, McLaughlin formed the Mahavishnu Orchestra, and two other members of the Miles Davis group, Joe Zawinul and Wayne Shorter, formed Weather Report, there was no doubt that the fusion of jazz and rock was here to stay.

John McLaughlin playing a Gibson 6/12 twin neck

THE MELODIC GUITARIST

This is the part of the book that explains scales. Scales are the basis of all melody and, to some extent, of all improvisation. Many guitarists — especially those that are self-taught — are suspicious of scales and regard them as an unattractive and unnecessary discipline. This is untrue. While some guitarists often get by without really knowing what they are playing, there are four reasons why it is worth learning scales: first, they teach you the fingerboard, so that you know where all the notes are on each string; second, they will give you the best kind of "ear training" you can have; third, they will — more than almost anything else — increase your speed, fluency and accuracy; and, fourth, they will provide you with a basis for understanding chords — both how they are built and how they relate to one another. In an interview, the guitarist Al DiMeola confirmed the truth of this:

Frank Zappa

"One thing I learned a long time ago was my fretboard, in terms of all the scales in all the positions . . . You have to learn it — there are no two ways about it. I shift between positions so easily now that I really don't have to think about them much . . . I would suggest starting your scale education with the major and minor scales, and after that, diminished, augmented and whole-tone. Then depending on what kind of music you want to play, the modes should be learned. My theory about this kind of thing is that you should learn it all. Once you've learned it you can play whatever you want to play, and I think that your playing will be more advanced, and you'll have a better understanding of the instrument."

Al DiMeola

All scales are essentially just different ways of dividing up the octave. In this section of the book, we begin by looking at the major and minor scales, and explain how they form the basis of the Western diatonic system and how key signatures are used to identify them. We then move on to look at the "modes" and at the "synthetic" scales such as the whole-tone, diminished and pentatonic — all of which can be used simply as alternatives to the familiar diatonic structure.

When learning or practising scales, you should aim to play them in as many positions and with as many different fingerings as you can. Start slowly, and increase your speed only when you can sound every note clearly. Familiarity with different scales in different fingerings and fingerboard positions is one of

the biggest assets a solo guitarist can have. Their importance goes beyond the question of pure technique. They will improve your ability to "hear" chords, and will help you identify the correct choice of scale intervals. These are the elements from which the ability to create melodies and to improvise your own solo lines is derived.

"My solos are speech-influenced rhythmically; and harmonically, they're either pentatonic, or poly-scale oriented. And there's the mixolydian mode that I also use a lot . . . But I'm more interested in melodic things. I think the biggest challenge when you go to play a solo is trying to invent a melody on the spot."

Frank Zappa

The range of the guitar

Modern flat-top steel-string acoustic guitars normally have clear access to the 14th fret, whereas the fingerboard of a traditional Spanish or classical guitar joins the body at the 12th fret. Electric guitars have cutaways that usually allow you to reach to at least the 19th fret fairly easily; some have as many as 24 clear frets — giving a two-octave range on one string, twice that of a classical guitar.

However, on any guitar, the note on the 13th fret is identical to the 1st fret but one octave higher. For this reason, the overall range of the guitar is considered to be from the open E on the 6th string to the high E on the 12th fret of the 1st string. This gives a span of three octaves, comprising 22 natural notes (not counting sharps and flats).

Unlike the keyboard, the fingerboard does not display the difference between the

natural notes and the sharps and flats, nor does it show the two places where there is only a semi-tone interval instead of a whole-tone (from E to F and from B to C). The big difference lies in the fact that many notes can be found on more than one string. This means that, in the great majority of cases, there is more than one place where you can play the same note.

Of the 22 natural notes contained within the 12-fret range, the three lowest and the three highest are the only notes that have just one position. Six notes can be played in two positions. The remaining ten notes, those in the centre of the range, are playable in three different positions. Including both natural notes and sharps and flats, the guitar has an overall 12-fret range of 36 different notes (three octaves at twelve semi-tones

per octave) which can be played in a total of 72 positions (six strings with twelve frets each). The guitar is one of the few instruments that can play so many notes in so many different places.

There are both advantages and disadvantages to this. Learning to play a piece of music on the guitar involves the extra step of deciding which position on the fingerboard is the most appropriate. With different fingerings, it is possible to play almost anything in at least two different ways. The same idea can therefore produce slightly different sounds, even though the actual notes are identical. This unique property of the fingerboard gives guitarists a great advantage over other musicians. The creative possibilities it allows far outweigh the extra difficulties.

Pitch

The first seven letters of the alphabet are used to represent the pitch of the notes that comprise the Western world's musical system. These are C–D–E–F–G–A–B. There are historical reasons why the musical alphabet starts at C instead of A.

There is also a system – used in many non-English-speaking countries – which replaces the letters with names. These are do–re–mi–fa–sol–la–ti (or si). The notes are the same in both systems; only the terminology differs.

In order to name the pitch of every note, from the very lowest to the very highest, the system of seven letters repeats itself. So the note that follows G is A. The distance or "interval" between one note and the next with the same name, either up or down, is described as an *octave*. Two notes an octave apart will sound the same but will have different pitches; one will be in a higher range or "register" than the other. This is a natural phenomenon based on a 2:1 ratio between the frequencies of the two notes.

The keyboard is the most immediate visual reference to the Western musical system. You will see that the seven "alphabetical" notes we have been describing are represented by the white keys. Starting from C, and playing the eight white keys that make up an octave demonstrates the *diatonic scale* of C major.

However, in the space of this octave, there are also five black keys. How do we identify these "extra" notes – called *accidentals* – since there are no alphabet letters left to label them? Each black note is named in relation to its closest white notes. The black note between the C and D, for example, is therefore known as C♯ (meaning a "sharpened" or "raised" C) or as D♭ (meaning a "flattened" or "lowered" D). A note referred to by two names is called *enharmonic*, and the context in which it is used will determine which name is appropriate. Unless the key signature (see p. 108) specifies otherwise, the general rule is to use a sharp when ascending to the note and a flat when descending to it.

The interval between a white note and a black note is called a *semi-tone*. Two semi-tones equal one *tone*. If you look at the keyboard, however, you will see that between the C and D and between the E and F, there is no black note. This is because the seven-note octave is not actually divided into equal intervals. C to D and E to F are semi-tones, not whole-tones.

Starting from C, and counting the interval to C♯ as the first semi-tone, there is a total of twelve equal semi-tones in one octave. Playing an octave in semi-tones (that is, playing all the white notes *and* all the black notes) demonstrates the *chromatic scale*. This system forms the basis of Western music.

The musical alphabet

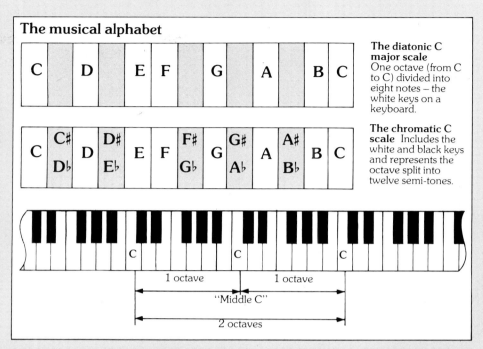

The diatonic C major scale One octave (from C to C) divided into eight notes – the white keys on a keyboard.

The chromatic C scale Includes the white and black keys and represents the octave split into twelve semi-tones.

Pitch notation

Pitch is conveyed in musical notation by placing note symbols on or between the parallel horizontal lines called the *staff* or *stave* (see p. 67). A *clef* at the start of each line of music determines what pitch value each line on the staff has. There are three different clefs – a G (or treble) clef, an F (or bass) clef, and a C clef which is only rarely used. Notes that will not fit on the staff are put on individual *leger lines* above or below.

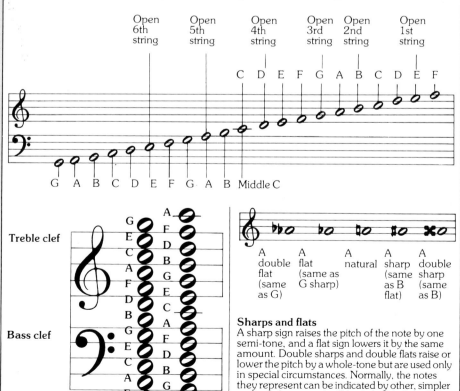

Sharps and flats
A sharp sign raises the pitch of the note by one semi-tone, and a flat sign lowers it by the same amount. Double sharps and double flats raise or lower the pitch by a whole-tone but are used only in special circumstances. Normally, the notes they represent can be indicated by other, simpler names – for example, G for A double flat or B for A double sharp.

The major scale

A *scale* is any consecutive series of notes that forms a progression between one note and its octave. The scale can go either up by an octave or down by an octave. The word comes from the Latin *scala*, meaning "ladder", and this is exactly what a scale is – a way of ascending or descending an octave, with each rung representing one of the notes in between.

There are many different scales, and the history of their development is complex. Any one scale can be distinguished from the others by its step-pattern – that is, by the way its notes divide up the distance represented by an octave. The most important scales in Western music are the diatonic major scale and the three relative minor scales.

The characteristic sound of any scale is determined by its number of steps, by the order in which they occur, and by their "size" – in other words, whether each step is a tone or a semi-tone. If this pattern remains consistent, the scale will have the same sound characteristics whatever note it starts from.

If we go back to the idea of the scale being like a ladder, we can see that the major scale has eight rungs (notes) and that it requires seven steps (intervals) to climb from the first rung to the eighth rung (the octave). In the major scale, the size of each step is as follows: tone (1st to 2nd), tone (2nd to 3rd), semi-tone (3rd to 4th), tone (4th to 5th), tone (5th to 6th), tone (6th to 7th), semi-tone (7th to 8th). The sound of the major scale is therefore

due to the fact that semi-tone steps occur between the 3rd and 4th notes, and between the 7th and 8th notes. Its "major" characteristic is the two-tone interval between the 1st and 3rd notes – this is called a *major third*.

The major scale, derived from the "Ionian mode" (see p. 110), was in use centuries before being accepted by serious composers. In medieval times, the Church strongly disapproved of it – condemning it as *Modus Lascivus* (meaning the "lustful mode") – and it was found primarily in folk songs and dances. However, since about the sixteenth century, when the laws of harmony were established, the major scale has come to represent the basic building material of contemporary music.

How to work out major scales

As we saw on p. 103, Western music divides the octave into twelve steps, each one being equal to a semi-tone. On the keyboard, this is reflected in the twelve different notes (seven white keys and five black keys) within an octave. On the guitar fingerboard, it is even simpler: one octave is divided into twelve frets – one for each note. So a semi-tone is one fret and a tone is two frets.

All major scales have a semi-tone interval between the 3rd and 4th and the 7th and

8th notes, so the pattern is easy to work out along one string: two frets, two frets, one fret, two frets, two frets, two frets, one fret. In the scale of C major, this step-pattern produces no sharps or flats. In fact, on the keyboard, C major is the diatonic scale which employs only the white keys. The scale of G major, however, has one sharp (see below), and the scale of F major has one flat. The scale of C♯ major, for example, actually has five sharps. This information is

contained in the "key signature" (see p. 108). The presence of the sharpened and flattened notes is essential if the step-pattern of the major scale is to be preserved whatever note it starts on. The notes of all twelve major scales are given in the chart opposite.

The individual notes that make up a major scale are often identified using the Roman numeral system. The way the notes are numbered (and named) is exactly the same as that described on p. 76.

The scale of C major
As an exercise in "hearing" the intervals of the major scale, try playing it up the length of a single string. Start from C on the 1st fret of the 2nd string, as shown below, and remember that one fret represents one semi-tone.

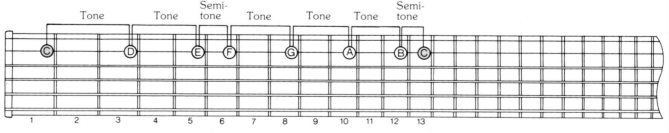

The scale of G major
To play a scale of G major, you must start from a G. Stick to the same step-pattern of tone (2 frets), tone (2 frets), semi-tone (1 fret), and so on. This time you will see that the tone (2 frets) step between the 6th and 7th notes in the scale brings you to F♯. The note F is not included in the scale of G major.

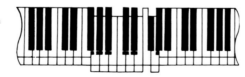

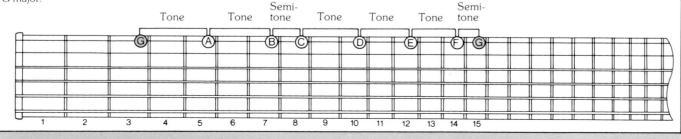

Major scale fingering patterns

It is impractical to play scales up and down the length of a single string. The examples on the opposite page are designed as exercises only, not as real fingerings. Instead, you must learn to play scales *across* the fingerboard, moving from string to string.

All three patterns shown below are within the span of four frets. This enables you to choose one hand position and make each of your four fingers responsible for one fret (see *The one-fret-per-finger rule*, p. 72). In

other words, you should play the complete scale (or scales) moving only your fingers, not your hand.

These are all *movable* fingering patterns that can begin at any note on the lowest string of the pattern. They can then be moved up and down the fingerboard without altering the pattern in order to play scales that start on different notes. The first note of the scale (the tonic or root note) is the first note of the fingering pattern. So, if

you begin on a C, the pattern will give you the scale of C major; if you begin on an A, it will give you the scale of A major. In the diagrams below, the numbers in the circles tell you which finger to use to play each note. The root notes are shaded green.

It is worth practising these patterns until they feel comfortable. They are not only useful for developing melodic speed, but they also form the foundations of understanding harmony.

Root note on 5th string
This is a one-octave pattern, with the root (I) notes on the 5th and 3rd strings. If you wanted to play a scale of C major, you would begin with your 2nd finger at the C on the 3rd fret of the 5th string.

Root note on 6th string
This is a two-octave pattern. The root (I) notes are on the 6th, 4th and 1st strings. The pattern begins with the 1st note of the scale you want to play. If this were C major, you would start with your 2nd finger at the C on the 7th fret of the 6th string.

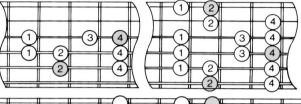

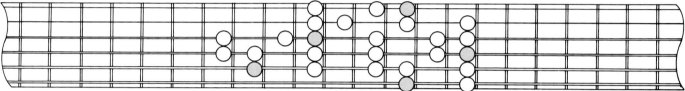

Green circle indicates root note of scale

Note These fingerings represent the shapes that guitarists often use – since they allow the scale to be played in the space of four frets. But, as you can see from the composite fingerboard pattern, almost any combination is, in fact, possible. It is helpful to have as many ways as you can of changing from one basic pattern to another.

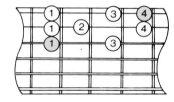

Root note on 3rd string
Another one-octave pattern, this scale has its root (I) notes on the 3rd and 1st strings. If you wanted to play a scale of C major, you would begin with your 1st finger at the C on the 5th fret of the 3rd string.

The major scale in all twelve keys

Note Read the scales from left to right.

	I		II		III		IV		V		VI		VII		I
Name of key (tonic or root note)	A		B		C♯		D		E		F♯		G♯		A
	B♭		C		D		E♭		F		G		A		B♭
	B		C♯		D♯		E		F♯		G♯		A♯		B
	C		D		E		F		G		A		B		C
	C♯		D♯		F		F♯		G♯		A♯		C		C♯
	D	Tone/2 frets	E	Tone/2 frets	F♯	Semi-tone/1 fret	G	Tone/2 frets	A	Tone/2 frets	B	Tone/2 frets	C♯	Semi-tone/1 fret	D
	E♭		F		G		A♭		B♭		C		D		E♭
	E		F♯		G♯		A		B		C♯		D♯		E
	F		G		A		B♭		C		D		E		F
	F♯		G♯		A♯		B		C♯		D♯		F		F♯
	G		A		B		C		D		E		F♯		G
	A♭		B♭		C		D♭		E♭		F		G		A♭

The minor scales

There are three different minor scales – the *natural* or *relative minor* scale, the *harmonic minor* scale and the *melodic minor* scale.

Each has its own individual step-pattern, but they all share one feature that differentiates them from the major scale. The interval between the 1st and 3rd notes in the scale is always a tone and a half (one whole-tone plus one semi-tone). This interval is called a *minor third*, and it contrasts with the *major third* interval (two tones) characteristic of the major scale. The minor scales differ from each other in terms of whether the 6th and 7th steps of the scale are raised (sharpened) or whether they are not.

The principle and formation of minor scales is easier to understand if we start by looking at how the natural minor scale is *related* to the major scale, and then go on to see how it is *altered* to produce the harmonic and melodic minor scales.

How to work out natural minor scales

Just as the "Ionian Mode" was the predecessor of the major scale, the natural minor scale is derived from what was called the "Aeolian Mode" (see p. 110). Both these modes were diatonic scales – played only on the white notes of the keyboard. But, whereas the Ionian started on C, the Aeolian started on A.

This means that the notes of the two scales are the same. However, because the natural minor scale has a different starting point, it has its own step-pattern: tone (1st note to 2nd), semi-tone (2nd to 3rd), tone (3rd to 4th), tone (4th to 5th), semi-tone (5th to 6th), tone (6th to 7th), tone (7th to 8th). The 8th note is the octave.

Compare the C major and the A minor scales. You will see that the 3rd note of the minor scale is the 1st note of the major scale (it is a C), and that the 6th note of the major scale is the 1st note of the minor scale (it is an A). This relationship is the key to understanding the connection between major and minor scales. Each major scale has a *relative* natural minor scale, and each minor scale has a relative major scale.

Working out the relative scales is easy. It is three semi-tones *down* from the major to the minor, and three semi-tones *up* from the minor to the major.

The major scale and its relative natural minor scale share the same "key signature" (see p. 108). They therefore share the same notes. However, because they start at different places, they have a different step-pattern and a different sound.

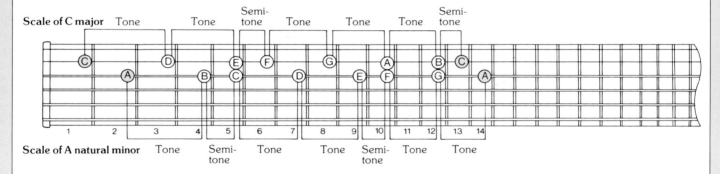

Scale of C major

Scale of A natural minor

The C major and natural A minor scales

The natural minor scale in A is the relative minor of C major. It contains the same notes as the scale of C major but starts from A. It is plotted here on the 3rd string of the guitar, starting from A three semi-tones below C (2nd string, 1st fret). You will see how the step-pattern therefore differs.

Natural minor scale fingering pattern

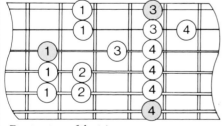

Root note on 6th string

C major scale

A natural minor scale

How the C natural minor scale differs from the C major scale

C major

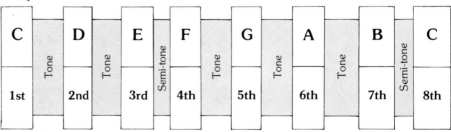

C natural minor

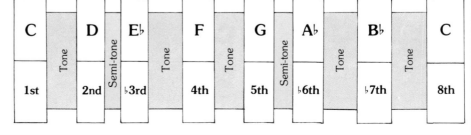

How to work out harmonic minor scales

The harmonic minor scale developed as a result of the principles of harmony applied to the construction of chords (see p. 124).

We have already seen (see p. 76-8) that a chord can be built on each note of the scale, and that the most important are those built on the 1st note (the "tonic" or I chord) and on the 5th note (the "dominant" or V chord). Now, one of the three notes that goes to make up the dominant chord is the 7th note of the scale. In the major scale, the 7th note is one semi-tone below the tonic. But, in the natural minor scale, the 7th note is a whole-tone below the tonic. This means that dominant chords built on the 5th notes of major and natural minor scales do not have the same effect. In order to overcome this problem the 7th note of the natural minor scale is raised (or "sharpened") by a semi-tone. The new scale is called the *harmonic minor*.

Harmonic minor scale fingering pattern

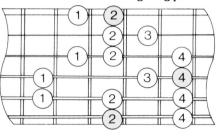

Root note on 6th string

C major scale

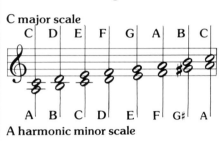

A harmonic minor scale

How the C harmonic minor scale differs from the C major scale

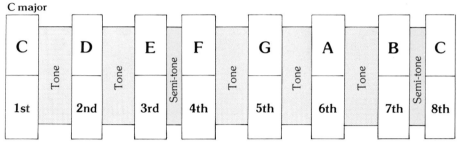

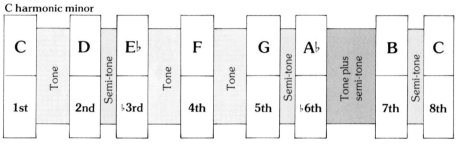

How to work out melodic minor scales

The only problem with the harmonic minor scale is that, by reducing the interval between the 7th and 8th notes to a semi-tone, the interval between the 6th and 7th is increased to *three* semi-tones (a minor third). When writing melody lines, this is an unacceptably big jump. The solution to this is to raise the 6th note of the scale by a semi-tone. In A minor, this means raising the F to an F♯, and it reduces the interval between the 6th and 7th notes to a tone. The result is a smoother melodic "flow". This method is used when ascending – going up in pitch – and the scale it produces is called the *melodic minor* for its improved melodic potential. When playing a descending melody, it is not important to have the semi-tone interval between the 7th and 8th notes, because the melodic flow is naturally smooth. Therefore, the ordinary natural minor scale is used.

Melodic minor scale fingering pattern

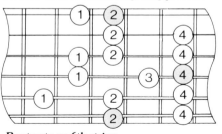

Root note on 6th string

C major scale

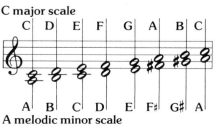

A melodic minor scale

How the C melodic minor scale differs from the C major scale

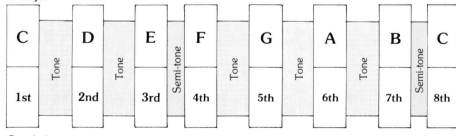

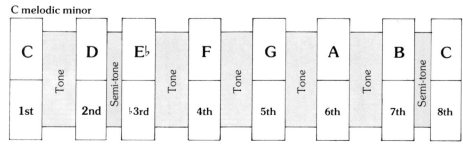

Key signatures

If we say that a scale or a piece of music is in a certain *key*, this defines what is called its "tonality". It tells us what tonic note all the other notes are related to. For example, a melody made up of notes from the scale of C major is said to be in the key of C major. The tonic note (the 1st note of the scale) is the *key-note*, and C major is the *key-centre*. Similarly, a melody made up of notes from the scale of E minor is said to be in the key of E minor. All the other notes in the melody will be heard in relation to E, the key-note.

As we saw on p. 86, it is possible to transpose a piece of music from one key to another without altering its sound characteristics. This is because, although the overall *pitch* of the music changes, the *intervals* between the notes or chords do not.

Key signatures are used to label keys and to indicate what notes must be raised or lowered in order to maintain the same intervals for the major and minor scales. If you want to transpose a melody in the key of C major to the key of G major, the new key signature will tell you that you must play an F♯ (instead of an F).

The key signature is indicated by putting the sharps or flats it contains on the staff between the clef and the time signature. So, an F♯ here will tell you that, unless there is a contrary instruction later, the music is in the key of G major (or E minor).

The key of C major is the simplest. It contains no sharps or flats at all. The next simplest are the key of G (which contains one sharp) and the key of F (which contains one flat).

How does the key of G major relate to the key of C major? G is the 5th note (the "dominant") in the scale of C major – it becomes the 1st note of the scale of G major. But, in order to maintain the standard step-pattern of the major scale, the 7th ("leading") note of the new scale must be raised by a semi-tone. This note is F – the 4th ("sub-dominant") note in the scale of C major – and

it must be raised to F♯. The rule is therefore this: the 5th (dominant) note of any scale can be used to start a new scale in which only one note need be raised – this is always the 4th note of the old scale, the one that becomes the 7th note of the new scale. As the chart below illustrates, this rule holds for all keys.

How does the key of F major relate to the key of C major? This time, F is the 4th note (the "sub-dominant") in the scale of C major, and the only note that differs is the 7th ("leading") note – B. It becomes the 4th note of the new scale, and, in order to maintain the step-pattern of the major scale, it must be lowered by a semi-tone – to B♭. This time the rule is different: the 4th (sub-dominant) note of any scale can be used to start a new scale in which only one note need be flattened – this is always the 7th note of the old scale, the one that becomes the 4th note of the new scale. As the chart below illustrates, this rule, too, holds for all keys.

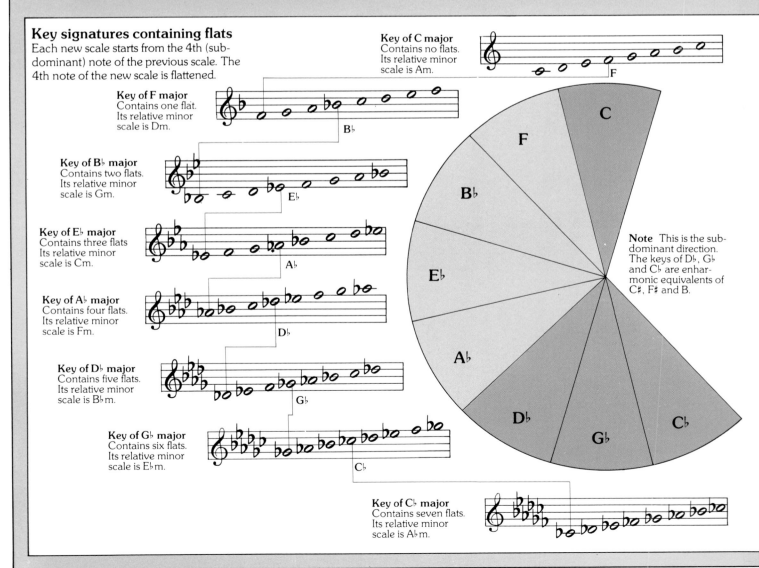

Key signatures containing flats
Each new scale starts from the 4th (sub-dominant) note of the previous scale. The 4th note of the new scale is flattened.

Key of C major
Contains no flats.
Its relative minor scale is Am.

F

Key of F major
Contains one flat.
Its relative minor scale is Dm.

B♭

Key of B♭ major
Contains two flats.
Its relative minor scale is Gm.

E♭

Key of E♭ major
Contains three flats
Its relative minor scale is Cm.

A♭

Key of A♭ major
Contains four flats.
Its relative minor scale is Fm.

D♭

Key of D♭ major
Contains five flats.
Its relative minor scale is B♭m.

G♭

Key of G♭ major
Contains six flats.
Its relative minor scale is E♭m.

C♭

Key of C♭ major
Contains seven flats.
Its relative minor scale is A♭m.

Note This is the sub-dominant direction. The keys of D♭, G♭ and C♭ are enharmonic equivalents of C♯, F♯ and B.

The circle of fifths

The key signatures can be combined to form what is called the *circle of fifths*. This device is often used in music theory to illustrate the relationship of the keys.

The method by which sharp key signatures are formed can be traced by moving clockwise around the circle. Each step in the "dominant" direction is an interval of a fifth (counting up from the tonic) and involves adding one extra sharp note to the new major scale.

Moving anti-clockwise traces the formation of flat key signatures. Each step in the "sub-dominant" direction is an interval of a fifth (counting *down* from the tonic) or a fourth (counting *up* from the tonic) and involves adding one extra flat note to the new major scale.

As the circle demonstrates, in theory, it is possible to continue right round in either direction. The key of C can therefore be represented theoretically as either B♯ (with twelve sharps) of D♭♭ (with twelve flats).

Sub-dominant direction
4th (sub-dominant) note of old scale becomes 1st note of new scale. 7th (leading) note of old scale becomes 4th (sub-dominant) note of new scale and is *flattened*.

Dominant direction
5th (dominant) note of old scale becomes 1st note of new scale. 4th (sub-dominant) note of old scale becomes 7th (leading) note of new scale and is *sharpened*.

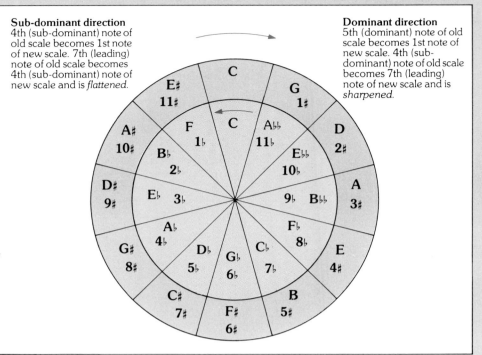

Note This is the dominant direction. The keys of C♯, F♯ and B are enharmonic equivalents of D♭, G♭ and C♭.

Key signatures containing sharps

Each new scale starts from the 5th (dominant) note of the previous scale. The 7th note of the new scale is sharpened.

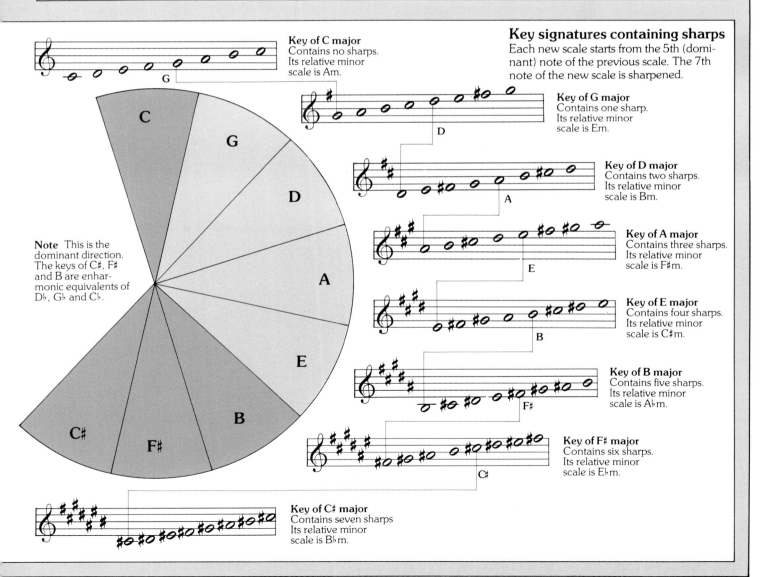

Key of C major
Contains no sharps.
Its relative minor scale is Am.

Key of G major
Contains one sharp.
Its relative minor scale is Em.

Key of D major
Contains two sharps.
Its relative minor scale is Bm.

Key of A major
Contains three sharps.
Its relative minor scale is F♯m.

Key of E major
Contains four sharps.
Its relative minor scale is C♯m.

Key of B major
Contains five sharps.
Its relative minor scale is A♭m.

Key of F♯ major
Contains six sharps.
Its relative minor scale is E♭m.

Key of C♯ major
Contains seven sharps
Its relative minor scale is B♭m.

Scales and modes

The ancient Greeks are credited with having the earliest form of scales. These were named after their most important tribes – the Dorian, Phrygian, Lydian and Mixolydian. They all contained eight notes (including the octave) which were equivalent to the notes on the white keys of a keyboard, and they were written in descending order. The Dorian scale descended from E, the Phrygian from D, the Lydian from C, and the Mixolydian from B.

In the Middle Ages, these scales were adopted by musicians in the Christian Church. But, for an obscure reason, they introduced various changes: first, they reversed the order, so that the scales ascended; second, they changed the notes from which they started; and, third, they substituted the term "mode" for "scale". This meant that the Greek Dorian scale became the Dorian Mode and went up from D to D, the Phrygian Mode went up from E to E, the Lydian Mode went up from F to F, and the Mixolydian Mode went up from G to G.

Furthermore, the old Greek Lydian scale, which had originally descended from C, now ascended from C and was renamed the Ionian Mode. And the Greek Mixolydian scale, which had descended from B, now ascended from B and was renamed the Locrian Mode. The scale that began on the note A was called the Aeolian Mode.

This meant that there were now seven modes – one for each of the white notes. We have already seen that the characteristic sound of any scale or series of notes is determined by its step-pattern of tone or semi-tone intervals. Since each mode has its own step-pattern, each mode has its own sound.

In the Middle Ages, the modal system was the source of melody. However, by the early sixteenth century, the increasing complexities of "polyphony" (music containing two or more harmonized melody lines) was leading to the breakdown of the modal system.

By the seventeenth century, a new harmonic language had been developed. The idea of "tonality" was expanded to include the *key* system (see p. 108). All music was written with a "key signature" which identified the tonic (or first) note of the scale as the "key-centre" or "home key". The intervals between notes were fixed by their distance from the tonic note or key-centre.

At the heart of the key system lay the concept of diatonic major and minor scales. A "diatonic" scale comprises the notes proper to the key. The diatonic major scale has the same pattern of tones and semi-tones as the medieval Ionian Mode (which started on C), and the diatonic natural minor scale has the same pattern as the Aeolian Mode (which started on A). However, the resemblance is one of structure, not usage.

The modal system

A *mode* is a series of notes, like a scale, in which there is one principal note to which all the others are related. The first and last note of the octave is always the principal note in any mode. It is this note that establishes the "tonality" of the mode, and it is the step-pattern of tones or semi-tones that establishes its "modality". Take the Aeolian Mode as an example. It begins and ends on A; therefore, A is its "tonality". Its intervals are tone, semi-tone, tone, tone, semi-tone, tone, tone; therefore, this step-pattern describes its "modality".

The staves below set out the seven modes, and show from which note each one starts. You can see that, because they are formed by playing only the white notes on the keyboard, each mode has its own different step-pattern. This gives it its own sound characteristic.

The C major scale (2 octaves of the white notes on the keyboard)
C D E F G A B C D E F G A B C

The Ionian Mode
From C to C.
C D E F G A B C

The Dorian Mode
From D to D.
D E F G A B C D

The Phrygian Mode
From E to E.
E F G A B C D E

The Lydian Mode
From F to F.
F G A B C D E F

The Mixolydian Mode
From G to G.
G A B C D E F G

The Aeolian Mode
From A to A.
A B C D E F G A

The Locrian Mode
From B to B.
B C D E F G A B

From modes to scales

The sound characteristic of each mode can be translated into any key as long as its original step-pattern is not altered. The scales below show the results of starting each mode on the note C.

In effect, this produces five new scales – not seven, since the Ionian and Aeolian are the same as the diatonic major and natural minor. These five new scales represent an *alternative* to the melodic and harmonic structure of the diatonic scales. In fact, modes and scales have different applications. Scales determine harmony and modes express melodic variation.

You can tell whether a mode is major or minor by looking at the interval between its 1st and 3rd notes (see p. 118). The Lydian and Mixolydian turn out to be major, and the Dorian and Phrygian are minor. The Locrian is unusual in that its tonic chord is "diminished" (see p. 121). The overall mood of the mode can be heard by playing chords built on its various steps, using only the notes which that mode contains.

Ionian Mode (in key of C)
This mode was the predecessor of the diatonic major scale. It has the same step-pattern and therefore the same sound.

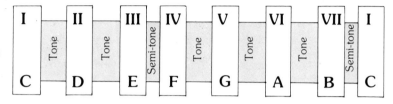

Note Fingering pattern is same as that of major scale (see p. 105).

Dorian Mode (in key of C)
This is a minor mode. It differs from the natural minor (Aeolian) scale in that the 6th note is sharpened. It suits minor chord sequences (e.g., I m, II m, III, IV, V m, and VII chords), and produces a jazz feel.

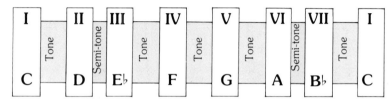

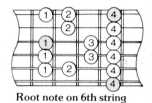

Root note on 6th string

Phrygian Mode (in key of C)
Also a minor mode, this is identical to the natural minor (Aeolian) scale except that it has a flattened 2nd note (the D♭). This note is heard as a "flattened 9th" when played against a tonic minor seventh chord.

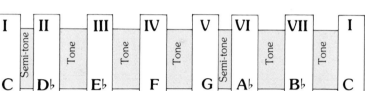

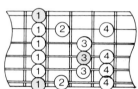

Root note on 6th string

Lydian Mode (in key of C)
This is a major scale. It differs from the diatonic major (Ionian) because it has a sharpened 4th note (the F♯). This means that it has the same notes as the major scale in the key of G – and G is the 5th (dominant) note in the C scale.

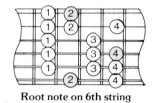

Root note on 6th string

Mixolydian Mode (in key of C)
The Mixolydian scale contains a flattened 7th note (the B♭). This is the only thing that differentiates it from the diatonic major (Ionian) scale. In fact, it is one of the most commonly used modes in blues and jazz improvisation.

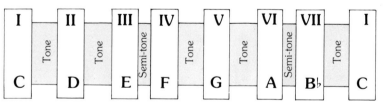

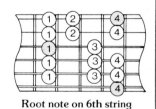

Root note on 6th string

Aeolian Mode (in key of C)
This mode was the predecessor of the diatonic natural minor scale. It has the same step-pattern and therefore the same sound.

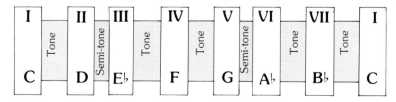

Note Fingering pattern is same as that of natural minor scale (see p. 106).

Locrian Mode (in key of C)
All the notes in this scale are flattened except for the tonic (1st) and the 4th (the F). Of the seven modes, it is the least often used in Western music, but it forms an important part of Japanese and Hindu music.

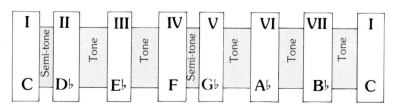

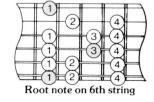

Root note on 6th string

Synthetic scales

The diatonic scales we have looked at so far – the major and three minors – are by no means the end of the story. While it is true that the major scale has dominated the theory and practice of melody and harmony, in fact, it is possible to create many other scales from the octave – simply by selecting a different step-pattern from the twelve equal semi-tone intervals of the chromatic scale. Some scales that fall outside the sphere of the major and minor scales and modes are called *synthetic*. Of these, the whole-tone, the diminished and the pentatonic scales are probably the most commonly used in contemporary music. They are all explained here.

The whole-tone scale

Also known as "augmented", the *whole-tone scale* is exactly what its name implies. It divides the octave into six equal intervals of a whole tone each. There are no semi-tone intervals at all.

The whole-tone scale has a "floating" sound characteristic, and establishes no specific key-centre. In fact, because of its unique step-pattern, with the absence of semi-tones, it sounds the same whatever note you start from. Therefore, only two whole-tone scales are needed in order to cover all twelve keys. One starts from C, and the other starts from C♯/D♭. The note you choose to play first gives the scale its name.

The whole-tone scale allows harmonic transitions not possible with conventional diatonic harmony, and as such is a very useful compositional device.

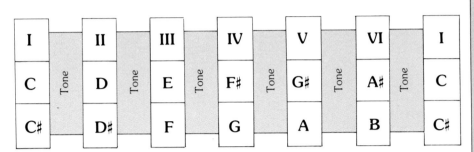

I		II		III		IV		V		VI		I
C	Tone	D	Tone	E	Tone	F♯	Tone	G♯	Tone	A♯	Tone	C
C♯		D♯		F		G		A		B		C♯

The two whole-tone scales All twelve notes in the octave are contained in these two scales. The starting note gives the name of the scale.

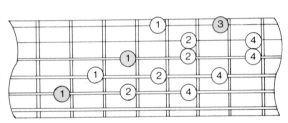

Fingering pattern Whole-tone scales do not really have root notes. If this pattern were used to play the whole-tone C scale, you would begin on the 3rd fret of the 5th string.

The diminished scale

This scale contains nine notes and divides the octave into eight intervals. Also called the "symmetric" scale, its step-pattern is based on alternate intervals of tone, semi-tone, tone, semi-tone, etc. Each diminished scale has four potential key-centres – the 1st, the 3rd, the 5th and the 7th notes in its scale. This means that only three diminished scales are needed in order to cover all twelve keys. One starts from C, the second starts from C♯/D♭, and the third starts from D. The scale that starts on C contains the same notes as the E♭, G♭ and A scales; C♯ is the same as E, G and B♭; and D is the same as F, A♭ and B (see *Diminished chords*, p. 128). The diminished is like the whole-tone scale in its potential to occupy or suggest more than one key-centre. Melodies and chords built on diminished scales are very unlike the familiar melodies built on diatonic harmony, and tend to have a powerful, disorienting effect on a key-centre. Playing the scales and the diminished "run" pattern shown below will illustrate this immediately.

The three diminished scales Each diminished scale has four key-centres – indicated by the 1st, 3rd, 5th and 7th notes of the scale. For example, the diminished scales of C, E♭, G♭ and A all share the same notes. Three scales alone can therefore cover all twelve keys.

I		II		III		IV		V		VI		VII		VIII		I
C	Tone	D	Semi-tone	E♭	Tone	F	Semi-tone	G♭	Tone	G♯	Semi-tone	A	Tone	B	Semi-tone	C
C♯		D♯		E		F♯		G		A		B♭		C		C♯
D		E		F		G		A♭		B♭		B		C♯		D

Fingering pattern for diminished scale The root note is on the 6th string. However, since diminished scales have four potential key-centres, starting this pattern on, say, D would also give the diminished pattern for F, A♭ and B.

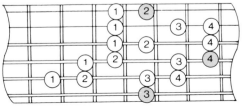

Fingering pattern for diminished "runs" This pattern is an "arpeggio" or "horizontal" form of a diminished seventh chord. It includes only the 1st, 3rd, 5th and 7th notes of the diminished scale – separated by minor thirds.

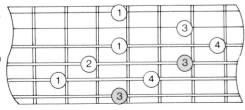

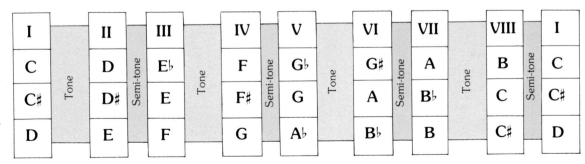

The pentatonic scales

One of the oldest and most widespread scales of all, the *pentatonic* is thought to have Mongolian and Japanese origins, and forms an important part of all far Eastern, African and Celtic music. It is a five-note scale, and differs from the diatonic major in that two notes are left out – the 4th and 7th.

There is also a *pentatonic minor* scale. It differs from the diatonic natural minor in that two notes are again left out – this time, the 2nd and 6th. Its minor characteristic can be identified by the three semi-tone interval (a minor third) between the 1st and 2nd notes of the scale.

The two pentatonic scales share the same relationship as the diatonic major and minor scales – three semi-tones *down* from the major to the minor, and three semi-tones *up* from the minor to the major (see p. 106). So the pentatonic C scale and the pentatonic A minor scale, for example, share the same notes and intervals. Pentatonic scales are used more widely than any other synthetic (or non-diatonic) scale – in particular, for their strong melodic feel. Several popular riffs and cliches used by rock and jazz guitarists are based around a pentatonic scale.

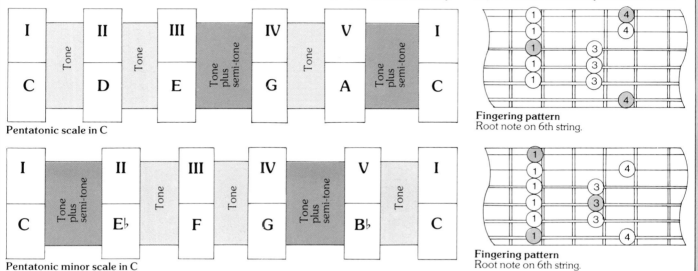

Pentatonic scale in C

Pentatonic minor scale in C

Fingering pattern
Root note on 6th string.

Fingering pattern
Root note on 6th string.

Other scales

The charts below illustrate four of the many other synthetic scales in use around the world. They all have a single key-centre and so, although written out here in C, they can be transposed easily to any other key provided their step-pattern remains intact. In comparison with conventional Western diatonic harmony, you may find them difficult to use, since they are considered in many ways to be "dissonant". However, they represent melodic alternatives, and the best policy is to experiment with them, familiarize yourself with their sound, and, if one catches your imagination, use it to create your own distinctive chords and melodies.

Enigmatic scale in key of C Differs from diatonic major scale in its flattened 2nd note and sharpened 4th, 5th and 6th notes.

Neapolitan scale in key of C Differs from diatonic major scale in its flattened 2nd and 3rd notes.

Neapolitan minor scale in key of C Differs from diatonic major scale in its flattened 2nd, 3rd and 6th notes.

Hungarian minor scale in key of C Differs from diatonic major scale in its flattened 3rd and 6th notes and sharpened 4th note.

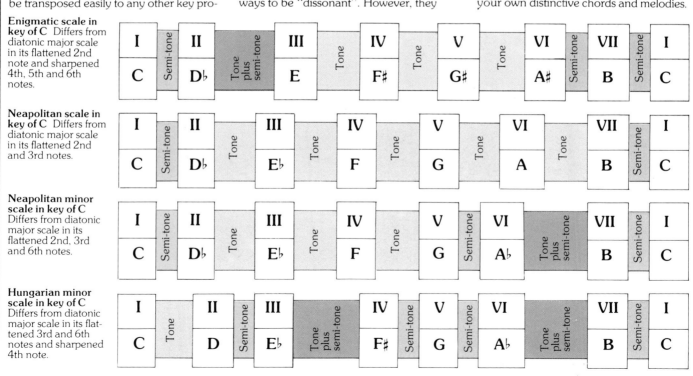

THE HARMONIC GUITARIST

This section of the book is concerned with *harmony*. We have already seen, in the preceding pages of *The Melodic Guitarist*, that melody represents the horizontal principle of music. All melodies are derived from scales, and all melodies move horizontally. Harmony, on the other hand, represents the vertical principle of music. Harmony is also derived from scales, but it is concerned with the effects produced by sounding two or more notes at the same time, not one after the other. It is the study of *chords*.

This section begins with the subject of *harmonics*. The reason for this is that the phenomenon of harmonics (or "overtones" as they are often called) lies at the heart of harmony. The harmonics that are present along with the fundamental whenever a note is played are not only responsible for the tonal characteristics of the sound. They are also responsible for the particular effect created whenever two or three or four different notes are played simultaneously.

"With a note of music, one strikes the fundamental, and, in addition to the root note, other notes are generated: these are called the harmonic series ... As one fundamental note contains within it other notes in the octave, two fundamentals produce a remarkable array of harmonics, and the number of possible combinations between all the notes increases phenomenally. With a triad, affairs stand a good chance of getting severely out of hand ..."
Robert Fripp

When you play any two notes together, you are playing what is called an *interval* (see p. 118). Intervals are built from scales and differ according to the distance between the two notes. When you play more than two notes together, you are playing a *chord*. Chords are built from intervals. The simplest type of chord is the *triad* (see p. 121-5), a three-note chord formed by stacking the 1st, 3rd and 5th notes of a scale on top of one another. This section of the book emphasizes the importance of understanding triads and will show you both how to play them and also why the four types — the major, minor, augmented and diminished — sound different.

From triads, we move on to look at slightly more complex chords — sevenths, sixths, suspended fourths, and so on — and explain how they are all built using the same principles of vertical construction, by stacking different notes of the scale one above the other. This basic principle applies to all chords. Once you have grasped it, seemingly difficult chords such as minor thirteenths, seventh diminished fifths or major ninth augmented elevenths will appear far less daunting.

"I practise all the scales. Everyone should know lots of scales. Actually, I feel there are only scales. What is a chord, if not the notes of a scale hooked together? There are several reasons for learning scales: one, the knowledge will unlock the neck for you — you'll learn the instrument; second, if I say I want you to improvise over G maj 7 +5, then go to E aug 9 −5, then to B maj 7 −5 — well, if you don't know what those chords are in scale terms, you're lost. It's not all that difficult, but you have to be ready to apply yourself ..."
John McLaughlin

Robert Fripp

The pages that follow will help you greatly increase your chord vocabulary. However, you should always bear in mind that understanding the chords is more important than simply being able to finger them. There is virtually no point in learning chords you do not know how to use. Chords are meaningless in isolation. They become interesting only when put together in sequences. This is why it is important to understand how chords move, how they create a sense of consonance, dissonance or resolution, and how chord voicings and cadences work. These principles are vital if you want to see how melody relates to chords. The thing to aim for is to know, whenever you play a chord, what notes it contains. This way, you will know, when you play a lead solo over the top which of the notes are part of the chord and which are not. Those that are not are called *passing notes*, and you should be aware of how they relate to the chord you are playing.

"I'm constantly thinking melodies. Now, to add interest to those melodies, obviously you have to know what things can be superimposed over a chord, and I will think of extended arpeggios and the upper extensions. If I'm playing very vertically, I will invariably start to include certain passing notes which imply certain scales — like a melodic minor scale against a C minor chord, or diminished scales, something like that. But I'm not thinking of a scale at that specific moment. I'm

John McLaughlin

thinking of the notes as surrounding that chord – because I know how each of the twelve notes in music sound against a C minor seventh, for instance.''

Lee Ritenour

This kind of theory always sounds more difficult than it really is. The way to master it is to play, and to think about what you are playing. Experiment with the chords that we have included, play them slowly one note at a time, and listen to the *sound* of the intervals from which they are constructed. With time, you will learn to recognize intervals instinctively.

For the sake of simplicity, the examples used in the following explanations of intervals, triads and chord-building are in the key of C major. The reason for this is that, in C major, the diatonic notes are natural, and the five chromatic notes are the five black keys on the keyboard. However, the same relationships and the same sound characteristics exist in any other key, and you should certainly make the effort to transpose them.

"I spent a lot of time teaching myself theory and harmony so I could be free to express myself on the instrument. I learned what relatives and substitutes could be played against a root of a chord, like E minor related to G, and so forth. I've also gathered all this knowledge because for ten years all I've done is play jazz, every day."

George Benson

George Benson

The principles of harmony

There are two sets of laws governing musical sounds. One stems from the natural properties of acoustics, and the other is based on the rules of mathematics. These laws are set out below as an introduction to this section of the book. They may be difficult to absorb at first, especially if intervals and chord construction are still a mystery to you. If so, do not worry. Come back to them as you work your way through the following pages. You should then find them easier.

Every note, regardless of the instrument on which it is produced, comprises a sound spectrum or "harmonic series". Within this spectrum are contained the tonic, the octave and the triad intervals (see p. 116). There is a mathematical relationship between them. Any two notes an octave apart have a frequency ratio of 2:1. Two notes separated by an interval of a fifth have a frequency ratio of 3:2. And two notes a fourth apart have a frequency ratio of 3:4. The fourth and the fifth have an inverse relationship; together, they make up one octave. These ratios and relationships form the basic harmonic structure present in the nature of sound. In a sense, they can be considered to be "the physics of the octave".

Historically, this harmonic structure has been organized in different ways by different cultures. Western music divides the octave into twelve equal divisions of a semi-tone each (see p. 103). But the octave has also been divided into as few as five and as many as twenty-four divisions. These steps or increments represent different scales.

It has been suggested that the number twelve (the basis of the Western system) was derived from ancient religions or from astrology. In terms of mathematics, however, twelve is quite simply the lowest common denominator for the fractions of a half, a third and a quarter. These are the fractions represented by the primary interval ratios – the octave 2:1, the fifth 3:2, and the fourth 3:4. This is one of the logical reasons why the number twelve has a special significance in terms of the natural harmonic structure.

The interval inversion chart on p. 120 illustrates the concept of the octave as a symmetric "sound prism". The tritone interval is at the centre, between the fourth and the fifth. It is unique in its ability to invert to itself, and can be seen as the neutral pivot on which the tonality of the octave is delicately balanced. Any vertical or horizontal combination of notes other than the tritone disturbs the balance and initiates a sense of *motion*. This motion is increased or counteracted by whatever intervals follow until it comes to rest – by resolving back to the tonic.

The further you go into a study of the principles of harmony, the more you will find that every aspect of tonal cause and effect is related to the number twelve. The following examples represent some of the many ways in which this can be demonstrated. They are presented simply to illustrate the mathematical balance that underlies the structure of Western harmony.

Interval inversions
Any interval plus the interval formed when it is inverted totals twelve semi-tones. Thus, an interval of x semi-tones will invert to an interval of 12−x semi-tones (see p. 120).

Triad inversions
A root position major triad spans seven semitones between the tonic and the 5th, five short of an octave (7+5=12). The first inversion spans eight semi-tones between the 3rd and the upper tonic, four short of an octave (8+4=12). The second inversion spans nine semi-tones between the 5th and the upper 3rd, three short of an octave (9+3=12). The sum of the semi-tones in all three inversions is twenty-four (7+8+9=24), and the sum of the semi-tones remaining from each inversion is twelve (5+4+3=12) (see p. 121-2).

The four triad types
There are four different kinds of triad – the major, minor, augmented and diminished (see p. 121). Each has three inversions. The result is 12 × 12 = 144 triads, 36 of each type. Each note in each type of triad can perform one of three different functions (it can be the tonic, 3rd or 5th). Considering the four kinds of triad in their root positions only, this means that each note can perform twelve different functions. For all twelve notes, there are 144 different uses.

Triad harmony
The four primary triads (those built on the tonic, the 4th, the 5th and the octave) use a total of twelve notes. So do the four secondary triads (those built on the 2nd, 3rd, 6th and 7th notes of the scale). The actual notes number seven (see p. 123).

Octave divisions
An octave divided into twelve equal steps produces a chromatic scale (see p. 103). An octave divided into six equal steps produces a whole-tone scale (see p. 112). An octave divided into four equal steps produces a diminished seventh chord (see p. 128). An octave divided into three equal steps produces an augmented chord. An octave divided in half produces the tritone interval (see p. 118-19).

Harmonics

Harmonics are an important part of *every* note. Each time a guitar string is struck it vibrates in a complex pattern, and the sound it generates is composed of several elements. The basic building block of the sound is the *fundamental*. This is the loudest element we hear, and the one by which we identify the pitch of the note. It is the sound generated by the string vibrating in a single loop along its entire length. At the same time, the string produces a series of *harmonics, overtones* or *upper partials*. These are simply tones with frequencies that are multiples of the frequency of the fundamental, and they are generated by the string also vibrating simultaneously in shorter loops. They begin one octave above the fundamental and then rise in pitch in specific intervals – the fifth, the next octave, the following third, and so on.

All musical instruments produce notes that consist of a fundamental and a number of harmonics. Together, these components of each note are known as its *harmonic series*, and, in this context, the fundamental is referred to as the *first harmonic*. The balance or blend of the fundamental and harmonics in relation to each other determines the "tone" of the instrument. In effect, the harmonic series therefore forms a unique "audio fingerprint". No two guitars – however similar – have exactly the same tone because they do not produce exactly the same balance of harmonics.

Artificial harmonics

There are several special techniques in guitar playing which enable you to sound one selected harmonic while at the same time silencing the louder fundamental and also the other harmonics. This is known as playing *artificial harmonics*.

Let's take the simplest example. By lightly fingering an open string over the 12th fret, you divide it into two equal lengths. When you then play the string, you get an artificial harmonic one octave above the open string. In the context of artificial harmonics, this octave note – not the fundamental – is called the *first harmonic*.

What happens is this. Fingering the string creates a *node* or *node point* where the string does not vibrate at all. This alters the vibration pattern that the open string would otherwise produce and stops the fundamental and other harmonics from sounding. On either side of the node, the two equal lengths of the string then vibrate out of phase with one another and produce the artificial harmonic. The points at which the string vibrates most are called the *anti-nodes*. As the drawing shows, there are several places on the string where artificial harmonics can be played.

Where to find open-string harmonics

If the length of the string is divided into two (exactly over the 12th fret), the frequency of the harmonic will be one octave higher than that of the fundamental on the open string. If you split the string length into three (exactly over the 7th or 19th fret), the frequency of the harmonic will be three times greater – one octave and a fifth above the open string. In theory, it is possible to go on producing higher and higher harmonics. In practice, you can only go so far before they become impossible to hear.

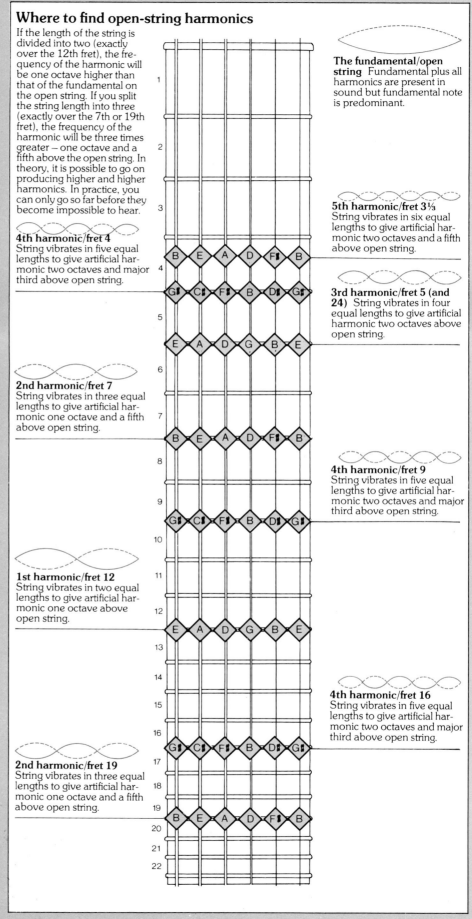

The fundamental/open string Fundamental plus all harmonics are present in sound but fundamental note is predominant.

5th harmonic/fret 3⅓ String vibrates in six equal lengths to give artificial harmonic two octaves and a fifth above open string.

4th harmonic/fret 4 String vibrates in five equal lengths to give artificial harmonic two octaves and major third above open string.

3rd harmonic/fret 5 (and 24) String vibrates in four equal lengths to give artificial harmonic two octaves above open string.

2nd harmonic/fret 7 String vibrates in three equal lengths to give artificial harmonic one octave and a fifth above open string.

4th harmonic/fret 9 String vibrates in five equal lengths to give artificial harmonic two octaves and major third above open string.

1st harmonic/fret 12 String vibrates in two equal lengths to give artificial harmonic one octave above open string.

4th harmonic/fret 16 String vibrates in five equal lengths to give artificial harmonic two octaves and major third above open string.

2nd harmonic/fret 19 String vibrates in three equal lengths to give artificial harmonic one octave and a fifth above open string.

How to play open-string harmonics

The first, second and third artificial harmonics are the easiest to play. More are available with varying degrees of practice. The right-hand technique is the same as normal: you pluck or strum the strings as usual. The left-hand technique – which is really the key to playing harmonics – differs from normal fretting in two ways. First, whichever finger you decide to use, you must only just touch the string. Do not push it down on to the fret. Second, you must place your finger directly over the fret in question, not slightly behind it as you would when playing a note normally. The only exception is the fifth harmonic – between the 3rd and 4th frets.

To get the first harmonic, place one of your left-hand fingers directly over the 12th fret. To get the second harmonic, place a finger directly over the 7th or 19th fret. For further harmonics, see the fingerboard opposite.

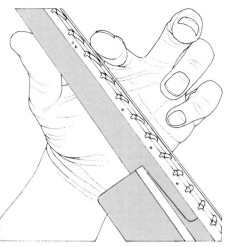

Left-hand technique
Place one left-hand finger on the string directly above the 12th fret. Pluck the string with your right hand. As soon as you feel the string being struck, remove your left-hand finger from the string.

Open-string harmonics technique

How to play fretted-string harmonics

There is a classical guitar technique for playing harmonics – also applicable to steel-string guitars – in which the fingers of the right hand are used to both touch and strike the string. As shown below, you touch the "node point" of the string with the 1st finger of your right hand, and then either pluck the string with your 4th finger or strike it with your plectrum. The great advantage of this technique is that it does not restrict you to playing harmonics on open strings. Your left hand is free to fret any note you wish. As long as you place the 1st finger of your left hand lightly on the string, exactly halfway

between the bridge and the fret on which you are holding down the string, you will get the octave harmonic of whatever note you are fretting. Using this method, melody or chord patterns can be picked out and played entirely in harmonics – for example, the notes of a G chord as shown below.

An alternative and favourite technique among rock and blues guitarists is that of "pinching" or "squeezing" harmonics between the right-hand thumb and the plectrum. Hold the plectrum so that it only just protrudes beyond your thumb. Then strike the string with your plectrum and

thumb virtually simultaneously. The effect of your plectrum hitting the string and your thumb damping it – in the right place – produces a dynamic harmonic shift. This works better on high fretted notes as it puts stronger harmonics in range.

To begin with, try the technique by fretting the 1st string at the 12th fret. Now "pinch" the string in the way described where the 24th fret would be – that is, midway along its length. You will hear immediately when you get it right. As soon as you can produce this first octave harmonic, go up to an F, a G and so on.

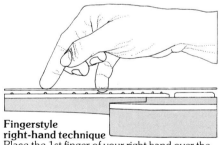

**Fingerstyle
right-hand technique**
Place the 1st finger of your right hand over the "node point" of the string and pluck it with your 4th (or 3rd) finger.

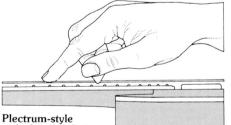

**Plectrum-style
right-hand technique**
Use your 1st finger to touch the string lightly in the correct place and strike it with the plectrum held between your thumb and 2nd finger.

Example: arpeggio harmonic G chord

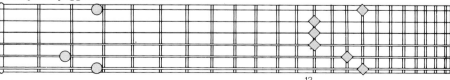

Left hand
Finger a G chord with your left hand as shown – pushing the strings down on to the frets.

Right hand
Using your right hand to locate the frets one octave (12 frets) higher than the fretted positions, play the notes of the G chord one at a time.

Fretted-string harmonics technique

Intervals

The difference in pitch between any two notes is called an *interval*. The interval is the same whether the notes are sounded together or one after the other.

Every different interval has its own specific sound quality. This is determined by the ratio between the frequencies of the two notes. We have seen how each note produces a harmonic series, made up of its fundamental plus a kind of "sound spectrum" of overtones or upper partials. Sounding two notes together therefore has the effect of combining two fundamentals and their two harmonic spectrums. The result is the creation of a third harmonic series – and it is this that is responsible for the specific sound of any interval.

In the case of two notes with the same pitch, the two harmonic series are doubled – this is called a *unison*. In the case of two notes an octave apart, the two harmonic series reinforce one another – this is the *octave*.

How intervals are named

Intervals can be identified by their position in the diatonic scale. The most fundamental of all intervals is, of course, the octave; it determines the first and last notes. All other intervals are then named according to their distance from the first note of the scale (the "tonic" or "root" note). They are called *seconds, thirds, fourths, fifths, sixths* and *sevenths*.

This system covers the eight notes (including the octave) that make up the diatonic major scale. However, as we have seen, the octave is divided into twelve semitones, producing thirteen different notes (including the octave). Since each of these has its own sound characteristic, there is a system of names which further defines each interval as being *perfect, major, minor, augmented* or *diminished*.

Of the diatonic intervals, the term "perfect" applies to the unison, the fourth, the fifth and the octave. The second, third, sixth and seventh intervals may be either "major" or "minor". The interval between the fourth and fifth is called the "tritone".

Because of enharmonic spellings, the same physical interval can have more than one name, so the tritone is called either an augmented fourth or a diminished fifth.

Here are the rules for identifying intervals.
- A major interval lowered by a semi-tone becomes a minor interval.
- A minor interval raised by a semi-tone becomes a major interval.
- A major interval raised by a semi-tone becomes an augmented interval.
- A minor interval lowered by a semi-tone becomes a diminished interval.
- A perfect interval raised by a semi-tone becomes an augmented interval.
- A perfect interval lowered by a semi-tone becomes a diminished interval.

Compound intervals

When the notes extend beyond the range of one octave, the diatonic scale numbering system simply continues.
- When the second is an octave higher, it is called a *ninth*. It is major naturally, minor if lowered, and augmented if raised.

- When the third is an octave higher, it is called a *tenth*. It can be major or minor.
- When the fourth is an octave higher, it is called an *eleventh*. It can be perfect, augmented or diminished.
- When the sixth is an octave higher, it is called a *thirteenth*. It can be major, minor or augmented.

Consonance and dissonance

The different sound quality possessed by each interval can be defined by using the terms *consonant* and *dissonant*. The reason for this is that some intervals seem to have a smooth, satisfying sound. These are the unison, the thirds, the fifth, the sixth and the octave. They are called either "open" or "soft" consonances. Others have an unsatisfying, "un-resolved" sound. These are the second and the seventh. They are called either "sharp" or "mild" dissonances. The fourth can be either consonant or dissonant. The tritone has an ambiguous quality which is considered neutral or restless on its own, but dissonant in a diatonic context.

Interval chart

							Enharmonic
Numerical symbol	I (1st)	ii (♭2nd)	II (2nd)	iii (♭3rd)	III (3rd)	IV (4th)	IV+ (♯4th)
Degree	Tonic	Supertonic		Mediant		Sub-dominant	Tritone
Pitch in key of C	C	D♭	D	E♭	E	F	F♯
Intervals from C	C to C	C to D♭	C to D	C to E♭	C to E	C to F	C to F♯
Distance of interval	Zero	1 semi-tone	2 semi-tones	3 semi-tones	4 semi-tones	5 semi-tones	6 semi-tones
Name of interval	Unison	Minor second	Major second	Minor third	Major third	Perfect fourth	Augmented fourth
Sound characteristic	Open consonance	Sharp dissonance	Mild dissonance	Soft consonance	Soft consonance	Consonance or dissonance	Neutral or

Fingerboard intervals

Intervals are the building blocks of all chords. If you are to understand the role of intervals in harmony and chord construction, you must learn to identify their sound by ear. They are set out in the large chart below, together with the names by which they are known.

The characteristic sound of each interval is always the same, whatever the two notes involved. So a minor third from C to E♭, for example, has the same sound quality as a minor third from D to F. A pattern of intervals can be plotted out on the guitar fingerboard. The pattern remains consistent wherever it is played. Any note can be considered as the tonic or root, and all the other intervals will then relate to this note. When playing in a specific key, the name of the key is the name of the tonic or root note.

Let's take an example. If you play the first pattern (below left) with your 1st finger on the 3rd fret of the 6th string, this identifies the tonic or root note as a G. All the other intervals then relate to G. If you start on the 5th fret, the tonic or root note will be an A. These patterns are invaluable for working out scale and chord fingerings.

Roman numerals are used to symbolize intervals in the same way as they are for chords (see p. 76). The only difference is that upper-case numerals are used specifically for major and perfect intervals, lowercase numerals are introduced for minor intervals, a plus sign means an augmented interval, and a small circle indicates a diminished interval.

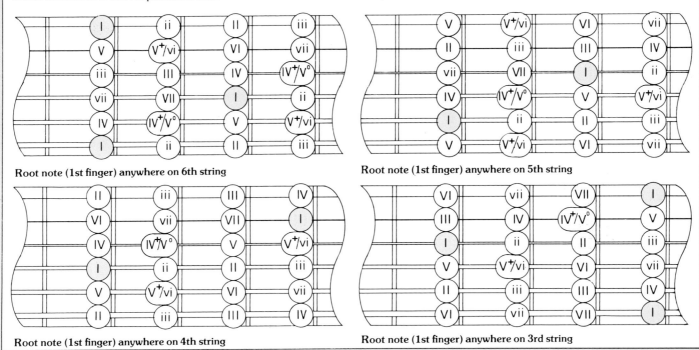

Root note (1st finger) anywhere on 6th string

Root note (1st finger) anywhere on 5th string

Root note (1st finger) anywhere on 4th string

Root note (1st finger) anywhere on 3rd string

	Enharmonic		Enharmonic		Enharmonic				
V° (♭5th)	V (5th)	V+ (♯5th)	vi (♭6th)	VI (6th)	vii° (♭♭7th)	vii (♭7th)	VII (7th)	I (1st)
Tritone	Dominant	Sub-mediant				Sub-tonic	Leading note	Tonic
G♭	G	G♯	A♭	A	B♭♭	B♭	B	C
C to G♭	C to G	C to G♯	C to A♭	C to A	C to B♭♭	C to B♭	C to B	C to C
6 semi-tones	7 semi-tones	8 semi-tones		9 semi-tones		10 semi-tones	11 semi-tones	12 semi-tones
Diminished fifth	Perfect fifth	Augmented fifth	Minor sixth	Major sixth	Diminished seventh	Minor seventh	Major seventh	Octave (8va)
restless	Open consonance	Soft consonance		Soft consonance		Mild dissonance	Sharp dissonance	Open consonance

Interval inversions

An interval is said to be *inverted* when the lower note becomes the higher, or the higher note becomes the lower. In effect, this is done either by raising the lower note or by lowering the higher note one octave.

When an interval is inverted it changes and becomes a new interval with a different value. The important thing to realize about inversions is that, in relation to an octave, the new interval is symmetrically equivalent to the old one. Let's look at an example in the key of C major. Take the interval between the 1st note (C) and the 4th note (F); it is a "perfect fourth". Now invert it so that the lower note is F and the higher note is C. You will see that, in its new form, it has become a "perfect fifth".

Together, the fourth and fifth make up an octave. This means that the note F is a fourth above C and a fifth below it.

Obviously, the same thing happens if you take an interval of a perfect fifth (in the key of C major, from C to G). When you invert it, it becomes a perfect fourth. Again, the two intervals add up to an octave. The note G is a fifth above C and a fourth below it.

The rules that govern other inversions work in the same way. This allows any note in a scale to be related to the tonic note either from *above* or from *below*.

For how inversions work in terms of chords, not just two-note intervals, see opposite and p. 122.

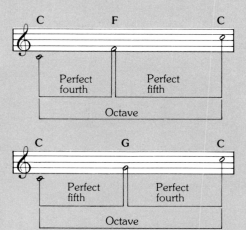

Rules governing interval inversions

When intervals are inverted their original quality of either consonance or dissonance may change. This is because the register of the two notes, and the spacing between them, has been altered. The degree of change depends on the interval in question.

We have seen that a perfect fourth becomes a perfect fifth and a perfect fifth becomes a perfect fourth. Although both remain perfect, inverting these two intervals alters their function considerably. The same

is true when a unison becomes an octave and an octave becomes a unison.

Inverting an interval of a second creates a seventh and inverting a seventh creates a second. The major and minor qualities change, but both intervals remain dissonant in character.

A third becomes a sixth and a sixth becomes a third when inverted. As before, major and minor change but both intervals remain consonant.

An augmented fourth becomes a diminished fifth when inverted, and vice versa. The sound qualities are exactly the same, however, since the intervals are enharmonic. Six semi-tones remain between the two notes, whether inverted or not.

This information is presented visually in the chart below. The scale of intervals can be considered as "pivoting" on the augmented fourth and diminished fifth, which are the same when inverted.

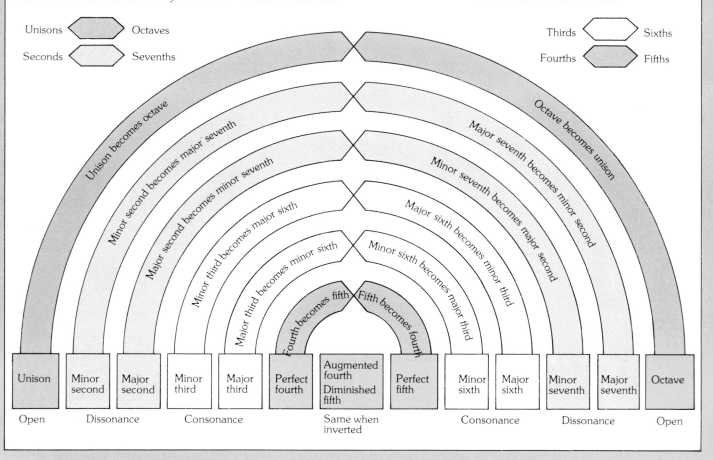

Triads

A *triad* is a simultaneous combination of three notes. It can be made up of any note plus the two notes a third and a fifth above it. This means that a triad has two intervals, each of a third. All triads are three-note chords, but not all three-note chords are triads.

The theory of triads dates back to the middle of the fifteenth century, when the diatonic major/minor tonal system was evolving. Before then, the horizontal effect of the intervals in the various "modes" (see p. 110) had established the tonic note and the 5th note of a scale as the most important. The triad was created when the 3rd was combined with the 1st and 5th to produce a vertical chord.

In the harmonic series of any note, the tonic is the fundamental, and the octave, the 5th and the 3rd are the most prominent "overtones" (see p. 116). These are the notes that make up the triad, and the reinforcement of these overtones gives it its strong sound.

The four different triads

There are four kinds of triad – major, minor, augmented and diminished. Although the intervals that make up the triad are always thirds, they differ in that they may be either major or minor thirds. They can also appear in a different vertical order.

In the context of triads (or, indeed, any chord), the tonic note is referred to as the root. Every interval has an effect on the sound of the chord, but it is the root that determines the chord's identity.

Major and minor triads both span an interval of a perfect fifth from the root note. It is the interval from the root to the middle note of the group (the 3rd) that determines whether they are major or minor. A major triad with a sharpened 5th is called augmented, and a minor triad with a flattened 5th is called diminished.

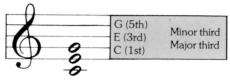

The C major triad
Derived from the 1st, 3rd and 5th notes of the diatonic major scale (see p. 104), the major triad consists of a minor third stacked on top of a major third. Overall this forms a perfect fifth.

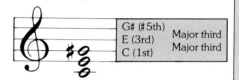

The C augmented triad
Derived from the 1st, 3rd and 5th notes of the whole-tone scale (see p. 112), this triad consists of two major thirds on top of one another. This forms an interval of an augmented fifth.

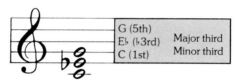

The C minor triad
Derived from the 1st, 3rd and 5th notes of the diatonic natural minor scale (see p. 106), the minor triad has a minor third on the bottom and a major third on top. It still forms a perfect fifth.

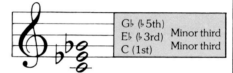

The C diminished triad
Derived from the 1st, 3rd and 5th notes of the diminished scale (see p. 112), this triad consists of two minor thirds which together form an interval of a diminished fifth.

Triad inversions

The four triads shown above are all in the *root position*. This means that the root or tonic note is the lowest note in the chord. If the lowest note is *not* the root, the chord is said to be *inverted* (see opposite). In this case, the term "root" may still be used to describe the lowest note – but it will no longer be the tonic.

If you take a C major root position triad and raise the tonic by an octave, the 3rd will

become the lowest note. This form of the triad is called the *first inversion*. If you now raise the 3rd by an octave, the 5th will be left as the root. This form is called the *second inversion*. Repeating the process once again brings you back to the root position triad one octave higher.

In this way, it is possible to get three different "sounds" from one triad – the root position, the first inversion and the second

inversion. Because the three notes have the same key-centre and tonality, whatever their arrangement, they have the same name – in the example below, C major. But, because of the influence of the root note, each inversion suggests a different "motion" and can have many different applications. An understanding of triad inversions, including where they can be played on the fingerboard, is important.

How major triad inversion works
In the root position, the tonic (C) is the lowest note. In the first inversion, the 3rd (E) is the lowest note. And, in the second inversion, the 5th (G) is the lowest note. The three forms are all C major triads, but each has a different sound and, therefore, a different use.

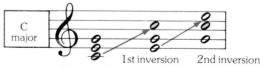

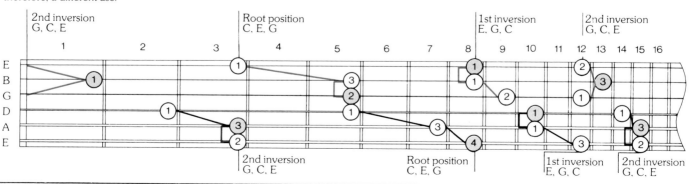

Further triad inversions

The principles of major triad inversion outlined on the previous page apply in exactly the same way to the other three kinds of triad – the minor, augmented and diminished. Each of these also has a root position, a first inversion and a second inversion. A sound knowledge of triads everywhere on the fingerboard is possibly one of the greatest assets to any guitarist wishing to work out chords and harmony. In the fingerboard drawings below and on the previous page, the triads shown are C major, A minor, C augmented and B diminished, but the shapes can be moved anywhere on the fingerboard to give triads with different names (or pitches).

It is important, not only that you learn these shapes and understand how they function, but also that you work out how to find triads and their inversions on any set of adjacent strings – on the 2nd, 3rd and 4th, or on the 3rd, 4th and 5th, for example. This will give you a thorough grounding for the theory and practice of all chord work.

How minor triad inversions work
In the root position, the tonic (A) is the lowest note. In the first inversion, the 3rd (C) is the lowest note. And, in the second inversion, the 5th (E) is the lowest note. The three forms are all A minor triads, but each has a different sound.

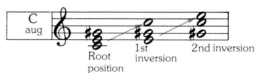

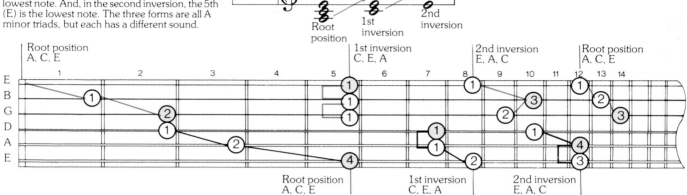

How augmented triad inversion works
In the root position, the tonic (C) is the lowest note. In the first inversion, the 3rd (E) is the lowest note. And, in the second inversion, the 5th (G♯) is the lowest note. The three forms are all C augmented triads, but each has a different sound.

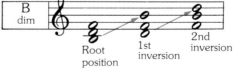

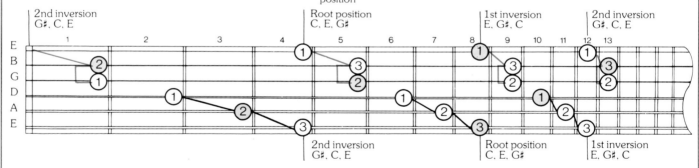

How diminished triad inversion works
In the root position, the tonic (B) is the lowest note. In the first inversion, the 3rd (D) is the lowest note. And, in the second inversion, the 5th (F) is the lowest note. The three forms are all B diminished triads, but each has a different sound.

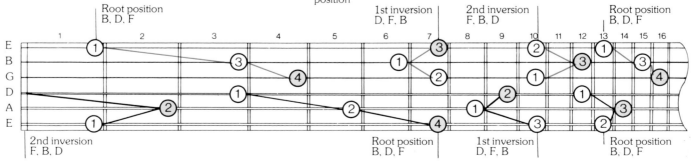

Triad doubling

The major and minor triads are the two most important basic chord forms in music. To use them in any chord in which more than three notes are sounded together requires *doubling* one or more of the three notes. Not surprisingly, the note most often doubled is the tonic. This reinforces the overall sound of the chord and stresses the key-centre. Doubling the 5th strengthens the "stability" of the chord, and doubling the 3rd emphasizes the tonality (that is, whether it is major or minor).

The choice of what notes are doubled and their vertical placement creates what is considered the *voicing* of the chord. The most important notes are always the highest and lowest. When one chord changes to another in the course of a progression, the highest notes establish a melodic relationship. The root note (the lowest) determines the "inversion" of the chord.

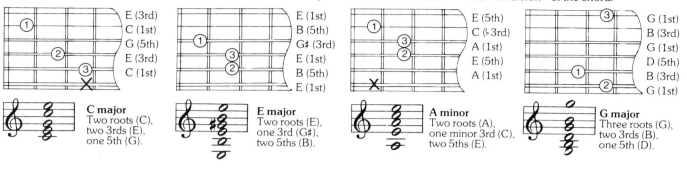

C major
Two roots (C), two 3rds (E), one 5th (G).

E major
Two roots (E), one 3rd (G♯), two 5ths (B).

A minor
Two roots (A), one minor 3rd (C), two 5ths (E).

G major
Three roots (G), two 3rds (B), one 5th (D).

Building triads on the notes of a scale

In any key, there are seven *diatonic triads*. They can be formed by building two intervals of a third on each note in the diatonic scale. Only notes included in the diatonic scale are used to build the thirds. The whereabouts of the semi-tone steps will determine whether the intervals are major or minor thirds, and will therefore dictate the type of triad.

Because each note in the scale represents an interval with its own sound in relation to the tonic, so the triads built on these notes also have their own sound in relation to the tonic triad. Changing from one chord to another within the scale creates an effect of movement that is considered in terms of "tension" and "resolution" within the key. This relationship between the seven different diatonic triads creates a sense of harmony which has been a characteristic feature of almost all Western music.

The harmonized C major scale
Building diatonic triads on each note of the diatonic major scale produces the following series: I major, II minor, III minor, IV major, V major, VI minor, VII diminished. The primary chords are the I, IV and V; the others are secondary. This "harmonized" scale is shown here on the staff and the guitar fingerboard in the key of C major.

The harmonized natural A minor scale
Building triads on each note of the diatonic natural minor scale produces the following series: I minor, II diminished, III major, IV minor, V minor, VI major, VII major. Again, the primary chords are the I, IV and V. The "harmonized" scale is shown this time in the key of A minor – the relative minor of C major.

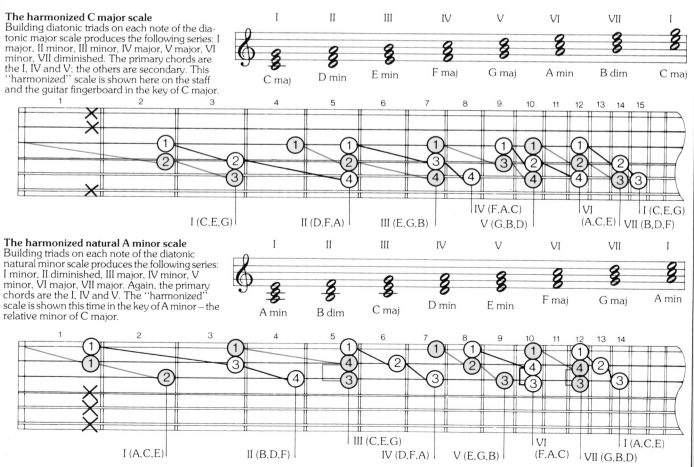

The theory of chord progressions

During the development of diatonic harmony, rules were established to govern the movement from one chord to another in progressions. These rules were based on a strict sense of consonance and dissonance (see p. 118), and their function was to organize chord changes within a key so that the tonic chord emerged clearly as the "home chord" and so that the best and most logical "horizontal" effect was created between two chords.

The role of the primary chords – the most important ones – was determined by what is called *cadence*. A cadence (from the Latin word meaning "to fall") describes a concluding phrase or a phrase suggesting conclusion. It normally occurs at or near the end of a melody or a section of music. There are four different cadences in primary chord progressions.

The *perfect cadence* is the resolution from the V (dominant) to the I (tonic) chord.

The *imperfect cadence* is the progression from the I (tonic) chord to the V (dominant). It normally occurs in the middle of a chord sequence, not at the end, and it can also be used to describe the movement of any chord to the V – usually the II, IV or VI.

The *plagal cadence* is the resolution from the IV (sub-dominant) to the I (tonic) chord.

The *interrupted cadence* is the progression from the V (dominant) to any chord other than the I (tonic). It is usually to the III, IV or VI.

In chord sequences in a major key, these cadences reflect a definite sense of motion, tension and resolution. However, in a minor key, the V (dominant) chord is a minor triad, not a major triad, and this means that it does not produce the same effect when used in cadences. It was for this reason that the 7th note in the minor scale was raised by a semi-tone to create the harmonic minor scale (see p. 107). Triads built on the notes of the harmonic minor scale could therefore produce a different series of chords: I minor,

II diminished, III augmented, IV diminished, V major, VI major, and VII diminished. The V chord was now major instead of minor, and the result was that the rules of cadences could be applied in the same way to both major and minor keys.

In traditional harmony, there is a system of general rules for how diatonic chords should be used in a progression. These rules reflect musical tastes at the time the diatonic system came into being.

- A I chord can change to any chord.
- A II chord can change to any chord except the I.
- A III chord can change to any chord except the I or VII.
- A IV chord can change to any chord.
- A V chord can change to any chord except the II or VII.
- A VI chord can change to any chord except the I or VII.
- A VII chord can change to any chord except the II or IV.

The harmonized harmonic A minor scale
In order to avoid the minor V chord that occurs when triads are built on the natural minor scale (see p. 123), the 7th note is sharpened to produce a major V chord. Using the harmonic minor scale allows primary chords in a minor key to follow the rules of cadence.

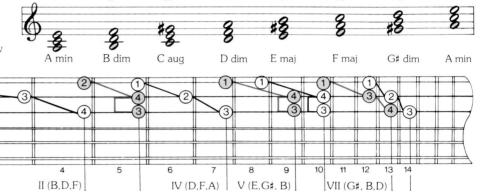

How chord voicings move in progressions

The basic rules of traditional harmony are usually illustrated in "four-part" writing. Triads become four-part chords when one of the notes is doubled (see p. 123). The doubled note is traditionally either the root or the 5th. In four-part progressions, both the vertical and horizontal effect of all four notes in each chord were conventionally subject to strict regulations.

Two or three parts moving in the same direction is called *similar motion*. Two parts moving in different directions is called *contrary motion*. And one part moving while the other stays at the same pitch is called *oblique motion*. In four-part harmony, the two most important parts are the lowest and highest. In vocal writing, the lowest is the bass, the highest is the soprano, and the two in between are the tenor and alto.

Some of the rules of traditional harmony

you are likely to encounter are as follows. No two parts are allowed to move in "consecutive" fifths or octaves. Less rigidly enforced is the rule forbidding "hidden" fifths or octaves. These occur when two parts move in similar motion (up or down together) to arrive at a fifth or octave; it is permissible only when the upper voice moves by no more than a single step. Wherever possible, common notes between two chords should be in the same voice, and, ideally, the movement of each should consist of the smallest intervals possible. The jump of a tritone (three tones) was strictly forbidden.

These rules form the basic framework of traditional harmony, and were established in the sixteenth century. However, even as they were being developed, they were being broken. Anything was considered

valid as long as the sound produced had a clear harmonic motive and met with popular acceptance. As musical taste broadened to include new concepts of consonance and dissonance, the many rules forbidding specific voice and chord movements were relaxed. By including non-diatonic notes, new chords were produced, and it became possible to "modulate" to another key (see p. 138).

In the eighteenth and nineteenth centuries, the fundamental rules of chord progression revolved around the tonal pillars of the I (tonic), IV (sub-dominant) and V (dominant) chords. Looking at the interval chart on p. 118-19, you can see that the IV and V chords balance the tonic on either side with perfect fifths. In any exploration of harmony, you will find that these relationships dominate all others.

Common or shared notes

It should now be apparent that, when building triads on the notes of a major or minor scale, each note has a variety of different functions. Since any triad contains three notes – the tonic, the 3rd and the 5th – and since any note can play any of these three roles, it follows that any note can belong in three different triads.

Take a look at the harmonic A minor scale on the opposite page. The 1st note (the A) shows up immediately as being included in three different triads – the A minor triad (I), the D diminished triad (IV), and the F major triad (VI).

In the examples on the right, the C major scale and its diatonic triads are used to show how the principle is applied. The note C is already familiar as the root note of a C major triad. It is also the minor third of the sub-mediant A minor triad, and it is the perfect fifth of the sub-dominant F major triad. The examples show each of the seven diatonic notes and indicate in which three triads each note appears. By transferring these principles to theory (using Roman numerals instead of specific pitches), they may be applied to any key and will give you a sound basis for understanding chord harmony.

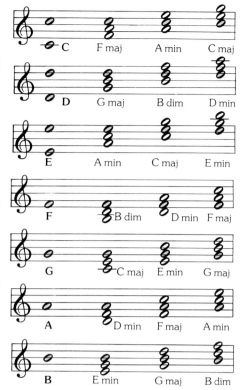

The tonic note (C)
The perfect fifth of the IV chord (F major).
The minor third of the VI chord (A minor).
The root of the I chord (C major).

The supertonic note (D)
The perfect fifth of the V chord (G major).
The minor third of the VII chord (B dim).
The root of the II chord (D minor).

The mediant note (E)
The perfect fifth of the VI chord (A minor).
The major third of the I chord (C major).
The root of the III chord (E minor).

The sub-dominant note (F)
The diminished fifth of the VII chord (B dim).
The minor third of the II chord (D minor).
The root of the IV chord (F major).

The dominant note (G)
The perfect fifth of the I chord (C major).
The minor third of the III chord (E minor).
The root of the V chord (G major).

The sub-mediant note (A)
The perfect fifth of the II chord (D minor).
The major third of the IV chord (F major).
The root of the VI chord (A minor).

The leading note (B)
The perfect fifth of the III chord (E minor).
The major third of the V chord (G major).
The root of the VII chord (B dim).

Choosing chords to create harmony

The principle of common notes shown above means that you can choose any one of three possible chords to use as a harmony for a particular melody note or bass note. If the bass note is C, for example, either C major, F major or A minor can be used as the chord. On p. 121-2, we also saw that it is possible to "invert" triads. Applying this principle gives you another possibility.

The four harmonized scales below show different chord progressions for the same series of bass or root notes – in this case, the notes of the C major scale. Compare them with the triads in their natural root positions – shown in the harmonized scale on p. 123. They demonstrate how the appropriate inversion can be used to treat the same material in a number of different ways.

Harmony using primary triads
By employing inversions, a harmonized scale is constructed using only primary (I, IV and V) triads.

Harmony using primary and secondary triads
The first example shows that further variation is possible by introducing inversions of the II and VI triads. The second example employs both inversions of the I (tonic) and II (supertonic) triads. In the last harmonized scale, inversions of the subtonic triad (B♭) are used to replace the II and IV chords – although, strictly, it is outside the diatonic major scale.

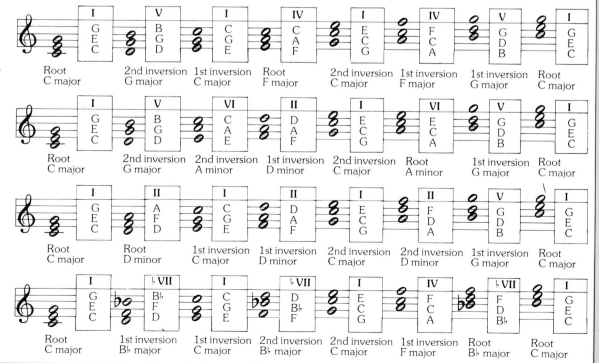

125

Seventh chords

The evolution of triad harmony established the prominent role of the dominant (V) chord. There is a strong resolution when it is followed by the tonic (I) chord. In four-part writing an extra note evolved on top of the dominant triad. Instead of simply doubling the root, the new note was considered to be a continuation of the construction of the triad; another minor third was added on top of the fifth so that the interval between the root note and the new note was a minor seventh. This produced a four-note chord called the dominant seventh, built on the 5th note of the diatonic scale.

As shown below, there are various other types of seventh chord created by adding to the triads built on each note of the scale – in all, there are ten different kinds. However, all seventh chords must consist of a root, a 3rd, a 5th and a 7th. And, when it is in its root position, each seventh chord must comprise three vertical thirds stacked on top of one another, totalling an interval of a seventh between the bottom and top note. The actual tonality of the thirds may be either major or minor. It is this variation that produces the ten different seventh forms.

How seventh chords are built from the diatonic major scale

Adding intervals of a third to each of the triads built on the notes of the major scale produces the following pattern: major seventh, minor seventh, minor seventh, major seventh, dominant seventh, minor seventh, half-diminished seventh.

The term *dominant seventh* came to apply not only to the chord built on the dominant note but to the type of seventh chord that it is. The usual abbreviation for a dominant seventh chord is simply to refer to it as the "seventh". Although the interval between the tonic and the extra note is a minor seventh, the term "minor seventh" is reserved for seventh chords built on a minor triad – for example, the supertonic (II), mediant (III) and sub-mediant (VI) seventh chords. The *triad* determines the name, not the interval between tonic and seventh.

When the extra note is added on top of the tonic (I) triad, it is an interval of a major seventh above the tonic note. Initially referred to as the "tonic seventh", this type of seventh chord is called a *major seventh*. The sub-dominant (IV) seventh chord is also a major seventh type.

The seventh chord built on the leading note of the scale (VII) produces an entirely new type of chord. It is made up of a major third on top of a diminished triad. This produces a minor seventh interval between the tonic note and the new note. The chord is called a *half-diminished seventh* because the triad is diminished but the seventh is not. It also has an alternative name – a "minor seventh diminished fifth".

The harmonized diatonic C major scale

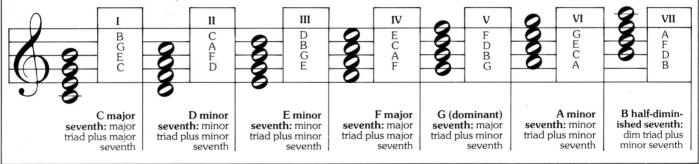

I	II	III	IV	V	VI	VII
B G E C	C A F D	D B G E	E C A F	F D B G	G E C A	A F D B
C major seventh: major triad plus major seventh	**D minor seventh:** minor triad plus minor seventh	**E minor seventh:** minor triad plus minor seventh	**F major seventh:** major triad plus major seventh	**G (dominant) seventh:** major triad plus minor seventh	**A minor seventh:** minor triad plus minor seventh	**B half-diminished seventh:** dim triad plus minor seventh

How seventh chords are built from the diatonic minor scales

Seventh chords built on the relative *natural* minor scale are identical to those derived from the major scale. Only their relative functions within the scale change. However, when the *harmonic* minor scale is used (see p. 107), three new kinds of seventh chord are produced. These are the "minor/major seventh", the "major seventh augmented fifth" and the "diminished seventh". The *minor/major seventh* is built on the 1st note of the scale, the tonic. It is made up of a major third on top of a minor triad – so that the interval from the root note of the chord to the 7th note is a major seventh. The *major seventh augmented fifth*, built on the mediant (III) note of the scale, is a minor third on top of an augmented triad. From bottom to top, the interval is actually an augmented major seventh, but, because this is a potentially confusing name, it is identified as a "major seventh sharp five". The *diminished seventh*, the chord built on the leading note (VII), is a special case. It is explained in more detail on p. 128.

The harmonized harmonic A minor scale

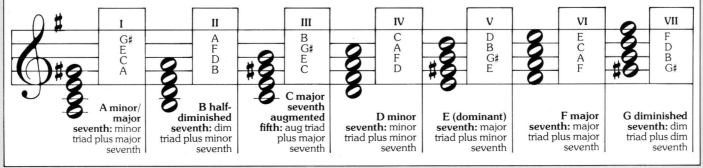

I	II	III	IV	V	VI	VII
G♯ E C A	A F D B	B G♯ E C	C A F D	D B G♯ E	E C A F	F D B G♯
A minor/major seventh: minor triad plus major seventh	**B half-diminished seventh:** dim triad plus minor seventh	**C major seventh augmented fifth:** aug triad plus major seventh	**D minor seventh:** minor triad plus minor seventh	**E (dominant) seventh:** major triad plus minor seventh	**F major seventh:** major triad plus major seventh	**G diminished seventh:** dim triad plus dim seventh

The dominant seventh chords

The three chords included in this family are all derived from major triads plus minor sevenths. They are the *dominant seventh* (usually just called the "seventh"), the *seventh augmented fifth* (or "seventh sharp five"), and the *seventh diminished fifth* (or "seventh flat five"). The dominant seventh is formed by adding a minor seventh on top of a major triad, the seventh augmented fifth is based on an augmented triad, and the seventh diminished fifth on a diminished triad. The fingering shapes below are all "movable" forms; the name of the chord is determined by the tonic or root note. The root note is coloured green.

Seventh chord fingerings
Usually abbreviated from "dominant seventh" to "seventh". Written simply as 7.

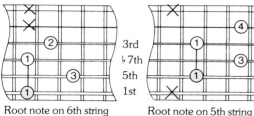
Root note on 6th string

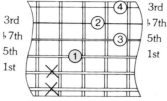
Root note on 5th string

Root note on 4th string

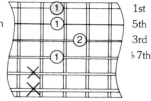
Root note on 1st string

Seventh augmented fifth chord fingerings
Also called "seventh sharp five". Written as 7+5.

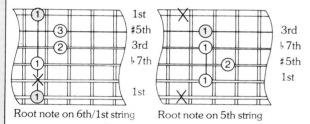
Root note on 6th/1st string

Root note on 5th string

Seventh diminished fifth chord fingerings
Also called "seventh flat five". Written as 7−5.

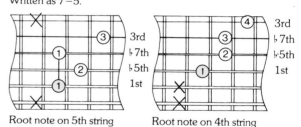
Root note on 5th string

Root note on 4th string

The minor seventh chords

There are also three chords in the minor seventh family. These are the *minor seventh* itself, the *half-diminished seventh* (or "minor seventh diminished fifth"), and the *diminished seventh*. The first two are shown here – with a choice of four different fingerings for each – and the third is dealt with separately on p. 128. The minor seventh is formed by adding a minor seventh interval on top of a minor triad. The half-diminished seventh is built on top of a diminished triad (one in which the 5th note is flattened).

Minor seventh chord fingerings
Written as m7.

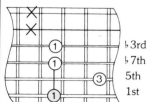
Root note on 6th string

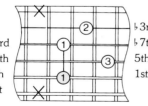
Root note on 5th string

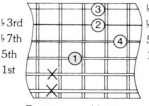
Root note on 4th string

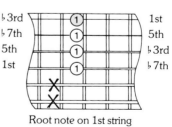
Root note on 1st string

Half-diminished seventh chord fingerings
Also called "minor seventh diminished fifth". Written as m7−5 or ⌀7.

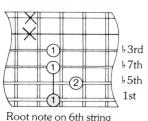
Root note on 6th string

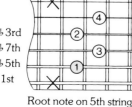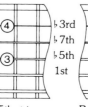
Root note on 5th string

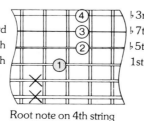
Root note on 4th string

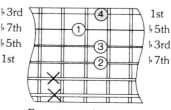
Root note on 1st string

The major seventh chords

The family of major sevenths includes four different chords. These are the *major seventh* itself, the *minor/major seventh*, the *major seventh augmented fifth* (or "major seventh sharp five"), and the *major seventh diminished fifth* (or "major seventh flat five"). These chords differ from those in the other families in that they all have an interval of a major seventh between the lowest and highest notes. Chords in the dominant and minor seventh families (see p. 127) both have an interval of a minor seventh.

The four major seventh chords are shown here in various fingering shapes, with their tonic or root notes on different strings. In most cases, they can be transformed from four-note chords into six-note chords (one note for each string) by "doubling" some of the notes (see p. 123). They can be doubled, inverted and spaced in any manner without affecting the chord.

Major seventh chord fingerings
Written as maj 7 or △ 7.

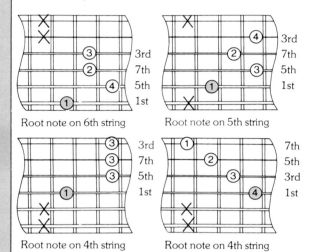

Root note on 6th string

Root note on 5th string

Root note on 4th string

Root note on 4th string

Minor/major seventh chord fingerings
Written as min/maj 7.

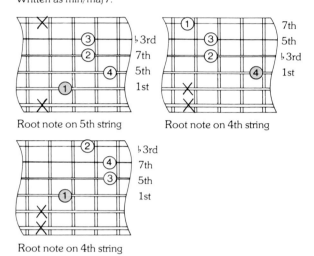

Root note on 5th string

Root note on 4th string

Root note on 4th string

The diminished chord

The seventh chord built on the leading note (VII) of the diatonic scale was considered to be an important musical discovery – the *diminished seventh*. This chord is often abbreviated to the name "diminished".

Because both the 5th in the existing triad and the new, added note are flattened, this seventh chord creates an interval of a diminished seventh to the tonic. The diminished seventh is a double flattened seventh – the enharmonic name for a major sixth (see p. 118). The most unusual feature of the diminished seventh chord is therefore the fact that it is made up of three minor thirds stacked on top of each other. And, when the tonic is doubled at the top, yet another minor third is formed. This means that, in effect, the octave is divided equally into four intervals of a minor third.

If each of the four notes (the root, the 3rd, the 5th and the 7th) is doubled in turn, so that two octaves are spanned, it is clear that any of the notes in the chord can be considered to be the root of a new chord that has exactly the same structure and tonality as the original. When viewed enharmonically, all four chords are, in fact, part of the same chord. In each inversion of the original chord, specific notes can be renamed as either the root, the 3rd, the 5th or the 7th to create the intervals necessary for forming a new diminished seventh chord.

The diminished chord was originally used to extend the properties of "resolution" that were a feature of leading note sevenths. However, it was soon realized that this was only part of its potential. Because it can be any one of four different chords, it occupies four different tonalities. This means that it is interchangeable between four separate keys, and that it represents a unique "gateway" between these keys. The sound of the chord quickly gained in popularity, and the effects it made possible opened up a new world of modulation (see p. 138).

For details of the "diminished scale" – also built on a series of minor third intervals – see p. 112.

The diminished seventh: four chords in one This example is in C and shows four inversions of a C diminished seventh chord. It illustrates the fact that, because the intervals remain the same from one inversion to the next, the notes C, E♭, G♭ and B♭♭ (A) give four diminished chords that are enharmonic equivalents of one another: they all share the same four notes.

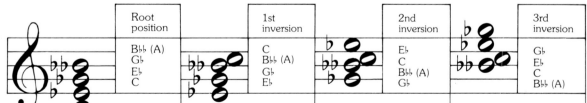

	Root position	1st inversion	2nd inversion	3rd inversion
	B♭♭ (A)	C	E♭	G♭
	G♭	B♭♭ (A)	C	E♭
	E♭	G♭	B♭♭ (A)	C
	C	E♭	G♭	B♭♭ (A)

C diminished
Each note of the chord represents an interval of a minor third. From C to B♭♭ (A) is a diminished seventh.

E♭ diminished
In the 1st inversion, E♭ is the root note. C is a minor third above B♭♭ (A) and still a diminished seventh above E♭, the new root.

G♭ diminished
In the 2nd inversion, G♭ is the root note. E♭ is a minor third above C and still a diminished seventh above G♭.

A diminished
In the 3rd inversion, B♭♭ (A) is the root note. G♭ is a minor third above E♭ and still a diminished seventh above B♭♭ (A).

Major seventh augmented fifth chord fingerings
Also called "major seventh sharp five".
Written as maj 7+5 or △7+5.

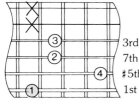

3rd
7th
♯5th
1st

Root note on 6th string

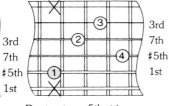

3rd
7th
♯5th
1st

Root note on 5th string

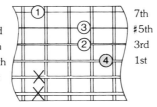

7th
♯5th
3rd
1st

Root note on 4th string

Major seventh diminished fifth chord fingerings
Also called "major seventh flat five".
Written as maj 7−5 or △7−5.

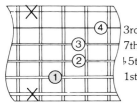

3rd
7th
♭5th
1st

Root note on 5th string

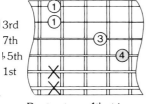

7th
♭5th
3rd
1st

Root note on 4th string

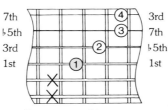

3rd
7th
♭5th
1st

Root note on 4th string

Diminished seventh chord fingerings
Usually abbreviated from "diminished seventh" to just "diminished".
Written as dim 7 or °.

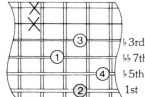

♭3rd
♭♭7th
♭5th
1st

Root note on 6th string

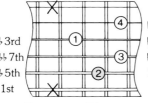

♭3rd
♭♭7th
♭5th
1st

Root note on 5th string

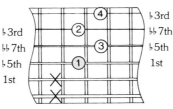

♭3rd
♭♭7th
♭5th
1st

Root note on 4th string

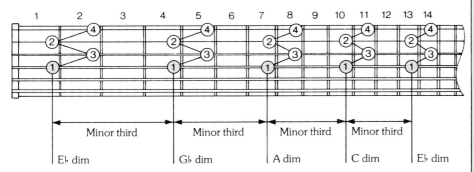

Minor third — E♭ dim
Minor third — G♭ dim
Minor third — A dim
Minor third — C dim
E♭ dim

Locating diminished chords
On the guitar fingerboard, a minor third equals three frets. Therefore, any diminished chord shape can be moved up or down the fingerboard by three frets to give a new chord that is an enharmonic inversion of the original one. Since four different chords share the same four notes, three chords can cover all twelve tones.

1	C dim, E♭ dim, G♭ dim, A dim
2	C♯ dim, E dim, G dim, B♭ dim
3	D dim, F dim, A♭ dim, B dim

A summary of the ten different seventh chords
The chords on the staves below represent all ten different seventh chords in the key of C. The pitch notation is accompanied by the names of the chords, their spellings, and the intervals from which they are built. Fingerings are shown on the previous few pages and in the *Chord Dictionary* (see p. 225-49).

C diminished (seventh)
C dim or C°
Spelling: 1st, ♭3rd, ♭5th, ♭♭7th. Intervals: root, minor third, diminished fifth, diminished seventh.

C half-diminished
C⌀7 or C m7−5
Spelling: 1st, ♭3rd, ♭5th, ♭7th. Intervals: root, minor third, diminished fifth, minor seventh.

C minor seventh
C m7
Spelling: 1st, ♭3rd, 5th, ♭7th. Intervals: root, minor third, perfect fifth, minor seventh.

C seventh diminished fifth C7−5
Spelling: 1st, 3rd, ♭5th, ♭7th. Intervals: root, major third, diminished fifth, minor seventh.

C seventh (dominant)
C7
Spelling: 1st, 3rd, 5th, ♭7th. Intervals: root, major third, perfect fifth, minor seventh.

C seventh augmented fifth C7+5
Spelling: 1st, 3rd, ♯5th, ♭7th. Intervals: root, major third, augmented fifth, minor seventh.

C major seventh
C maj 7 or C△
Spelling: 1st, 3rd, 5th, 7th. Intervals: root, major third, perfect fifth, major seventh.

C minor/major seventh
C min/maj 7 or C m/△7
Spelling: 1st, ♭3rd, 5th, 7th. Intervals: root, minor third, perfect fifth, major seventh.

C major seventh diminished fifth
C maj 7−5 or C△7−5
Spelling: 1st, 3rd, ♭5th, 7th. Intervals: root, major third, diminished fifth, major seventh.

C major seventh augmented fifth
C maj 7+5 or C△7+5
Spelling: 1st, 3rd, ♯5th, 7th. Intervals: root, major third, augmented fifth, major seventh.

Added ninths, suspended fourths, and sixths

We have now seen how four of the notes in the diatonic scale can be combined in various ways to form vertical chords. The 1st, 3rd and 5th notes form triads (see p. 121-5) and the 7th note, when added to the triad, forms seventh chords (see p. 126-9). We will now look at the remaining notes in the scale – the 2nd, 4th and 6th – and see what chords can be created by using them.

The three types of chords produced by using these notes are the "added ninths", the "suspended fourths", and the "sixths". In their root positions, these chords all remain within the span of one octave. They are the chords that we are concerned with here. However, if the notes are stacked in thirds on top of the existing chords, then chords that span more than one octave are created. When this happens, the 2nd, 4th and 6th are called the 9th, 11th and 13th respectively, and the chords are "extended" (see p. 132).

Added ninth chords

When the 2nd note of a scale is added to the major triad built on that scale's tonic note, it produces a chord made up of the 1st, 2nd, 3rd and 5th notes. Normally, it would be called a "second chord", but, to avoid confusion with second inversions and with chords in which the 2nd note actually replaces the 3rd, it is referred to by its ex-tended name – the "ninth" (the 9th note is the same as the 2nd but an octave higher). Because it is not an extended chord, this is made clear by using the prefix "added".

The 2nd note can be added to minor triads as well as to majors. In both cases, added ninths are clear, strong chords – due to the relationship of the I, II and V. In fact, the added ninth is often played without the third note. The minor added ninth features the most dissonant interval of all – the one semi-tone minor second – between the 2nd/9th note and the flattened 3rd. Yet, used creatively, this interval can produce simple chords of startling beauty, especially on the guitar.

How the "added ninth" is formed

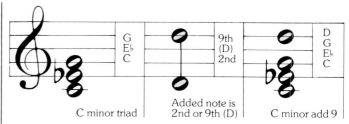

C major triad | Added note is 2nd or 9th (D) | C add 9

How the "minor added ninth" is formed

C minor triad | Added note is 2nd or 9th (D) | C minor add 9

Added ninth chord fingerings
Written as add 9.
Spelling: 1st, 3rd, 5th, 2nd/9th.

Added ninths in C, A and E
Open-string forms

Minor added ninth chords
Written as m add 9 or m/9.
Spelling: 1st, ♭3rd, 5th, 2nd/9th.

Minor added ninths in C, A and E
Open-string forms

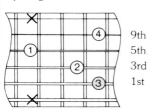

Root note on 5th string

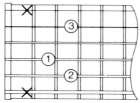

C add 9

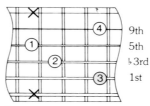

Root note on 5th string

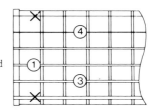

C minor add 9

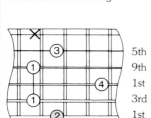

Root note on 6th string

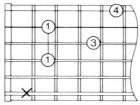

A add 9

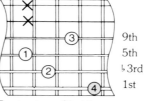

Root note on 6th string

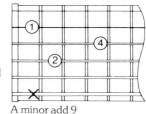

A minor add 9

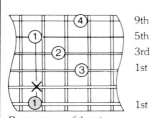

Root note on 6th string

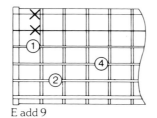

E add 9

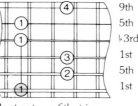

Root note on 6th string

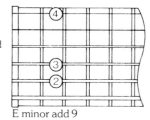

E minor add 9

Suspended fourth chords

When the 4th (sub-dominant) note of the scale is included in the major triad built on the tonic, it replaces the 3rd, and the resulting chord is called a *suspended fourth*. In fact, any chord in which the 3rd note has been replaced by the 4th is called suspended. The tension created by the 4th seeking resolution to the 3rd is clearly audible in the sound of the chord. When the 4th note replaces the 3rd in a dominant seventh chord, the new chord is called a *seventh suspended fourth*.

How the "suspended fourth" is formed

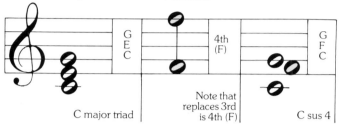

How the "seventh suspended fourth" is formed

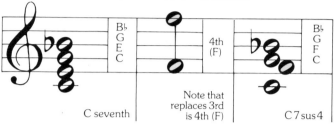

Suspended fourth chord fingerings
Written as sus 4 or abbreviated to sus.
Spelling: 1st, 4th, 5th.

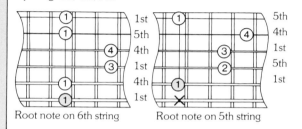

Root note on 6th string   Root note on 5th string

Seventh suspended fourth chord fingerings
Written as 7 sus 4 or 7 + 4.
Spelling: 1st, 4th, 5th, ♭7th.

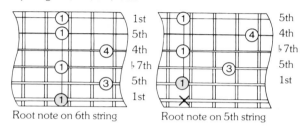

Root note on 6th string   Root note on 5th string

Sixths

When the 6th note of the scale, the sub-mediant, is added to a major triad, the resulting chord is called a *sixth*. When the 6th note is added to a minor triad, it produces a *minor sixth* chord. In both cases, the 6th is an extra note, not a replacement for the 5th. The fingerings below are all movable forms; the notes on the staves show each of the various sixth chords in C.

Sixth chord fingerings
Written as 6.
Spelling: 1st, 3rd, 5th, 6th.

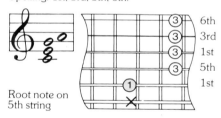

Root note on 5th string

Minor sixth chord fingerings
Written as m6.
Spelling: 1st, ♭3rd, 5th, 6th.

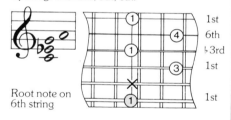

Root note on 6th string

Six nine chord fingerings
Also "major sixth added ninth". Written as 6/9.
Spelling: 1st, 3rd, 5th, 6th, 9th (i.e., 9th added to sixth chord).

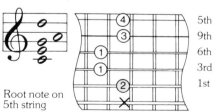

Root note on 5th string

Minor six nine chord fingerings
Also "minor sixth added ninth". Written as m6/9.
Spelling: 1st, ♭3rd, 5th, 6th, 9th (i.e., 9th added to minor sixth chord).

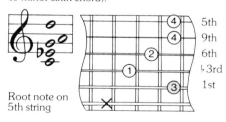

Root note on 5th string

Minor six seven chord fingering
Written as m6/7.
Spelling: 1st, ♭3rd, 5th, 6th, ♭7th (i.e., 6th added to minor seventh chord).

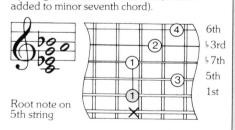

Root note on 5th string

Minor six seven eleven chord fingering
Written as m6/7/11.
Spelling: 1st, ♭3rd, 5th, 6th, ♭7th, 11th/4th (i.e., 11th added to minor 6/7 chord).

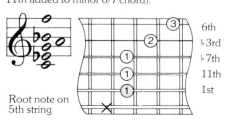

Root note on 5th string

Six seven chord fingering
Written as 6/7.
Spelling: 1st, 3rd, 5th, 6th, ♭7th (i.e., 6th added to seventh chord).

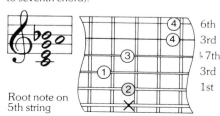

Root note on 5th string

Six seven suspended chord fingerings
Written as 6/7 sus.
Spelling: 1st, 4th, 5th, 6th, ♭7th (i.e., 4th replaces 3rd in 6/7 chord).

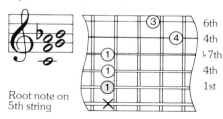

Root note on 5th string

Extended chords

Adding to a triad a note which is theoretically more than an octave above the root produces what is called an *extended chord*. If the 2nd note is inverted an octave above the root and added to a chord, the chord is called a *ninth*. If the 4th note an octave above the root is added, the chord is called an *eleventh*. And, if the 6th note an octave above the root is added, the chord is called a *thirteenth*.

Each extended chord belongs in one of three families – the dominant, major or minor. These are produced by adding the extra note to the four-note dominant seventh, major seventh or minor seventh. The tonality of the third and seventh intervals determines the tonality of the extended chord. When both are minor, the chord belongs to the minor family. When the third is major but the seventh is minor, the chord belongs to the dominant family. And, when both are major, the chord belongs to the major family.

By raising or lowering the 5th or the new, extra note, variations can be derived from the basic chord. These are called *altered chords*. However, it is vital that you learn how the basic chords function before you attempt to use the altered forms.

The three basic ninth chords

These ninths are five-note chords, all constructed by adding an extra note to the four-note seventh chords (see p. 126-9). The new note is actually a 2nd, but because it is added *on top* of the seventh chord, a third above the 7th, it is called a 9th. The 9th, in fact, equals a 2nd plus one octave; in other words, it is the same note but, as you can see below, it is an octave higher.

All three basic ninth chords comprise four intervals of a third stacked on top of one another. They can therefore be seen as two triads, the top one anchored to the upper note of the bottom one. The sound created by varying the five notes in a ninth chord will depend on which notes are omitted or doubled, and on how the notes are spaced (i.e., the chord's "voicing").

How the "ninth" is formed

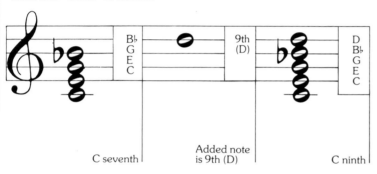

C seventh | Added note is 9th (D) | C ninth

Ninth chord fingerings
Written as 9.
Spelling: 1st, 3rd, 5th, ♭7th, 9th.
This chord differs from the added ninth (see p. 130) in that it contains the minor 7th note.

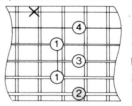

Root note on 6th string
5th, 9th, ♭7th, 3rd, 1st

Root note on 5th string
(5th can be added on 6th or 1st string)
(5th), 9th, ♭7th, 3rd, 1st, (5th)

How the "minor ninth" is formed

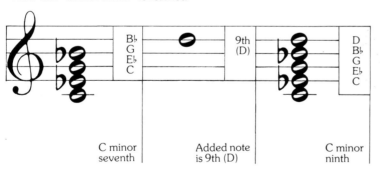

C minor seventh | Added note is 9th (D) | C minor ninth

Minor ninth chord fingerings
Written as m9.
Spelling: 1st, ♭3rd, 5th, ♭7th, 9th.
This chord differs from the minor added ninth (see p. 130) in that it contains the minor 7th note.

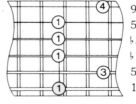

Root note on 6th string
9th, 5th, ♭3rd, ♭7th, 5th, 1st

Root note on 5th string
(5th can be added on 6th or 1st string)
(5th), 9th, ♭7th, ♭3rd, 1st, (5th)

How the "major ninth" is formed

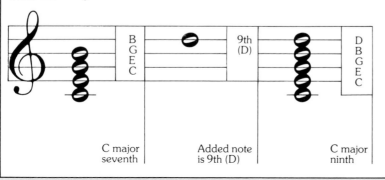

C major seventh | Added note is 9th (D) | C major ninth

Major ninth chord fingerings
Written as maj9 or △9.
Spelling: 1st, 3rd, 5th, 7th, 9th.

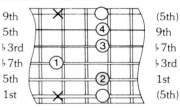

Root note on 6th string
9th, 5th, 3rd, 7th, 1st

Root note on 5th string
(5th can be added on 6th or 1st string)
(5th), 9th, 7th, 3rd, 1st, (5th)

Altered ninth chords

Within the structure of a ninth chord each of the four notes above the root (the 3rd, 5th, 7th and 9th) may be altered: the 3rd note may be either major or minor in relation to the root; the 5th may be diminished, perfect or augmented; the 7th may be diminished, minor or major; and the 9th may be minor, major or augmented. A simple mathematical calculation shows that these permutations can produce 27 different ninth chords. Many of these, however, are misspellings or "synonyms" (see p. 137) of other chords. Excluding the three basic chords on the opposite page, this leaves twelve altered ninth chords.

These chords can be grouped into the three families of dominants, minors and majors. The dominant family offers the greatest number of altered ninths. Eight are shown below. They can be divided into those that feature only one altered note (the 5th *or* the 9th) and those that feature two altered notes (the 5th *and* the 9th).

We have seen on p. 118 that, when the 5th note is altered, it becomes diminished if lowered by a semi-tone and augmented if raised by a semi-tone. In a chord, a diminished fifth is indicated by a minus (or a flat) sign before the five. The term "diminished" should be used only if it applies to the whole chord. An augmented fifth is indicated by a plus (or a sharp) sign before the five. A dominant ninth chord with an altered 5th note is therefore either 9−5 or 9+5.

When the 9th note is altered, the chord is named according to the four-note seventh chord that forms its foundation. The altered ninth is written after this as either −9 or +9. The term "minor ninth" and "major ninth" are generally reserved for ninth chords built on minor sevenths and major sevenths.

The 6th note of a scale can also be included in these ninth chords. However, if the 6th replaces the 7th, the chord is called a "six nine" chord (see p. 131) and, if the 6th, 7th and 9th are all present, the chord is called a thirteenth (see p. 135).

The chord fingerings shown below illustrate only one of the many possible positions and voicings for each chord. The notes on the staves show the chords in C. They illustrate the construction of each chord and not the spacing of the notes and intervals in the fingerings.

Seventh flat nine chord fingering
Written as 7−9.
Spelling: 1st, 3rd, 5th, ♭7th, ♭9th.

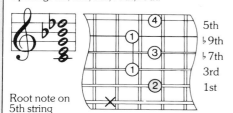

Root note on 5th string

5th
♭9th
♭7th
3rd
1st

Seventh augmented ninth chord fingering
Written as 7+9.
Spelling: 1st, 3rd, 5th, ♭7th, ♯9th.

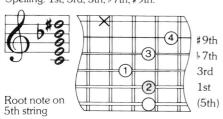

Root note on 5th string

♯9th
♭7th
3rd
1st
(5th)

Seventh augmented ninth diminished fifth chord fingering Written as 7+9−5.
Spelling: 1st, 3rd, ♭5th, ♭7th, ♯9th.

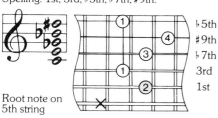

Root note on 5th string

♭5th
♯9th
♭7th
3rd
1st

Minor ninth diminished fifth chord fingering Written as m9−5.
Spelling: 1st, ♭3rd, ♭5th, ♭7th, 9th.

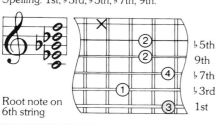

Root note on 6th string

♭5th
9th
♭7th
♭3rd
1st

Ninth diminished fifth chord fingering
Written as 9−5.
Spelling: 1st, 3rd, ♭5th, ♭7th, 9th.

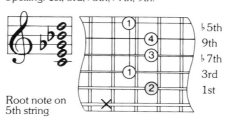

Root note on 5th string

♭5th
9th
♭7th
3rd
1st

Seventh flat nine diminished fifth chord fingering Written as 7−9−5.
Spelling: 1st, 3rd, ♭5th, ♭7th, ♭9th.

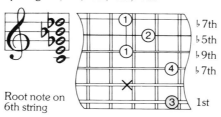

Root note on 6th string

♭7th
♭5th
♭9th
♭7th
1st

Seventh augmented ninth augmented fifth chord fingering Written as 7+9+5.
Spelling: 1st, 3rd, ♯5th, ♭7th, ♯9th.

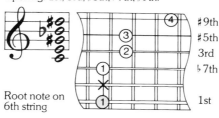

Root note on 6th string

♯9th
♯5th
3rd
♭7th
1st

Minor/major ninth chord fingering
Written as min/maj9 or m/△9.
Spelling: 1st, ♭3rd, 5th, 7th, 9th.

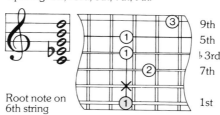

Root note on 6th string

9th
5th
♭3rd
7th
1st

Ninth augmented fifth chord fingering
Written as 9+5.
Spelling: 1st, 3rd, ♯5th, ♭7th, 9th.

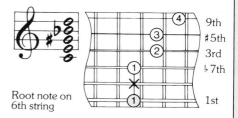

Root note on 6th string

9th
♯5th
3rd
♭7th
1st

Seventh flat nine augmented fifth chord fingering Written as 7−9+5.
Spelling: 1st, 3rd, ♯5th, ♭7th, ♭9th.

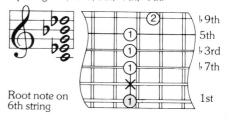

Root note on 6th string

♭9th
♯5th
3rd
♭7th
1st

Minor seventh flat nine chord fingering
Written as m7−9.
Spelling: 1st, ♭3rd, 5th, ♭7th, ♭9th.

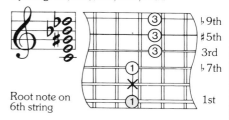

Root note on 6th string

♭9th
5th
♭3rd
♭7th
1st

Major ninth augmented fifth chord fingering Written as maj9+5 or △9+5.
Spelling: 1st, 3rd, ♯5th, 7th, 9th.

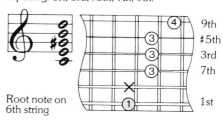

Root note on 6th string

9th
♯5th
3rd
7th
1st

Eleventh chords

When the 4th note of the diatonic scale is added to a ninth chord, an eleventh chord is created. It is called an eleventh because the 4th note is added *on top* of the original chord so that its distance from the root is an octave plus a fourth – an eleventh. It is placed a third above the 9th note.

If the 4th note is added lower down in the chord, it replaces the 3rd in the basic triad and produces a "suspended" chord (see p. 131). These are not the same as elevenths; elevenths include the 3rd note.

Elevenths are six-note chords. They can be seen as comprising two triads either a major or minor third apart. When played with all six notes, the sound is thick and definite, and requires careful handling in context. Often, the six notes are used as a basic structure from which only certain notes are selected. The sounds these chords produce give the effect of moving voices and harmonies over a pedal bass or against a moving bass line. Because each note contributes a part of the chord's sound, omitting it – or doubling it – will affect that part of the sound. Generally, leaving out the 5th removes the dissonance it creates against the 11th and sweetens the sound. The 9th is the note most often omitted.

How "elevenths" are formed

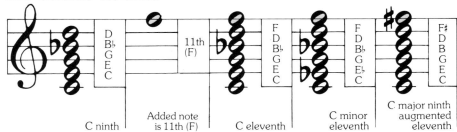

C ninth | Added note is 11th (F) | C eleventh | C minor eleventh | C major ninth augmented eleventh

The dominant eleventh chord family

Eleventh chord fingerings
Written as 11.
Spelling: 1st, 3rd, 5th, ♭7th, 9th, 11th.

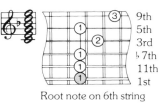

Root note on 6th string — 9th, 5th, 3rd, ♭7th, 11th, 1st

Root note on 6th string — 9th, 5th, 11th, ♭7th, 5th, 1st

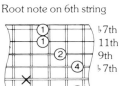

Root note on 6th string — ♭7th, 11th, 9th, ♭7th, 1st

Root note on 5th string — 5th, 9th, ♭7th, 11th, 1st

Seven eleven chord fingerings
Written as 7/11.
Spelling: 1st, 3rd, 5th, ♭7th, 11th.
This is a dominant seventh chord with an added 11th, but no 9th.

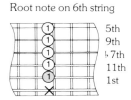

Root note on 6th string — 1st, 5th, 3rd, ♭7th, 11th, 1st

Root note on 5th string — 5th, 3rd, ♭7th, 11th, 1st

Eleventh diminished ninth chord fingering
Written as 11−9 or 11♭9.
Spelling: 1st, 3rd, 5th, ♭7th, ♭9th, 11th.
Differs from the dominant eleventh in that the 9th is flattened.

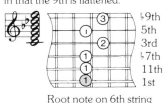

Root note on 6th string — ♭9th, 5th, 3rd, ♭7th, 11th, 1st

Seventh augmented eleventh chord fingering
Written as 7+11.
Spelling: 1st, 3rd, 5th, ♭7th, 9th, ♯11th.
Differs from dominant eleventh in that the 11th is sharpened.

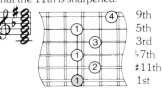

Root note on 6th string — 9th, 5th, 3rd, ♭7th, ♯11th, 1st

The minor eleventh chord family

Minor eleventh chord fingerings
Written as m 11.
Spelling: 1st, ♭3rd, 5th, ♭7th, 9th, 11th.

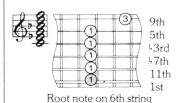

Root note on 6th string — 9th, 5th, ♭3rd, ♭7th, 11th, 1st

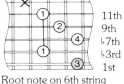

Root note on 6th string — 11th, 9th, ♭7th, ♭3rd, 1st

Minor seven eleven chord fingerings
Written as m 7/11.
Spelling: 1st, ♭3rd, 5th, ♭7th, 11th.
This is a minor seventh chord with an added 11th, but no 9th.

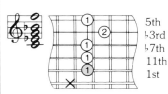

Root note on 5th string — 5th, ♭3rd, ♭7th, 11th, 1st

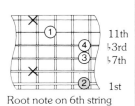

Root note on 6th string — 11th, ♭3rd, ♭7th, 1st

The major eleventh chord family

Major ninth augmented eleventh chord fingering
Written as maj 9+11 or △9+11.
Spelling: 1st, 3rd, 5th, 7th, 9th, ♯11th.

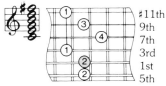

Root note on 5th string — ♯11th, 9th, 7th, 3rd, 1st, 5th

Major seventh augmented eleventh chord fingering
Written as maj 7+11 or △7+11.
Spelling: 1st, 3rd, 5th, 7th, ♯11th.
The thumb can play root note on 6th string.

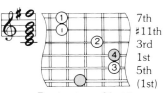

Root note on 6th string — 7th, ♯11th, 3rd, 1st, 5th, (1st)

Added augmented eleventh chord fingering
Written as add +11.
Spelling: 1st, 3rd, 5th, ♯11th.
The thumb can play root note on 6th string. The chord contains no 7th or 9th.

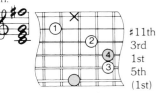

Root note on 6th string — ♯11th, 3rd, 1st, 5th, (1st)

Thirteenth chords

The 13th note is the 6th plus an octave. However, adding the 13th to a chord is not the same as adding a 6th. A sixth chord remains within the span of one octave (see p. 131), whereas a thirteenth chord extends beyond it. Thirteenths are built by enlarging the root position chord by a third. This means stacking the 13th note *on top*, a third above the 11th. Thirteenths are therefore seven-note chords.

Obviously, guitarists are restricted to six-note chords – one note per string. So, you will have to omit at least one note when playing thirteenth chords. In general, the most frequently omitted notes in thirteenth chords are the 9th or the 11th.

The number of possible variations on both eleventh and thirteenth chords is an interesting but somewhat daunting study. In fact, omitting, adding to or altering the notes in large chords of this kind eventually results in a version of a simpler chord with a less complicated name. The forms shown here are included to familiarize you with some of the sounds in common use.

How "thirteenths" are formed

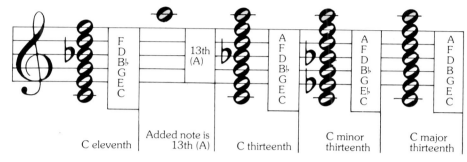

C eleventh | Added note is 13th (A) | C thirteenth | C minor thirteenth | C major thirteenth

The dominant thirteenth chord family

Thirteenth chord fingerings
Written as 13.
Spelling: 1st, 3rd, 5th, ♭7th, 9th, 11th (optional), 13th.

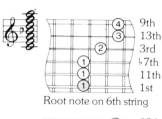

Root note on 6th string — 9th, 13th, 3rd, ♭7th, 11th, 1st

Root note on 6th string — 13th, 3rd, 9th, ♭7th, 1st

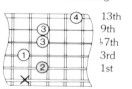

Root note on 5th string — 13th, 9th, ♭7th, 3rd, 1st

Root note on 5th string — 13th, 9th, ♭7th, 5th, 1st

Thirteenth diminished ninth chord fingering
Written as 13−9.
Spelling: 1st, 3rd, 5th, ♭7th, ♭9th, 11th, 13th. Differs from dominant thirteenth in that the 9th is flattened.

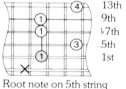

Root note on 6th string — ♭9th, 13th, 3rd, ♭7th, 11th, 1st

Thirteenth suspended chord fingering
Written as 13 sus.
Spelling: 1st, 4th, 5th, ♭7th, 9th, 13th. The 4th (same as 11th) replaces the 3rd.

Root note on 5th string — 13th, 9th, ♭7th, 4th, 1st, (5th)

Thirteenth augmented ninth chord fingering
Written as 13+9.
Spelling: 1st, 3rd, 5th, ♭7th, ♯9th, 11th, 13th. Differs from dominant thirteenth in that the 9th is sharp.

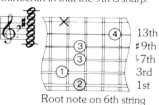

Root note on 6th string — 13th, ♯9th, ♭7th, 3rd, 1st

Thirteenth augmented eleventh chord fingering
Written as 13+11.
Spelling: 1st, 3rd, 5th, ♭7th, 9th, ♯11th, 13th. Differs from dominant thirteenth in that the 11th is sharp.

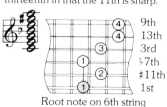

Root note on 6th string — 9th, 13th, 3rd, ♭7th, ♯11th, 1st

The minor thirteenth chord family

Minor thirteenth chord fingerings
Written as m 13.
Spelling: 1st, ♭3rd, 5th, ♭7th, 9th, 11th (optional), 13th.
These shapes contain no 11th.

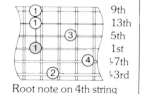

Root note on 6th string — 9th, 13th, ♭3rd, ♭7th, 1st

Root note on 4th string — 9th, 13th, 5th, 1st, ♭7th, ♭3rd

Minor thirteen eleven chord fingering
Written as m 13/11.
Spelling: 1st, ♭3rd, 5th, 9th (optional), 11th, 13th. No ♭7th.

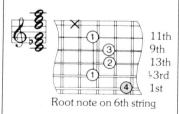

Root note on 6th string — 11th, 9th, 13th, ♭3rd, 1st

The major thirteenth chord family

Major thirteenth chord fingerings
Written as maj 13 or △13.
Spelling: 1st, 3rd, 5th, 7th, 9th, 11th (optional), 13th. These shapes contain no 11th.

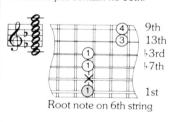

Root note on 6th string — 7th, 5th, 9th, 13th, 3rd, 1st

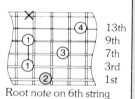

Root note on 6th string — 13th, 9th, 7th, 3rd, 1st

Root note on 5th string — 13th, 9th, 7th, 5th, 1st

Polychords

A *polychord* is defined as two chords sounding together. Polychords are also sometimes known as "polytonal" chords. A true polychord must contain at least the basic elements of its two constituent chords. Many of the extended chords that we have already described can, in fact, be considered as polychords. Take, as an example, C major ninth (see p. 132). If you look at the notes it contains – the 1st (C), 3rd (E), 5th (G), 7th (B) and 9th (D) – you will see that these actually represent a C major triad (C, E and G) and a G major triad (G, B and D). Playing the two triads together produces the effect of *one* chord and gives the C major ninth sound.

In contemporary usage, polychords can take many forms. One of the most common involves playing a chord over a different bass note – one that is not its normal root. Chords of this kind can be considered "bi-tonal" and can best be thought of as chords with *altered* bass notes. They are indicated using two symbols separated by an oblique stroke. The first (or top) symbol represents the chord, and the second (or bottom) symbol represents the bass note. So, D/C, for example, means you should play a D major chord with a C note in the bass.

Although these are not true polychords in the strict sense (because only the root note has changed), they are widely used. They provide a way of simplifying complicated information and of specifying the notes that are to be included or omitted.

All the chords shown on this page are formed by playing a simple triad over an altered bass note – that is, over a bass note that is neither part of the triad nor the note from which the triad is normally built (see p. 121-4). They produce a strong, clean sound in which both tonalities, the bass and the chord, can be clearly heard.

Polychords of this kind can all be analyzed and written out as extended or altered chords which have the bass note as their root. But there is an important distinction. The polychord does not contain *all* the notes included in the full extended or altered chord. The notes most often omitted from the extended chord are the 3rd and 5th.

Take C major ninth as an example again. If you leave out the 3rd (E) so that you are playing a G major triad over a C bass note, this can be indicated as the polychord symbol G/C. It is easier and more efficient than writing C maj 9 (no 3rd).

To take another, similar example, it is much simpler to write D/C than C 6/9/#11 (no 3rd or 5th) when you want to indicate that a D major triad should be played over the top of a C bass note.

If you are playing rhythm guitar and you come up against one of these polychord symbols, you immediately have two options. The obvious one is simply to play the top triad together with the altered bass note. But, if the bass note is being sounded clearly by either the bassist or the keyboard player, you need play only the top triad. However, you must take care to play an appropriate inversion, without altering or extending the chord.

The use of this type of polychord is on the increase in popular music. To familiarize yourself with their sound, try playing different triads over a common bass note – using an open bass string and sounding the triads on the higher strings.

Altered bass note chords

The polychords shown below are all major triads with an altered bass note. The two most commonly used are probably D/C and G/C. Although the bass note is always a C in the examples here, it can in fact be any note. Turn to the triad fingerings shown on p. 121-2 and experiment with adding altered bass notes to them.

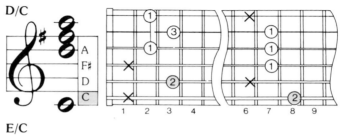

D major over C bass note If you look at this as a C chord, instead of a D chord, then D is the 9th, F# is the ♭5th or #11th, and A is the 6th. D/C is therefore C 6/9/♭5 with no 3rd, or C 6/9/#11 no 3rd or 5th.

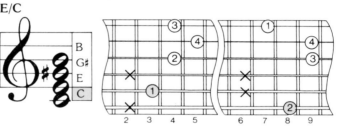

E major over C bass note If you look at this as a C chord, instead of an E chord, then E is the 3rd, C# is the #5th, and B is the 7th. E/C is therefore the same as C maj 7 +5.

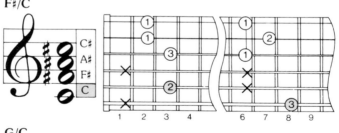

F# major over C bass note If you look at this as a C chord, instead of an F# chord, the F# is the ♭5th or #11th, A# is the ♭7th, and C# is the ♭9th. F#/C is therefore C 7−5−9 with no 3rd.

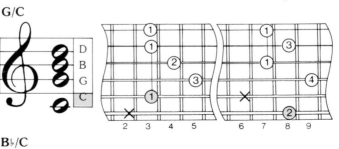

G major over C bass note If you look at this as a C chord, instead of a G chord, then G is the 5th, B is the 7th, and D is the 9th. G/C is therefore C maj 9 with no 3rd.

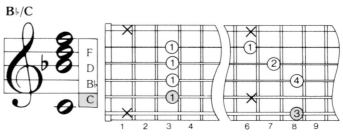

B♭ major over C bass note If you look at this as a C chord, instead of a B♭ chord, then B♭ is the ♭7th, D is the 9th, and F is the 4th or 11th. B♭/C is therefore C 11 with no 3rd or 5th.

Chord synonyms

Unlike keyboard players, guitarists are limited to playing a maximum of six notes at once, and – for chord work – a minimum of three. This means that you must choose carefully which notes you play and which you omit in any given chord progression. You must also consider how what you choose to play will complement the harmonic statements of the other instruments in a band. This ability is one of the principal skills of the harmonic guitarist.

The first step is obviously a solid understanding of how extended chords are constructed and how they can be altered. As soon as you begin to explore this area, you will see that the upper notes of extended chords often form separate chords with different names (although the notes may have to be inverted and re-arranged to make this clear). These are called *synonyms*. And synonyms are two or more chords made up of the same notes but with different names.

Let's take Am7 as a simple example. It is made up of the 1st (A), ♭3rd (C), 5th (E) and ♭7th (G). If you leave out the root note, then a C major triad remains. So, Am7 with no root and C major are chord synonyms. In practice, both chords are therefore interchangeable and either can be used as long as the bassist or keyboard player is clearly stating the bass note of A. This demonstrates that, if you understand the components of a chord, you will have more than one choice of harmony when playing in a band with other musicians. Due to the inherent limitations of the fingerboard, it is essential that you also understand the relationship between chords that have common or shared notes (see p. 125).

It is inevitable that, with only twelve notes to work with, there is a limit to the number of chords that can be formed without repetition, and also that all larger chords are composed of smaller ones. Because of the relationship between inverted intervals and chord construction, there are many ways in which the principles of chord synonyms can be applied. A few examples are given here to show how they work. But bear in mind that principles are useless without the ear to apply them. Unravelling the mysteries of related harmony can take years. However, once you understand even the most basic of these principles, you will find your existing chord vocabulary greatly expanded. A knowledge of chord synonyms and how they work also forms one of the necesssary skills required for chord substitution (see p. 150).

Examples of chord synonyms

Added ninths and suspended fourths
Omitting the 3rd from Cadd9 produces a three-note chord called C2 (C second). If the C is inverted so that G is the root, these three notes form a Gsus4 chord. (See p. 130-31 for these chords.)
Rule *Any add9 chord with no 3rd is the same as a sus4 chord whose root is a fifth higher.*

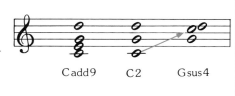

Cadd9   C2   Gsus4

Added ninth suspended fourths and seventh suspended fourths
This example is a variation on the one above. The 4th takes the place of the 3rd in the add9sus4 chord.
Rule *Any add9sus4 chord is the same as a 7sus4 chord whose root is a fifth higher.*

Cadd9   Cadd9   G7sus4
                sus4

Six nine chords and seventh suspended fouths
Omitting the 3rd from C6/9 and inverting the 9th (D) produces D7sus4. Omitting the root from C6/9 and using the 6th (A) as a new root produces A7sus4. (See p. 131 for these chords.)
Rule *Any 6/9 chord with no 3rd is the same as a 7sus4 chord whose root is one tone higher.*
Rule *Any 6/9 chord with no root is the same as a 7sus4 chord whose root is three semi-tones lower.*

C6/9   C6/9 (no 3rd)   D7sus4

C6/9   C6/9   A7sus4
            (no root)

Minor ninths and major sevenths
Omitting the root note from Cm9 produces E♭ major 7. No inversion is necessary. (See p. 128 and p. 132 for these chords.)
Rule *Any minor 9 chord with no root is the same as a major 7 chord whose root is three semi-tones higher.*

Cm9   Cm9   E♭maj7
            (no root)

Minor sevenths and sixths
Inverting the upper three notes of an Am7 chord produces a C6 chord. (See p. 127 and p. 131 for these chords.)
Rule *Any minor 7 chord is the same as a 6 chord whose root is three semi-tones higher.*

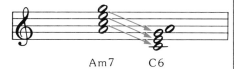

Am7   C6

Ninths and half-diminished chords
Omitting the root note from C9 leaves a four-note half-diminished chord with E♭ as its root. (See p. 127 and p. 132 for these chords.)
Rule *Any 9 chord with no root is the same as a half-diminished chord whose root is three semi-tones higher.*

C9   C9   E
          (no root)   half-dim

Seventh flat nines and diminished chords
Omitting the root note from C7−9 leaves a four-note diminished chord named according to any of its four notes – E dim, G dim, B♭ dim or D♭ dim. (See p. 128 and p. 133 for these chords.)
Rule *Any 7−9 chord with no root is the same as a diminished chord rooted on any of the remaining four notes.*

C7−9   C7−9   E dim
            (no root)

Ninth diminished fifths and seventh augmented fifths
Omitting the root note from C9−5 and inverting the 3rd (E) to its enharmonic equivalent (F♭) produces G♭7+5. (See p. 127 and p. 133 for these chords.)
Rule *Any 9−5 chord with no root is the same as a 7+5 chord whose root is a diminished fifth higher.*

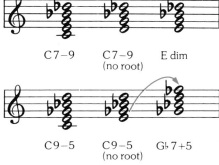

C9−5   C9−5   G♭7+5
            (no root)

Ninth diminished fifths and ninth augmented fifths
Inverting the various notes in C9−5 and using the 9th (D) as a new root produces D9+5. (See p. 133 for these chords.)
Rule *Any 9−5 chord is the same as a 9+5 chord whose root is one tone higher.*

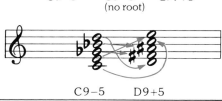

C9−5   D9+5

Modulation

Modulation can be defined as changing from one key to another in the middle of a piece of music. There are a number of rules and conventions designed to make the key change as smooth as possible.

Every major key is related to a minor key. The relative minor scale begins on the 6th note of the major scale, and the two scales share the same notes. They also share the same key signature (*see* p. 108-9). For this reason, the following explanation of modulation need deal only with major keys.

As the circle of fifths demonstrates (*see* p. 109), every major key is closely related to two other major keys. Only one note in their scales differs each time. These two other keys begin on the sub-dominant (4th) and dominant (5th) notes of the original key. Take the key of C major as an example: the two keys closest to it are F major and G major. F is the 4th note in the scale of C major, and G is the 5th. Only one note in the scale of F major differs from that of C major – Bb. And only one note in the scale of G major differs – F#.

Moreover, comparing the three major scales of C, F and G reveals that the primary intervals (I, IV and V) of all three keys are related by common notes. The note C is the root in C major, the sub-dominant (4th) in G major, and the dominant (5th) in F major. The note F is the root in F major and the sub-dominant (4th) in C major. The note G is the root in G major and the dominant (5th) in C major. This pattern is repeated throughout the twelve keys, and these primary relationships allow a smooth, natural modulation.

The primary modulation chart and how to use it

The vertical block of the three chords shown on the right represents the primary interval "link" that connects the key signatures. The primary intervals are the I, IV and V. They are colour-coded to indicate which note is which interval in every key. The rule when modulating from one key to another using primary interval links is: one horizontal step, then one vertical step. The chord in the vertical column is the "pivot" chord that allows the modulation.

		IV	Sub-dominant
I	Root or tonic
V	Dominant

Key	Signature													
Key of C#	7 sharps	A#	B#	C#	D#	E#	F#	G#	A#	B#	C#	D#	E#	F#
Key of F#	6 sharps	A#	B	C#	D#	E#	F#	G#	A#	B	C#	D#	E#	F#
Key of B	5 sharps	A#	B	C#	D#	E	F#	G#	A#	B	C#	D#	E	F#
Key of E	4 sharps	A	B	C#	D#	E	F#	G#	A	B	C#	D#	E	F#
Key of A	3 sharps	A	B	C#	D	E	F#	G#	A	B	C#	D	E	F#
Key of D	2 sharps	A	B	C#	D	E	F#	G	A	B	C#	D	E	F#
Key of G	1 sharp	A	B	C	D	E	F#	G	A	B	C	D	E	F#
Key of C		A	B	C	D	E	F	G	A	B	C	D	E	F
Key of F	1 flat	A	Bb	C	D	E	F	G	A	Bb	C	D	E	F
Key of Bb	2 flats	A	Bb	C	D	Eb	F	G	A	Bb	C	D	Eb	F
Key of Eb	3 flats	Ab	Bb	C	D	Eb	F	G	Ab	Bb	C	D	Eb	F
Key of Ab	4 flats	Ab	Bb	C	Db	Eb	F	G	Ab	Bb	C	Db	Eb	F
Key of Db	5 flats	Ab	Bb	C	Db	Eb	F	Gb	Ab	Bb	C	Db	Eb	F
Key of Gb	6 flats	Ab	Bb	Cb	Db	Eb	F	Gb	Ab	Bb	Cb	Db	Eb	F
Key of Cb	7 flats	Ab	Bb	Cb	Db	Eb	Fb	Gb	Ab	Bb	Cb	Db	Eb	Fb

Dominant direction (upward) / *Sub-dominant direction* (downward)

Modulation using primary chords

The chart on the opposite page illustrates how the primary intervals – the root or tonic (I), the sub-dominant (IV) and the dominant (V) – can be used to modulate between different keys. The relationships between the keys are those of the "circle of fifths" (see p. 109). Modulation based on these principles can work in two ways: it can either move in the dominant direction (up the chart) or in the sub-dominant direction (down the chart).

In the dominant direction, the dominant (V) of the old key becomes the root (I) of the new key. In the sub-dominant direction, the sub-dominant (IV) of the old key becomes the root (I) of the new key.

In the chart, each of the primary intervals appears in a different colour. For example, in the key of C, C itself (I) is coloured dark green, F (IV) is coloured light green, and G (V) is coloured grey. You will see that these three intervals occur throughout the chart in vertical columns. The root (I) is in the centre, the sub-dominant (IV) is above it, and the dominant (V) is below it. This demonstrates that the note C, for example, is the sub-dominant (IV) in the key of G major, the root (I) in the key of C major, and the dominant (V) in the key of F major. The vertical columns are therefore "pivots" which allow you to modulate directly from the key you are in to one of two others.

Take a simple example. Say you want to modulate from the key of C major to the key of G major. You might choose to do it one of two ways. You could change straight from C to G, since the vertical columns show that G is both the dominant (V) in the key of C and the root (I) in the key of C and the sub-dominant (IV) in the key of G. Alternatively, you could change from C to D to G. The vertical columns show that C is both the root (I) in the key of C and the sub-dominant (IV) in the key of G. Treating it as the latter, and then changing to the D, the dominant (V) in the key of G, introduces the F♯, heard for the first time. This chord then resolves to G.

If you want to modulate from C to F, the same principles apply, but you move in the opposite (sub-dominant) direction. You can therefore change straight from C to F, or you can go from C to B♭ (the pivot) to F.

Now take an example in which you want to modulate from your original key to one that is further away – say, from C to E. You can still use the primary intervals as your "pivot" chords and you can still follow the links indicated on the modulation chart. You might choose to do it like this: start at C and go horizontally to G; G takes you up one line; go horizontally to D; D takes you up one line; go horizontally to A; A takes you up one line; go horizontally to E (V in the key of A); E takes you up one line; go horizontally to B seventh (V in the key of E); go horizontally and resolve to E. The chord sequence is therefore C to G to D to A to E to B7 to E. You are, in effect, using primary intervals to travel round the circle of fifths in the dominant direction.

Travelling the opposite way uses the same principles. To modulate from C to A♭, for example, you might choose to go from C to F to B♭ to E♭ to A♭ to D♭ to A♭.

In other words, a modulating sequence may go through several key-centres before arriving at the new key. The keys passed en route are considered transitional.

Modulation using secondary chords

In the chart opposite, the secondary chords are the ones left white. They are based on the II, III, VI and VII intervals. These, too, can act as "pivot" chords when modulating from one key to another.

Take as an example a modulation from C major to G major. The difference between the two keys is that G major contains an F♯ instead of an F. Of the chords built on the notes of the C major scale, three contain the note F. These are D minor, F major and B diminished. When the F changes to F♯ in the key of G major, these chords change to D major, F♯ diminished and B minor. Any of these three chords can be used as the pivot chord in a modulation from C major to G major. This might produce any of the following chord sequences:
● C to D7 to G, or
● C to F♯dim to D7 to G, or
● C to Bm to D7 to G.
There is a principle here which applies to any modulation in the dominant direction. The II minor in the original key changes to major, and becomes the V chord in the new key; the IV major is sharpened by a semitone to produce a diminished chord based on the tritone, and becomes the VII chord in the new key; the VII diminished in the original key changes to minor, and becomes the III chord in the new key. The presence of the F♯ in these altered chords prepares the ear for the modulation to G major.

A similar principle operates for modulations in a sub-dominant direction. Take as an example a modulation from C major to F major. In this case, the difference between the two keys is that F major contains a B♭ instead of a B. This B♭ also affects three of the chords built on the notes of the C major scale – the three that contain the note B. When the B♭ is substituted, the result is that E minor changes to E diminished, G major changes to G minor, and B diminished changes to B♭ major. Again, any of these three altered chords can be introduced into a C major chord progression to act as a pivot for a modulation to F major. This might produce any of the following sequences:
● C to B♭ to C7 to F, or
● C to E dim to C7 to F, or
● C to Gm to C7 to F.
The pivot chord, in each case, precedes the dominant seventh of the new key – which then resolves to the new root or tonic.

Again, there is a principle at work which can be applied to other modulations in the sub-dominant direction. The III minor in the original key changes to diminished, and becomes the VII chord in the new key; the V major in the original key changes to minor, and becomes the II chord in the new key; the VII diminished is flattened by a semitone to produce a major chord, and becomes the IV chord in the new key. If any of these three altered chords are used in the key of C major, the presence of the B♭ can suggest a sense of motion which makes for a smooth, natural modulation to F major.

In either direction, the three altered chords may resolve directly into a progression based in the new key, or they may continue the modulation to a more remote key. In closely related keys, most chords remain unaltered – but their positions and functions in the scale change.

The study of modulation is complex. The explanations given here represent only some of the ways in which it is possible. The rules of modulation are governed not only by primary and secondary interval relationships, but also by the way in which individual notes in the chords move. Diminished (or diminished seventh) chords are particularly useful in this respect, since they can occupy four key-centres at once (see p. 128). Shown below are some other examples of modulations – all of which can be transposed to any key.
Key of C major to the key of F♯ major:
● C to Am to C♯7 to F♯, or
● C to Dm to C♯7 to F♯, or
● C to Bm to C♯7 to F♯.
Key of C major to E major:
● C to Em to B7 to E, or
● C to Am to B7 to E, or
● C to Dm to B7 to E.
Key of C major to A major:
● C to C♯dim to E dim to E to E7 to A, or
● C to C dim to E♭ dim to E7 to A, or
● C to D dim to F dim to A, or
● C to B dim to E7 to A.

IMPROVISATION

True improvisation consists of playing spontaneous variations on a musical theme. These variations are created actually during a performance. In this sense, improvisation provides a musician with an unequalled opportunity for personal expression. In contrast, unimprovised music is simply adhering note-for-note to a previously written or rehearsed arrangement.

There are essentially two ways of approaching an improvised solo: either you can start by playing the previously established melody and then go on to embellish it by altering the actual notes and the phrasing, or you can quite literally start from scratch with simply a feel or awareness of what is expected by the other musicians and by the audience.

"The only planning I do is about a minute before I play. I desperately try to think of something that will be effective, but I never sit down and work it out note for note."
Eric Clapton

"Improvisation" is a term with a wide usage: it can apply either to a player who is fluent, imaginative and truly creative, or to one who relies on a battery of standard licks that are rehearsed, memorized and then linked together. To some extent, most guitarists are a bit of both.

Playing a solo to fill a set number of bars somewhere in the middle of a song is not the same as just improvising endlessly until you are finished. In a set-piece, you would be more likely to look to the existing melody for

Jeff Beck

inspiration, and you would usually have some sort of structure to ensure that the right effect is created and that you can get out of the solo at the right place. In an extended "jam", there are few restrictions other than your own continual ability to think of fresh ideas to play. Opinions vary about which kind of solo is most valid.

"I've got no particular desire to play ten-minute solos. Those were never valid anyway in my book – never. It was just a cheap way of building up a tension in the audience ... A solo should do something; it shouldn't just be there as a cosmetic. It should have some aim, take the tune somewhere. I'm not saying I can do it, but I try and take the tune somewhere."
Jeff Beck

There is a rich tradition of guitar soloing which draws on every imaginable musical source. Two of the greatest guitar soloists, Django Reinhardt and Charlie Christian, established beyond doubt that the guitar was capable of almost anything that could be played on other instruments.

Aiming to play like Reinhardt or Christian might seem like an impossible ambition. Nevertheless, some kind of improvisation is well within the scope of every average guitarist. Approaches vary widely, and you can equally well construct a solo by connecting a series of licks or melodic phrases, by working from chord shapes, or by improvising on familiar scale patterns.

"I used to practise scales, but I think mainly in positions. I do runs that go from position to position, basically around chord shapes. I can get around pretty easily from one position to another, and on a good night it sounds pretty hot. I'll take chances. Sometimes I'll trip over myself, but most times I'm lucky."
Albert Lee

Knowing all the rock licks doesn't make you a lead guitarist, and simply being able to play any scale at blinding speed will rarely produce a good solo. The most common mistake made by aspiring guitarists is that of using a solo as a showcase for their technique. This is partly forgivable, since, as a guitarist, hearing a brilliant solo that is beyond your own ability is always impressive, but it will make little sense to the majority of an audience. A good solo, like any good art, stands out because it communicates. The secret is to *listen* – not only to your own playing and to the playing of the other musicians in the band, but to anything and everything.

"Listening to as many guitar solos as possible is the best method for someone in the early stages. But saxophone solos can be helpful. They're interesting because they're all single notes, and therefore can be repeated on the guitar. If you can copy a sax solo you're playing very well, because the average saxophonist can play much better than the average guitarist."
Ritchie Blackmore

Eric Clapton

Single-string lead techniques

One of the special features of the guitar is that – more than most other instruments – it allows you to manipulate the sound after a note has been played. With your left hand holding down a specific note, you have a choice of various special techniques which you can use to modify and control the sound as the note rings, or which you can use to go to the next note you want to play. These techniques can be divided into four broad categories – hammers, slides, bends, and vibrato. The first three are principally ways of changing the pitch without having to fret a new note and strike the string again – as you would normally have to. The fourth, the vibrato, is a technique that adds the guitarist's own personal signature to the overall sound.

We have included these single-string techniques here, in the section on improvisation, for two reasons. First, because they are an essential part of the lead guitarist's repertoire. And, second, because each technique has almost as many variations as there are guitarists. They form the basis of innumerable, individual tricks and licks that are an important and characteristic part of the *sound* of improvised guitar.

Hammering techniques

All these techniques involve sounding two or more notes while striking the string only once. They include hammer-ons, hammer-offs or pull-offs, and trills.

Hammer-ons

The simplest way to observe the effect of a *hammer-on* is with an open string. Play an E on the open 1st string and then, without striking the string again with your right hand, bring the 1st finger of your left hand firmly down on to the 1st fret. The note will keep ringing, but the pitch will rise from E to F.

Try the same thing with your 2nd finger on the 2nd fret (F♯), your 3rd finger on the 3rd fret (G), and your 4th finger on the 4th fret (G♯).

The effect of the hammer-on depends on two things: the length of time you leave

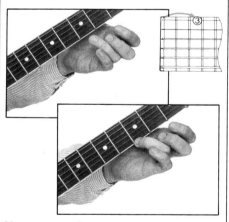

Hammering on from an open string

between playing the open string and hammering on with your left hand, and the speed and force with which you bring down your finger on to the ringing string.

Hammering on from a fretted note is essentially the same – although there is obviously a limit of around four frets, the span of the left hand in any one position. By starting with a note held down by your 1st finger, and then hammering on with each successive finger, it is possible to play four ascending notes with only one stroke of the right hand.

Hammering on from a fretted note

Pull-offs

Also called "hammer-offs", *pull-offs* are hammer-ons in reverse. This time, you start by playing a fretted note and then go down either to an open string or to a lower fret. The pitch of the note therefore drops.

Pull-offs require more care than hammer-ons if both notes are to be heard clearly. You must pull your left-hand finger away sharply and at an angle of about 45 degrees so that your fingertip virtually "plucks" the string and keeps the new note ringing. If you pull off too slowly or at the wrong angle, you will not catch the string and the second note will not sound clearly.

Pulling off from a fretted note to an open string is relatively easy, since you can move your whole hand. Pulling off from one fretted note to a lower fretted note needs more practice. There is less room for movement and more risk of accidentally hitting another string, yet your finger must pull off with enough force to sound the new note at the same volume.

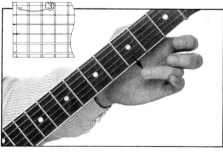

Pulling off from an open string

Pull-offs over four frets allow you to play four descending notes with only one stroke of your right hand. Start with all four fingers of your left hand on one string, with one finger per fret. Play the note held down by your 4th finger, and then pull off each finger in succession until the note held down by your 1st finger is left ringing. Four-fret pull-offs can be combined very effectively with four-fret hammer-ons. A descending pull-off using the 1st, 3rd and 4th fingers is a common lick that features in many blues and rock solos.

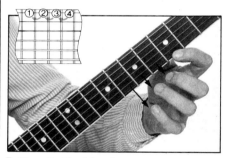

Pulling off with all four fingers

Trills

Alternating rapidly between the same two notes is called a *trill*. It is best done by fretting the lower of the two notes, playing it once, and then hammering quickly and regularly on and off the note above it. The string should keep ringing clearly.

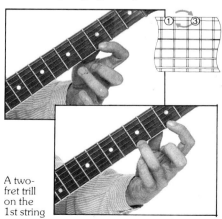

A two-fret trill on the 1st string

Slides

Slides are similar to hammer-ons and pull-offs in that more than one note is sounded but the string is only struck once. They differ in that *every* note between the first and last can be heard.

A slide is easier to perform on a guitar than on most other instruments; indeed, on some, it is impossible. Slides are best done with the 2nd or 3rd finger of your left hand, since this leaves your 1st and 4th fingers free to continue playing in either direction at the end of the slide.

Generally, ascending slides are easier than descending slides. This is because, as you slide your finger *up* the string, the volume tends to increase. No special skill is required other than accuracy; in other words, you should be able to stop exactly where you want to, without falling short of, or overshooting, the final fretted note. When you slide your finger *down* the string, you will find that you need more pressure to ensure that the last note rings properly.

Finger pressure is the key to sliding notes, whether ascending or descending. You must learn to release the grip of your left hand on the guitar neck so that the finger you are actually using is the only point of firm contact. When your finger reaches the note to which you are sliding, the rest of your left hand – especially your thumb – should tighten up on the guitar neck. This acts as a brake against the motion of your hand, and it should happen just before the

last note is sounded so that, from that moment, your left hand is once again in a stable playing position. You can, if you wish, finish the slide with a "vibrato" since this helps to keep the note ringing.

Sliding chords

The guitar is the only instrument on which it is possible to slide an entire chord up and down. Again, it is relatively easy when ascending but quite difficult when descending more than a couple of frets.

The principle of sliding chords is the same as that of single notes, but more control is required to keep all your fingers in the right place and to maintain each individual note of the chord. To start with, try sliding a simple F major shape (played on the top four strings) up and down over the space of one or two frets. Concentrate on keeping the chord under control, and avoid using so much pressure that you hurt your fingers. When you have mastered this, move on to various other full, six-string barre shapes. Ninth chords (see p. 132) are ideal for sliding, and can produce a jazz or funk feel.

The most *effective* chord slides are over an interval of a fourth (5 frets), a fifth (7 frets) and an octave (12 frets). Sliding fifths – especially with chords played on the lower strings – is a common feature of heavy metal; the sustain and distortion makes it easier to ascend and descend than it is if you hear only the pure sound of the strings.

A two-fret slide on the 6th string

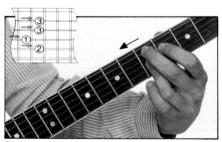

Sliding an entire ninth chord shape

String bending

This is one of the most basic of all techniques. It is used to some degree by virtually every guitarist playing a melody line or a lead break, and it is one of the most recognizable characteristics of modern guitar styles. James Burton, the pioneering country and rock session guitarist, is often credited as one of the first influential players to use string bending to alter one note in a chord. It was originally employed to imitate the sound of pedal-steel and bottleneck guitarists, and, as such, has its roots in blues and country music. Over the years, the technique has also been one of the major factors in the use of progressively lighter-gauge strings (see p. 163).

On modern electric guitars, the top three strings are the ones most commonly used for string bending – although, for special effects, any string can be bent. Usually, the pitch of the bent note is raised by the equivalent of one fret (semi-tone), two frets (tone) or three frets (tone and a half). It is possible to bend a string so that the pitch of the note rises by four frets (two tones), but this requires very light-gauge strings and considerable finger strength.

The most common problem associated with string bending is keeping the strings in tune. In general, bending a string beyond a tone tends to de-tune it – although this depends on the age of the string, whereabouts on the fingerboard you play the bend, how hard you strike the string with your right hand to begin with, how much finger pressure you apply, and, of course, exactly how far you bend the note. The way to avoid your strings de-tuning is to pay special attention to how they are wound on to the tuning heads, and to "stretch" them thoroughly when they are new (see p. 165).

3rd-finger bends

For beginners, the 3rd finger is the easiest to use for string bending. The leverage between your 3rd finger and your thumb will give you the pressure you need, especially if you hook your thumb over the top of

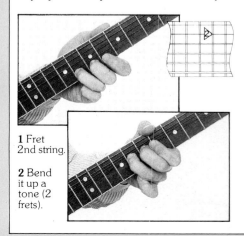

1 Fret 2nd string.

2 Bend it up a tone (2 frets).

Vibrato

Putting a slight "waver" into a note is called *vibrato*. It amounts to a rapid and slight variation in pitch. Vibrato increases a note's sustain and can add expression and feeling to the simplest melody or lead line. It is a technique that can be used in any situation, but is particularly effective when combined with string bending: you bend a string up, and apply vibrato when you reach the note you are bending to.

There are various ways of achieving vibrato, and *every* guitarist's method is slightly different. However, there are two basic techniques – horizontal and vertical

movement. The traditional method is the horizontal one. You move the whole of your left hand sideways (parallel to the guitar neck) while holding a note or chord. This is probably easier if you relax or even remove your thumb from the back of the neck. The contact between your finger and the string does not actually change, but the effect of it rolling back and forth produces a subtle variation in pressure that creates the vibrato.

The vertical technique is more often used with single-string bends. It, in fact, involves bending the string very slightly but very quickly up and down.

the neck. You should hold down the string with the middle of your fingertip so that it doesn't slide out underneath or catch on your fingernail.

On most guitars, the 2nd and 3rd strings are the easiest to bend. Although it can be bent in either direction, pushing a string upwards (towards the bass strings) generally gives you better control than pulling it down (towards the treble strings). When you push a string up, your whole hand can get behind it; when you pull a string down, one finger has to do all the work.

Two of the most important things on which to concentrate are pitch and noise. It is vital that, when you bend a string, it goes up to exactly the right pitch. Bending to a note that does not quite reach the desired pitch almost always sounds awful. How far you have to bend a string to get the note you want depends on the string gauge. It is not something you can measure, and only your ear will tell you whether you are getting it right. However, practising and *listening* will

A semi-tone (1-fret) bend

A whole-tone (2-fret) bend

A 3 semi-tone (3-fret) bend

A 4 semi-tone (4-fret) bend

soon give you the feel of the relationship between pressure and pitch.

Accidentally hitting other strings with the finger that is doing the bending can result in unwanted noise. It can ruin a perfectly good solo. There are several ways to cut out unwanted noise. One is to deaden other nearby strings by muting them with your 1st or 2nd finger, behind the fret on which the string is being bent. Another is to push the nearest strings clear with the protruding tip of the finger that is doing the bending.

Muting unused strings with 1st finger

Hooking 3rd finger beneath unused strings

Bends using your other fingers

Once you can control bends of up to three semi-tones with your 3rd finger, it is time to learn how to use the others. As with all guitar techniques, being able to use all your fingers equally well will increase your versatility.

Your 2nd finger should not prove too difficult once you have adjusted your hand so that your thumb still provides a fulcrum for the necessary leverage. Bends with your 1st finger can present problems: first, the fulcrum of your thumb is not as effective; second, you have no finger free to deaden strings behind the bend; third, you usually need your 1st finger to play other notes either immediately before or after the bend. However, you should be able to use your 1st finger for bends of at least a semi-tone on the 2nd and 3rd strings. 4th finger bends are obviously more difficult, since the 4th finger is much weaker than the others.

Descending string bends

All string bends can be done equally effectively in reverse. In other words, you start with a string bent up to a higher note, strike it, and then let it "relax" back to its normal pitch. The effect is of a single note falling in pitch. As when bending notes up, you can vary the speed at which the pitch drops. Descending string bends sound particularly

good if you put a vibrato on the note you bend down to.

The technique demands a good feel for tension and pitch, since you have to guess just how far to bend the string. You don't hear the note until it has been played. The answer is to practise, first with a one-fret bend, then with two, and then with three, to learn the differences in feel. Try playing a single note and bend it up and down two or three semi-tones while it is sounding. Remember that the tension differs from string to string.

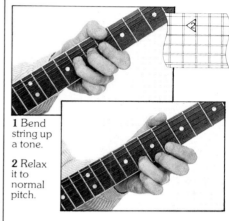

1 Bend string up a tone.

2 Relax it to normal pitch.

Double-string bends

It is possible to bend two strings at once to produce a slightly discordant effect which can nevertheless sound good in the right context. The most common double-string bends are on the 2nd and 3rd strings, bending both strings from the same fret, and on the 1st and 2nd strings, bending the 2nd string from one fret higher than the first. Both are illustrated here.

However, the technique is usually more effective if one string is bent and the other isn't. Common cliches employing this are shown on p. 145.

Bending 2nd and 3rd strings together

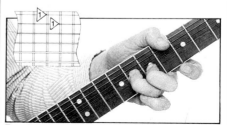
Bending 1st and 2nd strings together

Blues and rock guitar licks

Despite the fact that improvisation imposes no limits on what a guitarist can play, there is a strong tradition of popular guitar soloing. Certain licks and runs, established during the period when blues was evolving to rock, have become well-known cliches, and still form the basis of many lead solos. Of course, they are often adapted, changed, re-ordered, and used in a variety of different ways, according to the requirements of the music and the skill of the individual guitarists. But they are worth learning if only to understand how rock guitar solos are put together. Exactly when and where to use them is something that can be understood only by listening to how they

sound in the context of the ideas they connect. You should consider them as springboards to take you somewhere, not as thematic ideas in their own right. Once you have mastered them, you are quite free to throw them out altogether, and play something completely different. Remember that little individuality can be expressed simply by playing cliches.

Forms of improvisation can be found in black American music of around the turn of the century. This music, and the expressive qualities that it contained, formed the basis for the spirit of improvisation in both jazz and rock styles. Traditionally, a blues solo con-

tains a minimum of notes. It is the way the notes are played that produces the effect and creates the feeling of the blues. Rock guitarists have, in general, retained the essence of this approach but have expanded the formula — largely by introducing a feeling of speed and excitement.

The runs and licks in the following pages are just some of the elements that go into the making of a "classic" rock solo. Remember that there are no strict rules. Experiment with the examples given and try to see why and where they might work. Learn the basic fingering patterns and use them to invent your own lead lines.

Basic fingering patterns

By combining the notes that feature most often in a variety of soloing styles, it is possible to come up with a series of fingering patterns that you can use as the basis for your own solos. These are shown below —

one set of patterns for major solos and one for minor solos. We have plotted them here in the key of A, but you should learn to transpose them and to play them in as many different positions and situations as poss-

ible. They can be played in either ascending or descending order, and you can combine them in any way that gives you the right sound. Some notes can be left out, and others can be added.

Solo fingering patterns in A minor This pattern is based on a five-note pentatonic scale (see p. 113). All the notes indicated on the fingerboard with a triangle can be either fretted normally or bent up. In the third position, the A on the 2nd string can be bent up 3 frets to a C.

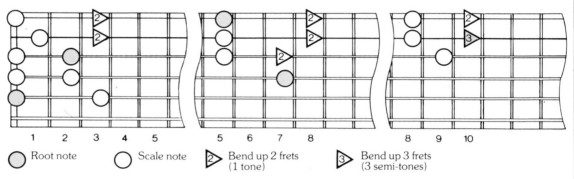

Note The scale steps are as follows: 1st (A), ♭3rd (C), 4th (D), 5th (E), ♭7th (G), 1st (A). The notes are the same as the pentatonic A minor scale and its relative pentatonic C major (see p. 113).

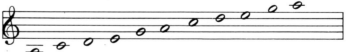

Solo fingering patterns in A major The position of the root note determines what key the pattern is in. Here, the root note is A. The bent notes are important: although most can be played either normally or bent, the C should be played only if bent up one semi-tone to C♯.

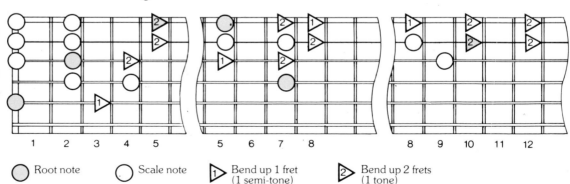

Note The scale steps are as follows: 1st (A), 3rd (C♯), 4th (D), 5th (E), 6th (F♯), ♭7th (G), 1st (A). This is not the same as a major scale (see p. 105).

Basic licks

String bending is an important factor in all rock solos, and it is one of the things that most strongly contributes to the sense of speed and the feeling that the guitarist creates. There are certain recognizable licks built around simple string bends which can serve as a starting point for discovering others of your own.

One of the most common of all licks is played on the top two strings (example 1).

One string is bent up and the other is fretted normally. There are two different places where this lick can be played within the context of one chord.

A variation of this technique can be played using three strings (example 2). Fret the 1st and 2nd strings in the same place, but hold them both down with your 4th finger. Use your 3rd finger to hold down the 3rd string one fret lower. Play all three

strings (together or separately) and bend the 3rd string up one tone. The sound this lick produces is similar to a pedal-steel guitar.

Two further licks exploit the major third relationship of the 3rd and 2nd strings (G and B). Examples 3 and 4 both feature bending the 3rd string up by a tone (2 frets) to produce the same note as the one you are holding on the 2nd string. The two strings can be played at once or one after the other.

Example 1
In key of A, hold down 1st string on either 12th fret (note will be 5th/E) or 3rd fret (note will be ♭7th/G). Bent note goes up from 2nd to major 3rd, or from 4th to 5th note of key.

2 Fret normally with 4th finger.

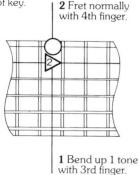

1 Bend up 1 tone with 3rd finger.

Example 2
In key of A, hold down 1st string on 5th fret (note will be 1st/A). Bent note on 3rd string goes up from 2nd to major 3rd in key.

2 Fret both notes with 4th finger.

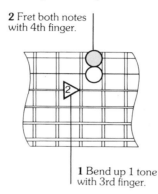

1 Bend up 1 tone with 3rd finger.

Example 3
In key of A, hold down 2nd string on 5th fret with 1st finger (note will be 5th/E). Bent note goes up from 4th to 5th note in key.

2 Fret normally with 1st finger. **3** Hammer on and off with 4th finger.

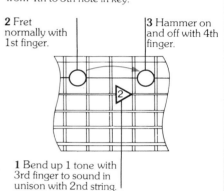

1 Bend up 1 tone with 3rd finger to sound in unison with 2nd string.

Example 4
In key of A, hold down 1st string on 5th fret (note will be 1st/A). Bent note on 3rd string goes up from 4th to 5th note in key.

2 Fret both notes with 1st finger. **3** Hammer on and off with 4th finger.

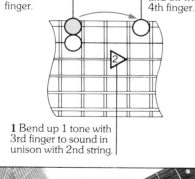

1 Bend up 1 tone with 3rd finger to sound in unison with 2nd string.

Example 5
In key of A, hold down 2nd string on 5th fret with 3rd finger (note will be 5th/E). Bent note goes up from 2nd to major 3rd in key.

3 Fret normally with 1st finger. **2** Fret normally with 3rd finger.

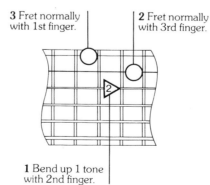

1 Bend up 1 tone with 2nd finger.

Example 6
In key of A, hold down 1st string on 5th fret (note will be 1st/A). Bent note on 3rd string goes up from 4th to 5th note in key.

3 Fret normally with 1st finger. **2** Fret normally with 3rd finger.

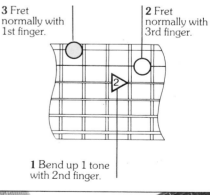

1 Bend up 1 tone with 2nd finger.

Ascending runs with 3rd-finger slides

To get from one position to another in the middle of a solo requires planning. Ideally, you should know the fingerboard well enough to give yourself plenty of options. So it is worth learning the ascending runs shown below. They are both based on pentatonic scales (see p.113). Written out here in the keys of E major and E minor, they both cover the three octaves of the first twelve frets. By beginning from a different root note, they can, of course, be transposed to other keys. The basic fingering

pattern remains the same; it is simply shifted intact up the fingerboard. The major run is often used in rock and country music, and the minor run in rock or jazz solos.

Both runs demonstrate a way of travelling smoothly and quickly up the fingerboard by sliding. In this case, the slide is done with the 3rd finger. Options are given which allow you to vary the fingering slightly when you cross from the 3rd to the 2nd string, or from the 2nd to the 1st string. It is important to remember that a certain series of notes can

be played in many different ways. The choice is up to you. Any difficult line can be made relatively easy when you locate the best fingering for it.

Obviously, what goes up must come down. Unfortunately, descending on the guitar is not quite as easy as ascending. For this reason, you may have to work out variations on these fingering patterns in order to run down the fingerboard as quickly as you can go up. Including pull-offs may be one answer (see p.141).

Ascending E major run
A pentatonic major run spanning three octaves: E, F♯, G♯, B, C♯, E, etc. The pattern can be moved anywhere on the fingerboard to start on a different root note and therefore play in any key.

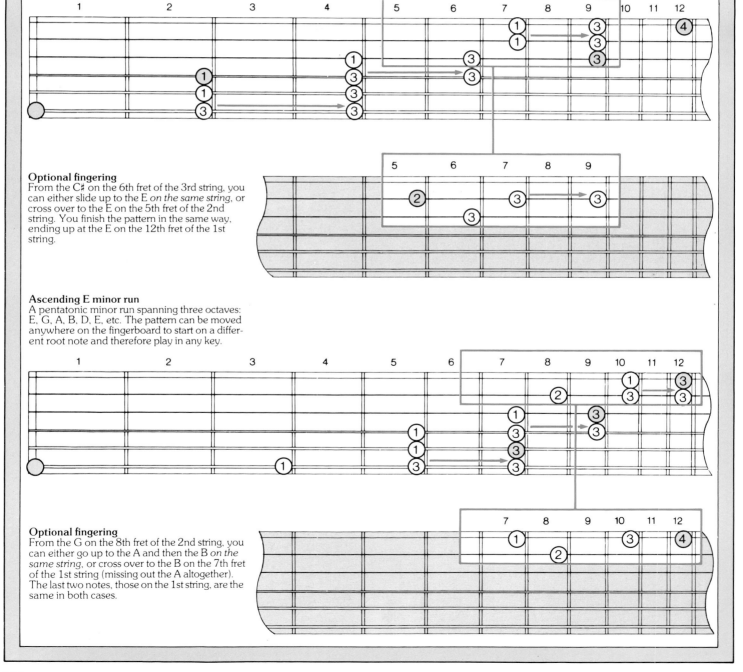

Optional fingering
From the C♯ on the 6th fret of the 3rd string, you can either slide up to the E *on the same string*, or cross over to the E on the 5th fret of the 2nd string. You finish the pattern in the same way, ending up at the E on the 12th fret of the 1st string.

Ascending E minor run
A pentatonic minor run spanning three octaves: E, G, A, B, D, E, etc. The pattern can be moved anywhere on the fingerboard to start on a different root note and therefore play in any key.

Optional fingering
From the G on the 8th fret of the 2nd string, you can either go up to the A and then the B *on the same string*, or cross over to the B on the 7th fret of the 1st string (missing out the A altogether). The last two notes, those on the 1st string, are the same in both cases.

Ascending runs with 4th-finger slides

Because it is so important that you should be able to play any run or scale in various different fingerings, two ascending runs in which the 4th finger not only starts the pattern but also slides to the next position are included here. The obvious advantage of this kind of fingering pattern is that it leaves you well placed to switch immediately to a fixed barre position — when playing a chord,

for example. The patterns are plotted out here in A major and A minor. They are, in fact, simply a diatonic major scale (see p. 104) and a natural minor scale (see p. 106) spread out horizontally up the length of the fingerboard. They can easily be transposed to any other key by moving the whole pattern up or down to a new root note. As with ascending runs where the 3rd finger slides,

you will have to adapt the fingering for a descending run.

It is good practice to be as comfortable with these patterns as with other scale fingerings. They will give you extra flexibility when working out solo lines. In classical guitar studies, all major and minor scales are practised starting from each finger, in every possible position.

Ascending A major run

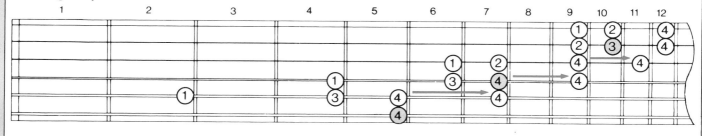

Ascending A minor run

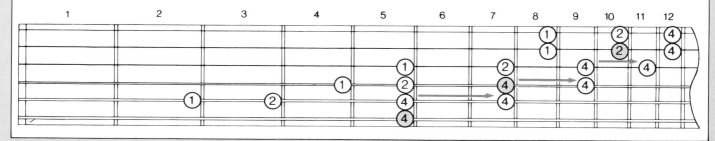

Ascending runs from fixed barre positions

One of the most effective ways of increasing speed and fluency is to learn fast runs from a fixed 1st-finger barre. All the notes other than those held by the barre are either hammered on or pulled off (see p. 141). This means that, when ascending and hammering on, you strike only the notes held by the barre. When descending, you strike only the notes held by your other fingers and pull off to those held by the barre.

Besides speed, one of the chief advantages of a fixed barre is that it reduces fret chatter behind the notes. You can see this for yourself by first playing a selection of notes anywhere between the 7th and 12th frets using normal fingering, and then playing them using a fixed barre. You should notice immediately how much clearer the overall sound is and how you are making more efficient use of your left hand. These are

among the reasons why the fixed barre technique is one of the principal features of classical left-hand posture.

The illustrations below show four fixed runs — in major and minor keys, and with the root note on the 6th and 5th strings. They are all movable forms, and, by adapting the fingering patterns to different chord inversions, they can be shifted up and down the fingerboard to play in any key you wish.

Major run with root note on 6th string
The pattern contains the dominant (or minor) seventh instead of the major seventh. In the key of C, this is B♭ instead of B.

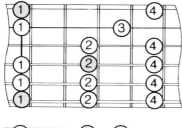

Minor run with root note on 6th string
The pattern contains a raised 6th note. In the key of A, this is F♯ instead of F.

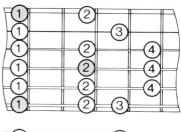

Major run with root note on 5th string
As above, this pattern contains the flattened 7th note of the major scale.

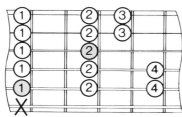

Minor run with root note on 5th string
This pattern skips the 6th note of the scale altogether. In A natural minor, this would be F.

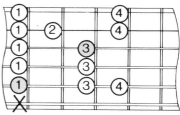

147

Descending pull-offs

Pull-offs (see p. 141) are a natural way of playing fast, descending runs. They can be used virtually anywhere on the fingerboard and will create a smooth, flowing effect. One of the best-known lead guitar cliches uses three descending pull-offs in quick succession. Starting on the 1st string, you pull off from your 4th finger to your 3rd and to your 1st. You repeat the same thing on the same frets of the 2nd string. Then, on the 3rd string, you pull off from your 3rd to your 1st finger. This means that you are sounding eight notes with only three strokes of your right hand. The note held by your 1st finger on the 1st string is the root note of the key you are playing in – so, if you want to play in A, for example, this will be the 5th fret.

The three pull-offs can be followed either by playing the root note an octave lower with the 3rd finger on the 4th string, or by hammering on or bending up to the major third on the 3rd string. If you hammer on, you do so with your 2nd finger; if you bend the string, you do so with your 1st finger.

Common cliche using descending pull-offs

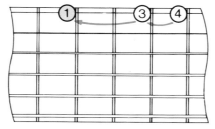

1 On 1st string, pull off from 4th to 3rd to 1st finger. Root note is held by 1st finger.

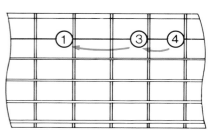

2 Repeat on same frets of 2nd string: pull off from 4th to 3rd to 1st finger.

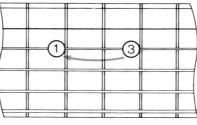

3 On 3rd string, pull off from 3rd to 1st finger – sounding only two notes, not three.

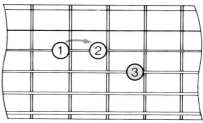

4 Either hammer on 3rd string with 2nd finger, or play root note on 4th string with 3rd finger.

Double-note licks

All the single-string techniques described on p. 141-3 can be applied equally well to two (or even three) strings – and, in rock solos, they often are.

The easiest is probably the *double pull-off*. You start by holding down both the 2nd and 3rd strings on the same fret with your 3rd finger. Play both strings together, pull off both notes to your 1st finger, holding down the strings two frets lower, and finish by hammering on to the 3rd string with your 2nd finger – as in the example above. The root note would be on the 1st string – on the same fret as your 1st finger. This lick can easily be adapted, embellished and used in numerous ways.

Double slides are commonly played on the 1st and 2nd strings. They can be done with the 1st, 2nd or 3rd finger – whichever is most convenient. Again, you play both strings together and slide your finger up and down over the space of two frets. The notes rise and fall by a whole-tone. This lick can

be played in two positions: either from the same fret as the root note when it is on the 6th string or from the same fret when it is on the 5th string.

Double bends are slightly more difficult. The technique is described on p. 143, but the way to fit them into a solo is as follows. Usually, you start by holding down the 2nd and 3rd strings with your first finger and playing both together. You then bring down your 3rd finger on to the 3rd string and your 4th finger on to the 2nd string two frets higher up. Play the strings again and bend both of them up. Because of the difference in string gauges, applying equal pressure to both strings will make the 3rd string go up by a whole-tone (two frets) and the 2nd string go up by a semi-tone (one fret).

This lick is particularly effective if you play it in reverse. Begin by bending the strings with your 3rd and 4th fingers, then strike them, let them relax back to their normal pitch, and, pull off down to your 1st finger.

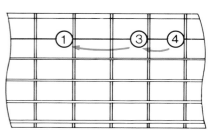

Root note on 5th or 6th string

1st finger on both strings

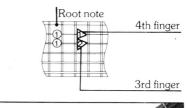

Double slide
Hold down and strike 1st and 2nd strings together. Slide up and down over two frets.

Root note

4th finger

3rd finger

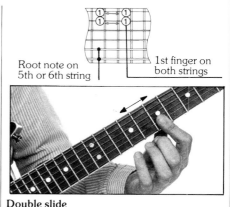

Double bend
Use 4th finger to bend 2nd string up a semi-tone (1 fret) and 3rd finger to bend 3rd string up a tone (2 frets).

Root note

Double pull-off

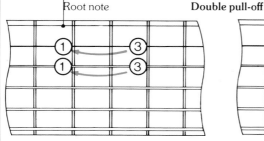

1 On 2nd and 3rd string, pull off from 3rd to 1st finger – playing both strings at once.

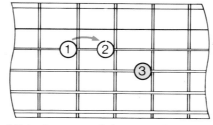

2 Either hammer on 3rd string with 2nd finger, or play root note on 4th string with 3rd finger.

Arpeggios

Fast arpeggios are a natural feature of many melodic guitar solos. The technique involves holding down a chord shape with your left hand and playing a simple strum or fingerstyle pattern with your right hand. Your left hand should then release the notes one by one, immediately after they have been struck. This produces the effect of hearing the notes in rapid succession.

Begin by trying an arpeggio with a major seventh chord shape on the top four strings. Sound each note individually, but release it at the same time as you hit the next note. At the end, only the 1st string should be ringing. When you can do this properly, with a single, quick stroke from your right hand, the four notes will sound as if they are being played very fast indeed.

Moving the shape up the fingerboard by three frets so that your 4th finger is no longer playing the root note changes the chord from a major seventh to a minor ninth.

Using only the top three strings of the same chord shape, you can follow the arpeggio with a hammer-on on the 1st string with your 4th finger. This is a common cliche in jazz guitar solos.

Once you feel comfortable with the arpeggio technique, you can apply it to almost any chord shape, and also combine it with hammers and bends. The remaining four examples below show these combinations applied to simple major and minor barre shapes. The only difference is that, where your 1st finger holds down three strings with a barre, you must learn to "roll" it off to create the same arpeggio effect.

The first example shows an arpeggio on the top four strings of a barre minor chord followed by a whole-tone (two-fret) bend on the 2nd string. This raises the note from a flattened seventh to the root. The second example uses the same minor arpeggio but finishes with a bend on the 1st string which raises the note from minor third to fourth.

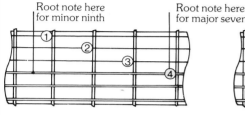

Major seventh/minor ninth arpeggio
Play 4th, 3rd, 2nd and 1st strings as shown. This is a major seventh or minor ninth chord shape according to where it is positioned.

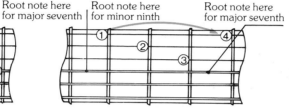

Major seventh/minor ninth arpeggio with hammer-on Play arpeggio on top three strings as shown, releasing each note as you strike the next. Finish by hammering on 1st string with 4th finger.

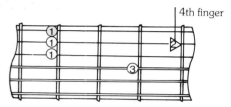

Minor arpeggio with 2nd-string bend
Play arpeggio on top four strings as shown. Finish by bending 2nd string up a whole-tone (2 frets) with 4th finger.

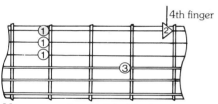

Minor arpeggio with 1st-string bend
Play arpeggio on top four strings as shown. Finish by bending 1st string up a whole-tone (2 frets) with 4th finger.

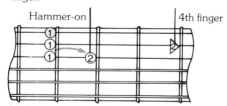

Major arpeggio with 2nd-string bend
Begin arpeggio with hammer-on as shown. Finish by bending 2nd string up a whole-tone (2 frets) with 4th finger.

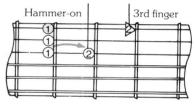

Major arpeggio with 1st-string bend
Begin arpeggio with hammer-on as shown. Finish by bending 1st string up a whole-tone (2 frets) with 3rd finger.

Octaves

The melodic content of a solo is its strongest quality, and the best way to emphasize a melodic line on the guitar is to use *octaves* — playing two notes at the same time but an octave apart. There are seven fingerings that create octaves, and you should aim to memorize them all.

The trickiest part about playing octaves is silencing the open strings in between the two you are sounding. If you play fingerstyle, the problem is immediately taken care of: you strike one string with your thumb and the other with one of your fingers. With a plectrum, it is possible to apply the same principle: your plectrum strikes the higher string (see p. 81). However, if you play only with a plectrum, you must learn to damp the strings in between with your left hand. This also applies when playing fast rhythms using only octaves.

The seven octave positions on the fingerboard These positions are not difficult to play in consecutive order, but, to improve your speed and versatility, try playing them in an ascending sequence: 1, 5, 2, 6, 3, 7, 4. Try working out melodies in octaves.

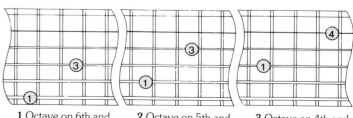

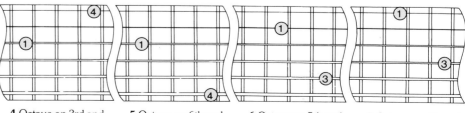

1 Octave on 6th and 4th strings.

2 Octave on 5th and 3rd strings.

3 Octave on 4th and 2nd strings.

4 Octave on 3rd and 1st strings.

5 Octave on 6th and 3rd strings.

6 Octave on 5th and 2nd strings.

7 Octave on 4th and 1st strings.

Chord substitution

The term *chord substitution* is something of a misnomer that throws many guitarists off the path to understanding what is, in fact, a relatively easy principle. Essentially, chord substitution is no more than the introduction of *variations* on an existing chord sequence. Once you understand the principles by which certain chords can be substituted for others, you will see that chord substitution offers a means of expression similar to that of improvisation. Whereas a guitarist improvising a solo is developing new melodic ideas, a rhythm guitarist substituting chords is experimenting with new harmonic ideas.

We have already seen that any chord progression consists of a succession of tonic or root notes (see p. 125). It is the notes stacked vertically above these that create the chords and "harmonize" the succession of root notes. Unless you intend to rearrange the original progression completely, these root notes always remain the same in their relation to time and melody. It is the other notes, the ones that create the chord harmony, which you alter in the process of chord substitution.

Chord substitution can work in two different ways: you can either choose to *change* some of the existing chords, or you can choose to *add* extra chords to the progression with which you start.

Changing existing chords
In a progression consisting of fairly simple chords, it is possible to extend or alter the chords you are given to produce a different type of harmony for what is essentially the same basic idea. A simple A minor chord, for example, could well become an A minor seventh, an A minor added ninth, a G suspended fourth, a C sixth, or a C major seventh. In the following pages, we will explain how this works, but, in each case, the substitution does not change the basic function of the A minor chord. You are simply choosing a different series of notes to create a new harmony for the root note of A. In other words, you are going beyond thinking of the chord just as an A minor triad.

Adding extra chords
Employing the same principle of introducing extended or altered chords that represent variations on the basic harmony, you can use the space or time between existing chord changes to play new chords chosen to complement the original progression. Taken to its logical extreme – as it is in some jazz styles – this can produce a progression in which you change chord on *every* beat of the bar.

The principles of substitution
Both the approaches to substitution outlined above – changing existing chords or introducing new ones to connect them – rely on your ability to create additional harmony. This works in two ways – vertically and horizontally. The vertical effect is determined by what notes you add on top of the root note. The horizontal effect is determined by when you play them.

When one chord changes to another, the two different root notes dominate the sound. The root note is always the strongest element in the chord, and the effect of the chord change depends on the interval between the two root notes. However, the other notes in each chord – called the "upper voices" – also play an important part. Of these, the highest note is the most prominent. In any chord progression, the changing top note of each chord can be heard as a melodic line. Of couse, when two chords share the same root note (as in a change from C major to C seventh, or C minor sixth to C minor seventh), then any change in the upper voices is more noticeable. In fact, harmonic variety can be achieved by changing just one note.

It is important both that you *understand* how chords are constructed and that you can *hear* how a chord changes when one or more of its constituent notes are altered. This lies at the heart of all chord substitution.

There are two further requirements. First, an understanding of how chords are generally divided into three families: major, minor and dominant. Chords are categorized according to whether the 3rd is major or minor (see p. 121) and whether the 7th is major or minor (see p. 127). The second requirement is a thorough grasp of "synonyms" – chords with the same notes but different names (see p. 137).

The only rules that exist in chord substitution are those of good taste, and these can only be determined by your own ear. The field is therefore open to experiment. However, there are some pointers, based on the principles of resolution, that should give you an indication of what is likely to work and what is not. It is these that we deal with in the following pages.

Substituting a dominant seventh chord

The simplest example of substitution occurs when you play a dominant seventh chord instead of a major chord – for example, a C seventh instead of a C major. However, this is not something that can be done randomly. There are some situations where it is appropriate, and others where it isn't. What is important is the context: you must learn to recognize what role the chord has (whether it is the I, IV, V or whatever) and to consider what chord it is going to change to.

Take a simple example of a chord change from C major to F major. There are two bars, with four beats in each. For the first bar you play C, and for the second bar you play F. For the substitution, you could play C seventh instead of C on the third and fourth beats of the first bar. The chord progression therefore becomes C major to C seventh to F major.

If you are in the key of F, the C is the dominant (V) chord and the F is the tonic (I) chord. When C resolves to F, a "perfect cadence" is observed (see p. 124). The root note descends by a fifth. Adding the extra note to the C major creates the C dominant seventh and enhances the sense of resolution.

If you are in the key of C, on the other hand, the C is the tonic (I) chord and the F is the sub-dominant (IV) chord. The root note ascends by a fourth. In this case, C seventh is actually a "tonic seventh" (built on the 1st, not the 5th, note of the scale), but it is still a dominant seventh *type* chord, and it resolves to F in the same way.

In each case, whether the root note goes up or down, substituting the dominant seventh is a way of *extending* the original chord. The dominant seventh acts as a "passing chord". There is a general rule here: *a dominant seventh can be formed on any chord when the root note of the next chord is a fourth higher or a fifth lower.*

Original progression

C	/	/	/	F	/	/	/
I				IV			
V				I			

Substitution

C	/	C7	/	F	/	/	/
I		I7		IV			
V		V7		I			

Principle Because F is a fourth above C or a fifth below it, the dominant seventh can be substituted in the first bar; in other words, C seventh can be played instead of C major to connect the two chords. This principle applies whether the progression shown above is in the key of C or the key of F.

Substituting minor seventh and dominant eleventh chords

A seventh chord acting as the dominant (V) chord in a progression presents you with the possibility of two common substitutions – a minor seventh or a dominant eleventh. In both cases, the dominant seventh is not completely replaced by the new chord; it is preceded by it. In other words, you are introducing an extra chord.

Take a simple example in the key of C – a chord progression from C major to F major to G seventh to C major. G seventh is the chord to focus on. It is a dominant seventh type and it is acting as the dominant (V) chord in the key.

Minor seventh substitutions

To substitute a minor seventh, you would replace the first and second beats on G seventh with two beats of D minor seventh. In other words, you substitute a minor

seventh built on the note one fifth higher than that of the dominant seventh chord. This minor seventh is, in fact, the supertonic (II) chord of whatever key you are playing in. The rule is therefore as follows: *any dominant seventh chord can be preceded by a minor seventh chord built on a root note a fifth higher.*

Dominant eleventh substitutions

Substituting a dominant eleventh works in the same way but is, if anything, even easier since the root note does not change. Using the same chord progression as an example, you would replace the first and second beats on G seventh with two beats of G eleventh. The rule is therefore: *any dominant seventh chord can be preceded by a dominant eleventh chord built on the same root.*

The interesting thing about the dominant eleventh is that it can be considered as a "polychord". If you turn to p. 136, you will see that B♭/C is basically C eleventh. It therefore follows that you can think of G eleventh as the polychord F/G – that is, F major played over a G bass note. This makes what is happening in the substitution more obvious: you are changing from F major to F major with a G in the bass, and then to G seventh.

It is possible to use both minor seventh and dominant eleventh substitutions in the same progression. Our third example illustrates this. The first two beats on the G seventh are replaced by two beats on G eleventh (or F/G), and the last two beats of F major are replaced by D minor seventh. It is worth noting that D minor seventh is actually the relative minor of F.

Original progression

C / / /	F / / /	G7 / / /	C / / /
I	IV	V7	I

Substitution

C / / /	F / / /	Dm7 / G7 /	C / / /
I	IV	IIm7 V7	I

Original progression

C / / /	F / / /	G7 / / /	C / / /
I	IV	V7	I

Substitution

C / / /	F / / /	G11 / G7 /	C / / /
I	IV	V11 V7	I

Original progression

C / / /	F / / /	G7 / / /	C / / /
I	IV	V7	I

Substitution

C / C7 /	F / Dm7 /	G11 / G7 /	C / / /
I I7	IV IIm7	V11 V7	I

Substituting a minor seventh

Principle The first two beats of G seventh (which is the dominant chord) are replaced by D minor seventh – the minor seventh chord built on the note a fifth higher than the root note of the original chord.

Substituting a dominant eleventh

Principle This time, the first two beats of G seventh are replaced by G eleventh – the dominant eleventh chord built on the same root note. G eleventh is, in fact, the same as the polychord F/G (see p. 136).

Substituting a dominant seventh, a minor seventh and a dominant eleventh

Principle This example illustrates all the three principles we have looked at so far – substituting dominant sevenths, minor sevenths and dominant elevenths. The newly introduced chords are C seventh, D minor seventh and G eleventh. The chord diagrams below illustrate one way in which the complete progression might be played.

C major	C7	F major	Dm7	G11 or F/G	G7	C major
2 beats	2 beats	2 beats	2 beats	2 beats	2 beats	4 beats

Extending and altering dominant chords

In theory, any simple chord can be "extended" to a ninth, eleventh or thirteenth form (see p. 132-5). In practice, however, the chords most frequently involved in substitutions come from the dominant family. All dominant chords contain a minor third *and* a minor or flattened seventh. There is scope for "altering" the remaining notes: the 5th can be sharpened to produce a seventh augmented fifth chord or flattened to produce a seventh diminished fifth (see p. 127); and the 9th can be sharpened to produce a seventh augmented ninth or flattened to produce a seventh flat nine (see p. 133). Essentially, other words, you are altering the ninth of a dominant chord. Alternatively, you could start by substituting C seventh for the C and F major seventh for F. You could then alter

What to do when a dominant chord is followed by one a fourth higher

Take as an example a bar of C followed by a bar of F. Here, C is about to change to a chord a fourth higher. You might decide to treat this first by substituting C ninth for the C and F seventh for the F. You could then introduce an altered chord – a C seventh augmented ninth or a C seventh flat nine – for the last two beats of the C ninth bar. In

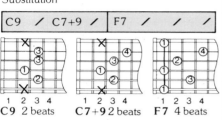

Principle C seventh augmented ninth can be substituted for the last two beats of the dominant chord C ninth, since it is followed by a chord a fourth higher.

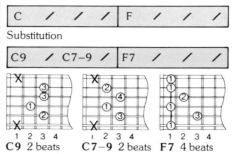

Principle C seventh flat nine can be substituted for the last two beats of the dominant chord C ninth, since it is followed by a chord a fourth higher.

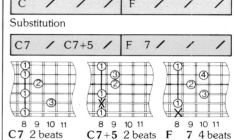

Principle C seventh augmented fifth can be substituted for the last two beats of the dominant chord C seventh, since it is followed by a chord a fourth higher.

What to do when a dominant chord is followed by one a semi-tone lower

This is the second situation where substituting altered dominant chords is possible. Take as an example a bar of C followed by a bar of B (in the key of F major). In this case, C is about to change to a chord one semi-tone lower. The same rules apply to this situation as they do to those above – where the dominant chord is followed by one a fourth higher. The dominant chord can be substituted for an extended one with various altered notes. In the examples below, the altered chord completely replaces the

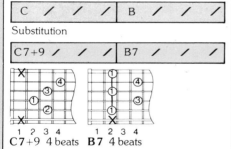

Principle C seventh augmented ninth can be substituted in the first bar, since it is followed by a chord a semi-tone lower.

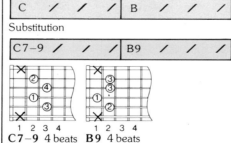

Principle C seventh flat nine can be substituted in the first bar, since it is followed by a chord a semi-tone lower.

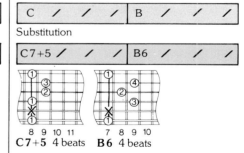

Principle C seventh augmented fifth can be substituted in the first bar, since it is followed by a chord a semi-tone lower.

Substituting minor "passing chords"

We have already seen on p. 151 how minor seventh chords can be used as substitutes in certain circumstances – in particular, how the supertonic (II) minor chord can be used to prepare a dominant (V) chord. Minor chords built on the mediant (III) note and on the sub-mediant (VI) note of the scale can also be introduced into simple chord sequences to add variety and sometimes to produce scale-like progressions. Take a simple example of a change from C to F. As a I to IV progression, it can be treated by substituting a D minor (the II chord) in the second half of the bar of C and an E minor (the III chord) in the first half of the bar of F. The two minor chords act as "passing chords" and serve to connect the two original chords. The sequence can be varied still further by substituting an A minor chord. This is the VI chord, the relative minor of C. Minor chords can be altered in substitutions. The most common alteration is to play the chord with a diminished fifth. For example, in a II–V–I progression such as D minor to G seventh to C major, the last two beats of D minor could be played as a D minor diminished fifth (Dm–5) or as a D half-diminished (Dm7–5).

Original progression

C	/	/	/	F	/	/	/
I				IV			

there are two situations where these chords can be substituted. First, when a dominant chord is followed by one that is a fourth higher, and, second, when it is followed by one that is a semi-tone lower.

the C seventh. In both cases, the rule is as follows: *a chord with an altered fifth or ninth can be substituted for a dominant chord if the next chord is a fourth higher.*

Original progression

C	/	/	/	F	/	/	/

Substitution

C7	/	C7−5	/	F9	/	/	/

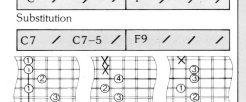

8 9 10 11	8 9 10 11	7 8 9 10
C7 2 beats	**C7−5** 2 beats	**F9** 4 beats

Principle C seventh diminished fifth can be substituted for the last two beats of the dominant chord C seventh, since it is followed by a chord a fourth higher.

original. The rule is as follows: *a chord with an altered fifth or ninth can be substituted for a dominant chord if the next chord is a semi-tone lower.*

Original progression

C	/	/	/	B	/	/	/

Substitution

C7−5	/	/	/	B7	/	/	/

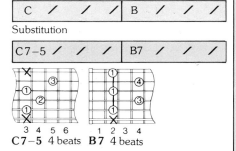

3 4 5 6	1 2 3 4
C7−5 4 beats	**B7** 4 beats

Principle C seventh diminished fifth can be substituted in the first bar, since it is followed by a chord a semi-tone lower.

Inserting new dominant chords

If you come across either of the situations described opposite – that is, a dominant chord followed by one either a fourth above or a semi-tone below – you have another option besides that of simply using an extended or altered version of the original chord. You can substitute in its place a dominant chord built on a root note that is a flattened fifth higher. As before, this new chord can be of any kind – extended or altered – as long as it comes from the dominant family, not from the majors or minors. Usually, it is a "partial" substitution. It does not replace the first chord completely but is played on the last two beats of the bar. In other words, it is introduced between the two original chords and acts as a link between them.

The rule is as follows: *when a dominant chord is followed by one either a fourth above or a semi-tone below, a new dominant chord built on a root note a flattened fifth above the first can be substituted.* The chord progressions shown here illustrate two examples of each situation. They work because, in the first case, C is a fourth above G (the chord it follows) and, in the second case, B♭ is a semi-tone below G.

Introducing a new dominant chord when the root note goes up by a fourth

Original progression

G	/	/	/	C	/	/	/

Substitution/example 1

G7	/	C♯9	/	C7+9	/	/	/

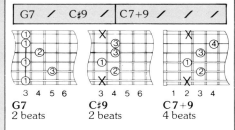

3 4 5 6	3 4 5 6	3 4 5 6
G7 2 beats	**C♯9** 2 beats	**C7+9** 4 beats

Substitution/example 2

G7	/	C♯7+9	/	C7	/	/	/

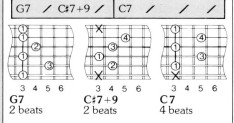

3 4 5 6	3 4 5 6	3 4 5 6
G7 2 beats	**C♯7+9** 2 beats	**C7** 4 beats

Principle C is a fourth above G. It is therefore possible to build a new dominant chord on C♯ – the root note a flattened fifth above G – and substitute it for the last two beats in the bar of G. The new chord can be extended and/or altered – to C♯ ninth or C♯ seventh augmented ninth, for example, as here – as long as it is dominant.

Introducing a new dominant chord when the root note goes down by a semi-tone

Original progression

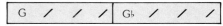

G	/	/	/	G♭	/	/	/

Substitution/example 1

G7	/	D♭7	/	G♭7	/	/	/

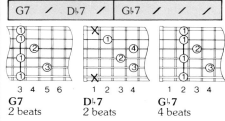

3 4 5 6	1 2 3 4	1 2 3 4
G7 2 beats	**D♭7** 2 beats	**G♭7** 4 beats

Substitution/example 2

G7	/	D♭9	/	G♭6	/	/	/

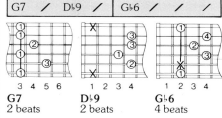

3 4 5 6	1 2 3 4	1 2 3 4
G7 2 beats	**D♭9** 2 beats	**G♭6** 4 beats

Principle G♭ is a semi-tone below G. It is therefore possible to build a new dominant chord on D♭ – the root note a flattened fifth above G – and substitute it for the last two beats of the bar of G. The new chord can be simply a dominant D♭7 or extended to a D♭9, for example, as long as it remains dominant.

Three examples of how to substitute minor chords

Principle The supertonic (II) minor chord is substituted for the last two beats of C, and the mediant (III) minor for the first two beats of F.

Substitution/example 1

C	/	Dm	/	Em	/	F	/
1		IIm		IIIm		IV	

Principle The relative minor (VI) chord is substituted for the last two beats of C, and the supertonic (II) minor chord for the first two beats of F.

Substitution/example 2

C	/	Am	/	Dm	/	F	/
I		VIm		IIm		IV	

Principle The relative minor (VI) chord is again substituted in the first bar. This time, however, the mediant (III) minor chord replaces the first two beats of F.

Substitution/example 3

C	/	Am	/	Em	/	F	/
I		VIm		IIIm		IV	

Substituting diminished seventh chords

The diminished seventh chord is probably the most useful of all chords when it comes to substitution. First, it can be introduced between any two chords. And, second, as explained on p. 128, there are only three different diminished chords covering all twelve keys. This means that one of the three will always fit.

In fact, when you are faced with a I–V progression, any of the three can be inserted. Of course, each one creates a different effect. In the first example shown below, a bar of C major (the I chord) is followed by a bar of G major (the V chord). Each of the three diminished chords (in this case, G diminished, G♭ diminished, and A♭ diminished) is shown replacing the last two beats of C. Play them through and listen to the difference in sound the choice of substituted chord makes.

Diminished chords are unique in that they repeat themselves every three frets as you move up or down the fingerboard. A diminished chord placed on one fret contains the same notes as one placed three frets lower or three frets higher. This makes them ideal for inserting en route when changing to higher or lower inversions of the chords that follow. The second two examples given below show how diminished sevenths can be substituted as passing chords in sequences that move up and then down the fingerboard. The first is in the key of C, and the second is in G. In the second example, you can play the root note of each diminished chord with your thumb on the 6th string. You will then see how the progression moves up the fingerboard, one fret at a time, before descending again.

Augmented chords, which repeat themselves every four frets, can be substituted as passing chords in a similar way.

How the three diminished chords can be substituted

Original progression

C	/	/	/	G	/	/	/
I	/	/	/	V	/	/	/

Principle In a I–V progression such as C to G, any of the three different diminished sevenths can be substituted between the two original chords. The effect created varies according to which diminished chord you choose.

Substitution/G diminished

C	/	G dim	/	G7	/	/	/
I	/	V dim	/	V7			

Substitution/G♭ diminished

C	/	G♭ dim	/	G7	/	/	/
I	/	♭V dim	/	V7			

Substitution/A♭ diminished

C	/	A♭ dim	/	G7	/	/	/
I	/	♯V dim	/	V7			

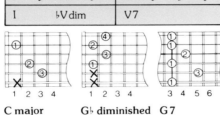
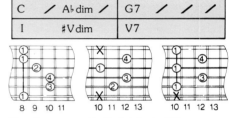

C major — 2 beats | G diminished — 2 beats | G 7 — 4 beats
3 4 5 6 | 1 2 3 4 | 3 4 5 6

C major — 2 beats · | G♭ diminished — 2 beats | G 7 — 4 beats
1 2 3 4 | 1 2 3 4 | 3 4 5 6

C major — 2 beats | A♭ diminished — 2 beats | G 7 — 4 beats
8 9 10 11 | 10 11 12 13 | 10 11 12 13

How to use diminished sevenths as "linking" chords
Example in key of C major

Original progression

C	/	/	/	Dm	/	/	/	Em	/	/	/	Dm	/	G7	/	C	/	/	/

Substitution

C	/	C♯ dim	/	Dm7	/	D♯ dim	/	Em7	/	E♭ dim	/	Dm7–5	/	G7	/	C	/	/	/

Principle The three diminished chords are introduced to create an ascending and descending progression. C♯ diminished is between C and D, and D♯ diminished and E♭ diminished (which are enharmonic names for the same chord) link D and E.

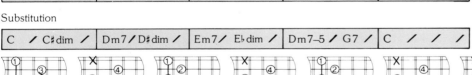

C major — 2 beats | C♯ diminished — 2 beats | D m 7 — 2 beats | D♯ diminished — 2 beats | E m 7 — 2 beats | E♭ diminished — 2 beats | D m 7–5 — 2 beats | G 7 — 2 beats | C major — 4 beats
3 4 5 6 | 3 4 5 6 | 5 6 7 8 | 5 6 7 8 | 7 8 9 10 | 5 6 7 8 | 5 6 7 8 | 3 4 5 6 | 3 4 5 6

Example in key of G major

Original progression

G	/	/	/	Am	/	/	/	Bm	/	/	/	Am	/	D7	/	G	/	/	/

Principle This example, in the key of G, illustrates three diminished seventh substitutions used to emphasize the same ascending and descending effect. G♯ diminished connects G and A, and A♯ diminished and B♭ diminished (enharmonic equivalents) link A and B.

Substitution

G	/	G♯ dim	/	Am7	/	A♯ dim	/	Bm7	/	B♭ dim	/	Am7	/	D7	/	G	/	/	/

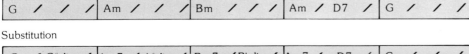
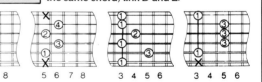
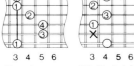

G major — 2 beats | G♯ diminished — 2 beats | A m 7 — 2 beats | A♯ diminished — 2 beats | B m 7 — 2 beats | B♭ diminished — 2 beats | A m 7 — 2 beats | D 7 — 2 beats | G major — 4 beats
3 4 5 6 | 3 4 5 6 | 5 6 7 8 | 5 6 7 8 | 7 8 9 10 | 5 6 7 8 | 5 6 7 8 | 3 4 5 6 | 3 4 5 6

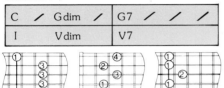

Choosing a different chord for every beat

So far, we have concentrated on introducing a substituted chord to connect two existing chords – for example, C to C7 to F. Since it is now clear that any two chords can be connected with a third chord, it follows that these three chords – C, C7 and F – can be connected by two more chords. In 4/4 time, this would mean that all four beats of the first bar could feature a different chord.

The examples on the right illustrate this kind of treatment. Both are based on an original progression of C to F. The first substitutes C sixth, C seventh and then C ninth for the last three beats in the bar of C. The second is similar but shows a slightly more linear approach: since the top note of the chords is the one that is altered, there is an ascending chromatic line which starts on the 5th of C major (G), goes up to the sharpened 5th of C augmented (G♯), to the 6th (A), to the 7th (B♭), and then resolves to the 3rd of F major (A). In other words, the top note (or upper voice) of the chord is raised by a semi tone at each chord change.

How one chord can be played for each beat of the bar
Original progression

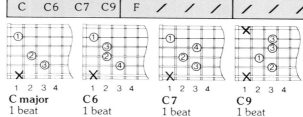

Substitution/example 1

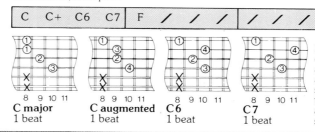

Principle Three new chords are substituted in the bar of C. They are all extended forms of the original C major chord. They produce a different chord for each beat, serving to link C and F, via C sixth, C seventh and C ninth.

Substitution/example 2

Principle The three substitute chords are chosen since their altered top notes create an ascending pattern rising one semi-tone at a time. In this case, then, C and F are linked via C augmented, C sixth and C seventh.

Varying a single chord over several bars

In essence, substitution means creating a new chord progression in between existing chords. Of course, if you come across several bars in an original sequence where the chord remains the same for some time, there is a wide scope for substitutions of all kinds. Even in a normal three-chord blues progression, there is plenty of time to create new harmonies using chord substitutions.

When there are several bars of the tonic (I) chord, it will invariably be a dominant type. You could treat this firstly by introducing various extensions and alterations of the dominant seventh, and, secondly, by alternating between the chord you are given and others built on different root notes – for example, the II minor seventh or the IV and IV minor seventh. Similarly, several bars of a tonic (I) minor chord could be varied by alternating from the I minor to the IV minor or the V seventh. In both cases, once you have decided on a substitute progression to fill out and relieve the monotony of a single chord, then the new chords can be altered to add more colour and interest to the sequence. As you become more familiar with the effects of different chord progressions, the potential for substitution will become gradually more obvious.

The chord sequence below illustrates one way in which you might treat several bars of A. The substitute chords, played in the appropriate inversions, create an ascending and descending sequence.

An example of chord substitutions on five straight bars of A
Original progression

Substitution

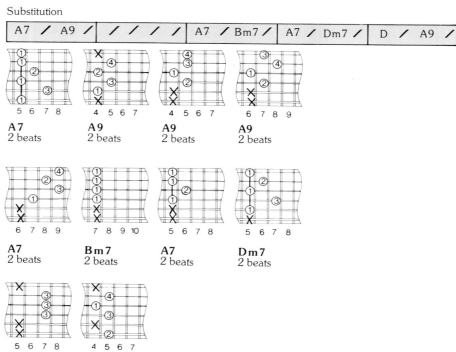

THE COMPLETE GUITARIST

As a guitarist, you are learning all the time. And the more you play, the more you'll improve. There are plenty of different hints, tips, exercises and practice methods around, but there are no short-cuts. Putting in the playing hours is the only real way to improve.

If you want to become an accomplished, all-round guitar player, you should be thinking about improvement in three directions – technique, theory and "taste". *Technique* is the mechanical part of guitar playing. It is essentially all about getting your fingers to do what you want them to. It is partly a question of developing coordination, strength and independent finger movement in your hands, and partly of memorizing chord shapes and fingering patterns. Ultimately, what you are aiming for is the ability to hit the notes you want when you want them, without fluffing them and without losing your timing. This is what is generally called "finger memory". Simple repetition is the key to acquiring it.

Theory is the intellectual part of guitar playing. It is all about understanding music and how it works. All guitarists pick up some theory as they go along – even if they don't think of it in those terms. Yet there is a certain mystique about music theory which convinces many guitarists that it is complex and difficult. In fact, it is easier than it looks. In this book, we have tried to emphasize the few basic principles which underlie it all and which, once you have grasped them, will help unlock such seemingly daunting concepts as extended and altered chords, substitution, modulation and scale theory. As the American jazz guitarist, Howard Roberts, has pointed out:

"There are books and educational programmes that tell the student, either directly or indirectly, that there are literally hundreds of tunes to learn. What they don't tell him or her is that those hundreds of tunes are put together with the same doggone chords, sequences, scale passages, and interval skips. It's constantly being suggested to the beginning

Time, harmony and melody – the three basic elements

All musical statements are heard as a combination of time, harmony and melody. Any sound that can be recognized as a musical form – whether a lead guitar solo or a symphony orchestra – displays all three elements. Previous sections of this chapter – on the *rhythm* guitarist, the *melodic* guitarist and the *harmonic* guitarist – have discussed the components within each separate element. All three are, of course, interdependent, and here we will attempt to provide some ideas on how these elements are put together.

Of all instruments, the guitar and the keyboard are best able to articulate all three elements at the same time. However, whenever musicians play together, it is understood that responsibility for the three elements is distributed. In most small bands, this means that the drummer's fundamental role is to keep *time* and accentuate rhythm patterns. The bass player assumes both a rhythmic and harmonic role – obviously involving *time* and *harmony*. The chordal interplay between the bass and the guitar or keyboards defines the harmonic setting but is also rhythmic – therefore involving *time* and *harmony* once again. The *melody* is the responsibility of the lead voice or soloist – which, at any one time, may be vocals, guitar, keyboards or even bass. The sound produced by the band is a result of how each musician interprets his or her role, and of how the three elements of time, harmony and melody are distributed between and accentuated by the different musicians.

Time is the *horizontal* effect in music. Think of it in terms of a stopwatch that starts the moment a note or chord is struck and stops when the sound dies away to silence. In a sense, time is the most independent of the three elements. When "un-pitched" instruments, such as most drums, are played alone, time is heard without melody or harmony – although, even in this case, the patterns established by the various different percussive sounds or textures can suggest a simple sense of harmony.

A single note is heard by the ear as a sound without musical motive. When a second note is played, two things happen: first, a sense of time is produced by the relative duration of the two notes; second, a horizontal interval is created by the difference in pitch. A third note further extends the feeling of time and creates another horizontal interval.

The primary effect of a series of single notes is of a *melody*. It is essentially a movement from pitch to pitch. The relative duration of the notes and the spaces between them create a sense of time which is as important to the identity of the melody as the notes themselves.

If melody and time represent the horizontal effect in music, then harmony is the *vertical* effect. In previous sections on scales, intervals and chords, we have seen how the relationship between the rules of melody and the rules of harmony evolved. In theoretical terms, harmony can be isolated from the element of time and considered vertically. A chord can be examined by "freezing" it in time and looking at the vertical structure of the intervals from which it is built.

When a series of chords is played on the guitar or keyboard, we hear the sound primarily as a combination of harmony and time. The vertical intervals in the chords create the harmony, and the attack and duration of the chords, as well as the spaces between them, determine the feeling of time. However, chord sequences also suggest melody as a result of the horizontal intervals between the top notes of each chord. This just goes to show how harmony and melody are interrelated. Through the basic rules of music theory, each can suggest the other.

How musical styles differ

Now that we have seen how the three basic elements combine to create form in music, we can look at a variety of styles to see how varying just one of the three elements can determine the identity of the style.

All folk, country, blues and rock music features chord progressions built from primary harmony – the tonic (I), sub-dominant (IV) and dominant (V) chords. This is the basis of what we have earlier called the *three-chord theory* (see p. 76). The relative minor (VI) and the supertonic minor (II) are the secondary chords most often used to introduce variety (see p. 78).

Many traditional folk melodies are almost entirely modal in origin. That is, they are based on the *modes* that pre-dated diatonic scales (see p. 110). They often involve only two different chords. More contemporary folk and country music is usually diatonic and employs the whole range of primary and secondary chords. In terms of rhythm, folk and country styles are played in 2/4, 3/4, 4/4 and 6/8 time signatures at all tempos (see p. 96). Blues and rock music tends to be restricted to 4/4 and 6/8 time signatures (see p. 97). It uses mainly primary chords, but employs them in different patterns. Melodically, one of the most important differences is its use of the Mixolydian mode (see p. 111), a major scale with a flattened 7th step, which complements dominant seventh type chords.

Modern popular music might be regarded as a combination of elements from various root styles put together to achieve a specific effect. This encompasses all time *student that there are a thousand things to learn – but there aren't.''*

Howard Roberts

In many areas of music theory, intellect overlaps with instinct. As your musical "ear" develops, you will get an instinctive feeling for what will sound right and what will not. All music theory can be considered as a method of simply analyzing what your ear tells you is or isn't correct.

Taste is the most difficult aspect of guitar playing to define. It is all about what you *choose* to play. There are no guidelines other than the importance of developing a feel for what other musicians in the band are playing and for what will sound appropriate in context. You should aim to think about your role as a guitarist, and listen critically to whether what you are playing works.

"The bits that the lead guitar might play could be bits you can't say – so the guitar says them . . . The song dictates what you play far more than your playing style – like in the old crying blues where the slide "talked" . . . It seems to me there's very little point in having a solo for its own sake in a song; it should come in naturally in context.''

Mark Knopfler

This brings us back full circle to the importance of practising (see p. 66). And remember that the best way to practise is simply to play.

"(When I practise) I usually put on a real hot record, crank it up and play along with it. It gives me that feeling of playing along with a band, gets the old adrenalin going.''

Albert Lee

Mark Knopfler of Dire Straits

signatures and tempos, both primary and secondary harmony, and modal or diatonic melody. The fusion forms — folk-rock, country-rock, jazz-rock, Latin-jazz and jazz-funk — represent some of the most important combinations. In recent years, elements from many varied styles have been combined to produce music that is original, interesting and also popular. More than ever, the ability to compose, arrange and play depends on an awareness of new ways in which the three basic elements of music can be put together.

The following chart gives an indication of the time signatures, tempos, harmony and scales used in various styles. There is, of course, a certain amount of crossover, and it should be taken as a general guide only.

A guide to the basic elements of time, harmony and melody in popular musical styles				
Styles	**Time**		**Harmony**	**Melody**
Folk	2/4, 3/4, 4/4, 6/8	All tempos	Primary chords	Modal
Country	2/4, 3/4, 4/4, 6/8	All tempos	Primary chords	Diatonic
Blues	4/4	All tempos	Primary chords	Mixolydian, pentatonic
Rhythm and blues	4/4, 6/8	Moderate to fast	Primary and secondary chords	Mixolydian, pentatonic, diatonic
Rock	4/4	Moderate to fast	Primary and secondary chords	Mixolydian, pentatonic, diatonic
Pop	2/4, 3/4, 4/4, 6/8	All tempos	Primary and secondary chords	Pentatonic, diatonic
Folk-rock	4/4	Slow to moderate	Primary and secondary chords	Modal, diatonic
Country-rock	4/4	Moderate to fast		
Jazz-rock	4/4, 6/8	All tempos	Extended and altered chords	Modal, diatonic, chromatic
Jazz-funk	4/4	Moderate to fast		
Jazz	4/4, 6/8, 5/4, 7/4, 9/8, 11/8	All tempos	Extended and altered chords	Modal, chromatic

Alternative tunings

The method we now use to tune the guitar – E, A, D, G, B, E from 6th string to 1st – is a convention that has developed over the centuries. Custom and practice have shown that it provides an acceptable range, a convenient placing of the intervals, and a manageable choice of basic chord fingerings. Of course, it is not the only system. There are countless other ways in which the strings can be tuned.

Alternative tunings generally fall into one of two categories. They are either "open" tunings, which means that the strings are tuned to sound a chord when they are all played open or unfretted, or they are adaptations of the standard tuning and are designed to feature one or more open strings as part of the piece for which they are used. Alternative tunings occur widely in folk, blues and ragtime styles, and, particularly, in bottleneck or slide playing (see p. 160).

The tunings illustrated here are presented as a selection of those used most often. You should remember that they are only suggestions. The field is wide open to experiment and to the discovery of new sounds.

Ry Cooder, renowned for his slide playing, much of which features alternative tunings

Open tunings

When the guitar is re-tuned so that you can play a chord on the open strings, this is known as an *open tuning*. The most common are open G (also known as "slack key", "Spanish" or "Hawaiian"), open D, open E and open C. These tunings give open-string chords of G major, D major, E major and C major respectively. One of the chief advantages of an open tuning is that other chords can be played simply by using a 1st-finger barre across all six strings, placed at any fret. In open G, for example, a 1st-finger barre on the 2nd fret will give the chord A major. You will, of course, have to discover fingerings for other chords yourself. A few examples in open G and open D are given below.

When choosing an open tuning, it is always better to go for one in which the altered strings are tuned *down*. Tuning strings *up* can break them.

Open G tuning ("slack key")					
6th	5th	4th	3rd	2nd	1st
D	G	D	G	B	D

How to tune
6th string *down* to D.
5th string *down* to G.
4th string as normal.
3rd string as normal.
2nd string as normal.
1st string *down* to D.

Open D tuning					
6th	5th	4th	3rd	2nd	1st
D	A	D	F♯	A	D

How to tune
6th string *down* to D.
5th string as normal.
4th string as normal.
3rd string *down* to F♯.
2nd string *down* to A.
1st string *down* to D.

Three chord shapes in open G tuning

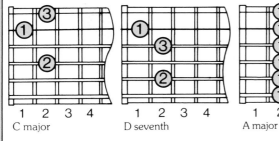

C major   D seventh   A major

Three chord shapes in open D tuning

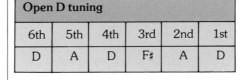

G major   A seventh   E major

Open E tuning					
6th	5th	4th	3rd	2nd	1st
E	B	E	G♯	B	E

How to tune
6th string as normal.
5th string *up* to B.
4th string *up* to E.
3rd string *up* to G♯.
2nd string as normal.
1st string as normal.

Open C tuning					
6th	5th	4th	3rd	2nd	1st
C	G	C	G	C	E

How to tune
6th string *down* to C.
5th string *down* to G.
4th string *down* to C.
3rd string as normal.
2nd string *up* to C.
1st string as normal.

Modal tunings

So-called *modal tunings* are, in a sense, "open" tunings. When all six strings are played open, the sound is of a suspended fourth chord (see p. 131). This gives a very distinctive feel and is ideal for fingerstyles. The example below shows a D modal tuning. It differs from open D in that the 3rd string remains on G instead of being tuned down to F♯. This means that the strings give the notes D (the 1st note in the scale of D major), G (the 4th note) and A (the 5th note). Together, the 1st, 4th and 5th produce a suspended fourth chord.

D modal tuning					
6th	5th	4th	3rd	2nd	1st
D	A	D	G	A	D

How to tune
6th string *down* to D. 5th string as normal. 4th string as normal. 3rd string as normal. 2nd string *down* to A. 1st string *down* to D. All modal tunings contain the 1st, 4th and 5th notes of the major scale in the key that gives them their name. In D modal, these notes are D (1st), G (4th) and A (5th).

Crossnote tunings

Open tunings in which the open-string chord is minor instead of major are called *crossnote tunings*. They differ from the ordinary open tunings in that one string is lowered by a semi-tone. This gives the minor third interval that characterizes minor chords. Thus, in crossnote D the 3rd string is tuned down to F instead of F♯, and in crossnote E the 3rd string remains at G instead of being tuned up to G♯. In both cases, fretting the 3rd string at the 1st fret will raise the open chord from a minor to a major.

Crossnote D tuning (open D minor)					
6th	5th	4th	3rd	2nd	1st
D	A	D	F	A	D

How to tune
6th string *down* to D. 5th string as normal. 4th string as normal. 3rd string *down* to F. 2nd string *down* to A. 1st string *down* to D.

Crossnote E tuning (open E minor)					
6th	5th	4th	3rd	2nd	1st
E	B	E	G	B	E

How to tune
6th string as normal. 5th string *up* to B. 4th string *up* to E. 3rd string as normal. 2nd string as normal. 1st string as normal.

Dropped tunings

A *dropped tuning* is the simplest and probably the most frequently used of all alternative tunings. Essentially, it involves lowering the pitch of just one or two of the strings. The most useful of all is dropped D: it is exactly the same as the standard E, A, D, G, B, E tuning except that the 6th string is lowered by a tone to D. It therefore sounds the same as the open 4th string but an octave lower in pitch. Dropped D tuning is ideal when playing in the key of D, since it means that the open 6th string can be used to play the bass. Alternating between the D on the 6th string and the D on the 4th string can produce an attractive rhythmic "drone" which underpins a melody played on the top strings. It is also useful when playing in the key of A, since the open 5th string acts as the bass for the tonic chord of A and the open 6th string for the sub-dominant chord of D. Dropped tunings are often used in blues for these reasons.

There is a variation on dropped D tuning that tunes the 2nd string down from B to A. It therefore sounds the same as the A on the open 5th string but an octave lower.

Dropped D tuning					
6th	5th	4th	3rd	2nd	1st
D	A	D	G	B	E

How to tune
6th string *down* to D. 5th string as normal. 4th string as normal. 3rd string as normal. 2nd string as normal. 1st string as normal. Tune either by lowering the 6th string so that it is an octave below the open 4th string or by lowering it so that the 7th fret on the 6th string gives the same note as the open 5th string.

Dropped D variation					
6th	5th	4th	3rd	2nd	1st
D	A	D	G	A	E

How to tune
6th string *down* to D. 5th string as normal. 4th string as normal. 3rd string as normal. 2nd string *down* to A. 1st string as normal. The variation on standard dropped D tuning lies in the fact that the 2nd string is tuned down from B to A.

Miscellaneous tunings

Example 1 is sometimes called "sawmill" tuning. It is in fact a G modal tuning – and differs from open G in that the 2nd string is tuned up to C. Examples 2 and 3 are variations on other D tunings. Example 4 is slightly more unusual. It involves tuning the 2nd string down from B to A and the 3rd string down three semi-tones from G to E. Example 5 is the same as 4 but with the 6th string dropped to D.

Example 1 ("sawmill")					
6th	5th	4th	3rd	2nd	1st
D	G	D	G	C	D

How to tune
6th string *down* to D. 5th string *down* to G. 4th string as normal. 3rd string as normal. 2nd string *up* to C. 1st string *down* to D.

Example 3					
6th	5th	4th	3rd	2nd	1st
D	A	D	F♯	B	D

How to tune
6th string *down* to D. 5th string as normal. 4th string as normal. 3rd string *down* to F♯. 2nd string as normal. 1st string *down* to D.

Example 5					
6th	5th	4th	3rd	2nd	1st
D	A	D	E	A	E

Example 2					
6th	5th	4th	3rd	2nd	1st
D	A	D	G	B	D

How to tune
6th string *down* to D. 5th string as normal. 4th string as normal. 3rd string as normal. 2nd string as normal. 1st string *down* to D.

Example 4					
6th	5th	4th	3rd	2nd	1st
E	A	D	E	A	E

How to tune
6th string as normal. 5th string as normal. 4th string as normal. 3rd string *down* to E. 2nd string *down* to A. 1st string as normal.

How to tune
6th string *down* to D. 5th string as normal. 4th string as normal. 3rd string *down to* E. 2nd string *down* to A. 1st string as normal.

Bottleneck and slide guitar

Bottleneck and *slide* are terms often used interchangeably for a style of guitar playing in which the strings are "stopped" by a small metal or glass tube held in the left hand or slipped over one of the left-hand fingers. Strictly speaking, "bottleneck" refers to glass, and "slide" refers to metal, but the technique is the same in both cases.

Slide guitar originated in America, in and around the Mississippi Delta. It was negro music, with its roots in the tradition of black slavery and therefore linked strongly to the evolution of the blues. At the outset, it was an attempt to imitate the expressiveness of the human voice. The term "bottleneck" comes from the fact that the earliest slides were made from the broken-off necks of beer bottles. Due to the Hawaiian influence, the first slide players laid their guitars flat across their laps with the strings facing upwards. They used anything from penknives to cigar tubes as makeshift slides. Later, when the slide was worn over one finger, the guitar was held in the normal way.

The history of slide guitar playing begins with some of the great American blues musicians – Charley Patton, Son House, Mississippi Fred McDowell, Big Joe Williams, Bukka White, Robert Johnson, Blind Lemon Jefferson, Leadbelly, Blind Willie McTell and Blind Boy Fuller. They created the style, set the standards, and passed on what they knew to the second generation – guitarists such as Muddy Waters and, primarily, Elmore James. They, in turn, took slide playing into the electric blues era and influenced the rock guitarists we now associate most strongly with slide playing – Eric Clapton, the late Duane Allman, the late Lowell George (of Little Feat), Rory Gallagher and Ry Cooder.

How to use a slide

It is in fact quite easy to make your own glass slide from the neck of a bottle, or improvise a metal one from a piece of tubing, but ready-made slides are available in most guitar shops and are not expensive. Metal and glass slides produce different sounds, so experiment with both to see which you prefer. The same goes for whether you choose to wear the slide on your 3rd or 4th finger. One advantage in wearing it on your 4th finger is that it leaves three other fingers free to play chords. A guitar with a high action is best for slide since it reduces the likelihood of fret buzz. The slide merely rests on the strings; it is *not* used to push them down to the frets. For this reason, it should come to rest directly over the frets, not slightly behind them. Many of the most effective slide guitar effects are created with open or dropped tunings (see p. 158), which allow whole chords to be slid up or down.

Slide technique
This close-up shows the left hand of Mississippi Fred McDowell, one of the greatest and earliest slide players. He wears an original glass bottleneck on his 3rd finger.

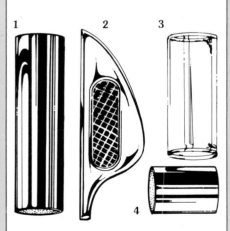

Four different types of slide
1 Full-length polished metal slide. 2 Metal lap slide used when guitar is rested flat on knees. 3 Glass slide. 4 Short polished-metal slide.

Big Joe Williams playing a 9-string Harmony Sovereign with a metal slide on his 4th finger.

GUITAR MAINTENANCE AND CUSTOMIZING

The information in this chapter should give you a good understanding of how to care for your guitar, how to set it up properly so that it plays well, and what to look for when buying a new one. It should also enable you to diagnose faults at an early stage and take the appropriate action before the situation gets progressively worse and more and more expensive to deal with. Although any vintage or valuable guitar in need of repair should be given to a specialist, there are many simple maintenance and repair jobs that can be carried out on more modest instruments by almost anyone willing to take time and care. If you are reasonably good with your hands, follow the instructions carefully and you should have no problems. But remember that many of the guitars which finally arrive on the professional repairer's workbench have been bodged by their owners and are often sadly beyond practical repair. Guitar electronics is also within the scope of the amateur. These pages contain all the basic information needed to open up a whole world of experimentation – from installing or re-wiring pick-ups to building a pre-amp. The growth of guitar customizing and "spare-part guitar surgery" has been astounding in the past few years. Nowadays, this can mean anything from fitting a special strap button to assembling a complete guitar from parts bought over the counter at a local music store. This chapter will tell you what's available, how to choose what you need, and how to fit what you've bought.

Strings

In the past, guitar strings were made of either wire or gut (called "cat gut" but, in fact, almost always the intestines of sheep). However, modern guitar strings divide into two basic types – steel and nylon. Steel strings are used on electric guitars and on flat-top and arch-top acoustics; nylon strings are used on classical and flamenco guitars.

Most guitars are strung with a set of six strings, each of a different thickness and each tuned to a different pitch. Of these six, the 1st and 2nd strings are "plain", and the 4th, 5th and 6th strings are "wound". On electric guitars, the 3rd string may be either plain or wound. Twelve-string guitars, of course, have twelve strings, normally tuned in pairs and octaves (see p. 68).

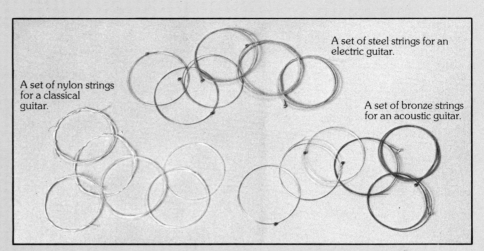

A set of nylon strings for a classical guitar.

A set of steel strings for an electric guitar.

A set of bronze strings for an acoustic guitar.

String types

Because it is impractical to make thick plain strings, the mass of the bass strings is increased by wrapping lengths of extra "wire" around a central core. These are *wound* strings. The central core may be either round or hexagonal. With steel strings, the core is made of steel; with nylon strings, the core is made of nylon.

The material from which the wire winding is made varies: they can be roughly classified as "white" or "silver" metal (stainless steel, nickel, nickel alloy, silver-plated copper) or "gold" or "yellow" metal (bronze, brass and various alloys). Either white or yellow strings can be used on acoustic guitars – although most players prefer the yellow bronze or brass strings. Only certain strings can be used on electric guitars with magnetic pick-ups. These are the magnetically responsive white metal ones. Neither yellow metal strings nor nylon strings will work with a magnetic pick-up. A guitar with a contact transducer or microphone can be fitted with any type of string.

The shape or profile which the winding gives the wound string varies according to whether the string is roundwound, flatwound or groundwound.

Roundwound strings

These are the most commonly used strings. To produce the bottom three (or four) wound strings, the steel or nylon core is wrapped round with a long, continuous length of round wire. The winding is done

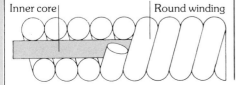

Inner core | Round winding

automatically, by a machine that spins the central core. Roundwound strings produce a good tone and volume, and when new give a clear ring suitable for both acoustic and electric guitars.

Flatwound strings

Also known as "tapewound" strings, flatwounds have a far smoother surface than that of roundwound strings. This is because the winding is made not from round wire

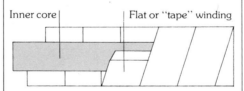

Inner core | Flat or "tape" winding

but from flat metal tape or ribbon.

Flatwound strings were designed to overcome the problem of "finger squeak" – the noise produced when the guitarist's left hand moves up and down the fingerboard while in contact with the strings. The smooth, flat surface of flatwound strings helps to reduce this noise.

Flatwounds have a more mellow sound than roundwound strings and are therefore

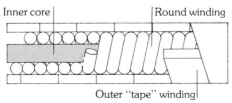

Inner core | Round winding

Outer "tape" winding

often preferred by jazz players. They tend not to be popular with rock guitarists, chiefly because they lack the bright, percussive tone of roundwounds – and also because

they tend not to last so well.

Some flatwound strings are made with both a round *and* a flat winding. The round winding goes on first and is then covered with a flat ribbon winding. Usually known as "compound flatwounds", these strings are sometimes used by jazz players.

Groundwound strings

These strings are an attempt to combine the different advantages of roundwound and flatwound strings. They are made in the same way as roundwound strings – that is, a round wire is wrapped around the core – but the winding is then ground down and polished so that the protrusions are removed and a flattened surface is left. Different makes are ground to different degrees. Groundwound (or "half-flat") strings therefore give some of the bright tone quality, projection and sustain of roundwounds while also offering the smoother feel of flatwounds.

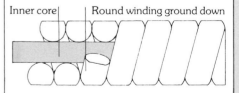

Inner core | Round winding ground down

Silk and steel strings

Sometimes called "compound strings", these are something of a special case, since the inner core is made of a combination of steel and silk. The two treble strings are plain, unwound steel. But the four bass strings comprise a steel core wrapped first with a fine layer of silk fibre and then with a regular metal winding. For use only on acoustic guitars, these strings have a sound and feel between that of steel and nylon.

String gauges and tension

The pitch of the note produced by a guitar string depends on three things: the tension placed on it (this is controlled by the tuning heads); the length of its vibrating section (determined by the distance between the nut and saddle); and its *mass*. When both the diameter and weight of a guitar string are increased, so is its mass. If two strings of equal length are placed under equal tension, the one with the greater mass will vibrate at a slower rate and produce a lower note. In short, this is why the bass strings get progressively heavier and thicker.

Steel-string diameters are expressed as *gauges* – usually measured as fractions of an inch. Sets of strings are graduated so that their tension is as consistent as possible

when they are in tune and so that they offer an even resistance when fretting notes with the left hand. They are available in sets, usually labelled "heavy", "medium", "light", "extra light" and "ultra light". Manufacturers' names for these basic sets may vary and you may find an intermediate set such as "medium light". Strings are also available individually – in almost all practical gauges – so you can make up your own combination if you wish.

Changing the strings on your guitar from one gauge to another will affect its sound and "feel". Light-gauge strings are easier to push down onto the frets (since the tension is lower) and make note bending easier. However, they can be hard to keep in tune,

they give less volume and sustain, and you may find that you tend to bend strings out of tune accidentally when playing chords. For the same reasons, using a set of heavy-gauge strings has all the opposite effects. The guitar may be slightly harder to play, but the strings will distort less when playing chords, will hold their pitch better, and will give longer sustain and more volume.

Classical nylon strings are available in different "tensions" as well as gauges. Varying the type of nylon will give a "hard", "medium" or "light" action. Flamenco strings (which are sometimes red) are generally "hard" since this suits the sound of flamenco music, the faster technique and the lower action of the guitars.

String gauges   A comparison of typical sets.

Note   W = wound 3rd string.

Ultra light	Extra light	Light	Medium	Heavy
.008	.010	.011	.013	.014
.010	.014	.015	.017	.018
.014	.020W	.022W	.026W	.028W
.022	.028	.030	.034	.040
.030	.040	.042	.046	.050
.038	.050	.052	.056	.060

Why do strings break?

Guitar strings can and do break for any of the following reasons.

● The string is over-tensioned. Guitar strings are designed to be tuned to concert pitch (see p. 69). They can be tightened only a little higher before there is a risk of them breaking or of the excessive tension distorting or damaging the guitar neck.

● The older a string, the more likely it is to break. Less elasticity, combined with wear and rust caused by sweat from the fingers, will weaken strings and may eventually cause them to snap.

● Strings are often broken by heavy right-hand technique, particularly hard strumming. This can cause the string to break at any point along its length. While many lead guitarists hardly ever break strings, some rhythm players – especially those who play hard – regularly do.

● A kink in a string can cause a weak spot. Before it breaks, it can be seen and felt as a small bump. When fitting strings, take care not to fold them back on themselves, since this is what causes the kinks.

● Sharp edges on the saddle, nut or tuning head capstans can cause strings to break. Check where the string has broken and file down any sharp edges.

How can I make strings last longer?

Strings stretch during their lifetime. They slowly lose their elasticity and their tone quality decreases. Eventually, they will stretch no more. Old, fully stretched strings produce notes which are no longer rich in harmonic overtones. As a result, the guitar becomes harder to tune and the sound is dull and lifeless.

Strings also wear, particularly at the points where they make contact with the frets. Wound strings suffer most; they develop "flat spots" where the undersides

Flat spot   Dirt and rust

of the windings are worn flat. Flat spots and broken windings will both impair tone, while the latter will also cause string "buzz".

With time, strings can become tarnished, dirty and rusty. Dirt and grease from sweaty hands build up quickly on the strings, especially on the undersides and between the windings. For this reason, you should clean and dry your strings immediately after playing (see p. 177).

"Snapping" the strings is a pro's trick which sometimes helps to dislodge dirt from beneath the windings. One at a time, pull each string away from the fingerboard and allow it to snap back. Repeat this a few times with each string.

"Boiling" the strings is an amateur's trick occasionally employed by impoverished professionals. The old strings are taken off the guitar and simply boiled in a pan of water for a few minutes to remove grease and dirt. Although this will never make the strings sound new again, some people claim that it gives them a slightly brighter tone.

Just how long you can expect a set of strings to last depends on several factors. A guitar player who works four hours a night, six nights a week, in a sweaty, smoke-filled club will get through far more sets of strings than someone who plays a twenty-minute party piece a couple of times a year. The more you sweat, the shorter the life of your strings. If you play hard with your right hand and fret notes heavily with your left, the same thing applies: you will wear out strings quickly.

How often you should change strings is also up to you. Some professional guitarists fit a new set of strings each night they play. Many amateurs, on the other hand, leave the same set on their guitar for years and regard replacing them as an unnecessary and exceptional circumstance.

Many people love the bright, "zingy" sound of new strings that have just been fitted. Most experienced guitarists, however, prefer the slightly more "played-in" sound that comes after playing for a couple of hours or so.

Fitting strings

Guitar manufacturers often advise you to fit new strings one at a time. The idea is that removing all the old strings at once will release the tension on the neck and risk it distorting. In fact, this is unlikely. What is more important, perhaps, is to de-tune the strings at a similar rate so that the tension on the neck is reduced evenly.

Occasionally, strings break while they are being tightened, and the whiplash of the sharp ends can be dangerous. For this reason, keep your face away from the string while you are tuning it up to pitch.

Never tune your strings more than a tone above concert pitch. Not only does this increase the chance of them breaking, it also exerts an excessive strain on the neck and may distort or damage it. Fitting one string at a time helps to avoid this, since you always have the other strings as an indication of the right pitch.

When you string any guitar, you can expect that by the time you have tuned the last string the first one you fitted will have gone down in pitch. New strings always take a couple of

days to stretch so that they stay reasonably in tune (see opposite).

Loose guitar strings are in fact quite easily damaged. They are usually sold coiled in separate envelopes, and when taking them out of their packets you should be careful not to get kinks in them. This will weaken them and may also hurt your left-hand fingers.

Various methods for fitting both steel and nylon strings are shown on these pages. It is most important that you *never* put steel strings on a classical or flamenco guitar. Nylon strings exert far less tension than steel, and classical and flamenco instruments are simply not constructed to withstand the extra forces. Putting steel strings on them will almost certainly damage the neck and, possibly, the soundbox.

You can, if you wish, put nylon strings on a steel-string guitar. There is little point, however, since their stronger, heavier construction means that the nylon strings will produce less volume and a tone which is neither as percussive as that of steel strings nor as rich as when they are fitted to a classical guitar.

Guitar stringwinders

A stringwinder is a gadget that slips over the button on the tuning head and enables you to wind the strings on or off the capstans quickly and easily. If several neat coils of string are wound on to the capstan, the extra string length will facilitate fine tuning and place a more even tension on the tuning head.

Using a stringwinder

Fitting steel strings to an acoustic guitar

Almost all steel strings have a small knob or ball attached to one end. This anchors the string to either the bridge or tailpiece, and it is the end that you should attach first. On most flat-top guitars, the strings are secured at the body by bridge pins. Bridge pins are tapered – as are the holes into which they fit – so that they will stay in place when pushed home. On most arch-tops, the strings are

attached to a tailpiece, not to the bridge. They each pass through a hole or slot large enough to allow the string through but not the knob on the end. The strings then simply pass over the bridge and saddle without being attached to them at all.

At the head of the guitar, the strings are secured to the tuning head capstans. Allow some slack so that they can be wound

round a couple of times before passing through the hole in the capstan. To prevent the treble strings from slipping, you may thread them once through the hole, once around the capstan, and then through the hole a second time. Tidy the ends and prevent them from rattling while you are playing by coiling them round or clipping them off with pliers or wire cutters.

Attaching the strings to the tuning heads

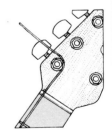

1 Bring the string over the nut and up the centre of the head. Wind it over the *top* of the capstan, towards the edge.

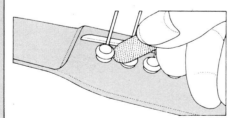

Removing bridge pins
The pins can be removed by gently prising them out with a coin or nail file. This is done *after* the string has been slackened.

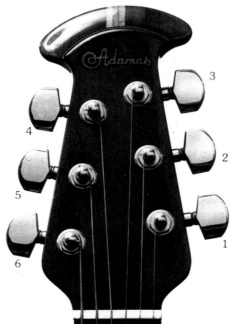

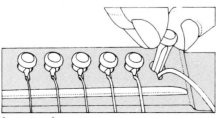

Inserting the string
The knob on the end of the string *must* be pushed to one side by the bridge pin, otherwise it will pull straight out again as the string is tightened. Bend the knob slightly to one side as it goes in.

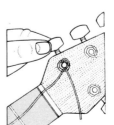

2 Thread the end of the string through the hole, pull it outwards and begin tightening the button to take up the slack.

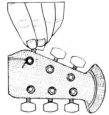

3 Continue winding so that the string coils neatly on to the capstan and the final wrap lies close to the head.

Fitting strings to an electric guitar

In the case of solid-body electrics, the strings are attached to the tuning heads in the same way as they are for steel-string acoustics. At the body, the fixing method varies with the design of the guitar. Sometimes the strings are secured by means of a tailpiece, sometimes a combined bridge and tailpiece, and sometimes they pass right through the body. The principle is usually the same: the string is threaded through a hole or slot small enough to retain the knob on the end of the string.

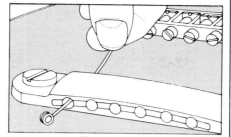

Tailpiece attachment
Electric guitars with tailpieces are simple to re-string. The ball-ends of the strings secure them in position at the holes in the tailpiece.

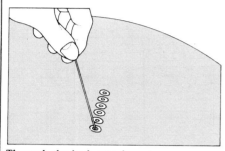

Through-the-body attachment
1 The strings are threaded through from the back of the body and are anchored to a bridge plate.

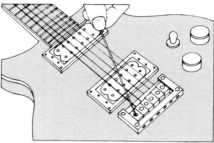

2 The strings are then pulled out from the front, up and over the bridge assembly, and are then fixed to the tuning head capstans.

"Stretching" the strings

Many guitarists, especially those new to performing in public, fit new strings too soon before a gig and consequently suffer severe tuning problems. If new strings must be fitted a few hours before a performance, playing them in or thoroughly stretching them as shown below will help to keep them in tune.

How to stretch strings
Tune the new string up to pitch, then pull it about an inch (2.5 cm) away from the guitar. It will have dropped in pitch slightly. Tune it back up and repeat until stretching it no longer puts it out of tune.

Fitting nylon strings to classical and flamenco guitars

Nylon strings have no ball-ends. Instead, they are fixed to the bridge with a simple knot. The wound bass strings usually have a loop made from the central nylon strands at one end. Originally, this was hooked on to the tailpieces fitted to early, rare instruments. The loop end is always the one which should be secured to the bridge since the last 2-3 in. (5-7.5 cm) of the string are usually more pliable and therefore easier to tie. There are various methods of tying the knot (see below), but in each case you should have only a short end of loose string left at the bridge. If the end is too long, it may rattle against the soundboard.

Flamenco guitars sometimes have wooden tuning pegs instead of geared tuning heads (see p. 43). The pegs stay in place because, like bridge pins, they have a taper fit. To replace a string, the peg must be pulled out slightly so that it can be turned. It is then pushed back to form a tight fit once the string is up to the right pitch. As there is no gearing, your fingers have to hold the tension that the string exerts on the peg until the peg is pushed back in. This is not easy and requires some practice.

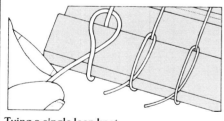

Tying a single loop knot
Thread end of string through bridge hole. Pass pliable end over top of bridge and under string. Make single loop knot and tighten.

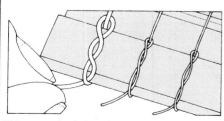

Tying a multiple loop knot
Begin in same way as above, leading string through, over bridge and under itself. This time, make two loop knots, threading string under, over and under itself.

Attaching the strings to the tuning heads

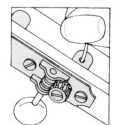

1 Bring the string over the nut and up the centre of the head. Thread it through the hole in the capstan from the top to the bottom.

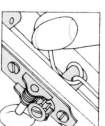

2 Bring the end of the string over the top of the capstan and pass it underneath itself.

3 Begin winding so that the string wraps neatly round the capstan as you take up the slack and come up to pitch.

Setting the action

The *action* of a guitar can be defined as its "playability". It determines how much pressure you have to exert on the strings in order to press them down on to the frets.

The strings on any guitar are always closest to the 1st fret and furthest away from the highest fret. So there is always a slight increase in the amount of pressure needed to fret strings as you go higher up the fingerboard. A guitar is said to have "good" action if it is possible to play in any position on the neck without having to exert any more than this slight increase in finger pressure – in other words, if the action is consistent. A guitar with "bad" action is noticeably more difficult – sometimes almost impossible – to play above the first few frets.

"High" or "low" action describes the actual distance between the top of the frets and the bottom of the strings. In general, a guitar with a low action is easier to play than one with a high action. However, if the action is *too* low, the strings may rattle against the frets and cause "fret buzz". A very low action also tends to reduce the guitar's volume and can impair its tone slightly. For this reason, and to prevent string rattle, you will probably

do best with a guitar that has its action set fairly high if you strum hard.

Most guitars, especially those in the cheaper price range, do not have their action set anywhere near the optimum. This can be very discouraging for beginners. Some simply give up learning to play because certain notes are too hard to fret or because "barre" chords are too difficult. Those who persevere on guitars with bad action risk developing faults in their technique that may be hard to correct later. Because bad action makes notes hard to fret, there is a tendency to tense up the left hand and also fret too heavily – even after graduating on to a better guitar.

How the action is adjusted

The action of any guitar is determined by the construction of the instrument, the condition of the neck and body, the scale length (see p. 40), the gauge of the strings, and the distance between the top of the frets and the bottom of the strings.

"Setting the action" is the term used for altering the distance between the frets and the strings. This adjustment can be done in any of four ways: by raising or lowering the bridge or

saddle; by altering the height of the nut; by adjusting the dip in the neck; and by changing the height or profile of the frets. The methods by which these adjustments are made are covered in the following pages. They should only be attempted *after* you have ruled out distortion and checked the glued joints between the guitar neck and body.

Sets of steel strings of different gauges will almost certainly have an effect on the profile of the guitar neck. The heavier the gauge of the strings, the greater the tension required to bring them up to pitch and the more strain is exerted on the neck. If the action of your guitar is correctly set for light-gauge strings, a change to a heavy-gauge set will probably mean that you will have to re-adjust the action slightly.

Many professional guitarists have their guitars set up by a specialist maker or repairer who will watch the guitarist playing in order to assess how high or low to set the action. The adjustment may take anything from a few minutes to a few hours, depending on what needs to be done. There may even be a "second fitting" after the guitar has been set up once and then played in for a while.

High action

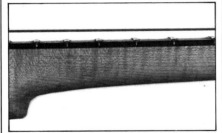

For
- More volume
- Likely to improve tone
- Ideal for rhythm chord playing

Against
- Notes harder to fret because more finger pressure required
- Fast runs are more difficult

Low action

For
- Notes easy to fret because less finger pressure required
- Facilitates fast lead playing

Against
- Risk of "fret buzz" when strumming
- Less volume
- Tone may be impaired slightly

Measuring the action

It is possible to measure the action on a guitar, but the adjustments are usually infinitesimally small and most guitarists and repairers are therefore concerned more with "feel" than with precise dimensions. Setting the action is normally a question of trial and error.

However, the figures given here can be taken as a rough guide. Action measurements are taken from at least two points on each string – usually at the 1st fret and at the "body fret" (the fret where the fingerboard joins the guitar body). Guitar necks are actually designed to have a slight dip (see p. 168). The action is always a little higher at the body fret to allow for the wide loop in which the string vibrates when played open or when low fretted notes are sounded.

The action is higher for the bass strings than it is for the treble strings. This, too, is to take account of the bass string's larger vibration loop.

All action measurements should be taken with the strings at concert pitch, although they may need to be slackened off while adjustments are made. The action at the body fret can be measured using a "feeler gauge" or by improvising one from several small pieces of card. The action at the 1st fret should be only slightly higher than the action at the 2nd fret when the string is held down on the 1st fret.

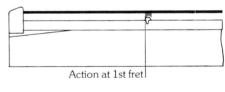

Action at 1st fret

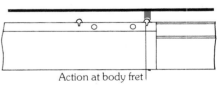

Action at body fret

A guide to action measurements
Measurements are for "medium" action. Adding or subtracting 1/64 in. (0.4 mm) will change the action to "high" or "low".

Type of guitar	Body fret	
	Bass E	Treble E
Electric	6/64 in. 2.38 mm)	4/64 in. (1.59 mm)
Flat-top acoustic	8/64 in. (3.18 mm)	6/64 in. (2.38 mm)
Classical	10/64 in. (3.97 mm)	8/64 in. (3.18 mm)

Adjusting the height of the nut

To set the action correctly, you *must* check the nut. Although you can sometimes *improve* the action simply by adjusting the bridge, you will never set up the guitar properly if the strings are too high or too low at the nut.

If your guitar has a "zero fret" (see p. 41), the action at that end of the neck should be correct – unless the frets need attention (see p. 170). If not, it may be that the grooves or notches in the nut are too high and that, as a result, the strings rest on the nut and not on the zero fret. This would put the intonation out as well. As long as the grooves in the nut are lower than the top of the zero fret, no problems should arise.

On guitars without a zero fret, the height of the nut is more critical. If the strings are set too high at the nut, you will find it hard to push them down on to the first two or three frets. A simple test will establish whether the nut is at fault. Play the guitar on and around the first three frets – including a bar F chord. Now put a capo on the 1st fret and play the same fingerings as before. If the guitar is much easier to play with the capo on, the action is too high.

The solution is usually to make the grooves in the nut a little deeper so that the strings sit closer to the fingerboard. Needle files and thin saw blades can be used for cutting the notches. However, be careful. The job must be done with precision. First, it is all too easy to make the grooves too deep. If this happens, you will get fret buzz and have to start all over again with a new nut. Second, the grooves should be semi-circular, providing a dish-shaped recess for each string to sit in, and should be of exactly the right diameter for each string. If they are too wide the string may rattle or slip out of position, and if they are too deep the tone

Groove height
Notches should be semi-circular, with no more than half the string's circumference below the top of the nut.

Nut profile
A curved fingerboard needs a curved nut. Otherwise, the strings will be closer to the fingerboard in the centre than at either edge.

will be impaired. Third, if the fingerboard is curved across the frets, the nut should have the same profile so that the height of all six strings will be correct. Fourth, because the scale length begins at the front of the nut, it is important that the grooves slope down slightly towards the head.

If the strings are set too low at the nut, they will rattle or buzz against the frets when you play them open (unfretted). The remedy is to fit a new nut. In most cases, the nut is lightly glued in position. Removing it is fairly simple, although it should be done with care. The glued joint can usually be freed by gently tapping the nut so that it comes out sideways, using a light hammer and a piece of wood to cushion the impact of the blows.

It is possible to make a temporary adjustment by putting thin veneers of wood or shims of plastic underneath the old nut to raise its overall height. But a new nut is better. Like saddles, nuts are made from plastic, ivory or bone (or in the case of some electric guitars, brass). Ivory is the best choice but may be difficult to obtain. New nuts must have grooves cut in them (see left) to match the guitar's string spacing.

Adjusting the height of the bridge

Since almost all electrics and many acoustic guitars have adjustable bridges, raising or lowering the height of the saddle is the most obvious way of adjusting the action. However, this should be done only *after* you have checked neck and body joints, the fret profile and dip in the neck, and the nut height. If any of these are at fault, no amount of bridge adjustment will improve the guitar's playability.

Electric guitars with bridges based on the design of the Fender Stratocaster can be adjusted by means of small Allen screws.

The two-footed adjustable bridge commonly fitted to f-hole arch-top guitars, and the "Tune-O-Matic" bridge fitted to most

Gibsons and many other electrics, both work in the same way. At each end of the saddle, there is a knurled metal adjuster threaded on to a metal shaft. When one adjuster is screwed up or down it raises or lowers its side of the saddle. With bridges of this type, you should adjust the height of the bass strings first and the height of the treble strings afterwards. You will find that you have to de-tune the strings in order to relax the tension on the saddle when raising it.

Guitars with fixed bridges – classical, flamenco and some flat-tops – are not so easily adjusted. The bridge is glued to the face of the soundboard. However, the saddle, over which the strings pass, sits in a

groove in the bridge and is usually held in position only by string tension. Once the strings have been loosened, the saddle comes out of its slot easily and can be re-shaped, re-positioned or replaced.

If the action is too low, you can insert thin "shims" of wood or veneer beneath the saddle to increase the string height. Alternatively, you can make a new saddle from a fresh piece of plastic, ivory or bone.

If the action is too high, you can either shave off the base of the saddle slightly or make the grooves in which the strings sit slightly deeper – in the same way as for the nut (see above). Take care not to damage the saddle's tight fit.

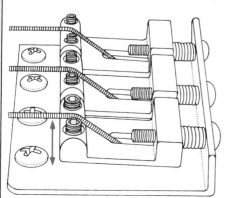

Fender Stratocaster bridge

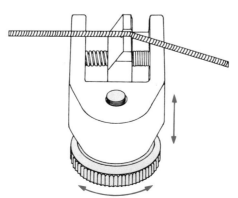

Gibson Tune-O-Matic bridge

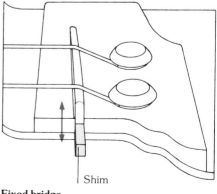

Shim

Fixed bridge

Adjusting the neck

Nine times out of ten, problems with the action of guitars can be traced to neck distortion of one kind or another. If a guitar is knocked about and not treated with care, the action will almost certainly suffer. Even the most expensive instrument is liable to distort if exposed to extreme changes in temperature or humidity.

It is impossible to set the action correctly if the joint between the neck and body is faulty (see p. 172) or if the shape of the neck itself is either "twisted", "bowed" or "warped". If the neck is badly distorted, the guitar will need the attention of a maker or repairer. However, if it is only slightly out of true and if it has an adjustable truss rod, you may be able to adjust it yourself. Only the very cheapest guitars – those that border on being toys – are so badly constructed that the action cannot be set in order and the instrument put in good playing condition.

It is a popular fallacy that all guitar necks should be perfectly straight. It is true that the fingerboard and the tops of the frets are usually level when first made but, as soon as the guitar is strung and the strings are tuned up to pitch, the tension should curve the neck very slightly – giving it a concave profile rather like an archer's bow. This has a beneficial effect on both the tone and the action: you are more likely to get a clean, ringing note and less likely to get fret buzz, because the dip in the neck corresponds to the point on the length of the open string where it vibrates in its widest arc.

Guitars fitted with adjustable truss rods (see p. 39) allow you to adjust the dip in the neck and therefore to compensate for the tension of the strings you select. They are also useful for any minor adjustments to the neck that may become necessary as a result of changes in humidity and temperature or the ageing of the instrument. Adjustable truss rods are fitted inside the guitar neck, below the fingerboard. One end is fixed (usually secured to the body of the guitar) and the other is threaded to accept a nut and washer. Because there is more wood in front of the rod than behind it, tightening the rod will reduce the dip in the neck and loosening the rod will increase the dip. Initially, before the guitar leaves its maker, the neck should be put under some compression – by tightening the adjusting nut on the rod – to act against the pull of the strings and to produce exactly the right amount of dip.

Most steel-string guitars (electric as well as acoustic) have adjustable truss rods of this type. However, Martin guitars do not, and several other famous makes have rods which work on different principles. Gretsch, for example, have fitted a geared arrangement in several of their guitar necks. Every guitar with an adjustable truss rod should be supplied with information on how to use it, but, if in doubt, always check with the manufacturer.

Guitars that do *not* have an adjustable truss rod must be taken to a professional repairer if the neck develops a bow, warp or twist. Correction of the fault may involve taking the neck apart, replacing or repairing certain parts, and then re-building it.

Adjusting the truss rod

Adjustable truss rods must always be used with great care. They are purely for *small* alterations in the dip of the neck. It is another popular fallacy that they can easily correct any degree of bow or warp. On anything other than a cheap copy guitar, you should attempt only very slight adjustments. Many guitar necks are ruined through incorrect truss rod adjustment, and any major alterations should be put in the hands of an experienced guitar repairer.

The actual dimensions of the dip in a neck depend on the type of guitar, the gauge and tension of the strings, and the way the instrument is played. Classical, flamenco, arch-top, flat-top and solid-body electric guitars all have different characteristics and will require different settings. Some makers and repairers do not take measurements at all, but instead work solely on visual assessment and "feel". However, as a general rule, the dip in the neck should measure about 1/64 in. (0.4 mm). If it is more than 1/32 in. (0.79 mm), it should probably be reduced slightly by adjusting the truss rod.

Before attempting any adjustment, check the maintenance instructions provided with the guitar to ensure that a standard type of truss rod is fitted. Then go over the joints between the neck and the body, and fit a new set of strings and bring them up to concert pitch.

There are two methods of measuring the dip in the neck. The first is as follows. Put a capo on the 1st fret and then hold down the bass E (6th) string one fret above the body fret. The string will then be in a perfectly straight line between these two frets. To check how much the neck dips, measure the distance between the bottom of the string and the top of the fret furthest from it. This will be the 5th, 6th, 7th or 8th fret, depending on the type of guitar and on the construction of the neck.

The second method is essentially the same but involves using a metal straight edge instead of the string itself. The metal edge is laid along the top of the frets and the dip measured as above.

If the dip is insufficient, increase it by rotating the adjusting nut on the truss rod by an eighth of a turn in an anti-clockwise direction. This will loosen the compression on the rod so that the string tension increases the "bow" of the neck very slightly. Take another measurement and, if the dip is still too shallow, give the nut another eighth of a turn. If you find that you have to turn the truss rod more than one complete rotation, consult a repairer before going any further. It is almost certain that some more major

Measuring the dip in the neck
If you have no straight edge to lay along the top of the frets, use the guitar strings themselves. Put a capo on the 1st fret and hold the string down on the fret one above the body fret. The dip in the neck is measured at its maximum, usually somewhere between the 5th and 8th frets.

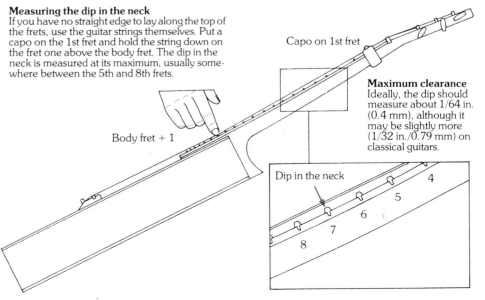

Capo on 1st fret

Body fret + 1

Maximum clearance
Ideally, the dip should measure about 1/64 in. (0.4 mm), although it may be slightly more (1/32 in./0.79 mm) on classical guitars.

Dip in the neck

Checking for a twisted neck

A twisted neck causes some of the frets – or, at least, parts of them – to be too close to the strings and others to be too far away. In other words, you may get fret buzz on some parts of the fingerboard while the action will be too high elsewhere.

You can check for a twist in the neck by "sighting a line" down the length of the fingerboard. The frets and the gaps should be perfectly parallel. If they are not, the neck is twisted and will need attention from a repairer before the action can be set. Some Rickenbackers and other guitars have "double adjustable truss rods" inside the neck which can be used to correct minor faults of this kind.

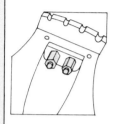

Dual truss rods
Rickenbacker build all their guitar necks with two adjustable truss rods. Each side can be adjusted separately so that it does not put the other out of alignment.

Correct
Frets perfectly parallel with one another indicate that neck is not twisted.

"Sighting a line"
Close one eye and look down the length of the neck towards the body. Hold the guitar at an angle which makes the frets look like sleepers on a railway track, with the gaps only just visible between.

Incorrect
Frets out of line with one another indicate that neck is twisted.

---

repair will be required.

If the dip is too great, first loosen the strings and then rotate the adjusting nut clockwise by an eighth of a turn. This will tighten the compression on the rod, thus straightening the neck against the pull of the strings and reducing the dip. Re-tune the strings, bringing them back up to pitch, and check the dip again. If it is still too great, repeat the operation – again going no further than one complete turn of the nut. Putting too much compression on the truss rod has often been known to break it.

Increasing the dip in the neck
If the dip in the neck is too shallow, the strings will be too close to the fingerboard and will probably cause fret buzz. To increase the dip, loosen the truss rod (anti-clockwise) so that compression on the neck is reduced.

When you have adjusted the dip between the neck and the bass E (6th) string, move on to the other side of the fingerboard and check the measurement from the treble E (1st) string. It can afford to be slightly smaller since the treble string does not vibrate in such a wide arc as the bass string.

Because the fingerboard above the body fret is usually secured to the body of the guitar, and the fingerboard below it is attached to the neck, there is sometimes a slight high point at the body fret. This does not usually present any problem.

Note In these drawings the bow and warp of the neck has been exaggerated for the purpose of explanation. Badly distorted necks cannot be repaired by adjusting the truss rod.

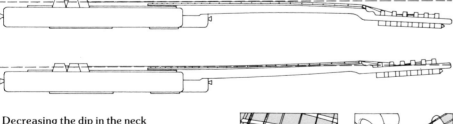

Decreasing the dip in the neck
If the dip in the neck is exaggerated, the action will be too high at certain frets. This makes the notes hard to play and may also affect the guitar's intonation (see p. 171). To reduce the dip, tighten the truss rod (clockwise) so that compression on the neck is increased.

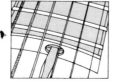

Screw adjustment   Nut adjustment

Neck tilt

With classical, flamenco and flat-top guitars, the fingerboard is usually more-or-less parallel with the face of the soundboard. Many electric guitars, however, have necks that tilt back slightly. This increases the space between the top of the body or soundboard and the bottom of the strings and provides sufficient room for mounting the pick-ups.

Most arch-top guitars also have tilted necks. This developed as a design feature of the instrument when it first appeared in the 1920s. The guitars were then played acoustically and players wanted as much volume as possible. Tilting the neck increases the height of the bridge – and this, in turn, increases the acoustic volume of the guitar. Some arch-top guitars have detachable necks which allow the angle of the tilt to be adjusted.

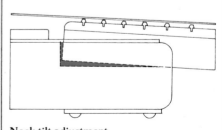

Neck tilt adjustment
Solid-body electrics with bolt-on necks can have "shims" (small pieces of wood veneer) inserted to adjust the neck angle. Some Fenders have their own built-in "Micro-Tilt" adjustment (see p. 51).

Fret care

Frets, which are cut from continuous lengths of metal "fretwire", are available in various shapes and sizes. In the early days of steel-string acoustic guitars, the tops of the frets were often fairly high off the fingerboard and somewhat square in profile. But, because guitarists felt that this slowed down their left-hand technique, there was a trend towards much lower frets. As an example, Gibson's Les Paul Custom, introduced in 1954, was nicknamed the "Fretless Wonder" because its frets were so low. (see p. 58).

More recently, slightly higher, more rounded frets have become popular on many electric guitars. They are still fast, but they make left-hand note-bending much easier. There is less friction because the tips of the left-hand fingers do not come into such close contact with the fingerboard and because there is more room to get a good "grip" on the string.

Levelling frets

When the strings are de-tuned and the tension on the neck is released, the tops of the frets should be in a straight line. If one fret is still higher than the others, the strings may well rattle against it and cause fret buzz. To find the fret or frets causing the problem, simply play each note on the string in question, moving up the fingerboard. As soon as you play a note *without* a buzz, you will have identified the fret immediately below it as the offender.

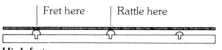

High frets
A high fret protrudes above the line of the others and will cause a rattle if you fret notes below it.

If the fret is not loose in its groove, if the action has been set correctly and if you have checked that the neck is not distorted, the fret must be too high. The answer is to level it down, and the procedure is as follows.

Loosen or remove the strings. Protect the wood of the fingerboard with masking tape and the face of the soundboard where the fingerboard ends with a piece of cardboard. Protect the nut with a piece of plastic or more tape so that you do not damage it while working. The tops of the protruding frets should be levelled with a very fine file about 10 in. (25 cm) long or with a carborundum stone. You must take care to exert an even pressure on the file or stone all the time and work along the length of the fingerboard. Work slowly and keep checking that you are not filing the frets too low.

The frets you have filed down will have a shiny, flat top surface and must now be "re-shaped" to the same rounded profile as the other frets. This is usually done using a small fine file – preferably a specially curved "fret file". The job is then finished by very carefully buffing the frets with fine-gauge wire wool or glasspaper.

On steel-string guitars, frets that have had grooves or notches cut in them by the strings can be ground down in the same way – although, in this case, *all* the frets must be filed to a new, uniform level, and badly worn frets will have to be replaced.

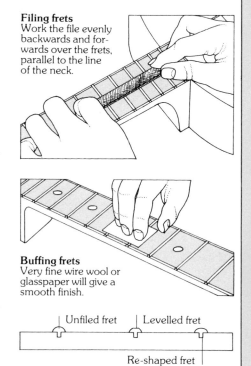

Filing frets
Work the file evenly backwards and forwards over the frets, parallel to the line of the neck.

Buffing frets
Very fine wire wool or glasspaper will give a smooth finish.

| Unfiled fret | Levelled fret |
| Re-shaped fret |

Re-fitting loose frets

Loose frets can affect intonation and tone, and can cause unwanted buzzes and rattles. They must be removed and either re-fitted or replaced. The job is tricky but within the capabilities of anyone prepared to take the necessary care.

The "tang" or stem of fretwire has small protrusions which grip the sides of the slot in the fingerboard when the fret is hammered into place. A filler (glue or polish) is then used to fill in the spaces between the fret and the wood of the fingerboard and to prevent rattles. Before a fret can be removed, this filler must be softened – either with steam, hot water on a rag, or a soldering iron run carefully along the fret. A special pair of flat-nosed pliers, a chisel or a knife with a thin blade can then be used to extract the fret. Frets are in fact easy to remove. The difficulty lies in avoiding damage to the fingerboard – and the only answer is to work with care.

It should be possible to re-fit the same fret if you roughen the tang so that it will grip firmly. Give it a coat of white glue or white polish before gently tapping it back into place. Putting a slight curve on the fretwire will help to seat the ends correctly. If the tangs will not bite, you must make a new fret or go to a repairer.

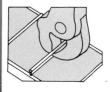

Removing frets
Guitar repairers often use a pair of pliers specially adapted for the job so that the jaws sit level on the surface of the fingerboard.

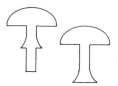

Re-shaping frets
Old frets can be re-fitted if the tangs are hammered and the bottom of the fret splayed out to give a good grip.

Filing down protruding frets

Sometimes the ends of the frets stick out slightly from the sides of the fingerboard. Brand new guitars may be faulty in this respect if they have not been properly finished, and on older instruments a slight shrinkage of the wood in the fingerboard may have the same effect. Protruding frets make a guitar uncomfortable – sometimes even painful – to play, and the sharp ends should be filed down.

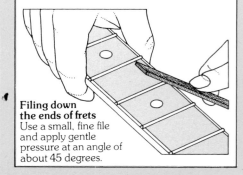

Filing down the ends of frets
Use a small, fine file and apply gentle pressure at an angle of about 45 degrees.

Setting the intonation

The *intonation* of a guitar is said to be correct when – once the open strings are tuned to concert pitch – the notes fretted at every point on the fingerboard all have the right pitch. That is to say, they are neither sharp nor flat.

Intonation is always a problem with guitars. Every time you fret a note, you stretch the string and increase its tension slightly as you push it down towards the fingerboard. This sharpens the pitch of the fretted note. It is more noticeable on a guitar with a high action and its effect increases with the thickness (gauge) of the strings. The result is that notes go progressively out of tune as you move up the fingerboard. If an open G chord sounds fine, but a barre G chord on the 10th fret sounds awful, then the guitar's intonation needs adjusting.

Assuming that the frets have been properly fitted in the right positions, that the neck is not distorted, and that the action is set correctly, the fault will almost certainly lie with the condition or length of the strings.

Old, tarnished or dirty strings can never be expected to play in tune. They will stretch with age, and dirt or damage will inhibit the notes' "harmonic series". The first thing to do before attempting to check the guitar's intonation is, therefore, to fit a new set and tune them up to concert pitch.

The length of the vibrating strings is determined by the guitar's *scale length* – the distance from the nut to the saddle (see p. 40). Increasing the scale length – by slightly more for the bass strings – will cancel out the rise in pitch of fretted notes.

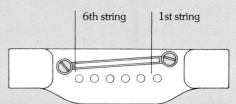

Slanted bridge
The bass strings, which go out of tune the most when fretted, are longer than the treble strings.

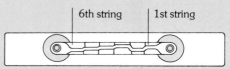

Compensating bridge
Each string has a different length. The 6th string is furthest from the nut and the 3rd string closest to it.

Checking the intonation

Tune the guitar to concert pitch and check the intonation of each string separately. First play the note on the 12th fret (one octave above the open string), then play the 12th fret harmonic (also an octave above the open string). The technique for playing harmonics is described on p. 116. If both notes have exactly the same pitch, the intonation is correct. If the pitch of the fretted note is higher than that of the harmonic, the scale length of the string is too short and the saddle should be moved away from the nut. If the pitch of the fretted note is lower than that of the harmonic, the scale length is too long and the saddle must be moved towards the nut so that the pitch of the fretted note is raised.

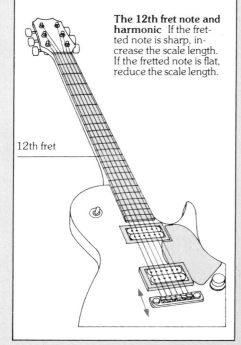

The 12th fret note and harmonic If the fretted note is sharp, increase the scale length. If the fretted note is flat, reduce the scale length.

12th fret

Adjusting the saddle

Classical, flamenco and most flat-top steel-string guitars have bridges which do not allow adjustment of the scale length – although most of them are "slanted" to improve intonation. If a slight adjustment is necessary, it may be possible by re-shaping the profile of the top of the saddle to increase or reduce the length of the vibrating string. If this is the case, however, you should probably take the guitar to an experienced repairer.

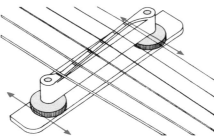

Floating bridge
The bridge is not fixed to the soundboard but is held in place only by the downward pull of the strings. If the intonation needs adjusting, set the bridge position for the treble E (1st) string first.

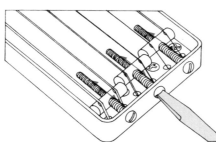

Fender Telecaster bridge
The bridge on a Telecaster allows the scale length of the strings to be adjusted in pairs. The strings to check and adjust are the treble E (1st), the D (4th) and the bass E (6th).

Almost all arch-top guitars and also most electrics have bridges that are adjustable both for string height and string length. This means that the action and the scale length – the two factors which most affect intonation – can be adjusted in relation to one another. Arch-tops usually have a floating bridge which can be moved freely backwards and forwards. Sometimes, there will be a mark on the soundboard indicating the correct position for the bridge.

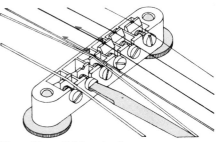

Gibson Tune-O-Matic bridge
Each string sits on a small metal insert that acts as its own saddle. These can be moved backwards and forwards individually by means of small adjustment screws.

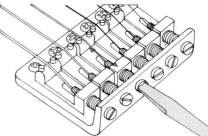

Fender Stratocaster bridge
Small screws mounted on the fixed base plate control the position of the separate saddle for each string. With bridges such as this, the string lengths need be set in no particular order.

Simple guitar repairs

If a guitar has been badly damaged or if it needs a complicated repair, you will probably need the skill and experience of a specialist repairer. However, some repairs can be made quite easily by any inexperienced player willing to work patiently and carefully. The most common of these are described here. They rarely require more than the right glue and a range of suitable clamps.

In essence, the procedure for repairing wood fractures, cracks and broken joints is always the same. The surfaces to be joined should marry up well and should be clean before the work begins. A liberal coating of glue should be applied to one or both surfaces (according to the glue manufacturer's instructions), and the surfaces should then be evenly and snugly pressed together.

When the pieces are aligned correctly, they should be clamped or secured in place, and any excess glue should be wiped away. The space between the two glued surfaces should be visible only as a hairline crack. If the repair is likely to be placed under stress when the guitar is re-strung and tuned up, it should be left for at least 24 hours for the glued joint to dry thoroughly.

Checking neck and bridge joints

The joints most likely to suffer with time are those between the neck and the body of the guitar and those between the bridge and the soundboard.

If the neck is of the glued-on type, the dovetail joint by which it is attached to the body is sometimes pulled open by the tension of the strings. If there are any signs of cracks appearing between the two, the guitar should be placed in the hands of a professional repairer.

Bridge joints are also placed under stress by string tension. If the bridge is glued to the face of the soundboard – as on classical, flamenco and flat-top guitars – it may either begin to pull away or distort the soundboard. And on guitars where the strings are anchored to a tailpiece, the soundboard may be pushed downwards, causing an indentation in the top of the guitar.

Distorted soundboards should be repaired professionally, but, if the bridge is simply peeling away, you may be able to prise it off carefully and re-glue it yourself.

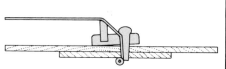

Faulty bridge joint
A gap may appear between the bridge and soundboard if the tension of the strings is pulling the glue joint apart.

Soundboard distortion
String tension acting on the glued bridge may sometimes pull the soundboard out of shape and affect the action.

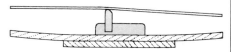

Soundboard indentation
On a guitar with a tailpiece, the downward pressure of the strings passing over the bridge may indent the soundboard.

Glues and clamps

The glue that guitar-repairers traditionally use is animal-based and called *hide glue* – although it may also be referred to as "Scotch", "cabinet-maker's", "gelatine" or "violin-maker's" glue. It can be used either hot or cold, and is sold in solid or powder form. It is also available as "fish glue", in which case it is fish- not animal-based.

Hot hide glue is the best. It is usually soaked in water and then heated to the required working temperature – either in an electric glue pot or a double boiler. The temperature and degree of dilution vary from repairer to repairer and job to job.

Hide glues have been used by instrument-makers for hundreds of years. Though not as strong as some modern adhesives, hide glues dry very hard and give a more rigid joint than more elastic resin glues. They also offer the advantage that the consistency can be controlled by varying the ratio of water to glue. Moreover, it is possible to separate a hide-glue joint. An eye dropper or teaspoonful of warm water, a controlled jet of steam, or a heated knife blade slipped into the joint, will usually break the seal. However, it might take half an hour or so for the glue to soften; time and patience are therefore essential.

Unfortunately, hide glues are not perfect. They are vulnerable to moisture in the air and to extremes of temperature. They are also popular with colonizing fungus spores who may set up home in a glued joint and will eventually weaken it.

Because all hide glues are quite time-consuming to prepare and sometimes difficult to obtain, *white woodworking glues* are used extensively throughout the industry – including guitar mass production. When set, white glue is softer and more elastic than hide glue, and some people feel this impairs the acoustic tone. Some makers are therefore happy to use white glue for joints such as the one between the neck and fingerboard, but prefer to use a traditional hide glue for the construction of the soundbox.

Modern "miracle" glues – those that set in a few seconds – are suitable for thousands of applications, but not for guitar repairs. The speed with which they bond and the fact that they are almost impossible to take apart mean that their use is very limited.

Both hide and white glues begin to set after a few minutes. They will then take several hours to dry completely and form a good bond. Excess glue forced out of cracks or joints as pressure is applied to them should be removed immediately with a damp cloth. In most cases, the repair will have to be clamped while the glue sets. As clamps are available in various shapes and sizes, make certain you have the right one for the job.

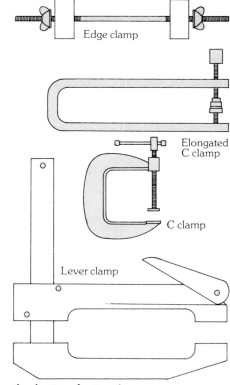

Edge clamp

Elongated
C clamp

C clamp

Lever clamp

A selection of guitar clamps
While glued joints are setting, a light, even pressure is required. Take care to use the correct clamps and not to overtighten them – otherwise you may damage the guitar still further.

Repairing a broken joint

Dropping or knocking a guitar will produce undue strain on the wooden joints. White glues are usually stronger than the woods they bind together, so the wood is likely to fracture before the joint gives way, but hide glues are fairly brittle and can break more easily. They can also be weakened by excess damp, extremes of temperature or attack by fungus spores.

If the joint has only partially come away, it must be dismantled and reset. One of the best methods is to apply small amounts of hot water to soften the glue – this may take half an hour or so. Once the glue is soft, the two pieces of wood can be pulled carefully apart. Scrape off the old glue while it is still soft, and, if water has been used, allow the wood to dry out thoroughly before re-gluing.

Although "keying" (or roughening) of the two surfaces to be joined is common practice among repairers who use traditional hide glues, wooden synthetic resin woodworking glues will work well with smooth surfaces. Once the new glue has been applied, the joint should be pressed gently together and clamped until set. Any glue that seeps out should be wiped off.

Repairing fractured wood

Wood fractures usually occur as a result of the guitar being dropped, knocked over or struck. Breaks of this kind tend to happen if a guitar is left propped up against a wall or speaker cabinet; the slightest vibration will send the guitar crashing to the floor.

One of the most common fractures occurs when the neck breaks somewhere between the nut and the first two machine heads – that is, at its weakest point. This is more likely with electric guitars (which are heavier than acoustics) and with any guitar that has a one-piece neck and truss rod.

If the wood has only partially split, or if it has broken into two separate pieces which can be fitted snugly together, the repair may be quite easy. As long as the two pieces of wood are aligned carefully and accurately, a simple gluing and clamping operation will be all that is required.

However, if the wood has splintered or broken so that the surfaces cannot be married up perfectly, the repair should be handed over to a professional.

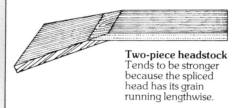

One-piece neck
Tends to be weaker because the grain runs across the headstock.

Two-piece headstock
Tends to be stronger because the spliced head has its grain running lengthwise.

Weak spots on the head The holes drilled for the tuning heads and the wood routed out for the truss rod make the head weakest just above the fingerboard, where it is tilted backwards.

Tinted area shows weak spot

Repairing splits and cracks

Splits and cracks in the woodwork are, once again, most often caused by accidentally dropping the guitar. But this kind of damage can also be the result of the wood ageing and changing its shape, or of the guitar being exposed to extremes of temperature and humidity. The thinner timbers of the soundbox are the most liable to split or crack, particularly if the wood originally used for the construction of the guitar was of low quality or poorly seasoned.

When making the repair, the most important thing is to align correctly the pieces of wood on either side of the crack and maintain this alignment while you make a tight, solid glued joint. This will almost certainly mean using a system of clamps or weights. It may also involve using "cleats" or "studs". These are thin slivers of wood which help to reinforce the crack and keep the wood aligned correctly. They are "patched" over the crack on the inside of the soundbox,

Re-aligning cracked wood
The two pieces of wood on either side of a crack or split are usually out of alignment. Cleats or studs attached to the underside will help to keep them together correctly.

Diamond cleats

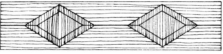

Rectangular cleats

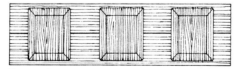

Fixing cleats
Cleats should be shaved or bevelled at the edges and glued over the inside of the crack with their grain running perpendicular to that of the damaged wood.

with their grain running at right angles to the wood of the guitar. In some cases, you may be able to work through the soundhole, using probes and an inspection light.

If you are willing to take the extra trouble, hot hide glue is the best sort to use for repairing cracks. It should be warmed until quite runny and then rubbed into the split with a piece of cloth. Apply the glue from the outside and work it in between the two edges of wood until it can just be seen on the inside. This will be sufficient.

Sometimes, a split may occur around the sides of an acoustic guitar soundbox. This can be treated in the same way, by working

glue into the crack and clamping the linings until set. Decorative edging that has come loose can be re-glued with hide glue or white glue if made of wood. But, if the edging is plastic, you should use an ordinary cement-type adhesive.

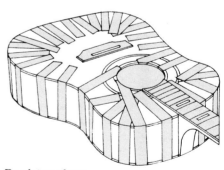

Re-gluing edging
While the glue dries, plenty of sticky tape can be used to keep the edging in place.

Repairs to simple splits and cracks are within the scope of most people and details of refinishing are given on p. 174-6. However, serious damage – a large crack or chip with a missing piece or a broken strut, for example – should be given to a repairer. The same is true for any repair work, however minor, that needs doing to valuable or older guitars.

Finishing

The finish on your guitar not only protects the instrument from accidental knocks and abrasions, but it also governs the aesthetic qualities of its appearance. If you are giving your guitar a brand-new finish to replace the existing one, it therefore makes sense to use the best possible materials and to put the maximum patience, care and hard work into the job. A careless mistake at any stage may mean having to strip off several painstakingly applied layers of finish and start again from scratch. But if you take your time, and follow instructions to the letter, you can create a high-quality finish individually tailored to your own taste and needs.

A wide range of finishes have been either adapted or designed for use on guitars. Some synthetic finishes, however, are suitable only for use on electric guitars, since they can have an adverse effect on the tone of acoustic instruments. A thick, heavy coat of finish will similarly impede high frequencies, thus depleting the treble sound. For this reason, you should always check, before buying finishing materials, that they will be suitable for your guitar. Contact the manufacturer if you are in any doubt.

Choosing the finish

A problem with some finishes – particularly synthetics such as polyester – is that they may contain chemicals which will react to other finishing materials, causing them to soften and blister. Manufacturers can often supply you with technical information sheets on their products. If you stick to the same range, the different materials are more likely to be compatible.

Modern spray finishes such as polyurethane are extremely tough, with a good resistance to scratches, impact damage, and corrosion by liquids which would destroy a more traditional finish. Their high gloss is popular with many people, although you may find it hard to carry out repair work on a finish which has been chosen primarily for its toughness. All hard-wearing synthetics must be applied with industrial spraying, smoothing and burnishing equipment, although there are many softer finishes which you can spray on yourself if you are willing to buy or hire the necessary equipment.

The accepted finish for classical guitars has traditionally been French polish. A well-applied finish of this sort has an attractiveness and depth of finish that is nothing short of stunning. However, compared with modern finishes, it is soft and vulnerable to wear from normal usage. Some leading makers of hand-crafted classical guitars now use carefully selected synthetic materials which have no adverse effect on the instrument's tone. As a compromise, the all-important soundboard is sometimes French-polished while the rest of the guitar is given a synthetic coating.

French-polished surfaces are easier to repair than tough synthetics, as are oil and spirit varnishes. Along with lacquer, these are the finishes most commonly used in hand-finishing, though they do not lend themselves so well to spraying. They consist of one or more natural substances combined with a volatile solvent called a "carrier". After application, the solvent evaporates, leaving a dry coat of finish on the surface. You can add extra solvent to thin down the finish and thus speed up its drying time.

French polish is basically "shellac", with a methylated spirit solvent. Traditionally dark brown, lighter versions are available under such names as "garnet", "button" and "white" polish. Shellac varnish is available with either alcohol or ethanol as the solvent. Spirit-based varnishes are ideal for use on acoustics, providing a more robust finish than French polish. Oil varnishes are easier for the beginner to use because of their relatively slow drying time. They do, however, tend to mute the sound of an acoustic.

Lacquers consist of either synthetics or natural resins combined with a solvent. They are available in clear or coloured finishes and can be applied by spray or by hand. If you are not using a spray, be sure you buy a lacquer suitable for hand finishing – spray lacquers dry faster and may be awkward to apply by hand. Clear lacquer is widely used in hand finishing and can be applied as a protective film on top of varnish, improving the gloss finish. Coloured lacquers are popular for solid-body electrics.

Aerosol sprays and custom car finishes (see the specialist magazines for details) can be used on solid-body guitars, though they will give neither the high gloss nor the durability of an industrial spray treatment.

Some guitarists like the "old" look of a matt or semi-matt wood-oiled finish. Small blemishes on the surface do not show up as much as with a high-gloss finish. With this natural finish, the instrument is stripped right down to the bare wood, which is then given a liberal coating of linseed or another similar oil. Boiled linseed oil will dry faster than raw, while petroleum jelly is an alternative material. Allow the oil or jelly to soak in for a day or two, then remove the surplus with a rag. No further treatment is necessary if you want a matt finish, but to achieve a slight sheen you can burnish the surface with a soft cloth. Further applications of oil can be made at any time.

The disadvantage of this type of finish is that the oil seeps into the wood, and is thus difficult to eradicate if you want to change the finish at a later date. Many finishes will not adhere to wood which has previously been oiled in this way.

The modern "sunburst" finish is a simulation of an aged and worn French polish, in which the areas that come in for most wear become progressively lighter as the finish wears off. Creating the subtle gradation of tone or colour is difficult and, unless you are proficient at French polishing, you must use spraying equipment. A spray with a fan setting is ideal. Sometimes experts also use chemicals to age the wood artificially. Graduate from unstained wood in the centre to quite heavily stained wood at the edges. If you prefer, two compatible colours of stain can be used – traditionally, the lighter central area fades into a darker tone or colour at the edges. With an opaque finish, you can apply the lighter colour as a base coat over the whole surface, then spray the darker colour or tone on top as required.

Gibson ES–345SV with sunburst finish.

Repairing existing finishes

Small indentations in the surface of the wood can sometimes be raised by applying heat and/or moisture. Use an eye-dropper or teaspoon to direct drops of hot water on to the spot, or attach a rubber tube to the spout of a boiling kettle. Another technique is to place layers of damp cloth over the affected area and turn the moisture to steam by pressing carefully with a domestic iron. Larger blemishes need some kind of fill-ing. If the finish is opaque, you can fill the indentation with wood filler. But with clear (tinted or translucent) finishes, this type of repair is unsightly, and you should use successive coats of sanding sealer instead. You can then touch up the finish using one of the techniques suggested below. If the surface is scratched right through to the bare wood, seal the wood first to prevent finish soaking into it and causing discolouration.

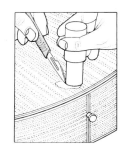

Using a shellac stick
This is a method used by instrument-makers to fill small indentations in the surface. Hold the stick against the blemish and melt the end with a heated knife. Push the melted shellac into the dent with the tip.

Preparing a guitar for refinishing

Before starting work on refinishing, you should first remove or mask components which may be damaged by the chemicals used, or may simply get in the way. This is better than trying to work round them. Tuning heads and electrical components can easily be unscrewed, remembering first to colour-code wires with tape to facilitate rewiring. Synthetic bindings and edgings which may be affected by the stripper should be carefully masked.

It is best to remove the bridge and finger-plate as well. Masking may be an unsatisfactory alternative if the bridge is made of rosewood, as the stripper may cause the natural colour of the wood to bleed into the lighter-coloured soundboard. Removing the flexible fingerplate is a straightforward

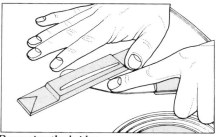

Removing the bridge
With a thin, blunt blade (a sharp knife may scratch the surface) work away at the glued joint between bridge and soundboard until you can insert the blade under the bridge and prise it off. Chip off and sand down any lumps of glue.

operation, but if the bridge is fixed with screws or bolts which can only be loosened from the inside, then the whole soundboard will have to be dismantled. This is a job which even the most experienced maker or repairer would try to avoid. All bridges must be refitted using elongated C clamps (see p. 172). Make sure you can get hold of the necessary number before starting the job.

With the normal type of glued joint between bridge and soundboard, you simply work away at breaking the joint with a thin, pliable table knife. Ease the knife under the bridge and lever it off carefully. With the bridge and fingerplate removed,

mask off their position. This stops finish getting on to these parts and impeding the re-gluing process.

Removing the existing finish
The final quality of the finish depends on the original surface being perfectly smooth and unscratched. Therefore, the existing finish must be completely removed before work can start on refinishing.

If your guitar has a natural wood finish, you may find that this is sufficiently thin for you to be able to remove it by sanding. As soon as you get down close to the wood, change to an abrasive paper no coarser than 340 or 400 grit. Sand down with the

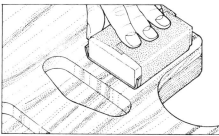

Sanding down
Wrap the abrasive paper around a block of wood after cushioning its base with felt or rubber to stop corners digging into the wood. Always work in straight lines, following the direction of the grain. Fine-grade wire wool can also be used.

grain, using progressively finer grades of glasspaper or abrasive paper until the surface is smooth. Follow the same basic technique for all subsequent sanding-down. Finally, clean down the wood with a rag dipped in benzine, turpentine or white spirit.

With coloured finishes, such as synthetic sprays or lacquers, you can use a paint or varnish stripper recommended for wood. Strippers of this type are usually neutralized by applying white spirit or water. Avoid the latter, because the amounts of water involved may be harmful to the wood of the instrument. It is a good idea to contact the maker or distributor of your guitar to check what type of finish has been used, and then to choose a suitable stripper. Some types

can actually melt the synthetic materials used for guitar edgings and bindings.

Strippers are caustic, and you should handle them with extreme care. Wear rubber gloves and work in a well-ventilated area. If you are working on the soundboard, pack the soundhole with rags to prevent blobs of stripper or discarded finish from falling inside the soundbox. Apply the stripper with an old paint brush. After ten minutes or so the finish will have softened and can be removed by wiping or using a scraper. This should be drawn carefully across the surface to shave the finish off.

When all traces of the old finish have been removed, sand down the surface. The wood is now ready for filling and sealing.

Grain filling and surface sealing
Slightly porous woods such as rosewood and mahogany must be filled to provide a sound, level surface on which the finish is built up. Spruce and maple do not need this treatment.

To prevent colouring from the filler and finish penetrating the surface, you should first seal the wood with one or more coats of shellac or a purpose-made sealing varnish. Fewer coats of finish need then be brushed on before the gloss starts to build up, and this may benefit the sound qualities of an acoustic guitar.

Filler usually dries slightly darker than the wood itself. You can buy proprietary fillers to match a particular wood, or darken them yourself with wood stain. Mix the filler to a thick, creamy consistency, thinning it if necessary. Pack it well down into the pores, using a rag or stiff brush and working initially across the grain. Finish by working with the grain. Do not apply subsequent coats of finish before the filler has dried properly. If you do, it may work loose and spoil the finish. Sand down to a smooth finish and give a second coat of sealer.

A more difficult way of building up a level surface – but one which produces a beautiful, deep lustre – is to omit the filler and apply successive coats of sealer, sanding down to a smooth finish between each.

Applying the finish

Whether you are using a spray or working by hand with a brush or rubber, finishing should always be carried out in a warm, dry environment. Some finishes are highly inflammable and may give off toxic fumes, so take precautions.

Make sure that the surface of the wood is perfectly smooth, and that all traces of stripper (which may attack the new finish) have been removed. Give several thin coats in preference to fewer, heavier applications. To familiarize yourself with a new technique, try it out first on a spare piece of wood – discarded furniture is ideal – before starting work on the guitar.

Lacquer, shellac and varnish can be applied with a soft, purpose-made varnishing brush no more than 1 in. (2.5 cm) wide. Buy a new brush rather than using an old one which you have previously used with a different kind of finish. To avoid overloading, dip only the tip of the bristles into the finish,

Sanding down between coats
After each layer of finish has been applied, it should be sanded down, using fine abrasive paper, before the next coat goes on. This technique is sometimes known as "cutting back".

and apply with regular, even strokes that follow the grain of the wood. Apply successive coats, sanding down in between until you have a smooth finish. Then give a couple of final coats without sanding.

Spray finishing

With practice, you can use spraying to give fine control, allowing you to achieve an even and regular finish. Industrial equipment gives the highest gloss, although you can use an artist's airbrush or a rented spraygun/compressor unit suitable for home use to achieve good results. Aerosol sprays are cheap and can give a passable finish if used with care.

Working into the light
If you work with your light source positioned so that the surface of the guitar catches the light, you will find it easy to spot any blemishes or irregularities in the finish.

Work on a dry day so that moisture in the air does not spoil the finish and slow down drying. Keeping the gun square-on to the surface, spray at a regular distance to give an even coating. Start moving the gun before you release the jet, otherwise the fluid may spurt and form blobs, and keep it moving at a constant rate. Spray thinly, and wear a face mask at all times.

Wood stains

Most people prefer to retain the attractive natural appearance of good quality timbers such as rosewood, mahogany, maple and spruce by using only a simple, clear finish. As woods like these have become expensive and harder to find, however, substitute

timbers have been used – often with great success – by many makers. These woods are frequently stained in order to enhance their appearance, as well as to give the traditional look of dark fingerboard, ribs and back against a light-coloured soundboard.

Stains can be bought in a variety of solid and liquid forms, and can be applied at any one of several stages in the finishing process. For example, a stain can be applied directly to the bare wood to darken it before finishing begins, using a brush, rag or rubber. It can also be added to grain filler to match a tone or colour, or it can be mixed with the finish itself. Different shades of varnish and French polish are available and are ideal for darkening existing finishes.

Since stain can sink deeper into some parts of the wood than others, care is needed in order to achieve an even tone. Generally speaking, it is best to use stain only when you wish to match an existing colour. Stained wood does not look as attractive as natural wood when finished.

French polishing

This technique must be used with great care, but results can be superior to brush finishing. You can use the method to apply other finishes besides French polish itself.

Take a piece of lint-free cotton or cloth 3-6 in. (7.5-15 cm) square. Dip a small ball of cotton wool into a tray of finish, shake off the excess, and then wrap it inside the cloth to form a pad or rubber. Apply coats of finish thinly. When the entire surface is covered, leave it to dry thoroughly and then give it a light rubbing down with garnet paper. Apply the next coat, repeating the process until a smooth, even finish is achieved. Finally apply two or three coats along the grain. If the rubber starts to stick or bind on the surface, add a drop of linseed oil to the pad.

If you want the highest possible gloss, add some methylated spirit to the finish before the final coats. Add more spirit to each coat and then finish off with a single coat of spirit on its own. For a matt finish, omit the spirit and simply burnish the surface with a soft, dry cloth.

Final rubbing down and polishing

Before giving a finish a final rub-down, it is best to put the instrument to one side for a week or so to dry. The exact drying time will depend on the type of finish you have used and the method you employed, as well as the temperature and humidity of the surroundings.

Rub down using very fine grades of abrasive paper or wire wool. Some makers

use 1000 or even 2000 grit when the instrument demands a first-class finish. Wet-and-dry papers are also useful, because they have less of a tendency to become clogged. They are commonly applied using water as a lubricant, although sometimes lemon oil is used instead.

Rubbing and polishing compounds are available in either paste or liquid form. A

rubbing compound paste contains a grinding agent which you rub evenly over the surface of the finish. Different grades are made, from coarse to fine, so make sure you buy the latter for work on guitars. Smoothing compounds are sold at motor spares dealers, as they are often used in restoring vehicle finishes which have lost their original high gloss.

Guitar care and travel

Always keep your guitar in its case when you are not using it, and clean the strings with a dry cloth as soon as you finish playing. This will remove any dirt, moisture or sweat and, more than anything else, will help make the strings last longer. It is also a good idea to wipe down the body and neck, including any metal parts – especially gold plating, which may tarnish if it is not kept clean.

Cleaning and polishing your guitar

Combined cleaner-polishers such as those made for use on household surfaces are suitable for all modern synthetic guitar finishes. Creams are probably better than aerosols since there is a danger that the spray will get into the pick-ups or tuning heads.

Guitars with a traditional finish such as French polish *must* be cleaned with a cream. The solvents used in aerosols have been known to have a harmful effect on these finishes. Some major guitar manufacturers market their own brands of hand-applied cream cleaner-polishers.

French-polish finishes can also be cleaned and polished with bees-wax, although many French polishers recommend that you simply wipe the surface with a damp cloth and a little vinegar or lemon oil, and then buff it up with a dry, soft cloth.

Varnished or lacquered fingerboards can be treated with the same cleaner-polisher as the rest of the guitar. But oiled fingerboards – such as those traditionally fitted to classical guitars – and oiled-wood bodies should be cleaned and oiled two or three times a year with linseed oil. This is rubbed into the wood, working with the grain, using fine-grade wire wool. A good time to do this is when you are changing strings.

It is worth noting that, if the guitar finish is scratched or damaged so that the wood shows through, the cleaner will penetrate the surface. Repair blemishes before applying any cream or aerosol.

Storing your guitar

Although a fairly constant temperature of 20-21°C (68-70°F) is desirable, it is more important to avoid sudden changes and extremes of temperature and humidity. Never leave a guitar near a radiator, close to hot water pipes, or in a damp cellar or basement.

Classical guitars are more vulnerable than other types to changes in humidity – as are old or antique instruments. If you intend to keep one in a centrally heated room, you should invest in a "room humidifier" to prevent the air from becoming too dry.

During most normal use, a guitar should be kept at concert pitch so that there is an even tension on the strings. But if you intend to store a guitar for a lengthy period, you should

de-tune *all* the strings and release the tension from the neck completely.

Travelling with your guitar

Advice about taking a guitar on a plane varies from airline to airline. Essentially, there are only two options: it either travels with you in the cabin – in which case you may have to book a seat for it – or it goes in the hold with the luggage. If the flight is not full, however, you may be allowed to take your guitar on board with you and store it in a closet in the cabin. Airline staff try to be as helpful as

possible, but obviously fare-paying passengers take priority. Guitars are frequently damaged in cargo holds. A proper flight case is the only way to give guaranteed protection. Even hardshell cases are often smashed, while a soft fabric or plastic case will mean almost certain disaster.

When travelling by road or rail, lay the guitar flat so it cannot fall forward. Avoid putting a heavy amp or speaker where a sudden jolt could tip it onto your guitar. Remember that guitar cases are very recognizable, and will readily attract thieves.

Guitar cases

Cheap fabric or plastic guitar cases give little protection other than keeping dust and rain off. Hardshell cases made from wood or fibreglass are essential if you intend to travel with your guitar. The inside of the case is usually covered with a soft felt or velvet-like material to protect the finish, and there is sometimes additional foam padding between the casing and the inner lining. A spare strings compartment is often positioned to give support to the neck and to stop movement once the case is closed.

If the case supplied with the guitar is unsatisfactory, buy one which fits the instrument as closely as possible, to stop it moving around in transit. Acoustic guitar cases usually follow the contours of the instrument. Because solid-bodies are considerably smaller, electric guitar cases are often

oblong. It is quite easy to make an oblong case yourself, but it may not be much cheaper than buying one ready-made.

A good hardshell case not only protects a guitar from knocks but also from excessive moisture and damp. An excessively warm, dry environment can be just as harmful, causing cracks and warping. Some owners of expensive, hand-made classical guitars put a small "guitar humidifier" in the string compartment of the case to ensure that the air is not too dry.

Touring bands and musicians usually invest in a complete set of "flight cases" for their equipment. These are similar to oblong hardshell cases but are larger, heavier and much more robust.

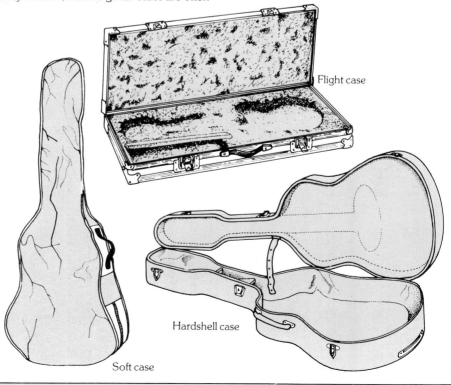

Flight case

Hardshell case

Soft case

Custom and customized guitars

A *custom* guitar is, strictly speaking, one that has been made to order or modified to suit a particular musician's requirements. Such instruments can either be hand-built or they can be standard production-line models which have been changed in some way by the manufacturer in response to a specific request. However, some makers also use the term loosely to distinguish between the basic production model and an instrument which has certain non-standard features. In the Gibson Les Paul range, for instance, the Les Paul Custom originally had three humbucker pick-ups and a special black finish which set it apart from other models.

A *customized* guitar is one which the owner has altered, or has had altered, to meet his own needs. Sometimes the modification is largely cosmetic, as with the use of brass control knobs to enhance the appearance of the instrument. More often, the motive is to combine the distinctive features of guitars made by different manufacturers to improve the sound and playing qualities. A custom modification which has been popular for many years is to fit a Gibson "PAF" humbucking pick-up (*see* p. 195) to the neck pick-up position of a Stratocaster. The Gibson pick-up can then be used on its own, or in conjunction with the two Fender single-coil pick-ups.

The growth of independent custom parts makers such as Schecter and DiMarzio in recent years has meant that guitarists are now able to improve or upgrade almost any type of instrument – Japanese copy guitars, for instance. Some players indeed prefer the tailor-made sound they can achieve with such instruments to the familiar, off-the-shelf properties of mass-produced guitars.

Hand-built guitar
Tony Zemaitis specializes in custom guitars. His early patrons included Keith Richards and Ron Wood. This guitar features an original Gibson "PAF" humbucking pick-up, and was given special mother-of-pearl inlays to the order of ex-Whitesnake guitarist, Micky Moody.

Spare parts and kits

Fender and Gibson have, for many years, produced a wide range of replacement parts for their guitars. Apart from the products of makers like Grover and De Armond, however, quality spares such as tuning heads and clip-on pick-ups have not always been so readily available. It was not until the growth of interest in customizing in the 1970s that alternative, custom parts could easily be bought over the counter. It was then that major custom parts makers such as DiMarzio, as well as smaller, specialist firms such as Seymour Duncan, began to offer precision equipment at reasonable prices. Seymour Duncan, himself, had made an extensive study of vintage pick-ups and had perfected the art of making them to match the requests of knowledgeable guitarists seeking particular vintage rock sounds, most of which could be traced back to the early products of Gibson or Fender. By the end of the 1970s, the range had been extended by companies such as Schecter Guitar Research, Mighty Mite and DiMarzio, among others, to include items such as tuning heads and bridges. The range has now become so extensive that it is possible to buy a complete set of guitar parts in a do-it-yourself kit form.

These kits and parts are still, by and large, based on Gibson Les Paul and Explorer guitars, Fender Telecasters, Stratocasters, and Jazz and Precision basses.

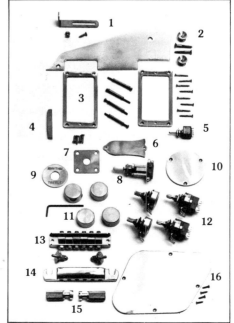

Guitar kit (*left*)
This is a replica Stratocaster in kit form from Mighty Mite. The body comes ready-sealed and primed, thus cutting down preparatory finishing work.

Custom spares (*right*)
Like several other makers, Mighty Mite offer a full range of high-quality fittings for custom guitars. This is their "Les Paul" range.
1 Fingerplate and mount. **2** Strap buttons. **3** Pick-up mounting rings. **4** Nut. **5** On–off switch. **6** Truss rod cover. **7** Jack plate. **8** Three-way switch with **9** mounting plate and **10** cover. **11** Control knobs. **12** Pots. **13** Bridge. **14** Tailpiece. **15** Studs. **16** Control cover back plate.

Custom modifications

The "spare-part surgery" market was mainly developed by American companies catering to guitarists who sought to enhance the performance of their instruments. In the early 1970s the emphasis was on quality, and this contrasted with the attitude of Japanese guitar-makers at the time.

Taking their chances with patent legalities, the Japanese had flooded the market with blatant copies of the most popular Gibson and Fender guitars. While some of these copies represented a genuine attempt at producing a replica that was as good as the original in every way, many more were made to be sold at very low prices, with a production and sound quality to match.

These Japanese copies brought electric guitars within almost everyone's reach, and even their rough sound quality found its adherents. Nevertheless, the higher-priced, better-made copies proved very popular, especially since musicians discovered that they could readily be upgraded by customizing. Tuning heads and pick-ups were often

of inferior quality, but with replacement spares from the American parts-makers' catalogues they could easily be rebuilt into high-quality instruments.

It is now common practice to use a Japanese copy guitar as the basis for a series of custom modifications. Replacement pick-

Pick-up modification
Rory Gallagher's Fender Esquire, as originally built, had only one single-coil pick-up in the bridge position. This has now been augmented by two new single-coils.

ups, bridges and hardware are based closely on the Fender, Gibson and (among others) Rickenbacker originals. Necks and bodies are also available if you wish to build up the whole guitar from scratch. If you take care over the work, you can produce a viable alternative to the "real" guitar, or you can improvise – building a guitar which will give a new range of characteristics.

Kit-built guitars
One of several similar instruments owned by Pete Townshend, this "Telecaster" was built entirely with Schecter parts. Though the basic assembly of a kit-built guitar is relatively easy, a great deal of care must be taken with setting the intonation and action. For instance, if you decide to fit a Fender-style single-coil pick-up to a Gibson model, you may have problems with setting the height of the strings in relation to the pick-up, or in matching the string spacings with individual pick-up pole pieces. Though many kits and parts are of excellent quality – as good as, if not better than, the products of established makers – they will be of little use if the basic guitar (a cheap Japanese copy, for instance) has faults which cannot be eradicated. The body or neck of a cheap guitar may be badly designed or made, in which case it may be impossible to get a good sound from the instrument, no matter how good the replacement parts.

Fitting new nuts and saddles

Most production-made acoustic and electric guitars have synthetic or plastic nuts; acoustics usually have a saddle made of a similar material. Only better quality guitars have bone, ivory or – in the case of electrics – brass nuts, which give a better tone and are less prone to wear.

If you want to upgrade your guitar you can buy slightly oversize pieces of bone or (more rarely) ivory from guitar shops and instrument-makers' suppliers, which you can then cut and file to the exact shape and size required. Brass nuts made by Mighty Mite, Schecter, and other customizing suppliers are made to suit stock models of electric guitars.

To fit a replacement nut, first remove the strings from the guitar, relaxing the tension gradually on all the strings at the same time so as not to put an uneven strain on the neck. If the finish has coagulated around the nut, scrape it off carefully with a knife. The nut will probably be held in place simply by a couple of spots of glue, in which case you can tap away gently at the sides of the nut with a hammer until the glue cracks. Hold a piece of wood against the nut to cushion the blows. If the nut is any more than slightly recessed, or if it will not come loose readily, you may damage the guitar by using force to remove it, and the job should really be given to a repairer to handle.

Saw the new nut to the rough shape of the old one, and then give it its final shape using fine, flat files. To finish, smooth down with 400-600 grit wet-and-dry abrasive paper before applying a burnishing cream or fine rubbing compound. The new nut should be glued in place with a couple of spots of epoxy resin; if you use too much, the nut may prove difficult to remove at a later stage. When the adhesive has set, you can cut grooves for the strings in the nut with fine needle files. Their depth determines the action of the guitar (see p. 167). Cutting too deeply will cause fret buzz.

If you are replacing a saddle, again use the original as a guide to shape and size. The saddle is usually held in its groove in the bridge solely by the downward tension of the strings.

Fitting replacement tuning heads

To make tuning easier and more accurate, many people like to upgrade their guitars by fitting better quality tuning heads. The best kind are the low-geared, enclosed, self-lubricating tuning heads of the type made by Schaller and Grover.

If you wish simply to replace heads which are worn or damaged, try to get an identical set from the maker of your guitar. If this is not possible, take the guitar or the old tuning heads along with you to a music shop. Look for a set that calls for the least amount of drilling of new holes in the head of the guitar. Tuning heads on two mounting plates, each with three machines, can be difficult to replace because, unless the new set has the same spacing between the cap-stans, the holes will have to be re-drilled. If this is the case, it is often better to replace them with the individual type, which also tend to be of higher quality.

Gradually reduce the tension on the strings and then remove the old tuning heads. If the old fixing holes do not match up, they must be filled. This is best done by plugging with small, matchstick-like strips of wood with a point at one end. Use a hardwood which matches the headstock. Put a good covering of glue (white woodworking glue will suffice) on to each piece and push them into the hole one by one. When the hole is almost full, tap the last strips of hardwood in place with a small hammer. After the glue has set, trim off the excess with a sharp knife, and touch up the spots with the appropriate finish.

Carefully mark the position of the new fixing screws and drill a pilot hole with a small hand drill or bradawl. Do not over-tighten the screws or you may strip the thread in the hole. If this happens, plug the hole and start again.

To prevent wear, good quality tuning heads have some type of sleeve or collar arrangement through which the capstan passes. If they are a tight fit, these sleeves can sometimes be simply tapped into position, and will stay firmly anchored. Otherwise, you will have to drill a bigger hole through the headstock. Use a hand drill and a drilling stand to ensure accuracy.

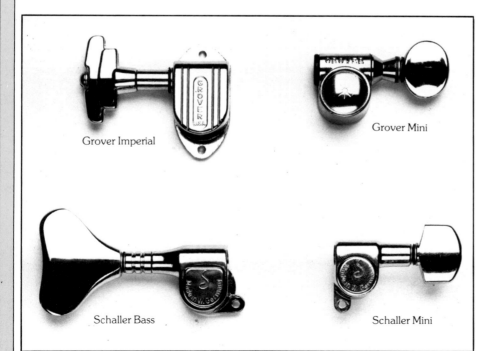

Grover Imperial

Grover Mini

Schaller Bass

Schaller Mini

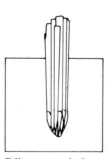 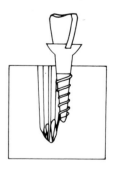

Filling screw holes
If the old holes are not covered by the machine heads, or if they are too close to the new positions, they should be filled. Plug the hole with pointed strips of hardwood which have been liberally coated with glue. Use the same technique to give grip to screws if the old holes are too large for them.

Tuning heads
The Grover Imperial has a gear ratio of 14:1 for very fine tuning. The smaller Grover model has a 12:1 ratio with sealed lubrication. Note the size difference compared to the butterfly-shaped Schaller machine head for bass guitars. Schaller's self-locking Mini is designed for guitarists who prefer a smaller and lighter machine head.

Fitting replacement bridges

Removing and replacing the glued-on bridge of an acoustic guitar is a tricky job which you should only attempt if you have an aptitude for working with wood. If not, you should entrust the job to an experienced maker or repairer. The bridge of an electric guitar is a more straightforward proposition. Fitting a new bridge can give better string-height and intonation adjustment, while a heavy brass bridge will markedly increase the sustain. You can also fit a Fender-type tremelo/bridge unit to many other makes of guitar. Choose the new bridge carefully, checking that it will give you the required string height after allowing for the size of the pick-ups.

If the new bridge is of the relatively simple surface-fixing type, and the intonation of your guitar was correct with the old one, use the position of the existing saddle (rather than the bridge itself) as a guide for fixing. Most quality bridges have a lengthways adjustment, which allows you to set the individual scale length of each string independently. The ideal bridge position should therefore give you maximum scale-length adjustment in both directions. If you position the bridge so that the intonation of the top E string is correct (see p. 171), you will have an equal amount of back and forward adjustment.

Surface-fixed bridges may be secured either by screws or, more likely, by a bolt-and-stud arrangement, in which the body is fitted with sunken metal studs into which are screwed the bolts securing the bridge or tailpiece. If the new fixing positions do not align with the old ones, or if the fixings have a different thread, you will need to change the studs. A special tool is available for removing them. The hole should then be filled. You can cut a length of dowel of the right diameter, or you can use a special plug-cutting tool of the appropriate size. Glue the new plug into the hole and, when it

is dry, trim the plug and smooth down to a level surface. To drill the new hole, make a small pilot hole and then drill with progressively larger bits until you have reached the correct size for the new plug. This can now be tapped into place; its fluted sides will grip the wood firmly.

As far as the guitar's appearance is concerned, it is best to find a replacement bridge which covers the old, plugged

mounting holes. If this is not possible, you should sand down the plug till it is level with the surface of the guitar body and then touch it up (as outlined on p. 175) to match the existing finish. This technique will be satisfactory for a guitar with an opaque finish, but unfortunately with a natural finish there is little you can do other than ensuring that the grain of the plug matches the direction of the grain on the body.

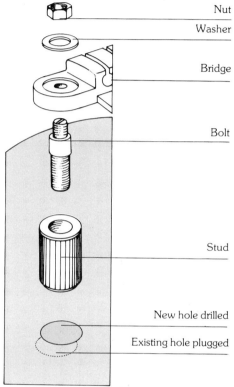

Nut
Washer
Bridge
Bolt
Stud
New hole drilled
Existing hole plugged

Bridge mounting
In the diagram above, the old stud holes have been filled in and new ones drilled. The stud (a screw-threaded brass collar with fluted sides) is tapped into position. A brass bolt is screwed into the stud and the bridge is mounted on this. It is then secured by a nut and washer.

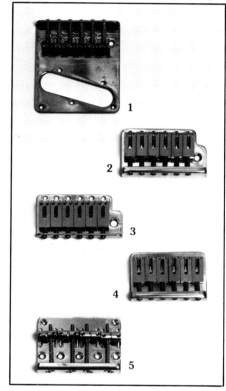

1
2
3
4
5

Replacement bridges
These are solid brass bridges for Fender guitars. **1** Bridge plate for a Telecaster. **2-3** Trax bridge for Stratocaster, with tremelo facility. **4** Stratocaster Trax bridge, without tremelo. **5** Bridge for Precision and Jazz model bass guitars.

String bender

Also known as a "pull-string", this is a mechanical system of levers and springs which allows you to raise the pitch of the top E or B string, according to type. It simulates some pedal-steel guitar techniques. The rods and springs are fitted into a cavity in the guitar body, and a pivoting arm is connected to the string at the bridge. A second arm is attached to the strap button, so that pushing down on the guitar at this point raises the pitch by a tone. Palm pedals such as those made by Bigsby also allow you to raise one or two notes without affecting the others, whereas a tremolo arm alters the pitch of all six strings.

☐ B string bender
☐ E string bender

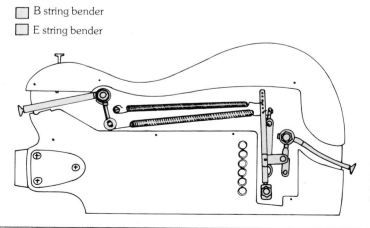

Parsons-White string bender
This Telecaster is custom-fitted with two benders, one working on the B string and the other on the top E. The device was invented by Gene Parsons and the late Clarence White when they were members of the Byrds. Though effective, the string bender requires considerable skill to make full use of its potential.

A guide to guitar electronics

The basic function of an electric guitar pick-up is remarkably simple. The pick-up generates a small alternating current (AC) across its windings when the strings are played, and this signal is subsequently amplified (see p. 52-3). You could plug the pick-up directly into an amplifier and the sound of the guitar would come through perfectly clearly, though with no variation in volume or tone, other than that achieved by adjusting the amplifier's controls. The controls wired into so-called "passive" guitar circuits simply enable you to modify the alternating current output from the pick-up in order to give variations of tone and volume. They work by altering and controlling the voltage, amperage and wattage of the signal generated by the pick-up before it is directed to the input of the amplifier.

Volume controls (potentiometers or "pots") control the amount of electrical energy delivered. Tone controls (incorporating potentiometers and capacitors or coils) modify the frequency distributions within the AC signal from the pick-up in a way which enables you to vary its harmonic content or balance.

"Active" guitar circuits make use of a battery-powered pre-amplifier mounted on the guitar itself. This permits tone settings to be cut or boosted by wider margins than are possible with passive circuits, which rely purely on power from the amplifier. All current in passive guitar circuitry is AC. Direct current (DC) is only present in active circuits.

Bearing in mind the increasing sophistication of guitar electronics, and the fact that you may wish to add electrical components to your guitar or make repairs and modifications, it is a good idea to have a working technical knowledge of the subject. In the following pages, we have assumed no prior knowledge of electronics. We therefore begin with a general introduction to electricity, electrical components and wiring diagrams, and follow with some practical information on soldering and screening before going on to look at particular guitar circuits.

What is electricity?

Electricity is a force which arises from the fundamental properties of matter, which is made up of atoms. The outer bands of some atoms are incomplete and unstable. As a result, electrons (elementary particles of atoms) within these bands can be made to pass from atom to atom and form a flow known as *electrical current*. Substances which have incomplete outer shells, permitting the passage of electrons, are called *conductors*.

Other substances – such as silicon – are formed in groups of atoms that have stable outer shells which block the passage of electrons. These are *non-conductors* or *insulators*. There are also *semi-conductors*, consisting of substances which, although normally insulators, are deliberately contaminated with atoms whose unstable outer shells permit a flow of electrons. As a result, electrons can be made to pass through a semi-conductor in a controlled fashion. The ability to regulate and modify the characteristics of a current by means of semi-conductors is an all-important part of electronic circuitry.

An electrical current flows through a conductor when a source of electrons is connected to one end and an "electron sink", into which the current is absorbed, is connected to the other. For example, a wire connected between the positive and negative poles of a battery will cause the electrons to flow from the minus connection to the plus connection. The pressure which pushes electrons through a conductor is called the *voltage*, and it is measured in volts, millivolts, etc. The quantity of electrons flowing through a conductor is called the current, and it is measured in amps, milliamps, etc. The power in the circuit is dependent on both the amperage and voltage and is measured in watts, milliwatts, etc. Voltage is multiplied by amperage to determine wattage.

To prevent connecting wires from melting, the flow of current must be controlled. This can be done by inserting a *resistor* into the circuit. As its name implies, this is a component with a more or less specific resistance to the flow of current. Resistance is measured in ohms (Ω). Ohm's law states that voltage = resistance × current. Conductors – even wiring components – have a very slight resistance to the flow of current, but no significant effect is likely to be noticed over short conductor lengths.

Reading wiring diagrams

Electrical wiring diagrams can, at first sight, appear frighteningly complicated. They are, however, quite simple to read. Each component in a circuit is represented by a standard symbol (see opposite). Intercommunications between components – which are either wires or copper tracks on a printed circuit board – are shown by solid, unbroken lines joining the component symbols together.

Wiring diagrams are generally arranged with the signal input or generation shown on the left of the diagram and the output shown on the right. So the signal flows from left to right. Across the bottom of the diagram, is the earth or "zero volts" line, while across the top is the DC (positive or negative) power line that powers the circuit. AC flows from left to right, while DC flows from top to bottom.

The components built into an electrical circuit are represented in wiring diagrams by standardized symbols. There are many variations of the basic types of components used in guitar and amplifier circuitry. One capacitor, for instance, can look totally different from another, in spite of the fact that they both perform the same function. Allowing for different values and tolerances, there are literally thousands of components to choose from. For the inexperienced, identifying components can be a problem at first. One reason is that the wiring diagram symbols for components are based on their internal structure, not their outward appearance.

On the opposite page are set out all the wiring diagram symbols you are likely to encounter, together with illustrations showing what the components actually look like.

Electronic abbreviations	
V	Volts
A	Amps
W	Watts
F	Farads
Ω	Ohms
H	Henries
Hz	Hertz (cycles per second)
K	Kilo (× 1,000)
M	Mega (× 1,000,000)
m	Milli (÷ 1,000)
μ	Micro (÷ 1,000,000)
p	Pico (÷ [1,000,000 × 1,000,000])

Electrical symbols

1 Fixed resistor.

2 (a) Variable resistor. **(b)** Potentiometer. (Both knob controlled.) **(c)** Preset variable resistor. **(d)** Pre-set potentiometer. (Both screwdriver controlled.)

3 Ganged variable resistors or potentiometers (two pots on one spindle).

4 (a) Capacitor (any non-polarized type). **(b)** Electrolytic capacitor. **(c)** Tantalum capacitor.

5 Fuse.

6 (a) Mono jack socket. **(b)** Stereo jack socket. **(c)** Stereo jack socket with one make switch. **(d)** Stereo jack socket with one break switch.

7 Coaxial socket.

8 (a) One-way (single-throw) switch. **(b)** Two-way (double-throw) switch.

9 Semi-conductor diode.

10 (a) P-N-P transistor. **(b)** N-P-N transistor.

11 (a) n-channel junction field effect transistor (J-FET). **(b)** p-channel FET. **(c)** n-channel I G FET. **(d)** p-channel I G FET.

12 (a) Diode valve. **(b)** Triode valve. **(c)** Tetrode valve. **(d)** Pentode valve.

13 (a) Wires crossed but not connected. **(b)** Wires connected.

14 (a) Earth connection. **(b)** Chassis. **(c)** Terminal.

15 Battery.

16 Microphones.

17 Loudspeaker.

18 Transformer.

19 Iron-cored choke or inductance.

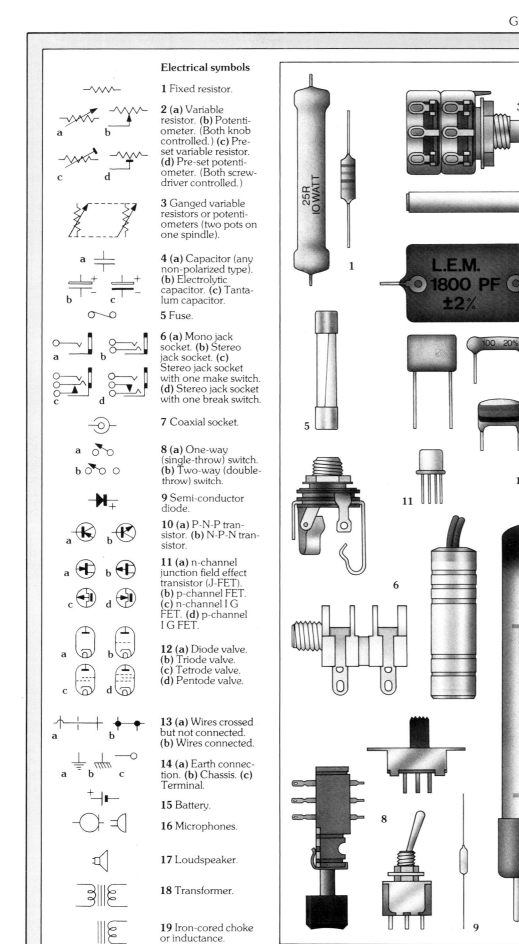

Electrical components

Choosing tools

Shown here is a selection of tools which should enable you to carry out almost any electrical work. You will find it useful to have two soldering irons, one for general work and the other for cases where heavy-duty soldering is involved. The multimeter is an invaluable item for measuring electrical currents and also enables you to carry out a large number of routine checks on electrical equipment. Your multimeter should be capable of measuring ohms from zero to 1 megohm and AC/DC volts from zero to at least 500 volts.

1 Multimeter.
2 Spanner with multiple jaws, used for potentiometer mounting nuts, etc.
3 Small electrical screwdriver.
4 Medium-sized, general-purpose screwdriver.
5 Cross-head screwdriver.
6 Small snipe-nosed or needle-nosed pliers.
7 Wire strippers with adjustable stop fitted to close over a cable so only the insulation is cut, the core remaining undamaged.
8 Wire cutter with sharpened tip. End cutters are the most useful type. The jaws are hollowed out for holding terminals.
9 40-60 W soldering iron for heavy-duty soldering, such as attaching earth leads to pot casings.
10 15-25 W soldering iron for most general work. Fit a 1 amp fuse in the plug of your soldering iron. Larger sizes of fuse may make the iron dangerous. Soldering irons are sometimes supplied with interchangeable tips of different sizes and shapes.

Soldering

Solder is an alloy which when heated – usually with an electric soldering iron – will melt so that it can be applied to two pieces of metal to make a fairly strong bond between them. The bonding occurs during the few seconds that the solder takes to cool. Solder is conductive, which means that it will carry electrical current. It is therefore ideal for many electrical connections of a semi-permanent nature, since the connection can easily be dismantled with the application of more heat from a soldering iron. This, of course, is useful for repair work.

You must always use an electrical solder in conjunction with a flux. Flux cleans the surface of pieces of metal which are to be joined together. It is needed because many metals oxidize when exposed to air, and the layer of oxidation left on the surface makes the joint weak and unreliable. Flux chemically removes this layer and prevents any re-oxidation during the soldering process.

The best type of solder to use in guitar and electronic work is that which has a built-in core or cores of flux. Remember that certain metals and metal platings will not accept solder: aluminium, for instance, needs a special purpose-made solder. Note, however, that plumbing solder is entirely unsuitable for any form of electrical soldering work.

Soldering is a relatively simple process and, in the long run, it is no more difficult to solder well than it is to solder badly. Since badly soldered joints will let you down sooner or later, it is only sensible to use the correct techniques from the outset.

For general-purpose work a 15–25 watt soldering iron with interchangeable tips is ideal. It is a good idea to have a second soldering iron of a fairly high power – 40–60 watts – to tackle those jobs involving soldering wires to larger pieces of metal which absorb far more heat: when you have to solder an earth connection to the outer casing of a pick-up, for example.

Selecting the size of tip to be used is simple. Choose the one with a tip contact size closest to the size of the joint to be made. Never change the tip of an iron while it is still plugged in or while it is still hot.

An important part of soldering is the technique of "tinning" the tip of the soldering iron bit before and after use to prevent it from becoming corroded and eventually unusable. Each time the soldering iron is switched on, hold the solder against the contact surface of the tip until the solder melts, giving the tip a thin coating. Surplus solder should always be removed from the tip by means of a quick wipe with a piece of damp foam, sponge or rag. Hot solder

should never be shaken or knocked off, because of the risk of damage to the iron, as well as the danger from flying molten metal.

After tinning, the iron should be used immediately. If you delay for even a couple of minutes, the iron should be wiped clean and tinned once again. Failure to do this will result in partially oxidized – and consequently much weakened – solder being applied to the joint. It is also sensible to do all pre-soldering preparation (cutting to length and stripping of wires, labelling of contacts, etc.) before switching on the iron.

Metal surfaces to be joined together should be clean, bright, dry and grease-free.

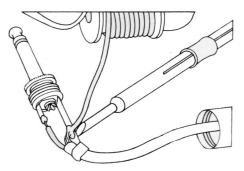

Soldering a jack plug connection
Use soldering iron to heat metal surface. Apply solder to connection, letting it flow over joint. Remove iron to let solder solidify.

Preparing screened cables for connections

Screened cable consists of one or more insulated central cores of wire around which a further screen of wires is wrapped or braided. A final external layer of insulation (rubber, plastic or fabric) encloses the complete cable. The central core is used to carry the signal transmitted from component to component, or for external connections such as the one between guitar and amplifier. The screening is connected to the earth side of the guitar's circuitry so that any rogue interference is sent to earth. Avoid the cheap, thinner types of wrapped screened cable; braided screen cables are far superior. For quality work such as recording – when it is desirable to keep background noise and interference to the minimum – "low-noise" screened cable is recommended.

To prepare wrapped screen cable for connections, use wire strippers or a sharp knife to remove 2 in. (5 cm) of the outer insulation. Unwind the screening wires and twist them into a core. Strip back about ½–1 in. (1.2–2.5 cm) of the insulation around the central core or cores. Insulate the part of the screening which is exposed, leaving ½ in. (1.2 cm) bare for the connection. Finally, tin the ends of the wires to be connected.

With braided cable, you should first remove about 2 in. (5 cm) of the outer insulation, and then push the braiding back from the cable end to form a bulge where the outer insulation now ends. Using a small screwdriver, push the wires aside and carefully part the braiding in the area of the bulge so that the insulated central core can be pulled through. Stretch out the braiding again into a fairly straight core, insulate the exposed screening and tin the ends.

Low-noise cables have an additional black layer of conductive synthetic material between the screening and the insulation around the central core or cores. As this layer is conductive and in contact with the main screening , it must be cut back so as not to short-circuit the signal connections carried by the central core or cores.

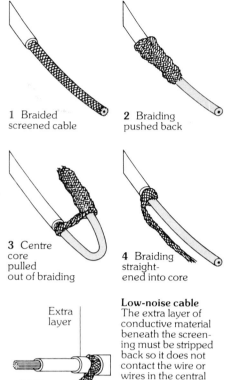

1 Braided screened cable

2 Braiding pushed back

3 Centre core pulled out of braiding

4 Braiding straightened into core

Low-noise cable
The extra layer of conductive material beneath the screening must be stripped back so it does not contact the wire or wires in the central core.

Extra layer

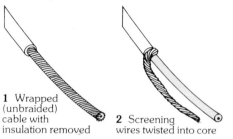

1 Wrapped (unbraided) cable with insulation removed

2 Screening wires twisted into core

When all the pre-soldering preparatory work has been carried out, the parts to be joined together should be tinned. This is done by applying heat directly to the parts being soldered, with the tip of the iron in contact with the cleaned metal surface. The solder is applied directly to the metal, not melted on the tip of the soldering iron first. Never carry a big blob of solder to the metal on the tip of the iron. Use the minimum amount of solder necessary to plate just the pieces of metal being joined. Now bring the parts together and, if possible, crimp wires to terminals to make a joint which is sound before it is soldered. Now apply the iron and add solder until it has flowed over the entire joint. Take the soldering iron away from the joint and allow it to cool, while at the same time ensuring that no movement of the components or wires occurs. A good soldered joint is bright and shiny. A crystalline or dull grey appearance implies that there was movement before the solder solidified, or that the solder has oxidized. In both cases, the joint must be completely re-soldered.

All components can be damaged by heat from a soldering iron, so it is wise only to apply the soldering iron to the joint for the minimum amount of time, without rushing the job.

Wiring an electric guitar circuit

In the following pages we shall explain the stages of installing the necessary circuitry for an electric guitar, beginning with a single pick-up plus tone and volume controls, and then going on to cover more sophisticated arrangements.

The physical layout of the components inside the guitar body will, of course, vary from make to make. For example, some solid-body guitars have recesses behind the fingerplates, and all the circuitry, except for the pick-up, can be fitted to the fingerplate itself. Other solid-body guitars have access plates at the back. Arch-top, hollow-body, f-hole guitars, on the other hand, do not have this recess and are best wired up by making up the circuit in the form of a wiring "harness" or "loom".

This is done by first deciding where to locate the components on the guitar, cutting all the connecting wires to the appropriate length, and then installing the assembly as a complete unit. (Some connections may have to be made once the components are fitted.) The wiring harness is then fed into the soundbox of the guitar through the openings in the body. A little manoeuvring and ingenuity (particularly in assessing the length of connecting wires) may be called for, depending on the design of the actual guitar.

"Screening" or "shielding" is the part of the guitar circuitry which reduces the amount of rogue interference picked up from outside sources such as radio waves. Many guitars employ no shielding materials other than those already built into the actual components and connecting wires. Though many manufacturers make guitars with circuits of this type, they are not ideal, since they leave the ends of wires, solder tags, capacitors and other components unshielded (see above for details of using screened cables).

Copper foil – available through some metal merchants or electrical components dealers – and purpose-made electrical shielding tape with an adhesive backing are the best types of material to use for lining a solid-body cavity. They can also be used to line the underside of plastic and synthetic fingerplates.

Also available are special screening paints – such as those that are carbon-based – but they must be used with great care if the shielding effect is to be consistent. The same must be said of domestic aluminium-based cooking foil, which some people use in the same way as copper foil.

Whatever materials or methods you employ, all shielding must be connected to the earth side of the guitar circuit.

How electric guitars are wired

Pick-ups and their associated controls form the heart of any electric guitar's sound characteristics. Though it is possible to make a modest adjustment to this by fitting custom brass hardware, it is really only through working on the actual electrical circuitry of the guitar that you can exploit its full potential.

In this section, the basic principles of pick-up and allied technology explained on p. 52 are developed to show you how, by making certain adjustments or by adding extra components, you can substantially alter the sound characteristics of your guitar. There are also

full notes on how to make checks to ensure that your equipment is functioning correctly. We begin with the rudimentary single pick-up circuit and then move on to more involved work. The pick-ups in this section are all single-coil types. Twin-coil "humbuckers" are dealt with on p. 194.

The single pick-up guitar is, in reality, something of a rarity. The only production guitars nowadays which do not have two or more pick-ups are either vintage models or the very cheapest "beginner's" guitars. While it is unlikely, then, that you would want to

make such a guitar yourself, it is important to understand the principle and assembly of the single pick-up wiring circuit. This is because the seemingly complicated circuitry involved in a two and three pick-up guitar is, in effect, a multiplication of the basic single pick-up circuit – with the addition of option switches that determine whether the pick-ups are used singly or in combination, in series or in parallel, and in or out of phase with one another. If you can grasp the basics of a single pick-up, you should have little difficulty in progressing to more sophisticated circuits.

A single pick-up guitar circuit

The single pick-up circuit shown below involves the following components: the pick-up itself, a capacitor, two potentiometers, screened cable, and a ¼in. (6mm) mono jack socket.

The potentiometers used in the tone and volume controls are shown with the same value of 500 K log. This means that they have a maximum resistance value of 500 Kilohms and that they are the logarithmic rather than linear type. They are good general-purpose pots which will work quite well in most passive guitar circuits.

If the value of the pot is too low, it will prevent your guitar from delivering the maximum volume of which it is capable, while too high a value will result in a loss of control sensitivity. In other words, your volume and tone controls will seem to have no effect over part of their range. The optimum result is – like so many things in electronics – a compromise. When it comes down to component values, the influencing factors should be the type and style of music you are playing as well as the situations in which you are playing it.

The capacitor is used in conjunction with one of the pots to form the tone control. This is, in effect, a treble-cut control. The capacitor's job is to set a frequency below which the tone control pot has no effect, but above which operation of the pot will progressively increase the proportion of high frequencies in the signal from the pick-up that it sends to earth.

The smaller the value of the capacitor, the higher the frequency "roll-off" point will be, and vice versa. To put it another way, the higher the value of the capacitor, the less noticeable it will be when high frequencies are sent to earth. The control will not cut off much treble. The lower the value of the capacitor, the more effective the tone control will be. It will cut off more of the treble.

The procedure for wiring a single pick-up guitar circuit is simplicity itself. As the

diagrams show, a screened lead comes from the pick-up to the volume pot, and another screened lead runs from the volume pot to the jack socket. The tone control is connected to the capacitor and an earth wire. Having prepared the ends of the screened leads as shown on p. 185; make the earth connections to the volume pot and solder them carefully. Then connect the short earth wire to the tone pot.

The next step is to solder the earth connections to the metal covers of the pots. You may need a more powerful soldering iron for this job, and, on some pots, you may have to use an aluminium solder. If you are unable to get a strong joint between the

earth wires and pot casings in this way, try wrapping a piece of bare wire several times through the shake-proof washer on the pot spindle and solder the other end of the wire to the earth tag on the pot.

Now attach and solder the cores of the two screened cables to the volume pot. Lastly connect the .02µF capacitor and the jack socket. Check the sound of the guitar both with and without the optional additional .001µF capacitor shown below. You can just crimp the wire for this component on to the volume control until you have decided whether or not you like the effect. If you then decide to keep it, the connections must be soldered.

Note Wires to earthed terminals on pots are extended past the terminals and soldered on to the cases of the pots as part of the necessary screening.

Treble by-pass capacitor
This capacitor is optional. It will give improved treble at lower volumes, but at full volume it will have no effect.

Components of single pick-up circuit with volume and tone controls

Wiring diagram for single pick-up circuit

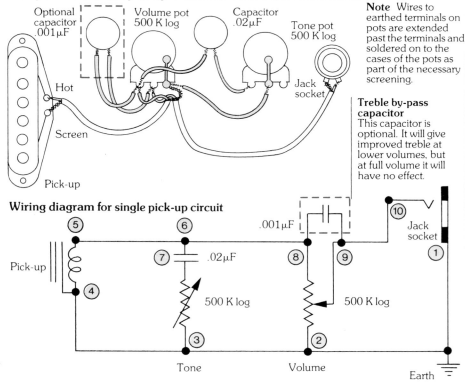

A two pick-up guitar circuit

The sound characteristics of an electric guitar are partially generated by the position of the pick-up under the strings – in the same way that different sounds can be produced from an acoustic guitar by playing at the bridge or directly above the soundhole. A single pick-up guitar, such as a Fender Esquire or Gibson Les Paul Junior, has a perfectly adequate sound, but because of the fixed position of the pick-up the only tonal variation comes from adjusting the tone control settings.

By using two pick-ups, you can amplify sound from two different sections of the strings. Either coil used on its own will give its own distinctive sound, or you can use the two pick-ups in phase together to produce a third variation in tone. By fitting the *phase switch* shown as an alternative in the diagram below, you can use the coils out of phase with one another, thus creating four basic options for single-coil pick-ups.

As can be seen from the wiring diagram,

the two pick-up circuit is, in effect, two single pick-up circuits wired in parallel, with the addition of a three-position selector switch. Consequently, apart from the switching, you can follow the basic wiring procedure described opposite.

A useful addition to wiring circuits of this type is the *coil tap*. This is attached to an extra output connection on the pick-up,

located in the centre of the coil. By wiring in a two-way switch, you can either use the pick-up as usual or you can take the output from one of the normal connections at either end of the pick-up and the centre coil-tap connection. This will effectively halve the impedence of the coil. The lower tap output produces a much cleaner tone with more high frequencies.

Components of twin pick-up circuit with individual volume and tone controls

Note The wiring for a two pick-up circuit is basically a duplication of the one opposite. The optional phase switch (inside the blue dotted line) can be added to pick-up 1.

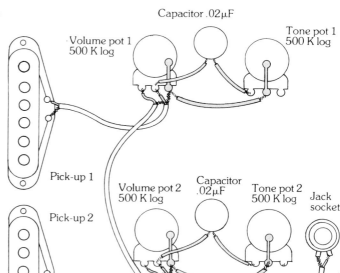

Capacitor .02μF

Volume pot 1
500 K log

Tone pot 1
500 K log

Pick-up 1

Volume pot 2
500 K log

Capacitor
.02μF

Tone pot 2
500 K log

Jack socket

Pick-up 2

Pick-up selector switch

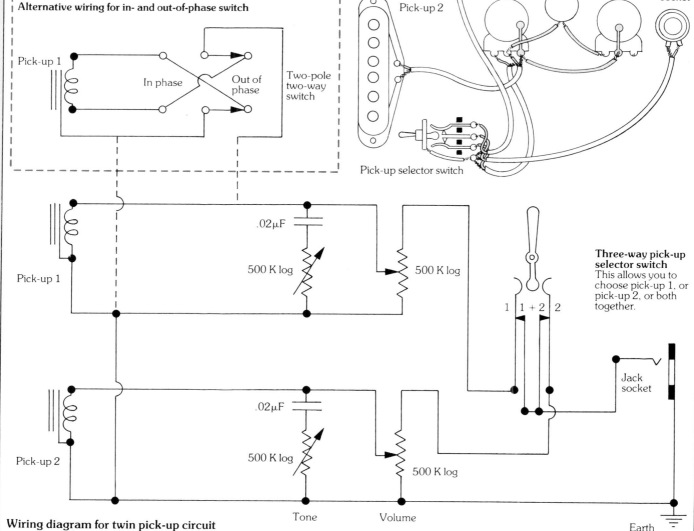

Alternative wiring for in- and out-of-phase switch

Pick-up 1

In phase

Out of phase

Two-pole two-way switch

.02μF

500 K log

500 K log

Pick-up 1

.02μF

500 K log

500 K log

Pick-up 2

Three-way pick-up selector switch
This allows you to choose pick-up 1, or pick-up 2, or both together.

1 | 1 + 2 | 2

Jack socket

Wiring diagram for twin pick-up circuit

Tone   Volume

Earth

A three pick-up guitar circuit

The use of a third single-coil pick-up dramatically increases the scope for tonal variations. Each single-coil pick-up can be used individually – giving three options – or any pair can be used in phase – giving three more options. Pairs can also be used out of phase with one another, producing a further three variations, while all three can be combined in phase to make an extra option. Bearing in mind the additional possibility of using all three pick-ups together, but with any one out of phase with the other two, there is a potential for many different switching positions, each with its own tonal characteristics.

With humbuckers (see p. 194), the choice can be almost infinite. If all the end connections for both coils are accessible, you have no less than six options for each pick-up. You can wire a humbucker to use either coil on its own, or with both coils in series (in or out of phase), or with both coils in parallel (again either in or out of phase). It should be pointed out, however, that some of these wiring options may negate the hum-cancelling properties of the pick-ups. The sound potential for three humbuckers, therefore, is enormous – as it would also be with three single-coil pick-ups fitted with "coil taps" (see p. 187). Of course, with this degree of choice the differences between tones may be so subtle that, in practice, they can scarcely be detected.

Wiring diagram for three pick-up multi-operation circuit

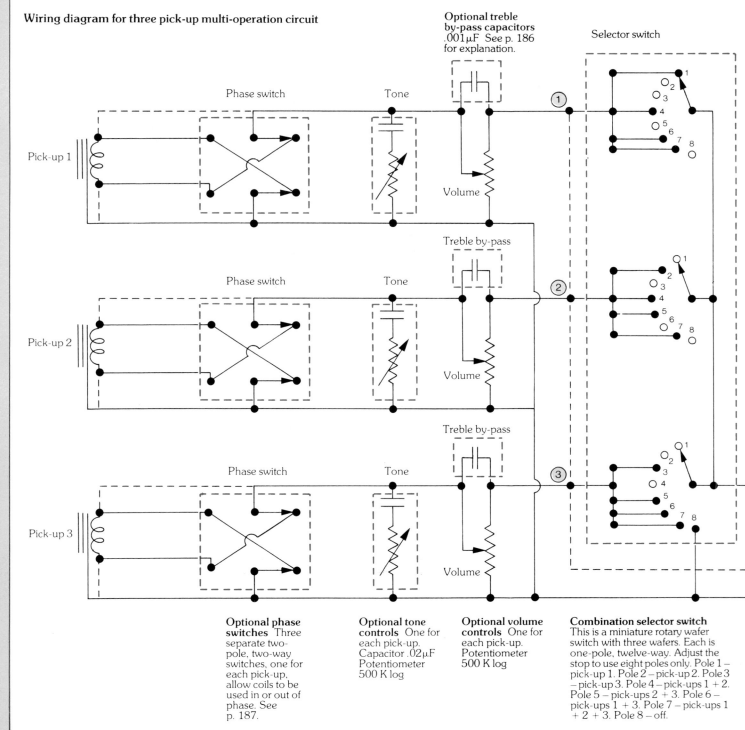

Optional phase switches Three separate two-pole, two-way switches, one for each pick-up, allow coils to be used in or out of phase. See p. 187.

Optional tone controls One for each pick-up. Capacitor .02μF Potentiometer 500 K log

Optional volume controls One for each pick-up. Potentiometer 500 K log

Combination selector switch This is a miniature rotary wafer switch with three wafers. Each is one-pole, twelve-way. Adjust the stop to use eight poles only. Pole 1 – pick-up 1. Pole 2 – pick-up 2. Pole 3 – pick-up 3. Pole 4 – pick-ups 1 + 2. Pole 5 – pick-ups 2 + 3. Pole 6 – pick-ups 1 + 3. Pole 7 – pick-ups 1 + 2 + 3. Pole 8 – off.

An important practical consideration is to think how you can accommodate all the necessary pick-up switches on one guitar. You may also find it difficult to remember how to select an individual sound from the hundreds available to you with such a set-up. Some degree of compromise is therefore necessary. The best thing to do is to experiment with different circuit connections to your switches until you get the results that you want.

Note All optional features are shown inside blue dotted lines. If they are not used, you should complete the black dotted circuitry. Individual volume controls can be used to fulfil the functions of the individual selector switches, which can then be left out (link points 1, 2, 3 and 4). However, a master volume control is useful if these selector switches are omitted. A master tone control may replace or supplement individual tone controls. If you fit treble by-pass filters to one or more of the individual volume controls, then you must also fit one to the master volume control.

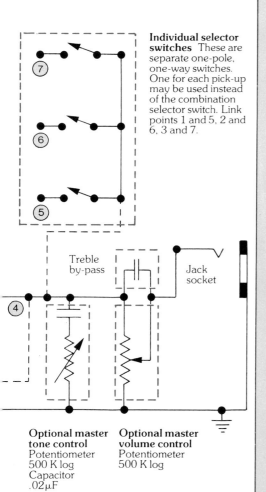

Individual selector switches These are separate one-pole, one-way switches. One for each pick-up may be used instead of the combination selector switch. Link points 1 and 5, 2 and 6, 3 and 7.

Optional master tone control
Potentiometer 500 K log
Capacitor .02 μF

Optional master volume control
Potentiometer 500 K log

Fault diagnosis

Use the table below as a guide to isolating faults which cannot be traced to the amplifier or lead. A number of faults can be located by testing the circuit with a multimeter, as detailed on the following pages.

Faults invariably occur when you least expect them to, so it is a good idea to follow the example of many roadies and make regular, systematic checks on your equipment. Always carry essential spares.

Fault	Remedy	Fault	Remedy
No output		**Hum or noise on output**	
Broken or detached internal wire	Find and replace broken wire or connection.	Earth line broken	Trace and repair break.
Short circuit	Locate short circuit and insulate or replace faulty wire or component.	Faulty screening	Use only high-quality braided screen cable. Screen the control compartment with copper foil, etc.
Pick-up, switch or volume control faulty	Replace faulty component. A faulty pick-up is likely to be nothing worse than a broken connection to the coil.	Local interference, especially on single-coil pick-up	This can be difficult to deal with. Interference can be mains or ether-borne. Mains filters can reduce interference to some extent, but the best solution is suppression at source , assuming you can gain access to this. Many venues today have a three-phase mains supply, so make sure your equipment is not plugged into the same phase as any lighting circuits which are often a prime cause of mains interference. Ether-borne interference, such as radio waves, can be even more troublesome. Try different locations and orientations of your equipment to minimize this, or short radio frequencies to earth before they can cause trouble. This can be done by inserting 250 μF capacitors in suitable places: between the pick-up hot wire(s) and earth; between the core and screen of your jack leads (you can easily fit a capacitor inside the jack plug); between grid and earth on all input and high-gain valves in the amp or the equivalent parts of a transistor amp. Note that capacitors used to modify amps in this way must be high-voltage working types with very low leakage, otherwise you will create problems worse than the ones you are trying to solve. Radio frequencies on valve grids can show up as excessive distortion.
Low output			
Section of pick-up wiring short-circuited	Simple single-section pick-ups should be replaced. Twin-coil or tapped-coil pick-ups are likely to be short-circuited at one of the internal connection points.		
Aged or faulty solder joint	Remove old solder with de-soldering braid and re-solder.		
Dirty switch	Clean with switch-cleaner.		
Muffled output			
Too high a value capacitor in tone control	Fit correct value capacitor. If in doubt, a 0.02 μF capacitor is generally satisfactory.		
Short circuit across tone pot	Find and remove cause of short circuit.		
Tone control acts as volume control			
Capacitor short circuited	Replace faulty capacitor.		
Capacitor has too large a value	Replace with correct value capacitor.		
Controls reversed			
Control wired wrong way round	Reverse connections to end of potentiometer track.		
Crackly or distorted output			
Faulty soldering (dry joint)	Remove old solder with de-soldering braid and re-solder.		
Dirty or loose pots or switches	Clean with switch-cleaner and re-solder.		
Worn jack plug	Replace socket.		
Poor-quality screened cable	Replace with high-quality cable.		

Testing components, connections and circuits

Over the next few pages are outlined a number of simple tests that should enable you to locate, diagnose and repair the faults that are most likely to stop an electric guitar from working properly. Some faults can be traced by sight or touch: for instance, soldered connections that have broken, or screws that have worked loose. There are, however, many other faults – such as damaged wires and components – which cannot be traced in the same way and require the use of special test equipment.

Most test equipment is costly, but it is possible to buy relatively inexpensively an accurate and efficient "multimeter", or "multi-tester" as it is sometimes called. This will enable you to carry out a number of useful tests and measurements; indeed it is impossible to carry out some circuitry work without using such a device. Very cheap meters are not recommended, both because they tend to be inaccurate (their own resistance is often low, and this will upset voltage readings), and because they may offer only a limited range of measuring facilities. Choose a meter which will measure from zero ohms to one megohm, and AC/DC volts from zero to 500 volts.

Safety precautions
Testing or metering any form of mains-powered equipment carries with it the risk of electrocution. This warning applies particularly to amplifiers, where very high (and potentially lethal) voltages are involved. None of the tests described in the following pages are to be used on equipment while it is still connected to the mains supply, or on any other devices (guitars, leads or pedals) while plugged into such equipment.

How to use a multimeter
Initially, your biggest problem is likely to be learning how to use the meter. At first glance, the multitude of markings and figures can be very confusing. However, here we shall only be using the meter for simple, basic tests, such as measuring resistance and measuring AC and DC voltage. For this reason, some of the controls normally found on a multimeter have been omitted from the diagram below, since they will not be used in the tests.

For this type of work, a multimeter with an indicator needle and scales is best. Meters with digital readouts can give very accurate readings but, if the voltage is fluctuating or if the resistance varies, you may see only a blur of unreadable figures. The way in which the needle moves across the scale can be useful information in itself.

Two test leads, sometimes called "banana jack leads", are usually supplied with the meter. One end of each lead is plugged into the meter, while the probes at the other ends are placed in contact with the component or connection being tested or measured. The function switch and range selector on the meter must be set according to the requirements of the test.

Zeroing the meter
Before carrying out any tests, you should first zero the meter. This involves getting the indicator to point to 0, showing that there is no resistance to the flow of current between the probes. Set the function switch to ohms and the range selector to the most sensitive setting (R × 1). Plug the test leads into the meter (the red lead always goes into the socket marked +) and touch the tips of the probes together. The needle should swing across the ohms scale, from maximum resistance to no resistance (zero). If this doesn't happen, turn the adjustment screw until it does.

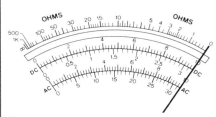

Range selector at R × 1

DC volts scale

Indicator needle

Adjustment screw

Ohms scale adjuster

Negative socket

Ohms scale

AC volts scale

Function switch

Range selector switch

Positive socket

Test leads
Two short jack leads each with a plug on one end and a probe on the other. The red lead goes into the positive socket and the black lead into the negative socket.

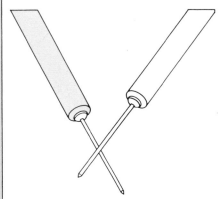

How to zero the meter
Function switch at ohms. Range selector at R × 1. Touch the two probes together and, if necessary, alter the ohms scale adjuster until the needle aligns exactly with 0 (zero ohms) on the ohms scale.

Testing a guitar lead

This is a test to ensure that the connections and cable of a standard screened mono guitar lead are not faulty. It will establish whether there is a short circuit between the outer screening and the central wire. This particular fault is caused by damage to the insulation between the earthing and the central core, and it allows electrical contact between the two. A short circuit can also occur in the region of the jack plug connecting tags or in the jack plug itself. The test measures the resistance to the flow of current in the lead.

Plug the test leads into the meter and set the range selector to its most sensitive setting. With the meter we are using as an example, use the R × 1 setting. As a result, a reading of 1 on the ohms scale will indicate a resistance of 1 ohm in the subject under test.

Testing for a short circuit

Zero the meter as described on the opposite page. Place one probe in contact with the earth sleeve of one of the jack plugs and the other in contact with the end central wire connection, as shown in the diagram below.

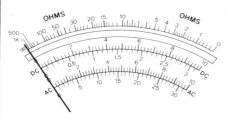

Range selector at R × 1

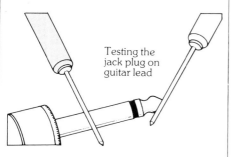

Testing the jack plug on guitar lead

The needle should point to the top end of the scale, indicating infinite resistance. If it does, there is no short circuit between the earth and central core connections allowing current to pass between them.

If the needle moves away from the top of the scale, this indicates a decrease in resistance. Current is able to pass between the earth and the central core. There is therefore a short circuit either through the insulation or between the internal connections of the jack plug. You should remedy this by repairing the insulation or replacing the faulty components.

If the original problem is that the sound of the guitar keeps cutting out intermittently,

and you suspect the lead may be at fault, pull the lead about in different directions while you are testing it. This should soon indicate whether a short circuit is causing the guitar to cut in and out.

Checking the plug connections

To check the central core connection of the lead, place the probes in contact with the jack plug end connections. Use the same settings as before. The needle should move from the high end of the scale to indicate

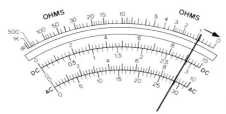

Range selector at R × 1

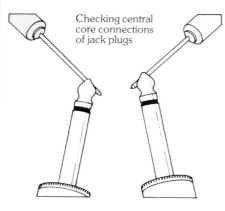

Checking central core connections of jack plugs

almost zero resistance to the flow of current (1 ohm or less is acceptable). The small resistance allows an unrestricted flow of current, so the lead is functioning correctly.

If the needle remains at the high end, indicating infinite resistance, then there is no flow of current. This means that there is a break in the connections or wires.

Repeat the above procedure, but this time place the probes in contact with the earth sleeve connections of each jack plug. This is to check that the screening and screen contacts are all in order. A reading of 0 (zero ohms) indicates that the connection is good. Less than 1 ohm is still acceptable.

If any fault is detected through these tests, you can narrow down its actual location by unscrewing the casing of the jack plugs and testing in the same way as before. Some faults can be isolated by taking readings from the point at which the wires are soldered on to the connecting tags.

Now that you have tested a guitar lead, you can apply the same principle and use the same method to test any lead, connection or passive resistive component.

Testing a mains lead

It is easy to test mains leads that have a plug (which goes into a wall socket) at one end and a cable socket (which plugs into the piece of equipment) at the other. If you think that the lead is malfunctioning, the first thing to test is probably the fuse. Set

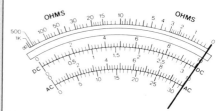

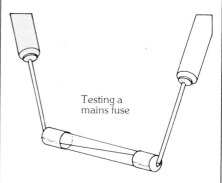

Range selector at R × 1

Testing a mains fuse

the function switch to ohms, and the range selector to R × 1. Zero the meter, and place the two probes in contact with opposite ends of the fuse. If the needle stays at the high end of the scale, indicating infinite resistance, the connection has broken and the fuse has blown. If the indicator swings across to measure zero, the fuse is good.

Assuming no problems with the fuse, the next thing is to test the lead for a short circuit. Set and zero the meter as above. Place one probe in the earth socket of the cable socket and the other in contact with the live socket. A reading of infinite ohms indicates that there is no short circuit.

Now repeat the check, but with one probe in the earth socket and the other in the negative socket of the cable socket. Analyze the readings as above. Finally, make the test with one probe in the positive socket and the other in the negative.

If the lead is not short-circuiting, you can go on to test the connections. Keeping the settings as above, zero the meter. Place one probe inside the earth socket of the cable socket and the other probe in contact with the earth pin on the plug at the other end of the lead. If the meter shows infinite resistance, there is a fault. If it registers zero or slightly above, the connection is in good order.

Repeat the process, checking first the positive connections and then the negative connections.

Checking the output signal

If there is no volume at all when the guitar is plugged into an amplifier, there may be no output signal coming from the guitar itself. First, make sure that the lead is functioning correctly (see p. 191). Then set the range selector to the most sensitive setting on the AC volts scale; with the meter shown, this is ACV 10. Plug the tested jack lead into the guitar output socket, and place one probe in contact with the centre connection of the jack plug at the other end of the lead. Place the second probe in contact with the earthing sleeve of the same plug.

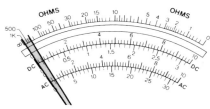

Range selector at AC volts 10

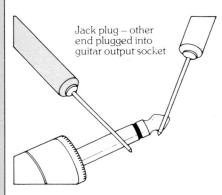

Jack plug – other end plugged into guitar output socket

As the output from the guitar is relatively small – in the region of 50-200 millivolts – even with the meter at its most sensitive setting, the needle will kick only very marginally at the bottom of the volts scale. To get the maximum output, turn the volume control full up and turn the treble and bass controls to maximum. Get someone else to play repeated chords with a plectrum, or use crocodile clips for the connections so you can play the guitar yourself. With all but the cheapest and least sensitive of meters, the output should be sufficient to nudge the indicator needle on the scale.

If there is plainly no output signal, you should locate the source of the fault by going through the circuit-testing procedure outlined on the opposite page. Once you have found the faulty component or connection, you should replace it with one which is working. You should then be able to plug the guitar into the amplifier and find that it is working normally.

Testing a pick-up

Testing the performance characteristics of a pick-up requires sophisticated measuring equipment capable of measuring AC impedance at all frequencies. This is beyond the scope of a multimeter. However, you can still use your meter to check that the pick-up is functioning, and also to measure its resistance. Because there is a correlation between its resistance and its AC impedance, this can give you a useful rule-of-thumb guide to the pick-up's.

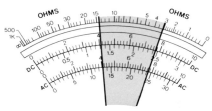

Range selector at R × 1K

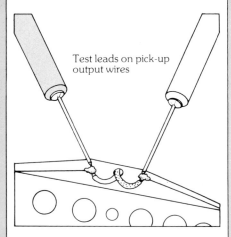

Test leads on pick-up output wires

tone and volume characteristics.

If the pick-up is wired into the circuit, you must first disconnect it. Set the meter's function switch to ohms (which will also measure DC resistance) and the range selector to a setting which can cope with between 3 and 14 K (R × 1 K is shown here). Zero the ohms scale, and place each test probe in contact with a pick-up output wire.

Generally, the resistance will lie between 3 K and 14 K. A pick-up with a 3 K resistance will have a very clear tone, but will not be capable of producing as much volume as a 12 K pick-up, which will have a correspondingly warmer tone as treble frequencies are increasingly impeded.

You can use DC resistance measurements to identify the coil-tap connection of a pick-up (if one is fitted). The coil-tap will have a lower resistance than the normal pick-up connections (see p. 187).

Testing components

These tests can be used to measure the resistance of components such as pots, capacitors and resistors. Their resistance values will affect their operation.

Testing pots

As we have seen (p. 186) a 500 K log pot is a good, general-purpose component for installation in guitar circuits. Here is a test for checking the efficiency of such a pot.

Set the function switch to ohms, and the range selector to R × 10 K. Zero the meter. Place the test probes in contact with the two

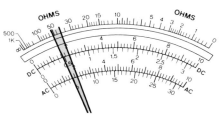

Range selector at R × 10K

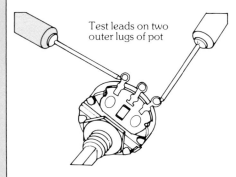

Test leads on two outer lugs of pot

outer lugs of the pot. Pots commonly used in guitar circuits usually have the resistance marked on the casing, along with a tolerance expressed as a percentage. Therefore, a pot marked 500 K (20%) should ideally have a maximum resistance of 500 K, but in practice may vary between 400 K and 600 K. Pots with 10%, 5% and 1% tolerances are also available, but 20% is the most common figure. If the needle shows a reading above 600 K, or whatever the upper tolerance limit may be, you should replace the pot. The resistive track has probably been damaged.

Now check from one outer lug to the central lug. Use crocodile clips to leave your hands free. Rotate the spindle smoothly from one end of its range to the other. As you do so, the indicator needle should also move smoothly from zero to the maximum value of the pot, or vice versa. Repeat this procedure, this time checking the other outer lug with the centre lug.

If the needle kicks during either of these tests, the pot may be dirty and you should clean it with special switch cleaner. If the needle still kicks, replace the pot.

Testing resistors

Whereas pots present variable resistance to the flow of current, resistors have just one set value which you can easily check by setting the function switch and selector as

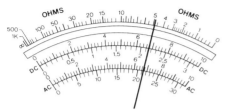

Range selector at R × 1K

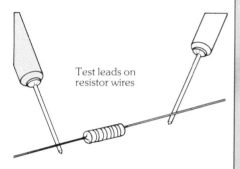

Test leads on resistor wires

above and placing the probes in contact with the wires of the resistor. There is a standard, colour-coded identification system for resistor values.

Testing capacitors

Specialized equipment is needed to test the actual capacitance of a capacitor; a multimeter cannot be used for this. However, the multimeter is useful for other tests on capacitors. If your guitar's tone control is totally ineffective, it may have gone "open circuit", meaning that the capacitor has a broken internal connection and must be replaced. If the tone control starts to act on both tone and volume, and then gradually loses its ability to alter the tone, the capacitor may be going "leaky" internally. Eventually it is likely to short circuit and behave purely as a volume control.

To test a capacitor, set the function switch to ohms, and the range selector to the highest ohms setting (R × 10 K here). Zero the meter and, if the capacitor is in a circuit, disconnect one wire. Place the probes in contact with the capacitor's wires. If the needle kicks momentarily across part of the scale and then returns slowly and smoothly to infinite ohms, then the capacitor is functioning correctly. If the needle stays on infinite ohms, then the capacitor has a broken connection; it should therefore be replaced. If the needle kicks across the scale but does not return to infinite ohms, the capacitor is leaking. A zero reading shows that the capacitor has short-circuited.

Testing a passive guitar circuit

The circuit test described here is for a single pick-up guitar (see p. 186); as we have seen, this is the basis for more complicated configurations, such as two and three pick-up circuits, and you can follow the same basic procedure for testing each of them.

The numbers refer to the test points on the circuit, shown in circles on the diagram. When testing the actual components, it is sometimes necessary to disconnect them by detaching one connection. Because these components behave as resistors wired in parallel, you may in some circumstances get a false reading if you do not do this.

Set the meter function switch to ohms, and the range selector to its most sensitive setting (R × 1 here). Zero the meter. Place the black (negative) probe in contact with point 1 (the outer screening connection of the jack socket); as it will remain in this position through most of the tests, you can use crocodile clips to hold it in place. Place the red (positive) probe in contact with point 2 (the earth tag of the volume pot). A reading of zero ohms indicates that the connection between the outer jack socket screening and the volume control is good. A reading of 1 ohm or more suggests a badly soldered connection or wire, which you should repair. A reading of infinite ohms indicates a broken or disconnected wire.

Now move the red probe so it is in contact with point 3, the earthed tag of the tone control. Interpret the readings as above. If no fault is indicated, move the red probe to point 4 (the earthed output of the pick-up). If this is satisfactory, turn the guitar volume control to the fully off position, and place the red probe in contact with point 9 (the centre tag of the volume control pot). Interpret the readings as above.

Now place the red probe in contact with point 10, and set the treble control to maximum. Operate the volume control through its range while watching the needle's movements. A zero reading throughout indicates a short circuit between the wire joining points 9 and 10 and the

earth wire. A reading of zero at the top and bottom of the scale with a reading of about half the value of the pot in between suggests a short circuit between the wire connecting point 5 (the hot connection of the pick-up) to point 8 (the third tag of the volume pot) and the earth wire. If the pot is operating correctly, with no short circuits, the needle will move smoothly across the scale. You will not, however, be able to read the value of the pot correctly, since it is wired in parallel with the pick-up. To do this, you should disconnect at either point 8 or 2 and then carry out the potentiometer value test described on the opposite page.

Having reconnected the pot, you can now continue with the circuit test. Leaving the volume pot set at maximum, the black probe in contact with point 1, and the red probe in contact with point 10, operate the treble control through its range. A zero reading indicates that the capacitor has short-circuited and must be replaced. If, the tone control does not work, then you should check the capacitor for an "open circuit".

To test the junction between the capacitor and the tone control pot, place the red probe in contact with point 7. Operate the control through its range. If the needle moves slowly from zero to the value marked on the pot, then all is in order. A reading of infinite ohms, though, indicates that the resistive track inside the pot is broken; zero ohms throughout indicates that the pot has short-circuited.

For the remaining tests you should unclip the black probe from point 1, and place it in contact with point 10 instead. Place the red probe in contact with point 5, and operate the volume pot from minimum to maximum through its range. A high reading, dropping smoothly to zero, shows that it is functioning correctly. If infinite ohms is indicated, the connection between points 5 and 8 is broken. A reading of 1 ohm suggests a suspect solder connection. To test the pick-up itself, disconnect one contact and proceed as described on the opposite page.

Wiring diagram for single pick-up passive guitar circuit
See p. 186 for an explanation of this circuit.

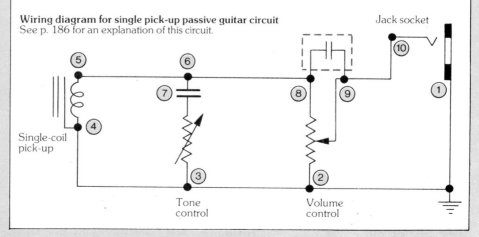

Humbucking pick-ups

Until now, we have been dealing only with single-coil pick-ups and how they are wired. Humbuckers, described on p. 53, contain two coils instead of one. Each coil has its own set of pole-pieces which are in contact with a single, central magnet. This means that, in effect, the humbucker can also be considered as though it were two separate pick-ups in one body. The fact that these two coils are wired in series and out of phase with one another means that mains hum or background noise picked up by the coils – not by the magnets – is cancelled out. Humbuckers have a characteristically warmer tone than single-coil pick-ups.

Wiring humbuckers

Humbuckers offer a wide variety of wiring options. One unit can be used either as a true humbucker, with its two coils in series, or as two separate single-coil pick-ups, with the coils working separately or together, in or out of phase. These different combinations can produce a formidable range of sounds.

Humbuckers can be bought already fitted with a four-core screened cable. This allows you immediate access to the individual coils and makes any or all of the above configurations possible. The first thing to do is to identify each of the four core wires. This is quite simple if you use a multimeter (see p. 190-93). To establish which wires come from the ends of the two coils, set your meter to read ohms and take readings until you have identified the two pairs. You must now find out which of each pair is the hot wire. To do this, set your meter to its smallest AC volts setting. Connect the ends of one coil to the meter, and tap the pick-up pole-pieces gently with a screwdriver blade. As you do so, you should see the needle of the meter kick slightly – either up or down off the scale. If the needle seems to kick down, reverse the connections to the meter. When you are quite certain that the needle is kicking upwards, the red wire of your meter will be connected to the hot wire of the coil. Repeat this procedure for the two wires from the other coil.

Humbuckers fitted with only a single-core screened cable can, with care and patience, be modified to produce the four separate core wires necessary for the options shown in the circuit below. However, you will have to open your pick-up to locate the connections. Unfortunately, this means unsoldering the pick-up cover from its base. The best way to do this is to use "de-soldering braid", which is flux-impregnated braided wire. Hold it against the solder you want to remove, and place a soldering iron on top of it to heat both the braid and the joint. The braid will take up the solder, and the cover will come free.

When the cover is off, you will see that there is insulation tape wrapping both coils together. Unwind the tape so that you can get to the soldered connection joining the two coils. Open this joint, so that the two ends become two of your cores. The third core wire will lead from the end of one of the coils to an earth connection on the pick-up base plate. This, too, should be disconnected. The fourth and final core wire is the one connected to the existing single-core cable. Detach this one as well.

Now connect the four ends that you have freed to the cores of the new four-core cable, and connect the screen wire of the cable to the base.

If you cannot get hold of four-core screened cable, you can use two lengths of two-core. Be sure, however, to connect the screen wire to the pick-up base (at one end) and to the potentiometer (at the other end) on only *one* of the two lengths. Leave the screen wire on the other length unconnected at the pick-up end.

Some humbuckers are available with wired-in "coil taps" (see p. 187). This increases their versatility still further, since each *section* of each coil can be used separately. Coil-tapped humbuckers have six core wires. When you come to identify which wires are connected to which coil, you will, of course, find that there are two sets of three linked wires. Of each three, one leads to one end of the coil, one leads to the other end, and one (the "tap") comes from the centre of the coil. If you use a meter to test each set of three wires in pairs (1 and 2, 2 and 3, 1 and 3), you will find that one pair has twice the resistance of the other two pairs. This pair will be connected to each end of the coil. The remaining one will be the coil-tap wire.

Wiring diagram for multi-option humbucker wiring

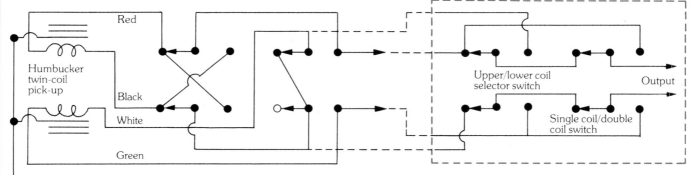

Note This entire circuit may be wired in place of any of the single-coil pick-ups in previous diagrams (see p. 186-9). However, the hum-cancelling property of the pick-up will not operate in all switch positions. The colours are based on the DiMarzio code.

Self-phase switch This two-pole, two-way switch puts the two coils of the pick-up either in or out of phase with one another.

Series/parallel switch Another two-pole, two-way switch changes the normal series wiring of the two coils to parallel.

Optional single-coil switching The two switches shown above allow you to choose between using only one or using both of the humbucker's coils. The selector switch chooses which of the two coils operates when you are switched to single coil. A simpler arrangement can be made by inserting a one-pole, one-way switch into the green wire. This will function as a single-coil switch when the series/parallel switch is set to parallel. When series is selected, it becomes an on/off switch.

Buying pick-ups

The two things that most affect the tone of pick-ups are the strength of the magnets and the way in which the coils are made.

In general, the stronger the magnet, the louder the sound and the more the treble frequencies are accentuated. Although magnets become gradually weaker over a period of years, this is not always regarded as a drawback. In fact, such is the demand for the sound of "vintage" pick-ups that the American manufacturer Seymour Duncan artificially "ages" the magnets in some of the pick-ups he makes. In recent years, manufacturers such as Alembic have begun using ceramic or piezo magnets. These are cheaper, more permanent and give a higher output.

Pick-up coils differ from one type to another in terms of the gauge of wire used and the number of turns or windings. Both these factors affect the impedance of the pick-up. Thin wire has a greater resistance to the flow of current than thick wire. Increasing the number of windings gives the coil a higher impedance and produces more volume – but a reduction in overall clarity because of the decrease in treble response.

The working impedance of a pick-up is difficult to measure without sophisticated equipment. For this reason, it is common practice when assessing a pick-up's likely performance to measure the coil's resistance to DC (see p. 192). However, some people regard the *resonant peak* or *resonant frequency* as the best indication of what a pick-up will actually sound like. A resonant peak occurs at the point in the audio spectrum where a pick-up is at its most efficient in reproducing the sound of the guitar. A graph showing a pick-up's frequency response would rise gradually before reaching a fairly sharp peak (representing the resonant peak) and would then fall off. If a pick-up has a resonant peak towards the higher end of its frequency spectrum, it will emphasize trebles. If the peak is lower down its frequency spectrum, then mid-range frequencies will be emphasized. Using a larger number of coil windings or weaker magnets will lower the resonant peak of the pick-up. Conversely, fewer windings or stronger magnets will result in a higher peak. Strong magnets can, however, inhibit or "choke" string vibration.

This all amounts to the fact that pick-up specifications can be, at the best of times, confusing and, at the worst, misleading. Judging a pick-up by its sound and by measuring its resistance to the flow of DC will give you the best indication.

Gibson pick-ups

The Gibson company has been making guitar pick-ups since the 1930s (see p. 54). However, perhaps the most famous of all their pick-ups are the "PAF" humbuckers fitted to Les Pauls between 1957 and 1960 (PAF stood for "patent applied for"). Something of a legend has grown up around these pick-ups, and originals are highly prized. Gibson make a current PAF model (see below) as well as many other humbuckers.

Gibson "PAF" humbucker

Gibson "Velvet Brick" humbucker

Custom pick-ups

Replacement pick-ups have played a prominent part in the custom-parts industry during the last ten years or so. Companies such as DiMarzio, Schecter, Mighty Mite, Seymour Duncan and Bill Lawrence now produce a wide variety of different pick-ups which vary in specification and design. It is now possible to simulate the vintage sounds of early Gibson and Fender pick-ups, or to switch instantly from the bright, clean sound of the classic single-coil to the fattest, dirtiest distortion of a powerful humbucker.

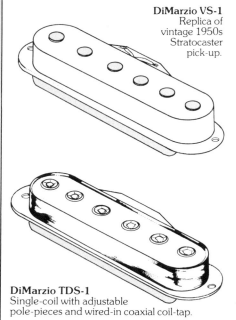

DiMarzio VS-1
Replica of vintage 1950s Stratocaster pick-up.

DiMarzio TDS-1
Single-coil with adjustable pole-pieces and wired-in coaxial coil-tap.

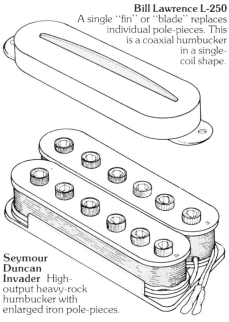

Bill Lawrence L-250
A single "fin" or "blade" replaces individual pole-pieces. This is a coaxial humbucker in a single-coil shape.

Seymour Duncan Invader High-output heavy-rock humbucker with enlarged iron pole-pieces.

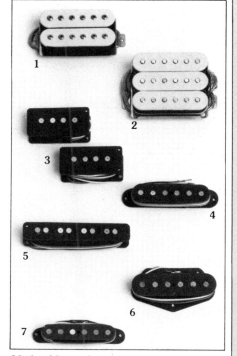

Mighty Mite pick-ups
1 Distortion humbucker with split-coil wiring. **2** Motherbucker triple-coil pick-up. **3** Offset single-coils for Precision-style bass. **4** Strat pick-up. **5** Lead pick-up for Jazz-style bass. **6** Lead pick-up for Tele. **7** Rhythm pick-up for Tele.

Active guitar circuitry

All the circuits discussed previously have been *passive*. There are, however, *active* guitar circuits as well. In electronics, an active circuit is one which includes a device that introduces *gain* (see p. 202) or allows current to flow in one direction only.

Active circuitry allows you to get a consistently high output signal, whatever type of pick-up is used. This is achieved by means of a *pre-amplifier*, which amplifies the signal from the pick-up. Boosting the signal level reduces the risk of extraneous noise being picked up by the guitar lead, improves the signal-to-noise ratio when pedals are in use, and makes it easy to drive a valve amplifier

into distortion. Active circuitry also lets you fit comprehensive tone controls of almost any level of sophistication – as well as many effects available as foot pedals – to your guitar.

Early pre-amps based on a single transistor suffered from the fact that, while guitar pick-ups and amplifiers are high-impedance units, transistors work better in low-impedance circuitry. Though the high-impedance *field effect transistor* is simple, cheap and performs tolerably well, today's trend is to use integrated circuits (ICs) in the form of an *operational amplifier*. When ICs containing several operational amplifiers are used, highly

complex circuits can be constructed in a very small space. Operational amplifiers amplify the difference between voltages fed to their two inputs. Either input can, however, be set at a fixed reference voltage and a signal applied to the other input. If this signal is fed to the non-inverting (positive) input, the output waveform will be in phase with the input waveform. If applied to the inverting (negative) input, the output will be 180 degrees out of phase. As it stands, the gain of the operational amplifier is unusably large; to bring it under control, some of the output is returned to the input in such a way as to subtract from the input (this is called *negative feedback*).

Building a pre-amplifier

This pre-amp uses a non-inverting circuit to preserve the phase relationship of the signal whether the unit is switched in or out of the circuit. It is constructed on "Veroboard", a readily available plastic board drilled every 0.1 in. (2.5 mm) and faced with copper strips on one side, which serves as a printed circuit. To build this pre-amp, your board should have 14 strips of 13 holes; identify these with letters and numbers respectively as in the diagram (right) where the strips on the reverse run left to right.

The first stage is to cut the strips into sections. Drill behind points A5, D9, E7, G7, H3, I8, J8 and K8. Assemble the components in the order suggested in the table. Bend the leads to fit through the holes and trim so about 1/8 in. (3 mm) protrudes. Bend these stubs flat along the copper strips and solder in place, being careful not to bridge the strips with solder. If the switch terminals are too large to fit through the holes, solder on short lengths of wire and feed these through instead. The potentiometer adjusts the gain of the unit to give an output of between twice and ten times the level of the input signal. The type used here is a 20-turn cermet preset resistor; it takes 20 turns of the screw to adjust from the minimum to maximum settings, thus giving precise adjustment. Set this to give the greatest distortion you wish to use. Turning down the volume on the guitar will give you the option of a clean sound or any amount of distortion up to the maximum you have set.

To fit the unit to your guitar, drill a 1/4 in. (6 mm) hole through the fingerplate and mount the switch through this. Detach the coaxial lead to the output socket from the volume control, and solder in its place a suitable length of coaxial, taking it to the unit's input terminals (E1 core, A1 screen). Rewire the lead to the output socket to the output terminals (E13 core, A13 screen).

Replace the output jack socket with a stereo jack socket using the sleeve and tip connections for the screen and core respectively of the signal cable. Solder a separate wire from

the ring connection on the stereo jack socket to point L1. The unit is switched on whenever the guitar is plugged in; the switch merely takes it in or out of the circuit.

Component layout (top view)

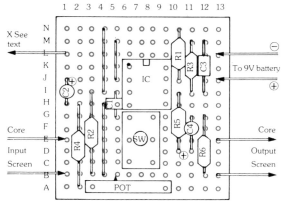

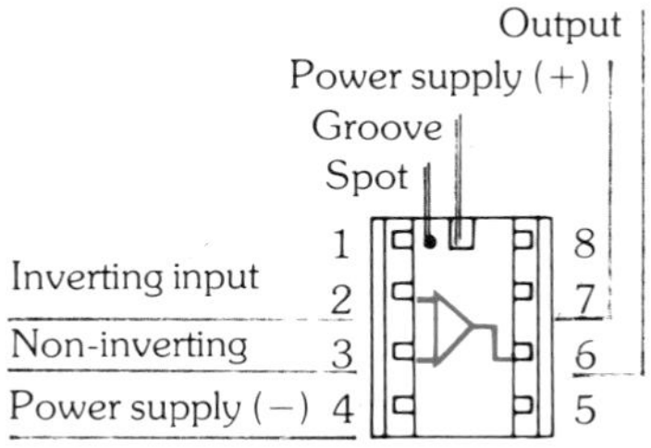

Operational amplifier (top view)
The device is in an 8-pin dual in-line (DIL) plastic package. Orientate the pins (un-numbered) by the spot above pin 1 or the groove between pins 1 and 8. The TL 071 version recommended has FET inputs and low noise and distortion.

Components list and assembly sequence		
Location	**Diagram**	**Component**
H/I/J/K 6 and 9	IC	IC socket (8-way low-profile DIL) with TL 071 (or 741 or 748) IC
J10–N10	R1	470K resistor, 5%, carbon film, ¼ watt
B3–I3	R2	470K resistor, 5%, carbon film, ¼ watt
I11–M11	R3	100K resistor, 5%, carbon film, ¼ watt
A2–H2	R4	10K resistor, 5%, carbon film, ¼ watt
D10–I10	R5	1K resistor, 5%, carbon film, ¼ watt
B12–G12	R6	100K resistor, 5%, carbon film, ¼ watt
B4–H4, I4–N4, J5–M5	–	Wire links (use offcuts from resistor wires)
G5–I5	C1	.022 µF capacitor (polyester or polystyrene)
H1–J1 (+)	C2	10 µF 25V DC capacitor (tantalum)
I12–M12	C3	100 pF capacitor
D11(+)–G11	C4	10 fd 25V DC capacitor (tantalum)
C/E/G 6 and 8	SW	DPDT miniature toggle switch
A3, A8, B5	POT	VRI 50K linear potentiometer
J13(+), L13	–	Battery connector for PP3 (9V)

AMPLIFICATION

A great deal of mystery and myth surrounds the subject of amplification. Quite simply, it is a method of boosting an electrical signal before feeding it to the loudspeaker which converts it into sound. Of course, in practice, amplification is much more complex – involving the most sophisticated of modern sound processing and sound reinforcement equipment. This chapter therefore explains all the basic principles in the belief that an understanding of them will help you get the best out of your equipment. Covering amps, speakers, special effects, and PAs and on-stage sound

systems, it explains the differences between types, describes what they do, and gives advice on when they might best be used. The enormous variety of names that manufacturers give to various effects and pieces of equipment can be bewildering, even to experienced musicians. The information in this chapter should help prevent you being blinded by science and give you a much better idea of what is happening when you play your guitar through a flanger into an overdriven valve amp with the reverb turned up and the treble boost switched on.

The role of the amplifier

An electric guitar relies on amplification to increase the signal generated by the pick-ups when the instrument is played. The guitar cannot be connected directly to a loud-speaker because it takes more energy to drive the moving parts of a speaker than the vibration of the strings can generate across the windings of the pick-up. Therefore, an amplifier has to be used. It takes electrical power from an external source (either mains or batteries) and uses the signal voltage derived from the guitar to control the delivery of that power to the speaker. The amplifier enables you to modify tone and volume, and to add qualities such as distortion and echo.

Many musicians think of amplification only in terms of power amplifiers used to drive loudspeakers. However, in the strict sense of the word, "amplifier" is equally applicable to many sound processing or "effects" devices usually referred to by other names – expanders, equalizers and limiters, for example. Therefore, with the exception of the terms "damping factor" and "power output", all the information in this section which concerns amplifier specifications can be taken as applying equally to these other devices.

Amplifiers operate in one of two ways – either by using valves or by using transistors. The processes differ, and so, to some extent, do the characteristics of the amplified sound.

Amplifiers can be designed to reproduce the input signal (the original sound) at the output (the speaker) with a very high degree of precision. This is, essentially, the meaning

of "high-fidelity". Hi-fi amplification is a fundamental requirement for amplifying acoustic guitars, bass guitars (when clean sound and projection are required), most keyboard, string and wind instruments, and, in particular, the human voice. The best PA systems and studio monitors embody state-of-the-art high-fidelity sound technology.

Amplifiers can also be designed to provide a harmonic enrichment of the signals fed into them. Many electric guitarists use this quality in preference to true hi-fi sound since it is an important factor in creating their own distinctive sound. The effect can also be of use to some electric keyboard instruments, but it is generally inappropriate for most other instruments unless some special effect is sought.

Amplifiers combined with the speaker(s) in one cabinet are known as combo amps. These are readily portable and easy to set up, but in cases where more flexibility is required (such as the need to add extra power) it is common practise to use separate amplifiers ("tops") and speakers ("bottoms"). The units can either be stacked on top of each other or the amplifier can be placed some way away from the speakers in order to minimize damage from vibration.

Combo amplifiers
Bill Nelson is seen here with two combo amps, both miked into the PA system. The output from both amplifiers can be mixed to give combinations of tone and distortion that would not be possible using either amplifier on its own.

How an amplifier works

The diagram opposite shows the various stages involved in the operation of a typical valve amplifier with two input channels and tremelo and reverb controls. The quality of the *power supply* governs the efficiency of all subsequent links in the chain. No matter how good the rest of the circuitry, the amplifier's performance will suffer if the power supply is sub-standard. At this pre-paratory stage, power taken from the AC mains is transformed to a higher voltage and rectified to DC current through valve or semi-conductor diodes. A network of resistors, capacitors and an inductor finally smooths the direct current and supplies different voltages to the various amplification stages.

The *first stage*, or pre-amplifier, consists of one valve and its associated components. These apply a fixed voltage gain to the input signal from the guitar (in other words, they amplify the signal voltage).

The *tone and volume controls* frequently use a passive network of resistors and capacitors, similar to the controls on a guitar. However, their operation can be slightly more complex because, by this time, the signal is at the higher voltage produced by the first stage. Some amplifiers have active controls which affect the gain of the second stage at suitable frequencies.

The *second stage* consists of one valve which, like the first stage, is a voltage amplifier. Its function is to make good the loss of signal voltage inherent in the use of passive tone controls, and in some cases to give additional voltage gain.

The *tremolo* consists of two valves arranged to make a low-frequency oscillator. The output waveform of this oscillator is superimposed on to the signal voltage to produce the tremolo effect of rapid, regular changes in volume.

The *reverberation* unit contains a pair of metal springs which are used to delay the signal. One or two valves are used as a current amplifier which drives a transducer connected to one end of the springs. This vibrates the springs, and the vibrations are picked up at the opposite end of the springs by a second transducer which feeds a one- or two-valve voltage amplifier. The reverb control is simply a volume control placed behind the first of these valves.

The *master volume* is a passive control acting on the overall signal level delivered from all the input channels to the power amplifier.

The *power amplifier* consists of three stages: the phase splitter or inverter, the driver, and the power stage. The phase splitter delivers two output signals, one of which is 180 degrees out of phase with the other. The voltage of these two signals is amplified by the driver stage. The two valves employed in the phase splitter are frequently used to achieve this amplification themselves, and so the two stages can be combined. Normally, all the valves used up to this point in the circuit are triodes. However, in order to save space, double triodes are usually employed, since these combine the function of two valves in one unit. Therefore, the function of one valve in theory may, in practice, be carried out by half a valve; the remaining capacity might be used for other purposes.

In the *power stage*, however, one or more pairs of valves (usually pentodes) are used to convert the large signal voltage into a large current flow. This current is drawn through the output transformer and is finally delivered to the loudspeaker.

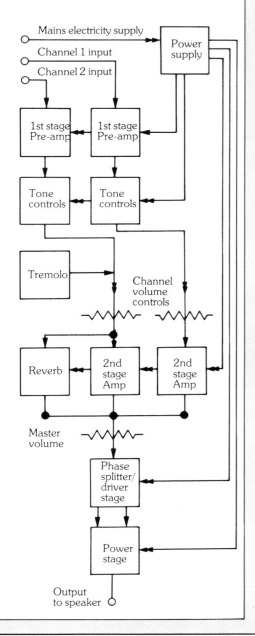

How a valve amplifies a signal

Valves or "tubes" work on the thermionic principle. A low voltage is passed through the heater filament which heats the cathode. This makes it possible for electrons to flow between the cathode and anode, so causing a current to flow from the power supply, through the valve and back to the power supply. The voltage signal from the guitar is fed to the control grid, where it regulates the flow of current between anode and cathode. As the controlling voltage rises and falls, so the flow of current rises and falls. The restrictive effect of the resistors feeding the anode and cathode causes a voltage fluctuation to appear at X and Y as a result of the variation in current flow. The voltage fluctuation is large compared to that on the control grid, so amplification has been achieved. Depending on requirements, the amplified signal can be taken from either X or Y. The signal at X is 180 degrees out of phase with that at Y.

Valves occasionally fail or "blow" and need replacement. The most common cause is the heater filament burning out. How long a valve will last before this happens depends on how often you use the amplifier. A hard-working professional musician may need to replace valves several times a year. Mechanical shock (typically caused by rough handling) may cause the glass envelope to fracture and thus destroy the vacuum within. Cracking of the glass

may also occur as a result of a sudden temperature change – as when cold drinks are spilt on to the glass. Internal short circuits can also occur. Another hazard is "microphony", caused by internal parts of the valve becoming loose enough to respond to vibration. This vibration will modulate the electrical signal, making the valve behave like a microphone.

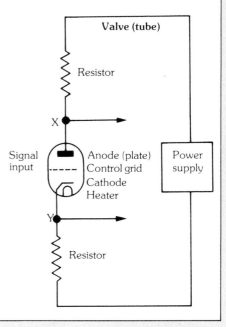

How a transistor amplifies a signal

Transistors consist of layers of different semi-conductor materials deposited on top of one another. Many contain toxic chemicals, so it is unwise to open them up to see what they are made of.

Unlike valves, transistors do not need heaters to make them work. Current flows from the power supply through the transistor, between the emitter and collector, and then back to the power supply. The fluctuating voltage of the signal from the guitar pick-up or microphone, applied to the base, controls the flow of current between emitter and collector. As with valves, the resistors feeding these cause current fluctuations to appear as voltage fluctuations at points X and Y. Amplifiers taking their output from point X are called "common emitter amplifiers", while those taking their output from Y are called "emitter follower amplifiers".

Transistor failure is almost always caused by the failure of associated components. This can mean that incorrect voltages or polarities are applied to the transistor or that too much current is passed through it. Short-circuiting the loudspeaker connec-

tions on a transistor amplifier will cause instant failure of the output transistors because it draws too much current through them, unless the amplifier has special circuitry to protect against this.

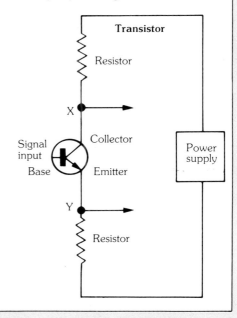

Comparing valve and transistor amplifiers

When a valve amplifier is turned up to a high volume level, it begins to distort in a characteristic way. The sound becomes rich and warm, caused by the amplifier generating a preponderance of even harmonics. This distortion is generally pleasing to the ear. Transistor amplifiers, on the other hand, tend to produce predominantly odd harmonics when overdriven, and this results in a harsh, unpleasant colouration of sound, at odds with such amplifiers' high-fidelity reproduction at lower volume.

The preference of most electric guitarists nowadays is to retain the harmonic enrichment of the valve amplifier. Many bass players also still use valve amplifiers, though an increasing number now prefer the clean, more controllable sound and projection that they can achieve with solid-state, transistorized equipment. Some players – epitomized by Stanley Clarke – use what amounts to a mini-PA system on stage.

Though solid-state equipment is smaller, more durable and generally more convenient to use on the road, the demand for the valve sound continues. This has led many manufacturers to try to combine the best of both worlds and produce a transistor amplifier that sounds like a valve model, though their success in this is questionable. Some hybrid amplifiers – notably the Boogie – give a variety of sounds by having both valve and transistor stages.

Switch-on characteristics

Valve amplifiers require a minute or two to warm up to operating temperature. This is because a valve cannot function until its heater filament has warmed the cathode to a temperature high enough to allow electrons to break free from its surface under the influence of the applied voltage. The standby switch found on many valve amplifiers disconnects the high operating voltages from the valve but leaves the low-voltage heater supply fully connected. This allows the amplifier to be held, fully warmed up, ready for instant use.

Transistor amplifiers respond instantly when switched on, and require no warm-up period. However, the initial surge of electricity rushing into the amplifier circuitry, charging the capacitors and establishing operating voltages throughout the circuit, causes a rushing noise or thump to be heard from the speakers. This is unpleasant and, in the case of high-powered amplifiers, can actually damage the speakers. To avoid this, many amplifiers incorporate automatic circuitry which inhibits the delivery of power to the speakers for a few seconds.

Matching speakers to the amplifier

Valve amplifiers must be accurately matched to the speaker impedances. These are normally either 8 ohms or 15-16 ohms. The various ways of connecting speakers to

achieve specific impedances are illustrated on p. 211. Valve amplifiers must never be switched on when they are not connected to speakers, otherwise the output transformer and output valves may be seriously damaged.

Transistor amplifiers are more robust in this respect, and most quality models are immune to both short and open circuits on the speaker outputs. Generally a minimum speaker impedance is quoted, which will give the greatest output at acceptable distortion levels. Fitting speakers with a larger impedance than specified will result only in reduced output – though perhaps also with reduced distortion levels.

If there is no standby switch on the amplifier it is good policy to turn the volume control to zero before switching on.

Solid-state amplification (*left*)
High-technology equipment used by Stanley Clarke: plexiglass dome with 24 small 4½ in. (11.5 cm) speakers, two cabinets with 15 in. (38 cm) speakers. The amplification equipment on the right comprises (from top to bottom) a flanger, two pre-amps, two power modules, crossover unit, mixer, mono amplifier, and power amplifier. A Carl Thompson Piccolo bass is flanked by two Alembics.

Valve amplification (*right*)
Pete Townshend opts for the traditional Hiwatt valve amplifiers and speaker stacks. Note that the stacks are miked up through the PA system. Townshend is playing a Schecter Telecaster (see p. 179).

A selection of typical combo amps

Vox AC 30 (30 watts)

Fender Twin Reverb (100 watts)

MESA/Boogie (100-60 watts)

Decibels

The decibel (db) scale is a logarithmic ratio between two numbers and exists in two forms. The first (10 x log R) is used when dealing with absolute units such as volts, amps, and watts; the second (20 x log R) is used when dealing with undefined things like a comparison between levels, responses, etc.

In a normal numerical ratio, 1 is the reference number. In decibels, however, 0 db is the reference. 0 db can be a minimum, with all references going positive. In the discussion of sound pressure, for example, 0 db is the threshold of hearing, 70 db represents average speech, 100 db is as loud as an orchestra is likely to play, and 110 db is about the level achieved by loud rock music. 0 db can also be a maximum, with all references going negative: when speaking of amplifier noise, 0 db is the maximum output of the amplifier, while −90 db may be quoted as the noise level at its maximum output. 0 db can also be centrally placed, with references going positive or negative from that point: in amplifier frequency response, 0 db is an arbitrary average output level of all audio frequencies, while ± 2 db might be the maximum deviation of any frequency from that average level.

10 x log ratio for decibel ratings	
db	ratio
0	1:1
20	10:1
30	50:1
40	100:1
60	1000:1
80	10,000:1
100	100,000:1
120	1,000,000:1

20 x log ratio for decibel ratings	
db	ratio
0	1:1
20	100:1
30	1000:1
40	10,000:1
60	1,000,000:1
80	100,000,000:1
100	10,000,000,000:1
120	1,000,000,000,000:1

Roland Jazz Chorus (120 watts)

HH Performer (150 watts)

A guide to amp specifications

The best way to judge the performance of a valve amplifier – if the way it can be used to enhance the sound of an instrument is important to you – is to listen to it. Distortion can be expressed in figures more accurately than in words (terms such as "dirty", "warm" or "rich" are invariably subjective), but neither gives the immediacy or subtlety of the evi-dence of your ears. Specifications which define technical performance are, however, of great importance in the case of transistor amplifiers designed for any kind of hi-fi appli-cation. Some manufacturers cloud the issue by publishing misleading figures but, if ex-pressed accurately, statistics can be an impor-tant and useful way of defining performance.

In the following pages, we will explain the various factors involved (gain, frequency response, input sensitivity, power output, rise time, slew rate, damping factor, noise and dynamic range are the most relevant) to give you an idea of what to look for in an amplifier. Most of these specifications also apply to sound-processing devices (see p. 204-207).

Gain, linearity and frequency response

In all amplifiers, there is a certain relation-ship between the waveform of the input signal (which comes from the guitar) and the waveform of the amplified output signal (which goes to the speaker). Unless other-wise stated, this relationship is *linear*. It can be plotted on a graph as a straight line, and it demonstrates that, if one part of the wave-form is multiplied (or amplified) by a factor of, say, 100 or 1,000, then all parts of the waveform at all frequencies are also multi-plied by the same factor. This factor is known as the *gain* of the amplifier. All ampli-fiers – whether tiny on-board pre-amps or

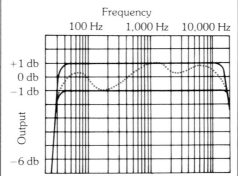

Gain and frequency
This three-dimensional graph shows the relation-ship between variations of gain with frequency. Note how gain falls off at the upper and lower ends of the audio spectrum.

complex units used in giant PA systems – are electronic devices designed to achieve voltage or current gain over the input signal.

In specifications, gain is expressed either as a factor or ratio (1,000 or 1,000:1), or by use of the decibel (db) scale. Gain factors may describe either voltage gain or power gain. Unfortunately, all you can glean from gain factors quoted in decibels is that, if two

channels of an amplifier are stated as having different gains, then the one with the greater gain will also have the greater sensitivity.

In the perfect amplifier, gain would remain constant at all frequencies. In prac-tice, however, this is not the case. At the extremes of the frequency range which the amplifier is capable of handling, gain tends to fall off – so that, ultimately, there is no output coming out whatever the level of the input. At intermediate frequencies, the gain factor fluctuates by only small amounts. These changes are deviations in what is called the *linearity* of the amplifier, and will cause volume distortion of the sound.

It is possible to draw a graph called a *frequency response curve* to show the amplifier's output level, derived from a con-stant, specific input level, at each frequency within the range at which it operates.

The hypothetically perfect amplifier – the one with constant gain at all frequencies – would have a frequency response curve that was, in fact, the zero db line in the graph below. The degree to which a real amplifier is able to respond in a linear fashion can be

Frequency

100 Hz	1,000 Hz	10,000 Hz

+1 db
0 db
−1 db

Output

−6 db

Typical amplifier frequency response curve
The graph shows the possible variations of ampli-fier output level at different frequencies throughout the audio spectrum. This amplifier has a frequency response specification of ± 1 db at 40-18,000 Hz, −3 db at 30 Hz and 20 kHz. The dotted line shows one possible curve within the specification.

assessed to some extent from the manu-facturer's stated frequency response. Typically, this might read "± 1 db from 40 Hz to 18,000 Hz, −3 db at 30 Hz and 20,000 Hz". This specification is shown on

the graph by the thick black lines. The frequency response curve falls within this area. Since the smallest volume change that the ear can detect is about 1 db, a specification of ± 1 db is acceptable. However, specifications can be misleading. Our example might describe an amplifier that has a suitably flat response between the stated frequencies but also an unwelcome 2 db "hump" somewhere in its range.

In addition, an amplifier may be less linear at some volume settings than at others. Frequency response curves such as the example relate only to one specific volume setting. Naturally many manu-facturers tend to quote the most favourable curve that their design can achieve.

All musical instruments produce notes which consist of a fundamental tone plus upper partial tones or harmonics (see p. 116). The lowest possible note on an organ has a fundamental with a frequency of just over 16 Hz, while the highest note of a piccolo has a frequency of 4,186 Hz. Because the harmonics of each note must be amplified along with the fundamental tone, amplifiers must be able to reproduce frequency ranges far higher than the highest fundamental: guitars can produce har-monics as high as 16,000 Hz. However, an amplifier may be unable to reproduce very low notes and yet can still be acceptable. This is because the ear has the remarkable property of being able to hear the funda-mental of a note in cases where an amplifier does not have the frequency range to repro-duce it. It deduces the fundamental from the presence and balance of the harmonics.

As well as an uneven frequency response, other non-linear distortions from which amplifiers suffer (and which modern tech-nology has tried to eradicate) are *harmonic distortion* and *intermodulation distortion*. The former is caused by the amplifier generating harmonics from the input signal – not just on the fundamental note, but on all that note's natural harmonics as well. Intermodulation distortion occurs when two different fundamentals are fed into an amplifier's input, causing beat notes and complex harmonics to form.

Input and output levels

For many guitarists, power output is the first consideration when comparing amplifiers. However, in practical terms, the actual input to the amplifier is also significant.

Input sensitivity

The sensitivity of an amplifier refers to the minimum voltage of input signal required to achieve the maximum specified power output from the amplifier (with the volume control at maximum and the tone controls set flat – i.e., giving neither boost nor cut). Thus it is easier to overdrive an amplifier with a low input sensitivity (of, say, 9 mV) in order to produce distortion (see p. 206).

Power output

No single amplifier is suitable for all potential uses. What you need will depend on the size of the venue, the type of mixing, the room's acoustics, the general sound level, and other factors. If you use an average 50 watt combo, this will give you sufficient volume on its own at small venues, and, when necessary, you can always increase your volume by miking up the combo through the PA or sound-reinforcement system at larger gigs. Using a powerful stack in a small club can be a problem, particularly if you want an overdriven sound, because the volume level needed to achieve this may be too much for the audience. In this case, the answer may be to use the amplifier with just one 4 x 12 cabinet and a pre-amp to achieve the overdriven sound.

There are several systems by which power output can be assessed, but the most useful is the RMS method. This indicates the sustained power load that the amplifier is capable of handling at various frequencies. Some manufacturers, however, invite confusion by using a variety of systems – often without stating which – in their performance statistics. Terms such as "music power" and "peak watts" can give misleadingly high figures, since they may refer not to sustained output over several cycles, but to moment-

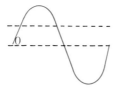

Peak power
Average power

Power ratings
Each system bases power output ratings on different sections of the sine wave.

ary peaks of high energy at a particular frequency. It is quite possible that an amplifier rated at 100 watts by such a system may, in practice, be drowned out by an amplifier rated at only 50 watts on the more meaningful (and universal) RMS system.

Rise time and slew rate

The *rise time* of an amplifier relates to the speed with which the amplifier can respond to a signal voltage. It is measured in microseconds. A slow rise time will change the

The effect of rise time on waveform

Square wave input

Fast rise time: slight signal deformation

Slow rise time: significant signal deformation

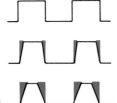

shape of the waveforms. The effect is most acute when square waves are being amplified. Therefore, faster rise times are desirable.

The *slew rate* of an amplifier refers to the maximum speed at which the voltage of the amplifier output can change. It is measured in volts per micro-second. A slow slew rate will change the wave shape, just as a slow rise time does. Slew rate affects the ability of the output stage of the amplifier to respond instantly to the input waveform. Consequently a slow slew rate will heavily distort any note that has a rapid attack.

Damping factor

A much overlooked, but nevertheless very important parameter of amplifier performance is the *damping factor*. This is a measure of the control that an amplifier has over the diaphragm of the loudspeaker it is driving. The signal voltage from the amplifier is a complex AC waveform. The diaphragm must respond instantly and follow this rapidly fluctuating voltage exactly. The momentum given by the signal must never cause the diaphragm to continue moving forward once the rising voltage that initially made it do so has changed to a falling voltage. In other words, the diaphragm must not overshoot the signal.

The higher the damping factor of an amplifier, the more efficiently it can control the speakers. Though damping factors vary between less than 10 and more than 200, performance can still be impaired when more than one speaker is being driven. Accordingly, multi-speaker arrangements will only perform well if the damping factor is very high.

Noise and dynamic range

Noise has two principal components: mains frequency hum, and white noise generated by random electron motion which has equal energy at all audio frequencies. An amplifier might have a noise figure or "signal-to-noise ratio" quoted as −60 db. This means that, when the amplifier is fed its maximum input voltage, the noise on the output will be 60 dbs quieter than the desired output signal. In other words, the maximum dynamic range of the amplifier is 60 dbs.

The *dynamic range* refers to the difference in volume between the loudest and quietest sounds that the equipment can reproduce. An orchestra, for example, has a dynamic range of around 60 db. An amplifier with the same range could just about cope with such a figure, but the quietest notes would be at the same level as the amplifier's own noise and would therefore be practically inaudible. The amplifier should really have a dynamic range at least 10 db greater than that of the sounds it is required to reproduce.

Rock music, though loud, has a surprisingly small dynamic range; the general volume level during a performance does not vary greatly. Though this might lead you to think that you could use an amplifier with an equally small dynamic range (such as 30 db), in practice such an amplifier would be unsatisfactory. While playing, the volume may reach quite high levels (110 db). As soon as you stop, however, the amplifier will still be at its full-volume setting but, with no signal from the guitar passing through, you will be able to hear mains hum and white noise which was previously drowned by the guitar. On an amplifier with a dynamic range of 30 db, that noise would come through at 80 db and would be uncomfortably audible above the ambient noise level of an audience (about 60-70 db) or a studio (20-25 db).

To be able to play loudly and not have amplifier noise above the ambient noise level, therefore, the dynamic range of the amplifier needs to be much greater than 30 db. 60 db can be considered an acceptable figure for a guitar amplifier, since hum and white noise will, if you have been playing at 110 db, come through at 50 db, which will obviously be inaudible above the audience. In the studio, sound processing devices such as noise gates (see p. 207) are used to minimize amplifier noise appearing above the ambient noise level.

PA systems need to have a dynamic range that is greater still if they are to handle anything from full-volume playing to whispered stage announcements. 90 db or more is quite common.

Sound processing

The alteration of the characteristics of sound in any way is known as *sound processing*. Sound processing techniques are employed whenever it is desirable to correct a deficiency, to improve audibility or to create special effects. Despite the many exotically-named effects units available for sound processing, both on-stage and for use in the studio, the ways in which sounds can be physically modified are, in practice, quite limited. Effectively, the options open to you are to alter the sound's frequency curve, volume, dynamics, phase or pitch, and to add to the basic sound the qualities of echo, reverberation or additional harmonics.

The principles of sound processing are always the same, whether the electronics are built into the amplifier (as is more and more the case) or whether they come in the form of effects units, foot pedals or studio devices (the degree of control given by each varies according to type). For this reason, all the various sound processors are covered together in the following pages. We begin by looking at the various ways in which the tone can be controlled – first, by simple treble, mid-range and bass controls, and, second, by more sophisticated equalizers – then move on to volume and distortion effects (see p. 206-7), and phasing, flanging and delay units (see p. 208-9).

Equalizers

Strictly speaking, the term "equalizer" applies to any form of tone control. The simplest uses a capacitor connected to a potentiometer to filter sound frequencies by cutting the signal. An amplifier may have several tone controls operating on bass, treble and mid-range frequencies. However, there are more sophisticated methods of altering frequency curves.

Sweep equalizers

Although some amplifier designs incorporate as many as three mid-range tone controls, a more elaborate method frequently used on mixing desks and available also as a foot pedal is to have one or two *sweep frequency controls*. A sweep equalizer has the usual lift/cut control, but also an additional control which allows you to shift the centre frequency of the control up or down the audio spectrum to a higher or lower frequency. This more flexible arrangement allows more accurate adjustment. The turnover frequency of treble and bass controls is also often sweepable on mixing desks.

On amplifiers fitted with two sweep frequency controls and two lift/cut controls, dramatic effects can be achieved if the area of operation of the controls is overlapped. A *wah-wah pedal* is simply a sweep equalizer with a fixed amount of lift.

Parametric equalizers

Parametric equalizers (as sweep equalizers are sometimes incorrectly termed) in fact have an additional control, the "band-width" or "Q" control. "Q" refers to the steepness of the slope on each side of the centre frequency. On cheaper parametric equalizers you simply switch from "low Q" to "high Q", but the best have a totally variable "Q" control (which allows you to select a suitable bandwidth) and also a frequency control as on a sweep equalizer, permitting precise shaping of the sound.

One way in which a parametric equalizer can be used on stage as well as in the studio is to remove a small peak of accentuated

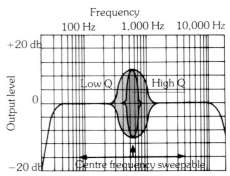

Effect of parametric equalizer
The wide, lightly shaded area shows the effect range of the mid-lift and cut of a parametric at low Q (wide bandwidth setting). Increasing Q narrows the bandwidth. The dark area shows a typical maximum Q setting.

Simple tone controls

Altering the frequency curve of an amplifier is achieved by the use of tone (or equalization) controls. The simplest tone controls act on the extremities of the audio frequency spectrum, namely the bass and treble. In a passive guitar circuit, the controls cut or reduce these frequencies. The tone controls on active guitar circuits, amplifiers and mixing desks, on the other hand, are also able to lift and increase these frequencies. The typical effect of these controls is shown in the graph below. The frequency at which the tone controls begin to take effect (X and Y on the graph) is known as the "turnover point". The curve which they produce is called the "slope".

A more sophisticated system can be produced by adding one or more mid-range controls, often termed "presence controls" by manufacturers. The effect of a mid-range control is shown in the second graph.

Some amplifiers also feature a *bright channel*. This is an additional channel which

Volume control
This controls the volume on channel A. The knob is pulled out to boost the mid-range sound.

Tone controls
Treble, middle and bass controls provide equalization on Channel A. The treble control can be pulled out to give added brightness.

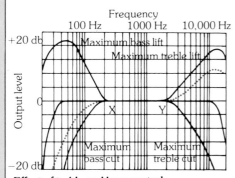

Effect of treble and bass controls
This typical graph shows the range of alteration of the output levels achieved by these controls. The dotted line shows the effect of setting an intermediate bass and treble cut.

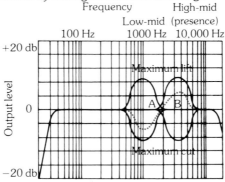

Effect of mid-frequency controls
Similarly, this shows the effect on mid-frequencies of two typical mid-range controls. The dotted line shows the effect of combining a small cut on one with a large lift on the other.

frequencies. In the studio, the peak might merely affect one note, or a group of notes, by making them louder, but on stage it may cause them to feed back. In both cases, a single note would require a high Q, whereas a group of notes is more likely to need the wider frequency bandwidth cut of a low Q.

Graphic equalizers
Originally designed for studio use, *graphic equalizers* can now be found on guitar amplifiers, foot pedals and domestic stereo systems. Technically more complex than parametric equalizers, they are paradoxically much easier to operate and can, if they offer sufficient facilities, do the job of all other kinds of equalizer.

The graphic equalizer uses sliding con-

trols called "faders" arranged with their tracks parallel to one another. Each fader controls a particular band of frequencies and is labelled with the centre frequency of that band. This may cover a full octave, a half, or a third, or even a sixth of an octave. Obviously, the more faders the equalizer has, the greater its versatility, although this creates design problems in trying to keep noise and harmonic distortion down to acceptable levels.

If you look at the fader knobs on a graphic equalizer as though they were points on a graph, and think of the curving line that would link them all together most smoothly, then this would recreate exactly the type of graph used to illustrate the effects of an equalizer. This is the feature that makes a

graphic equalizer so easy to use, and also explains its name.

Filters
Filters can be designed to remove or to pass any desired frequency or band of frequencies, although high-pass and low-pass filters are the types most frequently encountered. High-pass filters resemble bass-cut controls: all frequencies above their turnover frequency remain unchanged, while frequencies below the turnover point are sharply reduced. The chief difference is that the slope of the filter is generally invariable and much steeper than that of the bass control. A similar comparison can be made between the standard treble control and a low-pass filter.

Graphic equalizer
The design of this graphic equalizer shows clearly how frequency response can be visibly shaped by adjusting the faders, each of which controls a particular band of frequencies. Small graphic

equalizers are also available in pedal form, typically having between six and ten faders, operating across proportionally broader frequencies but giving less precise control.

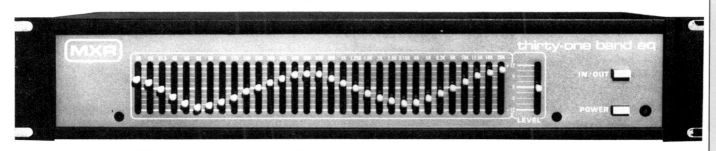

has an increased treble response, generally achieved by simply introducing a treble by-pass capacitor wired to the channel volume control in the same way as is shown on the

passive guitar circuits (see p. 186-9).

In recent years, tone controls on amps have become increasingly comprehensive, allowing greater flexibility and giving the

opportunity of "shaping" the sound far more precisely. It is not uncommon for modern amps to have built-in equalizers – simpler versions of the one shown above.

Input jacks and channel selector
The high and low inputs differ in sensitivity by 12 db. Either channel can be selected to give different sound characteristics.

Gain control
This adjusts the gain when using channel B. Pulling the knob out boosts the mid-range.

Master volume control
This control alters the volume of channel B, and can be used in conjunction with the gain control to vary distortion.

Tone controls
These act in the same way as those for Channel A.

Parametric equalizer
Level, Q and frequency controls divide up the audio spectrum into small bands for precise adjustment.

Built-in amplifier controls
These are the controls of a Yamaha G100-212 combo amplifier rated at 100 watts RMS and using two 12 in. (30 cm) speakers. The unit has two input channels: high (channel A) and low (channel B).

Reverb control
With this control the ratio of direct and delayed sound can be adjusted (see p. 209).

Volume modifiers

Volume and gain are terms often used interchangeably. This can lead to some confusion, especially with equipment (such as mixing desks) which has both. True gain controls are also found on many effects units, but only rarely on amplifiers.

As is shown on p. 202, all amplifiers have a property called gain. It is the number of times that the output of a circuit is greater than the input. As we have also seen (p. 199) amplifiers that drive loudspeakers embody, in the same box, a number of small amplifiers linked together to form a chain. Each of these – called amplification stages – has its own fixed gain. The total gain of the complete amplifier is the sum of the gain of these individual stages.

Volume controls act on either the input signal or the signal passing between two of these stages. They alter the level of the signal and can even reduce it to zero. They do not alter the actual gain of any of the stages. Gain controls, on the other hand, do alter the gain of an amplification stage. Their minimum setting is usually a gain of 1, which means that the level of the output signal is the same as the input. Their maximum setting may be designed to make the stage distort for special effect, although the normal use of these controls is to present an output level from the controlled stage which is at an optimum level for succeeding stages to operate at their maximum efficiency, no matter what the level of the input signal. In use, gain controls are turned up to give as high a signal level as possible to the following stages without causing distortion – unless, of course, distortion is required.

Volume controls are also available in pedal form. These are passive units containing a simple potentiometer wired up just like the volume control on the guitar.

Channel gain

Guitar amplifiers with more than one input channel (usually labelled "high" and "low") are frequently designed so that the different channels yield different overall gain figures. They therefore have different sensitivities. The higher-gain channel will have increased sensitivity and probably a reduced overload capability. Since the overall gain difference will almost certainly be caused by an alteration to the gain achieved by the first valve, the possibility of causing distortion in the first valve is increased. This is desirable because, if you can distort the first valve, you can have a distorted sound at any volume setting. Distortion in the second valve is not so desirable because the effect will vary depending on the setting of the tone controls.

Amplifiers with switchable gains carry this principle a stage further, giving increased versatility in terms of distortion levels.

Creating distortion effects

An electric guitar is capable of a sustained output of 50 millivolts or more; a signal of this level may overload (or overdrive) the amplifier. Guitar amplifiers are designed to withstand large, sustained overload conditions applied to their inputs. Nevertheless, this overload may cause distortion in the driver and/or power stages of the amplifier when the guitar is played at high volumes. The sound quality of an overdriven valve amplifier is, as we have seen, the prime reason why many guitarists choose this form of amplification.

If the first valve cannot be overdriven by the guitar alone, then you can use a *pre-amplifier* (see p. 196) to increase the voltage of the guitar output. This can either be built into the guitar (an "on-board" pre-amplifier), or be in the form of foot units, often called "overdrivers" or "boosters". They vary in the amount of gain they are able to achieve; some can achieve such high gains that part of the unit itself is driven into distortion.

This is also the basis of many *fuzz boxes* and other distortion devices. The majority of fuzz boxes are activated by an electronic trigger, usually of a type known as a "Schmitt trigger". This generates a square wave output at the same frequency as the input from the guitar. The output of the fuzz box is a blend of the amplified guitar output and the square wave. The proportion of undistorted signal to square wave is set by a mixing control usually labelled "distortion". Though many manufacturers have made strenuous attempts to evolve a fuzz box that can be adjusted to simulate the overdriven valve sound, it must be admitted that very few have succeeded in producing a device that sounds like anything other than a fuzz box.

When solid-state circuitry is overloaded, the waveform "clips" at a certain signal voltage depending on design criteria. Once the voltage of the input signal has reached a level that will cause clipping to occur, any further increase of input signal will not cause a change in the level of output signal. This phenomenon is utilized in producing *sustain* units. The unit gives its maximum output as soon as the guitar output rises above a very few millivolts, thus completely eliminating the normal attack and decay characteristics of a guitar note. Electronic trigger circuits producing square waves have the same characteristic since the output level of the square wave from the trigger is virtually independent of the input signal level.

Limiters and compressors

These two devices are both used to reduce the dynamic range of a sound signal before it is fed to a loudspeaker. Bearing in mind the importance of having an amplifier with a wide dynamic range (see p. 203), it may seem a little eccentric to reduce the dynamic range of a signal. In practice, however, it is one of the most important sound processing techniques, used in the recording studio and particularly by bass players.

Limiters

Limiting is the simplest of the techniques used in reducing dynamic range. It can be employed in any situation where sudden, excessively large signal voltages can be generated which, if uncontrolled, could result in serious damage to the musicians' ears and to loudspeakers and other equipment. Limiting is also the basis on which automatic volume and recording level controls function. The limiter is simply an amplifier which has variable gain. The gain is controlled by a circuit that senses the level of the incoming signal. The gain of the amplifier is linear until the input signal reaches a predetermined level. When the sensing circuitry detects a signal rising above this level, it instantly reduces the gain so that

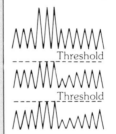

Input signal and un-limited output signal

Output signal with fast release

Output signal with slow release

Effect of signal limiting
Maximum volume output is held to the limiting threshold. Volume recovery after limiting is controlled by the release control.

the output level remains constant. The level at which this gain change occurs is called the "threshold". Most limiters have a threshold control which enables you to set this level. They also frequently have light-emitting diodes (LEDs) or a meter to indicate that limiting is occurring. When the input signal falls below the threshold once again, the gain of the amplifier returns to its original level.

A "release" control determines how quickly this happens. It may range from a few milliseconds to around a second or two. It should be set so that it causes the minimum disturbance to the sound of the music (distortion may become evident at very fast speeds, when the limiter has the least apparent effect on the dynamics of the signal). If the release time is extended beyond five seconds, the limiter will operate as an automatic volume control.

Compressors

Compressors are more subtle than limiters, but they both work in the same way. Most compressors can be set up as limiters, and some can both compress and limit a signal. Compression helps reduce the effect of variations in the output level from guitars and other instruments. These variations are produced by the differences between low and high notes, or between one string and another, or by irregularities in the way the right hand plays the strings. In this way, compression can improve audibility and contribute to a tight, punchy sound, invaluable to bass and rhythm players. Lead players will find that a compressor can increase sustain without increasing distortion.

Like a limiter, the compressor too has "threshold" and "release" controls, which act in a similar way. The difference lies in what happens when the sensing circuit detects an input signal that is above the threshold. Instead of altering gain to pre-serve a fixed output level, as the limiter does, the compressor changes the amplifier's ratio. Before compression occurs, the ratio is 1:1 (so, if the input voltage rises by 1 volt, the output voltage will also rise by 1 volt). If the ratio is changed to 2:1, for example, the output voltage would rise by only half a volt for each 1 volt rise in the input. The graphs below show the relationship between the input and output signals of a compressor, and how introducing a threshold alters the ratio. Different ratios can be selected, allowing you to make either subtle or dramatic changes to part (or the whole) of a signal's dynamic range.

The characteristics of different limiters and compressors vary. Some do not have variable thresholds, but achieve the same result through input and output volume controls. Others can be made to react only to specific frequencies in order to eliminate problems such as sibilance on vocals.

Tremolo units

A further modification to volume is the *tremolo* effect, often erroneously called vibrato. Both produce a fluttering sound, but while tremolo is a rapid, regular change of volume, vibrato is caused by changes of pitch. A tremolo unit (in pedal or built-in form) has two controls: speed, which controls the number of volume changes per second, and depth, which controls the amount of volume change that occurs.

Noise gates

The function of a *noise gate* is to shut off a signal line when no signal is being passed down it. This eliminates obtrusive background hiss which may be generated by a device somewhere in the signal line. Effectively, then, the dynamic range of the amplifier is expanded by the reduction of noise. As soon as the desired signal reaches the gate, it will open and pass the signal through unchanged. Though it also passes noise through with the signal, the masking effect of the signal itself generally makes the noise unobtrusive.

Noise gates, originally designed for studio use, are now available in pedal form. It is a good idea, when using a number of pedals, to install a noise gate as the last in line before the amplifier, to cut down the hiss that pedals generate.

A noise gate, technically the exact opposite of a limiter, has similarly named "threshold" and "release" controls. The first sets the signal level required to open the gate, while the release holds the gate open until the note has died away.

Ratio 1:1
(no compression)

Output level
Max
Min
Max
Input level

Ratio 2:1
(threshold at lowest level)

Output level
Max
Min
Max
Input level + threshold level

Ratio 1:1 (below threshold), 2:1 (above threshold)

Output level
Max
Min
Max
Threshold level
Input level

Effect of signal compression
Without compression the output:input relationship is linear. A threshold can be introduced above which dynamic range is reduced. Output voltage increase is proportionally reduced.

Compressor pedal
This simple unit, used to create undistorted sustain, has a fixed threshold. The sensitivity control brings the input signal up to threshold level. The final volume is set by adjusting the output control.

Noise gate
The threshold or sensitivity control adjusts the level at which the signal is cut off. The decay control allows you to set how long a decay each note will have before the gate cuts in.

Compressor/limiter
This sophisticated unit has adjustable threshold, compression, attack and release controls as well as variable gain indicated by metering.

Phasing and flanging

The phenomenon known as *phase shift* is of vital importance to the design, setting up and use of audio equipment. It can also be used to create dramatic "phasing" or "flanging" effects. In terms of sound processing, we are primarily concerned with the phase relationship between two signals, either electronic or acoustic, initially derived from the same source.

If you combine two signals of the same waveform at the same frequency and at the same amplitude (volume), but 180 degrees out of phase with each other, then the two will cancel each other out, and no signal voltage will result. This is why it is important to ensure that two speakers connected to the same amplifier are in phase with each other. If they are not, some of the frequencies – particularly those at the lower end of the spectrum – will be cancelled. In practice, however, total cancellation of all frequencies would not occur. This is because the physical separation between speakers changes the phase relationship in any case – although cancellation of low frequencies will still be quite marked. When setting up equipment, it is necessary to ensure that correctly phased connections are made. Occasionally, however, you can use phase shift to advantage: by reversing the phase of an acoustic guitar's contact transducer, for example, you can help reduce the sound it picks up from a nearby bass guitar.

In sound processing, special effects can be achieved by splitting a signal into two paths and introducing a variable phase shift to one of them before re-combining the signal. This is essentially what modern *phasers* and *flangers* do.

Though now achieved by pedals or special studio circuitry, flanging takes its name from a studio practice popular in the 1960s. An identical signal was recorded on two separate tape recorders running simultaneously. The two recordings were then played back and re-recorded, but this time the speed of one of the recorders was varied by the engineer pressing his finger on the flange (outer rim) of the spool. Phasers and flangers have controls to alter the effect manually and also automatically. A "speed" control alters the rate at which the effect sweeps through the frequency range from one extreme to the other, while the "depth" or "intensity" control defines the degree of phasing. Some units feature a control to give stereo output effects.

If the signal from a guitar is split so that it travels down two paths, and the signal on one path is put progressively out of phase with the signal on the other path, what actually happens is that the altered signal is *delayed* – it travels at a slightly lower speed. Speed difference also has the effect of creating changes in pitch. The principle is analogous with that of the "doppler effect". Because the two out-of-phase signals are, in effect, travelling at different speeds, one will sound higher or lower than the other. The larger the phase difference and the quicker it occurs, the more noticeable the change in pitch will be. This is, in fact, how flangers produce some of their remarkable effects.

Manual
Depth
Rate
Resonance
Pedal
OUTPUT
INPUT
Flanger BF-2
Output jack

Flanger pedal
This compact unit has four controls: manual (affecting the sound delay), depth (controlling sweep width according to delay time), rate (controlling the sweep frequency) and resonance (which controls the feedback level).

Delay, chorus and vibrato effects

By using the principle of phase shifting, it is possible to create electronically both delay effects and changes in pitch. If the speed is kept low but the path length is increased, then the two signals will eventually come back into phase again. However, the second signal will be one or more cycles behind the first. When the delay reaches a few milliseconds, an effect called *automatic double tracking* (ADT) or *doubling* is produced. It can make one guitarist sound like two playing in close unison. It is also the basis of electronic echo units (see opposite).

When delays of this kind are varied in a rapid and random way, the slight changes in pitch and delay can make one instrument sound like many playing together. This is called a *chorus* effect.

The rapid fluctuations of pitch caused by time-delay circuitry are also the basis of electronic *vibrato* units. All these effects units are available as pedals and may be either pre-set or may have controls similar to those on phasers and flangers.

OUTPUT
RATE
MXR
110mA
micro
chorus

Chorus pedal
This unit produces chorus and vibrato effects whose intensity is varied by the rate control. Sweep width decreases as sweep speed increases.

Rate
Depth
Intensity
INPUT
OUTPUT
Delay DM-2
BOSS
Pedal
Output jack

Delay pedal
The delay effect is controlled by adjustments to the rate (affecting the speed of repetition). intensity (the strength of the delayed signal), and depth (the amount of delay).

Phase relationship
Phasing depends on splitting a signal (the one that comes from the guitar pick-up, for example) into two. If the two signals remain in phase with one another, the sound will be unmodified. If the signals are 180 degrees out of phase, they will cancel each other out. But if they are 90 degrees out of phase, a "phasing" effect will be heard.

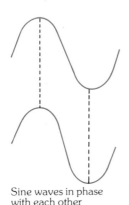

Sine waves in phase with each other

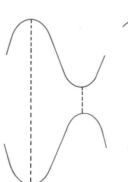

Sine waves 180 degrees out of phase

Sine waves 90 degrees out of phase

Echo units

If a signal is delayed for longer than a few milliseconds, a distinct repeat or *echo* is heard. This kind of delay can be achieved by using analogue circuitry similar to that used in the devices previously mentioned. Long delays may, however, result in a loss of high frequencies and a build-up of noise, although digital electronics can prevent these problems.

Such high-quality digital equipment is expensive, but cheaper systems based on tape recorders have been available for many years to produce similar echo effects. In these, the signal to be delayed is fed to a record head where it is recorded on a tape loop. The signal is then replayed after the desired delay, achieved either by changing the distance between record and replay heads, or by varying the speed at which the magnetic tape travels between these heads. Magnetic drums are sometimes used instead of tape. By placing a number of replay heads at different distances from the record head, multiple repeat echoes can be achieved.

The drawbacks of this kind of echo unit are that they cannot achieve the short delay times possible with analogue and digital units, and that they need regular maintenance to function correctly.

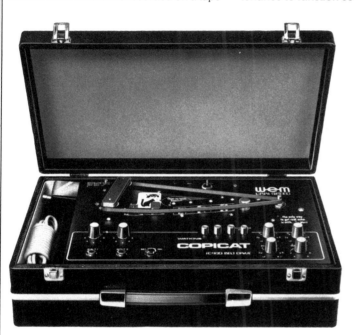

Tape echo unit
The WEM Copicat is a design which has been popular for many years. It is based on the tape-loop principle. Such units are inexpensive, but need regular care and attention. The heads require demagnetization and cleaning, while the tape loop has to be replaced periodically.

Reverb units

When echo repeats are so numerous and so close together that the ear cannot distinguish between them, you will hear instead a continuous sound which slowly dies away. This effect is called *reverberation*. Once again, analogue delay circuitry is limited in its ability to produce good, clean reverberation; as with repeat echo units, the frequency range drops and there is a build-up of noise. Much improved results come from digital equipment, which is of excellent quality but pricey. Simple mechanical devices are far cheaper; they employ a metal spring which is fastened to a transducer at each end. The incoming signal is fed to a small power amplifier driving one of the transducers. This causes the spring to vibrate, and the vibration travels rapidly up and down the spring many times. The second transducer senses the vibrations of the spring and converts them back into electrical energy; this forms the reverberation signal.

Mechanical reverb units – which are often built into amplifiers – suffer from a tendency to colour the sound. This is particularly evident in cheaper units. They can also be upset by sudden, dynamic sounds – which cause them to produce an unpleasant twanging noise – or by high sound levels or vibration nearby.

Reverb units partially simulate the natural effect of sound being reflected around a room (see p. 218-19). They come into their own in the recording studio, where much of the natural reverberation may have been removed by acoustic engineering.

Multi-effects units

Recent years have seen a trend towards larger, more flexible – and more expensive – effects units. These combine in one box various different functions previously available only as separate units. The best-known of these *multi-effects units* are probably those made by Roland, Yamaha, Ibanez and Korg. The Ibanez UE-405, for example, offers four different effects – a compressor/limiter, a stereo chorus, a parametric equalizer, and an analog delay. Although some of these multi-effects units look as if they might be more at home in a recording studio or as part of a domestic hi-fi rack system, they are being used on stage more and more often by professional bands.

Analog delay unit
The controls of the versatile unit shown below can be used in various combinations to produce echo, reverberation, chorus, vibrato and flanging effects. Like many pieces of sound processing equipment, it is designed for rack mounting in conjunction with other units for studio and on-stage use.

Speakers

The sound quality and volume of a speaker is governed by three factors: its efficiency, its size, and its use in combination with other speakers. The speaker's efficiency (the amount of energy delivered from the amplifier which is converted into sound) governs the volume which can be obtained from an amplifier of given power output. Highly efficient speakers (such as the horn-loaded type) can make a 50 watt amplifier louder than a 100 watt model put through less efficient speakers. The dimensions of the speaker (and of horns in particular) have a close relationship to its sound-handling characteristics: the larger the speaker, for example, the better it will handle low (bass) frequencies, the reproduction of which requires a larger volume of air to be moved. Similar speakers may be used in multiple to give an increase in overall volume, although the tone will remain substantially the same. Individual speakers are often used to handle particular frequencies – especially in PAs.

Bass speakers
Tina Weymouth, bassist with Talking Heads, playing through amplification which includes two 15 in. (38 cm) speakers. Though such large speakers can handle bass frequencies well, a certain loss of definition occurs. This can be compensated for by putting part of the amplifier output through additional, smaller speakers which are better able to produce the crisply defined sound sought by today's bass players. Note that only one of the twin speakers is miked into the sound reinforcement system: this is because both produce the same sound, and so it is only necessary to mike one.

How a loudspeaker works

A pick-up or microphone converts sound energy into an electrical signal, and a speaker is used to convert this signal back into sound again. An AC output signal from the amplifier is delivered to a "voice coil" wound around the neck of the cone and positioned between the poles of the magnet. The signal causes the coil to generate a magnetic field which interacts with the field of the fixed, permanent magnet in the speaker. When the voltage is rising on the voice coil, it is pushed away from the magnet, and thus the diaphragm moves forwards. With a falling voltage, the reverse occurs. The back-and-forth movement of the diaphragm causes the cone to vibrate on its suspension (by which the cone is held in place at each end). This in turn causes compression and rarefaction of the air in contact with it and the consequent generation of sound waves, whose dispersion is physically regulated by the shape of the enclosure. The degree to which the unit can move forwards is deliberately limited, and if the speaker is forced to exceed this (if an input signal greater than its handling capacity is applied, for instance), then damage may occur and the cone may break loose from its suspension. Since sound immediately expands away from the source (high-frequency sound is more directional than low-frequency), you will find that mounting the speaker on the front of the panel will make a significant difference to the sound compared to mounting it on the rear of the front panel.

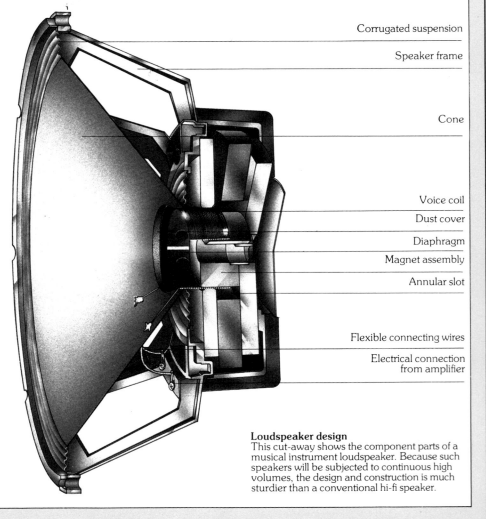

Corrugated suspension

Speaker frame

Cone

Voice coil

Dust cover

Diaphragm

Magnet assembly

Annular slot

Flexible connecting wires

Electrical connection from amplifier

Loudspeaker design
This cut-away shows the component parts of a musical instrument loudspeaker. Because such speakers will be subjected to continuous high volumes, the design and construction is much sturdier than a conventional hi-fi speaker.

Speaker cabinets

Speaker cabinets (or "enclosures") play an important role in the reproduction of sound. As air in front of the cone is compressed when the cone moves forwards, so air behind is rarified. The reverse happens as the cone moves backwards. If the air in front of the cone reaches the air behind quickly, then the difference in pressure is cancelled out, resulting in a loss of sound output. The pressures on the back and front of the cone are then said to be out of phase with each other. A function of the enclosure is to prevent or reduce phase cancellation. The cabinet also "loads" the cone in such a way as to optimize its coupling with the surrounding air. Ideally, it must not colour the sound in any way by adding its own resonance.

The materials from which enclosures are constructed should be thick and heavy, to reduce vibration of the cabinet walls. Sound-absorbing materials such as heavy felt are often used to cover all interior surfaces that could potentially reflect sound back on to the diaphragm or set up "standing waves" (see p. 219). Curtains of sound-absorbing material are also hung within the cabinet to damp out internal reflections.

There are four basic types of enclosure. An *infinite baffle* speaker is a sealed, air-tight box, filled with sound absorbers to soak up all internal energy. Since the air inside the cabinet is completely separated from that outside, there is no problem with phase cancellation. However, such speakers are comparatively inefficient, since only about 0.5-2 per cent of the electrical signal delivered to the speaker is actually converted into sound.

Open-backed (or *finite baffle*) speakers are more efficient than infinite baffle models (approximately 5 per cent). Since sound is projected from both the front and rear of the speaker, any wavelength longer than the minimum distance from the front of the

speaker around the cabinet to the rear will be attenuated by phase cancellation.

A third type of speaker is the *bass reflex* (or *tuned port*) cabinet. This has an opening, called a port, in the enclosure, through which bass frequencies from the rear of the cone are channelled. The port is "tuned" to cause low frequencies from the port to be added, in phase, to the front-of-cone output. Efficiency is again around 5 per cent, but the cabinet has to be relatively large if it is to handle low notes well.

The most efficient speakers currently available are the *horn-loaded* type. Though often very bulky, such speakers are capable of converting up to 50 per cent of the input energy into sound. The flared shape and the size of the horn are computed to regulate the dispersion and frequency range of the sound they project, and to give good coupling between the cone and the air. Many PA speakers are a combination of horn and bass reflex designs.

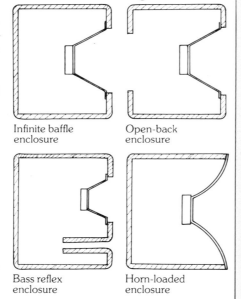

Infinite baffle enclosure

Open-back enclosure

Bass reflex enclosure

Horn-loaded enclosure

The Leslie speaker

Originally designed for use with electric organs, Leslie speakers are now used by many guitarists as well because of their unique sound quality. The distinctive pulsating vibrato is a result of a phase-shift phenomenon called the *Doppler effect*. Like the noise of a police car's siren as it passes in the street, the pitch of a moving sound source seems to rise and fall as the sound approaches and then travels away from the listener. The Leslie sound is produced by two rotating speakers which, as they move towards and then away from the audience, seem to produce pitch changes. One, a bass speaker, is mounted below a

rotating drum shaped to throw the sound out in a circle as it revolves. Another speaker handles the treble frequencies, which emerge from a rotating horn (there are actually two horns, one of which is a dummy whose rotation mechanically balances the other's). The horn and drum revolve at different speeds, and can be varied to produce complex simultaneous vibrato and tremolo effects, particularly when changing speeds on a held note. The pitch appears to rise when each speaker is sweeping towards the listener, and to drop as the speaker moves away – only to rise again as the speaker swings round.

Multiple speaker systems

To improve power handling, similar speakers can be connected together in the same cabinet and driven by one amplifier. This allows you to use a powerful amplifier to drive into speakers which individually have a moderate capacity. Methods of connecting speakers are shown below.

Large speakers cannot reproduce high frequencies very well, while small speakers have a similar problem with low-frequency sound. The *twin-cone speaker* is a compromise design which improves the treble response of a large speaker by having a smaller, secondary cone (giving treble output to around 16 kHz) mounted in front of the main cone and driven by the same voice coil. A superior two-way system is the *dual concentric speaker*, which is an attempt to eliminate the phase-shift problems caused by the physical separation of "woofer" (bass speakers) and "tweeter" (treble). It is possible, though technically very difficult, to build the latter into the centre of the voice coil/magnet arrangement of the bass speaker. This is the basis of the Tannoy speaker, a proven design used for many years.

Another solution to the problem of handling different frequencies is to use *passive frequency splitting*. The amplifier's output is split by a crossover network into high- and low-frequency components (the crossover frequency is generally around 1,000 Hz). Low frequencies are channelled into a bass speaker and high frequencies into a treble speaker. Three-way passive crossovers are also used, with the bass speaker handling frequencies up to around 850 Hz, treble speaker from 1,500 Hz-20,000 kHz, and a mid-range speaker being brought in to cover frequencies from 800-2,000 Hz. A high damping factor is necessary.

It is also possible to use *active crossovers* to split frequencies – a system employed in high-powered PAs and the best studio monitors. The pre-amp output is divided and each frequency range is fed into its own amplifier/speaker system; up to a five-way split can be employed.

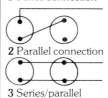

1 Series connection

2 Parallel connection

3 Series/parallel

Impedance
(1), combined impedance is the sum of individual impedances. In (2), total impedance R of speakers r1 and r2 is calculated thus:

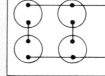

$$\frac{1}{R} = \frac{1}{r1} + \frac{1}{r2}$$

With four speakers of equal impedance connected as in (3), combined impedance is equal to the impedance of one speaker.

Sound reinforcement

Public address or PA systems have been in use for many years. Many "house" systems were originally installed in clubs and theatres to allow vocalists to be heard above the sound of other instruments. Rather than rely on these house systems – which could turn out to be of dubious quality – rock bands began from very early days to carry their own PA systems around with them. These handled only the vocals and acoustic instruments. Electric guitars and drums were considered to be sufficiently loud not to need further amplification.

As both volume levels and audience size increased, however, such simple set-ups were found lacking, and the concept of the modular *sound reinforcement* system evolved. As the name implies, such a system is used to boost a band's entire sound: guitars, keyboards, drums, vocals and everything else. Rather than use a huge stack of speakers – as a guitarist would have had to do at one time in order to be heard in a large auditorium – you can use a small combo amplifier at moderate volume levels in any size of venue. The speaker's output is picked up by a microphone and fed into the PA, where it is balanced with the input from other instruments. It is at this stage that the volume necessary to fill the venue is generated, using powerful PA amplifiers. As an extreme example, you could play through a small practice amplifier in a large hall and yet, by using the sound reinforcement concept, still deafen the audience. A modern, high-fidelity sound system can create a clean, undistorted sound which balances sound from various sources in a way which would be impossible with individually amplified instruments.

The design of today's sound reinforcement systems is modular; you can add to the basic unit in equal multiples. Thus a group working in small venues, for example, may use a mixer-amplifier of around 100 watts and augment this with similarly rated slave amplifiers to boost the PA output according to the demands of where they are playing, up to a total power output of around 500 watts. Larger PAs are rated in kilowatts. These are often referred to as "two-bin rigs", "four-bin rigs" and so forth, indicating a power output of 2 and 4 kilowatts respectively, each stack with its bass bin being assumed to have a handling capacity of around one kilowatt.

The growth of sound reinforcement The technology of the sound system has made enormous advances in recent years. In the 1960s "power trios" such as Cream or the Jimi Hendrix Experience made do with relatively simple "stacks" for the guitarists and a modest PA system for the vocals. The sound quality was often shockingly bad. Today's trios such as The Police (left) and The Jam use advanced, high-technology set-ups in which the sound of the whole group is put through the PA to re-inforce the sound sufficiently to enable it to be heard without excessive distortion in large halls or at outdoor venues. Complex monitoring systems (often using up to half the power of the out-front amplification) enable the musicians to hear themselves on stage. With larger groups, the degree of sophistication is even more marked.

The stage set-up

The diagram on the opposite page shows the sound reinforcement and monitoring system for a small group. It demonstrates three principal methods of amplification: miking acoustic instruments directly (which is explained in more detail on p. 216); miking the amplifier of an electric instrument and putting the signal through the sound reinforcement system for further amplification; and injecting the output signal directly into the sound system.

Miking up

This technique allows you to use a relatively low-powered amplifier at any volume setting, even in a large auditorium. The microphone is placed as close as possible to the speaker, to minimize the pick-up of sound from other instruments on stage. You should experiment to find the best position for placing the microphone: some guitarists place it centrally in front of the speaker, while others prefer an off-centre position. If you are using a cabinet containing several identical speakers, you need only mike up one, since the output from each will be the same. If you are using amplification which has individual speakers that each handle a different frequency range (a Leslie speaker, for example, or a high-fidelity multi-speaker bass rig) you must mike up each individual speaker. Microphones and their characteristics are discussed on p. 221.

Direct injection

This method of amplification takes the output signal directly from the transducer into the sound reinforcement system, producing a cleaner sound than is possible by amplifying through the musician's own speakers. Obviously, direct injection prevents you from using your amplifier to induce distortion and other effects, since final control is in the hands of the sound engineer operating the mix. The technique is commonly used for keyboards and other electronic instruments where a clean, crisp sound is required. Bass guitar is often amplified by a combination of direct injection and miking up, the engineer deriving a suitable sound from a balance of the two.

Many musicians using direct injection like to have a small combo amplifier which enables them to hear the signal from their instrument which is being fed to the PA. The combo's own tone and volume controls, of course, do not affect the overall output heard by the audience. A monitor speaker will also be used.

Before reaching the mixing stage, the signal is first channelled into a direct injection box. These convert the high impedance output of an electric instrument to match the low-impedance input requirements of mixing desks. This does not affect the instrument's ability to drive its amplifier. Direct injection boxes frequently use passive circuitry, although active units are becoming more common. Active circuits can give a low-impedance output without having to use a transformer, which can result in improvements in quality, weight and cost-effectiveness, as well as allowing you to achieve a higher output level than is possible with passive circuits. This in turn reduces the risk of extraneous noise being picked up.

Splitter boxes

As their name implies, these devices "split" the signal from microphones, or directly injected instruments. One signal is then directed into the main power amplifier in the sound reinforcement system. The other is fed into the monitor amplifier. Splitter boxes have a metal casing (used for screening purposes) and, at their simplest, contain three jack sockets wired in parallel. When an input signal is fed into one, the signal is available as an output from the other two.

More expensive splitter boxes use transformers or active circuitry to perform a similar function. The primary advantage of the active splitter box is that correct impedance matching is preserved, resulting in the optimum transfer of energy through the device. In addition, the isolation of the two outputs means that a fault on one output line will not affect the other.

PA amplifiers

Power amplifiers (which receive the signal from the splitter boxes) range from 100 watts output power upwards. They may offer mixing and tone control facilities, or be simply a slave amplifier which is used in conjunction with a mixer-amplifier to boost the PA output, or to amplify the output of a mixing desk. Large sound reinforcement or PA systems use a number of slave amplifiers driven from the mixing desk through an active "crossover" unit. This splits the signal into two or more frequency bands, each band having its own group of slaves which in turn drive the appropriate speakers.

The sound reinforcement system shown in the diagram on this page is one rated at 200 watts. It has a 100 watt mixer-amplifier and a 100 watt slave of the kind shown on the right. The power of the 100 watt mixer-amplifier used to drive the monitor speakers is not added to the system's power rating. The slave takes the final mix from the pre-amp stage of the mixer-amplifier (i.e., before it reaches the power stage) and feeds half the PA speakers, while the power stage of the mixer-amplifier feeds an identical signal to the other half.

Sound reinforcement and monitoring system
The diagram below shows the stage set-up for a small group featuring acoustic guitar, electric bass, keyboards and two vocal microphones. It can be adapted to suit most configurations of instruments, using direct injection, miking up and direct miking as appropriate.

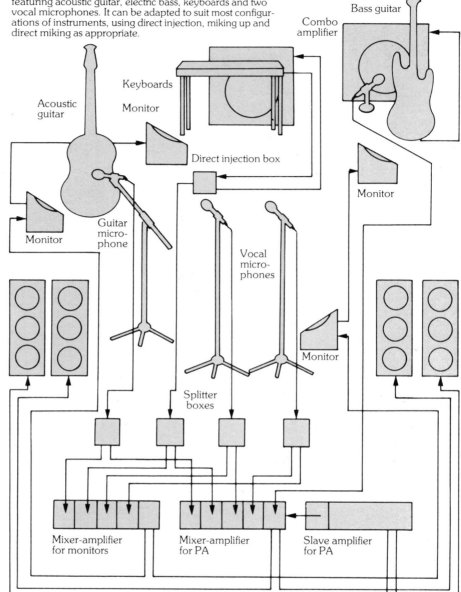

Mixer amplifier and slave
The HH MA–100 III is a versatile 120 watt PA mixer-amplifier. It has five channels, each with high/low impedance input and volume, bass, treble, effects send and reverb controls. The master volume and presence control the mix passing to the power amplifier. Slave amplifiers such as the 120 watt S–130 shown here can be used in conjunction with the MA–100.

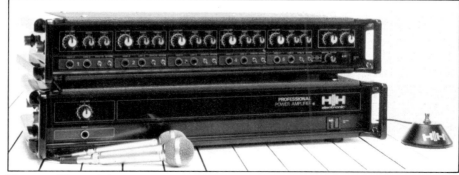

Working on stage

There are no golden rules about the best way to place your speakers, since each venue has its own characteristics. You will probably have to discover these for yourself while making a preliminary sound check. However, there are a number of useful guidelines which you can follow.

Keep each instrument's speakers as close together as possible to minimize phase problems. As a rough guide, any speaker which is out of the direct line of sight of part of the audience will, to those people, have reduced audibility and clarity. Your approach should be to try and fill the available space with sound, and balance it so that the sound quality is acceptable in any part of the auditorium. This is why most sound engineers stick to a mono mix (in which each side of the PA is producing an identical signal), since a stereo mix will be imbalanced to anyone not in a central position.

The type of PA speakers also has an effect on sound quality. Column speakers (containing a number of similar-sized speakers) are compact and disperse sound well in small venues. Their restricted frequency range, however, means that they cannot deliver a true high-fidelity sound. They are not ideally suited to large halls because their wide dispersion prevents them projecting adequate sound levels right to the back of the hall. In such a case, horn speakers with their good sound projection would be a much better choice. Horns are less suited to clubs as their dispersion of higher frequencies is limited (high frequencies are far more directional than low frequencies, which tend to disperse very easily). The fact that the physical dimensions and shape of each horn is closely related to the sound it handles accounts for the seemingly untidy appearance of many stacks. In fact, such equipment is arranged very carefully to make maximum use of dispersion characteristics, traditionally with the bass bins at the bottom, mid-range speakers in the middle and treble horns at the top.

Speakers need to be sufficiently high above the audience so that their output is not overtly absorbed by such acoustically "soft" surfaces as seating and the audience itself. They can be "flown" above the stage. Absorption is a particular problem if you are using a combo on a low stage. A combo tends to throw its sound directly forward, so you should either mount the unit on a firm stand of the appropriate height, or use the special legs with which some combos are fitted to tilt the amplifier backwards slightly. Without this adjustment, what to you seems a high volume level may be quite lost to the audience.

Monitor speakers

Monitor (or "foldback") speakers are an important part of the sound system. In almost any situation, *except* when only one or two musicians are playing through a small set-up, the performers are likely to experience difficulty in hearing each other (and themselves). To get over this problem, a system is needed which can deliver the missing sounds to the area of the stage in which each musician is playing. The simplest approach is to have a slave amplifier which drives a number of small speakers placed near each performer. This, however, is likely to be unsatisfactory because bringing the same signal that is going into the sound reinforcement system into the on-stage monitors can generate feedback. The problem can be reduced by arranging for the monitor amplifier and speakers to be fed from a separate mix to that sent to the PA.

Using a separate mixer-amplifier to power the monitors, you can adjust the controls to cope with the frequencies that are causing feedback. Larger systems employ a separate monitor mixing desk (positioned to one side of the stage) which usually permits each musician to have a mix specially prepared for him. It will then contain only those instruments which he has difficulty in hearing unaided.

Monitor speakers
Monitors such as the one being used by Peter Tosh (left) are usually wedge-shaped so that the sound can be directed upwards to the musician's ears. In larger systems, extra PA-type sidefill monitors are installed around the sides of the stage facing the musicians. Monitor speakers must have a very flat frequency response curve, since any peak will be liable to cause feedback – graphic equalizers are often used to control this.

Feedback

Feedback – a perennial problem for guitarists – is also something from which any kind of PA or sound reinforcement system may suffer if precautions are not taken. It occurs when a microphone or transducer (such as the pick-up of an electric guitar) picks up its own amplified sound and feeds it through the sound system once again. Feedback can be eliminated, but it is largely a matter of trial and error to find the best set-up for the venue you are playing. A system which performs perfectly in one hall may, when duplicated exactly in another, produce very unpleasant feedback effects.

Notes on feedback problems with amplified acoustic guitars are given on p. 216. You should not hold an electric guitar so that it directly faces the speakers, or stand too close to them. Use a long lead if necessary, but remember that this will also cut the treble response. With your PA system, make sure that the vocal microphones are positioned well behind the sound path of the PA speakers. This is especially important if you are using column speakers, since they can disperse the sound through an arc of 220 degrees or more. Consequently, a microphone placed within this field can set up feedback. Position the microphone pointing upwards and away from instruments to avoid pick-up of unwanted sound. If a vocal microphone is feeding back, reduce its volume level and move the singer closer to it. Use the bass-cut switch if the microphone is fitted with one; this will reduce pick-up of low frequencies, which are a problem because they are non-directional and cannot be avoided by pointing the microphone away from speakers. Similarly, avoid having monitors too close to a microphone. You should have few problems with feedback when you are close-miking a speaker using an omni-directional microphone. The very high sound levels involved mean that little microphone gain is required, thus minimizing the possibility of feedback.

Feedback is, of course, a property which many guitarists have used creatively. For some, such as Jimi Hendrix or Jeff Beck, it has formed an integral part of their playing style. If you want to exploit feedback, rather than minimize it, you can deliberately ignore all the suggestions made above. You should note, however, that your attempts to induce feedback can cause problems for the other musicians and vocalists. This is particularly evident when your guitar is miked through a sound reinforcement system. If you attempt to use feedback in this situation, the result will be pure mayhem.

Mixing desks

Stage mixers are either purpose-made units for road use or adapted versions of the consoles built into recording studios.

There are a number of points to bear in mind when mixing on stage. Use equalizers to remove all lower frequencies from each channel other than those actually needed for the sound of that particular instrument – this will cut out some of the extraneous sound picked up by the microphone. Do not turn up the input sensitivity or gain control so high that it can cause distortion in subsequent stages. Likewise, extreme equalization boosts can overload the subsequent stages, so it is best to turn down the input sensitivity to prevent this. Wide stereo spreads are often a problem because of the sound imbalance in different parts of the hall, and these should be avoided unless you want a particular panning effect. Use your ears to decide on the presence or absence of distortion in preference to relying completely on meters.

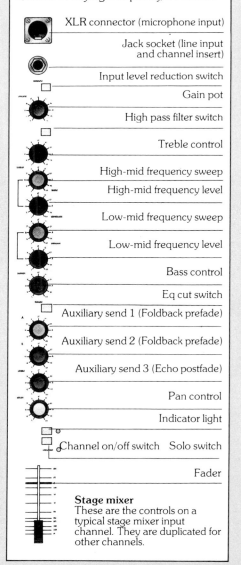

XLR connector (microphone input)

Jack socket (line input and channel insert)

Input level reduction switch

Gain pot

High pass filter switch

Treble control

High-mid frequency sweep

High-mid frequency level

Low-mid frequency sweep

Low-mid frequency level

Bass control

Eq cut switch

Auxiliary send 1 (Foldback prefade)

Auxiliary send 2 (Foldback prefade)

Auxiliary send 3 (Echo postfade)

Pan control

Indicator light

Channel on/off switch   Solo switch

Fader

Stage mixer
These are the controls on a typical stage mixer input channel. They are duplicated for other channels.

Cables and connections

Twin-core screened cable is standard for microphones. Mixing desks use three-pin connectors; this type of connection is called a balanced line. Two cores are taken to a transformer input (or its electronic equivalent) in the mixing desk. The signal voltages in the two cores are balanced on either side of earth potential (zero volts). This is useful because it allows external interference appearing in the cables to be cancelled out. Mixer-amplifiers use two-pin jack sockets; one of the two cores of the microphone cable is connected to the screening of the jack plug, while the tip is connected to the other core in the usual way. Unscreened twin-core cable is used for speakers. It is important to use high current-capacity carrying cable in high-powered systems. If you use cable which is too thin, a significant resistance will be added to the speaker circuit. This will result in a loss of volume and a reduction in the amplifier's effective damping factor.

Electrical safety

With any kind of mains-powered equipment there is the ever-present risk of electrocution. Earth connections and fuses are fitted so that when a fault arises and a dangerously high voltage develops, the voltage is carried safely to earth and the fuse blows, thus cutting off all power reaching the faulty equipment. However, faults sometimes develop in these safety precautions. Loose connections, or the corrosion or burning of pins, contacts, plugs, sockets and cable ends, can cause an earth line to break, or to show a high resistance to current flow. In both cases the flow to earth will be blocked and the fuse will not blow. If you touch equipment in this dangerous – but often undetectable – state, it could mean disaster.

Check that the earth circuitry is functioning correctly every time you use your equipment. For very little outlay you can buy a ring mains tester which plugs into a wall socket; the most useful have illuminated displays which indicate different kinds of faults. If you are expert at using a multi-meter, you can use this to test the mains supply and earth connections. If you find any fault, do not use your equipment until it has been rectified.

Check that fuses are correctly situated on the live line, and that they are only large enough to deliver the power that the equipment requires – any excess represents a risk. Special fuse devices can be obtained which fit between guitar and amplifier, to increase safety margins.

Amplifying acoustic guitars

Acoustic guitars have sufficient volume to allow them to be heard in a small room or folk club, but there are many situations when it becomes necessary to amplify the guitar in some way. This would include, for instance, playing an acoustic guitar in an amplified band, or playing in a larger room or venue where there is a problem with the dissipation of sound, or when background noise levels obscure the guitar.

Magnetic pick-ups

You can fit an acoustic guitar with a magnetic pick-up of the type used on electric guitars (see p. 52). The sound of an acoustic is generated by the resonance of the soundbox, but a magnetic pick-up responds primarily to the vibratory pattern of the strings instead. Therefore, the sound of an acoustic guitar amplified in this way lies somewhere between the natural sound of the instrument and the sound of an electric guitar. Some subtleties of acoustic tone are inevitably compromised in the process.

Using microphones

Modern PA equipment is capable of reproducing the sound of an acoustic guitar with a high degree of fidelity. Nevertheless, there are certain limitations when using a microphone to amplify an acoustic on stage. Once you have set up your equipment and obtained a sound balance, you must keep the guitar at a reasonably constant distance from the microphone. Any to-and-fro movement will cause fluctuations in volume, although this is something that, with practice, you can exploit creatively to control volume levels. There is also the danger of knocking the microphone and causing a loud bang through the speakers or feedback. If you are playing with an electric

Increasing your options John Martyn's acoustic guitar is amplified by means of both a magnetic pick-up and a contact device (partially obscured by his right hand). Using such a dual system, you can opt for either the "natural" sound from the contact device, the more "electric" quality of the magnetic pick-up, or a combination of the two. Magnetic pick-ups are usually fitted either across the sound-hole (as here) or at the end of the fingerboard.

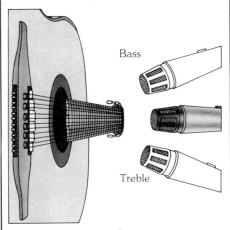

Positioning the microphone
Placing the microphone either above or below the central position will increase the emphasis on the bass and treble strings respectively. Close up, the picking noises will be heard more clearly.

Bass

Treble

band, place the mike as close to the sound-hole as possible; this will minimize the effect of sound being picked up from other sources nearby. You can use several microphones and balance the sound through the mix, although you may have phase problems caused by the microphones being at different distances from the soundhole.

Contact devices

Piezo-electric transducers (also known as "ceramic" transducers or pick-ups) consist of a small block of crystalline or ceramic material which is usually encased in metal or plastic. Two output wires are attached to two surfaces of the block. They are attached to the soundboard of an acoustic guitar, and work on the principle of the *piezo-electric effect*.

When the strings are not vibrating, the soundboard is at rest and the transducer is not subjected to any stress. The block is electrically neutral. When a note is sounded, however, the outward movement of the vibrating soundboard places the adjacent surface of the piezo block under compression and causes electrons to migrate to that face of the block, with the result that all the charges on that face become negative. When the soundboard vibrates inwards, the surface of the block is placed under tension. The electrons migrate to the opposite surface and the polarity is reversed. These small changes of polarity emerge, via wires attached to the two opposite faces of the block, as an alternating current signal. In some cases, because the output signal is not very strong, it is boosted by a pre-amplifier. Recent improvements in the design of piezo-crystal devices have resulted in a far more powerful output, thus doing away

with the need for a pre-amplifier.

This kind of contact transducer will reproduce the natural sound of an acoustic guitar very faithfully. It can be secured to the surface of the instrument with screws or adhesive, or it can be incorporated into the bridge (the area where the soundboard vibrates most) – as in the Barcus Berry "hot dot" arrangement. Other transducers fit directly under the saddle; some have a small block of piezo crystal under each string so that the sound of the strings can be split in stereo. Some guitarists like to fit both a transducer and a magnetic pick-up, so they can alternate (and mix) the resulting "acoustic" and "electric" sound as required.

Contact microphones vary in design. Some are fitted to the inside and others to the outside of the soundboard. However, the principle of reacting to the vibrations of the soundboard is common to all. The more centrally the microphone is placed on the soundboard, the stronger the vibrations.

Preventing feedback

You can experience problems caused by unwanted feedback with all the devices mentioned. As far as contact microphones and transducers are concerned, the closer the device is to the speaker, the more likely it is to feed back. And the louder the amplified sound, the greater the likelihood of feedback. You will also tend to get more trouble if the guitar is facing the speaker directly.

The solution is to stand as far as possible from the speaker. Make the maximum use of the length of your guitar lead, and experiment by playing in different positions. If this fails to eradicate the feedback problem, you must compromise by adjusting the volume, tone or equalization.

RECORDING

The art of good recording is fundamentally the same whether you are working with a simple home set-up or with the extensive facilities of a professional multi-track studio. An understanding of the capabilities and of the limitations of your equipment, as well as a grasp of how the acoustics of the room in which you are working "colour" the sound recorded on to tape, will help you achieve excellent results. The importance of understanding acoustics cannot be overstressed. Though it is an involved subject, the basic principles are easy to grasp and, with a degree of experimentation, you can soon have a room's

acoustics working for, not against, you. At a professional level, the standard of recordings can vary enormously from studio to studio – even between those with more-or-less the same equipment. One of the major reasons for this is that the ability of recording engineers differs. A good engineer can get excellent results from quite modest equipment and is therefore invaluable – both to the studio and to the musicians. This chapter, which deals with the technical aspects of recording, contains enough information to get you started on your own recording and will guide you through the complexities of a professional studio.

Recording techniques

The technical quality of any recording – whether it is a simple demo tape that you make yourself, or a professionally produced multi-track recording for commercial release – depends not so much on the specific equipment being used, but rather on the recording environment (especially its acoustics) and, more importantly, on the ability of the technician handling the session to use both to maximum effect. It is perfectly feasible that a

recording engineer with a thorough knowledge of his simple four-track studio can produce a better recording than an inexperienced engineer at the controls of a sophisticated 24-track machine whose intricacies he does not fully comprehend.

This section shows you how to understand acoustics and basic professional techniques so that you can apply this knowledge to making your own recordings at home.

The recording process

The first step in making a recording is to pick up the sound of each instrument on a microphone. Several microphones may be used on one instrument or, conversely, one microphone may be used to record several instruments in turn. The microphone signals are passed to a mixing desk where, along with the input from any directly injected instruments, they are subjected to any necessary sound processing. The sound of each instrument is then recorded on magnetic tape at the optimum recording level; if facilities permit, each instrument will be

allotted its own track on the tape.

Once the recording of the individual tracks is complete, the multi-track master tape must then be "mixed down" to stereo so it can be replayed on conventional hi-fi equipment. To do this, the tracks are fed back into the mixer where they are balanced against each other, given further sound processing, and then "reduced" to stereo. This is fed into a stereo (two-track) tape recorder to produce the master tape from which all subsequent copies (tape or disc) will be made.

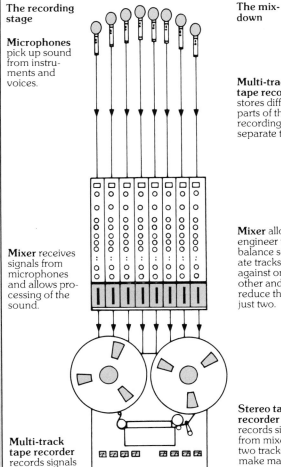

The recording stage

Microphones pick up sound from instruments and voices.

Mixer receives signals from microphones and allows processing of the sound.

Multi-track tape recorder records signals from mixer.

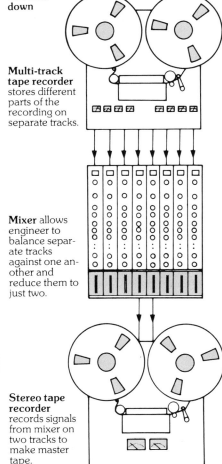

The mix-down

Multi-track tape recorder stores different parts of the recording on separate tracks.

Mixer allows engineer to balance separate tracks against one another and reduce them to just two.

Stereo tape recorder records signals from mixer on two tracks to make master tape.

Acoustics

Many home and demo tapes made in simple or makeshift studios sound inferior because the people who have made them lack a basic understanding of acoustics. You cannot simply set up your microphones and hope for the best; acoustics is one of the prime considerations taken into account when a new recording studio is being designed, and some knowledge of the way a room (be it your living room or a true studio) affects the sounds produced in it is essential to the quality of the finished recording.

If you sit in a room playing an acoustic guitar, you will hear both the sound coming directly from the instrument and the reflections of that sound which have been "bounced" off acoustically reflective surfaces around you (such as walls and ceilings). A microphone placed in the room would pick up both the direct and reflected sounds indiscriminately. In some circumstances, the reflected images could enhance the sound, but in others the effect may be detrimental.

A natural echo occurs when a soundwave is bounced off a reflective surface and is heard as a repeat of the original sound. Since some of the wave's energy will be lost in the process, the echo will not be quite as loud as the original sound. Because sound travels relatively quickly (approximately 1,130 ft/344m per second), the reflective surface must be some distance away from the source if the echo is to be delayed sufficiently for it to be heard as a distinct repeat *after* the original sound. A natural echo delay time of one second, for example, would involve the reflective surface being 565 ft (172m) away from the sound source. The fact that it would be impracticable to use rooms of such a size to generate natural echoes is, of course, one reason why electronic echo units (see p. 209) are used instead. Further successive echoes may be produced as a result of parts of the reflected sound striking other, more distant reflective surfaces before being bounced back to the listener. Successive echoes will always be of increasingly diminishing volume, until they finally die away altogether.

Reverberation occurs inside enclosures (such as rooms) and is caused by soundwaves travelling such a short distance before being reflected that, instead of being a separately distinct echo, the reflected sound image is heard so soon after the direct sound that it appears to be a part of it. When a series of reflected images or multiple reflections are heard as the decaying end of a sound, they are known collectively as *reverberation*. A long reverberation time in the average room is the result of soundwaves being successively bounced off several surfaces before being dissipated.

Again, reverberation effects can be produced artificially using sound processing equipment.

Recording studios and control rooms are designed to incorporate some degree of natural reverberation. However, this must be carefully controlled, since certain reflection conditions can result in an undesirable emphasis at one or more frequencies, thus giving unnatural coloration to the sound. This occurs when the room's shape and dimensions interact with specific frequencies to produce "standing waves".

A *standing* or *stationary wave* is the result of interference effects between the original and the reflected soundwaves. The most troublesome effect occurs when sound is reflected between two parallel surfaces, such as facing walls or between floor and ceiling. When the wavelength of a soundwave (or one of its equal fractions) coincides with the distance between such parallel, reflective surfaces, then a standing wave is set up. The original sound and all subsequent reflections add together in phase with each other, resulting in apparent amplification of that frequency and an increase in its reverberation time. When the distance between the walls is greater than 40 ft (12m), the frequency of the standing wave is so low (28 Hz in this case) that it is unlikely to cause trouble, but at shorter distances problems can and do occur and these are difficult to eradicate.

A solution sometimes attempted is to make one of the surfaces absorbent rather than reflective. Low frequencies are, however, difficult to absorb, and a booming sound caused by the absorption of high, but not low, frequencies is common. The most practical solution is to avoid parallel surfaces wherever possible. The unusual geometric shape of some studios is not the designer's folly but rather an attempt to eradicate standing-wave problems. This can also eliminate *flutter echo*, which is caused by regularly spaced multiple reflections between parallel surfaces at frequencies higher than those generating standing waves. It results in a very rapid repeat echo.

Though all echo and reverberation can be added to a recording electronically, in practice, some degree of natural reverberation and echo is retained in studios. Singers, especially, find it easier to pitch their voices if they can hear some reverberation, and it also aids ensemble players and, in particular, string sections. This is, of course, balanced with technical requirements. Modern multi-track studios offer the facilities to record with various degrees of natural reverberation, plus the alternative of a wide range of electronically created reverberation and echo.

Studio layout

The size of individual studios varies: reverberation times of between 0.2 and 0.35 seconds are to be expected. Different areas of the room may be given different acoustical properties, to make them suitable for recording particular instruments or for using special techniques.

The main studio is usually carpeted. Acoustic screens are used to provide separation between microphones on different instruments or amplifiers, or to control ambient sound. There may be a separate booth designed primarily to house the drummer and to prevent direct sound spilling on to the drum kit microphones from

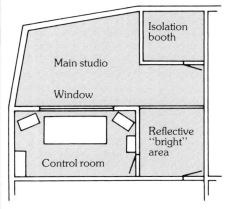

Multi-track studio
The main studio has non-parallel walls to minimize standing-wave problems. There are additional "bright" areas and isolation booths for particular recording techniques. The control room is acoustically isolated from these.

other instruments. Drums, acoustic guitars and strings are often recorded in a "live" or "bright" area, which is either a separate room or a screened area in the main studio. Such areas have reflective surfaces (uncarpeted wood flooring, tiling or glass are commonly used) to increase the natural reverberation time rather than adding it electronically.

Some studios have "adjustable" acoustics, made possible by altering the amount of exposed reflective surfaces in the room. A curtain may be hung in front of an acoustically "bright" wall, for example, so it can be drawn or opened as required to give a particular reverberation quality, or room dividers may be used to vary the actual size of the recording area and thus affect reverberation times.

The control room

In professional studios, the control room is acoustically isolated from the recording areas, in order to minimize sound-leakage problems. Its reverberation time is, however, similar to the main studio, and the general acoustic design is such that the

Inside the control room
The control room is the heart of the recording studio. As well as the mixing desk, here are all the sound processing devices, recording facilities, monitors and other equipment necessary to produce and mix down a multi-track recording.

engineer and producer can hear the sound being recorded without any deceptive acoustic coloration.

The control room houses the tape recorders, the mixing console, the electronic sound processing equipment and the monitor speakers. Monitors are usually large, of the highest quality and capable of producing high volumes. Small speakers are commonly placed on top of the recording console so that some idea can be gained of how the recording will sound when played on a radio or domestic hi-fi.

Sometimes – especially when recording overdubs – a musician will play in the control room rather than in the studio, using the direct injection method (see p. 212) to plug his instrument into the desk without the usual amplification. This enables him to hear any previously recorded backing track as well as the piece he is recording through the monitors, instead of the headphones used in the studio itself.

It also allows him better communication with the engineer and producer. Because the studio and control room are acoustically and structurally isolated from one another, communication has to be either by gestures through the glass screen separating them (some studios now use video systems) or verbally via a "talk-back" system. Not surprisingly, the interaction between the musicians in the studio and the technicians in the control room has a marked effect on the success (or otherwise) of the recording session.

You can adapt these principles of studio design to suit home recording (see p. 222). Since space is likely to be limited, you could use one room as the main studio and another as the control room. The effectiveness will be increased if you can provide some form of sound isolation, although the length of your leads and the need to improvise some form of talk-back may be limiting factors.

Mixing

The mixing desk is the heart of all but the most basic recording systems. In modified form (see p. 215), it is also used on the road as part of a sound reinforcement system. The mixer receives all microphone outputs and directly injected signals. It then allows extreme or subtle modifications to be made to the tonal characteristics of these signals. The mixer can send signals to, and receive returns from, all kinds of auxiliary "outboard" equipment such as echo devices, compressors, harmonizers, noise gates, etc. It directs the signals to the desired channels of the multi-track tape recorder at the optimum recording level while, at the same time, allowing the recording team to monitor any or all of the signals passing through it at any desired balance. One, or perhaps several, totally independent sound mixes can be sent back into the studio for the musicians to hear on headphones as they play (this facility is known as *foldback*). Further, it receives the playback signals from the multi-track recorder and permits any sound processing required to be carried out while the signals are mixed down to stereo and sent to the stereo tape machine.

How the mixing desk works

The vast majority of studio mixers are built on a modular basis. Each module is a vertical strip containing the various controls operating on one recording track. Duplicate modules act on each of the other inputs. Each vertical line, therefore, controls a single signal path; each horizontal line has the equivalent control for the other parts. This makes for easier operation and servicing, and also allows each mixer to be individually tailored by the manufacturer to suit a particular studio's requirements.

Each *input module* accepts a microphone (or directly injected) signal during recording, or one track of a multi-track recorder's playback during mix-down to stereo. A typical module might have facilities for microphone and line input gain control, input attenuation, equalization at various frequencies, foldback, auxiliary sends, panning controls and a fader. It will also accept a signal from an outboard source if the mixer has no (or insufficient) input modules for these tasks. Some mixer designs have input modules which give an output signal that will feed a tape recorder directly, while others can only feed the recorder through "group modules".

Group modules accept the output from one or more input modules. The routing of several inputs to one group allows the volume of all these inputs to be controlled by the one group fader, the balance between the inputs being adjusted by the individual input module faders. Group modules may be either very simple, having little more than the necessary fader, or they may have all the facilities found on the input channels. Many group modules incorporate the monitoring facilities of the mixer; if not, incorporated, separate monitor modules are used.

Monitor arrangements must allow the engineer to listen to any signal passing through the mixer. Any channel or group can be heard on its own by operating a switch on the appropriate module, which may be labelled "solo", "PFL" (pre-fade listen) or "AFL" (after-fade listen). Some mixers have all three, in which case "solo" means "solo in place", whereby the channel's position in the stereo picture is not altered. In other cases, operation of these switches generally directs the signal to only one of the monitor speakers. All auxiliary effects "sends" (additional mixed outputs, derived from the controls on input channels or groups, used to feed outboard effects units) can also be monitored in this way. The main monitoring arrangements allow the engineer to listen either to what is being recorded on tape or what is being played back from the tape. Monitoring by meter of all mixer outputs is also a feature. Not all outputs are permanently connected to meters, but generally one meter on the desk can be switched to read auxiliary outputs.

The *master module* is used during mixdown, when the recording on the multi-track master tape is mixed down to stereo (or mono for TV/radio broadcasts). The stereo recorder is fed from the master module, which receives its signals from all the input and group modules. It may also have master monitor volume controls.

Many mixing desks offer ancillary modules for facilities such as auxiliary output master volumes, auxiliary returns (from echo units, etc.) and studio "talkback". However, their arrangement is far from standardized and these relatively minor controls are often the prime source of confusion when one is confronted with an unfamiliar mixing desk.

Using the tape recorder

The art of good recording is to make full use of the dynamic range of the tape and equipment available to you. Sound levels vary during a piece of music. You should aim to get the highest level of sound on tape without the peak levels overloading and causing distortion, while ensuring that the quieter passages are not lost in electrical background noise or tape hiss.

VU meters give the best overall indication of recording levels, though they do not respond to very brief, instantaneous peaks. These are best monitored on special *peak meters*; there is a lot to be said for working with both. You should combine your reading of meter levels with subjective judgements based on listening to the recorded material (see p. 222). Tape recorders that have an "automatic record level" facility do so by means of a very long release limiting device (see p. 206-7).

Two-track recorder
1 Anti-flutter arm. **2** Tape-speed selector (15 ips). **3** Tape-speed selector (7½ ips). **4** Power on/off. **5** Monitor select (input off/tape). **6, 7** Headphone sockets. **8** Monitor volume levels. **9** Monitor mode selection. **10** Record ready (left). **11** Microphone input (left). **12** Record level (left). **13** Record source selector (left). **14** Record level (right). **15** Record source selector (right). **16** Microphone input (right). **17** Tape transport controls. **18** VU meters. **19** Record ready (right). **20** Tape splicer. **21** NAB hub. **22** Empty NAB spool. **23** Head cover. **24** Tape counter. **25** Full NAB spool.

Microphones

The microphone is the first link in any chain of sound recording equipment. Several basic types are used in recording: *capacitor* (also known as "condenser" types), *dynamic*, *ribbon* and *pressure zone* microphones. Only the first requires an outside source of power from mains or battery; they can also be "phantom powered" from mixing desks with suitable facilities.

Characteristics

A bewildering variety of microphones is available, making the selection of the right one for a particular situation a daunting task. However, there are a number of simple criteria which considerably ease the problem: frequency response, output level, dynamic range and polar response.

You can use the manufacturer's published *frequency response* figures to determine whether the microphone has a sufficiently wide frequency range to record a particular instrument. Always try to use a microphone that will respond to frequencies higher than you strictly need; this will keep the highs clean and transparent. Avoid using one which covers much lower frequencies than you need, however, since easily dispersed low-frequency sound from other sources can be picked up. Use the bass-cut switch if one is fitted. A study of frequency-response curves will show you how different models accentuate different frequencies; careful selection may therefore enable you to achieve an effect direct from the microphone which would normally require sophisticated equalization control.

Published figures for *dynamic range* are normally measurements taken with the microphone some distance from the sound source. Close to the instrument or speaker, however, the microphone receives a much wider dynamic range; if it is heavily overloaded, gross distortion will be apparent.

The greater the *output level* from the microphone, the smaller can be the gain of the microphone amplifier. Since the latter is responsible for almost all the electrically generated noise in a recording system, high microphone outputs are desirable. Capacitor microphones yield much higher output levels than any other type; the smallest output comes from ribbon microphones.

The *polar response* of a microphone is a measure of its sensitivity to sounds reaching it from different directions. It is shown by a graph or diagram detailing the directional characteristics at different frequencies (see simplified polar diagrams above, where the response line is a contour line joining points of equal volume or sensitivity). A microphone that responds to sounds equally, whatever direction they come from, is said to be *omnidirectional*. A *cardioid* microphone is one that accepts sound essentially from one direction only. This response can be varied in degree, giving a microphone known as a *hyper-cardioid* type which will accept sounds from narrower angles than the accepted pattern. You can buy capacitor and dynamic microphones with any of these polar responses. Ribbon microphones, however, will accept sound from both front and rear, but not from the sides (this is a "figure-of-eight" response). A few expensive capacitor microphones can achieve all these polar responses electronically by means of a switch, either built into

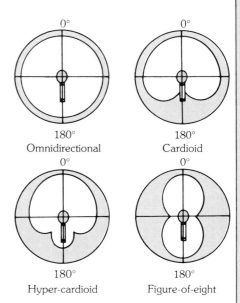

the microphone itself or on a remote control unit. The pressure zone microphone has a unique response which is hemispherical.

Microphones have their own characteristic *impedances*. There are two basic divisions: low-impedance and high-impedance. The performance of the latter is degraded when cables longer than about 10 ft (3 m) are used, thus rendering them unsuitable for most professional studio and stage applications. Low-impedance microphones have impedances ranging from 30 to 600 ohms, but the most versatile and commonly used impedance is around 200 ohms. This is a compromise between the lower noise of a 30 ohm model and the higher output of the 600 ohm microphone. There is no problem with cable length.

Tape hiss and noise reduction

Tape hiss is present on all analogue tape recordings. It is particularly evident when a recording is transferred from one tape to another, and it will build up cumulatively as the number of transfers increases. Using the full dynamic range helps make tape hiss less audible (see p. 203).

Noise-reduction units are used to combat tape hiss and other background noise. In the Dolby "B" system, high-frequency signals are boosted and compressed during recording and reduced and expanded during replay to improve dynamic range. In the DBX system, the signal dynamics, but not the noise, are compressed and the whole is then expanded on replay.

Tape drop-out and storage print-through

A *drop-out* is a momentary reduction in volume due to flaws in either the oxide coating or plastic tape base. If the tape is faulty, you have no choice but to roll the tape on to an unblemished section. Drop-out can also be caused by dust between the tape and record head. Regular cleaning of the heads and, if possible, the use of wider tape will minimize this problem. The narrower the width of tape (cassettes, for example) the greater the possible risk of drop-out will be.

A *print-through* occurs when the signal from part of a recording imprints itself on an adjacent layer of tape during storage, causing a faint echo (or pre-echo) during playback. Eradication is difficult, involving complex, specialist equipment, but you can reduce the risk of print-through by storing the tapes "end out" (though this means they have to be rewound before playback) in a cool place and avoiding any sudden, extreme changes of temperature.

Bias

An inaudible, very high frequency signal called the *bias frequency* is mixed in with the audio signal being fed to the record head. This enables the oxide particles with which the tape is impregnated to align themselves to the pattern dictated by the audio signal. Quality tape recorders (such as those designed for professional or semi-professional recording needs) have an adjustable bias signal level which allows the machine to be set to match the bias requirements of a particular tape. This is essential if the optimum machine/tape performance is to be obtained. Select a suitable brand and type of tape to give the best signal-to-noise ratio within your price range, and then have the bias adjusted to suit by professionals. Many cassette machines have switchable bias settings such as "normal", "chrome", "high" or "low".

Home recording

Making your own recordings gives you complete control over everything you do. You do not need to book studio time, and you can work far more cheaply than if you were using professional services. With care, and an awareness of the necessary limitations, you can produce a tape compatible with recordings made in many demo studios – which, in terms of acoustics and facilities, are often little more than home studios themselves.

Preparing to record

There are numerous acoustic and environmental problems associated with home recording. Outside noise will penetrate the recording room and be picked up by the microphones. And internal reflections of sound within the room are likely to cause unpleasant colouration of the sound through standing waves, flutter echo, etc. None of these problems are easy to deal with. Double glazing and heavy drapes may help to deal with sound leaking into or out of a room, while doors and windows should be made to shut airtight. A number of acoustic treatments have been suggested to deal with internal reflections, but, unfortunately, many sound-absorbent materials will only cope with very high frequencies. Polystyrene ceiling tiles and eggboxes are quite useless: though they bear a passing resemblance to materials used in recording studios, they have no effect on anything below 10 kHz. Heavy drapes, blankets or foam-backed carpet suspended a few inches from the wall are much more effective, and can absorb sound quite well down to below 500 Hz. Some acoustic tiles have an effect down to about 250 Hz. It is unlikely that you will record in a room which has non-parallel walls, but you could improvise with strategically sited bookcases or wardrobes (with the doors open and crammed with clothes) to break up standing waves.

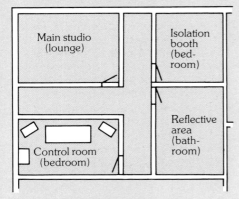

Adapting rooms for recording
Use the main bedroom for all recording and control facilities, the lounge can be used as the studio, with a smaller bedroom as an isolation booth for drums, etc. Make full use of the bathroom's bright acoustics.

Using VU meters

The correct use of microphone techniques and acoustics is, as we have seen, of fundamental importance to recording. Equally so is making full use of the possible dynamic range which you can obtain from the particular machine/tape combination you are using. This involves learning how to interpret the record-level meter. On the majority of tape recorders this will be a VU (volume unit) meter. PPMs (peak programme meters) are generally found only on professional mixing equipment. A vital point to remember about VU meters is that they do not respond to instantaneous peaks. This means that they may well fail to give any indication of sudden peaks that occur at the start of sounds from a percussive instrument such as a piano. Your object must at all times be to get the loudest parts of the music to drive the VU meter as high as possible without audible distortion being apparent on playback. It is not always correct to assume that distortion will occur when the needle is driven on to the red part of the scale; this depends on the type of tape in use, the type of instrument and the style of music, and it is largely a matter of trial and error to discover when distortion will occur.

Interpreting meter readings

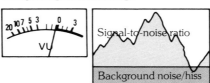

1 This is a good recording, making full use of the signal-to-noise ratio and dynamic range.

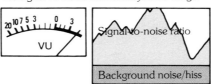

2 This has been over-recorded, resulting in peak clipping at certain frequencies.

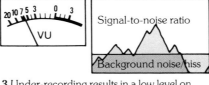

3 Under-recording results in a low level on playback, with accentuation of hiss and noise.

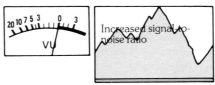

4 Effective use has been made of noise reduction to increase the signal-to-noise ratio and cut background noise and tape hiss.

Setting up the microphones

This simple technique uses two microphones and a stereo tape recorder to record an acoustic guitar with some degree of natural echo and reverberation. The principles and microphone techniques involved, however, are the same for recording virtually any instrument.

There are a number of approaches to positioning the two microphones needed in stereo recording. One is the *spaced-pair* technique, where the microphones are placed about 6-8 ft (1.8 – 2.4 m) apart, forming one side of an equilateral triangle with the guitar at the apex. It is rarely used professionally today because of technical problems in transferring such a recording to disc, though it can be used for home recording – particularly of a group. The

Coincident pair
Use figure-of-eight microphones to pick up the maximum environmental reverberation, or cardioid types to minimize this. You can further control environmental pick-up by moving the microphones closer or further away.

second approach, the *coincident pair* technique, uses microphones mounted together pointing inwards and is much more widely used; it is taken to its logical conclusion in the construction of stereo microphones. It also allows you to go as close as you wish to get the effect you require. With the microphones placed about 6-8 ft (1.8 – 2.4 m) in front of the guitar, they will give the most accurate representation of the sound that an ideally situated listener would hear. Moving in closer will increase the dynamic range that the microphones receive, and this will result in an apparent increase in definition. Since the instrument will also seem louder (which may cause problems with recording levels) but the reverberation from the room will be unchanged, less reverberation will appear on the recording. Conversely, moving further away will reduce the instrument's volume and increase the degree of reverberation.

Reverberation results from echoes of different lengths repeating and adding together until they die away. The smallest range of echo lengths will occur when you are playing in the centre of the room. If you play at one end of the room you will increase the echo lengths proportionally, while playing off-centre (in a corner, for example, or in an L-shaped room) will give the widest range.

Setting the recording level

Follow the instructions for your tape recorder to set the levels and controls. With the tape running, make a number of test recordings of the loudest section of the music you intend to record. Between each test, gradually increase the recording level until you begin to hear distortion on playback (its onset may be slow or sudden).

Even though the VU meter needle may move on to the red area of the scale, this does not necessarily mean that the overload is going to cause distortion. It is best to rely on the evidence of test recordings, rather than accept the meter's indications. You will also find that you can record at higher levels on some machines than on others – another reason for making tests rather than relying on formula.

The level you should use for the actual recording should be the highest you achieved before distortion became apparent. Now you can experiment with different placements of microphones and guitar, keeping the distance between the two constant. Once you have found the spot which, to you, gives the best combination of definition and reverberation, you can go ahead with the actual recording. It is helpful to make notes of levels, positioning and distances so you can use the same set-up again at a later date.

Improvising reverb effects

Connect the output of your tape recorder to the tape or auxiliary input of hi-fi amplifier (if you are using a cassette recorder without the appropriate sockets, use the headphone socket instead). If your tape recorder has only a two-head system, once you start recording the signal will be fed both to the record head and to the amplifier. Place your hi-fi speakers as far away from the microphone as possible, taking care not to turn up the amplifier volume so high that it causes feedback. Once you have the level correctly adjusted, the microphones will pick up both the original sound of the guitar and, at a lower level, the sound of the speakers. Since the speakers are further from the microphones than the guitar, the sound coming back from them will be slightly delayed. This signal is picked up by the microphone and routed through the speakers once more, inducing further delays until the signal decays below audibility, thus creating a reverberation effect.

You can use a tape recorder with three heads in the same way, or you can send the playback signal instead of the record signal to the amplifier. This will give a delayed echo effect which will repeat several times until it fades away. The length of delay depends on tape speed.

Two-channel mono recording

Rather than using your two microphones as a stereo pair, you can use one close up to the guitar and the other some distance away to capture the ambient sound. The recording level on the latter channel should be much higher than that recording the guitar directly, so that on playback the relative level of the two can be adjusted on the balance control to give the most pleasing mix. Place the guitar microphone in the same way as you would mike up an acoustic guitar on stage (see p. 216). The placing of the ambient microphone is largely a matter of experiment, since phase cancellation will occur at some frequencies. On the positive side, however, you may be able to use this technique to eradicate standing-waves.

Two-channel mono is the fundamental technique used in studios when miking up any instrument, not just an acoustic guitar, in multi-track recording sessions. If several instruments are being recorded together, normally only one ambient microphone, common to all, need be used. Acoustic keyboard instruments generally require two close microphones, one each on bass and treble strings; the same separation is used for split-speaker systems where one part of the PA handles the bass frequencies and the other the treble.

Sound-on-sound recording

This technique involves building up the recording, layer by layer, using the two tape tracks alternately. Each time a new line is recorded, the previously recorded material is then transferred and mixed in, leaving the second track free.

Your tape recorder must have separate erase, record and playback heads. It must be able to record on each track independently (because you need to record one track while playing back the other for synchronization); it must be possible to transfer a recording made on one track on to the other at the same time as new material is being recorded; and you must be able to monitor either channel separately on headphones.

As an example, we shall consider how to record successive rhythm, lead and vocal tracks. Only one microphone is used (since you will be recording each track in mono) and it should be placed just like the close-up microphone used in two-channel mono. Record the rhythm guitar on to track one – first being very careful to achieve the highest possible undistorted recording level. Switch the tape recorder (or use an external lead) to connect the playback of track one to the input of track two. Connect your micro-

phone to the input of track two and set your headphones to listen to the same input. Now switch to lead guitar. When you set the machine to record on track two only, you will hear on the headphones both the original track and whatever you are now playing. If your machine has track-transfer switching, then the level at which the track one is transferred to track two will be set by the first track's recording level control. If you are using an external lead, it will be set by the track one playback level, unless your machine has separate "mic" and "line" input-level controls, in which case the level will be set by the latter. The level of the lead guitar will be set by the microphone level control of track two. Once you are happy with the levels, you can record the lead guitar. If you make a mistake, you can always erase track two and start again. Some machines have a "drop-in" facility which allows you to record when the machine is already running, which will save you having to start again from the beginning if there is only a small section you are not happy with. Listen to the two tracks together and identify from the *rhythm* track the point at which the lead guitar starts to go wrong. Wind back to a point before the mistake

occurred and start the machine in playback. You will now hear only the backing track on the headphones, but you should be able to identify your "cue" quite easily. At this point, drop the machine into record while it is still running, and complete the lead guitar recording.

Having put down the lead and rhythm tracks, you can now add vocals by reversing all your connections so that this time you are recording on track one again. The mixed lead and rhythm guitars on track two are transferred to track one while the vocal is added, in exactly the same manner as before. Remember, though, that the original recording of the rhythm guitar on track one will now be erased, leaving you with just the track two version which has it mixed with the lead guitar. Once the original is erased, you can no longer make any adjustment to the balance between guitars.

This process can be repeated a number of times, although it is limited by the amount of noise build-up and the "cross-talk" between channels which, in sound-on-sound applications, results in bass notes sounding very woolly after a few transfers. With good equipment you can expect tolerable results from up to six transfers.

Multi-track recording

Multi-tracking gives both performer and technician the greatest possible flexibility. It allows you to make recordings in which you play all the instruments yourself, to record your part several times before choosing the best take, or to construct it from a combination of several takes. Recording engineers can treat the sound of each instrument individually during and after recording, and avoid committing themselves to a particular balance between instruments until all recording has been completed. The limiting factor is the number of tracks available on your tape recorder. You can, however, mix together a number of tracks and "bounce" them on to one track (as in the sound-on-sound technique), thus releasing them for making further recordings on the same tracks.

Recording techniques

Multi-tracking demands acoustic separation between the instruments. Each track should record sound from one instrument only, without "spillage" from others nearby. A lead guitarist, for instance, may play a perfect solo, only to find on playback that his rhythm guitarist has been playing slightly out of tune. With perfect acoustic separation, the rhythm track would simply be re-recorded later, the solo remaining unscathed. If there is spillage, however, some of the faulty rhythm playing may be picked up on the lead guitar microphone, in which case both will have to be recorded again. Even with perfect takes, there may be so much spillage that it is impossible to alter the relative balance between instruments.

When recording several instruments together you should make full use of isolation booths, screens, and close miking. All tracks should be recorded at as high a level as possible, irrespective of how loud the instruments will be in the final mix. This enables you to have the best possible basic recording on which to perform subsequent sound processing. To make overdubs the replay of the previously recorded track(s) is taken from the record head into the mixer. The musicians hear a rough mix of this in their headphones, and play new lines in time with what they hear. Since the replay comes from the same head that is recording the new material, synchronisation is preserved. Where a number of overdubs of the same part are recorded to give increased body to the sound, it is normal practice to bounce them down on to one track – either at the time they are recorded or afterwards. When doing this, avoid bouncing down on to a track adjacent to one involved in the bounce; "cross-talk" (electronic leakage) between channels can cause feedback.

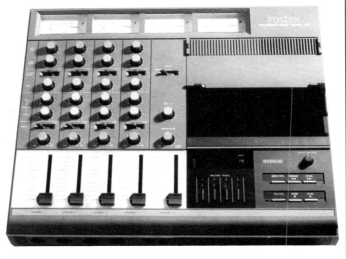

Multi-track recorder/mixer unit The Fostex 250 is a portable studio, recording on standard cassettes running at 3¾ ips. It has a built-in Dolby "C" noise-reduction system. There are four input channels with full mixing and bouncing facilities. A "trim" control matches any signal level to the input, and equalizers control tonal quality. "Patch points" allow you to add external sound processing to each channel.

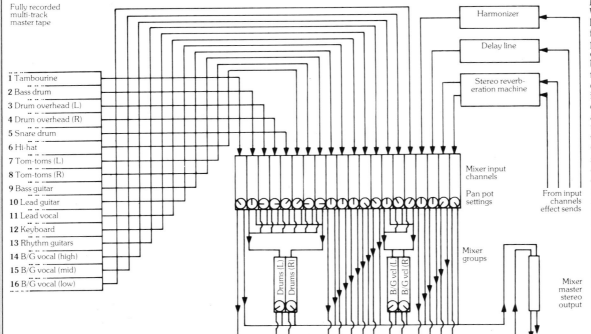

Fully recorded multi-track master tape

1 Tambourine
2 Bass drum
3 Drum overhead (L)
4 Drum overhead (R)
5 Snare drum
6 Hi-hat
7 Tom-toms (L)
8 Tom-toms (R)
9 Bass guitar
10 Lead guitar
11 Lead vocal
12 Keyboard
13 Rhythm guitars
14 B/G vocal (high)
15 B/G vocal (mid)
16 B/G vocal (low)

Harmonizer

Delay line

Stereo reverberation machine

Mixer input channels

Pan pot settings

From input channels effect sends

Mixer groups

Drums (L) Drums (R)

B/G vcl (L) B/G vcl (R)

Mixer master stereo output

Mixing down to stereo When all the tracks have been recorded final mixing takes place. The multi-track outputs from the playback head are fed to the mixer input channels. Equalization is checked on each channel and effects are added. The faders are used to balance the volume of the tracks with one another. By setting the pan controls either to left, right or centre, each instrument is positioned in the stereo picture. As many tracks as possible are sent through a group, as with the drums and backing vocals here. This enables them to be controlled by one fader. Now reduced to stereo, the signals are passed to a stereo tape recorder.

THE CHORD DICTIONARY

This Chord Dictionary is designed to serve two purposes: first, as a reference section to be used with the *Playing the guitar* chapter, second, as a collection on popular sounds.

It is not a complete catalogue of guitar chords. Instead, we have chosen just 23 chords in each of the twelve keys. The choice is, of course, subjective, but by and large these 23 chords are the first ones that the average guitarist is likely to encounter when playing with other musicians.

The first five chords in each key – the major, the seventh, the minor, the minor seventh and the major seventh – are the "workhorses" which guitarists use most often. The other eighteen are those most frequently combined with the first five; they form an introduction to more sophisticated chords. At first, some of these may sound awkward. But, once you begin to play them in context with other chords, as part of a progression, they will sound better, make more sense and gradually become part of your repertoire.

How to use the Dictionary
Each chord is identified first by its symbol

Cmaj7 (C△7)

then by its full name

C major seventh

and then by its spelling

1st(C), 3rd (E), 5th (G), 7th (B).

The spelling tells you which notes make up the chord and at what intervals they occur in the diatonic major scale of the key.

The fingerboard is divided into three sections to show three positions in which each chord can be played. The top E string is at the top of the drawing and the bottom E string is at the bottom. The head of the guitar is on the left; the bridge is on the right. In other words, you are seeing the fingerboard as if you were looking down at it while playing. Quite simply, the numbered green circles tell you where to put your fingers. The unnumbered white circles indicate extra notes which you can add once you know the basic chord. Strings without a circle are played open (unfretted) unless they have an "X" on them – in which case you do not play them at all.

Chords can be played on the guitar in an almost infinite variety of "voicings". Over the range of the twelve keys, this results in thousands of fingering positions. Getting to grips with the full harmonic potential of the fingerboard is a lifetime's study. Therefore, in this book, we have put more emphasis on *understanding* chords than on simply learning them by rote. A full explanation of chords together with additional forms that do not appear in the Dictionary is set out on p. 121-37.

Example: Cmaj7 in three positions

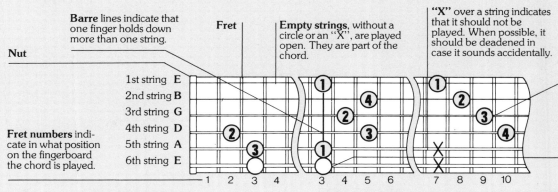

Barre lines indicate that one finger holds down more than one string.

Nut

Fret

Empty strings, without a circle or an "X", are played open. They are part of the chord.

"X" over a string indicates that it should not be played. When possible, it should be deadened in case it sounds accidentally.

Numbered green circles indicate the chord fingering. The number inside the circle tells you which finger to use.

Unnumbered white circles are optional notes which you can add to the chord if you wish – although you may need to alter the fingering.

1st string E
2nd string B
3rd string G
4th string D
5th string A
6th string E

Fret numbers indicate in what position on the fingerboard the chord is played.

1 2 3 4   3 4 5 6   7 8 9 10

First position
Follow the green circles: 2nd finger on 4th string, 2nd fret; 3rd finger on 5th string, 3rd fret (root note C); 1st, 2nd and 3rd strings are played open. Do not play 6th string unless you fret the extra G.

Second position
This is a "barre chord". 1st finger holds down both 1st and 5th strings on 3rd fret. Follow green circles for 2nd, 3rd and 4th fingers. You may add optional G on 6th string by extending barre.

Third position
In this form, the root note C is on 4th string, 10th fret. As before, numbered green circles show fingering position. 5th and 6th strings are not played.

Choosing the best fingering
The point of knowing at least three forms for each chord is so that you can interchange them. When you are playing a chord sequence, a form fairly high up the fingerboard may be much easier to get to than one at the bottom, down near the nut. Moreover, the different forms do not sound the same. Play them one after the other until you can hear the difference, and practise moving from one to the next – the smoother the better.

Most of the chord forms are "root positions" – that is, the lowest note is the root note of the chord. Once these forms have been learned, you should find it easy to move them up and down the fingerboard so that you can play the same chord in different keys (see p. 82). Sometimes the fingering of these basic forms can be altered slightly to accommodate open strings, to add optional notes or to substitute a different bass note.

Diminished chords occupy four "key-centres" and augmented chords occupy three. This means that one chord shape can be played in either three or four different places on the fingerboard. These chords are therefore a special case, and you should read the section on p. 128 to see how they work.

When playing chords consisting of more than four notes, you may not be able to play all the elements of the chord. In this case, you must select which notes to omit. Use the chord spelling to see which are the most important notes and experiment with different fingerings. Because the notes you choose will affect the sound of the chord, base your decision on the following factors: the arrangement of the notes in relation to one another (the bottom and top notes are predominant in the sound); the strings you wish to use; the position on the fingerboard; the function that the chord is to have between two others; and for how long it is to be heard in a progression.

Chords in **A**	Scale of A major						
	A	B	C♯	D	E	F♯	G♯
	1st	2nd	3rd	4th	5th	6th	7th
		9th		11th		13th	

A *A major*
Spelling: 1st (A), 3rd (C♯), 5th (E).

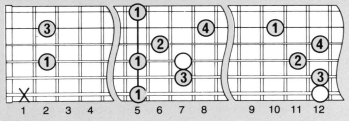

A 7 *A seventh*
Spelling: 1st (A), 3rd (C♯), 5th (E), ♭7th (G).

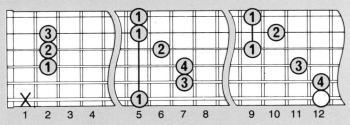

A m *A minor*
Spelling: 1st (A), ♭3rd (C), 5th (E).

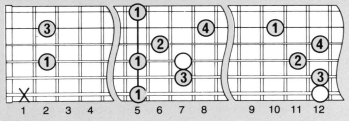

A m 7 *A minor seventh*
Spelling: 1st (A), ♭3rd (C), 5th (E), ♭7th (G).

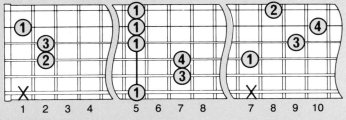

A maj 7 (A △ 7) *A major seventh*
Spelling: 1st (A), 3rd (C♯), 5th (E), 7th (G♯).

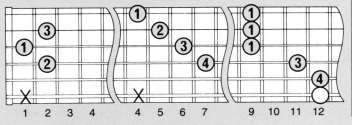

A sus 4 (A sus) *A suspended fourth*
Spelling: 1st (A), 4th (D), 5th (E). Note: no 3rd.

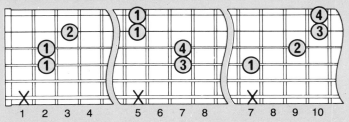

A 7 sus 4 (A 7+4) *A seventh suspended fourth*
Spelling: 1st (A), 4th (D), 5th (E), ♭7th (G). Note: no 3rd.

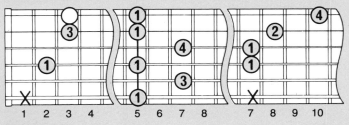

A 6 *A sixth*
Spelling: 1st (A), 3rd (C♯), 5th (E), 6th (F♯).

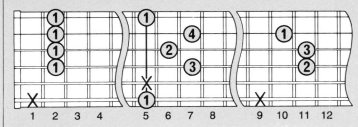

A m 6 *A minor sixth*
Spelling: 1st (A), ♭3rd (C), 5th (E), 6th (F♯).

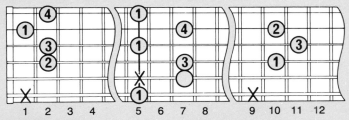

A 9 *A ninth*
Spelling: 1st (A), 3rd (C♯), 5th (E), ♭7th (G), 9th (B).

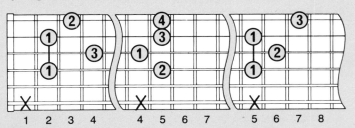

A m 9 *A minor ninth*
Spelling: 1st (A), ♭3rd (C), 5th (E), ♭7th (G), 9th (B).

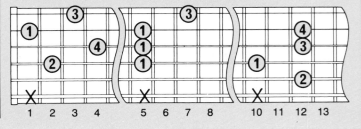

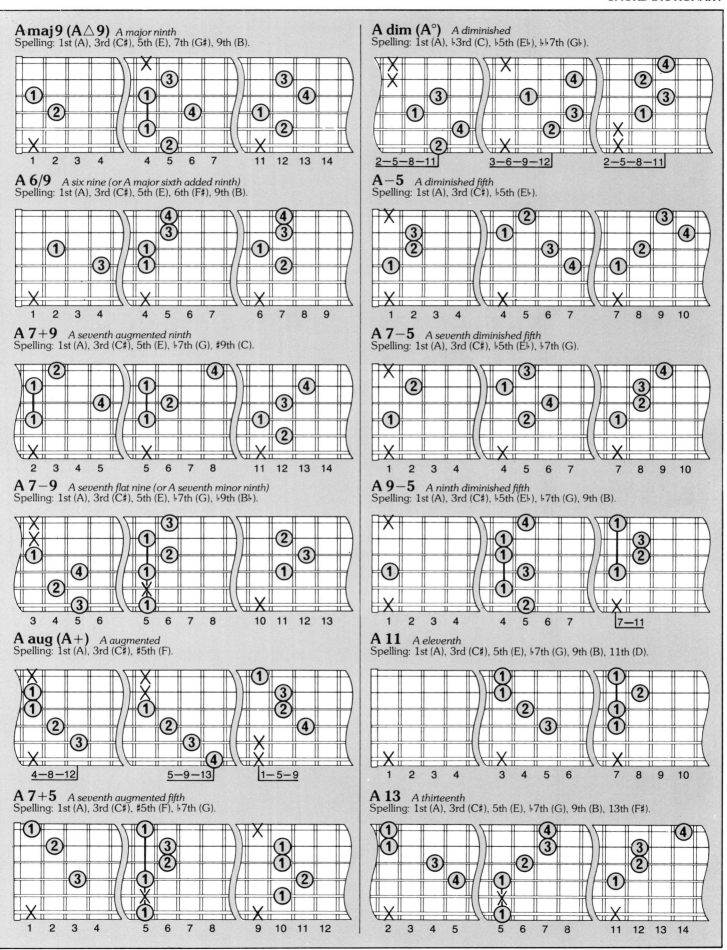

A maj9 (A△9) *A major ninth*
Spelling: 1st (A), 3rd (C#), 5th (E), 7th (G#), 9th (B).

A 6/9 *A six nine (or A major sixth added ninth)*
Spelling: 1st (A), 3rd (C#), 5th (E), 6th (F#), 9th (B).

A 7+9 *A seventh augmented ninth*
Spelling: 1st (A), 3rd (C#), 5th (E), ♭7th (G), #9th (C).

A 7−9 *A seventh flat nine (or A seventh minor ninth)*
Spelling: 1st (A), 3rd (C#), 5th (E), ♭7th (G), ♭9th (B♭).

A aug (A+) *A augmented*
Spelling: 1st (A), 3rd (C#), #5th (F).

A 7+5 *A seventh augmented fifth*
Spelling: 1st (A), 3rd (C#), #5th (F), ♭7th (G).

A dim (A°) *A diminished*
Spelling: 1st (A), ♭3rd (C), ♭5th (E♭), ♭♭7th (G♭).

A−5 *A diminished fifth*
Spelling: 1st (A), 3rd (C#), ♭5th (E♭).

A 7−5 *A seventh diminished fifth*
Spelling: 1st (A), 3rd (C#), ♭5th (E♭), ♭7th (G).

A 9−5 *A ninth diminished fifth*
Spelling: 1st (A), 3rd (C#), ♭5th (E♭), ♭7th (G), 9th (B).

A 11 *A eleventh*
Spelling: 1st (A), 3rd (C#), 5th (E), ♭7th (G), 9th (B), 11th (D).

A 13 *A thirteenth*
Spelling: 1st (A), 3rd (C#), 5th (E), ♭7th (G), 9th (B), 13th (F#).

Chords in A♯ B♭

Scale of A♯ major B♭ major						
A♯ B♭	C	D	D♯ E♭	F	G	A
1st	2nd	3rd	4th	5th	6th	7th
	9th		11th		13th	

Note A♯ and B♭ are two names for the same note (called "enharmonic"). Chords are shown here in B♭ because this tends to be the more commonly used key.

B♭ *B flat major*
Spelling: 1st (B♭), 3rd (D), 5th (F).

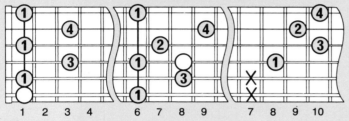

B♭ 7 *B flat seventh*
Spelling: 1st (B♭), 3rd (D), 5th (F), ♭7th (A♭).

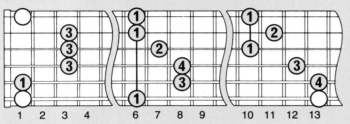

B♭ m *B flat minor*
Spelling: 1st (B♭), ♭3rd (D♭), 5th (F).

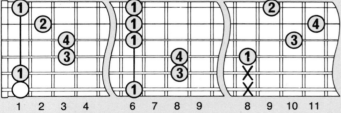

B♭ m7 *B flat minor seventh*
Spelling: 1st (B♭), ♭3rd (D♭), 5th (F), ♭7th (A♭).

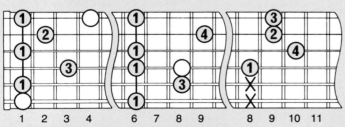

B♭ maj7 (B♭△7) *B flat major seventh*
Spelling: 1st (B♭), 3rd (D), 5th (F), 7th (A).

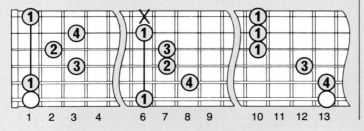

B♭ sus 4 (B♭ sus) *B flat suspended fourth*
Spelling: 1st (B♭), 4th (E♭), 5th (F). Note: no 3rd.

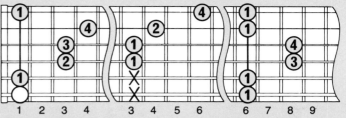

B♭ 7sus4 (B♭ 7+4) *B flat seventh suspended fourth*
Spelling: 1st (B♭), 4th (E♭), 5th (F), ♭7th (A♭). Note: no 3rd.

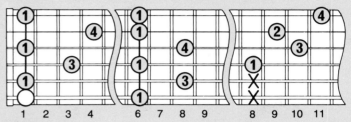

B♭ 6 *B flat sixth*
Spelling: 1st (B♭), 3rd (D), 5th (F), 6th (G).

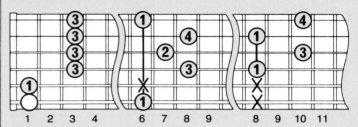

B♭ m6 *B flat minor sixth*
Spelling: 1st (B♭), ♭3rd (D♭), 5th (F), 6th (G).

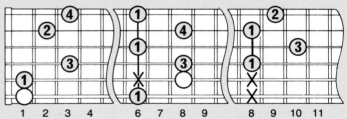

B♭ 9 *B flat ninth*
Spelling: 1st (B♭), 3rd (D), 5th (F), ♭7th (A♭), 9th (C).

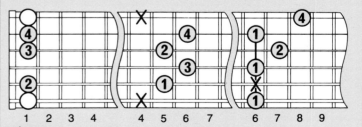

B♭ m9 *B flat minor ninth*
Spelling: 1st (B♭), ♭3rd (D♭), 5th (F), ♭7th (A♭), 9th (C).

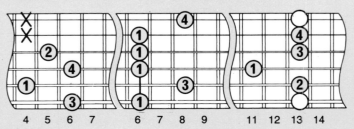

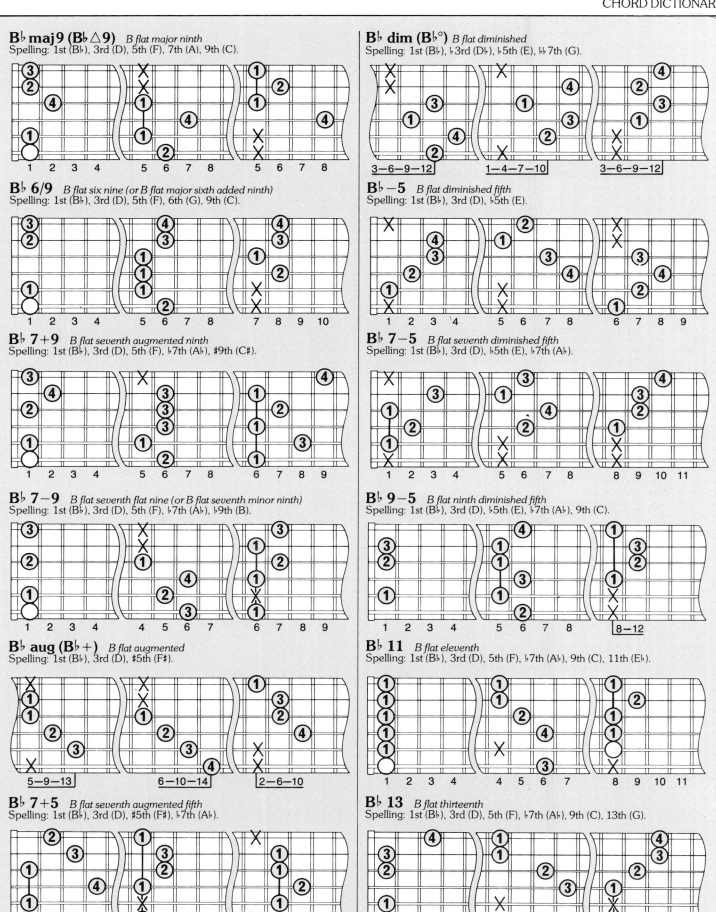

B♭ maj9 (B♭△9) *B flat major ninth*
Spelling: 1st (B♭), 3rd (D), 5th (F), 7th (A), 9th (C).

B♭ 6/9 *B flat six nine (or B flat major sixth added ninth)*
Spelling: 1st (B♭), 3rd (D), 5th (F), 6th (G), 9th (C).

B♭ 7+9 *B flat seventh augmented ninth*
Spelling: 1st (B♭), 3rd (D), 5th (F), ♭7th (A♭), ♯9th (C♯).

B♭ 7−9 *B flat seventh flat nine (or B flat seventh minor ninth)*
Spelling: 1st (B♭), 3rd (D), 5th (F), ♭7th (A♭), ♭9th (B).

B♭ aug (B♭+) *B flat augmented*
Spelling: 1st (B♭), 3rd (D), ♯5th (F♯).

B♭ 7+5 *B flat seventh augmented fifth*
Spelling: 1st (B♭), 3rd (D), ♯5th (F♯), ♭7th (A♭).

B♭ dim (B♭°) *B flat diminished*
Spelling: 1st (B♭), ♭3rd (D♭), ♭5th (E), ♭♭7th (G).

B♭ −5 *B flat diminished fifth*
Spelling: 1st (B♭), 3rd (D), ♭5th (E).

B♭ 7−5 *B flat seventh diminished fifth*
Spelling: 1st (B♭), 3rd (D), ♭5th (E), ♭7th (A♭).

B♭ 9−5 *B flat ninth diminished fifth*
Spelling: 1st (B♭), 3rd (D), ♭5th (E), ♭7th (A♭), 9th (C).

B♭ 11 *B flat eleventh*
Spelling: 1st (B♭), 3rd (D), 5th (F), ♭7th (A♭), 9th (C), 11th (E♭).

B♭ 13 *B flat thirteenth*
Spelling: 1st (B♭), 3rd (D), 5th (F), ♭7th (A♭), 9th (C), 13th (G).

229

Chords in

B

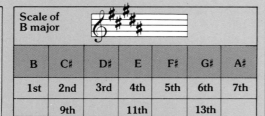

Scale of B major	B	C#	D#	E	F#	G#	A#
	1st	2nd	3rd	4th	5th	6th	7th
		9th		11th		13th	

B *B major*
Spelling: 1st (B), 3rd (D#), 5th (F#).

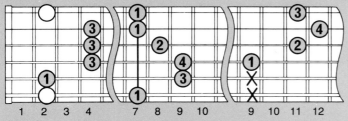

B 7 *B seventh*
Spelling: 1st (B), 3rd (D#), 5th (F#), ♭7th (A).

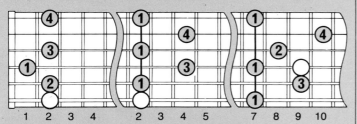

B m *B minor*
Spelling: 1st (B), ♭3rd (D), 5th (F#).

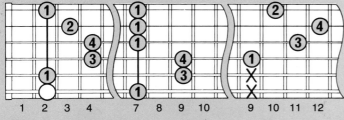

B m 7 *B minor seventh*
Spelling: 1st (B), ♭3rd (D), 5th (F#), ♭7th (A).

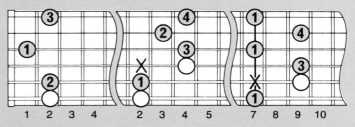

B maj 7 (B△7) *B major seventh*
Spelling: 1st (B), 3rd (D#), 5th (F#), 7th (A#).

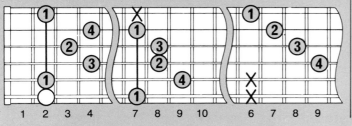

B sus 4 (B sus) *B suspended fourth*
Spelling: 1st (B), 4th (E), 5th (F#). Note: no 3rd.

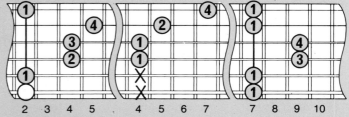

B 7 sus 4 (B7+4) *B seventh suspended fourth*
Spelling: 1st (B), 4th (E), 5th (F#), ♭7th (A). Note: no 3rd.

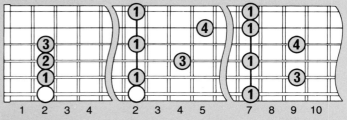

B 6 *B sixth*
Spelling: 1st (B), 3rd (D#), 5th (F#), 6th (G#).

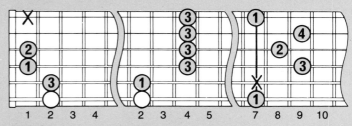

B m 6 *B minor sixth*
Spelling: 1st (B), ♭3rd (D), 5th (F#), 6th (G#).

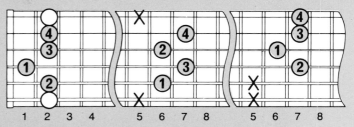

B 9 *B ninth*
Spelling: 1st (B), 3rd (D#), 5th (F#), ♭7th (A), 9th (C#).

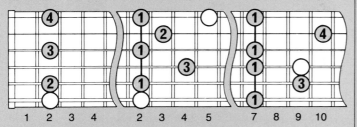

B m 9 *B minor ninth*
Spelling: 1st (B), ♭3rd (D), 5th (F#), ♭7th (A), 9th (C#).

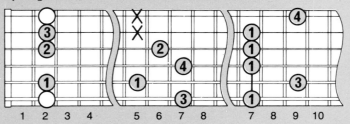

B maj9 (B△9) *B major ninth*
Spelling: 1st (B), 3rd (D♯), 5th (F♯), 7th (A♯), 9th (C♯).

B dim (B°) *B diminished*
Spelling: 1st (B), ♭3rd (D), ♭5th (F), ♭♭7th (A♭).

B 6/9 *B six nine (or B major sixth added ninth)*
Spelling: 1st (B), 3rd (D♯), 5th (F♯), 6th (G♯), 9th (C♯).

B−5 *B diminished fifth*
Spelling: 1st (B), 3rd (D♯), ♭5th (F).

B 7+9 *B seventh augmented ninth*
Spelling: 1st (B), 3rd (D♯), 5th (F♯), ♭7th (A), ♯9th (D).

B 7−5 *B seventh diminished fifth*
Spelling: 1st (B), 3rd (D♯), ♭5th (F), ♭7th (A).

B 7−9 *B seventh flat nine (or B seventh minor ninth)*
Spelling: 1st (B), 3rd (D♯), 5th (F♯), ♭7th (A), ♭9th (C).

B 9−5 *B ninth diminished fifth*
Spelling: 1st (B), 3rd (D♯), ♭5th (F), ♭7th (A), 9th (C♯).

B aug (B+) *B augmented*
Spelling: 1st (B), 3rd (D♯), ♯5th (G).

B 11 *B eleventh*
Spelling: 1st (B), 3rd (D♯), 5th (F♯), ♭7th (A), 9th (C♯), 11th (E).

B 7+5 *B seventh augmented fifth*
Spelling: 1st (B), 3rd (D♯), ♯5th (G), ♭7th (A).

B 13 *B thirteenth*
Spelling: 1st (B), 3rd (D♯), 5th (F♯), ♭7th (A), 9th (C♯), 13th (G♯).

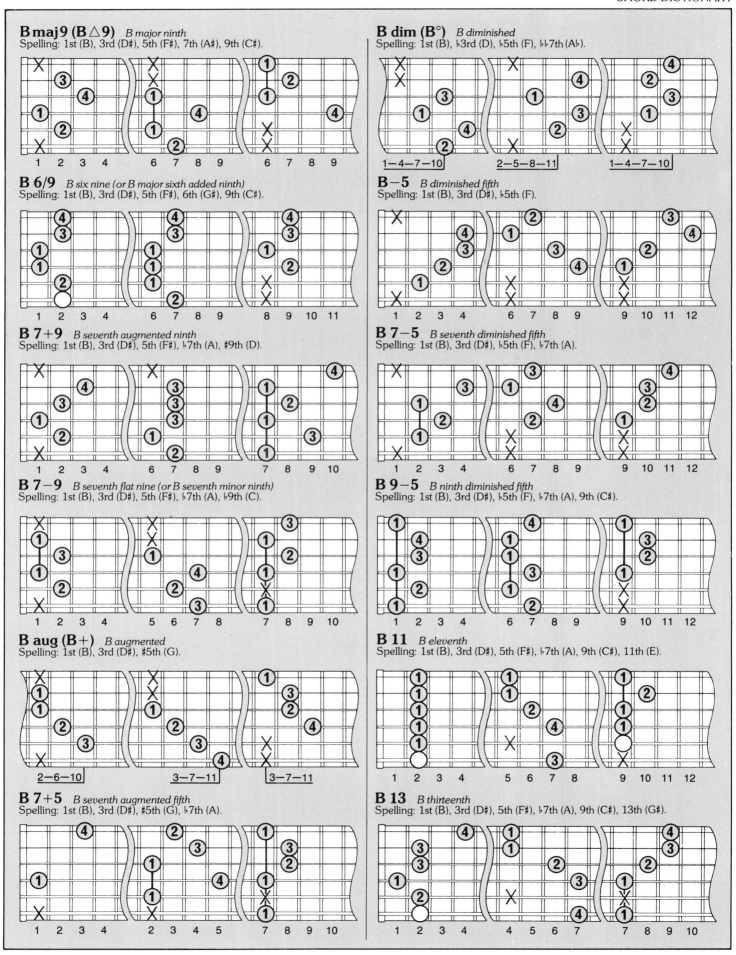

231

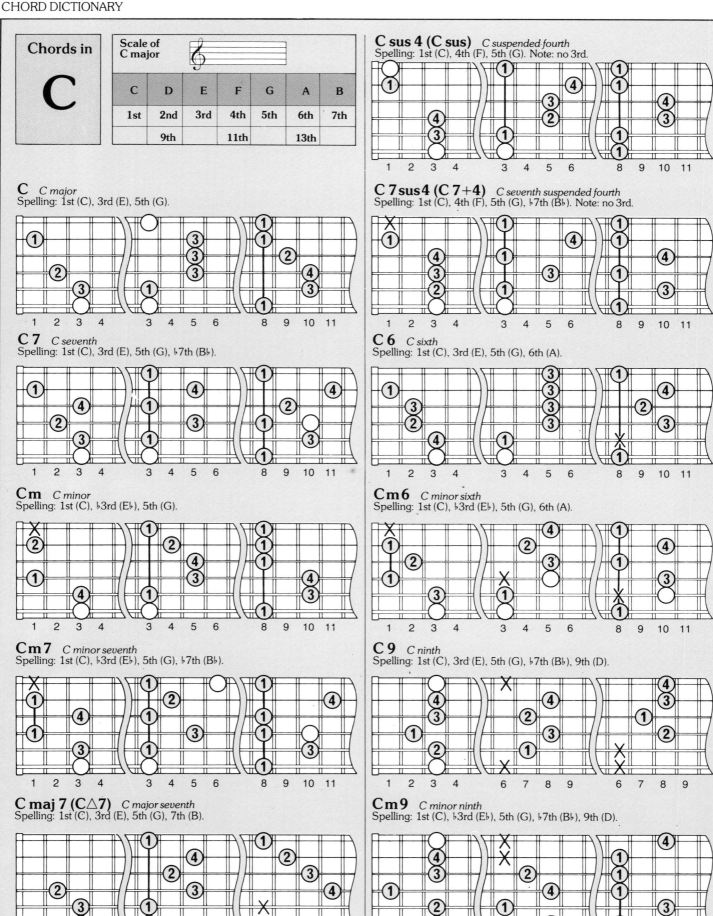

Chords in C

Scale of C major						
C	D	E	F	G	A	B
1st	2nd	3rd	4th	5th	6th	7th
	9th		11th		13th	

C *C major*
Spelling: 1st (C), 3rd (E), 5th (G).

C 7 *C seventh*
Spelling: 1st (C), 3rd (E), 5th (G), ♭7th (B♭).

Cm *C minor*
Spelling: 1st (C), ♭3rd (E♭), 5th (G).

Cm 7 *C minor seventh*
Spelling: 1st (C), ♭3rd (E♭), 5th (G), ♭7th (B♭).

C maj 7 (C△7) *C major seventh*
Spelling: 1st (C), 3rd (E), 5th (G), 7th (B).

C sus 4 (C sus) *C suspended fourth*
Spelling: 1st (C), 4th (F), 5th (G). Note: no 3rd.

C 7 sus 4 (C 7+4) *C seventh suspended fourth*
Spelling: 1st (C), 4th (F), 5th (G), ♭7th (B♭). Note: no 3rd.

C 6 *C sixth*
Spelling: 1st (C), 3rd (E), 5th (G), 6th (A).

Cm 6 *C minor sixth*
Spelling: 1st (C), ♭3rd (E♭), 5th (G), 6th (A).

C 9 *C ninth*
Spelling: 1st (C), 3rd (E), 5th (G), ♭7th (B♭), 9th (D).

Cm 9 *C minor ninth*
Spelling: 1st (C), ♭3rd (E♭), 5th (G), ♭7th (B♭), 9th (D).

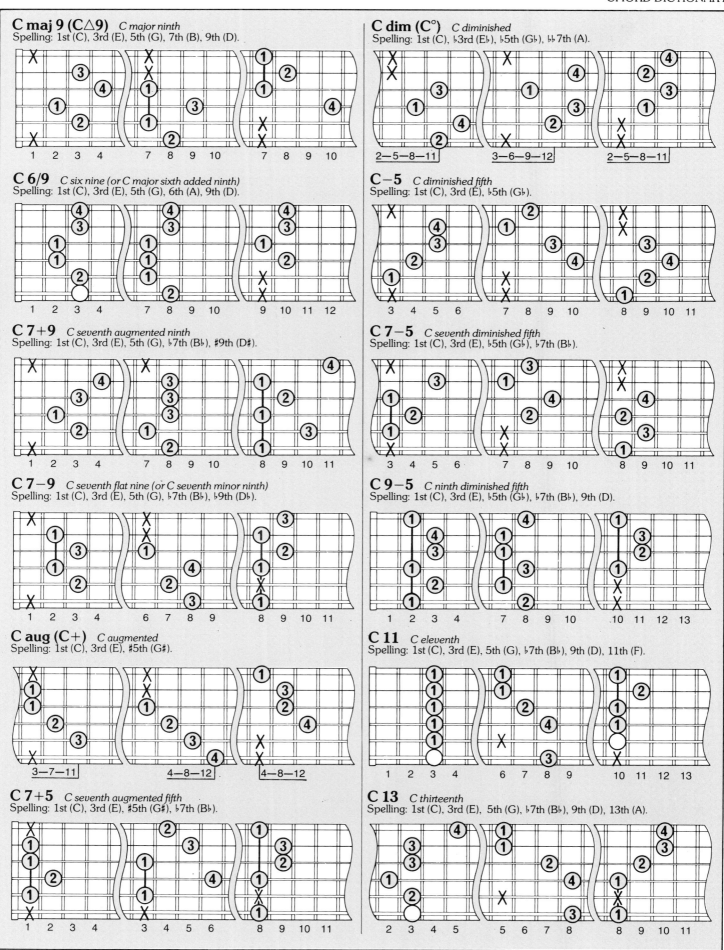

C maj 9 (C△9) *C major ninth*
Spelling: 1st (C), 3rd (E), 5th (G), 7th (B), 9th (D).

C 6/9 *C six nine (or C major sixth added ninth)*
Spelling: 1st (C), 3rd (E), 5th (G), 6th (A), 9th (D).

C 7+9 *C seventh augmented ninth*
Spelling: 1st (C), 3rd (E), 5th (G), ♭7th (B♭), ♯9th (D♯).

C 7−9 *C seventh flat nine (or C seventh minor ninth)*
Spelling: 1st (C), 3rd (E), 5th (G), ♭7th (B♭), ♭9th (D♭).

C aug (C+) *C augmented*
Spelling: 1st (C), 3rd (E), ♯5th (G♯).

C 7+5 *C seventh augmented fifth*
Spelling: 1st (C), 3rd (E), ♯5th (G♯), ♭7th (B♭).

C dim (C°) *C diminished*
Spelling: 1st (C), ♭3rd (E♭), ♭5th (G♭), ♭♭7th (A).

C−5 *C diminished fifth*
Spelling: 1st (C), 3rd (E), ♭5th (G♭).

C 7−5 *C seventh diminished fifth*
Spelling: 1st (C), 3rd (E), ♭5th (G♭), ♭7th (B♭).

C 9−5 *C ninth diminished fifth*
Spelling: 1st (C), 3rd (E), ♭5th (G♭), ♭7th (B♭), 9th (D).

C 11 *C eleventh*
Spelling: 1st (C), 3rd (E), 5th (G), ♭7th (B♭), 9th (D), 11th (F).

C 13 *C thirteenth*
Spelling: 1st (C), 3rd (E), 5th (G), ♭7th (B♭), 9th (D), 13th (A).

233

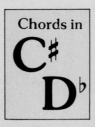

Chords in C♯ D♭

Scale of C♯ major D♭ major						
C♯ D♭	D♯ E♭	F	F♯ G♭	G♯ A♭	A♯ B♭	C
1st	2nd	3rd	4th	5th	6th	7th
	9th		11th		13th	

Note C♯ and D♭ are two names for the same note (called "enharmonic"). Chords are shown here in C♯ because this tends to be the more commonly used key.

C♯ *C sharp major*
Spelling: 1st (C♯), 3rd (F), 5th (G♯).

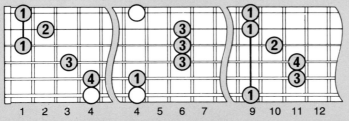

C♯ 7 *C sharp seventh*
Spelling: 1st (C♯), 3rd (F), 5th (G♯), ♭7th (B).

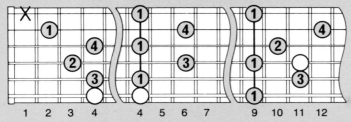

C♯ m *C sharp minor*
Spelling: 1st (C♯), ♭3rd (E), 5th (G♯).

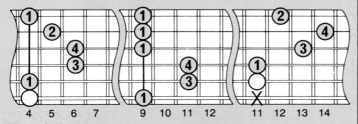

C♯ m 7 *C sharp minor seventh*
Spelling: 1st (C♯), ♭3rd (E), 5th (G♯), ♭7th (B).

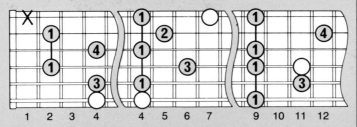

C♯ maj 7 (C♯ △ 7) *C sharp major seventh*
Spelling: 1st (C♯), 3rd (F), 5th (G♯), 7th (C).

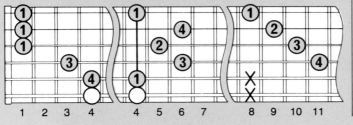

C♯ sus 4 (C♯ sus) *C sharp suspended fourth*
Spelling: 1st (C♯), 4th (F♯), 5th (G♯). Note: no 3rd.

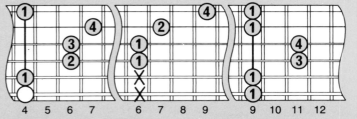

C♯ 7 sus 4 (C♯ 7+4) *C sharp seventh suspended fourth*
Spelling: 1st (C♯), 4th (F♯), 5th (G♯), ♭7th (B). Note: no 3rd.

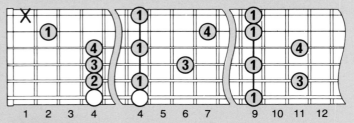

C♯ 6 *C sharp sixth*
Spelling: 1st (C♯), 3rd (F), 5th (G♯), 6th (A♯).

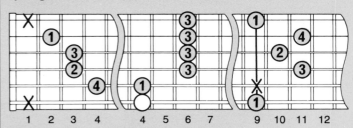

C♯ m 6 *C sharp minor sixth*
Spelling: 1st (C♯), ♭3rd (E), 5th (G♯), 6th (A♯).

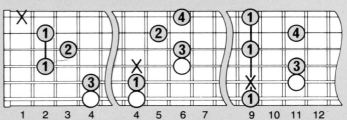

C♯ 9 *C sharp ninth*
Spelling: 1st (C♯), 3rd (F), 5th (G♯), ♭7th (B), 9th (D♯).

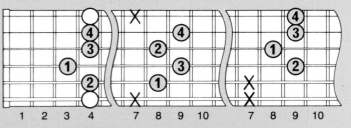

C♯ m 9 *C sharp minor ninth*
Spelling: 1st (C♯), ♭3rd (E), 5th (G♯), ♭7th (B), 9th (D♯).

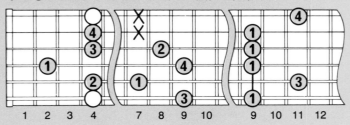

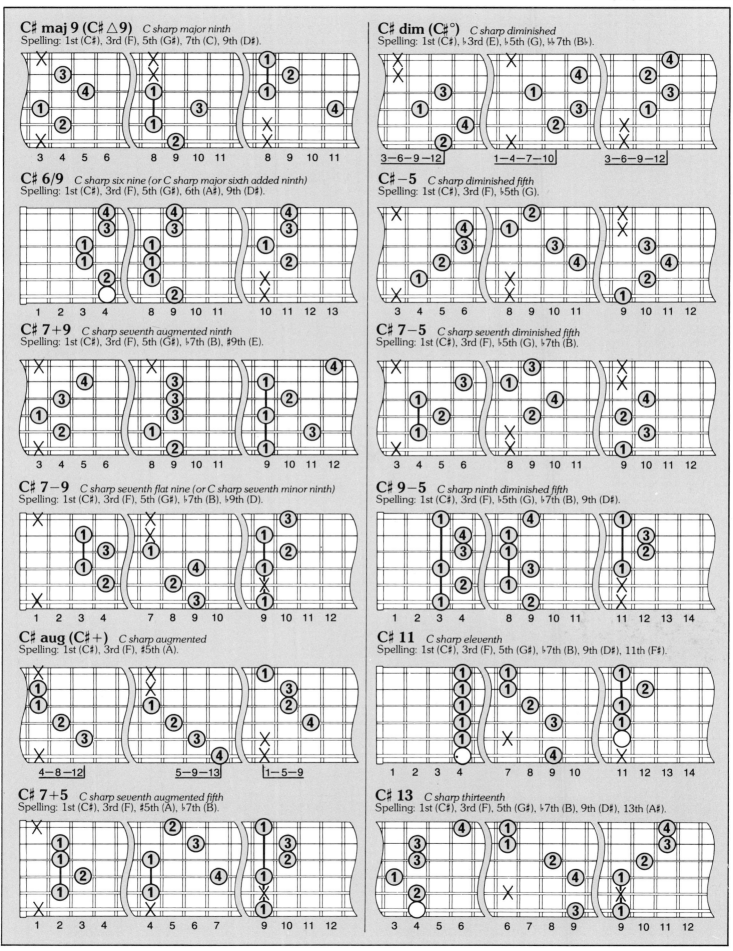

C♯ maj 9 (C♯△9) *C sharp major ninth*
Spelling: 1st (C♯), 3rd (F), 5th (G♯), 7th (C), 9th (D♯).

C♯ 6/9 *C sharp six nine (or C sharp major sixth added ninth)*
Spelling: 1st (C♯), 3rd (F), 5th (G♯), 6th (A♯), 9th (D♯).

C♯ 7+9 *C sharp seventh augmented ninth*
Spelling: 1st (C♯), 3rd (F), 5th (G♯), ♭7th (B), ♯9th (E).

C♯ 7−9 *C sharp seventh flat nine (or C sharp seventh minor ninth)*
Spelling: 1st (C♯), 3rd (F), 5th (G♯), ♭7th (B), ♭9th (D).

C♯ aug (C♯+) *C sharp augmented*
Spelling: 1st (C♯), 3rd (F), ♯5th (A).

C♯ 7+5 *C sharp seventh augmented fifth*
Spelling: 1st (C♯), 3rd (F), ♯5th (A), ♭7th (B).

C♯ dim (C♯°) *C sharp diminished*
Spelling: 1st (C♯), ♭3rd (E), ♭5th (G), ♭♭7th (B♭).

C♯ −5 *C sharp diminished fifth*
Spelling: 1st (C♯), 3rd (F), ♭5th (G).

C♯ 7−5 *C sharp seventh diminished fifth*
Spelling: 1st (C♯), 3rd (F), ♭5th (G), ♭7th (B).

C♯ 9−5 *C sharp ninth diminished fifth*
Spelling: 1st (C♯), 3rd (F), ♭5th (G), ♭7th (B), 9th (D♯).

C♯ 11 *C sharp eleventh*
Spelling: 1st (C♯), 3rd (F), 5th (G♯), ♭7th (B), 9th (D♯), 11th (F♯).

C♯ 13 *C sharp thirteenth*
Spelling: 1st (C♯), 3rd (F), 5th (G♯), ♭7th (B), 9th (D♯), 13th (A♯).

Chords in

D

Scale of D major						
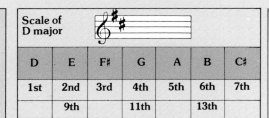
D	E	F#	G	A	B	C#
1st	2nd	3rd	4th	5th	6th	7th
	9th		11th		13th	

D sus 4 (D sus) *D suspended fourth*
Spelling: 1st (D), 4th (G), 5th (A). Note: no 3rd.

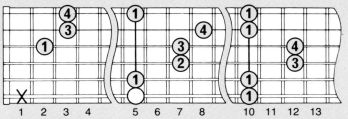

D *D major*
Spelling: 1st (D), 3rd (F#), 5th (A).

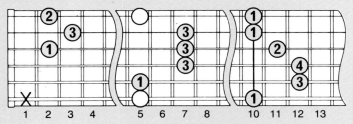

D 7 sus 4 (D 7+4) *D seventh suspended fourth*
Spelling: 1st (D), 4th (G), 5th (A), ♭7th (C). Note: no 3rd.

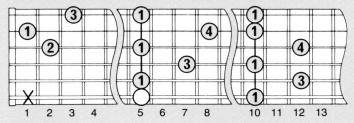

D 7 *D seventh*
Spelling: 1st (D), 3rd (F#), 5th (A), ♭7th (C).

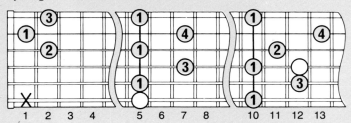

D 6 *D sixth*
Spelling: 1st (D), 3rd (F#), 5th (A), 6th (B).

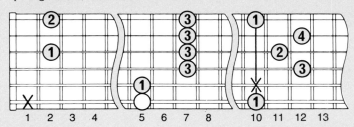

Dm *D minor*
Spelling: 1st (D), ♭3rd (F), 5th (A).

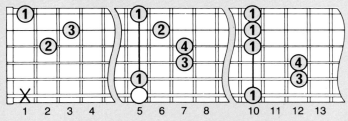

Dm 6 *D minor sixth*
Spelling: 1st (D), ♭3rd (F), 5th (A), 6th (B).

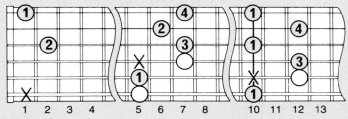

Dm 7 *D minor seventh*
Spelling: 1st (D), ♭3rd (F), 5th (A), ♭7th (C).

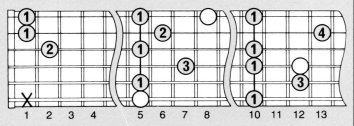

D 9 *D ninth*
Spelling: 1st (D), 3rd (F#), 5th (A), ♭7th (C), 9th (E).

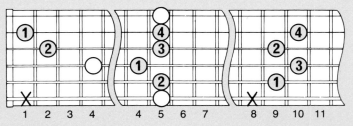

Dmaj 7 (D△7) *D major seventh*
Spelling: 1st (D), 3rd (F#), 5th (A), 7th (C#).

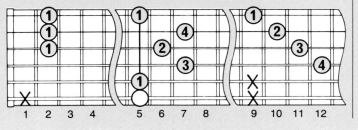

Dm 9 *D minor ninth*
Spelling: 1st (D), ♭3rd (F), 5th (A), ♭7th (C), 9th (E).

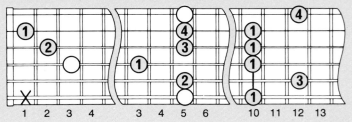

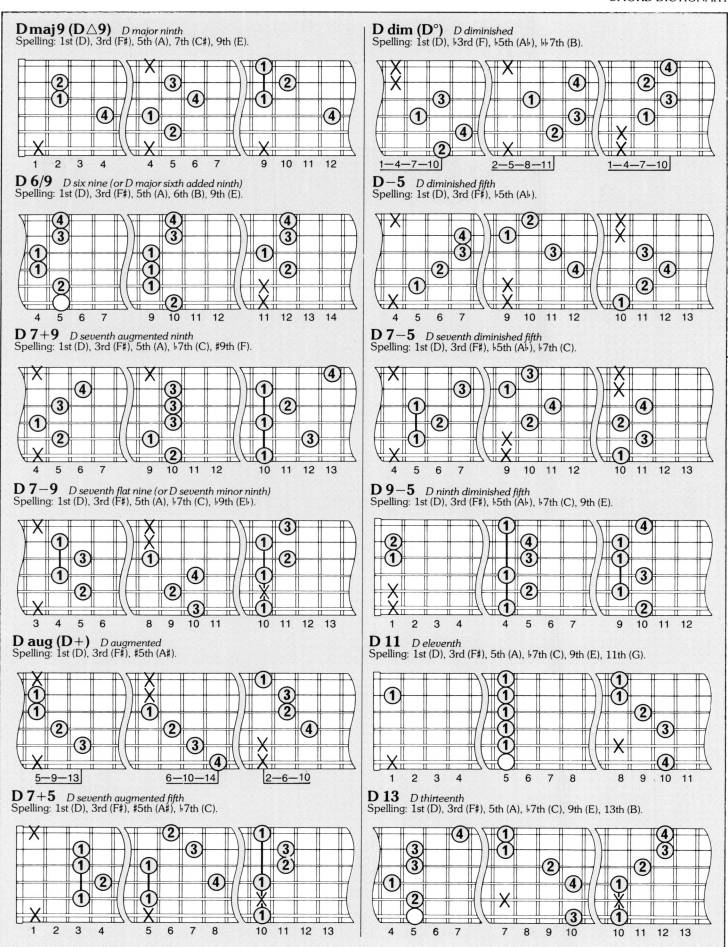

D maj 9 (D△9) *D major ninth*
Spelling: 1st (D), 3rd (F#), 5th (A), 7th (C#), 9th (E).

D 6/9 *D six nine (or D major sixth added ninth)*
Spelling: 1st (D), 3rd (F#), 5th (A), 6th (B), 9th (E).

D 7+9 *D seventh augmented ninth*
Spelling: 1st (D), 3rd (F#), 5th (A), ♭7th (C), #9th (F).

D 7−9 *D seventh flat nine (or D seventh minor ninth)*
Spelling: 1st (D), 3rd (F#), 5th (A), ♭7th (C), ♭9th (E♭).

D aug (D+) *D augmented*
Spelling: 1st (D), 3rd (F#), #5th (A#).

D 7+5 *D seventh augmented fifth*
Spelling: 1st (D), 3rd (F#), #5th (A#), ♭7th (C).

D dim (D°) *D diminished*
Spelling: 1st (D), ♭3rd (F), ♭5th (A♭), ♭♭7th (B).

D −5 *D diminished fifth*
Spelling: 1st (D), 3rd (F#), ♭5th (A♭).

D 7−5 *D seventh diminished fifth*
Spelling: 1st (D), 3rd (F#), ♭5th (A♭), ♭7th (C).

D 9−5 *D ninth diminished fifth*
Spelling: 1st (D), 3rd (F#), ♭5th (A♭), ♭7th (C), 9th (E).

D 11 *D eleventh*
Spelling: 1st (D), 3rd (F#), 5th (A), ♭7th (C), 9th (E), 11th (G).

D 13 *D thirteenth*
Spelling: 1st (D), 3rd (F#), 5th (A), ♭7th (C), 9th (E), 13th (B).

237

Chords in D♯ E♭

Scale of D♯ major E♭ major						
D♯ / E♭	F	G	G♯ / A♭	A♯ / B♭	C	D
1st	2nd	3rd	4th	5th	6th	7th
	9th		11th		13th	

Note D♯ and E♭ are two names for the same note (called "enharmonic"). Chords are shown here in E♭ because this tends to be the more commonly used key.

E♭ *E flat major*
Spelling: 1st (E♭), 3rd (G), 5th (B♭).

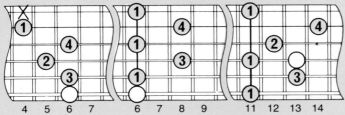

E♭7 *E flat seventh*
Spelling: 1st (E♭), 3rd (G), 5th (B♭), ♭7th (D♭).

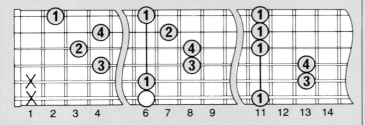

E♭m *E flat minor*
Spelling: 1st (E♭), ♭3rd (G♭), 5th (B♭).

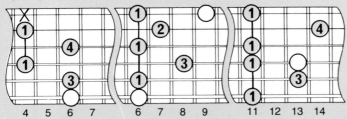

E♭m7 *E flat minor seventh*
Spelling: 1st (E♭), ♭3rd (G♭), 5th (B♭), ♭7th (D♭).

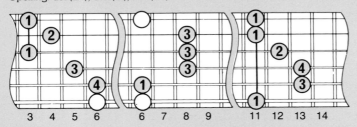

E♭maj7 (E♭△7) *E flat major seventh*
Spelling: 1st (E♭), 3rd (G), 5th (B♭), 7th (D).

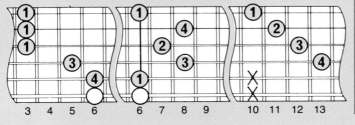

E♭sus4 (E♭sus) *E flat suspended fourth*
Spelling: 1st (E♭), 4th (A♭), 5th (B♭). Note: no 3rd.

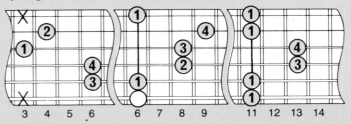

E♭7sus4 (E♭7+4) *E flat seventh suspended fourth*
Spelling: 1st (E♭), 4th (A♭), 5th (B♭), ♭7th (D♭). Note: no 3rd.

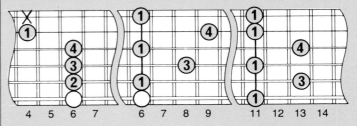

E♭6 *E flat sixth*
Spelling: 1st (E♭), 3rd (G), 5th (B♭), 6th (C).

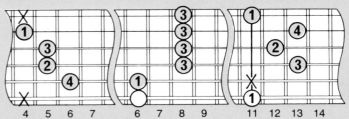

E♭m6 *E flat minor sixth*
Spelling: 1st (E♭), ♭3rd (G♭), 5th (B♭), 6th (C).

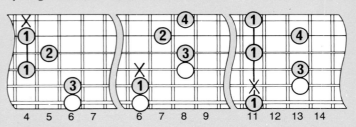

E♭9 *E flat ninth*
Spelling: 1st (E♭), 3rd (G), 5th (B♭), ♭7th (D♭), 9th (F).

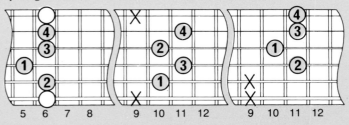

E♭m9 *E flat minor ninth*
Spelling: 1st (E♭), ♭3rd (G♭), 5th (B♭), ♭7th (D♭), 9th (F).

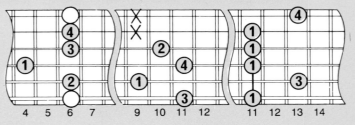

E♭ maj9 (E♭△9) *E flat major ninth*
Spelling: 1st (E♭), 3rd (G), 5th (B♭), 7th (D), 9th (F).

E♭ 6/9 *E flat six nine (or E flat major sixth added ninth)*
Spelling: 1st (E♭), 3rd (G), 5th (B♭), 6th (C), 9th (F).

E♭ 7+9 *E flat seventh augmented ninth*
Spelling: 1st (E♭), 3rd (G), 5th (B♭), ♭7th (D♭), ♯9th (F♯).

E♭ 7−9 *E flat seventh flat nine (or E flat seventh minor ninth)*
Spelling: 1st (E♭), 3rd (G), 5th (B♭), ♭7th (D♭), ♭9th (E).

E♭ aug (E♭+) *E flat augmented*
Spelling: 1st (E♭), 3rd (G), ♯5th (B).

E♭ 7+5 *E flat seventh augmented fifth*
Spelling: 1st (E♭), 3rd (G), ♯5th (B), ♭7th (D♭).

E♭ dim (E♭°) *E flat diminished*
Spelling: 1st (E♭), ♭3rd (G♭), ♭5th (A), ♭♭7th (C).

E♭ −5 *E flat diminished fifth*
Spelling: 1st (E), 3rd (G), ♭5th (A).

E♭ 7−5 *E flat seventh diminished fifth*
Spelling: 1st (E♭), 3rd (G), ♭5th (A), ♭7th (D♭).

E♭ 9−5 *E flat ninth diminished fifth*
Spelling: 1st (E♭), 3rd (G), ♭5th (A), ♭7th (D♭), 9th (F).

E♭ 11 *E flat eleventh*
Spelling: 1st (E♭), 3rd (G), 5th (B♭), ♭7th (D♭), 9th (F), 11th (A♭).

E♭ 13 *E flat thirteenth*
Spelling: 1st (E♭), 3rd (G), 5th (B♭), ♭7th (D♭), 9th (F), 13th (C).

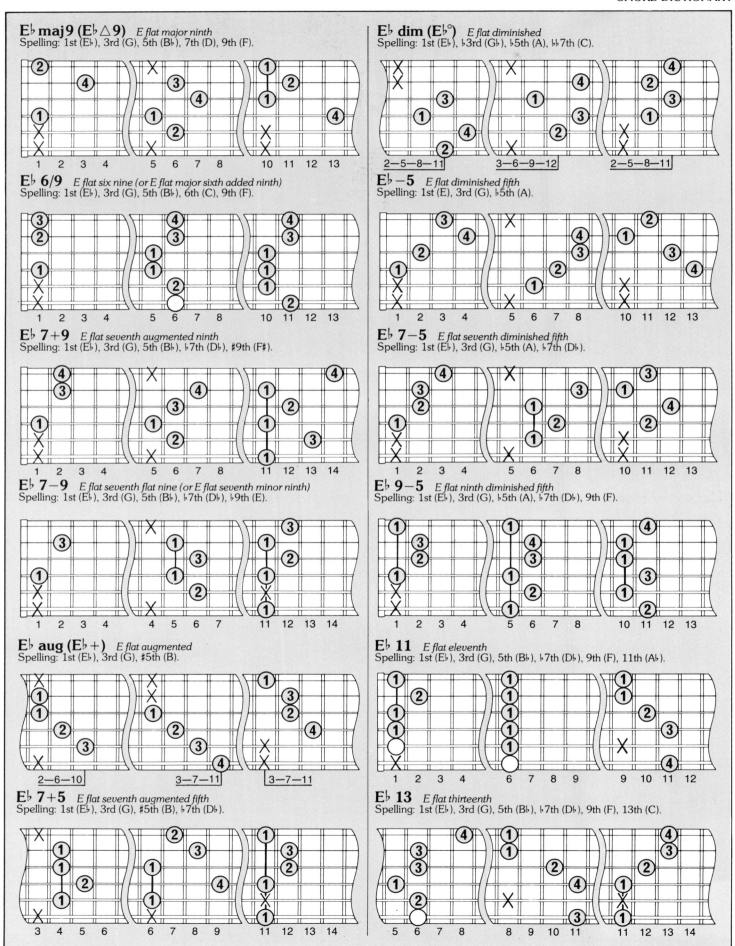

239

Chords in E

Scale of E major	E	F#	G#	A	B	C#	D#
	1st	2nd	3rd	4th	5th	6th	7th
		9th		11th		13th	

E sus 4 (E sus) *E suspended fourth*
Spelling: 1st (E), 4th (A), 5th (B). Note: no 3rd.

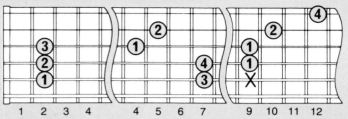

E *E major*
Spelling: 1st (E), 3rd (G#), 5th (B).

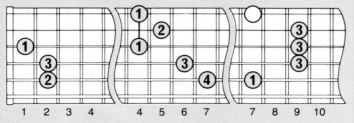

E 7 sus 4 (E 7+4) *E seventh suspended fourth*
Spelling: 1st (E), 4th (A), 5th (B), ♭7th (D). Note: no 3rd.

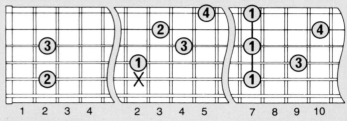

E 7 *E seventh*
Spelling: 1st (E), 3rd (G#), 5th (B), ♭7th (D).

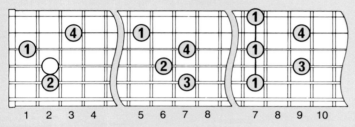

E 6 *E sixth*
Spelling: 1st (E), 3rd (G#), 5th (B), 6th (C#).

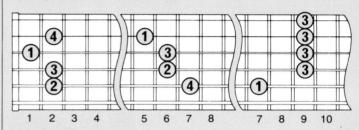

Em *E minor*
Spelling: 1st (E), ♭3rd (G), 5th (B).

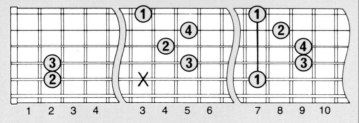

Em 6 *E minor sixth*
Spelling: 1st (E), ♭3rd (G), 5th (B), 6th (C#).

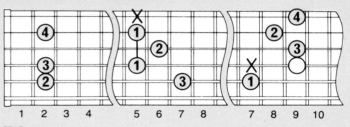

Em 7 *E minor seventh*
Spelling: 1st (E), ♭3rd (G), 5th (B), ♭7th (D).

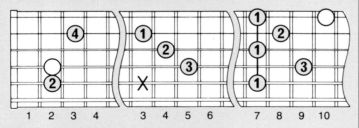

E 9 *E ninth*
Spelling: 1st (E), 3rd (G#), 5th (B), ♭7th (D), 9th (F#).

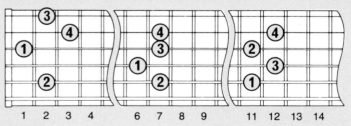

Emaj 7 (E△7) *E major seventh*
Spelling: 1st (E), 3rd (G#), 5th (B), 7th (D#).

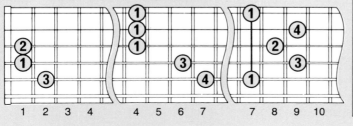

Em 9 *E minor ninth*
Spelling: 1st (E), ♭3rd (G), 5th (B), ♭7th (D), 9th (F#).

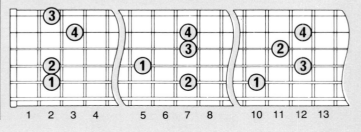

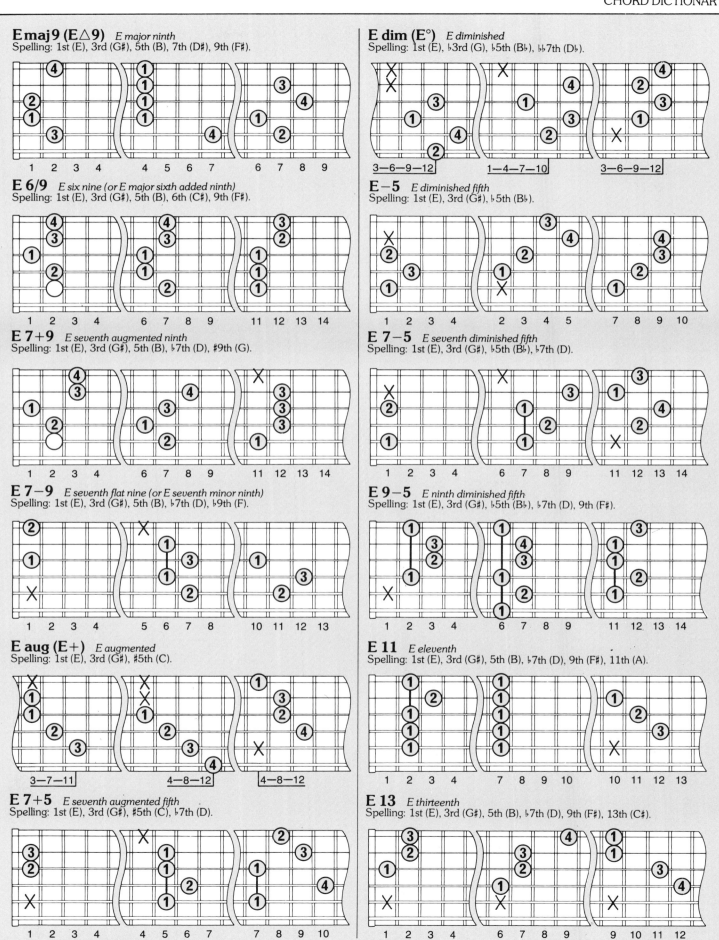

E maj 9 (E△9) *E major ninth*
Spelling: 1st (E), 3rd (G♯), 5th (B), 7th (D♯), 9th (F♯).

E 6/9 *E six nine (or E major sixth added ninth)*
Spelling: 1st (E), 3rd (G♯), 5th (B), 6th (C♯), 9th (F♯).

E 7+9 *E seventh augmented ninth*
Spelling: 1st (E), 3rd (G♯), 5th (B), ♭7th (D), ♯9th (G).

E 7−9 *E seventh flat nine (or E seventh minor ninth)*
Spelling: 1st (E), 3rd (G♯), 5th (B), ♭7th (D), ♭9th (F).

E aug (E+) *E augmented*
Spelling: 1st (E), 3rd (G♯), ♯5th (C).

E 7+5 *E seventh augmented fifth*
Spelling: 1st (E), 3rd (G♯), ♯5th (C), ♭7th (D).

E dim (E°) *E diminished*
Spelling: 1st (E), ♭3rd (G), ♭5th (B♭), ♭♭7th (D♭).

E−5 *E diminished fifth*
Spelling: 1st (E), 3rd (G♯), ♭5th (B♭).

E 7−5 *E seventh diminished fifth*
Spelling: 1st (E), 3rd (G♯), ♭5th (B♭), ♭7th (D).

E 9−5 *E ninth diminished fifth*
Spelling: 1st (E), 3rd (G♯), ♭5th (B♭), ♭7th (D), 9th (F♯).

E 11 *E eleventh*
Spelling: 1st (E), 3rd (G♯), 5th (B), ♭7th (D), 9th (F♯), 11th (A).

E 13 *E thirteenth*
Spelling: 1st (E), 3rd (G♯), 5th (B), ♭7th (D), 9th (F♯), 13th (C♯).

241

Chords in **F**	Scale of F major						
	F	G	A	B♭	C	D	E
	1st	2nd	3rd	4th	5th	6th	7th
		9th		11th		13th	

F sus 4 (F sus)   *F suspended fourth*
Spelling: 1st (F), 4th (B♭), 5th (C). Note: no 3rd.

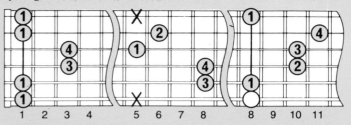

F   *F major*
Spelling: 1st (F), 3rd (A), 5th (C).

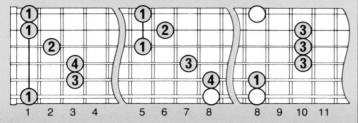

F 7 sus 4 (F 7+4)   *F seventh suspended fourth*
Spelling: 1st (F), 4th (B♭), 5th (C), ♭7th (E♭). Note: no 3rd.

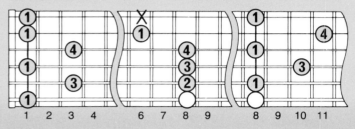

F 7   *F seventh*
Spelling: 1st (F), 3rd (A), 5th (C), ♭7th (E♭).

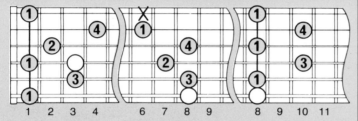

F 6   *F sixth*
Spelling: 1st (F), 3rd (A), 5th (C), 6th (D).

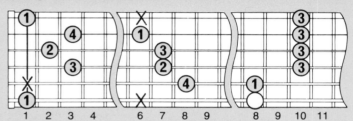

F m   *F minor*
Spelling: 1st (F), ♭3rd (A♭), 5th (C).

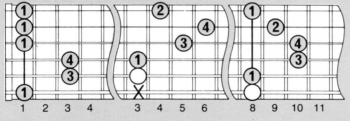

F m 6   *F minor sixth*
Spelling: 1st (F), ♭3rd (A♭), 5th (C), 6th (D).

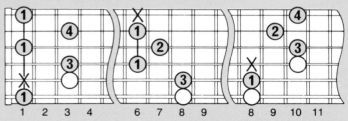

F m 7   *F minor seventh*
Spelling: 1st (F), ♭3rd (A♭), 5th (C), ♭7th (E♭).

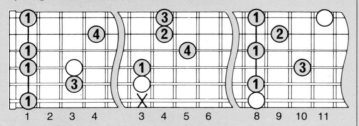

F 9   *F ninth*
Spelling: 1st (F), 3rd (A), 5th (C), ♭7th (E♭), 9th (G).

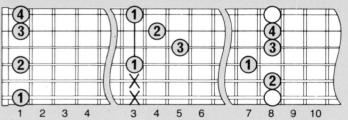

F maj 7 (F △7)   *F major seventh*
Spelling: 1st (F), 3rd (A), 5th (C), 7th (E).

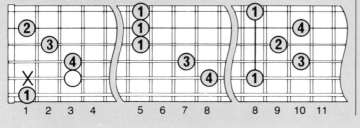

F m 9   *F minor ninth*
Spelling: 1st (F), ♭3rd (A♭), 5th (C), ♭7th (E♭), 9th (G).

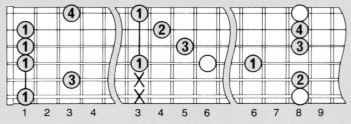

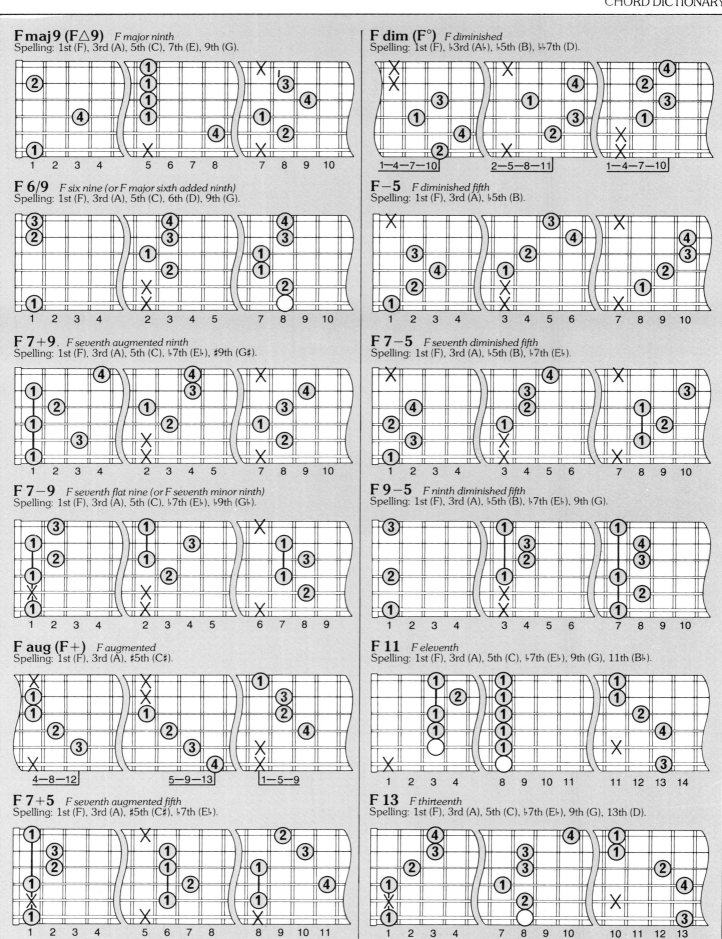

Fmaj9 (F△9) *F major ninth*
Spelling: 1st (F), 3rd (A), 5th (C), 7th (E), 9th (G).

F 6/9 *F six nine (or F major sixth added ninth)*
Spelling: 1st (F), 3rd (A), 5th (C), 6th (D), 9th (G).

F 7+9 . *F seventh augmented ninth*
Spelling: 1st (F), 3rd (A), 5th (C), ♭7th (E♭), ♯9th (G♯).

F 7−9 *F seventh flat nine (or F seventh minor ninth)*
Spelling: 1st (F), 3rd (A), 5th (C), ♭7th (E♭), ♭9th (G♭).

F aug (F+) *F augmented*
Spelling: 1st (F), 3rd (A), ♯5th (C♯).

F 7+5 *F seventh augmented fifth*
Spelling: 1st (F), 3rd (A), ♯5th (C♯), ♭7th (E♭).

F dim (F°) *F diminished*
Spelling: 1st (F), ♭3rd (A♭), ♭5th (B), ♭♭7th (D).

F−5 *F diminished fifth*
Spelling: 1st (F), 3rd (A), ♭5th (B).

F 7−5 *F seventh diminished fifth*
Spelling: 1st (F), 3rd (A), ♭5th (B), ♭7th (E♭).

F 9−5 *F ninth diminished fifth*
Spelling: 1st (F), 3rd (A), ♭5th (B), ♭7th (E♭), 9th (G).

F 11 *F eleventh*
Spelling: 1st (F), 3rd (A), 5th (C), ♭7th (E♭), 9th (G), 11th (B♭).

F 13 *F thirteenth*
Spelling: 1st (F), 3rd (A), 5th (C), ♭7th (E♭), 9th (G), 13th (D).

Chords in F♯ G♭

Scale of F♯ major G♭ major						
F♯ G♭	G♯ A♭	A♯ B♭	B	C♯ D♭	D♯ E♭	F
1st	2nd	3rd	4th	5th	6th	7th
	9th		11th		13th	

Note F♯ and G♭ are two names for the same note (called "enharmonic"). Chords are shown here in F♯ because this tends to be the more commonly used key.

F♯ sus 4 (F♯ sus) *F sharp suspended fourth*
Spelling: 1st (F♯), 4th (B), 5th (C♯). Note: no 3rd.

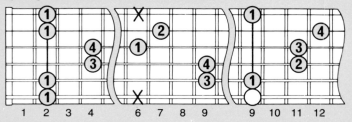

F♯ *F sharp major*
Spelling: 1st (F♯), 3rd (A♯), 5th (C♯).

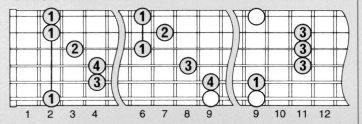

F♯ 7 sus 4 (F♯ 7+4) *F sharp seventh suspended fourth*
Spelling: 1st (F♯), 4th (B), 5th (C♯), ♭7th (E). Note: no 3rd.

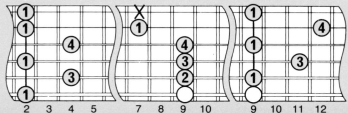

F♯ 7 *F sharp seventh*
Spelling: 1st (F♯), 3rd (A♯), 5th (C♯), ♭7th (E).

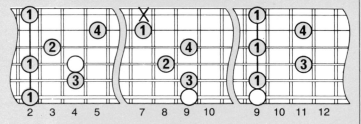

F♯ 6 *F sharp sixth*
Spelling: 1st (F♯), 3rd (A♯), 5th (C♯), 6th (D♯).

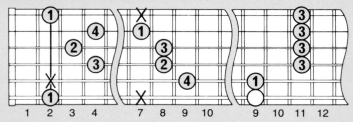

F♯ m *F sharp minor*
Spelling: 1st (F♯), ♭3rd (A), 5th (C♯).

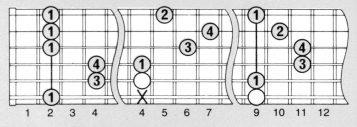

F♯ m 6 *F sharp minor sixth*
Spelling: 1st (F♯), ♭3rd (A), 5th (C♯), 6th (D♯).

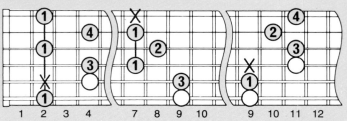

F♯ m 7 *F sharp minor seventh*
Spelling: 1st (F♯), ♭3rd (A), 5th (C♯), ♭7th (E).

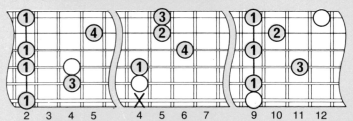

F♯ 9 *F sharp ninth*
Spelling: 1st (F♯), 3rd (A♯), 5th (C♯), ♭7th (E), 9th (G♯).

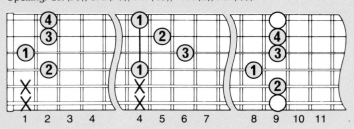

F♯ maj 7 (F♯△7) *F sharp major seventh*
Spelling: 1st (F♯), 3rd (A♯), 5th (C♯), 7th (F).

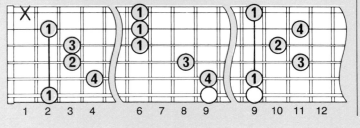

F♯ m 9 *F sharp minor ninth*
Spelling: 1st (F♯), ♭3rd (A), 5th (C♯), ♭7th (E), 9th (G♯).

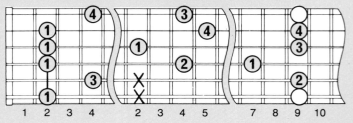

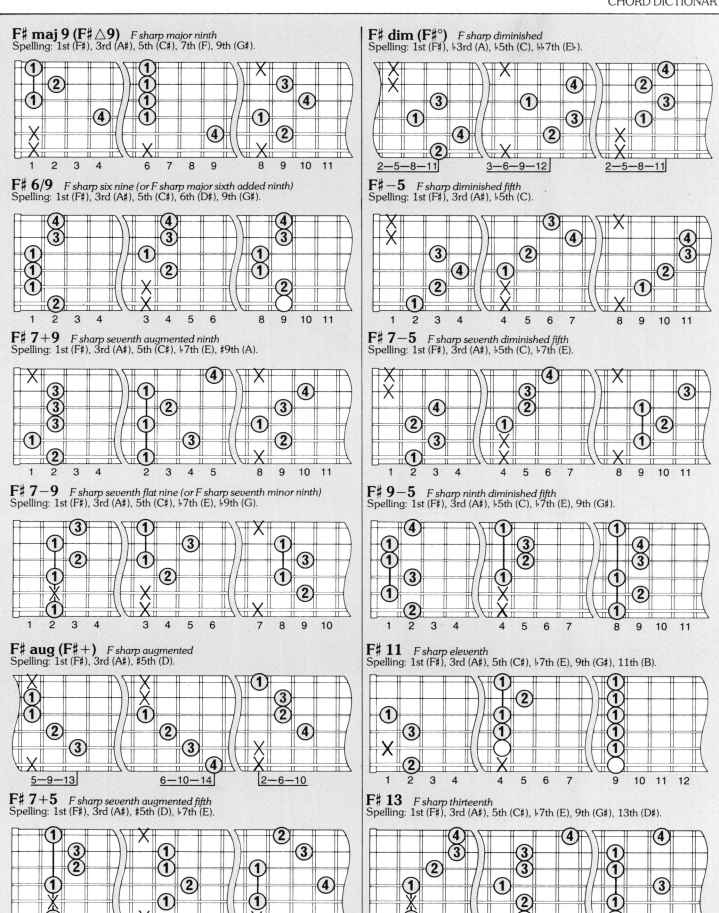

F♯ maj 9 (F♯△9) _F sharp major ninth_
Spelling: 1st (F♯), 3rd (A♯), 5th (C♯), 7th (F), 9th (G♯).

F♯ 6/9 _F sharp six nine (or F sharp major sixth added ninth)_
Spelling: 1st (F♯), 3rd (A♯), 5th (C♯), 6th (D♯), 9th (G♯).

F♯ 7+9 _F sharp seventh augmented ninth_
Spelling: 1st (F♯), 3rd (A♯), 5th (C♯), ♭7th (E), ♯9th (A).

F♯ 7−9 _F sharp seventh flat nine (or F sharp seventh minor ninth)_
Spelling: 1st (F♯), 3rd (A♯), 5th (C♯), ♭7th (E), ♭9th (G).

F♯ aug (F♯+) _F sharp augmented_
Spelling: 1st (F♯), 3rd (A♯), ♯5th (D).

F♯ 7+5 _F sharp seventh augmented fifth_
Spelling: 1st (F♯), 3rd (A♯), ♯5th (D), ♭7th (E).

F♯ dim (F♯°) _F sharp diminished_
Spelling: 1st (F♯), ♭3rd (A), ♭5th (C), ♭♭7th (E♭).

F♯ −5 _F sharp diminished fifth_
Spelling: 1st (F♯), 3rd (A♯), ♭5th (C).

F♯ 7−5 _F sharp seventh diminished fifth_
Spelling: 1st (F♯), 3rd (A♯), ♭5th (C), ♭7th (E).

F♯ 9−5 _F sharp ninth diminished fifth_
Spelling: 1st (F♯), 3rd (A♯), ♭5th (C), ♭7th (E), 9th (G♯).

F♯ 11 _F sharp eleventh_
Spelling: 1st (F♯), 3rd (A♯), 5th (C♯), ♭7th (E), 9th (G♯), 11th (B).

F♯ 13 _F sharp thirteenth_
Spelling: 1st (F♯), 3rd (A♯), 5th (C♯), ♭7th (E), 9th (G♯), 13th (D♯).

Chords in G

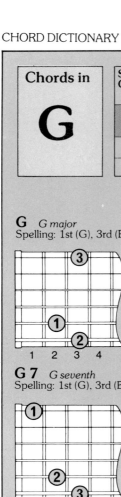

Scale of G major						
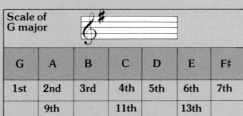
G	A	B	C	D	E	F♯
1st	2nd	3rd	4th	5th	6th	7th
	9th		11th		13th	

G *G major*
Spelling: 1st (G), 3rd (B), 5th (D).

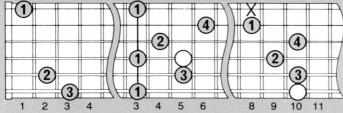

G 7 *G seventh*
Spelling: 1st (G), 3rd (B), 5th (D), ♭7th (F).

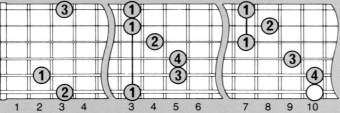

Gm *G minor*
Spelling: 1st (G), ♭3rd (B♭), 5th (D).

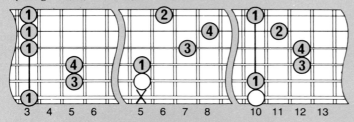

Gm7 *G minor seventh*
Spelling: 1st (G), ♭3rd (B♭), 5th (D), ♭7th (F).

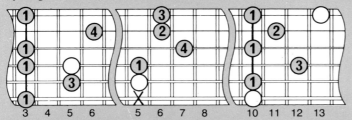

G maj 7 (G△7) *G major seventh*
Spelling: 1st (G), 3rd (B), 5th (D), 7th (F♯).

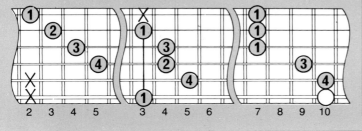

G sus 4 (G sus) *G suspended fourth*
Spelling: 1st (G), 4th (C), 5th (D). Note: no 3rd.

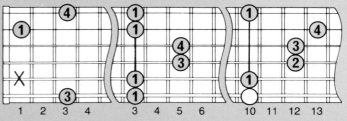

G 7sus4 (G 7+4) *G seventh suspended fourth*
Spelling: 1st (G), 4th (C), 5th (D), ♭7th (F). Note: no 3rd.

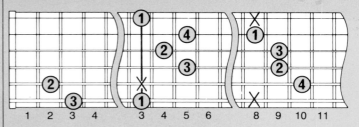

G 6 *G sixth*
Spelling: 1st (G), 3rd (B), 5th (D), 6th (E).

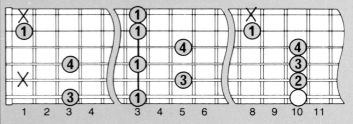

Gm6 *G minor sixth*
Spelling: 1st (G), ♭3rd (B♭), 5th (D), 6th (E).

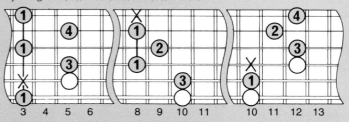

G 9 *G ninth*
Spelling: 1st (G), 3rd (B), 5th (D), ♭7th (F), 9th (A).

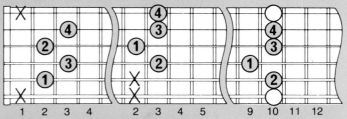

Gm9 *G minor ninth*
Spelling: 1st (G), ♭3rd (B♭), 5th (D), ♭7th (F), 9th (A).

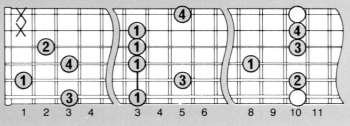

G maj 9 (G△9) *G major ninth*
Spelling: 1st (G), 3rd (B), 5th (D), 7th (F#), 9th (A).

G dim (G°) *G diminished*
Spelling: 1st (G), ♭3rd (B♭), ♭5th (D♭), ♭♭7th (E).

G 6/9 *G six nine (or G major sixth added ninth)*
Spelling: 1st (G), 3rd (B), 5th (D), 6th (E), 9th (A).

G−5 *G diminished fifth*
Spelling: 1st (G), 3rd (B), ♭5th (D♭).

G 7+9 *G seventh augmented ninth*
Spelling: 1st (G), 3rd (B), 5th (D), ♭7th (F), #9th (A#).

G 7−5 *G seventh diminished fifth*
Spelling: 1st (G), 3rd (B), ♭5th (D♭), ♭7th (F).

G 7−9 *G seventh flat nine (or G seventh minor ninth)*
Spelling: 1st (G), 3rd (B), 5th (D), ♭7th (F), ♭9th (A♭).

G 9−5 *G ninth diminished fifth*
Spelling: 1st (G), 3rd (B), ♭5th (D♭), ♭7th (F), 9th (A).

G aug (G+) *G augmented*
Spelling: 1st (G), 3rd (B), #5th (D#).

G 11 *G eleventh*
Spelling: 1st (G), 3rd (B), 5th (D), ♭7th (F), 9th (A), 11th (C).

G 7+5 *G seventh augmented fifth*
Spelling: 1st (G), 3rd (B), #5th (D#), ♭7th (F).

G 13 *G thirteenth*
Spelling: 1st (G), 3rd (B), 5th (D), ♭7th (F), 9th (A), 13th (E).

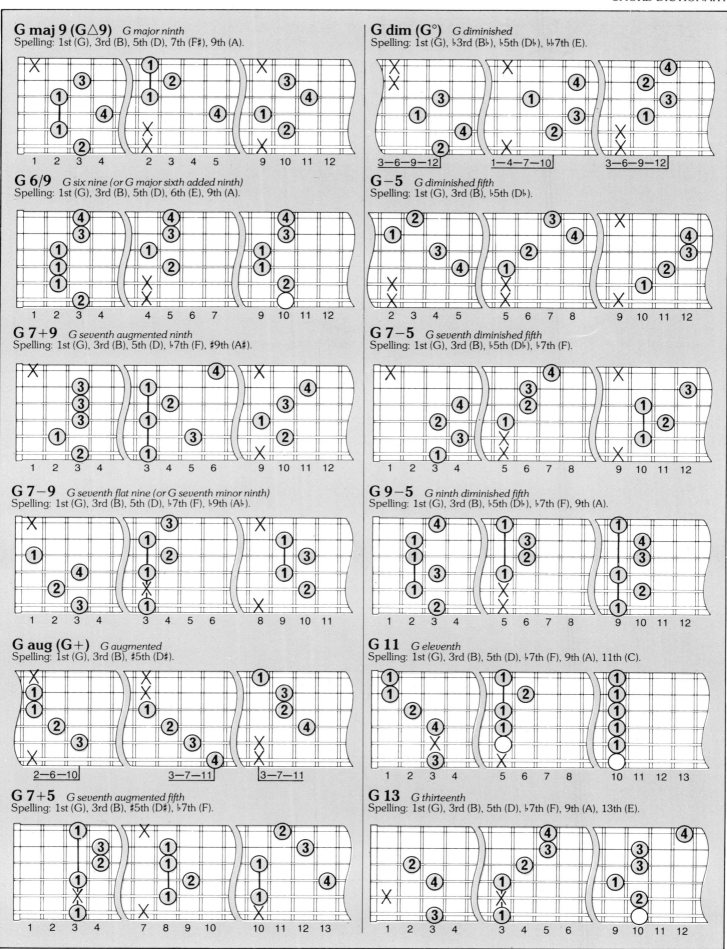

Chords in G♯ A♭

Scale of G♯ major A♭ major						
G♯ A♭	A♯ B♭	C	C♯ D♭	D♯ E♭	F	G
1st	2nd	3rd	4th	5th	6th	7th
	9th		11th		13th	

Note G♯ and A♭ are two names for the same note (called "enharmonic"). Chords are shown here in A♭ because this tends to be the more commonly used key.

A♭ *A flat major*
Spelling: 1st (A♭), 3rd (C), 5th (E♭).

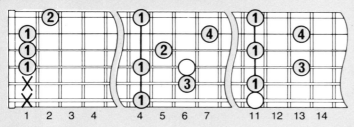

A♭ 7 *A flat seventh*
Spelling: 1st (A♭), 3rd (C), 5th (E♭), ♭7th (G♭).

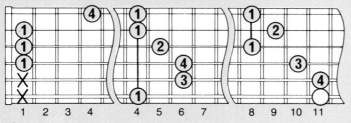

A♭ m *A flat minor*
Spelling: 1st (A♭), ♭3rd (B), 5th (E♭).

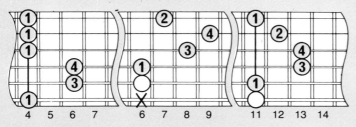

A♭ m7 *A flat minor seventh*
Spelling: 1st (A♭), ♭3rd (B), 5th (E♭), ♭7th (G♭).

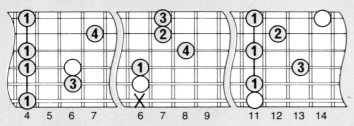

A♭ maj7 (A♭ △ 7) *A flat major seventh*
Spelling: 1st (A♭), 3rd (C), 5th (E♭), 7th (G).

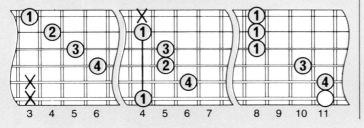

A♭ sus 4 (A♭ sus) *A flat suspended fourth*
Spelling: 1st (A♭), 4th (D♭), 5th (E♭). Note: no 3rd.

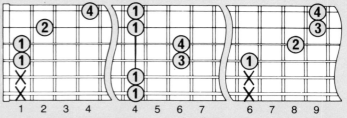

A♭ 7sus4 (A♭ 7+4) *A flat seventh suspended fourth*
Spelling: 1st (A♭), 4th (D♭), 5th (E♭), ♭7th (G♭). Note: no 3rd.

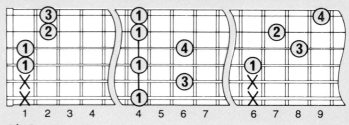

A♭ 6 *A flat sixth*
Spelling: 1st (A♭), 3rd (C), 5th (E♭), 6th (F)

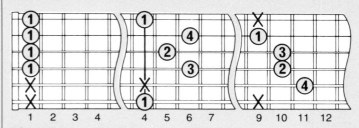

A♭ m6 *A flat minor sixth*
Spelling: 1st (A♭), ♭3rd (B), 5th (E♭), 6th (F).

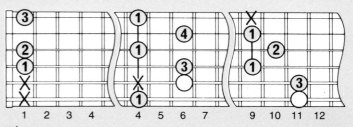

A♭ 9 *A flat ninth*
Spelling: 1st (A♭), 3rd (C), 5th (E♭), ♭7th (G♭), 9th (B♭).

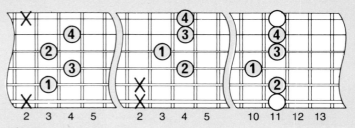

A♭ m9 *A flat minor ninth*
Spelling: 1st (A♭), ♭3rd (B), 5th (E♭), ♭7th (G♭), 9th (B♭).

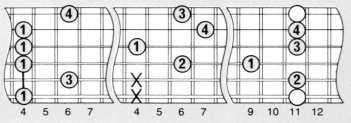

A♭ maj9 (A♭△9) *A flat major ninth*
Spelling: 1st (A♭), 3rd (C), 5th (E♭), 7th (G), 9th (B♭).

A♭ 6/9 *A flat six nine (or A flat major sixth added ninth)*
Spelling: 1st (A♭), 3rd (C), 5th (E♭), 6th (F), 9th (B♭).

A♭ 7+9 *A flat seventh augmented ninth*
Spelling: 1st (A♭), 3rd (C), 5th (E♭), ♭7th (G♭), ♯9th (B).

A♭ 7−9 *A flat seventh flat nine (or A flat seventh minor ninth)*
Spelling: 1st (A♭), 3rd (C), 5th (E♭), ♭7th (G♭), ♭9th (A).

A♭ aug (A♭ +) *A flat augmented ninth*
Spelling: 1st (A♭), 3rd (C), ♯5th (E).

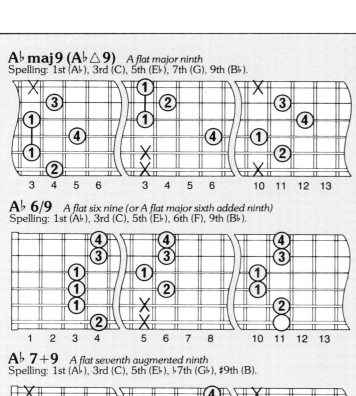

A♭ 7+5 *A flat seventh augmented fifth*
Spelling: 1st (A♭), 3rd (C), ♯5th (E), ♭7th (G♭).

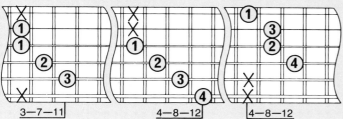

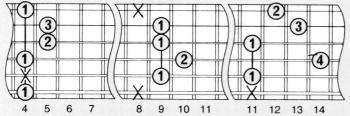

A♭ dim (A♭°) *A flat diminished*
Spelling: 1st (A♭), ♭3rd (B), ♭5th (D), ♭♭7th (F).

A♭ −5 *A flat diminished fifth*
Spelling: 1st (A♭), 3rd (C), ♭5th (D).

A♭ 7−5 *A flat seventh diminished fifth*
Spelling: 1st (A♭), 3rd (C), ♭5th (D), ♭7th (G♭).

A♭ 9−5 *A flat ninth diminished fifth*
Spelling: 1st (A♭), 3rd (C), ♭5th (D), ♭7th (G♭), 9th (B♭).

A♭ 11 *A flat eleventh*
Spelling: 1st (A♭), 3rd (C), 5th (E♭), ♭7th (G♭), 9th (B♭), 11th (D♭).

A♭ 13 *A flat thirteenth*
Spelling: 1st (A♭), 3rd (C), 5th (E♭), ♭7th (G♭), 9th (B♭), 13th (F).

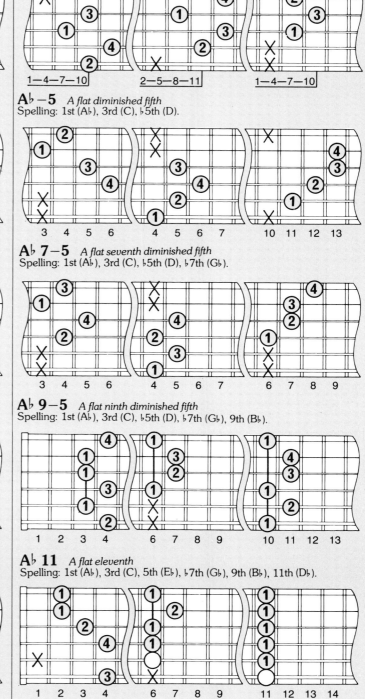

249

Index

Acknowledgments

Author's acknowledgments
I would like to extend my personal thanks to:
Alan Buckingham, Ron Pickless, Nick Harris,
Tim Shackleton and everyone at Dorling
Kindersley involed with the book; Felicity Bryan
of Curtis Brown Ltd and Brian Gascoigne;
Isaac Guillory for his work on the music section,
utilizing both the knowledge gained as a student
of composition and harmony at the Roosevelt
University, Chicago, and fifteen years'
experience as a professional guitarist with the
Cryin' Shames, Pacific Eardrum, Al Stewart,
Elkie Brooks and Barbara Dickson, as well as
many others as a solo artist in his own right;
Alastair Crawford for his work with me relating
to all things electric in the book, as well as for
his constant help and advice on various aspects
of the book; David Wernham, Pete Wingfield,
Frank Richmond and Dave Almond; guitarists
Andy Summers and Phil Palmer; bass guitarists
Mo Foster and Phil Childs; guitar-makers and
luthiers Tony Zemaitis, Chris Eccleshall, Mike
Cameron and Tom Mates; Richard Elen and
Noel Bell of *Studio Sound* magazine; Angus
Robertson of Link House Magazines
(Croydon) Ltd; freelance writer Tony Bacon;
Gwen Alexander; Dave Peterson of Vox Ltd
(for pre-amp design); Dave Green of Roland
(U.K.) Ltd; Christine Keiffer (for
information on Gibson guitars); Trevor
Newman of Rosetti Ltd; Trevor Cash of CBS/
Arbiter Ltd (for information on Fender
guitars); the London Rock Shop; Kelly Pike of
A & M Records Ltd; Mike Wilkie of Epic
Records Ltd; Hugh Attwool of CBS Records
Ltd. The views expressed in this book may not
necessarily be the same as the individual
opinions of those who contributed
information.

Dorling Kindersley would like to thank the
following for their help in the preparation of
this book: Warren Mitchell and Gordon Dungate
for their hard work on the typesetting and
make-up; Geoff Dann for much of the
special photography; Max Kay of EFR Guitars
for providing many of the photographs of
rare guitars; Judith More for picture research
and editorial assistance; Mark Richards, Calvin
Evans, Phil Wilkinson, Del Brenner and Lesley
Gilbert; Roddy MacDonald, Steve Parker and
Gary Marsh for the loan of equipment; Erica
of Keith Altham Publicity; David S. Harding of
Gibson; Mike Longworth of the C. F. Martin
Organization; M. J. Summerfield; David
Seville of Yamaha/Kemble Ltd; Gwen
Alexander and Adrian Legg of Rose-Morris;
Stuart Sawney and Robb Davenport of Guitar
Grapevine; Nick Martin of Scenic Sounds
Equipment Ltd; Anthony Macari of Macari's;
Fleur of Music Lab; Watkins Electric Music
(WEM) Ltd; Ken Achard of Peavey Electronics
(U.K.) Ltd; Roland (U.K.) Ltd; MESA/Boogie
Ltd.

Picture sources
Ralph Denyer
6, 30, 198, 200c, 201t, 201bl, 210t, 212, 214,
216, 219.
Geoff Dann
41, 48 l, 68, 69, 71, 72, 73, 74, 75, 82, 83, 84, 85,
87, 141, 142, 143, 145, 148, 162, 164, 165, 166,
169, 225.
E. F. R. Guitars/Geoff Dann
1, 46, 47r, 48r, 56, 57, 60, 61cl, 61b, 62l, 62c,
174, 176, 178t, 179t.
E. F. R. Guitars/Jack Durrant
38, 47l, 54, 58, 59, 62r, 63.
London Features International
7, 10, 11, 13r, 17t, 18, 19, 20, 21, 22, 23, 24, 25,
26, 29t, 32t, 88t, 102, 114, 115, 140, 158.
David Redfern
13l, 14, 15, 16, 27, 29b, 31, 66, 101.
Philip Dowell
2, 33, 49, 65, 161, 197, 217.
Rex Features
12, 28, 157.
Jazz Music Books
8, 9, 100.
Melody Maker
17b, 32b.
Summerfield
34, 47bc, 61t.
C. F. Martin Organization
37, 45.
Vox
61cr, 200bl.
Valerie Wilmer
160.
Daily Telegraph Colour Library
43.
Roland U.K. Ltd
64.
Ian O'Leary/Chandler Guitars
179b.
Rosetti
180, 181.
Mighty Mite/Rosetti
178b, 195b.
Gibson/Rosetti
195t.
H. H. Electronics
201bc, 213.
MXR
205c, 208cr.
Yamaha
205b, 209b.
MESA Boogie
200br.
DBX
207b.
Watkins Electronic Music
209c.
Revox
220.

Key t=top, c=centre, b=bottom, l=left, r=right.

Text quotations
GPI Publications, Cupertino, California.
Reprinted with permission: p.66 Howard
Roberts (*Rock Guitarists*, vol. 1); p.66 Ted
Nugent (*Rock Guitarists*, vol. 2); p.88 Keith
Richards (*The Guitar Player Book*, Nov. 1977);
p.88 Pete Townshend (*Guitar Player* magazine,
July 1981); p.102 Frank Zappa (*The Guitar
Player Book*, Jan. 1977); p.114 John
McLaughlin (*The Guitar Player Book*, Feb.
1975); p.114-15 George Benson (*The Guitar
Player Book*, Jan. 1974); p.140 Eric Clapton
(*Guitar Player* magazine, July 1981); p.140
Jeff Beck (*Guitar Player* magazine, July
1981); p.140 Ritchie Blackmore (*Guitar Player*
magazine, July 1981); p.156 Howard Roberts
(*Rock Guitarists*, vol. 1); p.157 Albert Lee
(*Guitar Player* magazine, May 1981).
Interview with Chuck Berry on p.10 and p.12 by
Patrick William Salvo from *The Rolling Stone
Interviews*, vol. 1, Rolling Stone Press & Arthur
Barker Ltd/Widenfeld Publishing C. 1981. All
rights reserved. Reprinted by permission.
Sphere Books Ltd, London. Reprinted with
permission: p.18 and p.20 Eric Clapton
(*Conversations with Eric Clapton* by Steve
Turner, Abacus, 1976).
Omnibus Press, London. Reprinted with
permission: p.26 Jimi Hendrix (*Hendrix: A
Biography* by Chris Welch, Omnibus Press,
1972).

Illustrators John Bishop, Gary Marsh,
Hayward and Martin, Alun Jones, Kong Kang
Chen and Nick Harris.

Photographic services W. Photo, Negs and
Photo Summit.

Reproduction F. E. Burman Ltd and Dot
Gradations Ltd.

Typesetting Rowland Phototypesetting
(London) Ltd.